AMERICAN DIARIES

An Annotated Bibliography of American Diaries
Written Prior to the Year 1861

COMPILED BY

WILLIAM MATTHEWS

WITH THE ASSISTANCE OF ROY HARVEY PEARCE

BOSTON, MASSACHUSETTS

J. S. CANNER & COMPANY · PUBLISHERS

1959

FIRST PUBLISHED, 1945, AS VOLUME 16

UNIVERSITY OF CALIFORNIA PUBLICATIONS IN ENGLISH

BY THE UNIVERSITY OF CALIFORNIA PRESS

SECOND PRINTING, 1959

PUBLISHED BY J. S. CANNER & COMPANY

BOSTON, MASSACHUSETTS

L.C. CATALOG CARD No. 59–13345

PRINTED IN THE UNITED STATES OF AMERICA

TO

MILES L. HANLEY

AND IN MEMORY OF

WILLIAM ELLERY LEONARD

PREFACE

A thought has struck me:—As I am about to enter
on an "adventurous career" *I will keep a journal.*
MAJOR MARTIN McLEOD, 1836

IN THE FALL OF 1938, I began to read American diaries and journals
in the Wisconsin Historical Society's library, intending to use them
for a study of the speech of the New England colonists. My guide
was the invaluable, but sometimes inaccurate, bibliography by Mrs.
Harriette M. Forbes, *New England Diaries, 1602–1800* (Topsfield,
Mass., 1923). As I read on, it became apparent that these astonishingly
numerous diaries were of great value for many kinds of historian, and
that many of them would interest the general reader. As Mrs. Forbes's
bibliography was both limited in scope and not always easily available
(it was privately published in a very small edition), I decided to collect
material for a bibliography that would be more comprehensive, covering all the states and going up to 1860, and would indicate the nature
and value of the individual diaries. The present list is the result. For its
limits and limitations I offer the following apologia.

As Mrs. Forbes's bibliography so well indicates, diaries are prone to
get published in the most divers forms and places, as separate books, in
every kind of periodical, in family histories, biographies, town and
county and state histories, in small private editions, and as public ven-
tures. Guides to their existence are far from satisfactory; indices and
lists of contents are all too apt to omit mention of the form, and such
characteristic titles as "Forty Years on the Frontier," or "How Many
Miles to St. Jo?" give little hint that a diary is being published. Cata-
logues, publishers' lists, even reviews, suffer from the same obscurant-
ism. The only working method I have devised to collect diaries is to
thumb through every available book that might be suspected of harbor-
ing a diary, relying upon the eye to catch the characteristic dates and
shapes of the diary form. The practice has its defects; the more popular
books are occasionally missing from the shelves when the searcher's
thumb arrives, his eye may not keep pace with his thumb, and even

the greatest libraries are far from complete—especially in privately printed books. Recognizing these dangers, I scanned such book lists, bibliographies, and reviews as were likely to mention diaries, hoping thereby not to overlook the obvious. To catch as many of the smaller fish as possible, I cast nets in different seas, one a large general library, the others scholars' libraries or special libraries in different parts of the country. Mrs. Forbes had made her list on the basis of libraries in New England; to supplement it, I worked in the Wisconsin State Historical Society's Library, the libraries of the University of California at Los Angeles and Berkeley, the Bancroft Library at Berkeley, the Henry E. Huntington Library, San Marino, and the public library of the City of Los Angeles. A good many items for which I had references, but which were not in these libraries, were checked in the Harvard University Library, the Boston Public Library, and the Library of Congress.

In the course of examining the books in the historical, periodical, biographical, literary, religious, and genealogical sections of these libraries, I have probably missed a number of diaries; I trust that they are fewer than I fear they may be. The Wisconsin State Historical Society's library and the Los Angeles Public Library have extensive genealogical and biographical sections, but I imagine that many diaries have been published in genealogies, town and county histories, and biographies which I have not seen. Neither my courage nor my leisure would permit me to scan newspapers, and I have examined thoroughly only the more promising popular weeklies and monthlies. Completeness is not claimed for this list; but I should be very grateful for references to diaries I have missed.

One group of omissions calls for special notice. There are innumerable manuscript diaries, published and unpublished, in the libraries of historical, genealogical, and antiquarian societies, in city and university libraries, and in private hands. Mrs. Forbes records about five hundred unpublished diaries for New England alone, not including diaries begun after 1800. Wishing to achieve some sort of completeness and to describe only those diaries that I had actually examined, I decided to omit manuscript diaries altogether. This may have been shortsighted, but it is the normal practice of cataloguing, and a list of unpublished diaries may always be prepared to supplement this one.

It will be discovered that some documents which appear in other bibliographies as "journals" or "diaries" do not appear in this list. These words are often misused; many works which are called journals by their authors, editors, or commentators should be known by other names. Religious "journals" are generally autobiographies, travel "journals" are frequently travel narratives; a historian's day-by-day record, if written as history, is a chronicle. Books of clippings and quotations should be called commonplace books, not journals; and annals, memoirs, reminiscences, minutes, orderly books, muster rolls, ships' logs, and extracts from the letters of even the most persistent letter writers should not be styled diaries and journals. To keep these sheep free from wolves, I have had to reject many hundreds from this fold.

I understand a diary to be a day-by-day record of what interested the diarist, each day's record being self-contained and written shortly after the events occurred, the style being usually free from organized exposition. Between a "diary" and a "journal" I have generally made a conventional distinction, that a diary is written for personal reasons, and that a journal, although otherwise similar to a diary, is kept as part of a job; in practice, there is often little or no difference, for journals are rarely altogether impersonal, many official journals being filled with the private opinions and affairs of the writers. Entry to this list has been only through the gateway of this definition. To have let in the miscalled "journals" and "diaries" would have transformed the list into a bibliography of miscellaneous documents which could never have been complete, and to which almost any kind of contemporary document could have been admitted with equal logic. More significantly, it would have obscured the motive of the collection. I believe the diary to be a unique kind of writing; all other forms of writing envisage readers, and so are adapted to readers, by interpretation, order, simplification, rationalization, omission, addition, and the endless devices of exposition. Although many diaries, too, are written with readers in mind, they are in general the most immediate, truthful, and revealing documents available to the historian. A comparison of a diary with a narrative based upon it, or of letters and diaries on the same subjects, will quickly show the essential differences.

I have also restricted the scope of the list to the English-speaking world of America. I have admitted diaries written by immigrants and foreign visitors, provided they were written in English or have been translated into English, but I have not included the journals of French and Spanish explorers and missionaries outside the areas controlled by English-speaking Americans. American missionaries are not pursued beyond the present territory of the United States, but the diaries written by American laymen visiting foreign parts have been brought in. After struggling for some time to separate the Canadians and Americans in the Northeast, the old Northwest, and the Pacific Northwest, I decided that, for my purposes, it was more profitable, as well as easier, to include all Canadian diaries written in English. As none of the libraries in which I worked was particularly strong in Canadian material, I fear that I may have missed many Canadian diaries.

The list is restricted to diaries and journals that have been published completely or in substantial part. Many items listed by Mrs. Forbes are omitted from this list because they are merely cited or briefly quoted in historical studies or biographies, or were published only through extracts of vital statistics. Diaries published only in quotation have been admitted only when the quotations were adequate to establish some idea of the diaries as separate entities.

I have given a few biographical details of the diarists whenever such information was available without special research. It has usually been derived from the diaries themselves or editorial notes, the Library of Congress catalogue, the *Dictionary of American Biography, Appleton's Cyclopaedia of Biography,* or Mrs. Forbes's bibliography.

The dates of the diaries are given by months and years, as actually published; these sometimes differ from Mrs. Forbes's dates, which are often the dates of manuscripts. All dates have been given in New Style.

The description of the diary and the notes of contents are intended to give a rough characterization of the document and to indicate the chief subjects, places, and persons dealt with therein; and whenever it seemed worth while to do so, a word of evaluation has been added. These notes and comments are those of a general reader, not of a specialist in American history. It is hoped that the evaluations may indicate where the chaff and where the grain lie, but no exactness is claimed for such spot judgments, the standard being higher when many diaries of the same type exist, as, for example, the Gold Rush diaries or the Revolutionary diaries and journals. Where no evaluation is given, the implication is usually that the diary is dull or conventional. In noting contents, I have usually indicated my own special interests in literature and language, as well as the subjects of more general and historical interest. The frequent note, "interesting spellings," is intended to indicate a general linguistic significance, for informal spellings are often accompanied by informal locutions.

When a diary has been published more than once, the publications are arranged chronologically, the last being usually the best and most reliable unless otherwise noted. Where the texts are complicated, as for George Croghan's diaries, the best text is given first, followed by notes on variations, etc. A complete text, if one has been published, is noted first, separated from other complete texts by semicolons. Extracts then follow. The texts have not been carefully compared; nor has every edition or selection from the more popular diaries always been cited, especially for George Washington's, Samuel Sewall's, and the like. Offprints have not been included. Asterisks mark those texts which have not been examined, but which are described by one or more reliable authorities. In giving the sources, I have rarely mentioned the editors unless the diaries are published as separate books; for this injustice, the necessity of saving space must be blamed.

The diaries are arranged chronologically, by years, according to the date of the first entries as published. Diaries beginning in the same year are arranged under that year alphabetically by the diarists' names. The reader seeking diaries about particular events or periods is reminded that to get in a full crop he must begin searching several years before the date of his interest, since diaries often cover many years.

It is a pleasant duty to acknowledge here the chief of my obligations. In compiling the list, I have been greatly helped by Mrs. Forbes's bibliography; something over a quarter of the items in this list also appear in hers. Nearly all her entries have been checked, however, and new sources have often been added. I have also found very helpful Grace G. Griffin's annual bibliographies published by the American Historical Association, Dr. W. S. Thomas's list of American Revolutionary diaries published in the *Bulletin* of the New York Historical Society, Volumes VI and VII, the bibliographies in the *Dictionary of American Biography,* Sabin's and Evans's bibliographies of American books, and Henry R. Wagner's *The Plains and the Rockies* (1937).

In compiling the list, I was fortunate enough to enlist the help of Mr. Roy Harvey Pearce, my friend and former student, now of Johns Hopkins. In the summers of 1941 and 1942 he spent long weeks checking entries, and finding some new items, in the Henry E. Huntington Library, the library of the University of California at Los Angeles, and the Los Angeles Public Library. The list owes much to his remarkable energy and care. I am also indebted and obliged to Mr. Thomas Wiener and Mr. N. H. Sand, who checked various items in libraries in Boston, Cambridge, and Washington; and to Dr. Louis B. Wright, Dr. Louis Koontz, and Dixon Wecter, who have all given advice at needed times. To Mr. Harold A. Small, Editor of the University of California Press, and his assistants, I am greatly indebted for the skill and care with which they saw the list through the press.

To the Regents of the University of California I tender my grateful thanks for generous research grants which made possible assistance in checking the list.

With genuine pleasure, I offer this list as a tribute of regard to my good friends Miles L. Hanley and the late William Ellery Leonard of the University of Wisconsin, and to the librarians in Wisconsin and California. The first set going and fanned my interest in the diaries, the second shared it, and the librarians made its gratification pleasant and easy.

WILLIAM MATTHEWS

Los Angeles, 1945

CONTENTS

Contents

AMERICAN DIARIES

1629

HIGGINSON, Rev. Francis (1588–1630) of Notts, Eng., and Salem, Mass.

Sea diary, April–May 1629; day-by-day narrative of voyage of fleet from England to New England; adventures at sea; God's providences, and description of New England; fairly good narrative.

Alexander Young, *Chronicles of the First Planters* (Boston, 1846) 213–238; *Massachusetts Hist. Soc. Proc.* LXII (1928–1929) 283–299.

1630

WINTHROP, John (1588–1649) of Boston, governor.

Historical journal, March 1630–January 1649; known as his "History of New England"; impersonal daily record of public events.

Originally published as *A Journal of the Transactions and Occurrences in the Settlement of Massachusetts* (Hartford, 1790) 364 pp.; republished with additional material as, James Savage (ed.), *The History of New England from 1630 to 1649* (Boston, 1825–1826); the best edition is that edited by J. K. Hosmer (New York, 1908) two vols. The first year (March 1630–March 1631) is corrected, supplementary to Hosmer's edition, in *Massachusetts Hist. Soc. Proc.* LXII (1928–1929) 325–361.

1631

EASTON, Peter (1622–1694) of Newport, R. I.

Private diary, 1631–1678; notes about his family and settlement in New England, and brief notes of events in Newport history.

Newport Mercury, December 26, 1857, and January 2, 1858; some Rhode Island items in *Rhode Island Hist. Soc. Colls.* XI (1918) 78–80.

1634

CURLER, Arent van (*d.* 1667) of Rensselaerwyck colony.

Travel diary, December 1634–January 1635; early journey among Iroquois Indians; personal notes and descriptions of Indian customs and vocabulary; fairly good narrative, and valuable as first account of the Iroquois. Translated from the Dutch.

Edited by J. G. Wilson, *Ann. Rep. Amer. Hist. Assoc.* (1895) 81–101.

HULL, John (1624–1683) of Market Harborough, Eng., and Boston.

1. Public journal, 1634–October 1681; notes of "publick occurrences."
Trans. and Colls. Amer. Antiq. Soc. III (1857) 167–265. Extract in *Proc. Amer. Antiq. Soc.* (April 1856) 14–15.

2. Personal diary, November 1647–March 1682; examples of God's providence

toward New England and himself; typical religious diary, with some personal and weather notes, and items about the Dutch and the Quakers; fair.

Trans. and Colls. Amer. Antiq. Soc. III (1857) 141–164.

[VAN DEN BOGAERT, Harmen Meyndertsz, surgeon.]

Travel journal, December 1634–January 1635; journey from Fort Orange into the Mohawk country; Mohawk vocabulary. Translated from the Dutch.

John F. Jameson (ed.), *Narratives of New Netherland* (New York, 1909) 137–162.

1635

HOBART, Rev. Peter (1604–1679) of Hingham, Mass.

Clergyman's diary, June 1635–December 1678; scattered entries of births, marriages, and deaths; some war items, massacres, etc.

Diary of William Bentley (Salem, 1911) III 282–284.

MATHER, Richard (1596–1669) of Lowton, Warwickshire, and Dorchester, Mass.

Sea diary, April–August 1635; voyage to New England; narrative in day-by-day form of life at sea, storms, hardships, etc.; good narrative.

Alexander Young, *Chronicles of the First Planters* (Boston, 1846) 445–481; *Dorchester Antiq. and Hist. Soc. Colls.* III (1850) 5–34.

1638

DE VRIES, David Peterson (*fl.* 1618–1655) of New Netherland, merchant skipper.

Diary, December 1638–1642; life in New Netherland; interesting but narrative type.

Old South Leaflets VII No. 168, 20 pp. (from his *Short Historical and Journal Notes*).

1639

BUTLER, Nathaniel, governor of Providence Island.

Journal, February–March 1639 (extracts); "diary of my present employment," dealing with privateers off New England coast.

John F. Jameson, *Privateering and Piracy in the Colonial Period* (New York, 1923) 3–8.

1640

SHEPARD, Rev. Thomas (1605–1649) of Cambridge, Mass.

Religious diary, November 1640–March 1644; religious experiences and self-analysis.

Three Valuable Pieces (Boston, 1747) Part III.

1641

DE HOOGES, Antony.

Travel journal, July–November 1641; from Holland to New Netherland; a passenger's logbook; statistics. Translated from the Dutch.

A. J. F. Van Laer (ed.), *Van Rensselaer Bowier Manuscripts* (Albany, 1908) 580–603.

1643

ELIOT, Rev. John (1604–1690) of Roxbury, Mass.

Clergyman's journal, March 1643–April 1677; mostly church records and notes of outstanding yearly events; weather, Indian affairs, etc. Narrative type.

New England Hist. Geneal. Reg. XXXV (1881) 21–24, 241–247.

1645

WINTHROP, John (1606–1676) of Boston.

Travel diary, November–December 1645; trip from Boston to Nameaug via Springfield and Hartford, and back along coast through Providence; brief notes of stages, travel difficulties, weather, visits. Mostly in Latin.

Massachusetts Hist. Soc. Proc. 2d Ser. VIII (1892–1894) 4–12. Extracts translated, with editorial interpolations, in *New England Quar.* XIII (1940) 494–510.

1649

DANFORTH, Rev. Samuel (1626–1674) of Roxbury, Mass.

Clergyman's journal, March 1649–July 1674; affairs of First Church in Roxbury, local affairs, weather, etc.

New England Hist. Geneal. Reg. XXXIV (1880) 85–89, 162–166, 297–301, 359–363.

1650

BLAND, Edward (*d.* 1653) of Kimages, Va.

Travel diary, August–September 1650; long entries of a week of travel in the country and rivers behind Fort Henry, Va.; fairly good descriptions.

Published as *The Discovery of New Brittaine* (London, 1651) 16 pp.; reprinted in C. W. Alvord and L. Bidgood, *The First Explorations of the Trans-Allegheny Region by the Virginians* (Cleveland, 1912) 114–130.

JEFFERAY, William (1591–1675) of Chiddingly, Eng., and Newport, R.I.

Private diary, 1650–January 1669 (preceded by autobiographical notes); a fake diary of the life of an actual inhabitant of Providence, recently written.

John O. Austin, *The Journal of William Jefferay* (Providence, 1899) 189 pp.

1653

FLYNT, Rev. Josiah (1645–1680) of Dorchester, Mass.

Clergyman's journal, October 1653–November 1674; a few brief entries, mostly about church affairs and troubles with the deacon.

Dedham Hist. Reg. X (1899) 19–25.

MINOR, Thomas (1608–1690) of Stonington, Conn.

Private diary, November 1653–July 1684; brief notes of personal matters, farming, and local affairs; some linguistic interest.

The Diary of Thomas Minor (New London, 1899) 221 pp.

NUTON, Capt. Brian.   1656
Travel diary, December 1656–January 1657; from New Amsterdam to East-
chester; brief description of a four days' trip. Translated from the Dutch.
E. B. O'Callaghan, *Doc. Hist. State New York* III (1850) 557–559.

ANON.   1659
Slave-ship journal, March–November 1659; scattered entries from business
journal of the slaver "St. John." Translated from the Dutch.
E. B. O'Callaghan (ed.), *Voyages of the Slavers St. John and Arms of Amsterdam* (Albany, 1867) 1–9.

HERRMAN (or Heermans), Augustine.
Dutch diplomatic journal, September–October 1659; "touching the pretensions
set up by Colonel Nathaniel Utie to the South River"; journey from New Amstel
to South River; negotiations. Translated.
E. B. O'Callaghan, *Docs. Rel. Col. Hist. State New York* II (1858) 88–98;
revised translation in Clayton C. Hall (ed.), *Narratives of Early Maryland
(Original Narratives of Early American History)* (New York, 1910) 311–333.

WIGGLESWORTH, Rev. Michael (1631–1705) of Malden, Mass.
Private diary, July 1659–October 1669; brief, scattered extracts of no particular
value; literary and personal affairs.
Hist. Mag. VII (1863) 361–363.

1660

GOFFE, Col. William (*ca.* 1605–*ca.* 1679) of Westminster, Eng.
Private diary, March–July 1660 (a brief and pointless extract); social and
religious affairs at Boston.
Massachusetts Hist. Soc. Proc. 1st Ser. VII (1863–1864) 280–283.

1661

SPÖRI, Felix Christian (*b.* 1601?) of Zurich (?), surgeon.
Travel diary, February 1661–February 1664 (extract from second half of journal); voyage from Bermuda to America; detailed account of New England;
Rhode Island; whale hunt; voyage to London and Amsterdam. (First part, not
published, is of voyage from Amsterdam to Bermuda.) Irregular entries, many
apparently *post facto*. Translated from the German.
New England Quar. X (1937) 536–548.

1662

BOWNE, John (1628–1695) of Flushing, Quaker.
Quaker journal, July 1662–January 1664; persecutions by Dutch; seminarrative.
Amer. Hist. Rec. I (1872) 4–8.

1663

ANON.

Slave-ship journal, April–October 1663; scattered entries; recapture of slaver "Arms of Amsterdam."

E. B. O'Callaghan (ed.), *Voyages of the Slavers St. John and Arms of Amsterdam* (Albany, 1867) 89–95 (*New York Colonial Tracts* No. 3).

ANON.

Official exploration journal, September–November 1663; "Report of Commissioners Sent from Barbadoes to Explore the River Cape Fear"; entries are of fair interest.

J. Sprunt, *Chronicles of the Cape Fear River* (Raleigh, N.C., 1916) 26–30.

ANON. (Dutchman).

Travel journal, December 1663; voyage from Gravesend, L. I., to the Nevesinks in search of a place to settle.

John E. Stillwell, *Historical and Genealogical Miscellany* (New York, 1914) III 248–249.

KREGIER, Capt. Martin.

Military journal, July 1663–January 1664; official report of second Esopus War; attack by Indians and massacre at Wildwyck, N. Y. Translated from the Dutch.

E. B. O'Callaghan, *Doc. Hist. State New York* IV (1851) 33–62.

VAN RUYVEN, Cornelis (and Burgomaster Cortlandt and John Laurence).

Official journal, October 1663; voyage and horseback journey of delegates from New Netherland to the General Assembly at Hartford; territorial dispute. Translated from the Dutch.

E. B. O'Callaghan, *Docs. Rel. Col. Hist. State New York* II (1858) 385–393; John F. Jameson, *Narratives of New Netherland* (New York, 1909) 432–445 has a new translation.

1664

BRADSTREET, Simon (1640–1683) of New London, Conn.

Private diary, November 1664–August 1683; notes of important local happenings and providences; fires, flood, accidents, fevers; a few fairly interesting entries each year.

New England Hist. Geneal. Reg. VIII (1854) 325–333 and IX (1855) 43–51, 78–79.

1667

ADAMS, Rev. William (1650–1685) of Dedham, Mass.

Private diary, August 1667–April 1682; written partly while author was student at Harvard; later, brief local notes, with a good supernatural story.

Massachusetts Hist. Soc. Colls. 4th Ser. I (1852) 8–22.

1668

TAYLOR, Rev. Edward (1642–1729) of Westfield, Mass.

Private diary, April 1668–January 1672; voyage from Wapping to New England; entry at Harvard, study, and comments on teachers; journey through New England; an interesting document.

Massachusetts Hist. Soc. Proc. 1st Ser. XVIII (1880–1881) 5–18; John H. Lockwood, *Westfield and Its Historic Influences* (n.p., 1922) 130–136.

1669

GOULD, Daniel (*ca.* 1626–1716) of Newport, R. I.

Quaker travel journal, October 1669–October 1693; brief notes of travel in Maryland, Virginia, Pennsylvania, and New England; visits, meetings, distances, weather; quite impersonal.

Rebecca G. Mitchell, *The Goulds of Rhode Island* (Providence, 1875) 10–31.

GRAVE, John (1633–1695) of Guilford, Conn.

Journal, March 1669–1794; accounts, births, deaths, family, and farm memoranda; kept up by his descendants; interesting spellings.

Connecticut Mag. X (1906) 18–24.

PENN, William (1644–1718), Quaker leader.

Travel journal, August 1669–April 1670; second visit to Ireland; London to Ireland; brief, factual entries.

Pennsylvania Mag. Hist. Biog. XL (1916) 46–84.

1671

ANON.

Travel journal, September 1671; official report, in third person; exploration in western Virginia.

E. B. O'Callaghan, *Docs. Rel. Col. Hist. State New York* III (1853) 193–197.

BATTS, Thomas (*d.* 1691) of Charles City Co., Va.

Exploring journal, September–October 1671; from Virginia across the Appalachians, and discovery of Kanawha River falls; a rather dull surveying journal.

The Ohio River in Colonial Days (New York, 1890) 220–229; C. W. Alvord and L. Bidgood, *The First Explorations of the Trans-Allegheny Region by the Virginians* (Cleveland, 1912) 183–193; L. P. Summers, *Annals of Southwest Virginia* (Abingdon, 1929) 1–7; E. B. O'Callaghan, *Docs. Rel. Col. Hist. State New York* III (1853) 193–197; *William and Mary Coll. Quar.* 1st Ser. XV (1906–1907) 234–241.

1673

ANON.

Sea journal, October–November 1673; cruise aboard frigate "Zeehond" from New Orange to east end of Long Island; description of storm. Translated from the Dutch.

E. B. O'Callaghan, *Docs. Rel. Col. Hist. State New York* II (1858) 654–656.

SEWALL, Samuel (1652–1730) of Boston.

Private diary, December 1673–October 1729; beginning at Harvard and ending shortly before his death; an invaluable record of Boston life in the period of the Mathers, and an intimate picture of the diarist; probably the best American diary; some linguistic interest.

Massachusetts Hist. Soc. Colls. 5th Ser. V (1878) VI (1879) VII (1882); best abridgment in one volume by Mark Van Doren (New York, 1927). Extracts in most anthologies of American literature.

1675

MATHER, Rev. Increase (1639–1723) of Boston.

Religious diary, January 1675–December 1676; religious observations and self-analysis; some public and family matters, illness, Indian affairs; pious and ejaculatory style.

Massachusetts Hist. Soc. Proc. 2d Ser. XIII (1899–1900) 340–374. Another version of his diary (November 1674–May 1687), which is somewhat less theological and of more general interest, *Massachusetts Hist. Soc. Proc.* 2d Ser. XIII (1899–1900) 398–411.

RANDOLPH, Edward (1632–1703) of Canterbury, Eng.

Diary letters, March 1675–November 1700 (with numerous gaps); written to Sir Robert Southwall; account of his proceedings and voyage to and from New England; survey in America; travels in Virginia, Maryland, Rhode Island, Massachusetts, and New Hampshire.

Massachusetts Hist. Soc. Proc. 1st Ser. XVIII (1880–1881) 258–261. Extracts in *Andros Tracts* (Boston, 1874) III 214–218.

SCOTTOW, Capt. Joshua (*d.* 1698) of Boston.

Military travel journal, October–December 1675; notes of "diverse marches & improvement of Boston souldiers sent to Black Point."

New England Hist. Geneal. Reg. XLIII (1889) 68–70.

SHEPARD, Hety (*b.* 1660) of Rhode Island.

Private diary, December 1675–November 1677 (extracts); life of a young woman in Rhode Island; social and family life; pleasant, personal picture of Puritan influences on feminine pleasures. The genuineness of the diary, however, has been doubted.

Edited by A. E. H. Slicer, *New England Mag.* XI (1894–1895) 20–25.

WILTON, David (1633–1678) of Northampton, Mass.

Private diary, June–September 1675 (extracts); mostly accounts, with a few farming and social notes; interesting spellings.

J. R. Trumbull, *History of Northampton* (Northampton, 1898) I 280–283.

1677

HAMMOND, Capt. Lawrence (*d.* 1699) of Charlestown, Mass.

Diary and commonplace book, March 1677–April 1691 (some dates disordered); personal and social notes, outstanding local and public events, deaths, weather; recipes; fairly amusing antiquarian material, with some linguistic interest.

Massachusetts Hist. Soc. Proc. 2d Ser. VII (1891–1892) 144–172; brief additional entry, *ibid.* 2d Ser. XIII (1899–1900) 411.

MANNING, Mr.

Sea journal, July–August 1677; from Salem to Cape Sable in the ketch "Supply" against Indians who had stolen boats; mainly log entries; interesting spellings.

Doc. Hist. State Maine (Maine Hist. Soc.) VI (1900) 179–184.

STOCKWELL, Quentin (*d.* 1714) of Deerfield, Mass.

Captive's diary, 1677–1678; capture in Deerfield by Indians and journey to Canada; seminarrative.

Edited by S. G. Hubbard, *Hist. and Proc. Pocumtuck Valley Mem. Assoc.* II (1880–1889) 462.

WALDERNE, Maj. Richard (1615?–1689) of Dover, N.H.

Military journal, February–March 1677; expedition to Maine in King Philip's War; Arrowsick, Pemaquid, etc.

William Hubbard, *The History of the Indian Wars in New England* (Roxbury, 1865; ed. S. G. Drake) II 212–245.

1678

PIKE, Rev. John (1653–1710) of Dover, N.H.

Private diary, November 1678–June 1709 (earliest entries autobiographical); brief local notes; in three sections, personal, weather, providences; impersonal and disjointed, but with fair genealogical and local interest, and some interesting language.

Massachusetts Hist. Soc. Proc. 1st Ser. XIV (1875–1876) 121–150; *New Hampshire Geneal. Rec.* III (1905–1906) 77–85, 97–104, 145–153; *New Hampshire Hist. Soc. Colls.* III (1832) 40–67.

1679

DANKERS (or Danckaerts), Jasper (*b.* 1639), and SLUYTER, Peter, of Wiewerd, Friesland, Labadists.

Travel journal, June 1679–October 1680; journey from Friesland to England, New York (New Netherland); in New York and vicinity, Delaware and Maryland, Hudson River country, Boston; return to Friesland. Seeking a site for a Labadist colony. Detailed but rather formalized accounts of travel and descriptions of country; lengthy and valuable account of the early colonial scene.

Translated and edited by Henry C. Murphy, *Memoirs Long Island Hist. Soc.* I (1867) 1–428; translated and edited by B. B. James and J. F. Jameson, *Journal of Jasper Danckaerts* (New York, 1913). Extract concerning Albany, *Munsell's Colls. on Hist. Albany* (Albany, 1867) II 358–373.

HOBART, David (*ca.* 1651–1717) of Hingham, Mass.

Private diary, March 1679–May 1740; brief notes of local, parish, and church affairs; the later entries are by his son Nehemiah.

Diary of William Bentley (Salem, 1911) III 284–286.

THACHER, Rev. Peter (1651–1727) of Milton, Mass.

Private diary, April 1679–February 1699 (with gap); brief but varied entries, partly in cipher; personal and local affairs of some interest; language interesting.

A. K. Teele, *The History of Milton, Mass.* (1887) App. B 641–657.

1681

MATHER, Rev. Cotton (1663–1728) of Boston.

Religious journal, March 1681–February 1724 (some gaps); religious work and experiences; very important, but the monotony of its endless introspection restricts its interest.

Massachusetts Hist. Soc. Colls. 7th Ser. VII, VIII (1911–1912); extracts relating to the *Magnalia, Massachusetts Hist. Soc. Proc.* 1st Ser. VI (1862–1863) 404–414; extracts relating to Calef, *ibid.* 1st Ser. III (1855–1858) 289–293.

1682

PIERPONT, Rev. Jonathan (1665–1709) of Reading, Mass.

Religious diary, July 1682–February 1707; brief, scattered, and rather dull personal and religious notes.

New England Hist. Geneal. Reg. XIII (1859) 255–258.

RUSSELL, Rev. Noadiah (1659–1713) of Harvard College and Middletown, Conn.

1. Tutor's diary, March 1682–March 1684; miscellaneous happenings at Harvard and elsewhere, fire at Harvard, supernatural incident; fairly interesting.

New England Hist. Geneal. Reg. VII (1853) 53–59.

2. Private diary, March 1687–February 1688; includes account of Andros and his taking over government of Connecticut.

Diary of the Reverend Noadiah Russell . . . , published by Connecticut Hist. Soc. (Hartford, 1934) 18 pp.

1683

KNEPP, John, of England.

Sea journal, September 1683–June 1684 (abstract); journey from England to Boston on H.M.S. "Rose"; stay in Boston, and return to England.

Frederick Lewis Gay, *A Rough List of a Collection of Transcripts Relating to the History of New England, 1630–1766* (Brookline, Mass., 1913) 135–139.

1684

VAUGHAN, Maj. William (1640–1719) of Portsmouth, N.H., merchant.

Prison diary, February–April 1684 (in a letter); trial and imprisonment at Great Island, N.H., for noncompliance; details of public affairs in New England and details of prison life; good narrative in literary style.

George E. Hodgdon, *Reminiscences and Genealogical Record of the Vaughan Family* (Rochester, N.Y., 1918) App. I 75–91.

1687

DUNLOP, Capt.

Sea journal, April 1687; voyage to the southward by periago [piragua, or pirogue], from Charlestown to St. Catherine's Island.

South Carolina Hist. Geneal. Mag. XXX (1929) 127–133.

1688

COIT, Mehetabel Chandler (1673–1758) of New London, Conn.

Private diary, May 1688–September (1749?); commonplace book and family notes, of genealogical interest.

Mehetabel Chandler Coit, Her Book, 1714 (Norwich, Conn., 1895) 5–12.

PYNCHON, Maj. John (*d.* 1705) of North Brookfield, Mass.

Diary and account book, August–September 1688 (extracts); measures against attack by Quabaug Indians; brief notes.

J. H. Temple, *History of North Brookfield* (North Brookfield, 1887) 140.

1689

BAYARD (or Beyard), Col. Nicholas (1644?–1707).

1. Military journal, June–July 1689; official notes of public matters, disturbances, and riots in New York; rather interesting.

E. B. O'Callaghan, *Docs. Rel. Col. Hist. State New York* III (1853) 599–604.

2. Military journal, February 1692 (with Charles Lodowick); French attempt on the Mohawk country.

A Narrative of an Attempt Made by the French of Canada ... (Boston, 1693) 14 pp. fol.; reprinted as *A Journal of the Late Actions of the French of Canada;* London edition reprinted (New York, 1868) 55 pp.; facsimile of first American edition edited by A. R. Hasse (New York, 1903).

3. Military journal, February–March 1693 (with Charles Lodowick); Governor Fletcher's expedition to New York frontier against French and Indians of Canada; brief military notes.

E. B. O'Callaghan, *Docs. Rel. Col. Hist. State New York* IV (1854) 14–16.

HOMES, Rev. William (1663–1746) of Chilmark, Mass.

Clergyman's journal, February 1689–June 1746 (extracts); weekly entries on sermons, church affairs, marriages, deaths, etc.

New England Hist. Geneal. Reg. XLVIII (1894) 446–453, XLIX(1895) 413–416, L (1896) 155–166.

KELSEY, Henry (1670?–1724?), governor of York Fort.

Fur trader's journal, June 1689–August 1721; journeys for Hudson's Bay Company in Canada, and work in fur trade; some accounts of Indian superstitions and customs; considerable human interest, and valuable as account of early exploration of Hudson's Bay country; many interesting spellings and an introduction in verse.

A. G. Doughty and C. Martin (eds.), *The Kelsey Papers* (*Pubs. Archives Canada,* Ottawa, 1929) 128 pp. Account of journal (1691–1692, Hudson's Bay to Saskatchewan River) by C. N. Bell, *Hist. Scientific Soc. Manitoba Trans.* n.s. No. 4 (1928) 43 pp.

NEWBERRY, Benjamin (1653–1711?) of Newport, R.I.

Private diary, August 1689–June 1706 (extracts); brief and dullish notes on religion and public alarms.

Mag. New England Hist. III (1893) 203–206.

1690

ANON.

Military journal, August–October 1690; narrative and journal of expedition against Quebec; some religious notes.

S. A. Green, *Two Narratives of the Expedition against Quebec,* A.D. *1690* (Cambridge, 1902) 27–42.

BULLIVANT, Dr. Benjamin, of Boston.

Private diary, February–May 1690; lengthy notes on public affairs in New England.

Massachusetts Hist. Soc. Proc. 1st Ser. XVI (1878) 103–108.

LYNDE, Benjamin (1666–1745) of Salem, Mass.

Private diary, August 1690–November 1742; brief notes of private affairs; mostly dull, but some interesting details of food and drink; some linguistic interest.

Fitch E. Oliver (ed.), *The Diaries of Benjamin Lynde and Benjamin Lynde, Jr.* (Boston, 1880) 251 pp.

NATSTO, Joshua, naval clerk.

Naval journal, April–May 1690; voyage and proceedings in expedition against Port Royal; ship movements.

A Journal of the Proceedings in the Late Expedition to Port-Royal (Boston, 1690) 3–8.

PHIPS, Sir William (1651–1695) of Boston.

Sea journal, August 1690–November 1691; notes on expedition against Quebec.

A Journal of the Proceedings in the Late Expedition to Port-Royal (Boston, 1690) 16 pp.

POTTER, Capt. Cuthbert (*d.* 1691) of Lancaster Co., Va.

Travel journal, July–September 1690; mediocre account of voyage from Virginia to New England and stay at Boston.

Calendar of State Papers, Col. Ser. 1690, 341–344; Newton D. Mereness, *Travels in the American Colonies* (New York, 1916) 3–11.

SCHUYLER, Capt. John (1668–1747) of Albany, N.Y.

1. Military journal, August 1690; activities of volunteers fighting in Canada. Translated from the Dutch.

E. B. O'Callaghan, *Doc. Hist. State New York* II (1850) 160–162; *New Jersey Hist. Soc. Proc.* I (1845) 72–74.

2. Travel journal, August–September 1698; report of journey to Canada and discussions with Frontenac, etc.

E. B. O'Callaghan, *Docs. Rel. Col. Hist. State New York* IV (1854) 404–406.

WALLEY, Maj. John (1644–1712) of London, Eng., and Bristol, Mass.

Military journal, September–October 1690; expedition against Quebec; long and pedestrian entries; fairly good but impersonal.

L. S. Mayo (ed.), *Hutchinson's History of the Colony and Province of Massachusetts Bay* (Cambridge, 1936) I, App.; also in Ernest Myrand, *Sir William Phipps devant Québec* (Quebec, 1893) and *Year-Book of Soc. Col. Wars in Massachusetts* No. 4 (1898) 116–130.

WINTHROP, Maj. Gen. Fitzjohn (1639–1707) of New London, Conn.

Military journal, July–September 1690; march from Albany to Canada; councils with Indians.

Massachusetts Hist. Soc. Colls. 5th Ser. VIII (1882) 312–318; *Calendar of State Papers,* Col. Ser. 1696, 117; E. B. O'Callaghan, *Docs. Rel. Col. Hist. State New York* IV (1854) 193–196.

1691

SCHUYLER, Maj. Peter (1657–1724) of Albany.

1. Military journal, June–August 1691; expedition against Canada; march from Albany to Chambly River; interesting details of raid.

2. Military journal, February 1693; notes of skirmishes and pursuit of French near Schenectady.

3. Treaty journal, January 1694; journey to Five Nations at Schenectady and negotiations.

4. Treaty journal, May–June 1698; journey with Dellius, and report of negotiations in Canada; discussions at Montreal with Frontenac.

5. Treaty journal, April–May 1711; negotiations with Onondaga Indians; minutes and speeches.

E. B. O'Callaghan, *Docs. Rel. Col. Hist. State New York* III (1853) 800–805, IV (1854) 16–19, 81–83, 347–351, V (1855) 245–249.

1693

WESSEL, Maj. Dirck.

1. Treaty journal, August 1693; embassy from New York to Onondaga, exchange of prisoners, negotiations and festivities; report.

2. Treaty journal, August–September 1698; negotiations with sachems of Five Nations.

E. B. O'Callaghan, *Docs. Rel. Col. Hist. State New York* IV (1854) 59–63, 372–374.

1694

COTTON, Hon. Josiah (1680–1756) of Plymouth, Mass.

Private diary, June 1694–July 1698; mostly reminiscences, but partly diary at Harvard; fairly interesting.

Pubs. Col. Soc. Massachusetts XXVI (1925) 277–280.

KELPIUS, Johannes (1673–1708) of Transylvania.

Travel journal, January–June 1694; journey of a German pietist to America; Pennsylvania; Germantown; religious notes.

Translated by J. F. Sachse, *Proc. and Addresses Pennsylvania German Soc.* XXV (1917) 11–28.

SCHUYLER, Capt. Arent.

Travel journal, February 1694?; report of journey to Minisinck country; brief, but with interesting spellings.

E. B. O'Callaghan, *Docs. Rel. Col. Hist. State New York* IV (1854) 98–99.

WADSWORTH, Rev. Benjamin (1670–1737), president of Harvard.

Travel diary, August 1694 (extract); journey from Boston to Albany to treat with Five Nations; fairly pleasant descriptions of journey and conference; amusing "literary" style.

Massachusetts Hist. Soc. Colls. 4th Ser. I (1852) 102–110.

1695

PAINE, Deacon John (1660–1731) of Eastham, Mass.

Private diary, 1695–1718; rather dull personal and religious notes in a flowery clerical style; interesting for its doggerel verses.

Mayflower Descendant VIII (1906) 180–184, 227–231, IX (1907) 49–51, 97–99, 136–140.

PRATT, Elder William (1659–1713) of Easton, Mass., and Dorchester, S.C.

Travel diaries, December 1695–June 1701 (extracts); miscellaneous notes of no great value; two voyages to South Carolina, and some odd items.

A. S. Salley (ed.), *Narratives of Early Carolina* (New York, 1911) 191–200; W. L. Chaffin, *History of Easton* (1886) 67–68.

1696

FLETCHER, Col. Benjamin, governor of New York.

Travel and treaty journal, September–October 1696 (kept by David Jamison); brief notes of journey to Albany, and negotiations for renewal of treaty with Five Nations; minutes and speeches.

E. B. O'Callaghan, *Docs. Rel. Col. Hist. State New York* IV (1854) 235–241; *A Journal of What Passed in the Expedition of His Excellency Col. Benjamin Fletcher* (New York, 1906) 11 pp.

RUDMAN, Rev. Andrew John (1668–1708) of Wilmington and Philadelphia.

Travel diary, July 1696–June 1697; journey from Stockholm to London, Virginia, Maryland; descriptions of places, religious observances, and life on board ship; fair interest. Swedish and English text.

Translated and edited by Luther Anderson, *German American Annals* VIII (1906) 282–312, 315–334, 355–376, IX (1907) 9–18.

1697

CARERI, Dr. Gemelli (1651–1725) of Naples.

Travel journal, 1697–1698; from the Philippines to America; hardships of a voyage of "204 days and 5 hours."

Originally published at Naples (1700) seven vols.; translated in Awnsham and John Churchill's *Collection of Voyages* (London, 1704) IV; undated extracts in *Jour. Amer. Hist.* II (1908) 579–586.

MARSHALL, John (1664–1732) of Braintree, Mass.

Private diary, January 1697–December 1711 (extracts); brief notes of personal, religious, and local affairs; deaths, notes on Indians; rather dull.

Massachusetts Hist. Soc. Proc. 2d Ser. I (1884–1885) 148–163; further extracts, *ibid.* 2d Ser. XIV (1900–1901) 16–34.

MINOR, Manasseh (1647–1728) of Stonington, Conn.

Personal diary, January 1697–April 1720 (with gaps); brief but extended notes of personal affairs and farming; linguistic interest.

F. D. Miner (ed.), *The Diary of Manasseh Minor* (Jersey City, 1915) 196 pp.

ROBERTS, Hugh (*d.* 1702) of Merion, Pa.

Travel diary, December 1697–March? 1698; voyage from Pennsylvania to England and Wales; brief and moderate interest.

Pennsylvania Mag. Hist. Biog. XVIII (1894) 199–205.

1699

ANON.

Military journal, February 1699; official journal "taken down upon order of Capt. Samuel Mason"; expedition from New London to settle unrest among Indians; carefully detailed.

Massachusetts Hist. Soc. Proc. 1st Ser. IX (1866–1867) 473–478.

BRATTLE, Rev. William (1662–1717) of Cambridge, Mass.

Clergyman's private diary, April 1699–March 1748; scattered brief notes of weather, farming, and gardening. (Diary continued by N. Appleton.)

Geneal. Mag. 4th Ser. I (1905–1906) 358–361.

CALLEY, Robert, of Charlestown, Mass.

Diary, 1699–1765; partly an earlier record of church affairs in Malden, and items of genealogical interest; author was cabinetmaker and schoolmaster.

New England Hist. Geneal. Reg. XVI (1862) 34–40, 129–133.

COOTE, Richard, Earl of Bellomont (1636–1701).

1. Travel journal, August–September 1699; journey from Boston to Rhode Island.

2. Conference journal, August–September 1700; conference with Indians at Albany.

Calendar of State Papers, Col. Ser. 1700, XVIII 584–591.

GLEN, Johannes.

Treaty journal, March–April 1699; with Nicholas Bleeker; negotiations with Indians at Onondaga. Translated from the Dutch.

E. B. O'Callaghan, *Docs. Rel. Col. Hist. State New York* IV (1854) 558–560, 562–563.

VIELE, Arnout Cornelisse (1640–1704?) of Albany.

Interpreter's journal, April–May 1699; journey from Long Island to Onondaga and Indian transactions there. Translated from the Dutch.

E. B. O'Callaghan, *Docs. Rel. Col. Hist. State New York* IV (1854) 560–562.

1700

BROWN, Rev. Richard (1675–1732) of Reading, Mass.

Clergyman's journal, February 1700–September 1719 (extracts); religious work, reflections and introspection; earlier autobiographical notes.

L. Eaton, *Genealogical History of the Town of Reading* (Boston, 1874) 53–55.

BRUGH, Peter van.

Treaty journal, September–October 1700; journey with Hendrik Hansen to Onondaga and negotiations with Indians.

E. B. O'Callaghan, *Docs. Rel. Col. Hist. State New York* IV (1854) 802–807.

DU RU, Paul (1666–1741), Jesuit missionary.

Travel and missionary journal, February–May 1700; Jesuit's journey from Biloxi Bay up the Mississippi, with events on journey. Translated from the French.

Journal of Paul du Ru (Chicago 1934) 74 pp.

GREEN, Rev. Joseph (1675–1715) of Salem, Mass.

Clergyman's diary, March 1700–June 1715; notes on local, church, family, and personal affairs; farming and weather; a pleasant local, social diary.

Essex Inst. Hist. Colls. VIII (1866) 215–224, X (1869) 73–104, XXXVI (1900) 325–330.

LAWSON, John (*d.* 1712) of New Bern, N.C., surveyor.

Travel journal, December 1700–(January 1701?); notes of a journey along the Catawba Path in North Carolina; journey of about a thousand miles; interesting descriptions of back country, and Indians and their customs. He was surveyor general of North Carolina.

First published in *A New Voyage to Carolina* (London, 1709); reprinted in Lawson's *History of Carolina* (London, 1714); *History* reprinted (Richmond, Va., 1937), journal on pp. 1–60.

ROMER, Col.

Treaty journal, September 1700; negotiations with Indians at Onondaga, etc. Translated from the Dutch.

E. B. O'Callaghan, *Docs. Rel. Col. Hist. State New York* IV (1854) 798–801.

BLEEKER, Capt. Johannes.   1701

Treaty journal, June 1701; journey with David Schuyler to Onondaga and negotiations with Indians.

E. B. O'Callaghan, *Docs. Rel. Col. Hist. State New York* IV (1854) 889–895. (See also 1699, GLEN.)

[MAHER, John, mate of sloop "Mary"?]

Sea journal, October–November 1701; voyage of the "Mary" from Quebec and account of her wreck off Montauk Point, L.I.

E. B. O'Callaghan (ed.), *Journal of the Voyage of the Sloop Mary* (Albany, 1866) 1–28.

MICHEL, Francis Louis, of Switzerland.

Travel journal, October 1701–December 1702; report, partly in narrative form, of journey from Berne to Virginia; interesting account of travel, geographical, social, and religious conditions. Translated from the German.

Virginia Mag. Hist. Biog. XXIV (1916) 1–43, 113–141, 275–288.

1702

KEITH, Rev. George, of Edburton, Sussex, Eng.

Missionary travel journal, April 1702–August 1704; voyage from England to Boston; travel and ministry among the Quakers in the American colonies, especially in New England and Pennsylvania; preaching, religious life and disputes, comments on clergymen, account of churches appended. Formal style, but useful account of early Quakers in New England.

A Journal of Travels (London, 1706) 92 pp.; reprinted in *Protestant Episc. Hist. Soc. Colls.* I (1851) 5–51.

SANDEL, Rev. Andreas, of Philadelphia.

Lutheran journal, March 1702–July 1719 (extracts); journal of the pastor of the Swedish Lutheran Church at Philadelphia; rather dull church affairs and visits, but an excellent ghost story. Translated from the Swedish.

Pennsylvania Mag. Hist. Biog. XXX (1906) 287–299, 445–452.

1703

CAMPBELL, John (1653–1728) of Boston.

Diary-letters, April–September 1703; news of public affairs at Boston and ship movements, written to Governor Winthrop of Connecticut; rather lively.

Massachusetts Hist. Soc. Proc. 1st Ser. IX (1866–1867) 485–501.

1704

HASTINGS, Dr. Thomas (1679–1728) of Hatfield, Mass.

Public journal, February 1704–May 1746; the town clerk's notes on Indian troubles: Queen Anne's War, Father Rasle's War, French and Indian War.

D. W. and R. F. Wells, *A History of Hatfield* (Springfield, 1910) 150–152.

HILTON, Maj. Winthrop (1671–1710) of Dover, N. H.

Military journal, February–March 1704; expedition against Indians to Saco River.

Maine Hist. Soc. Colls., Doc. Hist., 2d Ser. IX (1907) 140–142.

KNIGHT, Sarah Kemble (1666–1727) of Boston, schoolteacher.

Travel diary, October 1704–January 1705; journey from Boston to New York and back; remarkable for its lively descriptions, character sketches, conversation pieces, sharp-tongued wit, romanticism, and literariness; one of the best feminine diaries extant.

First published in *The Journals of Madame Knight and Rev. Mr. Buckingham* (New York, 1825) 1–70; separate editions (Albany, 1865, and Norwich, 1901); edited from MS (Boston, 1920, reprinted New York, 1935) by G. P. Winship, 72 pp. Extracts in most anthologies of American literature.

PALMER, ESTHER (*d.* 1714) of Flushing, L.I.

1. Quaker travel diary, 1704 (with Susanna Freeborn); from Rhode Island to Pennsylvania; rather dull itinerary but some interesting spellings.

2. Travel diary, 1705 (with Mary Lawson); from Philadelphia to Maryland, Virginia, Carolinas, and return to Philadelphia; similar to No. 1.

3. Travel diary, 1705 (with Mary Banister); in Maryland and Virginia; similar to No. 1.

Jour. Friends' Hist. Soc. (London) VI (1909) 38–40, 63–71, 133–139.

SHARPE, Rev. John (*b.* 1680).

Clergyman's journal, March 1704–March 1713 (with prior autobiographical entries); line-a-day notes of clerical work; rather dull.

Pennsylvania Mag. Hist. Biog. XL (1916) 257–297, 412–425.

1707

BARNARD, Rev. John (1681–1770) of Marblehead, Mass.

1. Diary, May–July 1707; experiences with French and Indians at Port Royal.
Massachusetts Hist. Soc. Colls. 3d Ser. V (1836) 191–195; W. A. Calzek, *History of the County of Annapolis, N.S.* (Toronto, 1897) 54–58.

2. Travel diary, August–November 1710; trip from England to Boston.
Massachusetts Hist. Soc. Colls. 3d Ser. V (1836) 211–212; *Congregational Quar.* IV (1926) 380–381.

1708

MAY, John (1686–1770) of East Woodstock, Conn.

Private diary, December 1708–May 1717 (extracts); very brief notes of work, farming, building, etc., and some local items.
Lyman M. Paine, *My Ancestors* (1914) 94–96.

1709

BALDWIN, William (1677–1720) of Marsden, Lancs, Eng.

Travel diary beginning March 1709; southern states and New England.
Abstract in *Jour. Friends' Hist. Soc.* XV (1918) 27–30.

BYRD, William (1674–1744) of Westover, Va.

1. Private diary, February 1709–September 1712; a detailed daily record of the life of a Virginia gentleman; manners, customs, politics, domestic affairs, and above all, his personal life; an interesting diary, sometimes almost a Virginia counterpart to Sewall's diary, but often dull. Kept in shorthand.
Louis B. Wright and Marion Tinling (eds.), *The Secret Diary of William Byrd of Westover 1709–1712* (Richmond, Va., 1941) 622 pp.

2. Secret journal, February–November 1728; running the dividing line between Virginia and North Carolina; this journal, a kind of veiled narrative, is the basis for the later *History of the Dividing Line,* and it contains some rather outspoken material omitted in the *History*.
William K. Boyd (ed.),*William Byrd's Histories of the Dividing Line Betwixt Virginia and North Carolina* (Raleigh, 1929) 13–325; the journal and the *History* are printed in parallel texts.

3. Private diary, August 1739–August 1741; similar to No. 1; very formal and rather dull.
Maude H. Woodfin (ed.), *Another Secret Diary of William Byrd of Westover, 1739–1741* (Richmond, Va., 1942). 490 pp.

HOLYOKE, Rev. Edward (1689–1769) of Marblehead, president of Harvard.

Private diary, April 1709–December 1768; line-a-day notes of personal, religious, and Harvard matters; fair interest.
G. F. Dow (ed.), *The Holyoke Diaries* (Salem, 1911) 1–30.

ANON.   1710

Military journal, 1710; expedition against Port Royal under General Nicholson.
Journal of an Expedition Performed by the Forces of Our Sovereign (London, 1711) 24 pp.

ANON. (English).

Military journal, July–September 1710; expedition from Massachusetts against Port Royal; articles of capitulation given.
Year-Book Soc. Col. Wars in Massachusetts III (1897) 84–94.

BUCKINGHAM, Rev. Thomas (1671–1731) of Hartford, Conn.

1. Chaplain's journal, October–November 1710; naval expedition against Port Royal; brief entries of moderate interest.

2. Chaplain's journal, August–October 1711; expedition against Crown Point.
The Journals of Madam Knight and Rev. Mr. Buckingham (New York, 1825) 71–129; reprinted in *The Roll and Journal of Connecticut Service in Queen Anne's War* (Acorn Club Pubs. XIII, New Haven, 1917) 12–43.

FARWELL, Joseph (*b.* 1696) of Groton, Mass.

Private diary, 1710–1775; a few scattered, brief, and dullish notes of private, church, and war matters.
New England Hist. Geneal. Reg. XXXV (1881) 275–276; John D. Farwell, *The Farwell Family* (n.p., 1929) I 72–73.

NICHOLSON, Gen. Sir Francis (1660–1728) of Boston and England.

Military journal, July–October 1710; expedition against Port Royal; daily happenings in siege, mixed with letters and orders.
Journal of an Expedition (London, 1711); *Nova Scotia Hist. Soc. Colls.* I (1879) 59–104.

WEISER, Conrad (1696–1760) *b.* Germany, of Schoharie, N.Y., and Lancaster Co., Pa.; official interpreter for Pennsylvania.

1. Journal, 1710; translated from the German.
Olde Ulster II (1906) 199–204, 229.

2. Travel journal, February–October 1737; from Tulpehocken to Onondaga.
Pennsylvania Hist. Soc. Colls. I (1853) 6–33.

3. Travel journal, January–February 1743; to Shamokin, with reports of negotiations with Indians.
Col. Recs. Pennsylvania IV 640–646.

4. Travel journal, July–August 1743; to Onondaga.
Ibid. IV 660–669.

5. Travel journal, May 1744; to Shamokin.
Ibid. IV 680–685.

6. Travel journal, August–October 1748; journey to the Ohio.
Ibid. V. 348–358; *Pennsylvania Hist. Soc. Colls.* I (1853) 23–33; R. G.

Thwaites (ed.), *Early Western Travels* (Cleveland, 1904) I 21–44; *Early History of Western Pennsylvania* (Pittsburgh, 1846) App. 23–33.

7. Travel journal, August–September 1750; to Onondaga.

Col. Recs. Pennsylvania V 470–480.

8. Journal at Onondaga, June–July 1751.

Ibid. V 541–543.

9. Travel journal, July–August 1753; from Heidelberg, Berks Co., to Mohawks, and negotiations.

E. B. O'Callaghan, *Docs. Rel. Col. Hist. State New York* VI (1855) 795–799; *Col. Recs. Pennsylvania* V 642–647.

10. Journey to Aucquick (Auckwick?), August–September 1754.

Col. Recs. Pennsylvania VI 150–160.

11. Treaty journal, January 1756; proceedings with Indians at John Harris' Ferry.

Ibid. VII 33–35.

12. Journal, November 1756 (extract); concerning Indians at Bethlehem and Easton.

Pennsylvania Archives 1st Ser. III 32–33.

13. Journal at Fort Allen, November 1756.

Ibid. 1st Ser. III 66–68.

Most of the diaries of Conrad Weiser are reprinted in: C. Z. Weiser, *The Life of (John) Conrad Weiser* (Reading, Pa., 1876), and William M. Beauchamp, *Life of Conrad Weiser* (Syracuse, 1925).

1711

BARNWELL, Capt. John (*d.* 1724) of South Carolina.

Scouting journal, January–May 1711; letters describing expeditions against Tuscarora Indians.

Virginia Mag. Hist. Biog. V (1897–1898) 391–402, VI (1898–1899) 42–55; *South Carolina Hist. Geneal. Mag.* IX 28–54.

CRANE, Benjamin (*ca.* 1656–1721) of Berkeley, Mass.

Surveyor's journal; January 1711–July 1721 (extensive fragment); surveying and statistical notes at New Bedford, Dartmouth, etc.

The Field Notes of Benjamin Crane, Benjamin Hammond, and Samuel Smith (New Bedford, 1910) 1–618.

HEMPSTEAD, Joshua (1678–1758) of New London, Conn.

Farming diary, September 1711–November 1758; mainly local, personal, business, and farming notes; journey from New London to Maryland; mainly brief notes, but its lengthy span and details make it an interesting and valuable diary of farming life.

New London County Hist. Soc. Colls. I (1901) 750 pp.

SPOTSWOOD, Alexander (1676–1740), lieutenant governor of Virginia.

Travel journal, 1711–1717; travels and expeditions in the public service; single entry for each journey, with distances, statistics, etc.; very dull.

William and Mary Coll. Quar. 2d Ser. III (1923) 40–45.

VETCH, Gov. Samuel (1668–1732) of Boston and Nova Scotia.

Sea journal, July–October 1711; expedition from Boston to Quebec in fleet commanded by Sir Hovenden Walker; brief but fairly good.

Nova Scotia Hist. Soc. Colls. IV (1884) 105–110.

WALKER, Adm. Sir Hovenden (*ca.* 1656–1726) of Ireland.

Naval journal, April–October 1711; expedition from Boston to Quebec, and appendix of orders, etc.

A Journal; or Full Account of the Late Expedition to Canada (London, 1720) 304 pp.

1712

EDWARDS, Rev. Timothy (1669–1758) of East Windsor, Conn.

Diary, August 1712–April 1724; scattered extracts from his notebook; purchases, and domestic and family notes.

Yale Review n.s. XV (1926) 621–624.

SEWALL, Samuel, Jr. (1678–1750) of Brookline, Mass.

1. Travel journal, October 1712; trip from Boston to Martha's Vineyard; visits and stages.

New England Hist. Geneal. Reg. XVIII (1864) 74–75.

2. Private diary, January–December 1714; brief notes of weather, and local and personal affairs.

Massachusetts Hist. Soc. Proc. 2d Ser. VIII (1892–1894) 221–225.

1713

GRIFFITH, John (1713–1776) of Chelmsford, Eng., and Darby, Pa.

Quaker autobiography and journal, 1713–1770; journeys and meetings in New England and Pennsylvania.

A Journal of the Life, Travels, and Labours in the Ministry of John Griffith (London, 1779; Philadelphia, 1780) 426 pp; reprinted *Friends' Library* V (Philadelphia, 1842) 329–468.

HANSEN, Hendrik.

Treaty journal, September 1713; mission with John Bleeker and Lowrens Clasen to Onondaga; journey to Oneida, negotiations, and speeches; translated from the Dutch.

E. B. O'Callaghan, *Docs. Rel. Col. Hist. State New York* V (1855) 372–376.

MAYHEW, Rev. Experience (1673–1758) of Martha's Vineyard, Mass.

Missionary journals, 1713–1714; missionary visits to Indians; seminarrative.

In *Some Correspondence between the ... New England Company in London and the Commissioners of the United Colonies in America* (London, 1896) 97–127.

STODDARD, Capt. John (1681–1748) of Northampton, Mass.

Journal, November 1713–September 1714; negotiations with the Governor General of Canada; full entries of discussions, and letters; moderate general interest.

New England Hist. Geneal. Reg. V (1851) 26–42.

1714

FONTAINE, John (*b.* 1693) of Taunton, Eng., and Virginia.

Travel diary, December 1714–December 1718; journey from England to America, trading and travel in Virginia; notes on colonial and Indian customs, scenery, coffee houses, clubs, religious practices; rare contemporary account of Spotswood's expedition; a well-written and interesting diary.

Ann Maury, *Memoirs of a Huguenot Family* (New York, 1852) 247–310.

CAPON, Peter, of Bordeaux.   # 1715

Sea journal, August–November 1715; from Annapolis Royal to Cape Breton to investigate Indian depredations.

Hist. Mag. 3d Ser. III (1875) 18–20.

COOPER, Rev. William (1693–1743) of Boston.

Clergyman's journals, February 1715–December 1730 (extracts); church and personal affairs, and notes of sermons; extracts of genealogical interest.

New England Hist. Geneal. Reg. XXX (1876) 435–441, XXXI (1877) 49–55.

MASON, Joseph (*d.* 1761) of Warren, Mass.

Private diaries, April 1715–November 1794 (latter part by his son Marmaduke); brief, erratic extracts of genealogical interest, and notes of public affairs.

A. H. Mason, *Genealogy of the Sampson Mason Family* (East Braintree, 1902) 49–56.

READING, John.

Surveying journals, April–June 1715, May 1716, June–July 1716; survey notes and statistics; a very good section describes the adventures of the surveyors.

New Jersey Hist. Soc. Proc. 3d Ser. X (1915) 35–46, 90–110, 128–133.

1716

BODFISH, Mrs. Mercy Goodwin (1752–1803) of Pownalborough, Me.

Private diary, January 1716–1816; scattered extracts of births, marriages, deaths, genealogy of her family, some personal notes; interesting spellings.

New England Hist. Geneal. Reg. LXVII (1913) 28–32.

PAINE, Moses (1695–1764) of Truro, Mass.

Private diary, May 1716–July 1719 (extracts); very brief entries about family affairs, weather, etc.; little value.

New England Hist. Geneal. Reg. LIV (1900) 87–88.

1717

BAXTER, Rev. Joseph (1676–1745) of Medfield, Mass.

Missionary journal, August 1717–September 1721; kept while author was missionary to Indians at Arrowsic Island, Me.; mainly notes of where he preached, but some interesting notes on travel, Indians, and missionary rivalry.

New England Hist. Geneal. Reg. XXI (1867) 46–59.

KNIGHT, Capt. James (*d.* 1720?) of York Fort.

Fur trader's journal, July–September 1717; voyage from York Fort to Churchill River to found a post for Hudson's Bay Company; excellent daily narrative of dangers, hardships, and daily life.

James F. Kenney, *The Founding of Churchill* (Toronto and London, 1932) 111–189.

1718

FRANKLIN, Benjamin (1650–1727) of Boston.

Antiquarian diary, 1718–May 1724; a few almanac and commonplace-book jottings; antiquarian notes about Boston by uncle of Benjamin Franklin.

Pubs. Col. Soc. Massachusetts X (1904–1906) 191–205.

HADWEN, Isaac (1687–1737) of Sedbergh, Eng.

Quaker travel journal, March 1718–May 1719 (extracts); brief scattered notes of travel to and in the American colonies; rather dull subject-matter but many interesting spellings.

Bull. Friends' Hist. Soc. Philadelphia XV (1926) 29–31.

WIEGNER, Christopher (*ca.* 1712–1746) of Germany, and Towamencin, Pa.

Religious diary, 1718–1739; account of and few extracts from a diary of religious introspection, etc.

Montgomery County Hist. Soc. Sketches (Pa.) III (1905) 271–289.

1719

DES URSINS (French intendant of the Illinois country).

Travel journal, June 1719; Kaskaskia to Mine la Motte (lead mines in what is now Madison Co., Mo.); official report and descriptions. Translated.

Missouri Hist. Rev. XX (1925–1926) 205–207.

FISKE, Rev. Samuel (1689–1770) of Salem, Mass.

Clergyman's journal, March 1719–March 1721 (extracts); rather dull notes of church and local affairs, and notes of preaching.

Essex Inst. Hist. Colls. LI (1915) 282–289.

CLAWSON, Lawrence. 1720

Interpreter's journal, April–May 1720; journey to Niagara country and negotiations with Senecas.

E. B. O'Callaghan, *Docs. Rel. Col. Hist. State New York* V (1855) 550–551.

DEXTER, Rev. Samuel (1700–1755) of Dedham, Mass.

Private diary, July 1720–December 1752; occasional entries of private and public affairs; long descriptions of deaths and an earthquake; a pleasant diary of clerical life, mainly at Medford.

New England Hist. Geneal. Reg. XIII (1859) 305–310, XIV (1860) 35–40, 107–112, 202–205.

LORD, Rev. Joseph (1670–1748) of Chatham, Mass.

Diary, 1720–1748 (extracts); "they are a wonder" (H. M. Dexter).

Yarmouth Register, December 17, 1846. [Forbes.]

MOODY, Rev. Joseph, "Handkerchief" (1700–1753) of York, Me.

Clergyman's journal, August 1720–November 1724 (mostly in Latin cipher); brief and poor entries; marriages, deaths, a few general entries of weather, Indians, pirates, etc.

Maine Hist. Soc. Colls. 2d Ser. III (1892) 317–324.

RHODES, John (*b.* 1658) of Newport, R. I.

Private diary, October 1720–July 1731; very brief extracts of personal and public matters, and recipes.

Newport Hist. Mag. I (1880–1881) 234.

SCHUYLER, Myndert.

Treaty journal, April–May 1720; with Robert Livingston; negotiations with Senecas at Albany; minutes and speeches.

E. B. O'Callaghan, *Docs. Rel. Col. Hist. State New York* V (1855) 542–545.

WOOLMAN, John (1720–1772) of Mount Holly, N. J.

Quaker autobiography and journal, June 1720–April 1772; personal life, religious work and travels; journey to England in 1772.

The Works of John Woolman (Philadelphia, 1774) Part I; best edition is A. M. Gummere, *Journal and Essays of John Woolman, 1720–72* (New York, 1922) 151–333.

1721

FOTHERGILL, Rev. John (1676–1744) of Wensleydale, Yorkshire.

Quaker travel journal, July 1721–August 1722, and July 1736–November 1737 (these are the American sections); visits to Quaker meetings in America, travel in most of the Atlantic states; conventional journal of a ministering Quaker.

Friends' Library XIII (Philadelphia, 1849) 378–396, 418–425.

LYNDE, Benjamin, Jr. (1700–1781) of Salem, Mass.

Private diary, April 1721–April 1780; apparently summarized from almanacs; dull notes of personal affairs.

Fitch E. Oliver (ed.), *The Diaries of Benjamin Lynde and of Benjamin Lynde, Jr.* (Boston, 1880) 251 pp.

SMITH, Rev. Thomas (1702–1795) of Falmouth (later Portland), Me.

Clergyman's diary, May 1721–May 1788; mostly brief, impersonal notes, but its span and consistency make it a valuable New England record of foreign and domestic news, especially at Falmouth.

William Willis (ed.), *Journals of the Rev. Thomas Smith and the Rev. Samuel Deane* (Portland, 1849) 39–284.

1722

ASHTON, Philip (1703–1746) of Marblehead, Mass.

Captive's journal, June 1722–April 1725; or rather, a narrative with daily entries; account of capture by pirates and life on a desert island; a highly interesting story of an unwilling pirate and a new Robinson Crusoe.

Ashton's Memorial (Boston, 1725); reprinted in B. F. Dow and J. H. Edmonds, *Pirates of the New England Coast, 1630–1730* (Salem, 1923) 218–269; shortened version in Ralph D. Paine, *Ships and Sailors of Old Salem* (New York, 1909) 46–59.

BLANCHARD, Joshua (1692–1748) of Boston.

Private diary, 1722–1730; brief yearly entries of family affairs and principal public events in Boston.

New England Mag. n.s. XIII (1895–1896) 396–398 ("The Builder of the Old South Meeting-House").

BUMSTEAD, Jeremiah (1678–1729) of Boston.

Private diary, January 1722–December 1727 (with gaps); brief notes of Boston news; births, deaths, and marriages; interesting language.

New England Hist. Geneal. Reg. XV (1861) 193–204, 305–315.

COGAN, Capt. John (*b.* 1699) of East Sudbury, Mass.

Scouting journal, September–October 1722; brief notes of expedition to Pigwacket, and vain search for Indians.

New England Hist. Geneal. Reg. XXXIV (1880) 382–383.

COMER, Rev. John (1704–1734) of Newport, R.I.

Baptist journal, February 1722–March 1734 (with autobiographical notes from birth); brief impersonal notes of religious and public affairs, providences, preaching; interesting language.

Rhode Island Hist. Soc. Colls. VIII (1893) 132 pp.

D'ARTAGUIETTE, Diron, inspector for Western Company in Louisiana.

Travel journal, September 1722–September 1723; from New Orleans up the Mississippi to the Illinois country; report on conditions in the country, complaints, etc.; some notes on travel difficulties and personal affairs; fairly interesting. Translated from the French.

Newton D. Mereness, *Travels in the American Colonies* (New York, 1916) 17–92.

EDWARDS, Rev. Jonathan (1703–1758) of Northampton, Mass.

Religious journal, December 1722–June 1735; religious meditations and self-analysis, spiritual life and resolutions.

Sereno E. Dwight, *The Life of President Edwards* (New York, 1830) 74–106.

JOHNSON, Rev. Samuel (1696–1772) of West Haven, Conn.

Travel diary, October 1722–November 1723 (extracts); visit to England.

E. Edwards Beardsley, *Life and Correspondence of Samuel Johnson* (New York, 1874) 18–53.

TAITT, David.

Travel journal, January–June 1722; from Pensacola to and through the country of the Upper and Lower Creeks; arranging secession of land on Scamba River; brief travel notes, and longer notes of meetings with Indians about Tucka-batchi, etc.; good descriptions of Indian ceremonies.

Newton D. Mereness, *Travels in the American Colonies* (New York, 1916) 497–565.

1723

ELIOT, Rev. Jacob (1700–1766) of Boston.

Clergyman's diary, September 1723–September 1764; scattered extracts on weather and on personal and miscellaneous affairs.

Hist. Mag. n.s. V (1869) 33–35.

FAIRBANK, Lieut. Jabez (*ca.* 1674–1758) of Lancaster, Mass.

Scouting journal, December 1723–April 1724; scouting expeditions from Lancaster sent out by Fairbank; brief notes of movements.

Henry S. Nourse (ed.), *The Early Records of Lancaster* (Lancaster, 1884) 218–220.

HAMMOND, Benjamin (1673–1747) of Rochester, Mass.

Surveyor's journal, January 1723–June 1741; field notes around New Bedford.

The Field Notes of Benjamin Crane, Benjamin Hammond, and Samuel Smith (New Bedford, 1910) 647–659.

MOULTON, Capt. Jeremiah (*b.* 1688) of York, Me.

Scouting journal, May–June 1723; expedition to York; brief and dull notes.

Maine Hist. Geneal. Recorder I (1884) 204–207.

PECKER, Capt. Daniel (1690–1750) of Haverhill, Mass.

Scouting journal, November–December 1723; brief notes of expedition to New Hampshire; stages of march.

William B. Trask (ed.), *Letters of Col. Thomas Westbrook and Others* (Boston, 1901) 187–188.

SAYWARD, Joseph (1684–1741) of York, Me.

Scouting diary, November–December 1723; very brief notes of expedition to Salmon Falls River, Me., under Capt. Bragdon.

Charles A. Sayward, *The Sayward Family* (Ipswich, 1890) 49–50.

WESTBROOK, Capt. Thomas (*d.* 1744) of Portsmouth, N.H.

Military journal, May–June 1723; at garrisons in Maine; notes of executive work in camp, sickness, etc.

William B. Trask (ed.), *Letters of Col. Thomas Westbrook and Others* (Boston, 1901) 16–26.

1724

BARLOW, Jonathan, of Newport, R.I.

Seaman's journal, June 1724–January 1725; notes on personal affairs and adventures, by a sailor captured by pirates.

New England Quar. II (1929) 658–663.

BROWN, Sergt. Allison, of Arundel, Me.

Military journal, May 1724; brief notes of a march to Saco River and Arundel.

William B. Trask (ed.), *Letters of Col. Thomas Westbrook and Others* (Boston, 1901) 58–59.

JEFFRY, James (*ca.* 1706–1755) of Salem, Mass.

1. Private diary, January–December 1724; line-a-day entries of personal and local affairs; subject matter poor, but some linguistic interest.

2. Private diary, January 1727–September 1749; scattered extracts of local and personal notes.

Essex Inst. Hist. Colls. II (1860) 64–67, XXXVI (1900) 331–338.

KELLOGG, Capt. Joseph (1691–1756) of Northfield, Mass.

Scouting journal, November–December 1724; very brief notes of stages of expedition.

J. H. Temple and G. Sheldon, *A History of the Town of Northfield* (Albany, 1875) 207.

SIMMONS, Nicholas, of Newport, R.I.

Seaman's journal, 1724–January 1725; notes on personal affairs and adventures of a sailor captured by pirates.

New England Quar. II (1929) 658–669.

SKINNER, Richard (*ca.* 1666–1727) of Marblehead, Mass.

Diary, March 1724–November 1725; notes from family Bible; sermons and odd family items.

New England Hist. Geneal. Reg. LIV (1900) 413–415.

WARNER, Sergt. Eleazar (1687–1776) of Brookfield, Mass.

Scouting journals, April 1724–July 1725; military service near Brookfield; very brief notes of guards and marches.

J. H. Temple, *History of North Brookfield* (North Brookfield, 1887) 204–205.

WHEELWRIGHT, Capt. Samuel (*b.* 1692) of Wells, Me.

Scouting journal, November–December 1724; very brief notes of expedition to Pigwacket in search of Indians.

E. E. Bourne, *The History of Wells and Kennebunk* (Portland, 1875) 323; H. M. Sylvester, *Indian Wars of New England* (Boston, 1910) III 245–246.

WRIGHT, Capt. Samuel (1670–1740) of Rutland, Mass.

Scouting journals, November 1724–June 1725, June–November 1725; brief notes on expeditions around Rutland.

Worcester Soc. Antiq. Proc. VII (1885) 53–61.

1725

ATKINSON, Hon. Theodore (1697–1779) of Portsmouth, N.H.

Indian commissioner's travel journal, January–May 1725; journey from Portsmouth to Montreal; visits to Indians and captives; treaty with the French Mohawks; interesting spellings.

Edited by G. A. Gordon, *Register Soc. Col. Wars New Hampshire* (Concord, 1907) 25–53.

BLANCHARD, Col. Joseph (1704–1758) of Dunstable, N.H.

Scouting journal, July–August 1725; march from Dunstable to Penacook Falls and back in search of Indians; brief and dull.

New England Hist. Geneal. Reg. VII (1853) 184.

CHICKEN, Col. George, Indian commissioner in South Carolina.

Travel journal, June–October 1725; visit to Cherokees; largely negotiations and reports of talks; letters, etc.

Newton D. Mereness, *Travels in the American Colonies* (New York, 1916) 97–172. Extracts in S. C. Williams, *Early Travels in the Tennessee Country* (Johnson City, 1928) 97–104.

FITCH, Capt. Tobias, Indian commissioner.

Travel journal, June–December 1725; journey to Creek Indians in Alabama; negotiations and lengthy reports mainly in direct speech; some interesting language.

Newton D. Mereness, *Travels in the American Colonies* (New York, 1916) 176–212.

LOVEWELL, Capt. John (1691–1725) of Dunstable, Mass.

Military journal, January–February 1725; notes of the second campaign against the Indians.

Frederic Kidder, *Expeditions of Capt. John Lovewell* (Boston, 1865), reprinted with slight revisions in *Mag. Hist.* Extra No. 5 (New York, 1909) 16–18; *New England Hist. Geneal. Reg.* VII (1853) 62–63.

TYNG, Capt. Eleazar (1690–1782) of Chelmsford, Mass.

Scouting journal, March–April 1725; brief notes of scouting in Lovewell's War; stages about Penacook, etc.

Granite Monthly XV (1893) 183–186.

WHITE, Capt. John (1684–1725) of Lancaster, Mass.

Scouting journals, February–August 1725; first with Lovewell; marches from Groton to Contookook, etc., notes on weather; interesting spellings.

Henry S. Nourse, *The Early Records of Lancaster, Massachusetts* (Lancaster, 1884) 230–234; *Granite Monthly* XIV (1892) 207–209.

WILLARD, Col. Samuel (1690–1752) of Lancaster, Mass.

Scouting journals, July–October 1725; brief notes of distances and Indian affairs; language interesting.

Henry S. Nourse, *The Early Records of Lancaster, Massachusetts* (Lancaster, 1884) 237–242.

WRIGHT, Capt. Benjamin (1660–1743) of Northfield, Mass.

Scouting journal, July–September 1725; expedition to Lake Champlain; brief notes of marches, etc.

J. H. Temple and G. Sheldon, *A History of the Town of Northfield* (Albany, 1875) 210–212.

1726

FRANKLIN, Benjamin (1706–1790) of Philadelphia.

1. Travel diary, July–October 1726; "Journal of Occurences in my Voyage to Philadelphia on board The Berkshire, Henry Clark, Master, from London." Descriptions of Portsmouth, Cowes, Newport, etc.; life at sea, and interesting observations of natural phenomena.

A. H. Smyth (ed.), *The Writings of Benjamin Franklin* (New York, 1907) II 53–86.

2. Personal diary, October 1778, with three later entries, January 14 and February 28, 1779, and January 16, 1780; notes on his health in France; illnesses, and treatment for them.

E. E. Hale and E. E. Hale, Jr., *Franklin in France* (Boston, 1887–1888) 246–250.

3. "Part of a Journal," December 1780–January 1781; primarily notes on political activities in France; commercial entanglements.

Ibid. 437–446; Franklin's *Works,* ed. Bigelow (New York, 1888) VII 172–183.

4. Political journal, March–July 1782; negotiations for peace with Great Britain; letters and documents included.

Smyth (ed.), *Writings* VIII 459–560; Bigelow (ed.), *Works* VIII 1–118.

GODDARD, Edward (1675–1754) *b.* Watertown, Mass., of Boston.

Official treaty journal, July–August 1726; peace commission to eastern Indians; journey, proceedings, treaty in Maine, some social items.

Pubs. Col. Soc. Massachusetts XX (1917–1919) 128–147.

WAINWRIGHT, John (1690–1721) of Haverhill, Mass.

Surveying journal, May 10–21, 1726; journey from Haverhill of a committee to lay out lands in Penacook.

Nathaniel Bouton, *The History of Concord* (Concord, 1856) 64–77.

1727

LANE, Joshua (*d.* 1766) of Hampton, Mass.

Private diary, January 1727–December 1755 (MS dates); religious activities and reflections, providences, local and family affairs; account and a few brief extracts.

James P. Lane, *Lane Families of the Massachusetts Bay Colony* (n.p., 1886) 50–53.

WHIPPLE, Rev. Joseph (1701–1757) of Hampton Falls, N.H.

Clergyman's journal, January 1727–October 1754; brief notes of church events and proceedings.

Warren Brown, *History of the Town of Hampton Falls* (Manchester, N.H., 1900) 33–40.

1728

BUSS, Stephen (1718–1790) of Leominster, Mass.

Private diary, June 1728–December 1762; church affairs, necrology, and local history; brief extracts.

R. P. Stebbins, *Centennial Discourse* (Leominster, 1843) 90.

WALKER, Dr. Benjamin, of Boston, shopkeeper.

Private diary, July 1728–July 1729; extracts relating to Governor Burnet; rather good picture of official ceremonies.

Pubs. Col. Soc. Massachusetts XXVIII (1930–1933) 238–244.

WHITE, Timothy (1700–1765) of Nantucket, Mass.

Missionary journal, July 1728–February 1756; very brief notes of missionary work among Indians, school accounts, etc.

Bull. Nantucket Hist. Assoc. I (1898) No. 2, 15–26.

WOODBRIDGE, Dr. Dudley (1705–1790) of Groton and Stonington, Conn.

Travel diary, October 1728; journey from Cambridge in Massachusetts; long entries; stages and scenery.

Massachusetts Hist. Soc. Proc. 1st Ser. XVII (1879–1880) 337–340.

1729

CLINTON, Charles.

Travel journal, May–October 1729 (brief extracts); voyage from Ireland to Pennsylvania; list of deaths.

Pennsylvania Mag. Hist. Biog. XXVI (1902) 112–114.

FESSENDEN, Rev. Benjamin (1701–1746) of Sandwich, Mass.

Diary, June–October 1729 (extracts); brief entries, mostly about building his house.

New England Hist. Geneal. Reg. XIII (1859) 31–33.

SANFORD, William (1676–1760) of Portsmouth, R.I.

Diary, January–October 1729; very brief almanac entries; mostly necrology, births, etc.

Pubs. Col. Soc. Massachusetts VII (1900–1902) 198–202.

1730

CORSE (or Cross), James (1694–1783) of Deerfield, Mass.

Travel diary, April 1730; brief account of trader's journey on the old Crown Point road, from Fort Dummer to Lake Champlain.

Black River Gazette (Ludlow, Vt.) August 5, 1870; George Sheldon, *A History of Deerfield, Massachusetts* (Deerfield, 1895) I 518; *Manchester Hist. Assoc. Colls.* IV (1908–1910) 235–236; *Vermont Hist. Soc. Proc.* II (1931) 165–167.

CUMING, Sir Alexander (1692–1775) of Scotland.

Travel diary, March–April 1730; from Charleston, S.C., to the Cherokees; with an account of these Indians.

Historical Register (London) LXI (1731) 1–18; S. C. Williams (ed.), *Early Travels in the Tennessee Country* (Johnson City, 1928) 115–143.

ROBBINS, Rev. Philemon (1709–1781) of Branford, Conn.

Clergyman's journal, November 1730–August 1745; a very few notes of religious and parish affairs, and family matters; worthless extracts.

E. D. and G. S. Dickerman, *Dickerman Genealogy* (New Haven, 1922) 510–511.

1731

HALE, Robert (1703–1767) of Beverly, Mass.

Sea journals, June 1731–September 1732 (with gaps); journeys to Maine and Nova Scotia; mainly descriptions of scenery, character and habits of people, and stopping places; fairly good.

Essex Inst. Hist. Colls. XLII (1906) 217–241.

1732

TUDOR, Deacon John (1709–1795) of Boston.

Private diary, June 1732–October 1793; occasional entries of private and public affairs; war, riots, weather, massacre; long span and fairly interesting.

William Tudor (ed.), *Deacon Tudor's Diary* (Boston, 1896) 110 pp.

YEAMANS, John (*d.* 1749) of Noddle's Island, Mass.

Political diary, November 1732–May 1733; brief parliamentary notes on progress of sugar bill.

William H. Sumner, *A History of East Boston* (Boston, 1858) 724–729.

ANON.   1733

Travel journal, 1733–1734; voyage to Georgia, travels in the Carolinas; semi-narrative.

A New Voyage to Georgia (London, 1735, reprinted 1737) 62 pp.; reprinted *Georgia Hist. Soc. Colls.* II (1842) 37–60.

ANON.

Travel journal, April–September 1733; journey of Schwenckenfelders to Pennsylvania; Rotterdam, Plymouth, Philadelphia; usual descriptions and sailing details.

Pennsylvania Mag. Hist. Biog. X (1886) 167–179.

ANON.   1734

Travel diary, November 1734; voyage from Red Bank, N.J., to New York City (six days); loading goods; return; fair interest.

John E. Stillwell, *Hist. and Geneal. Misc.* I (New York, 1903) 222–224.

BOLZIUS (or Boltzius), Rev. John Martin (1703–1765) *b.* Germany, Lutheran
pastor.

Travel diary, March–May 1734 (extract); with the Salzburgers led by Von Reck, from Charleston to Ebenezer, Ga.; descriptions of scenery, religious and moral observations.

First printed in *An Extract of the Journals of Mr. Commissary Von Reck ... and the Rev. Mr. Bolzius* (London, 1734); reprinted in Peter Force, *Tracts* IV No. 5 (Washington, 1846) 17–37.

SERGEANT, John (1710–1749) of Stockbridge, Mass.

Missionary journal, October 1734–February 1749 (scattered extracts); missionary work among Housatonic Indians.

In Samuel Hopkins, *Historical Memoirs Relating to the Housatunnuk Indians* (Boston, 1753), which is reprinted *Mag. Hist.* Extra No. 17 (New York, 1912), where journal is on pp. 21–89 *passim*.

VON RECK, Baron Philipp-Georg Friedrich.

Travel journal, January–May 1734; voyage of the Salzburgers from Dover, Eng., to Charleston, S.C., and thence to Ebenezer, Ga., to establish a settlement; notes on Indians and worship.

An Extract of the Journals of Mr. Commissary Von Reck ... (London, 1734); reprinted in Peter Force, *Tracts* IV No. 5 (Washington, D.C., 1846) 1–16.

ANON.   1735

Official travel journal, August–September 1735; Governor Belcher's journey to council with Indians in Deerfield, Mass.; mainly distances.

Mary C. Crawford, *Old New England Inns* (Boston, 1924) 55–61.

CHECKLEY, Rev. Samuel (1696–1769) of Boston.

Clergyman's journal, January–December 1735; records of church affairs, local events at Boston, weather; mainly local interest.

Pubs. Col. Soc. Massachusetts (1908–1909) 270–306.

MORRIS, Robert Hunter (1713–1764) of New Jersey and New York.

Private diary, April 1735–January 1736; kept while author was accompanying his father, Lewis Morris, on business venture in England; business and social life in London, domestic affairs, travel, reading; lengthy and interesting entries. Some interesting spellings, but "certain changes" made by editor.

Edited by Beverly McAnear, *Pennsylvania Mag. Hist. Biog.* LXIV (1940) 164–217, 356–406.

WESLEY, Rev. John (1703–1791), Methodist.

Missionary diary, October 1735–February 1738; voyage to Georgia; work, travel, and evangelizing; return to England.

Nehemiah Curnock (ed.), *The Journals of the Rev. John Wesley, A.M.* (London, 1909–1916) I 79–426.

1736

LORING, Rev. Nicholas (1711–1763) of North Yarmouth, Me.

Clergyman's journal, January 1736–November 1762 (extracts); very brief notes of journeys and sermons, but mainly necrology.

Old Times, Yarmouth, Me. VIII (1884) 1105–1109.

SECCOM, Thomas (1711–1773) of Medford, Mass.

Private diary, July 1736–October 1743; brief notes of local news, sermons, etc.

New England Hist. Geneal. Reg. XII (1858) 267–268.

1737

BALLANTINE, Rev. John (1716–1776) of Westfield, Mass.

Private diary, February 1737–November 1774 (extracts); an interesting record of domestic and family matters, work, local news, teaching; a good varied diary of minor local matters.

John H. Lockwood, *Westfield and Its Historic Influences* (1922) 380–437.

HOLMES, Jonathan (1704–1778) of Monmouth Co., N.J.

Private diary, January 1737–April 1738; personal affairs, reading, illness; public news and local events; law, trade, farming, amusements, church; a most interesting record of local affairs.

John E. Stillwell, *Historical and Genealogical Miscellany* III (New York, 1914) 362–375.

PARKMAN, Rev. Ebenezer (1703–1782) of Westborough, Mass.

Clergyman's diary, February–November 1737 and November 1778–December 1780; an excellent diary of the quiet life of a country parson and his parish; detailed and intimate; local news and gossip, notes on Indians and Acadians.

The full manuscript dates are August 1723–October 1780 (with gaps): for location of manuscripts, see Harriette M. Forbes, *New England Diaries* (1923) 220.

Harriette M. Forbes (ed.), *The Diary of Rev. Ebenezer Parkman* (Westborough, Mass., 1899) 327 pp. An extract for July 1744 in *New England Hist. Geneal. Reg.* XIV (1860) 239.

PRINCE, Rev. Thomas (1687–1758) of Boston, pastor of Old South Church.

Clergyman's journal, January–December 1737; mainly notes of preaching and church affairs; some local and Harvard notes.

Pubs. Col. Soc. Massachusetts XIX (1916–1917) 331–364.

STEPHENS, Col. William (1671–1753), secretary to the trustees in Georgia.

Official journal, October 1737–October 1741; a lengthy and detailed investigation of the complaints arising from the discontents of the colonists with the plan of government in Georgia. A huge daily survey, with some personal details.

A Journal of the Proceedings in Georgia (London, 1742) three vols.; reprinted in *Col. Recs. Georgia* IV (1906) 698 pp. and supplement (1908) 285 pp.

TOBLER, John, leader of Swiss colony in South Carolina.

Diary, February–March 1737 (fragment); record of colony and journey to Savanaton (Fort Moore); factual details. Translated from the German.

Jour. Southern Hist. V (1939) 85–97.

WADSWORTH, Rev. Daniel (1704–1747) of Hartford, Conn.

Clergyman's journal, May 1737–February 1747; short notes of work as pastor of First Church in Hartford, study, weather, and local affairs; moderate interest.

George L. Walker (ed.), *Diary of Rev. Daniel Wadsworth* (Hartford, 1894) 149 pp.

WESTON, Mary (1712–1766) of Wapping, Eng.

Quaker travel journal, June 1737–April 1752 (extracts); notes of meetings and preaching in Rhode Island, Boston, Nantucket, Connecticut, and southern colonies in 1750–1751.

Eliot Howard, *Eliot Papers* (London, 1895) 93–110.

1738

ADAMS, Eliphalet (1677–1753) of New London, Conn.

Travel diaries, April–October 1738; very brief memoranda of trip among the Indians; bits of earlier diary, August 1699, added.

Massachusetts Hist. Soc. Colls. 4th Ser. I (1852) 27, 35–36.

EGMONT, John Perceval, First Earl of (1683–1748).

Official journal, June 1738–May 1744; first president of Board of Trustees of Georgia; largely official and administrative minutes, but much political and social interest; historically valuable.

Col. Recs. Georgia V (1908) 783 pp. Extracts from his journal for 1730–1733, which is mainly British but contains some items about Georgia and Oglethorpe's colony, in Hist. MSS. Comm., *MSS. Earl of Egmont* (London, 1920) I, 477 pp., *passim.*

GREEN, Capt. Jonathan (1719–1795) of Melrose, Mass.

Private diary, July 1738–June 1744; brief extracts concerning public and local affairs.

E. H. Goss, *The History of Melrose* (Melrose, 1902) 98.

SMITH, Rev. William (1702–1783) of Weymouth, Mass.

Clergyman's journals, 1738–1768 (outside years, extracts with many gaps); almanac notes; church work, religious introspection, some verses; rather dull.

Massachusetts Hist. Soc. Proc. XLII (1908–1909) 444–470.

WHITEFIELD, Rev. George (1714–1770), English Methodist.

Missionary journals 1738–1770 (outside dates of American sections); travels throughout the colonies during various missionary tours; innumerable meetings, sermons, etc.; in the exuberant and ejaculatory style of this Calvinistic branch of Methodism; important but rather dull reading. American sections deal with tour in Georgia, 1738; more extended tours through the colonies in 1738–1741, 1744–1748, 1751–1752, 1754–1755, 1763–1764, 1769–1770.

Frequently printed, but most easily available in John Gillies (ed.), *Works of the Rev. George Whitefield* (London, 1771–1772) six vols. A diary for October 1744–spring 1745, describing a tour in New England, has recently been published in *Church Hist.* VII (1938) 297–345.

WILLIAMS, Rev. Stephen (1693–1782) of Longmeadow, Mass.

1. Clergyman's journal, 1738–1742; quotations in biography; personal activities.

Connecticut Valley Hist. Soc. Papers and Proc. (1876–1881) 36–61.

2. Chaplain's journal, July 1745–January 1746; siege of Louisburg; military, religious, and personal items, and notes on sufferings of the men; fairly interesting.

L. E. de Forest (ed.), *Louisbourg Journals, 1745* (New York, 1932) 121–169.

3. Clergyman's journal, May 1754–July 1761 (extracts); clerical work and local affairs at Longmeadow, varied incidents, news, gossip, and moral reflections; fair interest.

Proceedings at the Centennial Celebration ... of the Town of Longmeadow (Longmeadow, Mass., 1884) 221–229.

1739

ANON. (a ranger with Gen. Oglethorpe).

Travel journal, July 1739–September 1742; journey to Indian assembly at Cowete on Chattahoochee River; operations against St. Augustine and in defense of Georgia coast against Spaniards; scattered and impersonal entries at long intervals; some good descriptions of Indian ceremonies.

Newton D. Mereness, *Travels in the American Colonies* (New York, 1916) 218–236.

LANE, Samuel (1718–1806) of Stratham, N.H., farmer.

Private diary, October 1739–October 1803; notes of family affairs and work as farmer and tanner; notes on war, and yearly notes on events of public interest; reading; mainly weather and farming notes; brief entries but an interesting record; some vocabulary interest.

Charles L. Hanson (ed.), *A Journal for the Years 1739–1803* (Concord, N.H., 1937) 115 pp.

1740

BRAINERD, Rev. David (1718–1747) of Crosswicks, N.J.

Missionary journal, October 1740–1747; perfervid and ejaculatory religious journal; self-analysis; work among the Indians; interesting for picture of frontier missionary life in New York, New Jersey, and Pennsylvania, and as a picture of a man wholly occupied with God and the Devil.

Mirabilia Dei inter Indios (Philadelphia, 1746) 253 pp.; often reprinted and abridged; among the most easily accessible editions are: *An Abridgement of Mr. David Brainerd's Journal* (London, 1748) 110 pp.; "Mirabilia," in Jonathan Edwards, *An Account of the Life of David Brainerd* (Edinburgh, 1765) 321–472; Oswald Smith (ed.), *David Brainerd, the Man of Prayer* (Grand Rapids, Mich., 1941) 86 pp.

BRINGHURST, John (1691–1750) of Philadelphia, merchant.

Travel diary, August 1740–September 1744 (extracts); brief and scattered notes of visit to Tortola and Barbados.

C. F. Jenkins, *Tortola, a Quaker Experiment* (London, 1923) 87–88.

DUDLEY, Paul (1675–1751) of Roxbury, Mass.

Private diary, January–December 1740; brief notes of weather and public affairs.

New England Hist. Geneal. Reg. XXXV (1881) 28–31.

GLADDING, John (1717–1785) of Bristol, R.I.

Private diary, 1740–October 1779; a few brief extracts, mostly news of Revolutionary War.

Henry C. Gladding, *The Gladding Book* (Providence, 1901) 45–46.

HAZEN, Richard (1696–1754) of Haverhill, Mass.

Surveyor's journal, March–April 1740; surveying Massachusetts boundary at Pentucket; notes of scenery, some personal matters, and a duel.

New England Hist. Geneal. Reg. XXXIII (1879) 323–332.

HOPKINS, Dr. Samuel (1721–1803) of Great Barrington, Mass.

Clergyman's diary, 1740–1800; religious work and meditations; some personal items; some cipher.

Stephen West, *Sketches of the Life of the Late Rev. Samuel Hopkins* (Hartford, 1805) 43–72 *passim*.

SALLEY, John Peter (*d.* 1755) of Augusta Co., Va.

Journal and recollections, 1740–1744 (scattered entries and dates); exploration on the Ohio and Mississippi; with John Howard; capture by French, imprisonment in New Orleans; and escape.

W. M. Darlington (ed.), *The Journals of Christopher Gist* (Pittsburgh, 1893) 253–260; *Louisiana Hist. Quar.* V (1922) 323–332 ("The Virginians on the Ohio and the Mississippi in 1742").

SEWARD, William.

Religious travel journal, April–June 1740; voyage from Savannah to Philadelphia and thence to England; accompanying Whitefield; preaching and religious reflections in Whitefieldian style.

Journal of a Voyage from Savannah to Philadelphia (London, Boston, 1740) 87 pp.

STORER, Col. John (1694–1768) of Wells, Me.

1. Official journal, October 1740–January 1741; report as agent of government in building of Fort Richmond, Me.

Maine Hist. Soc. Colls. and Proc. 2d Ser. V (1894) 142.

2. Military journal, April 1745; brief details of siege of Louisburg.

Portsmouth Journal, May 6, 1854; reprinted in Benjamin and W. R. Cutter, *A History of the Cutter Family of New England* (Boston, 1871) 310.

1741

BONNEFOY, Antoine.

Captive's diary, August 1741–May 1742; capture by Cherokees when on a journey from New Orleans, and journey to French post; seminarrative.

Newton D. Mereness, *Travels in the American Colonies* (New York, 1916) 241–255; S. C. Williams (ed.), *Early Travels in the Tennessee Country* (Johnson City, 1928) 149–162.

BRYENT, Walter (1710–1807) of Newmarket, N.H.

1. Surveying journal, March–April 1741; surveying boundary between Maine and New Hampshire.

Hist. Mag. n.s. IX (1871) 17–19; *New Hampshire Provincial and State Papers* VI (1872) 349–351.

2. Military journal, January–February 1747; march from New Hampshire to Canada; dull apart from incident of tapping rum cask.

New England Hist. Geneal. Reg. XXXII (1878) 297–302.

BURR, Esther (1732–1758) of Northampton, Mass., and Princeton, N.J.

Private diary, February 1741–September 1757; child's notes on religion and religious figures, Hopkins, Brainerd, etc.; household notes in a religious home; marriage and children; an interesting diary.

Esther Burr's Journal (Washington, 1903) 92 pp. Extensive extracts in *New England Quar.* III (1930) 297–315 (Josephine Fisher, the editor, strongly attacks the text of the earlier edition).

SMITH, John (1722–1771) of Burlington, N.J., and Philadelphia.

Private diary, October 1741–March 1752; voyage to Barbados, journey to New York, work as merchant in Philadelphia; courtship of Hannah Logan; later years in Philadelphia; a charming diary of Quaker social and business life.

Albert C. Myers (ed.), *Hannah Logan's Courtship* (Philadelphia, 1904) 65–324, 326–345. Myers gives an account of missing portions and a single extract, in *Bull. Friends' Hist. Soc. Philadelphia* XII (1923) 26.

VEZIAN, Peter, quartermaster of sloop "Revenge."

Sea journal, June–October 1741; a very interesting journal of cruising against pirates and Spanish privateers off the American coast.

John F. Jameson, *Privateering and Piracy in the Colonial Period* (New York, 1923) 381–429. Extracts in *Atlantic Monthly* VIII (1861) 353–359, 417–424.

WHEELOCK, Rev. Eleazar (1711–1779) of Hanover, N.H.

Travel journal, October–November 1741; long entries describing a journey to Boston.

Hist. Mag. n.s. V (1869) 237–240.

1742

ARREDONDO, Don Antonio de.

Military journal, June 1742; details of Spanish expedition against Georgia, by chief engineer. Translated from the Spanish.

Georgia Hist. Soc. Colls. VII (1913) Part 3, 52–64.

CARY, Mrs. Margaret (1719–1762) of Charlestown, Mass.

Private diary, 1742–1759; occasional entries about the chief family, personal, and religious matters.

C. G. Curtis (ed.), *Cary Letters* (Cambridge, 1891) 59–64. Extracts in Bayard Tuckerman, *Notes on the Tuckerman Family* (Boston, 1914) 122–123.

CASINAS, Marquess of.

Military journal, July–August 1742; account of failure of Spanish expedition against Georgia. Translated from the Spanish.

Georgia Hist. Soc. Colls. VII (1913) Part 3, 65–87.

CURTIS, Rev. Philip (1717–1797) of Sharon, Mass.

Clergyman's journal, January 1742–March 1797; private church records, births, marriages, deaths; genealogical interest only.

Sharon Hist. Soc. Pubs. No. 5 (1908) 5–53.

GOODHUE, Joseph (*b.* 1720) of Newbury, Mass.

Diary, 1742–1763; extracts of vital records and some miscellaneous notes.

Essex Inst. Hist. Colls. LXVII (1931) 401–407.

HOLYOKE, Edward Augustus (1728–1829) of Cambridge, Mass.

Private diaries, January 1742–1747 (lacking 1745); almanac notes, partly in shorthand; brief cryptic entries; college life at Harvard, preaching, etc.

G. F. Dow (ed.), *The Holyoke Diaries* (Salem, 1911) 31–43.

PECKOVER, Edmund (1695–1767) of Fakenham, Eng.

Quaker travel journal, September 1742–January 1743; journeys in New England, southern states, and Barbados. Abstract.

Jour. Friends' Hist. Soc. I (1904) 95–109.

SOULE, Capt. Cornelius (1703–1755) of North Yarmouth, Me.

Travel diary, July 1742; journey from Boston to eastern frontier; a few brief personal entries.

Old Times, Yarmouth, Me. VI (1882) 862–863 (reprinted from *Massachusetts Archives* XXXVIII).

1743

BANGS, Benjamin (1721–1769) of Harwich and Eastham, Mass.

Private diary, September 1743–September 1744; brief, varied notes of daily life at Harwich; fishing, local events, visits, ship movements, whaling, journeys to Boston, etc.; fair interest.

Dean Dudley, *History and Genealogy of the Bangs Family in America* (Montrose, Mass., 1896) 4–8.

DOOLITTLE, Rev. Benjamin (1695–1749) of Northfield, Mass.

Public diary, March 1743–October 1748; accounts of leading events in French and Indian War; interesting Indian episodes, although the work is not a private diary; possibly selected items from a private diary.

A Short Narrative of the Mischief Done by the French and Indian Enemy (Boston, 1750) 1–19; reprinted in J. H. Temple and G. Sheldon, *A History of the Town of Northfield* (Albany, 1875) 370–382, and in *Mag. Hist.* Extra No. 7 (New York, 1907) 1–23.

EMERSON, Rev. John (1707–1774) of Topsfield, Mass.

Clergyman's journal, January–December 1743 and January–December 1754 (extracts); brief almanac entries, mostly church work, baptisms, etc., and a few personal affairs.

Benjamin K. Emerson, *The Ipswich Emersons* (Boston, 1900) 424–428.

JOHNSTON, Andrew (1694–1762) of Perth Amboy, N.J., merchant.

Surveying journal, April 1743–1754; journeys to and surveying at Pepack, and other details concerning the Pepack patent, leases, rents, etc.; only local topographical interest.

Somerset County Hist. Quar. I (1912) 190–196, 262–265, II (1913) 35–38, 120–125, 186–188, 277–280, III (1914) 19–26, 106–109, 193–197, 261–267.

KIMBER, Edward (1719–1769) of London, Eng., novelist.

Military journal, February–March 1743; Oglethorpe's expedition to St. Augustine, Fla.; literary description of the campaign, and defense of Oglethorpe's conduct; effusive style.

A Relation, or Journal, of a Late Expedition to the Gates of St. Augustine (London, 1744); reprinted with notes by S. A. Kimber (Boston, 1935) 36 pp.

MacSparran, Rev. James (*d.* 1757) of Narragansett, R.I.

Clergyman's journal, May 1743–December 1751; religious, missionary services outside his parish, and personal affairs at Narragansett; some social notes; fair.

Daniel Goodwin (ed.), *A Letter Book and Abstract of Out-Services* (Boston, 1899) 1–67.

Mills, William (*b.* 1718) of Needham, Mass.

Diary, May 1743–September 1778; extracts arranged by subject; accounts, weather, family, and local affairs.

G. K. Clarke, *History of Needham, Massachusetts* (Cambridge, 1912) 49–51.

Preston, John (1717–1771) of Salem and Danvers, Mass.

Private diary, December 1743–March 1760; entries of important public events, family affairs, weather, etc.; rather dull.

New England Hist. Geneal. Reg. LVI (1902) 80–83; *Essex Inst. Hist. Colls.* XI (1871) 256–262.

Reed, Rev. Solomon (1719–1785) of Titicut, Mass.

Religious journal, October 1743–January 1745 (brief extracts); notes on religious work and Whitefield's preaching.

S. H. Emery, *History of Church of North Middleborough* (Middleborough, Mass., 1876) 31–32.

Schnell, Leonard, of Bethlehem, Pa., Moravian presbyter.

1. Moravian travel journal, November 1743–April 1744; journey with Robert Hussey to Georgia; daily life and worship; social and travel notes; one of the best of the Moravian journals. Translated from the German.

Virginia Mag. Hist. Biog. XI (1903–1904) 370–393.

2. Travel journal, May–July 1747; journey with V. Handrup to Maryland and Virginia.

Ibid. XII (1904–1905) 55–61.

3. Travel journal, October–December 1749; with John Brandmueller from Bethlehem, Pa., to Virginia; notes on worship and brethren; some interesting German-English spellings.

Ibid. XI (1903–1904) 115–131.

Whiting, John (1716–1784) of Dedham, Mass.

Private diary, June 1743–May 1784; brief and uninspiring entries of weather, local affairs, and public events; fires, epidemics, war news, etc.; a few entries each year.

New England Hist. Geneal. Mag. LXIII (1909) 185–192, 261–265.

1744

Anon.

Diary, June 1744–May 1756 (extracts); brief notes of remarkable providences, prodigies, and coincidences.

Ebenezer Clapp, *The Clapp Memorial* (Boston, 1876) 377–378.

BLACK, William, of Virginia.

Travel diary, May–June 1744; journey as secretary to commissioners in Maryland and Pennsylvania; personal and social side of the trip; feasts, flirtations, ceremonies; an entertaining account in a flowery, epic style.

Pennsylvania Mag. Hist. Biog. I (1877) 117–132, 233–249, 404–419, II (1878) 40–49.

GREEN, Benjamin (1713–1772) of Danvers, Mass. (See 1744, PEPPERELL 1, below.)

HAMILTON, Dr. Alexander (1712–1756) of Scotland, and Annapolis, Md.

Travel diary or "Itinerarium," May–September 1744; health trip from Annapolis to New Hampshire and back; extensive and vigorous descriptions and ironical comments on social and religious life, with many excellent scenes involving medicos and sectarians; some literary matters and conversation pieces; an excellent diary by a skeptical Scottish physician.

Dr. Albert Bushnell Hart (ed.), *Hamilton's Itinerarium* (St. Louis, Mo., 1907) 263 pp.

MACK, Rev. John Martin (1713?–1784?) *b.* Leysingen, Germany; Moravian bishop in West Indies.

1. Moravian travel journal, April 1744; trip with Christian Froelich from Bethlehem to Wyoming.

Wyoming Hist. Geol. Soc. Proc. & Colls. VIII (1902–1903) 149–155.

2. Travel journal, July–November 1752; journey to Onondaga with Zeisberger and Rundt; interesting for Moravian life and work.

William M. Beauchamp, *Moravian Journals Relating to Central New York, 1745–1766* (Syracuse, N. Y., 1916) 112–156. Partly in *W. H. Egle's Notes and Queries* (Pa.) 3d Ser. I (1885) 345–350, 351–355; *Pennsylvania Mag. Hist. Biog.* XXIX (1905) 343–358.

3. Travel journal, August 1753; Bethlehem to Shamokin; missionary work.

Hist. Jour. (Pa.) I (1887) 93–97.

OSBORN, Mrs. Sarah (1714–1796) of Newport, R.I.

Religious diary, September 1744–July 1768; God's dealings with her; self-analysis, prayers, religious reading, etc.

Samuel Hopkins, *Memoirs of the Life of Mrs. Osborn* (Catskill, 1814) 65–322.

PEPPERELL, Sir William (1696–1759) of Kittery Point, Me.

1. Military journal, March 1744–August 1745; a kind of log of the siege of Louisburg; in hand of Benjamin Green, Pepperell's secretary.

An Accurate Journal and Account of the Proceedings of the New-England Land Forces (London, 1746) 40 pp.; reprinted *Amer. Antiq. Soc. Proc.* n.s. XX (1909–1910) 139–183.

2. Official military journal, March–June 1745; siege of Louisburg and other military operations in expedition against Cape Breton; full day-to-day narrative, signed by a committee.

Appended to *A Letter from William Shirley, Esq.* (London, 1746) 17–32.

PIERCE, Daniel (1709–1773) of Portsmouth, N.H.

Private diary, June 1744–July 1772; brief scattered extracts from almanac notes; public and private events.

C. W. Brewster, *Rambles about Portsmouth, First Series* (Portsmouth, 1873) 360–361.

1745

ANON.

Travel journal, 1745; "through several towns in the country, and to Boston again, in the Winter past; containing many strange and remarkable occurrences. Which may be of singular advantage to the public if rightly improved in the present day. In the method of Mr. Whitefield's Journal, but vastly more entertaining."

Journal of Travels (Boston, 1745). [Evans.]

ANON.

Military journal, March–June 1745; from Boston to Louisburg and siege.

L. E. de Forest (ed.), *Louisbourg Journals 1745* (New York, 1932) 67–72.

ANON. (of Massachusetts contingent).

Military journal, March–June 1745; siege of Louisburg.

L. E. de Forest (ed.), *Louisbourg Journals 1745* (New York, 1932) 73–79.

ANON. (of Second Massachusetts Regiment).

Military journal, March–July 1745; from Charlestown to Louisburg; details of siege; interesting spellings and language, and doggerel verses.

L. E. de Forest (ed.), *Louisbourg Journals 1745* (New York, 1932) 80–96.

ANON. (of Fourth Massachusetts Regiment, probably of Springfield).

Military journal, March–October 1745; siege of Louisburg; intelligent, detailed observation, and colloquial style.

L. E. de Forest (ed.), *Louisbourg Journals 1745* (New York, 1932) 1–54.

ANON.

Sea journal, March–August 1745; journal of sloop "Union," Capt. Elisha Mayhew; expedition against Cape Breton; ship movements and engagements; interesting spellings.

H. M. Chapin (ed.), *A Journal of the Voige in the Sloop Union* (Providence, 1929) 26 pp.

ANON. (member of crew of the "Hector").

Military journal, August–September 1745; siege of Louisburg.

L. E. de Forest (ed.), *Louisbourg Journals 1745* (New York, 1932) 61–66.

ANON. (Frenchman).

Military journal, November 1745–November 1746; military and other operations in Canada; official abstracts in form of journal, military affairs affecting the colonies, and news from abroad. Translated.

E. B. O'Callaghan, *Docs. Rel. Col. Hist. State New York* X (1858) 38–75.

ANON. (Frenchman).

Military journal, December 1745–August 1746; military operations of French in New England and New York; brief abstracts; scalpings, etc. Translated.

E. B. O'Callaghan, *Docs. Rel. Col. Hist. State New York* X (1858) 32–35.

ANON. (British sailor).

Captive's diary, December 1745–October 1748; a most entertaining account of a sailor's capture, journey to Quebec, imprisonment there, and subsequent travel in West Indies. Lively details, and vigorous criticism of the colonists.

Isabel M. Calder, *Colonial Captivities, Marches, and Journeys* (New York, 1935) 3–136.

BIDWELL, Rev. Adonijah (1716–1784) of Hartford, Conn.

Sea chaplain's journal, April–October 1745; expedition to Cape Breton; brief notes of ship movements, deaths, bombardments, etc.

New England Hist. Geneal. Reg. XXVII (1873) 153–160.

BRADSTREET, Col. Dudley (1708–*ca.*1750) of Groton, Mass.

Military journal, April 1745–January 1746; naval and military details of siege of Louisburg; camp life, weather, private comments.

Massachusetts Hist. Soc. Proc. XI (1896–1897) 417–446; S. A. Green (ed.), *Three Military Diaries* (Groton, 1901) 3–39.

BUCHANAN, Col. John, deputy surveyor of Augusta Co., Va.

Surveying journal, October 1745; with Peter Salley, laying claim in Smyth Co., Va.; amusing meeting with Dunkers.

Goodridge Wilson, *Smyth County History and Traditions* (n.p. 1932) 10–15.

CHANDLER, Rev. Samuel (1713–1775) of Gloucester, Mass.

1. Clergyman's diary, November 1745–December 1764 (extracts); parish work at Scotland and Gloucester, journeys, visits; domestic and family affairs, weather, etc.; varied short notes of fair interest.

George Chandler, *The Descendants of William and Annis Chandler* (Worcester, Mass., 1883) 192–198.

2. Military journal, September 1755–April 1756; expedition to Crown Point; scenery, estates, camp life.

New England Hist. Geneal. Reg. XVII (1863) 346–354. Extract in *Munsell's Colls. on Hist. Albany* II (Albany, 1867) 373–375.

CLEAVES, Benjamin (1722–1808) of Beverly, Mass.

Military journal, March–July 1745; siege of Louisburg; fairly good, with interesting language.

New England Hist. Geneal. Reg. LXVI (1912) 113–124.

CRAFT, Benjamin (1706–1746) of Chebacco (now Essex), Mass.

Military journal, April–November 1745; siege of Louisburg; short and rather dull notes of camp life, religious reflections, etc.

Essex Inst. Hist. Colls. VI (1864) 183–194. Partly in J. M. and W. F. Crafts, *The Crafts Family* (Northampton, 1893) 659–670.

CURWEN, Samuel (1715–1802) of Salem, Mass.

1. Military journal, March–July 1745 (extracts); siege of Louisburg.

G. A. Ward (ed.), *Journal and Letters of the Late Samuel Curwen* (New York, 1842) 12–14.

2. Travel journal, May–June 1755; from Salem to Philadelphia; distances, roads, taverns.

Essex Inst. Hist. Colls. LII (1916) 76–83.

3. Loyalist diary, May 1775–April 1784; interesting and important record of life in London with other loyalists; travel in England.

G. A. Ward (ed.), *Journal and Letters of the Late Samuel Curwen* (New York, 1842) 25–418 (with letters); this reprinted (Boston, 1845, 1864).

EMERSON, Rev. Joseph (1724–1775) of Pepperell, Mass.

1. Naval chaplain's journal, March–August 1745; siege of Louisburg; quite interesting.

Massachusetts Hist. Soc. Proc. XLIV (1910–1911) 65–84.

2. Private diary, August 1748–April 1749; the everyday rounds of a clergyman; quiet and pleasant details, with interesting language.

Massachusetts Hist. Soc. Proc. XLIV (1910–1911) 262–282; extract in *Jour. Amer. Hist.* III (1909) 120–127.

EVANS, Rev. Joshua (1731–1798) of Newton Township, West Jersey.

Quaker diary and autobiography, 1745–1798 (diary March 1793–June 1798); New England journeys, meetings, New York, Carolina, Canada; notes on slaves, Indians, racial problems, schools.

Friends' Miscellany X (Byberry, Pa., 1837) 7–212, diary being on pp. 43–212. Account of MS with extracts in *Bull. Friends' Hist. Assoc.* XXVIII (1939) 30–36.

GIBSON, Col. James (1690?–1752) of Boston.

Military journal, April–July 1745; notes of a gentleman volunteer at the siege of Louisburg; clear but impersonal.

A Journal of the Late Siege (London, 1745) 49 pp.; L. D. Johnson (ed.), *A Boston Merchant of 1745* (Boston, 1847) 102 pp.; reprinted as *A Journal of the Siege of Louisburg and Cape Breton* (Washington, 1894) 35 pp.

GIDDINGS, Lieut. Daniel (*ca.* 1704–1771) of Ipswich, Mass.

Military journal, March–November 1745; journey to Louisburg; notes on siege, camp life, religion; interesting spellings.

Essex Inst. Hist. Colls. XLVIII (1912) 293–304.

GORHAM, Col. John (1709–1746) of Barnstable, Mass.

Sea journal, June 1745; kept during siege of Louisburg; very brief military details, with some family and genealogical notes.

Mayflower Descendant V (1903) 172–180.

How, Rev. Nehemiah (1693–1747) of Putney, Vt.

Captive's diary, October 1745–May 1747; capture by Indians, journey to Quebec, and imprisonment there; begins as narrative; a good record of captivity.

A Narrative of the Captivity of Nehemiah How (Boston, 1748) 23 pp.; reprinted in Samuel G. Drake, *Indian Captivities* (Auburn, 1850) 127–138; edited by V. H. Paltsits (Cleveland, 1904) 72 pp.

LAMB, Caleb.
Military journal, November 1745–April 1746; continuation of Mygate's diary of siege of Louisburg.
L. E. de Forest (ed.), *Louisbourg Journals 1745* (New York, 1932) 106–108.

LOGAN, William (1718–1776) of Philadelphia.
Travel diary, September 1745–January 1746; business journey to Georgia; interesting details of social life in the South by a cantankerous Quaker; some interesting spellings.
Pennsylvania Mag. Hist. Biog. XXXVI (1912) 1–16, 162–186.

MYGATE, Pvt. George (*d.* 1745) of Springfield, Mass.
Military journal, May–September 1745; a fairly interesting account of siege of Louisburg, with some personal notes; language interesting.
L. E. de Forest (ed.), *Louisbourg Journals 1745* (New York, 1932) 97–106.

NORRIS, Isaac (1701–1766) of Philadelphia.
Treaty journal, September–October 1745; trip to Albany and treaty negotiations there.
Pennsylvania Mag. Hist. Biog. XXVII (1903) 20–28.

POMEROY, Gen. Seth (1706–1777) of Northampton, Mass.
1. Military journal, March–August 1745; siege of Louisburg; a well-written and valuable account; some interesting spellings.
2. Military journal, June–October 1755; Lake George expedition; well-written and valuable account.
L. E. de Forest (ed.), *The Journals and Papers of Seth Pomeroy* (New York, 1926) 14–51, 100–127; J. R. Trumbull, *History of Northampton* (Northampton, Mass., 1902) II 121–146, 260–280.

POTE, William (1718–1755) of Falmouth (later Portland), Me.
Prison diary, May 1745–August 1747; capture by French and Indians off coast, journey to Quebec, and imprisonment there; interesting notes of Indian customs and barbarities, daily life in prison; lively and highly personal account, with interesting language.
J. F. Hurst (ed.), *The Journal of Captain William Pote, Jr.* (New York, 1896) 223 pp.

REINCKE, Rev. Abraham (1712–1760) of Sweden.
Moravian travel journal, March–April 1745; visit of a Swedish Moravian to the Swedes of West Jersey; some interesting comments on miscegenation and language.
Pennsylvania Mag. Hist. Biog. XXXIII (1909) 99–101.

SHERBURNE, Joseph (*b.* 1694?) of Portsmouth, N.H.

Military journal, May–June 1745; siege of Louisburg; brief military details.

L. E. de Forest (ed.), *Louisbourg Journals 1745* (New York, 1932) 55–60.

SHIRLEY, Lieut. Gen. William (*ca.* 1693–1771) of Roxbury, Mass.

Military journal, March–June 1745; siege of Louisburg.

A Letter from William Shirley, Esq. (Boston, 1746) 31 pp.; other editions, New York, 1746, London, 1748; L. E. de Forest (ed.), *Louisbourg Journals 1745* (New York, 1932) 109–120.

SPANGENBERG, Bishop August Gottlieb (1704–1792) of North Carolina.

1. Moravian travel journal, May–July 1745; notes of travel to the Onondaga; missionary work among Indians. Translated from the German.

Pennsylvania Mag. Hist. Biog. II (1878) 424–432, III (1879) 56–64; William M. Beauchamp (ed.), *Moravian Journals Relating to Central New York, 1745–1766* (Syracuse, 1916) 5–16.

2. Travel journal, September 1752–January 1753; from Bethlehem to North Carolina; topographical notes and description of government; interesting German spellings of place names. Translated from the German.

Adelaide L. Fries (ed.), *Records of the Moravians in North Carolina* (Raleigh, 1922–1941) I 30–64. Partly in *Southern Hist. Assoc. Pubs.* I (1897) 99–111.

[STEARNS, Benjamin (1714–1755) of Concord and Boston.]

Military journal, March–August 1745; siege of Louisburg; interesting language.

Massachusetts Hist. Soc. Proc. XLII (1908–1909) 135–144; *Acadiensis* VIII (1908) 317–329.

WOLCOTT, Roger (1679–1767) of Windsor, Conn., governor.

Military journal, May–July 1745; siege of Louisburg; military affairs, documents, recapitulation.

Connecticut Hist. Soc. Colls. I (1860) 131–161.

1746

ANON.

Official treaty journal, July–August 1746; journey from Boston to Albany; conference of a Massachusetts commission with the Six Nations.

Bull. Boston Public Library 4th Ser. IV (1922) 127–130 (facsimile).

ANON. (Frenchman).

Military journal, November 1746–September 1747; notes of the most interesting occurrences in Canada, especially military movements and foreign news; official record, but interesting. Translated.

E. B. O'Callaghan, *Docs. Rel. Col. Hist. State New York* X (1858) 89–132.

CLOUGH, Abner (1720–1786) of Exeter, N.H.

Military journal, July–September 1746; march with Capt. Ladd's company to protect Rumford, N.H., against Indians; rather good narrative of Indian skirmishes; colloquialisms.

New Hampshire Hist. Soc. Colls. IV (1834) 201–214.

CUSHING, Rev. John (1709–1772) of Boxford, Mass.

Clergyman's journal, January–December 1746; moderate brief notes of private and town affairs.

New England Hist. Geneal. Reg. XIX (1865) 237–239; *Essex Antiquarian* IV (1900) 155–156.

DE BEAUCHAMPS, of Mobile.

Travel journal, September–October 1746; journey from Mobile to Choctaw Indians to settle for assassinations of Frenchmen; mainly inquiries and discussions. Translated from the French.

Newton D. Mereness, *Travels in the American Colonies* (New York, 1916) 261–297.

HEYWOOD, Col. William (1728–1803) of Charlestown, N.H.

Military journal, July 1746–April 1751 (extracts); marches through Deerfield to Fort Dummer, Canada, and Fort Massachusetts; brief extracts.

H. H. Saunderson, *History of Charlestown, N.H.* (Claremont, N.H., 1876) 402–406.

LEWIS, Thomas.

Surveying journal, September–November 1746; surveying in Augusta County, Va.; selections of genealogical interest.

Joseph A. Waddell, *Annals of Augusta County, Va.* (Richmond, 1886) supplement 467–471, second edition (Staunton, 1902) 84–88.

NICHOLSON, Rev. Thomas (1715–1780) of Perquimans Co., N.C.

Quaker journal, April 1746, February 1749–November 1750, November–December 1771; visits to Friends at Cape Fear; 2,500 miles' travel in England, visiting Quakers; visit to North Carolina Assembly; long, rather dull entries.

Southern Hist. Assoc. Pubs. IV (1900) 172–186, 233–247, 301–315.

NORTON, Rev. John (1716–1778) of Bernardston, Mass.

Journal, August 1746–August 1747; seminarrative describing capture of Fort Massachusetts by the French and Indians, and the author's captivity.

The Redeemed Captive (Boston, 1748) 40 pp.; S. G. Drake, *A Particular History of the Five Years' French and Indian War* (Albany, 1870) 253–295; S. G. Drake (ed.), *Narrative of the Capture and Burning of Fort Massachusetts* (Albany, 1870) 51 pp.

PRINGLE, Robert (1702–1776) of Scotland, and Charleston, S.C.

Merchant's journal, May 1746–November 1747; line-a-day notes on trade and domestic affairs, and accounts; rather dull.

South Carolina Hist. Geneal. Mag. XXVI (1925) 21–30, 93–112.

RICE, Capt. William (1708–1747) of Warwick, R.I.

Military journal, May–December 1746; military movements of Rhode Island company during expedition against Canada; some good details, gambling, sickness, etc.

Nine Muster Rolls (Soc. Col. Wars Rhode Island, Providence, 1915) 45–53.

SCHLATTER, Rev. Michael (1716–1790) of St. Gall, Switzerland, and Philadelphia.

Moravian journal, June 1746–1751; pastor of First Reformed Church in Phila-delphia; notes of work among the Moravians in Pennsylvania, New Jersey, Maryland, and Virginia; and notes during French and Indian War. Translated from the Dutch.

Rev. H. Harbaugh, *The Life of Rev. Michael Schlatter* (Philadelphia, 1857) 87–234. Extract in *Jour. Presbyterian Hist. Soc.* III (1905) 105–121, 158–176.

WALKER, Rev. Timothy (1705–1782) of Concord, N.H.

Clergyman's diary, April 1746–December 1780 (with large gaps); brief notes of local and personal affairs, church work, and farming; interesting picture of life in an interior pioneer village.

Joseph B. Walker (ed.), *Diaries of Rev. Timothy Walker* (Concord, N.H., 1889) 80 pp.; *New Hampshire Hist. Soc. Colls.* IX (1889) 123–191.

WRIGHT, Deacon Noah (1716–1797) of Deerfield, Mass.

Diary, June 1746–April 1747; extracts (normalized) giving news of Indian raids.

New England Hist. Geneal. Reg. II (1848) 208–210.

1747

ANON. (official French).

Official journal, November 1747–October 1748; notes of "whatever occurred of interest at Quebec in regard to the operations of the war and the various intelligence received there." Translated from the French.

E. B. O'Callaghan, *Docs. Rel. Col. Hist. State New York* X (1858) 137–179.

BATCHELDER, Deacon David (1736–1811) of Hampton Falls, N.H.

Private diary, December 1747–July 1811; brief scattered notes of weather, farming, etc., at Portsmouth.

Warren Brown, *History of the Town of Hampton Falls* (Manchester, N.H., 1900) 476–481.

BOWEN, Silas (1722–1790) of Woodstock, Conn.

Private diary, June 1747–April 1787; brief extracts of births, marriages, etc.; mainly family notes, with some public items.

Daniel Bowen, *The Family of Griffith Bowen* (Jacksonville, Fla., 1893) 188–194.

DE BOISHEBERT, Charles Deschamps.

Military journal, June 1747; French and Indian expeditions against Fort Clinton. Translated from the French.

E. B. O'Callaghan, *Docs. Rel. Col. Hist. State New York* X (1858) 79–80.

GOELET, Capt. Francis, of New York, mariner.

Travel journal, January 1747–January 1754; very lively account of voyages along New England coast, and social life at the ports, feasts, parties, etc.

New England Hist. Geneal. Reg. XXIV (1870) 50–63.

PHILBROOK, Jonathan (1721–1801) of Brunswick, Me.

Scouting journal, March–April 1747; brief notes on expedition up the Kennebec River, by the clerk of the expedition.

G. A. and H. W. Wheeler, *History of Brunswick, Topsham, and Harpswell, Maine* (Boston, 1878) 58–60.

1748

CAMMERHOFF, Bishop John Christopher (1721–1756) *b.* Hillersleben, Germany, Moravian bishop of Bethlehem, Pa.

1. Travel journal, January 1748; journey from Shamokin, Pa.; fair account of Moravian life and worship. Translated from the German.

Pennsylvania Mag. Hist. Biog. XXIX (1905) 160–179.

2. Travel journal, May–August 1750; journey with Zeisberger from Bethlehem to Onondaga; excellent full narrative; travel, religion, and Indian notes. Translated.

William M. Beauchamp, *Moravian Journals Relating to Central New York, 1745–1766* (Syracuse, 1916) 24–112.

GOTTSCHALK, Matthias Gottlieb (*d.* 1748) of Bethlehem, Pa.

Moravian missionary journal, March–April 1748; journey through Virginia and Maryland; religious life and preaching.

Virginia Mag. Hist. Biog. XII (1904–1905) 62–76.

HOLYOKE, John (1734–1753) of Cambridge, Mass.

Private diary, January–December 1748; brief notes of social life and study at Harvard; language interesting.

G. F. Dow (ed.), *The Holyoke Diaries* (Salem, 1911) 44–46.

MELVEN (or Melvin), Capt. Eleazar (1703–1754) of Concord, Mass.

Military journal, May 1748; march to Crown Point; fairly well-written but brief notes of Indian skirmishes.

New Hampshire Hist. Soc. Colls. V (1837) 207–211; *Vermont Hist. Soc. Proc.* II (1931) 167–168.

PARSONS, Rev. Moses (1716–1783) of Byfield, Mass.

Private diary, 1748–1783 (extracts); brief notes of weather, farming, social and family affairs; longer notes on important public affairs.

John L. Ewell, *The Story of Byfield* (Boston, 1904) 101–158 *passim*.

ROGERS, Rev. John (1692–1773) of Eliot, Me.

Clergyman's journal, February–June 1748; notes of religious work and self-analysis, with some local items; moderate interest.

Old Eliot VII (1906) 15–20.

SPANGENBERG, Rev. Joseph (1704–1792) of Bethlehem, Pa.

Moravian travel journal, June–August 1748 (extracts); journey through Maryland and Virginia with Matthew Reutz; missionary work. Translated from the German.

Virginia Mag. Hist. Biog. XI (1903–1904) 235–242.

WASHINGTON, George (1732–1799), first President of the United States.

Diaries and journals, March 1748–December 1799 (with some big gaps, especially 1754–1759 and during Revolution and Presidency); mostly brief notes on farming, sport, and social life at Mount Vernon.

John C. Fitzpatrick (ed.), *The Diaries of George Washington, 1748–1799* (Boston and New York, 1925) four vols. This edition supersedes the myriad earlier editions of separate journals and parts of journals; on pp. xv–xviii, Mr. Fitzpatrick gives a complete list of the different journals and diaries with notes of their principal contents.

ZEISBERGER, David (1721–1808) b. Zauchenthal, Moravia.

1. Journal, July 1748 (extract); description of Indian famine. Translated, as are all his journals, from the German.

Pennsylvania Mag. Hist. Biog. XVI (1892) 430–432.

2. Travel journal, April–November 1753; journey to Onondaga with Henry Frey, and missionary work there; notes on travel, religious life, and Indians.

William M. Beauchamp (ed.), *Moravian Journals Relating to Central New York, 1745–1766* (Syracuse, 1916) 156–197.

3. Travel journal, October 1766; with Gottlob Senseman on mission from Friedenshuetten to Onondaga and Cayuga; Indian conferences.

Ibid. 222–240.

4. Travel journal, September–November 1767; journey to the Monsey town at the mouth of Tionesta Creek on the Allegheny River; narrative in journal form; meetings, accounts of Indians, religious discussion.

Ohio Archaeol. and Hist. Quar. XXI (1912) 8–32. Extracts in *W. H. Egle's Notes and Queries (Pa.)* 4th Ser. I (1893) 351–352.

5. Travel journal, May 1768–January 1769; journey with Gottlob Senseman to Goschgoschinck and their sojourn there; notes on travel, meetings, councils, topography.

Ohio Archaeol. and Hist. Quar. XXI (1912) 42–104.

6. Travel and missionary journal, August 1781–May 1798; life and work at missions at Muskingum, Upper Sandusky, Detroit, Clinton River, Cuyahoga, Huron River, New Salem, mouth of Detroit River, and Fairfield on the Thames; similar content and interest to most Moravian journals.

E. F. Bliss (ed.), *Diary of David Zeisberger* (Cincinnati, 1885) two vols. Extracts (1782–1798, relating to Delaware Indians) in *Ontario Hist. Soc. Papers* XII (1914) 176–198.

1749

ANTHONY, Susanna (1726–1791) of Newport, R.I.

Quaker journal, June 1749–June 1769; extracts for biography and character; religious meditations.

Samuel Hopkins, *The Life and Character of Miss Susanna Anthony* (Worcester, 1796) 193 pp. *passim*.

BRAINERD, Rev. John (1720–1781) of Haddam, Conn.

Missionary journal, August–November 1749; work among Indians at Bethel, near Cranberry, N.J.; religious reflections and introspection; journeys in New Jersey, Elizabethtown, Newark, Brunswick, Gnadenhuetten, etc.; impressions of Moravians.

Thomas Brainerd, *The Life of John Brainerd* (Philadelphia, 1865) 160–226.

CELORON DE BLAINVILLE, Pierre Joseph.

Exploration journal, June–November 1749; expedition from Quebec down the Allegheny and Ohio rivers.

Ohio Archaeol. and Hist. Quar. XXIX (1920) 335–396.

KALM, Pehr (1716–1779) of Sweden.

Travel diaries, 1749–1750; an excellent travel record; descriptions of places and his activities in great detail. Translated.

Translated by John R. Foster as *Travels into North America* (London, 1770–1771) three vols.; reëdited by Adolph B. Benson, *The America of 1750* (New York, 1937) two vols. Sections of 1748 journal in *Amer. Scandinavian Rev.* X (1922) 350–355, relating to travel in New York, New Jersey, Pennsylvania; extracts relating to New Jersey (1748) in *Somerset County Hist. Quar.* V (1916) 29–33. For a bibliography of Kalm's travel journals, see *Scandinavian Studies and Notes* XII (1933) 89–98.

PHILLIPS, Catherine (1727–1794) of Worcestershire, Eng.

Quaker journal, May 1749–August 1785; memoirs in journal form; visit to America; North Carolina, Virginia, Maryland, New York, New England; sociological and religious notes.

Memoirs of the Life of Catherine Phillips (London, 1797) 384 pp. (with narrative and letters); reprinted (Philadelphia, 1798).

STEVENS, Capt. Phineas (1706–1756) of Charlestown, N.H.

1. Official travel journal, August–December 1749 (extracts); journey to Canada, via Deerfield, Albany, Crown Point, Montreal; brief notes.
New Hampshire Hist. Soc. Colls. V (1837) 199–205.

2. Travel journal, April–November 1752; journey to Canada to treat about prisoners; later part domestic; cryptic.
Newton D. Mereness, *Travels in the American Colonies* (New York, 1916) 302–322.

1750

BEVERLEY, William (1698–1756) of Blandfield, Va.

Travel diary, June–October 1750; visit to England; social and public details; impersonal notes of things done and seen, and places visited.

Virginia Mag. Hist. Biog. XXXVI (1928) 161–169.

BIRKET, James, of Antigua.

Travel diaries, July 1750–April 1751; voyage from Antigua, B.W.I., to Portsmouth, N.H., and travels in New England, New York, and Pennsylvania; long descriptions of places, people, and trade; impersonal style.

Some Cursory Remarks Made by James Birket (New Haven, Conn., 1916) 74 pp.

FITCH, Jabez (1737–1812) of Norwich, Conn., and Hyde Park, N.Y.

Private diary, September 1750–February 1812 (with a few added prior entries from 1749); social life, and service in French and Indian wars; settlement in northern Vermont; lengthy, detailed diary of private affairs, in intimate and entertaining style; interesting spellings and language.

Mayflower Descendant I (1899)–XV (1914), continued in *Pilgrim Notes and Queries* II–V. Extracts (1750–1788), *Vermont Hist. Gazetteer* II (1871) 638–653; extracts relating to the Revolution, *Massachusetts Hist. Soc. Proc.* 2d Ser. IX (1894–1895) 40–91; a facsimile of part of the manuscript relating to imprisonment on prison ship published by Prison Ship Martyrs' Monument Assoc. as *Diary of Captain Jabez Fitch* (Brooklyn, 1897?).

GIST, Col. Christopher (*ca.* 1706–1759) of Will's Creek, Pa.

1. Explorer's journal, September 1750–May 1751; exploring for Ohio Company beyond Allegheny Mountains as far as Falls of Ohio, searching for level lands; meetings with Indians, Indian customs, but mainly official and surveying notes.

W. M. Darlington (ed.), *Christopher Gist's Journals* (Pittsburgh, 1893) 31–66; L. P. Summers, *Annals of Southwest Virginia* (Abingdon, 1929) 29–57; J. S. Johnston, *First Explorations of Kentucky* (Louisville, 1898) 101–164. Extracts in Charles A. Hanna, *The Wilderness Trail* (New York, 1911) II 143–152.

2. Exploration journal, July 1751–March 1752; exploring for Ohio Company for route between Will's Creek and Monongahela, and down Ohio River to Big Kanawha.

Darlington, *op. cit.,* 67–79.

3. Exploration journal, October 1753–January 1754; visit with George Washington to French forts on the Ohio.

Ibid. 80–87; *Massachusetts Hist. Soc. Colls.* 3d Ser. V (1836) 101–108.

HAZARD, Thomas (1720–1798) of South Kingston, R.I.

Diary and account book, January (?) 1750–1790 (extracts); a few rather dull farming and personal notes.

Caroline Hazard, *College Tom* (Boston, 1893) 324 pp. *passim.*

JONES, Sarah, of Falmouth (later Portland), Me.

Private diary, July 1750–January 1766; social life, sleighing parties, etc. Editor notes that authenticity is doubtful, as language is too modern.

New England Family Hist. IV (1911–1912) 577–587, 599–604.

MITTELBERGER, Gottlieb, of Entzweilingen, Germany.

Moravian travel journal, May 1750–October 1754; journey to Pennsylvania and return to Germany; Moravian religious life, topography, natural history, and trade of Pennsylvania. Translated.

Translated by Carl T. Eben as *Gottlieb Mittelberger's Journey to Pennsylvania in the Year 1750* (Philadelphia, 1898) 129 pp.

WALKER, Dr. Thomas (1715–1794) of Fredericksburg, Va.

Travel journal, March–July 1750; first exploration of Kentucky; stages and distances; a few descriptions of places; generally impersonal; account of snake-bite of horses; important in history of the frontier.

J. S. Johnston (ed.), *First Explorations of Kentucky* (Louisville, 1898) 33–75; W. C. Rives (ed.), *Journal of an Exploration in the Spring of the Year 1750* (Boston, 1888) 69 pp. Partly in L. P. Summers, *Annals of Southwest Virginia* (Abingdon, Va., 1929) 8–26; A. B. Hulbert, *Historic Highways of America* VI (Cleveland, 1903) chap. ii; and S. C. Williams (ed.), *Early Travels in the Tennessee Country* (Johnson City, Tenn., 1928) 169–174.

WATSON, John (1720–1761).

Surveying journals, September 1750–March 1751; Pennsylvania-Maryland boundary dispute; topographical descriptions, with some personal notes; fairly interesting.

Pennsylvania Mag. Hist. Biog. XXXVIII (1914) 385–406, XXXIX (1915) 1–47.

WINSLOW, Joshua (1727–1801) *b*. Boston, paymaster of British forces in Nova Scotia.

Military journal, March–December 1750; with Maj. Lawrence on two expeditions to Chignecto, N.B.; brief entries, mostly military and naval movements.

J. C. Webster (ed.), *The Journal of Joshua Winslow* (Pubs. New Brunswick Museum, 1936) 40 pp.

ANON.   1751

Travel journal, April 1751; from Oxford Furnace in the Jerseys to Moravian settlements at forks of the Delaware; narrative account of Moravians and the settlements.

The Jerseyman III (1895) 8–11.

BLAIR, John (1687–1771), President of the Council of Virginia.

Private diary, January–December 1751; line-a-day almanac notes on outstanding local and private items; plantation life; some longer political items.

William and Mary Coll. Quar. 1st Ser. VII (1898–1899) 133–153, VIII (1899–1900) 1–17.

CROGHAN, George (*d*. 1782) *b*. Dublin, Ireland, Indian agent.

Journals of travel and transactions with the Indians; mostly containing minutes and speeches.

1. May 1751; treaty with the Ohio Indians.

R. G. Thwaites (ed.), *Early Western Travels* (Cleveland, 1904) I 58–69; also in *Pennsylvania Col. Recs.* V 530–536; Israel D. Rupp, *Early History of Western Pennsylvania* (Pittsburgh and Harrisburg, 1846) App. 75–98. An extract in N. B. Craig, *The Olden Time* I (1846, reprinted Cincinnati, 1876) 135–136.

2. January 1753–February 1754; at Logstown, O.
Americana X (1915) 677–683.

3. January 1754; conditions on the Ohio.
Thwaites I 72–81; *Pennsylvania Col. Recs.* V 731–735; Rupp, App. 59–53.

4. May–August 1757; journey from Lancaster and negotiations for a treaty with Teedyuscung and other Indians at Easton, Pa.
Pennsylvania Archives 2d Ser. VI 560–569.

5. November–December 1758; from Pittsburgh to the Delaware Indians.
Ibid., 1st Ser. III 560–563 (N.B., author given as Christian Frederick Post; but Thwaites [I 101 note] identifies him as Croghan).

6. July 1760; Fort Pitt to Presque Isle.
Massachusetts Hist. Soc. Colls. 4th Ser. IX (1871) 283–289.

7. October 1760–January 1761; expedition under Major Robert Rogers to secure possession of Detroit and other western posts.
Thwaites I 100–125; *Massachusetts Hist. Soc. Colls.* 4th Ser. IX (1871) 362–379.

8. February–May 1765; negotiations with Indians at Fort Pitt.
Illinois Hist. Colls. XI (1916) 1–23; *Pennsylvania Col. Recs.* IX 250–256.

9. May–September 1765; down Ohio River to Shawneetown; capture by Indians and release; meeting with Pontiac; return to Detroit.

There are two versions: (*a*) "personal," detailed, omitting meeting with Pontiac and Indian affairs; largely topographical; (*b*) official report emphasizing Indian affairs. A combined version, emphasizing (*a*), in Thwaites 1 126–166. Version (*a*) is printed in *Illinois Hist. Colls.* XI (1916) 23–38 (where dates are given as May–October 1765); *Monthly Jour. Amer. Geol.* I (1831) 257–272; separately at Burlington, N.J. (1857) 38 pp.; Mann Butler, *History of the Commonwealth of Kentucky* (Louisville, 1834) Appendix; N. B. Craig, *The Olden Time* (1846, reprinted Cincinnati, 1876) I 404–415. Version (*b*) is printed in *Illinois Hist. Colls.* XI (1916) 38–52; Samuel P. Hildreth, *Pioneer History of the Ohio Valley* (Cincinnati, 1848) 68–85; E. B. O'Callaghan, *Docs. Rel. Col. Hist. State New York* VII (1856) 779–788.

10. October–December 1767; from Fort Pitt to Detroit and return; council with Indians.

Howard H. Peckham (ed.), *George Croghan's Journal of His Trip to Detroit in 1767* (Ann Arbor, 1939) 61 pp. (with letters).

CUTHBERTSON, Rev. John (1720–1791) of Lancaster Co., Pa.

Clergyman's travel journals, December 1751–September 1790 (extracts arranged geographically); a covenanting minister's horseback journeys; preaching and clerical work; mostly in Pennsylvania, but also in Maryland, Delaware, Virginia, New Jersey, New York, Connecticut, and Massachusetts; dull and genealogical arrangement.

S. Helen Fields, *Register of Marriages and Baptisms Performed by Rev. John Cuthbertson* (Washington, D.C., 1934) 69–260.

Mason, Jonas (1708–1801) of North Yarmouth, Me.
Private diary, February–November 1751; a few brief, miscellaneous notes of local affairs.
Old Times, Yarmouth, Me. VIII (1884) 1188–1189.

Willis, Benjamin (1686–1767) of Medford, Mass.
Private diary, July 1751–February 1764; brief notes of weather, sickness, prayers; little value.
Medford Hist. Reg. V (1902) 95.

1752

Anon.
Treaty journal, October 1752; conference held with the eastern Indians at St. George's.
A Journal of the Proceedings of Jacob Wendell ... (Boston, 1752) 16 pp.

Balch, Ebenezer (1723–1808) of Wethersfield, Conn.
Religious diary, 1752–1757; "gives us a very good insight of the religious fervor of the time."
Balch Leaflets I. [Forbes.]

Billing, Rev. Edward (1707–1760) of Greenfield, Mass.
Clergyman's diary, October 1752–April 1756; a few dullish extracts of personal and local affairs.
David Willard, *History of Greenfield* (Greenfield, 1838) 119–122.

Mueller, Joseph.
Moravian travel journal, August 1752–January 1753; written *post facto* but arranged by dates; from Bethlehem to North Carolina and return; difficulties of trip; nursing fever-stricken Brethren. Translated from the German.
Adelaide L. Fries (ed.), *Records of the Moravians in North Carolina* (Raleigh, 1922–1941) II 521–525.

Ramsour (or Ramsauer), David (d. 1785) of Lincoln Co., N.C.
Farming diary, August 1752–February 1759 (with gaps); partly financial memoranda, partly record of work on plantation; very interesting language, German-English combinations.
Pennsylvania Germania n.s. II (1913) 22–25.

Ravenel, Henry (1729–1785) of Hanover, S.C., and an unknown continuator.
Private diary, March 1752–February 1822; domestic work, farming, weather, family affairs, local events, and memoranda of births and deaths.
Henry E. Ravenel, *Ravenel Records* (Atlanta, 1898) 212–220, 223–225.

Trent, Capt. William (1715–1787?) b. Philadelphia(?), Indian trader.
1. Travel journal, July–August 1752; from Wastown to Pickawillany; rather good account of Twightee (Miami) Indians in Ohio; largely reports of speeches, but many descriptions.

Alfred T. Goodman (ed.), *Journal of Captain William Trent* (Cincinnati, 1871) 83–105; Charles Hanna, *The Wilderness Trail* (New York, 1911) II 291–298.

2. Trading journal, May–September 1763; trade at Fort Pitt; trouble with Indians; fairly interesting.

M. C. Darlington, *Fort Pitt and Letters from the Frontier* (Pittsburgh, 1892) 84–110 (where it is ascribed to Capt. Ecuyer); *Mississippi Valley Hist. Rev.* XI (1924–1925) 393–413.

ANON.   1753

Moravian travel journal, October–November 1753; from Bethlehem, Pa., to Bethabara, N.C.; extensive details of travel, services, etc. An interesting record; translated from the German, with some interesting German spellings of place names.

Newton D. Mereness, *Travels in the American Colonies* (New York, 1916) 325–356; *Virginia Mag. Hist. Biog.* XII (1904–1905) 134–153, 271–281.

BAILEY, Rev. Jacob (1731–1808) of Pownalborough, Me.

Clergyman's diary, January 1753–June 1779 (extracts); begun at Harvard, with visits and journeys to New England towns; schoolmastering at Kingston; later, mostly church affairs and records.

William S. Bartlett, *The Frontier Missionary, Colls. Protestant Episc. Church Hist. Soc.* II (1853) 11–171 *passim*.

BETHABARA MORAVIAN CONGREGATION. (See also WACHOVIA, 1754.)

Moravian congregational journals; notes of travel between the various Moravian settlements, domestic and civic life of the community, religious observances, troubles with Indians; notes on newcomers, "love-feasts," etc.; in all, "work and worship." Very interesting records of religious and frontier life, with some German-English spellings of place names, etc.

Published in Adelaide L. Fries (ed.), *Records of the Moravians in North Carolina* (Raleigh, 1922–1941) five vols.; in progress.

October–December 1753, I 75–87; January–December 1756, I 161–174; January–December 1758, I 184–194; January–December 1759, I 209–215; January–December 1760, I 229–233; January–December 1761, I 235–238; January–December 1762 (with Bethania) I 243–253; January–December 1763, I 268–278; January–December 1764, I 283–293; January–December 1765, I 297–309; January–December 1766, I 323–338; January–December 1772 (written by Johann Michael Graff) II 726–742; January–December 1773, II 776–783; January–December 1774, II 831–839; January–December 1775 (written by Lorenz Bagge) II 900–908; January–December 1776, III 1091–1103; January–December 1777, III 1182–1194; January–December 1778, III 1267–1270; January–December 1779, III 1331–1338; January–December 1780, IV 1613–1637; January–December 1781, IV 1739–1764; January–December 1782, IV 1810–1816; January–December 1783 (largely weather) IV 1859–1866; January–December 1784 (by Lorenz

Bagge and Simon Peter) V 2046–2058; January–December 1785, V 2103–2107; January–December 1786, V 2149–2155; January–December 1787, V 2196–2200; January–December 1788, V 2245–2252; January–December 1789, V 2284–2286; January–December 1790, V 2311–2313; January–December 1791, V 2339–2341; January–December 1792, V 2371–2373.

COOPER, Rev. Samuel (1725–1783) of Weston and Waltham, Mass.
Clergyman's diary, January 1753–January 1754, and 1769; rather dull, line-a-day entries; baptisms, notes for sermons, some personal and public affairs.
New England Hist. Geneal. Reg. XLI (1887) 388–391, LV (1901) 145–149; *Hist. Mag.* X (1866), Supplement 82–84.
2. Diary, April 1775–May 1776; notes relating to Revolutionary War; Lexington, siege of Boston; travel and religious work in Massachusetts.
Amer. Hist. Rev. VI (1900–1901) 303–341.

DAVIES, Samuel (1723–1761) *b.* Hanover Co., Del., president of Nassau Hall.
Travel diary, July 1753–February 1755; travel to England as delegate to advance interests of New Jersey College; preaching and visits in London, travel through England, and return; literary style, with poetical quotations and evidence of wide reading; a good diary.
William H. Foote, *Sketches of Virginia* (Philadelphia, 1850) 228–281.

GRUBE, Rev. Bernard Adam (1715–1808) *b.* Thüringen, Moravian missionary.
Moravian travel journal, August 1753; tour of Shamokin and notes of Moravian affairs in Indian towns along West Branch.
Pennsylvania Mag. Hist. Biog. XXXIX (1915) 440–444.

HAWLEY, Rev. Gideon (1727–1807) of Bridgeport, Conn., missionary.
Clergyman's travel journal, May–June 1753; journey to Oquago (now Windsor), N.Y.; missionary work by a newly ordained clergyman.
E. B. O'Callaghan, *Doc. Hist. State New York* III (1850) 1031–1046.

PRINCE, Dr. Jonathan (1734–1759) of Danvers, Mass.
Clergyman's journal, January–December 1753; very brief notes of births, deaths, weather, visits, sickness, and local affairs.
Geneal. Quar. Mag. II (1901) 51–53.

1754

ANON.
Treaty journal, June–July 1754; two conferences held at Falmouth, Mass. (later Portland, Me.), between William Shirley and the Norridgewock Indians.
A Journal of the Proceedings at Two Conferences (Boston, 1754) 27 pp.

ANON.
Military journal, June–July, 1754; notes by officer in command at "Fort on Northkill"; trouble with marauding Indians; good frontier journal.
Pennsylvania Archives 1st Ser. II (1852) 159–166.

BARBER, John (1708–1754?) of Medfield, Mass.

Military journal, May–August 1754; with Eleazar Melven's company on Shirley's expedition; scattered and dull notes.

New England Hist. Geneal. Reg. XXVII (1873) 281–285.

BROWN, Charlotte, hospital matron with British forces.

Military journal, November 1754–August 1756; with Braddock's army during French and Indian War; entertaining record of personal affairs, hardships, illness, travel through Atlantic states.

Isabel M. Calder, *Colonial Captivities, Marches and Journeys* (New York, 1935) 169–200. Extracts relating to Maryland and Virginia in *Virginia Mag. Hist. Biog.* XXXII (1924) 305–320.

DE LÉRY, Lieut. Joseph Gaspard Chaussegros (1721–1797) *b.* Toulon, France, engineer of Quebec.

Military journal, March 1754–April 1755; march from Quebec to Detroit; military operations; relations with Indians around Detroit; routes, marches, conferences, topography. Translated from the French.

S. K. Stevens and D. H. Kent (eds.) (Harrisburg, Pa., 1940) 118 pp. mimeographed; French text in *Rapport de l'archiviste de la province de Québec pour 1928–1929.*

DE VILLIERS, Neyon (French officer in Canada).

Military journal, July 1754 (extract); defeat of English by French and Indians at the "Beautiful River." Translated.

E. B. O'Callaghan, *Docs. Rel. Col. Hist. State New York* X (1858) 261–262.

FREDERICK, Charles.

1. Moravian travel journal, June 1754–June 1755; journey with David Zeisberger from Bethlehem to Onondaga; residence, missionary work, and return.

2. Travel journal, April–May 1766 (extracts); journey and mission to Cayuga.

William M. Beauchamp, *Moravian Journals Relating to Central New York 1745–1766* (Syracuse, 1916) 197–222.

FRIIS, Rev. John Jacob, pastor of Bethabara.

Moravian diary, April–July 1754; diary-letter written originally in English, giving intimate glimpse of Moravian life at Bethabara.

Adelaide L. Fries (ed.), *Records of the Moravians in North Carolina* (Raleigh, 1922–1941) II 529–533.

HENRY, Anthony, of Isle of Wight, Eng., and York Fort.

Fur trader's journal, June 1754–June 1755; journey from York Factory (H.B.C.) to the Blackfeet country in the Southwest, stirring up trade and offsetting French competition; 1,000 miles inland to South Saskatchewan River; important geographically, and interesting for details of Blackfeet Indians; good, simple style.

Edited by L. P. Burpee, *Proc. and Trans. Royal Society Canada* 3d Ser. I (1907) Sec. II 307–354.

MANIGAULT, Mrs. Ann (1703–1782) of Charleston, S.C.

Private diary, January 1754–1781; half-line entries of social, domestic, personal, and religious affairs; rather dull.

South Carolina Hist. Geneal. Mag. XX (1919) 57–63, 128–141, 204–212, 256–259, XXI (1920) 10–23, 59–72, 112–120.

PATTEN, Matthew (1719–1795) of Bedford, N.H., judge.

Private diary, June 1754–July 1788; short entries of his everyday affairs and local events; a farmer's view of the Revolution. The length and consistency of the diary make it a valuable counterpart to the diaries of Joshua Hempstead and "Nailer" Tom Hazard.

The Diary of Matthew Patten of Bedford, N.H. (Concord, 1903) 545 pp.

POWERS, Capt. Peter (1707–1757) of Hollis, N.H.

Military journal, June 1754 (extracts); expedition from Massachusetts to explore the northern country, as far as Dalton.

R. W. Musgrove, *History of the Town of Bristol* (Bristol, N.H., 1904) I 25–26.

POWNALL, Thomas (1722–1805) of Boston, governor.

1. Travel journal, 1754; notes on Pennsylvania roads.

Almon's Remembrancer V (London, 1778) 486–490; *Pennsylvania Mag. Hist. Biog.* XVIII (1894) 211–218.

2. Treaty journal, May 1759; voyage to Penobscot; notes on negotiations with Indians, and on Fort Pownall; official journal probably written by Pownall's secretary but signed by Pownall himself.

Maine Hist. Soc. Colls. V (1857) 365–387.

SEWALL, David (1735–1825) of York, Me.

Diary, June 1754; journey with his tutor, Henry Flynt, from Harvard to Portsmouth; very entertaining, although slight.

Massachusetts Hist. Soc. Proc. 1st Ser. XVI (1878) 5–11.

SPICER, Jacob (*d.* 1765).

Memorandum book, 1754–1764; domestic affairs.

New Jersey Hist. Soc. Proc. III (1848–1849) 103–104, 192–198; *Cape May Co. Hist. Geneal. Reg.* I (1933–1934), II (1934–1935).

STILES, Ezra (1727–1795) of New Haven, Conn., president of Yale.

1. Travel journal, September–October 1754; horseback journey from New Haven to Philadelphia and return; charming social details.

Massachusetts Hist. Soc. Proc. 2d Ser. VII (1891–1892) 338–345.

2. Travel diaries, November 1755–November 1794; notes of persons and places made during his many journeys in New England, etc.

F. B. Dexter (ed.), *Extracts from the Itineraries and Other Miscellanies of Ezra Stiles* (New Haven, 1916) 620 pp.

3. Literary diary, January 1769–May 1795; social news and gossip; religious, scholarly, and literary interests; very detailed and consistent entries; a most valuable diary.

F. B. Dexter (ed.), *The Literary Diary of Ezra Stiles* (New York, 1901) three vols. Account of the diary, with extracts, *Jour. Amer. Hist.* XXVI (1932) 146–170; extracts in "References to Jews in the (Literary) Diary of Ezra Stiles," *Pubs. Amer. Jewish Hist. Soc.* X (1902) 5–36; extracts in George A. Kohut, *Ezra Stiles and the Jews* (New York, 1902) 155 pp. *passim.* Extracts (March–August 1776) in *New England Mag.* n.s. XIV (1896) 317–322.

WACHOVIA (N.C.) MORAVIAN CONGREGATIONS (various).

Moravian congregational journals; typical contents described in entry for Bethabara congregation, *q.v.* 1753.

In Adelaide L. Fries (ed.), *Records of the Moravians in North Carolina* (Raleigh, 1922–1941) January–December 1754, I 89–113; January–November 1755, I 122–140; November–December 1755 (by Dr. Bachhof), I 147–153; January–December 1757, I 177–182; January–December 1767, I 350–362; January–December 1768, I, 372–381; January–December 1769, I 386–395; January–December 1771 (with other congregations), I 437–473; August–November 1780, IV 1653–1654.

WINSLOW, Col. John (1703–1774) of Marshfield, Mass.

1. Travel journal, 1754; journey to Kennebec to build forts and maintain Indian alliance.

S. M. Pargellis, *Military Affairs in North America, 1748–1765* (New York, 1936) 54–58.

2. Military journal, summer and autumn 1755; siege of Fort Beauséjour and deportation of French Acadians; an orderly book with brief diary entries.

Nova Scotia Hist. Soc. Colls. IV (1884) 113–246, III (1883) 71–196.

ANON. (naval officer).   **1755**

Military journal, April–August 1755; one of thirty sailors with Braddock's expedition; march of Dunbar's brigade through Maryland and Virginia; military details, accounts of Indians and their customs, account of the battle; some long and fairly good descriptions; some notes *post facto.*

A. B. Hulbert, *Historic Highways of America* IV (Cleveland, 1903) 83–107. An expanded version, by Capt. Harry Gordon, published as *The Morris Journal* (London, 1854), reprinted in Winthrop Sargent, *The History of an Expedition against Fort Du Quesne in 1755* (Philadelphia, 1855) 359–389.

ANON.

Military journal, June–August 1755? (fragment); activities at Fort North Kill; principally scouting notes.

Israel Daniel Rupp, *History of Northampton, Lehigh, Monroe, Carbon, and Schuylkill Counties* (Harrisburg, 1845) App. 463–477.

ANON. (official French).

Military journal, July–September 1755; operations of the French army, march from Quebec to Lake Champlain, and battle there.

E. B. O'Callaghan, *Docs. Rel. Col. Hist. State New York* X (1858) 337–340; *Pennsylvania Archives,* 2d Ser. VI 334–338.

ANON. (official French).

Official journal, October 1755–June 1756; journal of occurrences in Canada; military details and news.

E. B. O'Callaghan, *Docs. Rel. Col. Hist. State New York* X (1858) 401–406.

ADAMS, John (1735–1826) of Braintree, Mass., second President of the United States.

1. Diary, November 1755–November 1777; fragmentary notes of his public work and private activities.

2. Travel diary, February 1778–September 1796; journey abroad, residence in France, and return.

The Works of John Adams (Boston, 1850–1856) II and III. Extract (with facsimile) relating to Boston Tea Party in *Massachusetts Hist. Soc. Proc.* 1st Ser. XIII (1873–1875) 191–192.

BURK, Maj. John (1717–1784) of Barnstable, Mass.

Military journal, July–September 1755; brief notes of marches, camp life; Saratoga, Crown Point.

L. C. Kellogg, *History of the Town of Bernardston* (Greenfield, Mass., 1902) 42–46.

DE FIEDMONT, Jacau (*ca.* 1720–post 1792) *b.* Louisburg, N.S.

Military journal, March–June 1755; attack on Beauséjour by officer in charge of French artillery; military details. Translated from the French.

John C. Webster, *The Siege of Beauséjour in 1755* (Pubs. New Brunswick Museum, 1936) 42 pp.

DE MONTREUIL, Chevalier, adjt. gen. to Baron Dieskau.

Military journal, August–September 1755; battle of Lake George. Translated from the French.

E. B. O'Callaghan, *Docs. Rel. Col. Hist. State New York* X (1858) 335–337.

DE VAUDREUIL, M.

Sea journal, May–June 1755 (abstract); journey of fleet under De la Mothe from Brest to Quebec. Translated from the French.

E. B. O'Callaghan, *Docs. Rel. Col. Hist. State New York* X (1858) 297–299.

DWIGHT, Capt. Nathaniel (1711–1784) of Belchertown, Mass.

Military journal, September–December 1755; battle of Lake George; Crown Point; building of Fort William Henry.

New York Geneal. Biog. Rec. XXXIII (1902) 3–10, 65–70.

FISHER, Daniel, of Williamsburg and York, Va.

Private diary, May–August 1755 (extracts); mainly kept at Philadelphia; long entries of fair interest, describing persons and places.

Pennsylvania Mag. Hist. Biog. XVII (1893) 263–278.

FLEET, Mary (*b.* 1729) of Boston.

Private diary, November 1755–October 1803; social and church affairs of the Old South Church; brief, scattered notes.

New England Hist. Geneal. Reg. XIX (1865) 59–61.

FRANKLAND, Sir Charles Henry (1716–1768) of Boston.

Travel diary, March 1755–December 1767 (extracts); stay in Lisbon, Portugal, etc.; notes on business, private, and social matters in New England; fashions and current events; fair interest.

Elias Nason, *Sir Charles Henry Frankland* (Albany, 1865) 51–97.

FROST, Edmund (1715?–1775) of Cambridge, Mass.

Private diary, November 1755–July 1759; a few notes of outstanding family events; little general interest.

New England Hist. Geneal. Reg. LV (1901) 441–442.

GATES, John (1713–1797) of Stow, Mass.

Private diary, March 1755–October 1789; few occasional entries, mostly on religion and public affairs.

Worcester Soc. Antiq. Proc. (1898) 267–280.

GILBERT, James (*b.* 1730) of Morton, Mass.

Military journal, July–September 1755; march from Albany to Lake George; marches, skirmishes, battle; very interesting spellings.

Mag. New England Hist. III (1893) 188–195.

GODFREY, Capt. Richard (*b.* 1711) of Taunton, Mass.

Military journal, June–October 1755; with Major Godfrey's company on expedition to Crown Point; Taunton, New York, Albany, Saratoga; interesting details of camp life and discontents; vigorous account of the victory; some interesting spellings.

Samuel H. Emery, *History of Taunton, Massachusetts* (Syracuse, 1893) 419–424; Ebenezer W. Peirce, *The Peirce Family of the Old Colony* (Boston, 1870) 109–114.

GORDON, Capt. Harry, of 48th Artillery. See 1755, ANON. (1) above.

HAWLEY, Lieut. Elisha (1726–1755) of Northampton, Mass.

Military journal, June–September 1755; brief military details of expedition against Crown Point; Fort Lyman.

J. R. Trumbull, *History of Northampton* (Northampton, Mass., 1902) II 254–258.

HERVEY, Hon. William (1732–1815) of Suffolk, Eng.

Military and private journals, June 1755–December 1814; American sections are dated 1755 (brief journal of march with Shirley's regiment from Boston to Lake Ontario), summer 1756 (work on roads and forts under Shirley), 1758 (journal of Ticonderoga campaign), 1760–1763 (full journal of Amherst's campaign, and orderly books at Montreal).

Journals of the Hon. William Hervey (Bury St. Edmunds, 1906) 548 pp. American sections pp. 1–17, 18–46, 47–52, 65–184.

HILL, James (1735–1811) of Newbury, Mass.

Military journal, May–December 1755; private soldier's account of first Crown Point expedition; battle of Lake George; brief entries; interesting spellings.

New England Quar. V (1932) 602–618.

JOHNSON, Sir William, and his scouts.

Journals of scouts, September 1755–July 1756; brief reports in journal form; reconnoitering from Lake George to Fort Frederick and Crown Point fort, etc. The scouts include Robert Rogers, Israel Putnam, William Symes, James Connor, Samuel Angell, Michael Thorley, Lieut. Waterbury, and others.

E. B. O'Callaghan, *Doc. Hist. State New York* IV (1851) 167–185.

KING, Titus (*ca.* 1729–1791) of Northampton, Mass.

Captive's diary, June 1755–June 1758 (with some narrative); capture by Indians, journey to Canada; hardships; Indian customs; a rather good diary, with interesting spellings and language.

Narrative of Titus King (Hartford, 1938) 21 pp.

LAWRENCE, Lieut. Eleazer (1708–1789) of Littleton, Mass.

Scouting journal, July–August 1755; scouting expedition from Lunenburg, between Connecticut River and Merrimac; little interest.

Robert M. Lawrence, *Historical Sketches of the Lawrence Family* (Boston, 1888) 33.

LEWIS, Col. Charles (*d.* 1774) of Staunton, Va.

Military journal, October–December 1755; march to Fort Cumberland after Braddock's defeat; notes on drunkenness and discipline of troops, marches, weather, Indian atrocities; fairly interesting.

Virginia Hist. Soc. Colls. n.s. XI (1891) 203–218; *West Virginia Hist. Mag.* IV (1904) 109–116.

ORME, Lieut. Robert (*ca.* 1725–1781) of Hertford, Eng.

Military journal, February–July 1755; with the Coldstream Guards on Braddock's expedition; mostly military details, vicissitudes of troops, topography.

Winthrop Sargent, *The History of an Expedition against Fort Du Quesne in 1755* (Philadelphia, 1855) 281–358.

OWEN, Nicholas (*d.* 1759), slave trader.

Slave trader's journal, July 1755–June 1758 (last few entries kept by Blayney Owen); begins as narrative in 1746 (?); interesting account of hardships and philosophy of slave trader between Africa and America.

Eveline Martin (ed.), *Journal of a Slave Dealer* (London, 1930) 120 pp.

ROGERS, Maj. Robert (1731–1795) of Portsmouth, N.H.

1. Scouting journals, September 1755–February 1761; scouting expedition during French and Indian War; fair but impersonal.

Journals of Major Robert Rogers (London, 1765) 236 pp.; Franklin B. Hough (ed.), *Journals of Major Robert Rogers* (Albany, 1883) 297 pp.

2. Scouting journal, October 1760–February 1761; journey to renew occupation of western French posts.

Edited by V. H. Paltsits, *Bull. New York Pub. Lib.* XXXVII (1933) 265–276, which corrects errors in previous editions.

3. Military journal, May–July 1763 (fragment); siege of Detroit.

Franklin B. Hough (ed.), *Diary of the Siege of Detroit* (Albany, 1860) 121–135.

4. Journal, September 1766–July 1767; kept while author was officer at Fort Michillimackinac; good picture of Indian trade.

Amer. Antiq. Soc. Proc. n.s. XXVIII (1918) 224–273.

SAUTER, Johann Michael.

Moravian travel journal, September–November 1755; Bethlehem to Wachovia, N.C.; Moravian religious details. Translated from the German.

Adelaide L. Fries (ed.), *Records of the Moravians in North Carolina* (Raleigh, 1922–1941) I 140–147.

STACKPOLE, Lieut. John (1708–1796) of Biddeford, Me.

Military journal, July 1755; brief notes of a march in Maine; some interesting spellings.

Maine Hist. Soc. Colls. 3d Ser. II (1906) 241–242.

STUART, Charles, of Cumberland Co., Pa.

Captive's diary, October 1755–August 1757; day-to-day narrative of captivity among Indians; apparently copy of a statement; fair.

Mississippi Valley Hist. Rev. XIII (1926–1927) 58–81.

THOMAS, Dr. John (1724–1776) of Kingston, Mass.

Surgeon's journal, April–December 1755; Winslow's expedition to remove the Acadians; fairly well told; interesting spellings.

John C. Webster (ed.), *Journals of Beauséjour* (Sackville, N.B., 1937) 11–39; *New England Hist. Geneal. Reg.* XXXIII (1879) 385–398; *Nova Scotia Hist. Soc. Colls.* I (1877–1878) 119–140.

WALTON, Josiah (1736–1831) of New Ipswich, N.H.

Military journal, June–October 1755; a few brief entries on the expedition to Crown Point.

New England Hist. Geneal. Reg. V (1851) 42.

WILLARD, Capt. Abijah (1724–1789) of Lancaster, Mass.

Military journal, April 1755–January 1756; Monkton's expedition to Nova Scotia, and siege of Fort Beauséjour; mainly military details, but good narrative and description, some of a general kind on people, camp life, etc.; very interesting spellings.

Edited by John C. Webster, *New Brunswick Hist. Soc. Colls.* No. 13 (1930) 1–75. Extracts in *Mag. Hist.* IX (1909) 10–12.

Anon. (British officer). 1756

Military journal, April–November 1756; march from Boston to Schenectady, Oneida, and Oswego; siege of Oswego; journey to Canada; description of Montreal and Quebec; letter-diary.

The Military History of Great Britain for 1756, 1757 (London 1757) 26–50.

Anon. (French).

Military journal, August 1756; siege of Chouaguen (Fort Pepperell).

E. B. O'Callaghan, *Doc. Hist. State New York* I (1850) 315–319.

Bacon, Capt. William (1716–1761) of Dedham, Mass.

Military journal, May–December 1756; a rather dull record of a march from Dedham to Albany.

The Dedication of a Monument to the Memory of the Men of Walpole (Walpole, 1901).

Beatty, Rev. Charles (*ca.* 1715–1772) *b.* county Antrim, Ireland.

Missionary journal, May–June 1756; travel and preaching in Pennsylvania, among Indians west of the Alleghenies.

Journal of a Two Months' Tour (London, 1768) 110 pp. Extracts in *W. H. Egle's Notes and Queries* (Pa.) 1st Ser. Part 5 (1881) 205–208.

Bethlehem (Pa.) Moravian Congregation.

1. Moravian journal, 1756; religious life and work. Translated.

Pennsylvania Germania n.s. II (1913) 187–193 (reprinted from *The Moravian,* July 6 and 13, 1910.)

2. Journal, April 1775–July 1782; extracts relating to the Revolution; largely notes on affairs of church and its members, but many interesting and well-written passages of general description.

Pennsylvania Mag. Hist. Biog. XII (1888) 385–406, XIII (1889) 71–89.

Burd, Col. James (1726–1793) of the Augusta Regiment.

1. Military journal, December 1756–October 1757 (with a few scattered prior entries); building Fort Augusta at Shamokin, Pa.; some notes on Indian affairs; a few interesting spellings.

Pennsylvania Archives 2d Ser. II 641–704.

2. Military journal, February–March 1758; inspection of Pennsylvania frontier forts, Fort Henry, Fort William, Fort Hamilton; official report.

Ibid., 1st Ser. III 352–357; Israel D. Rupp, *History of Northampton, Lehigh, Monroe, Carbon, and Schuylkill Counties* (Harrisburg, 1845) App. 449–459.

3. Military journal, February–March 1760; Indian affairs at Fort Augusta; brief, factual notes.

Pennsylvania Archives 2d Ser. VII 441–444.

4. Military journal, July–November 1760; at Pittsburgh; brief, factual notes.

Ibid., 2d Ser. VII 447–456.

5. Military journal, June–December 1763; at Fort Augusta; most of entries signed by Burd, others by various lieutenants.

Ibid., 2d Ser. VII 459–484.

CHESNEY, Alexander (*b.* 1756) of Pacolet River, S.C.

Loyalist diary, 1756–January 1820 (first part autobiography); vicissitudes of a Carolina loyalist in the Revolution; battle of King's Mountain; last part in Ireland; quite interesting.

Edited by E. A. Jones, *Ohio State Univ. Stud.* XXVI No. 4 (1921) 1–56. Extracts relating to King's Mountain (July–October 1780) in S. C. Williams, "The Battle of King's Mountain," *Tennessee Hist. Mag.* VII (1921) 54–61; and in Kathrine K. White, *The King's Mountain Men* (Dayton, Va., 1924) 108–112.

CROSS, Stephen (1731–1809) of Newburyport, Mass.

Private diary, March 1756–January 1757; adventures of a shipwright who went to build boats at Oswego to transport a British army for the attack on Montreal and Niagara; Lake Ontario, Quebec; excellent details of hardships; imprisonment in France; a good diary.

Essex Inst. Hist. Colls. LXXV (1939) 334–357, LXXVI (1940) 14–42.

CUTTER, Dr. Ammi Ruhamah (1735–1820) of North Yarmouth, Me.

Surgeon's military journal, June 1756–June 1758; with New Hampshire regiment; stages to Albany, Ticonderoga, Fort Edward; military details, casualties, etc.; in Connecticut and Massachusetts; siege of Louisburg; brief businesslike entries.

Benjamin Cutter, *A History of the Cutter Family of New England* (Boston, 1871) 61–70.

FRIZZELL, John (1730–1815).

Prison journal, August 1756–October 1760 (extracts); capture at Oswego, journey to Canada, exchange; a fairly interesting, naïve journal; interesting spellings.

Mag. Hist. XXIII (1916) 88–94.

GRAHAM, Rev. John (1694–1774) of Suffield, Conn.

Chaplain's journal, June–August 1756; with Connecticut troops in expedition against Crown Point and Fort William Henry.

Mag. Amer. Hist. VIII Part I (1882) 206–213.

HUTCHINSON, Thomas (1711–1780) of Boston, governor.

1. Travel diary, October–November 1756; journey to Rhode Island and Albany.

2. Travel diary, June 1774–April 1780; journey to England; domestic, personal, and political notes.

Extracts, combined with letters and editor's narrative, in Peter O. Hutchinson, *Diary and Letters of His Excellency Thomas Hutchinson, Esq.* (Boston, London, 1884–1886) two vols. Extract (July 1774, conversation with George III) in *Massachusetts Hist. Soc. Proc.* 1st Ser. XV (1876–1877) 326–334.

JOHNSON, Sir William (1715–1774), superintendent of Indian affairs.

1. Journals of Indian transactions, March 1756–December 1762; nine journals of public conferences held with Indians at Fort Johnson, Onondaga, Canajoharie, etc.; mostly minutes and speeches, with some brief notes of ceremonials. Reports to the Lords of Trade, signed by Peter Wraxall, secretary.

E. B. O'Callaghan, *Docs. Rel. Col. Hist. State New York* VII (1856) 91–116, 130–161, 171–200, 229–244, 244–254, 254–265, 324–333, 378–394; July–September 1756, April 1757, June 1757 also in *Pennsylvania Archives* 2d Ser. VI 489–527, 530–548.

2. Private diary, July–October 1759; kept at Niagara and Oswego; Indian affairs during the war, with some notes on weather, hunting, entertainment, etc.

William L. Stone, *The Life and Times of Sir William Johnson* (Albany, 1865) II App. 394–429; reprinted in A. G. Doughty (ed.), *Appendix to an Historical Journal of the Campaigns in North America ... by Captain John Knox* (Toronto, 1916) 187–232.

JONES, Col. John (1716–1801) of Dedham, Mass.

1. Diary, July 1756–March 1767; affairs as justice of the peace.

2. Surveying journal, 1762–1763; surveying at Mount Desert.

Amos Perry (ed.), *Book of Minutes of Col. John Jones* (Boston, Providence, 1894) 42 pp.

LOWRY, Jean, of Pennsylvania.

Captive's journal beginning April 1756; capture, with her children, by Indians at Rocky-Spring, Pa., and notes of hardships; religious disputes with French.

A Journal of the Captivity of Jean Lowry (Philadelphia, 1760) 31 pp.

MORTON, Thomas, of New Kent Co., Va.

Military journal, March 1756; expedition against Shawnee Indians; notes of movements, discipline, etc.; some interesting spellings.

Virginia Hist. Reg. IV (1851) 143–147.

POND, Peter (1740–1807) of Milford, Conn.

Fur trader's autobiography and journal, beginning 1756; a most lively and entertaining account of fur trade and travel in Old Northwest, mainly Wisconsin; interesting details of Wisconsin Indians and vivid portrayal of himself, his life, and his milieu; very interesting spellings and vocabulary.

Charles M. Gates (ed.), *Five Fur-Traders of the Northwest* (Univ. Minnesota, 1933) 11–59; *Connecticut Mag.* X (1906) 239–259; *Wisconsin Hist. Soc. Colls.* XVIII (1908) 314–354; extracts in articles in *Jour. Amer. Hist.* I (1907) 89–93, 357–365.

SECCOMBE, Rev. Joseph (*b.* 1732) of Medford, Mass.

Clergyman's journal or "textbook," January 1756–February 1777; scattered notes of sermons, births, deaths, weather, public events.

Essex Inst. Hist. Colls. XXXIV (1898) 23–39; extracts in *Danvers Hist. Soc. Colls.* IX (1921) 112–115.

SMITH, Maj. John.

Military journal, 1756–1757; brief extracts relating to French and Indian War.
Isabel M. Calder, *Colonial Captivities, Marches and Journeys* (New York, 1935), 137–139.

VAN ETTEN, Capt. John (in command of Fort Hyndshaw).

Military journal, December 1756–July 1757; events at Forts Hyndshaw and Hamilton; scouting, duties, Indian encounters; some interesting spellings.
Israel D. Rupp, *History of Northampton, Lehigh, Monroe, Carbon, and Schuylkill Counties* (Harrisburg, 1845) App. 423–445; *Pennsylvania Archives* 1st Ser. III 222–235; Thomas L. Montgomery, *Frontier Forts of Pennsylvania* (Harrisburg, 1916, 2d ed.) I 305–321.

WYMAN, Capt. Isaac (1725–1792) of Keene, N.H.

Military journal, May–July 1756; brief notes of military activities at Fort Massachusetts, guards, etc.; rather dull.
A. L. Perry, *Origins in Williamstown* (New York, 1896) 278–280.

YOUNG, James, of Pennsylvania, commissary general.

Military journal, June 1756; from Reading to forts in northern Pennsylvania, North Kill, Lebanon, etc.; descriptions and details.
Pennsylvania Archives, 1st Ser. II 675–681; Israel D. Rupp, *History of Northampton, Lehigh, Monroe, Carbon, and Schuylkill Counties* (Harrisburg, 1845) App. 410–420.

1757

ANON. (officer in command of Fort North Kill).

Military journal, June–August 1757; march from Reading to Fort North Kill; Indian affairs around the fort; official report.
Thomas L. Montgomery, *Frontier Forts of Pennsylvania* (Harrisburg, 1916, 2d ed.) I 107–117.

ANON. (official French).

Military journal, July–August 1757; expedition against Fort William Henry.
E. B. O'Callaghan, *Docs. Rel. Col. Hist. State New York* X (1858) 598–605.

BANCROFT, Deacon Samuel (1715–1782) of Reading, Mass.

1. Military journal, August 1757; expedition to Brookfield.
2. Private diary, September–October 1766 and April–June 1769; personal and religious notes, farming, etc.
Frank D. Andrews (ed.), *Family Record of Deacon Samuel Bancroft* (Vineland, 1922) 24 pp.

BANYAR, Goldsbrow, of New York, deputy secretary of New York.

Official journal, August 1757; mostly official military business in French and Indian War; impersonal notes, orders, statistics.
Mag. Amer. Hist. I Part I (1877) 25–33.

CLINTON, George (1739–1812) of New York, soldier and statesman.

Sea journal, October 1757–January 1758; on board the "Defiance," privateer of New York, during French and Indian War; brief notes.

New York History XVI (1935) 89–95.

DARLING, Jonathan (1741–1763) of Bluehill, Me.

Military diary, July 1757–October 1772; mostly military items, Louisburg campaign of 1759; other notes on life in Andover, Mass., and Bluehill, Me.

Bangor Hist. Mag. II (1886–1887) 76–78.

ENGLE, Lieut. Andrew.

Military journal, December 1757; very brief notes of stationing men about Lehigh during French and Indian War.

W. H. Egle's Notes and Queries (Pa.) (1897) 13 pp.

FREEMAN, Capt. Joshua (1717–1794) of Truro, Mass.

Scouting journal, May–July 1757; brief notes of march to Meduncook.

Cyrus Eaton, *Annals of the Town of Warren* (Hallowell, Me., 1877) 106–108.

GAINE, Hugh (1727–1807) *b.* Ireland, of New York City, printer.

1. Diary, January 1757–March 1758; notes of public occurrences, political and military.

2. Diary, January 1777–December 1782; news of war; short notes, mainly of naval and military movements.

3. Diary, March 1797–December 1798; notes on weather, news, local affairs and gossip in New York, ship movements.

Paul L. Ford (ed.), *The Journals of Hugh Gaine* (New York, 1902) II 3–15, 16–163, 164–213.

GRIDLEY, Pvt. Luke (*b.* 1734) of Farmington, Conn.

Military journal, March–November 1757; fairly interesting notes of military life at Fort Edward during French and Indian War; interesting spellings.

Luke Gridley's Diary of 1757, Acorn Club Pubs. X (Hartford, 1906) 64 pp.

HERRICK, Capt. Israel (1721–1782) of Topsfield, Mass.

Scouting journal, May–July 1757; expedition between the Androscoggin and Kennebec rivers; mainly notes of movements; some interesting spellings.

Maine Hist. Soc. Colls. and Proc. 2d Ser. II (1891) 219–224.

HINCHMAN, Dr. Joseph, of Long Island.

Surgeon's journal, August–November 1757; kept while author was surgeon on the "Prince George," privateer; log with many private entries; wreck, landing on Tortuga Island; first part very good; interesting spellings.

Pennsylvania Mag. Hist. Biog. XXIX (1905) 268–281.

KELSEY, Sergt. Moses (*d.* 1758) of New Hampshire.

Military journal, July 1757–May 1758; brief notes of movements and discipline; mainly kept during Loudon's expedition against Louisburg; interesting spellings.

Granite State Mag. II (1906) 95–101.

KNOX, Capt. John (*d.* 1778) *b.* Ireland, of 43d Foot Regiment.

Military journal, February 1757–September 1760; a most copious journal of campaigns in the French and Indian War, including sieges of Louisburg and Quebec; many general notes and character sketches. "The most valuable record of those eventful times" (Doughty).

An Historical Journal of the Campaigns in North-America (London, 1769) two vols.; edited by A. G. Doughty (Toronto, 1914) two vols. Extracts (Sept. 1759, battle of Quebec) in *Old South Leaflets* III No. 73, 16 pp.

METCALF, Seth (*b.* 1735) of Rutland, Mass.

1. Military journal, April 1757–January 1758; kept at Fort Edward; brief notes, with some interesting spellings.

2. Personal diary, November 1755–January 1807; actually scattered notes of memorable events, weather, and providences.

Diary and Journal (1755–1807) of Seth Metcalf (Boston, 1939) 31 pp. mimeo.

MONTRESOR, Capt. John (1736–1799) of London, Eng., engineer.

Military journals, January 1757–December 1778; extensive notes of journeys and campaigns; Fort Edward, Louisburg, Quebec, Bradstreet's expedition; building fortifications in New York 1757–1759; Albany and New York 1765; Boston 1770; Long Island 1771; Revolutionary War. An important journal.

New York Hist. Soc. Colls. (1881) 11–520. Diary of journey from Quebec to Maine, June–July 1760, which was used as guidebook on Arnold's expedition to Quebec, in *Maine Hist. Soc. Colls.* I (1865) 448–466; Kenneth Roberts (ed.), *March to Quebec* (New York, 1938) 5–24. Journal of expedition to Detroit, 1763, in *Trans. Royal Soc. Canada,* 3d Ser. XXII (1928) 10–29. Extracts for July 1777–July 1778 (Brandywine, occupation and evacuation of Philadelphia) in *Pennsylvania Mag. Hist. Biog.* V (1881) 393–417, VI (1882) 34–57, 189–206, 284–299.

MORGAN, Capt. Jacob (1716–1792) of Schuylkill Valley, Pa.

1. Military journal, July 1757; kept at Fort Lebanon, Pa.; notes of daily routine.

Pennsylvania Archives 1st Ser. III 252–254; Thomas L. Montgomery, *Frontier Forts of Pennsylvania* (Harrisburg, 1916, 2d ed.) I 129–133; *Pubs. Hist. Soc. Schuylkill County* (Pa.) III (1911) 47–48.

2. Military journal, April 1758; fort life in Pennsylvania during French and Indian War.

Pennsylvania Mag. Hist. Biog. XXXIX (1915) 186–191.

OLIVER, Peter (1741–1822) of Middleborough, Mass.

Private diary, October 1757–June 1821; begins with autobiographical sketch; notes of personal affairs, life in New England and England, and public affairs.

Extracts in Thomas Weston, *History of Middleborough* (Boston, 1906) 148–150, and in Peter Oliver (ed.), *The Diary and Letters of Thomas Hutchinson* (Boston, 1883) 68–69 etc.

PUTNAM, Gen. Rufus (1738–1824) of Brookfield, Mass.

1. Military journals, March 1757–December 1760; kept in northern New York

during four campaigns of French and Indian War; military movements, hardships, atrocities.

E. C. Dawes (ed.), *Journal of Gen. Rufus Putnam* (Albany, 1886) 115 pp.

2. Travel and exploration journal, December 1772–August 1773; reconnoitering and exploring around the Mississippi; a long and a shorter journal; fairly good, with interesting spellings.

The Two Putnams, Israel and Rufus (Hartford, 1931) 143–262.

[REMILLY, Capt. Matthias, of Waldoborough, Me.]

Scouting journal, May–June 1757; brief and mediocre notes of service at Broad Bay; one good Indian story and some interesting spellings.

Cyrus Eaton, *Annals of the Town of Warren* (Hallowell, Me., 1877) 111–114.

WITHERSPOON, John, of Annapolis, N.S.

Prison diary, November 1757–September 1759; capture by French and imprisonment at Quebec; a rather good diary with varied events, hardships, siege, religion, etc.

Nova Scotia Hist. Soc. Colls. II (1879–1880) 31–62.

1758

ANON. (of Windsor, Conn.).

Military journal, May–June 1758; brief extracts concerning the French and Indian War.

S. W. Adams and H. R. Stiles, *The History of Ancient Wethersfield, Connecticut* (New York, 1904) I 406.

ANON.

Military journal, May–August 1758; rather dull notes of Amherst's expedition against Louisburg.

New York Hist. Soc. Colls., Cadwallader-Colden Papers V (1921) 265–281.

ANON. (provincial officer).

Military journal, May–November 1758; kept in northern New York.

Hist. Mag. n.s. X (1871) 113–122.

ANON.

Military journal, June–July 1758; full day-to-day account of the siege of Louisburg by a spectator.

An Authentic Account of the Reduction of Louisbourg (London, 1758) 60 pp.

ANON. (official French).

Military journal, July 1758; battle of Ticonderoga. Translated from the French.

E. B. O'Callaghan, *Docs. Rel. Col. Hist. State New York* X (1858) 741–744.

ALEXANDER, Ens. Thomas (1727–1801) of Northfield, Mass.

Military journal, May–October 1758; Ticonderoga expedition; brief notes of movements and military affairs.

J. H. Temple and G. Sheldon, *A History of the Town of Northfield* (Albany, 1875) 303–305.

AMES, Dr. Nathaniel (1741–1822) of Dedham, Mass.

Private diary, September 1758–June 1821; extensive and sustained personal, social, local, and national notes; a valuable and entertaining diary, with interesting vocabulary and some verse (several prepared for his almanacs).

Dedham Hist. Reg. I (1890) to XIV (1903) *passim.* Extracts, with a narrative on the conflicts of the parties of Hamilton and Jefferson, in Charles Warren, *Jacobin and Junto; or, Early American Politics as Viewed in the Diary of Dr. Nathaniel Ames* (Cambridge, 1931) 324 pp.

AMHERST, Maj. Gen. Jeffery (1717–1797), governor general.

1. Military journal, 1758–1763; military affairs during French and Indian War.

John C. Webster (ed.), *The Journal of Jeffery Amherst* (Chicago, Toronto, 1931) 324 pp.

2. Military journal, 1758–1760 (with Col. William Amherst); French and Indian War.

A Journal of the Landing of His Majesty's Forces on the Island of Cape-Breton (Boston, 1758, 3d ed.) 22 pp.; A. G. Doughty (ed.), Appendix to *An Historical Journal of the Campaigns in North-America by Captain John Knox* (Toronto, 1916) 1–96.

AMHERST, Lieut. Gen. William (1732–1781) *b.* Sevenoaks, Eng.

1. Military journal, March 1758–September 1760; journey to America, military affairs up to surrender of Montreal, including an important account of siege of Louisburg; military details only.

John C. Webster (ed.), *Journal of William Amherst in America* (Frome and London, 1927) 82 pp.

2. Military journal, August–October 1762; recapture of St. John's, N.F.

John C. Webster (ed.), *The Recapture of St. John's, Newfoundland, in 1762* (n.p., 1928) 15 pp.

BARROWS, Abner (1732–1818) of Middleborough, Mass.

Military journal, July 1758 (extract); service in French and Indian War; engagement at Lake George; interesting spellings.

Thomas Weston, *History of the Town of Middleboro* (Boston, 1906) 95–98.

BASS, Lieut. Benjamin.

Military journal, August–October 1758; expedition under Bradstreet against Fort Frontenac; linguistically interesting.

New York History XVI (1935) 449–452.

BIGELOW, Rev. Silas (1739–1769) of Shrewsbury and Paxton, Mass.

Schoolmaster's diary, March 1758–February 1761; short personal entries; clothes, illnesses, remedies, a startling dream.

Worcester Soc. Antiq. Proc. XVII (1900) 260–268.

CALLENDER, Hannah (1737–1801) of Philadelphia.

Private diary, August 1758–June 1762; social, personal, and topographical notes.

Pennsylvania Mag. Hist. Biog. XII (1888) 432–456.

CHAMPION, Col. Henry (1723–1797) of Colchester, Conn.

Military journal, June–November 1758; march from Colchester to Ticonderoga; mostly brief notes of march, camp life, discipline, military details, and return home.

F. B. Trowbridge, *The Champion Genealogy* (New Haven, 1891) 417–435.

CHEW, Colby.

Scouting journal, August 1758; official report of expedition; frontier scouting methods; report to Washington.

Stanislaus M. Hamilton (ed.), *Letters to Washington and Accompanying Papers* III (Boston, 1901) 39–43.

COBB, Capt. Elisha (1736–1794) of Gorham, Me.

Scouting journal, May–July 1758 (extracts); with Preble's regiment in French and Indian War; notes of army movements.

H. D. McLellan, *History of Gorham, Me.* (Portland, 1903) 66–68.

COBB, Capt. Samuel (1718–post 1789) of Falmouth Neck, Me., shipwright.

Military journal, May–November 1758; march from Falmouth to Kittery, New York, Schenectady, Ticonderoga; military details; interesting language.

Reg. Soc. Col. Wars State of Maine (Portland, 1905) 90–113.

DORR, Ens. Moses.

Military journal, May–October 1758; expedition against Canada in Capt. Parker's company; Roxbury and Fort Stanwix; military movements; some interesting spellings.

New York History XVI (1935) 452–464.

DRINKER, Mrs. Elizabeth (1734–1807) of Philadelphia.

Private diary, October 1758–November 1807; private and social life in Philadelphia; notes on the Revolution.

Henry D. Biddle (ed.), *Extracts from the Journal of Elizabeth Drinker* (Philadelphia, 1889) 423 pp. Extracts (1771) in James B. Nolan, *Early Narratives of Berks County* (Reading, Pa., 1927) 54–56; *Pennsylvania Mag. Hist. Biog.* XIII (1889) 298–308.

FOSTER, Capt. Asa (1710–1787) of Andover, Mass.

Military journal, June–October 1758; rather dull notes kept during French and Indian War, in New York State.

New England Hist. Geneal. Reg. LIV (1900) 183–188.

FULLER, Col. Archelaus (1727–1776) of Middleton, Mass.

Military journal, May–November 1758; expedition to Ticonderoga; interesting for sympathy toward victims; many very interesting spellings.

Essex Inst. Hist. Colls. XLVI (1910) 209–220.

GORDON, Capt., of Royal Artillery.

Military journal, April–August 1758; combined with order book; siege of Louisburg; very little of nonmilitary or personal interest.

Nova Scotia Hist. Soc. Colls. V (1886–1887) 97–153.

GORDON, Col. James (1713–1768) of Lancaster Co., Va.

Plantation diary, December 1758–December 1763; life in Lancaster Co.; rather brief notes on domestic, business, local, plantation, social affairs; fairly interesting.

William and Mary Coll. Quar. 1st Ser. XI (1902–1903) 98–112, 217–236, XII (1903–1904) 1–12. Extracts in *Jour. Amer. Hist.* III (1909) 81–89.

GORDON, William Augustus, of Highland Infantry.

Military journal, April–August 1758; siege of Louisburg; statistics.

Royal United Services Inst. Jour. LX (1915) 117–152.

GUILD, Ens. Aaron (1728–1818) of Dedham, Mass.

Military journal, May–July 1758; march with Nichol's regiment to Fort Edward.

*The Dedication of a Monument to the Memory of the Men of Walpole and Vicinity (Walpole, 1901). [Forbes.]

HAYDEN, Augustin (1740–1823) of Windsor, Conn.

1. Military journal, May–November 1758; brief notes of march from Windsor to Ticonderoga and back.

2. Military journal, April–December 1759; kept at Fort Edward and Crown Point.

J. H. Hayden, *Records of the Connecticut Line of the Hayden Family* (Windsor Locks, 1888) 120–123.

HOLT, Joseph (1718–1789) of Wilton, N.H.

1. Military journal, May–October 1758; expedition to Canada; brief notes of army movements.

2. Travel journal, June–July 1676 (*sic*); journal of voyage to Penobscot; ascribed to Holt, but must be by someone else. [Forbes.]

New England Hist. Geneal. Reg. X (1856) 307–311.

JEWETT, Benjamin.

Military journal, April–November 1758; expedition from Windham against Canada; interesting spellings.

National Mag. XVII (1892–1893) 62–64.

KENNY, James, of Philadelphia.

1. Travel journal, 1758–1759; journey "to the Westward"; trading at Pittsburgh.

Pennsylvania Mag. Hist. Biog. XXXVII (1913) 395–449.

2. Travel and trading diary, January 1761–April 1763; journey to Pittsburgh and trade there; excellent description of frontier life by a shrewd and humorous Quaker; interesting language.

Ibid. XXXVII (1913) 1–47, 152–201.

KERN, Lieut. Jacob.

Travel journal, January–February 1758; journey from Reading to Delaware and back; fairly interesting.

W. H. Egle's Notes and Queries (Pa.) 3d Ser. II (1896) 124–125.

KNAP, Nathaniel (1736–1816) of Newbury, Mass.

Military journal, March 1758–July 1759; brief and rather dull military and naval notes of the siege of Louisburg.

Soc. Col. Wars Massachusetts Pub. No. 2 (1895) 1–42; extracts in J. J. Currier, *Ould Newbury* (Boston, 1896) 485–487.

LYON, Capt. Lemuel (*b.* 1738) of Woodstock, Conn.

Military journal, April–November 1758; expedition against Canada; fairly good personal and military notes, some of them amusing.

Abraham Tomlinson (ed.), *The Military Journals of Two Private Soldiers* (Poughkeepsie, 1855) 11–45.

MALARTIC, Adjt.

1. Military journal, June–July 1758; French operations before Ticonderoga on frontier of Lake St. Sacrament; translated from the French.

2. Military journal, October 1757–October 1758; occurrences in camps occupied by the Béarn Regiment; quite interesting.

E. B. O'Callaghan, *Docs. Rel. Col. Hist. State New York* X (1858) 721–725, 835–855.

MONCKTON, Col. Robert, of Royal American Regiment.

Military journal, September–November 1758; expedition up St. John's River; destroying Acadian settlements; military details only.

New Brunswick Hist. Soc. Colls. No. 5 (1904) 165–174.

NOYES, Capt. John (1740–1784) of Newbury, Mass.

Military journal, April–November 1758, and odd later items; Ticonderoga expedition; marches, distances, some unremarkable general notes; a few interesting spellings.

Essex Inst. Hist. Colls. XLV (1909) 73–77.

PARKMAN, William (1741–1832) of Concord, Mass.

Military journal, July–August 1758 (extracts); a few entries relating to battle of Ticonderoga; Howe's death; capture of Putnam.

Massachusetts Hist. Soc. Proc. 1st Ser. XVII (1879–1880) 243–244.

POST, Christian Frederick (1710–1785) *b.* Prussia, Moravian missionary.

Missionary travel journals; official negotiations with Indians; language normalized from an extraordinary German-English (sample in Thwaites I 183–184).

1. July–September 1758; tour to the Ohio Indians with Charles Thomson.

R. G. Thwaites (ed.), *Early Western Travels* (Cleveland, 1904) I 185–233; (Charles Thomson), *An Enquiry into the Causes of the Alienation of the Delaware and the Shawanese Indians* (London, 1759) 130–171; Robert Proud, *History of Pennsylvania* (Philadelphia, 1798) II App. 65–95; N. B. Craig, *The Olden Time* I (1846, reprinted, Cincinnati, 1876) 99–125; Israel D. Rupp, *Early History of Western Pennsylvania* (Pittsburgh, Harrisburg, 1846) App. 75–98; *Pennsylvania Archives* 1st Ser. III 520–544 (with slight variations from original MS).

2. October 1758–January 1759; second journey to the Ohio.

Thwaites I 234–291; *The Second Journal* . . . (London, 1759); Proud, II App. 96–132; Craig, I 145–177; Rupp, App. 99–126.

3. July–August 1762; leading Indians from Tuscarora to Lancaster.
Pennsylvania Archives 1st Ser. IV 92–98.
(The journal for November–December 1758 which is listed in *Pennsylvania Archives* as Post's is by Croghan, *q.v.*[1751]; see Thwaites I, 101 note.)

REA, Dr. Caleb (1727–1760) of Danvers, Mass.
Surgeon's diary, May–November 1758; Ticonderoga expedition; long medical, general, and personal notes; camp life; fair interest.
Essex Inst. Hist. Colls. XVIII (1881) 81–120, 177–205.

RICHARDSON, William (1729–1777) *b.* England, of Waxhaw settlement, S.C.
Missionary journal, November 1758–February 1759; mission to the Overhill Cherokees; preaching and baptizing; fall of Fort Loudon; fairly interesting.
Tennessee Hist. Mag. 2d Ser. I (1931) 125–138.

SHUTE, Rev. Daniel (1722–1802) of Hingham, Mass.
Chaplain's journal, May–October 1758; expedition against Canada; from Boston through Albany and Schuyler's Farm; religious, social, personal details; fairly interesting.
Essex Inst. Hist. Colls. XII (1874) 132–151.

SMITH, Joseph (1735–1816) of Montville, Conn.
Military journal, June–September 1758; brief notes of expedition to Ticonderoga and Crown Point; skirmishes, camp life, hardships; fairly interesting; some spellings of interest.
Connecticut Soc. Col. Wars Proc. I (1896) 303–310.

SPAULDING, Lieut. Leonard.
Military journal, July–October 1758; Crown Point expedition; marches, discipline, camp life; moderate, but very interesting spellings.
Vermont Hist. Gazetteer V Part II (1891) 28–32.

SPICER, Abel (1746–*ca.* 1787) of Groton, Conn.
Military diary, June–September 1758; enlistment, expedition with Stanton's company; New London to Lyme and New York, Tappan Bay, Albany, Fort Edward; marches, skirmishes, news from other fronts, camp life; details of Major Rogers; solid entries; fairly interesting.
Susan S. and Susan B. Meech, *History of the Descendants of Peter Spicer* (n.p., 1911) 388–408.

THOMPSON, Charles, secretary to Chief Teedyuscung.
Travel journal, March 1758; with Christian Post on journey to northern frontiers of Pennsylvania; report of conferences with Indians.
Hazard's Reg. Pennsylvania VIII (1831) 85–87, 97–98, 113–116, 129–130, 145–148.

THOMPSON, Sergt. James (1732–1830) *b.* Tain, Scotland, of Quebec.
Diary 1758–1830 (dates of MS); undated extract relating to Montgomery's sword.

Lit. Hist. Soc. Quebec Trans. No. 22 (1898) 57–62; *Lit. Hist. Soc. Quebec Hist. Docs.* 7th Ser. (1905).

THOMPSON, Lieut. Samuel (1731–1820) of Woburn, Mass.

Military journal, May–November 1758; expedition against French at Lake George; marches, camp life; moderate interest.

Samuel Sewall, *The History of Woburn* (Boston, 1868) App. IX 547–558. An account of Thompson's diaries in *New England Hist. Geneal. Reg.* XXXIV (1880) 397–401.

TINKHAM, Sergt. Seth, of Middleborough, Mass.

Military journal, May–September 1758; march of Pratt's company to join Col. Bradstreet; Lake George and Ticonderoga; battle of Lake George; marches, camp life, casualties, hardships; fair interest; some spellings of interest.

Ebenezer W. Peirce, *The Peirce Family of the Old Colony* (Boston, 1870) 119–128.

TITAMY, Moses, and HILL, Isaac.

Travel journal, June–July 1758; to Minisink Indians; dealings with Indians. *Pennsylvania Archives* 1st Ser. III 504–508.

WHEELER, Jonathan (1741–1811) of Grafton, Mass.

Private diary, April 1758–March 1796; a few scattered notes of weather, accidents, news of French and Indian War.

F. C. Pierce, *History of Grafton* (Worcester, 1879) 71–73.

ZANE, Isaac, of Philadelphia.

Private diary, May–June 1758; journey to Wyoming to build an Indian town; a carpenter's adventures among the Indians; some interesting spellings. *Pennsylvania Mag. Hist. Biog.* XXX (1906) 417–426.

1759

ANON. (Sergt. Maj. in Hopson's Grenadiers).

A Journal of the Expedition up the River St. Lawrence: containing a true and most particular account of the transactions of the fleet and army under the command of Admiral Saunders and General Wolfe from the time of their embarkation at Louisbourg 'til after the surrender of Quebeck (Boston 1759) 24 pp. Reprinted *Mag. Hist.* Extra No. 24 (New York, 1913) 97–113.

ANON.

Military journal, 1759; expedition up the St. Lawrence; apparently based on the preceding journal.

Lit. Hist. Soc. Quebec Hist. Docs. 2d Ser. No. 6 (1868) 19 pp., reprinted from *New York Mercury,* December 31, 1759.

ANON. (official French).

Military journal, May–August 1759 (fragment); siege of Quebec; narrative with daily entries. Translated.

E. B. O'Callaghan, *Docs. Rel. Col. Hist. State New York* X (1858) 993–1001.

ANON.

Military journal, May–September 1759; expedition up the St. Lawrence; purely military details; found among papers of George Alsop, secretary to Wolfe's quartermaster general.

Lit. Hist. Soc. Quebec Hist. Docs. 4th Ser. No. 1 (1875) 21 pp.

ANON. (officer in Fraser's regiment?).

Military journal, June–August 1759 (extracts); siege of Quebec; at anchor opposite Isle of Orleans; detailed description of operations.

Hist. Mag. IV (1860) 321–326.

ANON. (official French).

Military journal, June–September 1759; operations of the French army under Montcalm before Quebec; discursive entries. Translated.

E. B. O'Callaghan, Docs. Rel. Col. Hist. State New York X (1858) 1016–1046.

ANON.

Military journal, June–September 1759; siege of Quebec; military and naval movements, bombardments; historical and dull.

An Accurate and Authentic Journal of the Siege of Quebec (London, 1759) 44 pp.; reprinted by Arthur Doughty, The Siege of Quebec IV (1901) 279–294.

ANON. (French soldier?).

Military journal, July 1759; siege of Niagara; British victory; translated from the French.

New York Mercury, August 20, 1759; Hist. Mag. n.s. V (1869) 197–199.

BACKUS, Rev. Isaac (1734–1806) of Titicut, Mass.

Baptist journal, November 1759–1804 (extracts); rather dull journal of religious work, mainly in and around Titicut.

Alvah Hovey, A Memoir of the Life and Times of the Rev. Isaac Backus (Boston, 1859) 73–305 passim.

BAILY, Joshua (1737–1774) of Bradford, Mass.

Military journal, March–July 1759; brief notes of events on expedition to Fort Penobscot.

Quoted in New England Hist. Geneal. Reg. XIV (1860) 4–10 ("Building and Occupancy of Fort Pownall").

BAYLEY, Capt. Jacob (1726–1815) of Newbury, Vt.

Military journals, July–October 1759 and August 1760; fragments of letter-journals, describing journey to and siege of Ticonderoga, and camp life at Isle aux Noix.

F. P. Wells, History of Newbury, Vermont (St. Johnsbury, 1902) 376–380.

BOWEN, Ashley (1727–1813) of Marblehead, Mass.

1. Sea journal, April–November 1759; voyage from Boston to Halifax to join fleet for expedition to Quebec; military and naval details at Quebec.

Essex Inst. Hist. Colls. LXX (1934) 227–266.

2. Private diaries, June 1773–December 1774; almanacs with notes of important events at Marblehead; local affairs, ship movements, necrology.

Massachusetts Mag. I (1908) 174–176, 260–265, II (1909) 109–114, III (1910) 240–245, V (1912) 29–35.

BOYLE, John (1746–1819) of Boston, printer and publisher.

Public journal, January 1759–April 1778; journal of public occurrences, compiled from news items; public affairs; important for social history and genealogy.

New England Hist. Geneal. Reg. LXXXIV (1930) 142–171, 248–272, 357–382, LXXXV (1931) 5–28, 117–133.

BURNABY, Rev. Andrew (1734–1812) of Greenwich and Leicester, Eng.

Travel journal, April 1759–October 1760; travels through Pennsylvania, New York, Rhode Island, Massachusetts, New Hampshire, and especially Virginia; account of the colonies; acute Tory observations on colonial politics and policies; an important sourcebook.

Travels through the Middle Settlements in North America (London, 1775) 106 pp. R. R. Wilson (ed.), *Burnaby's Travels through North America* (New York, 1904; reprinted from third edition, 1798) 265 pp. Extracts relating to Virginia (April–May 1759) in *Virginia Hist. Reg.* V (1852) 27–38, 81–93, 144–157.

BURRELL, Sergt. John (*b.* 1717) of Abington, Mass.

Military journal, August 1759–July 1760; with Parke's company during French and Indian War; brief notes at St. John's, N.B., Fort La Tour; very interesting spellings.

New England Hist. Geneal. Reg. LIX (1905) 352–354; *Acadiensis* V (1905) 287–294; *Jour. Amer. Hist.* XX (1926) 375–381.

CLARK, Thomas (1737–1809) of Gloucester Co., N.J.

Private diary, *ca.* 1759–1804 (summary, with obscured dates); farm life; as prisoner of British; life as judge and influential citizen.

Frank H. Stewart, *Notes on Old Gloucester County* I (Camden, N.J., 1917) 303–306.

CLEAVELAND, Rev. John (1722–1799) of Salem, Mass.

Chaplain's journal, June–August 1759; siege of Louisburg; clerical and military details.

Essex Inst. Hist. Colls. XII (1874) 85–103, 179–196, XIII (1875) 53–63.

CLOUGH, Gibson (1738–1799) of Salem, Mass.

Military journal, April 1759–January 1761; march from Salem to Louisburg, and siege; mediocre journal, but has a few interesting episodes.

Essex Inst. Hist. Colls. III (1861) 99–106, 195–201.

DIBBLE, Ens. Ebenezer (*d.* 1784) of Cornwall, Conn.

1. Military journal, May–December 1759; Amherst's campaign against Ticonderoga and Crown Point; brief notes of marches and hardships.

2. Military journal, May–November 1762; in garrison at Crown Point; very interesting spellings.

Connecticut Soc. Col. Wars Proc. I (1896) 311–329. Extracts in Edward C. Starr, *A History of Cornwall, Connecticut* (New Haven, 1926) 179–184.

FOBES, Perez (1742–1812) of Harvard and Brown University.

Diary and commonplace book, August 1759–1760 (dates obscure in text); his reading, and philosophical and introspective observations; extempore Latin.

New England Quar. II (1929) 654–658.

FRASER, Col. Malcolm (of Fraser's Highlanders).

Military journal, May 1759–May 1760; a fairly interesting account of the siege of Quebec.

Lit. Hist. Soc. Quebec Hist. Docs. 2d Ser. (1927) 1–37; *Jour. Soc. Army Hist. Research* XVIII (1939) 135–168; George M. Wrong, *A Canadian Manor and Its Seigneurs* (Toronto, 1908) 249–271.

GARDNER, Samuel (1740–1762) of Salem, Mass.

Private diary, January–December 1759; begins with a flippant account of Harvard life; long description of voyage to Portugal and Algiers.

Essex Inst. Hist. Colls. XLIX (1913) 1–22.

HARDY, Constantine (1737–1777) of Westborough, Mass.

Military journal, April–September 1759 (extracts); Crown Point expedition; skirmishes; very interesting spellings.

New England Hist. Geneal. Reg. LX (1906) 236–238.

HAWKS, Maj. John (1707–1784) of Deerfield, Mass.

Orderly book and journal, July 1759–September 1760; Ticonderoga and Crown Point campaign; mostly military details and orders.

Orderly Book and Journal of Major John Hawks, Soc. Col. Wars New York, Pub. No. 15 (New York, 1911) 92 pp.

HENSHAW, Col. William (1735–1820) of Leicester, Mass.

Military journal, May–November 1759; service at and about Ticonderoga under Gen. Amherst; brief notes.

Worcester Soc. Antiq. Proc. XXV (1912) 46–63.

HURLBUT, John (1730–1782) of New London, Conn.

1. Military journal, May–December 1759; Crown Point expedition, with private items for 1775.

Mag. Amer. Hist. XXIX (1893) 395–396.

2. Travel diary, May–June 1773; journey from Connecticut to Wyoming Valley, Pa., and Delaware, to inspect lands.

Historical Record (Wyoming Valley, Pa.) I (1886–1887) 213–214.

LANE, Daniel (1740–1811) of Buxton, Me.

1. Military journal, July–December 1759; siege of Quebec; journeys to Halifax to work on fortifications.

2. Travel journals, May–November 1761 and May–June 1762; few, dull notes.

New England Hist. Geneal. Reg. XXVI (1872) 238–243.

MacKellar, Patrick (1717–1778), engineer.

1. Military journal, April–September 1759; siege of Quebec; known as "Journal of Major Moncrief."

"A Short Account of the Expedition against Quebec," *Jour. Corps Royal Engineers* (1848); reprinted in A. G. Doughty, *The Siege of Quebec* V (1901) 33–58.

2. Military journal, June–August 1762; military landing at Cuba; siege of Havana; military, engineering, and artillery details.

A Correct Journal of the Landing His Majesty's Forces (London, Boston, 1762) 19 pp.

Merriman, Samuel (1723–1803) of Northfield, Mass.

Military journals, May 1759–September 1760; one official and one personal; at Albany, Ticonderoga, Crown Point, etc.; rather dull, apart from interesting spellings.

George Sheldon, *A History of Deerfield, Mass.* (Deerfield, 1895) I 661–668.

Murray, Gen. James (1719?–1790), governor of Quebec.

1. Military journal, September 1759–May 1760; military and political activities at Quebec after its surrender; official entries, but many items of general interest.

Lit. Hist. Soc. Quebec Docs. 3d Ser. No. 4 (1871) 45 pp.

2. Military journal, May–September 1760; mainly notes of military and naval movements at and about Quebec and Montreal.

Arthur G. Doughty (ed.), *An Historical Journal of the Campaigns in North America . . . by Captain John Knox* (Toronto, 1916) Appendix Vol. III 306–334.

Pouchot, Capt.

Military journal, July 1759; siege of Niagara. Translated from the French.

E. B. O'Callaghan, *Docs. Rel. Col. Hist. State New York* X (1858) 977–992.

Procter, Capt. Jonathan (1739–1821) of Danvers, Mass.

Military journal, May 1759–November 1760; siege of Louisburg, and return home; notes on terrain and works; ship movements; weather, and some personal items; very interesting language.

Essex Inst. Hist. Colls. LXX (1934) 31–57.

True, Rev. Henry (1726–1782) of Hampstead, N.H.

Chaplain's journals, June–October 1759; Ticonderoga, Fort Edward, Crown Point; mediocre, although some amusing Latin entries.

Journal and Letters of Rev. Henry True (Marion, O., 1900) 36 pp.

Warner, Samuel "Clark" (1708–1783) of Wilbraham, Mass.

Military journal, June–November 1759; march from Albany to Fort Edward, Lake George, and return; hardships, military details, news of war; very interesting spellings and language.

Chauncey E. Peck, *History of Wilbraham* (Wilbraham, 1913) 86–89; Rufus P. Stebbins, *An Historical Address Delivered at the Centennial Celebration . . . of the Town of Wilbraham* (Boston, 1864) 208–213.

WEBSTER, Robert, of 4th Connecticut Regiment.

Military journal, April–November 1759; march from Woodstock on Amherst's campaign; Lake George, Crown Point, Saratoga; brief, factual details of hardships and camp life.

Fort Ticonderoga Museum Bull. II (1931) 120–153. Extracts in *Vermont Hist. Soc. Proc.* II (1931) 173–175.

WOOD, Lemuel (1741–1819) of Boxford, Mass.

Military journal, May 1759–May 1760; Amherst's expedition against Canada; fairly interesting and extensive journal of march, taverns, ordinary camp life and incidents; many interesting spellings.

Essex Inst. Hist. Colls. XIX (1882) 61–74, 143–152, 183–192, XX (1883) 156–160, 198–208, 289–296, XXI (1884) 63–68.

WOODS, John (1735–1816) of Marlborough, Mass.

Military diary, June–November 1759; march from Worcester, Mass., to Lake George and Ticonderoga via Albany; military details, guards, etc., personal details of daily camp life and work; some interesting language and spellings.

Geneal. Mag. 4th Ser. I (1905–1906) 307–312, 339–342.

1760

ANON.

Military journal, August–September 1760; mediocre historical journal of Amherst's campaign and reduction of Montreal.

All Canada in the Hands of the English (Boston, 1760) 20 pp.

ANON.

Military journal; with plan of environs of Quebec and the battle on September 13, 1759, executed by Thomas Jefferys.

A Journal of the Siege of Quebec (London, 1760) 16 pp.

BOOTH, Capt. Joseph (1736–1810) of Enfield, Conn.

Military journal, July–October 1760; French and Indian War.

Charles E. Booth, *One Branch of the Booth Family* (New York, 1910) 142–144.

BRADBURY, Lieut. John (1736–1821) of York, Me.

Military journal, April 1760–August 1762; brief notes of war services; march from Saco to Crown Point, Lake George, and Montreal, with Moulton's company; camp life, casualties, engagements, discipline, weather; return to Boston, and journey to Kittery; rather intimate and very readable; some interesting spellings.

J. M. Bradbury, *Bradbury Memorial* (Portland, 1890) 261–295.

BREHM, Lieut. Diederick, of Royal American Regiment.

Travel journal, November 1760–February 1761; report of journey up St. Lawrence; Niagara, Detroit, Sandusky, etc.; notes on countryside and its condition.

New England Hist. Geneal. Reg. XXXVII (1883) 22–26.

BUCK, Abijah (*ca.* 1742–*ca.* 1829) of Buckfield, Me.

Private diary, June 1760–October 1785; scattered notes of family affairs, journeys, and accounts; little interest.

A. Cole and C. F. Whitman, *A History of Buckfield* (Buckfield, 1915) 509–512.

COFFIN, Rev. Paul (1737–1821) of Buxton, Me.

1. Travel journal, July–August 1760; from Wells to the Connecticut River; visits to meetings and relatives.

2. Travel journal, July–August 1761; preaching tour to Rhode Island.

3. Travel journal, September–October 1768; ride to Pigwacket; some good stories and notes on charms of countryside.

4. Travel journal, October 1795; to Hanover, to enter his son at Dartmouth College.

5. Missionary tour, June–August 1796; tour in Maine, with account of Sandy River, and remarks on Methodists.

6. Missionary journal, August–November 1797; in Maine; travels, sermons, comments on people and places.

7. Missionary journal, August–October 1798; in Maine; accounts of Methodists and Baptists.

8. Missionary journal, August–October 1800; in Maine.

Maine Hist. Soc. Colls. 1st Ser. IV (1856) 261–405; C. Woodman (ed.), *Memoirs and Journals of Rev. Paul Coffin* (Portland, 1855). First journal also in *New England Hist. Geneal. Reg.* IX (1855) 340–342.

EVANS, Henry (1725?–1782) of Annapolis, N.S., judge.

Travel journal, April–November 1760; rather dull, brief notes of voyage from Marblehead to Halifax, and his activities there.

W. A. Calnek, *History of the County of Annapolis* (Toronto, 1897) 148–151.

EYRE, Col. Jehu (1738–1781) of Burlington, N.J.

Travel diary, May–December 1760; brief, but fairly interesting notes of travel in the western parts of Pennsylvania, etc.

Pennsylvania Mag. Hist. Biog. III (1879) 296–307.

FROST, Lieut. John, Jr. (1738–1810) of Eliot, Me.

Military journal, May–November 1760; march to St. John's and return to Crown Point; brief entries, with interesting spellings.

Old Eliot VIII (1908) 109–117.

HAYS, John.

Journal, May–June 1760; notes of Indian trouble in Wyoming, Pa.

Pennsylvania Archives 1st Ser. III 735–741.

HOLDEN, Sergt. David (1738–1803) of Groton, Mass.

Military journal, February–November 1760; expedition against Canada; Crown Point, Ticonderoga; notes on campaign, camp life; impersonal, but has some spellings of interest.

Massachusetts Hist. Soc. Proc. 2d Ser. IV (1887–1889) 384–406; Samuel A. Green, *Three Military Diaries* (Groton, 1901) 47–74. Extracts in *Vermont Hist. Soc. Proc.* n.s. II (1931) 178–179.

HOLYOKE, Mrs. Mary (née Vial) (1737–1802) of Salem, Mass.

Private diary, January 1760–December 1799; brief notes of domestic, personal, and social affairs; interesting record of a woman's life in Salem.

G. F. Dow (ed.), *The Holyoke Diaries* (Salem, 1911) 47–138.

HUTCHINS, Capt. Thomas (1730–1789) *b.* Monmouth County, N.J., engineer.

1. Military journal, July 1760; march from Fort Pitt to Venango; rather dull.
Pennsylvania Mag. Hist. Biog. II (1878) 149–153.

2. Travel journal, April–September 1762; journey to posts on western lakes, Wabash and Scioto, to hold councils with Indians; sent by Croghan.

Charles A. Hanna, *The Wilderness Trail* (New York, 1911) II 362–367.

JENKS, Capt. Samuel (1732–1801) of Chelsea, Mass.

Military diary, May–November 1760; campaign against Canada; highly personal record; camp life, hardships, campaign; a vigorous and entertaining diary, with substantial entries and much linguistic interest.

Massachusetts Hist. Soc. Proc. 2d Ser. V (1889–1890) 352–391.

KENT, Col. Jacob (1726–1812) of Newbury, Vt.

Military journals, May–October 1760; scattered notes, with later entries to February 1791; notes of military movements during Amherst's campaign; later entries include Burgoyne's surrender, and farming notes.

F. P. Wells, *History of Newbury, Vermont* (St. Johnsbury, 1902) 380–382.

SOELLE, George (1709–1773) *b.* Denmark, Moravian pastor.

1. Moravian travel journal, August–September 1760; journey with Samuel Herr, seeking site for Moravian settlement in New England; Boston to New Hampshire; long entries describing travel and religious life; fairly interesting. Translated.

New England Quar. XII (1939) 747–759.

2. Travel journals, March 1771–April 1773; "editorial compilation" from diaries of pastoral tours; straightforward notes of travel, meetings, work; conveys good picture of missionary zeal.

Adelaide L. Fries (ed.), *Records of the Moravians in North Carolina* (Raleigh, 1922–1941) II 784–803.

WALKER, Capt. James (*d. ca.* 1786) of Bedford, N.H.

Military journal, June–September 1760; brief notes of work as sutler in French and Indian War; Crown Point and Ticonderoga.

History of Bedford, New Hampshire (Boston, 1851) 122–123.

WATERMAN, Asa (*b.* 1743) of Norwich, Conn.

Military journal, June–September 1760; march against Canada; list of casualties.

Published by W. F. Eddy in *Leaflet* (Brooklyn, N.Y., 1904) 4 pp. Also in *Hartford Times*, May 24, 1904; *Bridgewater Daily Standard*, Sept. 13, 1904.

WEKQUITANK (PA.) MORAVIAN INDIAN MISSION.

Moravian congregation diary, April 1760–August 1763 (extracts); particularly interesting notes on missionary work and worship.

W. H. Egle's Notes and Queries (Pa.) (1899) 123–126, 129–132, 134–138, 140–142.

WHITALL, Mrs. Ann (1716–1797) of Gloucester Co., N.J., Red Bank, N.J., and Philadelphia.

Quaker diary, February 1760–May 1783; notes of Quaker meetings, weather, children's pranks, overeating; quite lively.

Hannah W. Smith, *John M. Whitall: The Story of His Life* (Philadelphia, 1879) 14–21. Extracts in F. H. Stewart, *Notes on Old Gloucester County* (1917) I 315–316.

ANON. (Quaker of Philadelphia).   1761

Travel journal, August 1761; narrative with dates; Philadelphia to Easton, Pa.; Indian treaty; Quaker relations with Indians interestingly outlined.

Indiana Mag. Hist. XXXII (1936) 266–274.

ANON. (sailor on sloop "Betsey" of Dartmouth).

Sea journal, August–September 1761 and September 1762 (extracts); brief notes of whaling voyages from Dartmouth to Newfoundland Banks.

Daniel Ricketson, *The History of New Bedford* (New Bedford, 1858) 62–64.

DEANE, Rev. Samuel (1733–1814) of Portland, Me.

Clergyman's diary, February 1761–October 1814 (extracts); relating principally to local, domestic, and religious affairs; impersonal, but useful as a local record.

William Willis, *Journals of the Rev. Thomas Smith and the Rev. Samuel Deane* (Portland, 1849) 301–406. Brief extracts in *Sprague's Jour. Maine Hist.* II (1914–1915) 27–28.

GORRELL, Lieut. James.

1. Military journal, September 1761–August 1763; beginning at Detroit and ending at Montreal; councils with Puans, Chippewas, etc.; account of attempts of French to turn Indians against the English; Indian trade; fairly interesting.

Wisconsin Hist. Soc. Colls. I (1903 reprint) 24–48.

2. Military journal, August 1763–January 1764; Wilkins's expedition from Montreal; brief, scattered notes of military affairs.

Maryland Hist. Mag. IV (1909) 183–187.

GRANT, Lieut. Col. James (1720–1806) of Ballindaloch, Scotland.

Military journal, June–July 1761; report to Lord Amherst on expedition against Cherokees from Fort Prince George; moderate and purely military.

Florida Hist. Soc. Quar. XII (1933) 25–36.

NEWTON, Rev. Roger (1737–1816) of Greenfield, Mass.

Clergyman's diary, November 1761–December 1812 (extracts); moderate notes on personal, social, and church affairs, but mainly baptisms, deaths, etc.

New England Hist. Geneal. Reg. LXII (1908) 263–273; F. M. Thompson, *History of Greenfield* II (1904) 700–748; David Willard, *History of Greenfield* (Greenfield, 1838) 121–130.

PIERCE, Col. Samuel (1739–1815) of Dorchester, Mass.

Private diary, November 1761–January 1787 (with gap); personal, local, and public affairs in and around Dorchester; fishing, farming, religion; Boston Tea Party, burning of Charlestown, troop movements around Boston; a varied and quite interesting diary; some interesting language.

History of ... Dorchester, Massachusetts (Boston, 1859) 358–371, 588.

SMETHURST, Gamaliel (1738–1826) of Marblehead, Mass.

Travel diary, October–December 1761 and December 1763–1765; first part, travel in Nova Scotia; second part, fisheries in the St. Lawrence; quite good narrative and details of his adventures.

New Brunswick Hist. Soc. Colls. No. 6 (1905) 365–390.

TILESTON, John (1735–1826) of Boston.

Diary, September 1761–November 1766; meager notes on neighbors, schools, politics, expenses.

D. C. Colesworthy, *John Tileston's School* (Boston, 1887) 71–80. Extracts (February–April 1775) in *New England Hist. Geneal. Reg.* XX (1866) 11.

WINTHROP, John (1714–1779) of Cambridge, Mass.

Scientific travel journal, June 1761; voyage from Boston to Newfoundland to observe transit of Venus.

Relation of a Voyage from Boston (Boston, 1761) 24 pp.

1762

ANON. (of Wachovia, N.C., Moravian).

Moravian travel journal, April–June 1762; from Bethlehem to Wachovia, via Philadelphia, Wilmington, Bethabara; sea, river, and land journey; difficulties of voyage; mistaken for pirates.

Adelaide L. Fries (ed.), *Records of the Moravians in North Carolina* (Raleigh, 1922) I 256–263.

BALDWIN, Rev. Ebenezer (1745–1775) of Yale.

Private diary, March–May 1762; brief notes kept while author was a student at Yale; lively picture of college social life, curriculum, etc.

William L. Kingsley (ed.), *Yale College* (New York, 1879) I 444–446.

BERNARD, Sir Francis (1712–1779), governor of Massachusetts Bay.

Surveying journal, September–October 1762; surveying journey to island of Mount Desert, Me., and voyage from Boston.

Bangor Hist. Mag. II (1887) 185–188.

Brown, Beriah (1714–1792) of North Kingston, R.I.

Travel journal, September 1762; horseback journey with Christopher Gardiner and Benoni Gardiner, from North Kingston to the Susquehannah River; stages, taverns, meals, trade; moderate, but some interesting spellings.

Narragansett Hist. Reg. II (1883–1884) 219–221.

Calhoun, William, of Long Cane Creek, Abbeville Co., S.C.

Journal and accounts, December 1762–1770, with some earlier and later family records; mostly accounts and memoranda.

Southern Hist. Assoc. Pubs. VIII (1904) 179–195.

Chouteau, Auguste (1750–1829) of St. Louis, Mo., merchant.

Diary, 1762–1764; written as recollections, with a few dates; founding of St. Louis. French and English texts.

St. Louis Mercantile Lib. Assoc., 12th Ann. Rep. (1858) App.; reprinted *Missouri Hist. Soc. Colls.* III (1908–1911) 335–366.

Forbes, Rev. Eli (1726–1804) of Brookfield, Mass.

Clergyman's journal, January–December 1762; church affairs and visits; journey to council with Tuscarora Indians in western New York; brief entries of fair interest.

Massachusetts Hist. Soc. Proc. 2d Ser. VII (1891–1892) 384–399.

Foulke, Samuel (1718–1797) of Bucks Co., Pa.

Diary, September 1762–February 1764 (fragments); brief and mediocre political notes.

Pennsylvania Mag. Hist. Biog. V (1881) 60–73.

Gorham, Maj. Gen. Joseph (1725–1790) of Barnstable, Mass.

Military diary, June–August 1762; expedition of corps of rangers from New York to Havana; capture of city; and return; a brief general diary with personal comments on Havana, sickness, etc.

Year-Book Soc. Col. Wars Massachusetts (Boston, 1899) 159–161.

Graham, Rev. John (1722–1796) of Suffield, Conn.

Chaplain's journal, September–October 1762; with 1st Connecticut regiment during siege of Havana.

Extracts from the Journal of the Rev. John Graham (New York, 1896) 18 pp.

Hoyt, Capt. Samuel (1744–1826) of East Guilford, Conn.

Sea journal, 1762–1800; really narrative written up from journal and memory; adventures of a sailor's life; interesting.

Connecticut Mag. X (1906) 631–646, XI (1907) 275–284. Extracts in article by T. W. Pease, *Jour. Amer. Hist.* I (1907) 81–88, 485–493, II (1908) 64–73.

Johnson, Lieut. Guy (1740?–1788), deputy agent for Indian affairs.

Official journal, November–December 1762; meeting with Indians at Onondaga to settle for murders in Seneca country; minutes and speeches.

E. B. O'Callaghan, *Docs. Rel. Col. Hist. State New York* VII (1856) 511–515.

KNIGHT, Capt. Nathaniel, of Salem.

Sea journal, May–July 1762; voyage from St. Martins toward Salem; captured by Spanish privateer off Porto Rico.

New England Hist. Geneal. Reg. XLIV (1890) 200–202.

MAXWELL, Hugh (1733–1799) of Bedford, Mass.

Private diary, October 1762–February 1795 (extracts); personal experiences and reflections; partly during French and Indian War, partly during Revolution.

*The Christian Patriot (New York, 1833). [Forbes.]

MIFFLIN, Benjamin (*b.* 1718) of Philadelphia, merchant.

1. Travel diary, July–August 1762; Philadelphia to Delaware and Maryland; some good observations on people, towns, taverns, trade.

Edited by V. H. Paltsits, *Bull. New York Pub. Lib.* XXXIX (1935) 423–438.

2. Travel diary, June–July 1764; journey from Philadelphia to Cedar Swamps and back; vigorous comments on inns; expenses; religious discussion; fairly interesting.

Pennsylvania Mag. Hist. Biog. LII (1928) 130–140.

PARK, Roswell (1726–1762) of Preston, Conn.

Military journal, May–August 1762; notes of expedition against Havana.

Univ. Buffalo Stud. I (1920) 231–244.

ROBERTSON, Lieut. Gen. Archibald (*ca.* 1745–1813) *b.* Scotland, of Royal Engineers.

Military journals, January 1762–November 1780 (with gap, 1762–1775); five journals, mainly relating to Revolutionary War, Havana expedition, siege of Boston, White Plains, Danbury expedition, Cornwallis' expedition, etc.; surveying and engineering work; mainly military notes, with many interesting drawings.

H. M. Lydenberg (ed.), *Archibald Robertson—His Diaries and Sketches in America, 1762–1780* (New York, 1930) 300 pp.; reprinted in *Bull. New York Pub. Lib.* XXXVII (1933) 7–37, 113–143, 181–199, 277–290, 479–503, 577–608, 660–694, 775–795, 865–901, 953–969.

SMITH, Rev. Hezekiah (1737–1805) of Haverhill, Mass.

Missionary journal, October 1762–December 1805 (with gaps); abundant, brief notes of missionary work in South, experiences as chaplain in Nixon's regiment; Saratoga, Burgoyne's surrender, White Plains, etc.; very detailed.

Reuben A. Guild (ed.), *Chaplain Smith and the Baptists* (Philadelphia, 1885) 429 pp. *passim.*

STARR, Lieut. William (*b.* 1730) of Middletown, Conn.

Sea journal, May–November 1762; expedition against Havana in British fighting ship.

Jour. Amer. Hist. III (1909) 113–117.

WILKINSON, Elizabeth (1712–1771), English ministering Quaker.

Quaker journal, March 1762–January 1763 (extracts); visits to Friends in America; meetings on Long Island and in Pennsylvania; some ecstatic religious entries.

Bull. Friends' Hist. Soc. Philadelphia XVIII (1929) 87–90.

1763

ANON. (officer).

Military journal 1763–1764; siege of Fort Detroit.

*Journal of an Officer during the Siege of Fort Detroit (London, 1858). [Sabin.]

DYER, John (*d.* 1811) of Plumsted, Pa.

Private diary, November 1763–August 1805; brief notes, mostly of births, marriages, deaths, removals; a few local affairs.

Pubs. Geneal. Soc. Pennsylvania III (1906) 38–72.

GRAYDON, Lieut. C. (commandant at Fort Augusta, Pa.).

See 1756: BURD, 5.

HAY, Lieut. Jehu (*d.* 1785) *b.* Chester, Pa., later lieutenant governor of Detroit.

Military journal, May 1763–June 1765; daily events of siege of Detroit; full details; an extremely valuable journal of Pontiac's siege.

F. B. Hough (ed.), *Diary of the Siege of Detroit* (Albany, 1860); discussed and quoted by W. L. Jenks in *Michigan Hist. Mag.* XII (1928) 437–442.

HUNTER, Lieut. Samuel.

See 1756: BURD, 5.

[NAVARRE, Robert, keeper of notarial records at Detroit?]

Military journal, 1763; record of Pontiac's Conspiracy; parallel French and English texts.

M. A. Burton (ed.), *Journal of Pontiac's Conspiracy, 1763* (Michigan Soc. Colonial Wars, 1912) 243 pp.

PHELPS, Mrs. Elizabeth (1747–1817) of Hadley, Mass.

Private diary, October 1763–April 1812 (extracts with editorial comments); texts of sermons; notes on household, social, and some public affairs.

Arria S. Huntington, *Under a Colonial Roof-tree* (New York, 1891) 26–105.

WALKER, Timothy, Jr. (1737–1822) of Concord, N.H., judge.

Private diary, January 1763–July 1766 (with gaps); very brief notes of personal affairs, journeys, visits, preaching.

James O. Lyford, *History of the Town of Canterbury* (Concord, 1912) I 96–97.

WISWALL, Rev. John (1731–1821) of Portland, Me.

Private diary, April 1763–1797; notes of private affairs, war news, journey to England; quotations.

Nova Scotia Hist. Soc. Colls. XIII (1908) 1–73 *passim*.

1764

ANON. (agent of French government).

Travel journal, December 1764–September 1765; French traveler in the Colonies; voyage to West Indies; journey through southern colonies, and through Annapolis, Philadelphia, New York; accounts of country and its resources; notes on topography, towns, trade, agriculture, weather; written in English, with part redaction in French; a very interesting journal, with some interesting spellings in English portion.

Amer. Hist. Rev. XXVI (1920–1921) 726–747, XXVII (1921–1922) 70–90.

BOUQUET, Col. Henry (1719–1765) b. Switzerland, of Long Meadow, Md.

Military journal, August–October 1764; expedition against the Ohio Indians.

N. B. Craig, *The Olden Time* I (Cincinnati, 1846, reprinted 1876) 217–221, 241–260.

[GORDON, Adam, Lord (*ca.* 1726–1801) of 66th Foot Regiment.]

Travel diary, April 1764–October 1765; tour in West Indies and North America; Georgia, Carolina, Virginia, Maryland, New York, New England, Canada; interesting descriptions of places, persons, trade, routes, etc., but impersonal.

Newton D. Mereness, *Travels in the American Colonies* (New York, 1916) 365–453.

KIRKLAND, Rev. Samuel (1742–1808) of Norwich, Conn., and New York City.

1. Missionary journal, November 1764–April 1765 (extract); visit to Seneca Indians.

William Ketchum, *An Authentic and Comprehensive History of Buffalo* I (Buffalo, 1864) 212–239.

2. Missionary journal, September–November 1776; among Oneida Indians.

Hist. Mag. n.s. III (1868) 37–39.

3. Missionary travel journal, September–December 1788; Fort Stanwix to the Five Nations.

Ketchum II (1865) 97–110.

MITCHELL, Capt. John, of Chester, N.H.

Surveying journal, May–June 1764; notes of surveying on Massachusetts and New Brunswick border; some personal details, and some interesting spellings.

New Brunswick Hist. Soc. Colls. No. 5 (1904) 180–187.

MORGAN, Dr. John (*b.* 1736) of Philadelphia, physician.

Travel journal, September 1764; extract concerning visit with Voltaire.

Pennsylvania Mag. Hist. Biog. X (1886) 43–50.

MORRIS, Capt. Thomas (*b.* 1732?), of 17th Infantry.

Military travel journal, August–September 1764; journey to Miami Indians; narrative arranged as a diary; amusing account of adventures and self-glorification of an insignificant hero.

Published in his *Miscellanies in Prose and Verse* (London, 1791); *Mag. Hist. Extra No.* 76 (1922) 1–29; R. G. Thwaites (ed.), *Early Western Travels* I (Cleveland, 1904) 301–328.

MOSLEY, Father Joseph, of Talbot Co., Pa.
Catholic journal, August 1764–January 1768 (extracts); brief notes concerning period of foundation of St. Joseph's Mission, Talbot Co., Pa.
Amer. Cath. Hist. Soc. Recs. XVII (1906) 196–200.

ROGERS, Rev. John (1724–1779) of New London, Conn.
Religious journal, June 1764–December 1766; religious notes; Quaker meetings and opposition.
*A Looking Glass for the Presbyterians of New-London (Providence, 1767). [Evans.]

ROWE, John (1715–1787) of Boston, merchant.
Private diary (with letters), September 1764–July 1779 (with gaps); social and public life of a Boston merchant; political disturbances, dinners, clubs; impersonal, but of considerable genealogical interest.
Anne R. Cunningham (ed.), *Letters and Diary of John Rowe* (Boston, 1903) 453 pp. Extracts in *Massachusetts Hist. Soc. Proc.* X (1895) 60–108.

1765

AULD, James (*d.* 1780) of Anson Co., N.C.
Travel diary, February 1765–August 1766; erratic and poor notes of travel, mostly in the South; a few genealogical notes by a later writer.
Southern Hist. Assoc. Pubs. VIII (1904) 253–268.

BARTRAM, John (1699–1777) *b.* Marple, Pa., naturalist.
Botanical journal and narrative, December 1765–February 1766; travel from St. Augustine, Fla., up River St. John to the Lakes; travel notes and natural history observations.
William Stork, *A Description of East Florida* (London, 1769) Part 2, 35 pp.; extract concerning antiquities of Florida in *Smithson. Inst. Ann. Rep.* 1874 (Washington, 1875) 393.

CUTLER, Rev. Manasseh (1742–1823) of Dedham, Mass., and Marietta, O.
Private diary, December 1765–July 1819 (nine years missing); preaching journeys, personal and local affairs at Dedham, Marietta, etc.; notes on social life, religious work, etc. A very good diary.
W. P. and J. P. Cutler, *Life, Journals and Correspondence of Rev. Manasseh Cutler* (Cincinnati, 1888) two vols. Extracts (August–September 1788; Ohio journey) in *New England Hist. Geneal. Reg.* XIV (1860) 105–106, 234–236, 364–366, XV (1861) 45–49; scattered extracts relating to New Jersey, Ohio, and Pennsylvania, in *New Jersey Hist. Soc. Proc.* 2d Ser. III (1872–1874) 75–96.

GREGORY, William (1742–1817) *b.* Ayrshire, of Fredericksburg, Va., and New Haven, Conn.

1. Travel diary, September–October 1765; journey from Fredericksburg to Philadelphia on business, and return; fairly interesting.

William and Mary Coll. Quar. 1st Ser. XIII (1904–1905) 224–229.

2. Travel diary, September–October 1771; journey in New England; Hartford, Sudbury, Cambridge, Boston, voyage to Newport, Yale; substantial and well-written entries, describing towns and places, taverns, and social life; a very readable diary.

New England Mag. n.s. XII (1895) 343–352.

HENFIELD, Joseph (1743–1809) of Salem, Mass.

Private diary, February 1765–December 1800; almanac notes of weather, local affairs in Salem, vital statistics.

Joseph B. Felt, *Annals of Salem* (Boston, 1849) II 108–109, 138–139.

HILTZHEIMER, Jacob (1729–1798) of Philadelphia.

Private diary, September 1765–September 1798 (with gaps 1771, 1775–1776); public affairs, and private and domestic life in Philadelphia; mostly brief entries, but extent and consistency give a full picture of Philadelphia life; plays, amusements, sports, journeys, visits, religion; a very attractive diary.

Jacob C. Parsons (ed.), *Extracts from the Diary of Jacob Hiltzheimer* (Philadelphia, 1893) 270 pp. Extracts in *Pennsylvania Mag. Hist. Biog.* XVI (1892) 93–102, 160–177, 412–422 (Philadelphia entries); James B. Nolan, *Early Narratives of Berks County* (Reading, Pa., 1927) 42–50 (visits to Reading and Gen. Mifflin).

IZARD, Ralph (1742–1804) of Charleston, S.C.

Travel diary, June 1765; travel in upper New York; description of Niagara.

Published anonymously as *An Account of a Journey to Niagara . . . in 1765* (New York, 1846) 30 pp.; extract in *Buffalo Hist. Soc. Pubs.* XV (1911) 339–346.

LEACH, Mrs. Christiana, of Kingsessing, Pa.

Private diary, February 1765–May 1796; scattered notes, mostly of family matters; rather dull. Translated from the German.

Pennsylvania Mag. Hist. Biog. XXXV (1911) 343–349.

QUINCY, Josiah (1744–1775) of Braintree, Mass.

1. Diary, August 27, 1765 (extract); description of Stamp Act riot.

Massachusetts Hist. Soc. Proc. IV (1858–1860) 46–51.

2. Travel diary, February–May 1773; journey to South Carolina; good description of country and towns, etc.

Ibid. XLIX (1915–1916) 424–481.

3. Travel diary, September 1774–March 1775; voyage to England, and residence there; interesting details of social life and etiquette; amusing high-flying style.

John Quincy (ed.), *Memoir of the Life of Josiah Quincy, Jr.* (Boston, 1825)

498 pp. *passim*; other editions, Boston 1874, 1875; *Massachusetts Hist. Soc. Proc.* L (1916–1917) 433–470.

WEBSTER, Pelatiah (1725–1795) *b.* Lebanon, Conn., of Philadelphia.

Travel diary, May–June 1765; voyage from Philadelphia to Charleston, S.C., and return; mainly descriptions of Charleston and environs; interest in Southern plants; fairly interesting.

Southern Hist. Assoc. Pubs. II (1898) 131–148.

WESTON, Warren (1738–1799) of Duxbury, Mass.

Private diary, January 1765–April 1766; brief notes on personal affairs of a ship's carpenter; rather dull, but interesting spellings.

Pilgrim Notes and Queries II (1914) 1–3.

1766

CLARKSON, Matthew (1733–1800) of Philadelphia, agent for Indian traders.

Travel diary, August 1766–April 1767; from Philadelphia to Fort Pitt, Fort Chartres, and Kaskaskia; Indian vocabulary; fur prices; social details of frontier.

In H. R. Schoolcraft, *Information Respecting the History . . . of the Indian Tribes of the United States* IV (Philadelphia, 1854) 265–278; C. W. Alvord and C. E. Carter, *The New Regime 1765–1767,* in *Illinois Hist. Soc. Colls.* XI (1916) 349–363.

GORDON, Capt. Harry (*d.* 1787) of Royal Engineers, of Knockespeck, Scotland.

Surveying journal, May–December 1766; surveying trip down Ohio River, Illinois, and Mississippi, to New Orleans, and thence to Mobile and Pensacola; descriptions of places, distances, trade, weather, fur trade. Accompanied by George Croghan.

C. W. Alvord and C. E. Carter, *The New Regime 1765–1767,* in *Illinois Hist. Soc. Colls.* XI (1916) 290–311; Newton D. Mereness, *Travels in the American Colonies* (New York, 1916) 464–489. Partly in T. Pownall, *A Topographical Description . . . of North America* (London, 1766) App. 2–5; Charles Hanna, *The Wilderness Trail* II (New York, 1911) 40–55; *Missouri Hist. Soc. Colls.* III (1908–1911) 437–443; *Illinois Hist. Soc. Jour.* II (1909–1910) 55–64.

HASEY, Rev. Isaac (1742–1812) of Lebanon, Me.

Clergyman's diary, February 1766–September 1808 (extracts); brief, scattered notes of personal and parish affairs, and war news.

Maine Hist. Soc. Colls. and Proc. 2d Ser. IX (1898) 132–136; Benjamin K. Emerson, *The Ipswich Emersons* (Boston, 1900) 431–432.

JENNINGS, John (*ca.* 1738–1802) of Northampton Co., Pa.

1. Travel diary, March–April 1766; from Fort Pitt to Fort Chartres; trading expedition down Ohio and up Mississippi; descriptions of French villages.

Pennsylvania Mag. Hist. Biog. XXXI (1907) 145–156; C. W. Alvord and C. E. Carter, *The New Regime 1765–1767,* in *Illinois Hist. Soc. Colls.* XI (1916) 167–177.

2. Travel journal, May–July 1768; Fort Chartres, and trip down the Mississippi to New Orleans; some fair descriptions of scenery and forts.

Pennsylvania Mag. Hist. Biog. XXXI (1907) 304–310. Extract in C. W. Alvord and C. E. Carter, *Trade and Politics 1767–1769,* in *Illinois Hist. Soc. Colls.* XVI (1921) 336–339.

McCLURE, Rev. David (1748–1820) of Boston and Yale.

1. Private diary, June 1766–May 1819; written up and expanded from earlier diary; long entries of Indian affairs and adventures; fairly good.

F. B. Dexter (ed.), *Diary of David McClure* (New York, 1899) 219 pp.; extract (April 1775; Lexington alarm) in *Massachusetts Hist. Soc. Proc.* 1st Ser. XVI (1878) 157–158; extract (July–August 1772, description of Lancaster, Pa.) in *Lancaster County Hist. Soc. Papers* V (1901) 106–112.

MORGAN, George (1743–1810) b. Philadelphia, Indian agent.

1. Travel diary, November–December 1766; remarkable occurrences during voyage down Mississippi; starting at Kaskaskia village; to Fort Bute; notes on forts, villages, etc.

C. W. Alvord and C. E. Carter, *The New Regime 1765–1767,* in *Illinois Hist. Soc. Colls.* XI (1916) 438–447. Extracts in S. C. Williams, *Early Travels in the Tennessee Country* (Johnson City, 1928) 216–218.

2. Travel diary, September–November 1767; journey from Philadelphia to Mingo town; trading details.

C. W. Alvord and C. E. Carter, *Trade and Politics 1767–1769,* in *Illinois Hist. Soc. Colls.* XVI (1921) 67–71.

OWEN, Capt. William (d. 1778) of Campobello Island.

Travel diary, July 1766–May 1770 and April–June 1771; journey along the Nova Scotia and Maine coast; early history of Campobello; some interesting long entries.

Bull. New York Pub. Lib. XXXV (1931) 76–98, 139–162, 263–300, 659–685, 705–751; *New Brunswick Hist. Soc. Colls.* I (1894) 195–208, II (1899) 8–27.

WADSWORTH, Dr. Joseph Bissell (1747–1784) of East Windsor, Conn.

College diary, January–September 1766; college affairs at Yale.

Yale College Courant, September 12, 1868, pp. 131–133; **Alumni Weekly,* June 17, 1896. [Forbes.]

WOOD, Solomon (1722–1766) of Boxford, Mass.

Surveying journal, August–October 1766; surveying around Bridgeton, Me.; brief notes.

New England Hist. Geneal. Reg. XXVIII (1874) 63–67.

1767

ANON.

Official journal, July–September 1767; fairly interesting official report of transactions with Indians about stealing at Niagara.

E. B. O'Callaghan, *Doc. Hist. State New York* II (1850) 504–511.

BAYLEY, Mrs. Abigail (1746–1815) of Bath, N.H.

Private diary, April 1767–June 1792; partly memoirs; her marriage and a lengthy account of her sufferings at the hands of a "depraved and deceitful man," with notes of Christian consolation.

Memoirs of Mrs. Abigail Bailey (Boston, 1815) 275 pp. *passim*; extracts in Peterson, *Abigail Goodhue Bayley* (New Castle, N.H., 1917) 11–182.

GRANT (Francis, of Monymusk, Scotland?).

Travel diary, April–July 1767; New York to Canada, via Albany, Schenectady, Ontario, Niagara, Montreal, Quebec; return by Lake Champlain and Lake George; long descriptions of towns, scenery, and such notabilia as maple sugar, Indians, Niagara Falls, and the Indian government.

New York History XIII (1932) 181–196, 305–322.

1768

CRAFT, James (1743–1808) of Burlington, N.J.

Private diary 1768–1785 (extracts); brief, scattered notes of local affairs.

Hist. Mag. I (1857) 300–302.

ETTWEIN, Rev. John (1721–1802) *b.* Freudenstadt, Germany, Moravian missionary in North Carolina.

Moravian journal, April–May 1768; journey with David Zeisberger and Gottlob Senseman to Friedenshuetten; residence there, religious journeys and work; scenery.

Ohio Archaeol. and Hist. Quar. XXI (1912) 32–42.

2. Travel journal, June–August 1772; with Christian Indians from Susquehanna to Beaver River, Pa.; fairly interesting.

Pennsylvania Mag. Hist. Biog. XXV (1901) 208–219; *W. H. Egle's Notes and Queries* (Pa.) (1898) 49–51, 58–59, 68–70, 77–79.

GOODWIN, Dr. Francis LeBaron (1762–1816) of Winterport, Me.

Private diary, 1768–1816 (brief extracts); rather dull notes of local and personal affairs.

A. D. Littlefield, *An Old River Town* (New York, 1907) 119–129.

JONES, Joel (1764–1845) of Lanesborough, Mass.

Private diary and record, March 1768–July 1844; mostly notes of his own activities, chief family affairs, deaths of friends, etc., moral reflections, and notes on weather; genealogical interest.

Elbert Smith, *The Descendants of Joel Jones* (Rutland, Vt., 1925) 279–291.

LEES, John, of Quebec, merchant.

Travel diary, April–October 1768; New England, New York, Michigan, Montreal, etc.; descriptions from mercantile viewpoint; disjointed but interesting details.

Soc. Col. Wars Michigan Proc. (Detroit, 1911) 55 pp.

PAINE, Robert Treat (1731–1814) of Taunton, Mass., lawyer.

Private diary, September 1768–July 1776 (extracts); personal affairs, war news, Congressional affairs, visits, weather; some political interest.

Sarah C. Paine, *Paine Ancestry* (Boston, 1912) 31–40.

SIMITIÈRE, Pierre Eugène du (*d.* 1784) of Switzerland and Boston.

Travel diary, June 1768; tour through New England; descriptions of towns, etc.; mostly in French.

Rhode Island Hist. Soc. Colls. XII (1919) 47–52.

SUMNER, Rev. Joseph (1739–1824) of Shrewsbury, Mass.

Clergyman's journal, January 1768–December 1822 (with many gaps); brief notes of sermons, visits, illnesses, births, marriages, deaths.

*Privately published (Worcester, Mass., 1888). [Forbes.]

TYLER, Rev. John (1742–1823) of Norwich, Conn.

Sea journal, May–November 1768; voyage from New York to England; brief notes of what he saw and did.

*Published at San Francisco, Calif. [Forbes.]

1769

HEMPSTEAD, John, of New London, Conn.

Diary, September 1769–June 1779; a few brief notes.

New London County Hist. Soc. Proc. I (1901) 711 (appended to edition of Joshua Hempstead's diary).

LEE, Maj. Gen. Charles (1731–1782) *b.* Cheshire, Eng.

1. Military diary, June 1769; fragment describing his service in Russia.

New York Hist. Soc. Colls. (1871) 85–86.

2. Travel diary, June 1784 (fragment, of uncertain date); Fredericksburg, Md., to Pittsburgh; itinerary and notes on taverns.

New York Hist. Soc. Colls. (1874) 73–75.

MARRETT, Rev. John (1741–1813) of Woburn, Mass.

Private diary, January 1769–December 1812 (scattered extracts); weather, journeys, parish work, public events; Boston Massacre and Tea Party, Lexington, Bunker Hill; moderate interest.

Samuel Dunster, *Henry Dunster and His Descendants* (Central Falls, R.I., 1876) 81–94.

PEMBERTON, John (1727–1795) of Philadelphia.

Quaker journal, June 1769–January 1795; first part in New England and Virginia during Revolution; arrest by Revolutionaries; greater part of journal describes his ministry in England, Ireland, Scotland, and Holland; an interesting and sometimes exciting record of an active and troubled life.

Friends' Library VI (Philadelphia, 1842) 284–374.

SMITH, Elizabeth Murray (1726–1786) of Boston.

Loyalist diary, October 1769–July 1770; journey to England; brief notes.

Letters of James Murray, Loyalist (Boston, 1901) 124–131.

SMITH, Richard (1735–1803) of Burlington, N.J., member of Congress.

1. Travel diary, May–June 1769; surveying lands from Burlington to Otsego Lake; on the Hudson, Mohawk, Susquehannah, and Delaware rivers; fairly good descriptions of topography.

A Tour of Four Great Rivers (New York, 1906) 80 pp.; extracts in Charles A. Hanna, *The Wilderness Trail* II (New York, 1911) 61–64.

2. Political diary, September 1775–March 1776; kept while author was member of Congress for New Jersey; political and war news.

Amer. Hist. Rev. I (1895–1896) 288–310, 493–516.

THOMAS, William (1725–1810) of Lancaster, Mass.

Private diary, January 1768–December 1769 (with gaps and a few later entries); farming, weather, religion, local and some public news; brief and dull notes.

Essex Inst. Hist. Colls. XIV (1877) 257–267.

1770

ALLEN, James (1742–1778) of Philadelphia.

Diary, November 1770–July 1778; personal and political notes; author member of Congress; fairly interesting.

Pennsylvania Mag. Hist. Biog. IX (1885) 176–196, 278–296, 424–441.

BALDWIN, Bethiah (*b.* 1743) of Norwich, Conn.

Travel diary, September–October 1770 (extracts); lively notes on the rigors of a horseback journey to Danbury.

New Haven Colony Hist. Soc. Colls. IX (1918) 162–169.

CARTER, Col. Landon (*b.* 1709) of Sabine Hall, Richmond Co., Va.

Plantation diary, January 1770–July 1776; extensive and detailed notes; personal affairs, farming, social, Negro life, law matters; visits to and from famous Southerners; a very interesting record.

William and Mary Coll. Quar. 1st Ser. XIII (1904–1905) 45–53, 157–164, 219–224, XIV (1905–1906) 38–44, 181–186, 246–253, XV (1906–1907) 15–20, 86–87, 205–221, XVI (1907–1908) 149–156, 257–269, XVII (1908–1909) 9–18, XVIII (1909–1910) 37–44, XX (1910–1911) 173–186, XXI (1911–1912) 172–181.

CARTWRIGHT, Capt. George (1739–1819) *b.* Marnham, Notts, Eng.

Pioneer diary, March 1770–October 1786; daily record of his life and adventures during a residence of nearly sixteen years on the Labrador coast; an excellent diary of pioneer life, with extensive notes on the topography, inhabitants, etc.; literary style.

Journal of Transactions and Events (Newark, 1792) three vols.; same, edited by C. W. Townsend (Boston, 1911) 385 pp.

COLLIN, Nicholas (1746–1831) of Philadelphia.

Moravian journals, May 1770–June 1786; kept while author was pastor of the Swedish mission at Raccoon, N.J.; scattered entries, but fairly interesting religious and personal notes, with a few passages about the Revolution.

Amandus Johnson, *The Journal and Biography of Nicholas Collin* (Philadelphia, 1936) 207–296.

ENS (SOUTH FORK, N.C.) MORAVIAN CONGREGATION.

Moravian congregational journals, January–December 1770. (For analysis of type, see 1753: BETHABARA).

Adelaide L. Fries (ed.), *Records of the Moravians in North Carolina* (Raleigh, 1922–1941) I 408–410.

HUNT, John, ministering Quaker of Evesham, N.J.

Private diary, July 1770–May 1800 (extracts; only scattered notes after November 1770); religious work and worship, civil and domestic life; brief notes, but gives excellent cumulative picture of Quaker life; intimate and revealing; many interesting spellings.

New Jersey Hist. Soc. Proc. LII (1934) 177–193, 223–239, LIII (1935) 26–43, 111–128, 194–209, 251–262.

MEASE, Edward.

Official travel journal, November 1770–April 1771; journey through West Florida from Pensacola; topography, notes on population and economy.

Mississippi Hist. Soc. Pubs. Cent. Ser. V (1925) 58–90.

PARKER, Pvt. James (1744–1830) of Shirley, Mass.

Private diary, January 1770–December 1829 (extracts); personal and local affairs at Shirley and Groton; farming, weather, visits, preaching, law, neighbors; a few military entries at Lexington, etc.; a few brief entries for each month, but the consistency of the diary builds up an excellent picture of New England country life and a portrait of a shrewd Yankee farmer; interesting linguistically. A valuable companion to Hempstead's and Hazard's diaries.

New England Hist. Geneal. Reg. LXIX (1915) 8–17, 117–127, 211–224, 294–308, LXX (1916) 9–24, 137–146, 210–220, 294–308.

POWELL, William Dummer (1726–1805) of Boston.

Private diary, September 1770–December 1782; brief notes of journeys around Boston; death of Whitefield; Boston affairs.

Maine Hist. Soc. Colls. 1st Ser. VII (1876) 235–238.

RUSSELL, Barnabas (1745–1812) of New Bedford, Mass.

Travel diary, August–September 1770; brief notes kept in London; sightseeing, visits to coffee houses, etc.

Daniel Ricketson, *The History of New Bedford* (New Bedford, 1858) 197–198.

1771

ANON. (diarist's name not given by editor).

Social diary, May 1771–November 1785 (extracts); social and farming life in Connecticut, building of meetinghouse, war news; fair interest.

Connecticut Quar. Mag. I (1895) 265–270.

ASBURY, Rev. Francis (1745–1816), Methodist bishop.

Methodist journal, August 1771–December 1815; the endless travels of a Methodist minister in America on preaching tours over the whole country east of the Mississippi; notes religious and personal, meetings and work, the people he meets and his entertainment; perhaps the best record of early Methodism in America.

The Journal of the Rev. Francis Asbury (New York, 1821) three vols. E. S. Tipple, *The Heart of Asbury's Journal* (New York, 1904) 720 pp. Extracts relating to Tennessee in S. C. Williams, *Early Travels in the Tennessee Country* (Johnson City, 1928) 291–313.

FAIRFAX, Sally Cary, of Fairfax Co., Va.

Private diary, December 1771–January 1772; amusing domestic notes of a spirited Virginia child; interesting spellings.

Virginia Mag. Hist. Biog. XI (1903–1904) 212–214; W. M. Cary, *Sally Cary* (New York, 1916) 59–65.

HELFRICH, Rev. John H. (1739–1810) *b.* Mosbach, Germany.

Sea journal, September 1771–January 1772; journey from Amsterdam to New York; storms, etc.; work as German Reformed minister in Pennsylvania; fairly interesting. Translated.

Pennsylvania Mag. Hist. Biog. XXXVIII (1914) 65–82.

HUBBARD, Joshua (1744?–1807) of Eliot, Me.

Private diary, February 1771–September 1779; personal and business affairs, and journeys.

Old Eliot VIII (1908) 22–28 (account and quotations).

MUHLENBERG, Rev. Frederick Augustus Conrad (1750–1801) *b.* Trappe, Pa., Lutheran.

Travel journal, June–July 1771; journey of a young minister to Shamokin; descriptions of scenery, towns, etc.; life of Irish Lutheran assembly.

Northumberland Co. Hist. Soc. Proc. (Pa.) IX (1937) 208–226.

NEALE, Samuel (1729–1792) of Ireland, ministering Quaker.

Quaker journal, January 1771–September 1772 (American section); visiting Friends' meetings in Southern and New England states; Salem, Philadelphia, Oswego, etc.; meeting with John Woolman; moderate interest.

Friends' Library XI (Philadelphia, 1847) 49–61.

RICHARDSON, Lieut. William (1748–1772) of Royal Navy.

Journal, beginning May 1771; visit to and account of Labrador; seminarrative.
Canadian Hist. Rev. XVI (1935) 54–61.

WIGHT, Sergt.

Travel journal, November–December 1771; journey from Pensacola to the
Upper Creek Indians; stages, and notes on Creek customs.
Isabel M. Calder, *Colonial Captivities, Marches and Journeys* (New York,
1935) 236–243.

WILLARD, Rev. Joseph (1741–1828) of Mendon, Mass.

Clergyman's journal, October 1771–June 1783 (extracts); scattered notes of
sermons, ordinations, church affairs, etc.
Worcester Soc. Antiq. Proc. XIV (1895) 161–164.

WINSLOW, Anna Green (1759–1779) of Boston.

Private diary, November 1771–May 1773; girl's record of domestic life; naïve,
but vivid details; excellent picture of the social life of the Old South congregation.
Alice M. Earle (ed.), *Diary of Anna Green Winslow* (Boston, 1894) 121 pp.

1772

ANON. (of Dorchester, Mass.).

Diary, June 1772–October 1785 (extracts); local affairs at Dorchester, Mass.,
and some personal items; extraordinary spellings.
Ebenezer Clapp, *The Clapp Memorial* (Boston, 1876) 376–377.

ANDREWS, John (1743–*ca.* 1822) of Boston.

Journal-letters, February 1772–April 1775; Boston life and public affairs.
Massachusetts Hist. Soc. Proc. VIII (1864–1865) 316–412.

COCKING, Matthew, of Hudson's Bay Company, second factor at Fort York.

Fur trading and travel journal, June 1772–June 1773; journey from York Factory to the Blackfeet country to the southwest, stirring up trade; stages, and
details of Indians; fairly interesting.
Edited by L. P. Burpee, *Proc. and Trans. Royal Soc. Canada,* 3d Ser. II (1908)
Sec. II 91–121. Extracts (1776–1777) in W. S. Wallace, *Documents Relating to
the North West Company* (Toronto, 1934) 44–47. Wallace says Burpee's version
is "abbreviated and garbled."

CONDICT, Jemima (1754–1779) of Orange, N.J.

Private diary, 1772–1779; personal, family, and local affairs in Essex County,
N.J.; a very attractive journal of the conflict of love and religion in a Puritan
society; interesting language.
Jemima Condict, Her Book (Newark, N.J., 1930) 73 pp.

DILLWYN, William.

Travel diary, October 1772–January 1773; visit from Burlington, N.J., to
Charleston; poorly written but of some sociological interest.
South Carolina Hist. Geneal. Mag. XXXVI (1935) 1–6, 29–35, 73–78, 107–110.

Eve, Sarah (1759–1774) of Frankford, Pa.

Private diary, 1772–1773; personal, family, and social affairs near Philadelphia; visits; an intimate, genteel diary; very well written and attractive.

Pennsylvania Mag. Hist. Biog. V (1881) 19–36, 191–205.

Friedberg (N.C.) Moravian Congregation.

Congregational journals; usual details of Moravian life and work. (For analysis of type, see 1753: Bethabara.)

Adelaide L. Fries (ed.), *Records of the Moravians in North Carolina* (Raleigh, 1922–1941).

January–December 1772 (written by L. G. Bachhof) II 742–745; January–December 1775 (written by same; selections emphasize duties of pastor) II 911–914; January–December 1776, III 1110–1120; January–December 1777, III 1199–1201; January–December 1778, III 1274–1278; January–December 1779, III 1339–1340; January–December 1780 (with interpolations from the *Extract der Diarii der Gemeiner in der Wachau*) IV 1647–1652; January–December 1781, IV 1774–1779; January–December 1781 (also Hope; *Extract der Diarii der Gemeiner in der Wachau*) IV 1780–1783; January–December 1782, IV 1827–1831; January–December 1782 (also Hope; items from *Extract der Diarii der Gemeiner in der Wachau*) IV 1831–1833; January–December 1783, IV 1870–1872; January–December 1784, V 2063–2064; January–December 1785, V 2112–2115; January–December 1786, V 2160–2163; January–December 1787, V 2206–2209; January–December 1788, V 2258–2260; January–December 1789, V 2289–2290; March–December 1790, V 2316–2317; January–December 1791, V 2343–2344; January–December 1792, V 2375–2376.

Hearne, Samuel (1745–1792) of Hudson's Bay Company, explorer.

1. Travel journal, 1772; journey to northern regions; Indian affairs.
Jour. Amer. Hist. V (1911) 76–80.

2. Travel journal, June 1774–June 1775; inland journey from Fort York toward Basquiau; interesting details of travel, fur trade, Indians, weather, etc.; some linguistic interest.

3. Travel journal, July–October 1775; remarkable transactions and occurrences on journey from and to Fort York and at Cumberland House; similar to 2.

J. B. Tyrrell (ed.), *Journals of Samuel Hearne and Philip Turnor* (Toronto, 1934) 95–194.

Horton, Samuel (1731?–1808) of Newburyport, Mass.

Private diary, January 1772–1781 (extracts); brief entries about ship movements, etc.

Essex Inst. Hist. Colls. XLIII (1907) 285–286.

Jones, Rev. David (1736–1820), minister at Freehold, N.J.

Missionary journal, May 1772–April 1773; journeys to Indians on Ohio and Sciota rivers; fair narrative of his work; some concluding poems.

A Journal of Two Visits Made to Some Nations of Indians on the West Side of the River Ohio in the Years 1772 and 1773 (Burlington, N.J., 1774) 95 pp.; reprinted in *Sabin's Reprints* No. 11 (New York, 1865) 127 pp.

PUTNAM, Gen. Israel (1718–1790) of Brooklyn, Conn.

Travel journal, December 1772–March 1773; voyage from New York to the Natchez; entertaining journal of cruise round West Indies, interesting spellings and language.

The Two Putnams, Israel and Rufus (Hartford, 1931) 113–138.

SALEM (N.C.) MORAVIAN CONGREGATION.

Congregational journals; usual details of Moravian life and work. (For analysis of type, see 1753: BETHABARA.)

Adelaide L. Fries (ed.), *Records of the Moravians in North Carolina* (Raleigh, 1922–1941).

January–December 1772 (written by Paul Tiersch) II 666–693; January–December 1773, II 755–763; January–December 1774 (written by Paul Tiersch and Br. Graaf) II 813–822; January–December 1775 (written by Graaf) II 862–894; January–December 1776, III 1044–1081; January–December 1777, III 1136–1172; January–December 1778, III 1216–1255; January–December 1779, III 1287–1321; January–December 1780, IV 1520–1580; January–December 1781 (some items English in original) IV 1666–1708; January–December 1782, IV 1787–1799; January–December 1783, IV 1836–1845; January–December 1784 (prob. by the Rev. Christian Ludwig Benzien) V 2008–2025; January–December 1785, V 2071–2089; January–December 1786, V 2119–2129; January–December 1787, V 2168–2176; January–December 1788, V 2215–2227; January–December 1789, V 2264–2272; January–December 1790, V 2294–2302; January–December 1791, V 2321–2329; January–December 1792, V 2356–2368.

THACHER, Rev. Peter (1752–1802) of Malden and Boston.

Clergyman's journal, January 1772–March 1785 (extracts, with large gaps); notes of domestic and social life, weather, work and studies, visits, journeys; pleasant record of a quiet life.

Malden Hist. Soc. Reg. I (1910) 38–59.

THURSTON, Edward (1729–1782) of Newport, R.I.

Private diary, February–November 1772; brief almanac notes of personal and local affairs.

Newport Hist. Mag. I (1880–1881) 125–126.

TUFTS, Dr. Cotton (1732–1815) of Weymouth, Mass.

Private diaries, January–December 1772 and January–December 1784; brief notes, at first largely of weather and some social affairs, later mainly local affairs.

Massachusetts Hist. Soc. Proc. LXII (1908–1909) 444, 470–478.

ANON. [W. in text].   1773

Travel journal, August 1773; tour from Philadelphia to Bethlehem, Nazareth, Allentown, Lancaster; summer jaunt, seeing how Moravians lived; notes on inns, sights, etc.

Pennsylvania Mag. Hist. Biog. X (1886) 205–213; James B. Nolan, *Early Narratives of Berks County* (Reading, Pa., 1927) 38–42.

BARTRAM, William (1739–1823) of Kingsessing, Pa., traveler and naturalist.

Travel journals, beginning April 1773; travels in search of natural history specimens; Philadelphia to Florida, West Carolina, and Georgia; descriptions of country, manners and customs of Indians; a valuable and entertaining record.

Travels through North and South Carolina . . . (Philadelphia, 1791) 520 pp. Frequently reprinted. Modern edition, Mark Van Doren (ed.), *The Travels of William Bartram* (New York, 1928, 1940) 414 pp.

CHANDLER, Samuel (1753–1786) of Gloucester, Mass.

College diary, February 1773–December 1774; a year's life at Harvard College; naïve but interesting notes on reading, studies, student life, fires; some interesting spellings.

S. E. Mulliken, "Harvard on the Eve of the Revolution," *Harvard Graduates' Mag.* X (1901–1902) 376–381, 529–535.

DUNBAR, Rev. Asa (1745–1787) of Weston, Mass.

Private diary, July 1773–June 1776 (quotations); brief notes of his journeys; a poem.

Amer. Antiq. Soc. Proc. XIX (1908–1909) 66–76 ("Thoreau's Maternal Grandfather, Asa Dunbar").

FINLAY, Hugh (*ca.* 1731–1801) *b.* Scotland, surveyor of post roads.

Surveying journal, September 1773–May 1774; surveying journeys between Portsmouth and Savannah; mainly in Canada and New England; quite impersonal, but some pleasant topographical descriptions.

F. H. Norton (ed.), *Journal Kept by Hugh Finlay* (Brooklyn, 1867) 94 pp. Quoted in A. B. Hulbert, *Historic Highways of America* VII (Cleveland, 1903) 112–115.

FISH, Maj. Thomas (1743–1782) of Oxford, Mass.

Surveyor's journal, April 1773–May 1774; journeys from Oxford to Androscoggin River, Falmouth, Port Royal; camping and travel experiences; fairly interesting, and very useful linguistically.

Notes, Historical, Descriptive, and Personal, of Livermore (Portland, 1874) App. D 132–141.

FITHIAN, Philip Vickers (1747–1776) *b.* Greenwich, N.J.

1. Tutor's diary, October 1773–October 1774; tutor in Carter family; first-rate diary of social life in a great Southern family; detailed picture of Southern life by a scholarly and disapproving Northerner.

Philip Vickers Fithian, Journal and Letters I, J. R. Williams, ed. (Princeton, 1904) 47–274.

2. Religious diary, October 1774–March 1775; preaching in New Jersey.

Ibid. II, R. G. Albion and L. Dodson, eds. (Princeton, 1934) 245–258.

3. Religious and military diary, May 1775–October 1776; missionary work on

Virginia-Pennsylvania frontier, and in army around New York; details of back-country poverty; extremely interesting.

Ibid. II 1–243. Extracts in *Hist. Reg.* (Pa.) I (1883) 91–94, 177–181, 285–288, II (1884) 13–18, 99–119, 194–201, 241–247.

FRISBIE, Judah (1744–1829) of Wolcott, Conn.

Military journal, April–December 1773 and May–September 1776; weather notes; march to New York; Ticonderoga; brief notes of marches and military affairs.

Samuel Orcutt, *History of the Town of Wolcott* (Waterbury, Conn., 1874) 306–310.

GNADENHUETTEN MORAVIAN CONGREGATION (Ohio-to-be).

Congregation journals, January–October 1773 and May–August 1776; extracts to show their character; usual Moravian work and life.

Ohio Archaeol. and Hist. Soc. Pubs. XVIII (1909) 203–207 (in an article by A. B. Hulbert which gives a lengthy list of such journals in manuscript).

HARROWER, John, *b.* Scotland.

Private diary, December 1773–1776; notes of an indentured servant in Virginia; private affairs, the Revolution, original poems, letters; fairly interesting.

Amer. Hist. Rev. VI (1900–1901) 65–107.

KEMBLE, Lieut. Col. Stephen (1740–1829) of New Brunswick, N.J., loyalist officer.

1. Military journal, June 1773–December 1779 and June 1784–January 1789; includes siege of Boston; first part, social and political life in London and English counties; second part, military affairs during the Revolution.

New York Hist. Colls., Kemble Papers I (1883) 1–247.

2. Military journal, January 1780–April 1781; expedition from New York to Nicaragua.

Ibid., Kemble Papers II (1884) 1–64.

KENNEDY, Patrick.

Travel journal, 1773; Kaskaskia village in the Illinois country to the head of the Illinois River in search of copper mines; topographical notes.

Thomas Hutchins, *A Topographical Description of Virginia* (London, 1778) 51–64; reprint, Frederick C. Hicks, ed. (Cleveland, 1904) 122–134.

LACEY, John, of Pennsylvania.

Quaker missionary journal, July–September 1773; from Pennsylvania to the Indians of the Ohio.

Hist. Mag. n.s. VII (1870) 103–107.

McAFEE, James (1736–1811) *b.* Ireland, of Mercer Co., Ky.

Pioneer journal, June–August 1773; from Botetourt Co., Va., to Ohio River, Kentucky River, through wilderness of Kentucky, to Salt River; exploring and surveying; notes on topography, soil, prospects, timber, rivers, weather; notes for settlers; impersonal, but interesting historically; complements Robert McAfee's journal.

N. M. Woods, *The Woods-McAfee Memorial* (Louisville, Ky., 1905) App. A 425–437.

McAFEE, Robert (1745–1795) of Mercer Co., Ky.

Pioneer journal, May–August 1773; journey from Botetourt Co., Va., to Ohio River, mouth of Kentucky River, through wilderness of Kentucky, to Salt River; exploring and surveying; practical notes on topography, soil, weather, prospects, Indians, timber, animals; plain and impersonal; complements James McAfee's journal.

N. M. Woods, *The Woods-McAfee Memorial,* (Louisville, Ky., 1905) App. A 425–437.

NEWELL, Thomas (*b.* 1749) of Boston.

Private diary, January 1773–December 1774; brief notes, mostly weather, deaths, public affairs; Boston Tea Party; rather dull.

Massachusetts Hist. Soc. Proc. 1st Ser. XV (1876–1877) 335–363. Extracts relating to Boston Tea Party, etc., *ibid.* 1st Ser. IV (1858–1860) 216–224.

PARRISH, John.

Quaker travel journal, July–September 1773 (extracts); missionary journey from Lancaster down Ohio, around Pittsburgh; Indian council; return; mostly stages and visits, but also notes on some well-known Indians.

Pennsylvania Mag. Hist. Biog. XVI (1892) 443–448.

WHITELAW, Gen. James (1748–1829) of Ryegate, Vt.

Travel diary, April 1773–June 1783 (a few later notes); journeys to Nova Scotia, New York, Pennsylvania, Maryland, North Carolina, Virginia, etc.; descriptions of places and people; notes on settlement of Ryegate.

Vermont Hist. Soc. Proc. (1905–1906) 119–157.

1774

ANON. (Lieut. Thorne or Lieut. Hamilton of 4th ["King's Own"] Regiment).

Military journal, November 1774–March 1776 (extracts); siege of Boston; military affairs, general news, riots; strong feeling against Yankees; some fair description of engagements.

Mag. Hist. XVIII (1914) 1–15.

ASHLEY, Dr. Elihu (1750–1817) of Deerfield, Mass.

Private diary, September 1774; brief but entertaining social notes at Deerfield, while author was a medical student; some political notes.

George Sheldon, *History of Deerfield* (Deerfield, 1896) II 686–691.

BARKER, Lieut. John, of Clare Priory, Suffolk, Eng.

Military journal, November 1774–May 1776; in King's Own Foot Regiment, stationed at Boston; valuable account from British side; military and political affairs; anti-Yankee sentiment; good narrative.

Atlantic Monthly XXXIX (1877) 389–401, 544–554; E. E. Dana, *The British in Boston* (Cambridge, Mass., 1924) 73 pp.; reprinted in *Soc. Army Hist. Research Jour.* VII (1928) 83–109, 145–174.

CARPENTER, Jonathan (1757–1837) of Rehoboth, Mass., and Pomfret, Conn.
Prison diary, September 1774–January 1783; imprisonment on prison ship and in Forton Prison, Eng.; interesting but poorly written diary of an angry and patriotic American prisoner.
Vermont Hist. Soc. Proc. (1872) vii–xi.

CRESSWELL, Nicholas (1750–1804) of Edale, Derbyshire, Eng.
Travel journal, 1774–1777; voyage to Virginia; travel in Virginia, Kentucky, Pennsylvania, New York; unsuccessful attempt to settle, unsuccessful trading trip along Ohio; misadventures in the Revolution; vigorous abuse of Revolutionaries and propaganda; some good observations on places and people by a disillusioned young Englishman; a very good diary.
The Journal of Nicholas Cresswell, 1774–1777 (New York, 1924) 287 pp. Summary with extracts in *National Review* (London) XC (1927) 122–132; selection in Mark Van Doren, *An Autobiography of America* (New York, 1929) 108–121.

EVANS, David, of Philadelphia.
Journal, September 1774–January 1810; brief business notes, really from a cabinetmaker's daybook.
Pennsylvania Mag. Hist. Biog. XXVII (1903) 49–55.

FITCH, Ebenezer (1756–1833) of Yale and Williams College.
College diary, May 1774–September 1777; notes of chief events of each day; college life; a college student and the war.
Rev. Calvin Durfee, *Sketch of the Late Rev. Ebenezer Fitch, D.D.* (Boston, 1865) 20–33.

FOBES, Timothy (1740–1803) of Bridgewater, Mass.
Private diary, August 1774–December 1786; brief notes of births, deaths, local affairs; genealogical interest.
Pilgrim Notes and Queries II (1914) 152–154.

FRISBIE, Rev. Levi (1748–1806) of Hanover, N.H.
Treaty journal, June–September 1774; mission to Quebec Indians to recover boy prisoners.
Eleazar Wheelock, *A Continuation of the Narrative of the Indian Charity School* (Hartford, 1773) App. 44–68; facsimile as *Rochester Reprints* VIII (Rochester, N.Y., 1910?).

HARE, Robert, of Philadelphia.
Travel journal, May–July 1774; from Philadelphia to Canada and back, via Massachusetts; notes on places and people, Indians, and Canadian Jesuits.
Pennsylvania Hist. Soc. Colls. I (1853) 363–376.

HARVEY, Col. Alexander (1747–1809) b. Scotland, of Barnet, Vt.

Business journal, May 1774–November 1775; agent of Scottish Company of farmers; journey with company of emigrants from Scotland to Barnet, Vt.; survey of site, development of community; interesting picture of growth of an early community; interesting spellings.

Vermont Hist. Soc. Proc. (1921–1923) 201–262.

LITCHFIELD, Deacon Israel (1753–1840) of Scituate, Mass.

Private diary, November 1774–August 1775; journeys to Boston, etc., pleasant details of provincial life, religion, work, amusement, news, war, wreck; some doggerel verses; some linguistic interest.

The Litchfield Family in America, Part I No. 5 (1906) 313–351.

LITTLE, Deacon Enoch (1763–1848) of Boscawen, N.H.

Private diary, April 1774–December 1819; brief scattered entries, beginning as autobiography; many entries in verse form.

C. C. Coffin, *The History of Boscawen and Webster* (Concord, N.H., 1878) 403–406.

LOTT, Abraham, treasurer of colony of New York.

Travel journal, June–July 1774; voyage from New York City to Albany; tours; rather dull.

Hist. Mag. VIII (1870) 65–74.

McKEE, Alexander, Sir William Johnson's resident on the Ohio.

Journal, March–May 1774; meetings with Indians; news of Indian disturbances

E. B. O'Callaghan, *Docs. Rel. Col. Hist. State New York* VIII (1857) 461–467. Extract in N. B. Craig, *The Olden Time* II (1847, reprinted Cincinnati, 1876) 13–26.

McMILLAN, Rev. John (1752–1833) of western Pennsylvania, Presbyterian minister.

Presbyterian diary, October 1774–August 1776; life and work of the first Presbyterian minister in western Pennsylvania; notes on frontier life.

Jour. Presbyterian Hist. Soc. XV (1933) 222–238.

M'ROBERT, Patrick.

Journal-letters, August 1774–May 1775; a visiting Scotsman's tour through northern provinces of America; acute and judicious observations based on actual experience; farming, industry, commerce, general social observations; one of best travel books of the period.

Pennsylvania Mag. Hist. Biog. LIX (1935) 134–180; reprinted in *Pennsylvania Hist. Soc. Pamphlet Ser.,* No. 1.

MARSHALL, Christopher (1709–1797) of Philadelphia, patriot.

Historical journal, January 1774–September 1781; public affairs in New England; historically valuable but impersonal jottings of newspaper kind, political and public events.

William Duane (ed.), *Passages from the Remembrancer of Christopher Marshall* (Philadelphia, 1839) 124 pp.; William Duane (ed.), *Passages from the Diary of Christopher Marshall, Volume I 1774–1777* (Philadelphia, 1849) 174 pp. (Vol. II never issued); William Duane (ed.), *Extracts from the Diary of Christopher Marshall* (Albany, 1877) 330 pp.

NEWELL, Lieut. James.
Orderly book and journal, September–October 1774 (fragment); a rather dull account of the Point Pleasant campaign; a poem.
Virginia Mag. Hist. Biog. XI (1903–1904) 242–253.

SANGER, Abner, of Keene, N.H.
Private diary, 1774–1776; written by one of the early settlers of Keene, during the Revolution.
Repertory (Keene, N.H.) I (1926) II (1927).

WARD, Samuel (1725–1776) of Westerly, R.I., governor.
Political journal, August 1774–March 1776; notes of politics, Congressional activities, war news.
Mag. Amer. Hist. I (1877) Part 2 438–442, 503–506, 549–561.

WATSON, Elkanah (1758–1842) of Providence, R.I.
1. Quaker travel journal, April 1774–1784; march to Lexington, journeys to the South; rather dull.
New England Hist. Geneal. Reg. XVII (1863) 97–105 (brief quotations); a more extensive version of his travels in America and Europe is in Winslow Watson (ed.), *Men and Times of the Revolution* (New York, 1856) 460 pp. (*passim,* verbatim journal extracts).
2. Travel journal, May–June 1784; letter form; in Holland.
A Tour in Holland (Worcester, Mass., 1790), 191 pp.

WETMORE, William (1749–1830) of Salem, Mass.
Diary, May 1774–October 1778 (extracts); brief notes, war news, etc.; rather dull.
Essex Inst. Hist. Colls. XLIII (1907) 115–120.

WHITE, John (*b.* 1729) of Salem, Mass.
Private diary, August 1774–October 1789; almanac notes with large gaps; weather, domestic and public affairs; mediocre.
Essex Inst. Hist. Colls. XLIX (1913) 92–94.

1775

ANON. (sailor, of "Preston").
Sea journal, April–October 1775 (extracts); kept while "Preston" was in Boston Harbor; British account of incidents about time of Bunker Hill.
Massachusetts Hist. Soc. Proc. V (1860–1862) 53–55.

ANON. (British side).

Military journal, November 1775–May 1776; apparently adapted from Thomas Ainslie's journal; most remarkable occurrences in Quebec after Arnold appeared before the town; interesting and often amusing.

Lit. Hist. Soc. Quebec Hist. Docs. 7th Ser. (1905) 93–154.

ANON. (British garrison officer).

Military journal, November 1775–May 1776; most remarkable incidents of siege of Quebec; well-written, lively narrative.

Almon's Remembrancer (London, 1778) 1–34; reprinted in William Smith, *History of Canada* (1815) and in *New York Hist. Soc. Colls.* (1880) 173–236.

ANON. (British side).

Military journal, December 1775–May 1776; siege of Quebec; notes on artillery activities by a British artillery officer.

Lit. Hist. Soc. Quebec Hist. Docs. 8th Ser. (1906) 11–53.

AINSLIE, Thomas, collector of customs at Quebec.

Military journal, June 1775–May 1776; siege of Quebec; entertaining notes on the siege from the British side; good narrative and interesting details.

Lit. Hist. Soc. Quebec Hist. Docs. 7th Ser. (1905) 11–89.

ALLINE, Rev. Henry (1748–1784) of Newport, R.I., and Cornwallis, N.S.

Missionary diary, March 1775–November 1783; "some accounts of my travels, and the dealings of God with me."

Benjamin Rand (ed.), *The Life and Journal of Rev. Henry Alline* (Boston, 1806) 180 pp.

AMORY, Mrs. Katherine (1731–1777) of Boston.

Private diary, May 1775–March 1777; passage to London and record of her life there until her death; interesting notes of a loyalist in London; social, religious, theatrical notes.

Martha C. Codman (ed.), *The Journal of Mrs. John Amory* (Boston, 1923) 3–56.

ARNOLD, Gen. Benedict (1741–1801), Revolutionary patriot and renegade.

1. Regimental Memorandum Book, May–June 1775; jottings while author was at Ticonderoga and Crown Point; military movements, etc.

Pennsylvania Mag. Hist. Biog. VIII (1884) 363–376.

2. Military journal, 1775–1776; expedition against Quebec.

Justin H. Smith, *Arnold's March* (New York, 1903) 467–483; Kenneth Roberts (ed.), *March to Quebec* (New York, 1938) 45–61.

AVERY, Rev. David (1746–1818) of Groton, Conn.

1. Chaplain's journal, April–May 1775; siege of Boston; brief notes.

Amer. Monthly Mag. XVII (1900) 342–347.

2. Chaplain's journal, June 1776; in Paterson's regiment during northern campaign; battle of Trenton; services, visits to sick, marches, hardships.

Ibid., XIX (1901) 20–23, 151–156, 260–262, 375–378.

BALDWIN, Col. Jeduthan (1732–1788) of North Brookfield, Mass.

Military diary, 1775–1778; military affairs, with some personal notes; siege of Boston; New York campaign; expedition against Crown Point; march to Canada; Burgoyne's surrender; mostly brief entries but some good long ones; good picture of life of troops; some interesting spellings.

Thomas W. Baldwin (ed.), *The Revolutionary Journal of Col. Jeduthan Baldwin* (Bangor, 1906) 164 pp. Journal for July 1776–July 1777 (maneuvers around Ticonderoga) in *Bull. Fort Ticonderoga Museum* IV (1938) 10–40; extracts in *Jour. Military Service Inst.* XXXIX 257–273.

BARLOW, Sergt. Aaron (*b.* 1750) of Redding, Conn.

Military journal, June–December 1775 (extracts); expedition of Schuyler and Montgomery against Montreal and Quebec; march from Redding to Stamford to join Connecticut regiment; Ticonderoga, Lake Champlain, St. John's, etc.; military details; hardships; daily life of a common soldier.

Amer. Hist. Reg. II (1895) 641–649.

BEDINGER, Sergt. Henry (1753–1843) of Shepherdstown, Va.

Military journal, July 1775–June 1776; march to Roxbury, in camp there and at Staten Island; movements, engagements, news.

Danske Dandridge, *Historic Shepherdstown* (Charlottesville, Va., 1910) 97–144.

BELKNAP, Rev. Jeremy (1744–1798) of Dover, N.H.

1. Travel journal, October 1775; tour to camp at Cambridge, Mass.; siege of Boston; some interesting details of sufferings of Revolutionary soldiers.

Massachusetts Hist. Soc. Proc. 1st Ser. IV (1858–1860) 77–86.

2. Travel journal, July 1784; tour in the White Mountains.

Journal of a Tour to the White Mountains (Boston, 1876) 21 pp.

3. Travel journal, June–July 1796; from Boston to the Oneidas to examine Hamilton Oneida academy; interesting travel details, scenery, hardships, Indian life.

Massachusetts Hist. Soc. Proc. 1st Ser. XIX (1881–1882) 393–423.

BETHANIA (N.C.) MORAVIAN CONGREGATION.

Congregational journals; usual details of Moravian life and work. (For analysis of type, see 1753: BETHABARA.)

Adelaide L. Fries (ed.), *Records of the Moravians in North Carolina* (Raleigh, 1922–1941).

January–December 1775 (written by Rev. John Jacob Ernst) II 908–911; January–December 1776, III 1103–1110; January–December 1777, III 1194–1199; January–December 1778, III 1271–1274; January–December 1779, IV 1889–1892; January–December 1780, IV 1639–2646; January–December 1781, IV 1764–1773; January–December 1782 (travel journal) IV 1817–1826; January–December 1783, IV 1866–1870; January–December 1784, V 2058–2062; January–December 1785, V 2107–2112; January–December 1786, V 2155–2160; January–December

1787, V 2201–2206; January–December 1788, V 2252–2258; January–December 1789, V 2286–2289; January–December 1790, V 2313–2316; April–December 1791, V 2341–2342; January–December 1792, V 2373–2375.

BIXBY, Samuel (*b.* 1755) of Sutton, Mass.
Diary, May 1775–January 1776; moderate account of siege of Boston.
Massachusetts Hist. Soc. Proc. 1st Ser. XIV (1875–1876) 285–298.

BOARDMAN, Rev. Benjamin (1731–1802) of Middle Haddam, Conn.
Chaplain's journal, July–November 1775; with 2d Connecticut Regiment; siege of Boston; news, casualties, camp life; dinner with Washington and Franklin; rather dull chronicle of camp life.
Massachusetts Hist. Soc. Proc. 2d Ser. VII (1891–1892) 400–413.

BOUDINOT, Col. Elias (1740–1821) *b.* Philadelphia, statesman.
Historical journal, 1775–1789; "historical recollections of American events during the revolutionary war," memoirs of the Revolution and extracts from private journal.
Historical Recollections of American Events during the Revolutionary War (Philadelphia, 1894) 97 pp. Extracts in *Pennsylvania Mag. Hist. Biog.* XV (1891) 27–34, XXIV (1900) 453–466.

BURTON, Lieut. Jonathan (1741–1811) of Wilton, N.H.
1. Military diary, December 1775–January 1776; encampment at Winter Hill; very brief entries.
2. Military diary, August–November 1776; Canada expedition; a few personal entries; record of route.
New Hampshire Provincial and State Papers XIV (Concord, 1885) 667–702.

CALK, William (*b.* 1740) of Prince William Co., Va.
Travel diary, March–May 1775; interesting details of hardships of a pioneer; journey from Prince William Co., Va., to Boonesboro, Ky., and settlement there; interesting language.
Mississippi Valley Hist. Rev. VII (1920–1921) 363–377; S. Dunbar, *A History of Travel in America* (Indianapolis, 1915) I 142–146; A. B. Hulbert, *Historic Highways of America* VI (Cleveland, 1903) 107–117; T. Speed, *The Wilderness Road* (Louisville, 1886) 34–38.

CHANDLER, Rev. Thomas Bradbury (1726–1790) of Elizabethtown, N.J.
Missionary journal, May 1775–April 1786 (extracts); notes of his work at the mission in New Jersey.
Extracts in article by F. Gavin, *Church Hist.* I (1932) 90–106.

CHEEVER, William (1752–1786).
Military journal, May 1775–March 1776; battle of Bunker Hill; evacuation of Boston.
Massachusetts Hist. Soc. Proc. LX (1926–1927) 91–97.

CRAFT, Lieut. Benjamin (1738–1823) of Manchester, Mass.

Military journal, June–November 1775; siege of Boston; camp life; personal details; brief but lively notes.

Essex Inst. Hist. Colls. III (1861) 51–57, 133–140, 167–174, 219–220.

CRUGER, Henry (*d.* 1780) of New York, and Bristol, Eng.

Diary abroad, August 27, 1775; extract concerning his life in England; opinions of Burke and North about settlement with colonies.

Mag. Amer. Hist. VII (1881) 358–363.

DEARBORN, Gen. Henry (1751–1829) of Nottingham, N.H.

1. Military journal, September 1775–July 1776; Arnold's expedition to Quebec; military details, with some personal items and a detailed account of siege of Quebec.

Massachusetts Hist. Soc. Proc. 2d Ser. II (1885–1886) 275–305; *Mag. Hist.* Extra No. 135 (Tarrytown, 1928) 45 pp.; Kenneth Roberts (ed.), *March to Quebec* (New York, 1938) 129–168.

2. Military journal, July 1776–March 1783 (with some gaps); mostly brief details of the campaigns in which he was engaged, with many personal notes; interesting spellings.

Massachusetts Hist. Soc. Proc. 2d Ser. III (1886–1887) 102–133. Extracts (Sullivan's campaign) in F. Cook, *Journals of the Military Expedition of Major-General John Sullivan* (1887) 62–79; *Cayuga County Hist. Soc. Colls.* I 76–81.

DEMING, Mrs. Sarah (1722–1788) of Boston.

Letter-diary, April 1775; her adventures on retreat from Boston to Providence; fair interest.

Amer. Monthly Mag. IV (1894) 45–59; repeated, *ibid.* V (1894) 67–70.

DUDLEY, Dorothy, of Cambridge, Mass.

Private diary, April 1775–July 1776; siege of Boston, affairs in Cambridge; notes of social life, war news, sketches and opinions of various great men; a substantial and good diary.

A. G. (ed.), *Theatrum Majorum. The Cambridge of 1776* (Cambridge, Mass., 1876) 24–88.

EDES, Peter (1756–1840) of Boston, printer.

Prison diary, June 1775–January 1776; imprisonment in Boston by British after Bunker Hill; notes about his schoolhouse; simple, straightforward style; quite interesting.

A Diary of Peter Edes (Bangor, 1837) 24 pp.; Samuel L. Boardman, *Peter Edes, Pioneer Printer in Maine* (Bangor, 1901) 93–109.

EMERSON, Rev. Daniel (1716–1801) of Hollis, N.H.

Chaplain's journal, July–September 1775; at Crown Point; march, services, prayers, religious reflections; rather dull.

Benjamin K. Emerson, *The Ipswich Emersons* (Boston, 1900) 86–91.

EMERSON, Rev. William (1743–1776) of Concord, Mass.

Diary, April 19, 1775 (extract); battle of Lexington and Concord; a good description.

James L. Whitney, *The Literature of the Nineteenth of April* (Concord, 1876) Appendix.

EWING, George (1754–1824) of Greenwich, Conn.

Revolutionary journal, November 1775–May 1778; expedition against Canada; Valley Forge; clear but somewhat dull.

Thomas Ewing (ed.), *George Ewing, Gentleman* (Yonkers, 1928) 1–54.

FARNSWORTH, Corp. Amos (1754–1847) of Groton, Mass.

Military journal, April 1775–April 1779 (with gaps); notes on camp life and events of the war; Concord, Lexington, siege of Boston, Bunker Hill; much religious self-analysis; more personal than the usual military journal.

Samuel A. Green, *Three Military Diaries* (Groton, 1901) 77–113; *Massachusetts Hist. Soc. Proc.* 2d Ser. XII (1897–1899) 74–107.

FASSETT, Capt. John (1743–1803) of Bennington, Vt.

Military journal, September–December 1775; march of the Green Mountain Boys to Canada and return; Montgomery's campaign; full entries and rather good narrative of hardships and adventures.

Harry P. Ward, *The Follett-Dewey-Fassett-Safford Ancestry* (Columbus, O., 1896) 215–243.

[FINLAY, Hugh?]

Military journal, November 1775–May 1776; siege and blockade of Quebec; nontechnical military details; fair interest.

Lit. Hist. Soc. Quebec Hist. Docs. 4th Ser. (1875) 25 pp.

FISHER, Pvt. Elijah (*b.* 1758) of Turner and Livermore, Me.

Military diary, May 1775–February 1785; notes of a laborer during the Revolutionary War and later; siege of Boston; Burgoyne's campaign; captivity; matter-of-fact attitude to hardships and adventures; later, farming in Sylvester; interesting spellings.

Elijah Fisher's Journal (Augusta, 1880) 29 pp.; reprinted *Mag. Hist.* Extra No. 6 (New York, 1909) 76 pp.

FISHER, Pvt. John (1756–1840) of Killingly, Conn.

Military journals, July–October 1775 and June–July 1777; New York campaign; battle of Long Island; and in Connecticut; brief notes; some interesting spellings.

Mag. Hist. XIII (1911) 184–186.

FOBES, Simon (1756–1840) of Canterbury, Conn.

Military diary, April 1775–April 1780; mainly devoted to a narrative of Bunker's Hill and Arnold's expedition against Quebec; interesting.

Mahoning Valley Hist. Soc., Hist. Colls. Mahoning Valley (1876) 345–394;

reprinted *Mag. Hist.* Extra No. 130 (Tarrytown, 1927) 53 pp. Partly in Kenneth Roberts (ed.), *March to Quebec* (New York, 1938) 575–613.

FOGG, Maj. Jeremiah (1749–1808) of Kensington, N.H.
  1. Military journal, 1775–1776.
  *Journal of Major Jeremiah Fogg (Exeter, N.H., 1879) 24 pp.
  2. Military journal, August–September 1779; longish entries of Sullivan's campaign.
  F. Cook, *Journals of the Military Expedition of Major-General John Sullivan* (Auburn, N.Y., 1887) 92–101.

FULLER, Rev. Daniel (1740–1829) of Gloucester, Mass.
  Clergyman's journal, March 1775–December 1797; notes on journeys, public affairs; Charlestown and Boston during the Revolution; domestic, parish, and personal affairs.
  The Diary of the Reverend Daniel Fuller (New York, 1894) 49 pp.

GERRISH, Capt. Henry (*b.* 1742) of Boscawen, N.H.
  Military journal, April 1775–October 1777 (extracts); march to Cambridge; auction at which plunder from Fort Edward was sold.
  C. C. Coffin, *History of Boscawen and Webster* (Concord, N.H., 1878) 247, 265.

HALE, Capt. Nathan (1755–1776) of Coventry, Conn.
  Military journal, September 1775–August 1776; occasional and brief entries, mostly of moderate interest.
  Henry P. Johnston, *Nathan Hale* (New York, 1914) 240–257.

[HAMILTON, Sir J., captain of H.M.S. "Lizard"?]
  Military journal, December 1775–May 1776; principal events of siege of Quebec; military details; some personal; literary style, with poetical quotations; perhaps the best British journal of the siege.
  W. T. P. Short (ed.), *A Journal of the Principal Occurrences during the Siege of Quebec* (London, 1824) 111 pp.; F. C. Würtele, *Blockade of Quebec in 1775–1776, Lit. Hist. Soc. Quebec Hist. Docs.* 8th Ser. (Quebec, 1906) 55–101.

HASKELL, Pvt. Caleb (*b.* 1723) of Newburyport, Mass.
  Military journal, May 1775–May 1776; Arnold's expedition; siege of Boston; hardships of soldiers; moderate interest.
  Newburyport Herald (1881); *Mag. Hist.* Extra No. 86 (1922) 49 pp.; Kenneth Roberts (ed.), *March to Quebec* (New York, 1938) 459–499.

HASLEWOOD, Capt. John, of 63d British Infantry.
  Military journal, April 1775–May 1778; from Cork to Boston; notes on campaigns, Charlestown, Long Island, Rhode Island, New York; Bunker Hill, siege of Boston; brief military details; some interesting spellings and vocabulary.
  Mississippi Valley Hist. Rev. VII (1920–1921) 51–58.

HAWS, Pvt. Samuel (1743–1795?) of Wrentham, Mass.

Military journal, April 1775–February 1776; Lexington, siege of Boston; camp life of ordinary soldier; colloquial and humorous.

Abraham Tomlinson, *The Military Journals of Two Private Soldiers* (Poughkeepsie, 1855) 49–90.

HEATH, Gen. William (1737–1814) of Roxbury, Mass.

Military journal, June 1775–November 1803; military affairs during the Revolution; a valuable source book.

Memoirs of Major-General William Heath (Boston, 1798) 388 pp.; reprinted (New York, 1904) 422 pp. Extract (siege of Boston) in *Massachusetts Hist. Soc. Proc.* 1st Ser. IV (1858–1860) 294–296.

HEBRON (PA.) MORAVIAN CONGREGATION.

Congregational journals, 1775–1783 (extracts); life and work of Moravians at New Lebanon; some very interesting general entries; quarrels with the Hessians.

W. H. Egle's Notes and Queries (Pa.) 4th Ser. II; further extracts in *Lebanon Co. Hist. Soc. Pubs.* I (1898) 8–16, and in *Pennsylvania Mag. Hist. Biog.* XVIII (1894) 449–462.

HENDERSON, Richard (1735–1785) of Hanover Co., Va.

Travel diary, March–July 1775; trip to Kentucky, and events in settlement of Boonesborough; interesting details of frontier life.

G. W. Ranck, *Boonesborough* (Louisville, 1901) 169–180. Extract in A. B. Hulbert, *Historic Highways of America* VI (Cleveland, 1903) 101–107.

[HENDRICKS, Capt. William (*d.* 1776) of Harrisburg, Pa.]

Military journal, July–December 1775; Arnold's march to Quebec; Carlisle, Boston, Quebec, siege; notes of hardships; a valuable journal. Justin H. Smith thought author might have been Sergeant William McCoy, although it is usually called "Hendricks' Journal."

A Journal of the March of a Party of Provincials from Carlisle to Boston (Glasgow, 1776) 36 pp.; reprinted in *Pennsylvania Archives* 2d Ser. XV 25–58.

HENRY, John Joseph (1758–1811) of Lancaster, Pa.

Military journal, September 1775–September 1776; mainly describes Arnold's campaign against Quebec; the author's own military career; captivity; written up for his children in a literary and occasionally heroic style; very detailed and perhaps the most extensive journal of Arnold's campaign.

An Accurate and Interesting Account . . . (Lancaster, 1812) 221 pp.; reprinted as *Campaign against Quebec* (Watertown, 1844) 212 pp., and *Account of Arnold's Campaign against Quebec* (Albany, 1877) 198 pp.; *Pennsylvania Archives* 2d Ser. XV 59–191; Kenneth Roberts (ed.), *March to Quebec* (New York, 1938) 299–429.

HONYMAN, Dr. Robert (1747–1824) of Hanover Co., Va.

Travel journal, March–April 1775; visit to northern colonies from Virginia; longish entries; touristic descriptions; a very pleasant diary.

Philip Padelford (ed.), *Colonial Panorama, 1775* (San Marino, Calif., 1939) 86 pp.

How, Pvt. David (1758–1842) of Methuen, Mass.

1. Military journal, December 1775–January 1777; siege of Boston, Harlem Heights, Trenton, White Plains; many details of ordinary camp life of private soldier; brief notes, but they give interesting picture; interesting spellings.

2. Military journal, September–November 1777; march to Fort Edward and return to Methuen.

G. W. Chase and H. B. Dawson (eds.), *Diary of David How* (Morrisania, N.Y., 1865) 51 pp.

Howe, John, British spy.

Journal and narrative, April 1775 and 1812–1813; adventures in New England; first part kept while author was British spy during the Revolution, second part while he was engaged in smuggling business during War of 1812.

A Journal Kept by Mr. John Howe (Concord, N.H., 1827) 44 pp.; reprinted *Mag. Hist.* Extra No. 132 (Tarrytown, 1927) 5–36; facsimile of original edition in *Photostat Americana, Second Series* No. 82 (Boston, 1939) 44 pp.

Humphrey, Lieut. William, of Thayer's company.

Military journal, September 1775–August 1776; Arnold's campaign against Quebec; largely weather notes and accounts of hard marches; quite interesting.

Mag. Hist. Extra No. 166 (Tarrytown, 1931) 5–42.

Ingalls, Pvt. Phineas (1758–1844) of Andover, Mass.

Military journal, April 1775–December 1776 (with gap); siege of Boston, army movements and camp life in Cambridge, Lake Champlain campaign, Ticonderoga, Saratoga; moderate interest.

Essex Inst. Hist. Colls. LIII (1917) 81–92.

Jeffry, James (1733–1807) of Salem, Mass.

Private diary, January–October 1775; long entries of war news at Quebec, where diarist was postmaster; mostly historical interest.

Essex Inst. Hist. Colls. L (1914) 97–150.

Kimball, M[oses].

Military diary, September 1775–September 1776; Arnold's campaign against Quebec; extracts published as footnotes to James Melvin's journal.

Kenneth Roberts (ed.), *March to Quebec* (New York, 1938) 435–454.

Knox, Maj. Gen. Henry (1750–1806) of Boston.

Military journal, November 1775–January 1776; journey to Stillwater, transferring ordnance; includes a description of Niagara and the frozen Cohoos Falls.

New England Hist. Geneal. Reg. XXX (1876) 321–326.

Leach, John (*ca.* 1724–1799) of Boston.

Prison diary, June–October 1775; civilian prisoner of British; a good account of life in Boston Jail.

New England Hist. Geneal Reg. XIX (1865) 255–263; Samuel L. Boardman, *Peter Edes, Pioneer Printer in Maine* (Bangor, 1901) 115–125.

LEMPRIERE, Capt. Clement, of sloop "Commerce."
Sea journal, July–August 1775; log notes of voyage of the "Commerce" toward New Orleans.
R. W. Gibbes, *Documentary History of the American Revolution* I (New York, 1855) 121–123.

LINDSAY, Lieut. William, of British militia.
Military journal, September–December 1775; siege and blockade of Quebec.
*Canadian Rev. II and III (1826), incomplete.

LITCHFIELD, Rev. Paul (1752–1827) of Carlisle, Mass.
College diary, March–July 1775; kept while author was, a student at Harvard, but mostly war news at Scituate.
Massachusetts Hist. Soc. Proc. 1st Ser. XIX (1881–1882) 376–379.

LITTITZ (PA.) MORAVIAN CONGREGATION.
Congregational journals, February 1775–May 1786 (extracts); items relating to Revolutionary War and the life and work of the congregation. Translated.
Pennsylvania Germania n.s. I (1912) 849–862. Extracts relating to the hospital, *Lancaster Co. Hist. Soc. Papers* XXIII (1919) 5–14.

LIVINGSTON, Maj. Henry (1748–1828) of 3d N.Y. Continental Line.
Military journal, August–December 1775; Montgomery's expedition against Canada; some independent descriptions and observations.
Pennsylvania Mag. Hist. Biog. XXII (1898) 9–33.

LUKENS, Jesse (1748–1776) of Franconia, Pa.
Letter-diary, September 1775; incidents of siege of Boston, and Arnold's departure for Quebec; fairly good descriptions.
Amer. Hist. Rec. I (1872) 546–550; *Boston Pub. Lib. Bull.* (1900) 23–29.

LUNT, Paul (1747–1824) of Newburyport, Mass.
Military journal, May–December 1775; travel to camp at Cambridge, notes on camp life.
Massachusetts Hist. Soc. Proc. 1st Ser. XII (1871–1873) 192–206.

LYMAN, Pvt. Simeon (1754–1780) of Sharon, Conn.
Military journal, August–December 1775; march to Boston, siege, return to Sharon; lively, amusing record of common soldier's life; mostly personal details; originally interesting spellings normalized (sample, p. 99).
Connecticut Hist. Soc. Colls. VII (1899) 111–134.

McCURTIN, Pvt. Daniel, of Pennsylvania.
Military journal, July 1775–May 1776; siege of Boston, camp at Cambridge and Roxbury; details, but some amusing general observations and adventures.
Thomas Balch, *Papers Relating Chiefly to the Maryland Line* (Philadelphia, 1857) 1–41.

MACKENZIE, Adjt. Frederick (*d.* 1824) *b.* Dublin, of Royal Welch Fusiliers.

Military journal, 1775–1781; a daily narrative of his service as an officer during the Revolution; campaigns in Massachusetts, Rhode Island, New York; vivid account of burning of New York; a most valuable journal from the British side.

Diary of Frederick Mackenzie (Cambridge, Mass., 1930), two vols. Extracts in *Newport Hist. Soc. Bull.* No. 86 (1933) 5–36, 93 (1934) 3–31; portion describing Concord and Lexington published as Allen French (ed.), *A British Fusilier in Revolutionary Boston* (Cambridge, Mass., 1926) 83 pp.

MEIGS, Maj. Return Jonathan (1740–1823) of Middletown, Conn.

Military journal, September 1775–January 1776; Arnold's expedition against Quebec; military details; some descriptions of Montgomery and other leaders.

Originally published in part in *Almon's Remembrancer* (London, 1776) Part III 295–301; *Massachusetts Hist. Soc. Colls.* 2d Ser. II (1814) 227–247 (printed from MS); C. J. Bushnell (ed.), *Journal of the Expedition against Quebec, Crumbs for Antiquarians* I No. 6 (New York, 1864) 57 pp.; *Annual Papers Winchester Hist. Soc.* (Va.) I (1931) 119–155; Kenneth Roberts (ed.), *March to Quebec* (New York, 1938) 173–192.

MELVIN, Pvt. James (*b.* 1754) of Hubbardston, Mass.

Military journal, September 1775–August 1776; Arnold's expedition against Quebec; first part fairly interesting; imprisonment; then mostly weather notes.

Journal of the Expedition to Quebec in 1775 (Philadelphia, 1864) 34 pp.; Andrew A. Melvin (ed.), *The Journal of James Melvin* (Portland, 1902) 90 pp. Partly in Kenneth Roberts (ed.), *March to Quebec* (New York, 1938) 435–454.

MORGAN, Ens. Nathaniel (*b.* 1717) of Voluntown, Conn.

Military journal, April–December 1775; Lexington alarm, siege of Boston; fairly interesting, but disjointed.

Connecticut Hist. Soc. Colls. VII (1899) 99–110.

MORISON, George, of Cumberland Co., Pa.

Military journal, July 1775–September 1776; Arnold's expedition against Quebec; Bunker Hill; notes on camp life; fairly good.

An Interesting Journal of Occurrences (Hagerstown, Md., 1803); *Mag. Hist.* Extra No. 52 (Tarrytown, 1916) 44 pp.; Kenneth Roberts (ed.), *March to Quebec* (New York, 1938) 505–539. Extract in *Pennsylvania Mag. Hist. Biog.* XIV (1890) 434–439.

NAZARETH (PA.) MORAVIAN CONGREGATION.

Congregational journals 1775–1776 (extracts); details of Indian warfare on the frontier.

Pennsylvania Mag. Hist. Biog. XXXIX (1915) 345–352.

NEWELL, Deacon Timothy (1718–1799) of Boston.

Private diary, April 1775–March 1776; siege of Boston; good, vivid descriptions of misfortunes of inhabitants after the siege, pillage, etc.

Massachusetts Hist. Soc. Colls. 4th Ser. I (1852) 261–276.

NICHOLS, Lieut. Francis (*d.* 1812) of Pennsylvania Rifles.

Military journal, December 1775–September 1776; expedition against Quebec; prisoner; scattered brief entries.

Pennsylvania Mag. Hist. Biog. XX (1896) 504–514.

NOURSE, James.

Travel diary, April–July 1775; from Virginia to Kentucky; fairly interesting narrative of early journey into the interior.

Jour. Amer. Hist. XIX (1925) 121–138, 251–260, 351–364.

OGDEN, Maj. Matthias (*b.* 1754) of Elizabethtown, N.J.

Military journal, October–November 1775; Arnold's expedition; failure to take Heights of Abraham; hardships of campaign; good style; modernized.

New Jersey Hist. Soc. Proc. n.s. XIII (1928) 17–30.

OSWALD, Capt. Eleazer (1755–1795) of New Haven, Conn.

Military journal, September–October 1775; Arnold's expedition; a journal similar to Arnold's own, and called "the missing pages of Arnold's journal."

Peter Force, *American Archives* 4th Ser. III 1058–1062.

OXNARD, Edward (1747–1803) of Portland, Me.

Loyalist diary, August 1775–June 1785 (extracts); a very good account of social and public life in England, as a loyalist exile; meetings with public and literary figures, notes on London sights, theaters, etc.; allusions to public affairs in New England.

New England Hist. Geneal. Reg. XXVI (1872) 8–10, 115–121, 254–259.

PREBLE, Gen. Jedidiah (1707–1784) of Falmouth (later Portland), Me.

Military journal, August 1775–November 1782; notes of campaigns; Roxbury, Boston, etc.; a few social entries.

G. H. Preble, *Genealogical Sketch of the Prebles in America* (Boston, 1868) 61–91.

PRICE, Ezekiel (1728–1802) of Boston and Stoughton.

1. Private diary, May 1775–August 1776; long and detailed notes on siege of Boston and author's personal affairs; quite interesting.

Massachusetts Hist. Soc. Proc. 1st Ser. VII (1863) 185–262.

2. Private diary, December 1777–November 1778; war news, mainly about the French in Rhode Island.

New England Hist. Geneal. Reg. XIX (1865) 331–338.

RITZEMA, Col. Rudolphus (*d.* 1803) of 1st New York Regiment.

Military journal, August 1775–March 1776; Montgomery's expedition against Canada; visit to Congress.

Mag. Amer. Hist. I (1877) Part I 98–107.

SCHAUKIRK (or Shewkirk), Rev. Ewald Gustav (1725–1805) *b.* Stettin, Germany, Moravian bishop in New York.

Moravian journal February 1775–November 1783; extracts from the journal of the New York congregation, kept by him; the selections relate to the occupation of New York by the British, war news, and the life and work of the congregation; good narrative. Translated.

Pennsylvania Mag. Hist. Biog. X (1886) 418–445. Extracts relating largely to campaigns around New York and Brooklyn in *Long Island Hist. Soc. Proc.* III (1878) Part II 101–127.

SENTER, Dr. Isaac (1753–1799) of Cranston, R.I.

Surgeon's journal, September 1775–June 1776; kept during Arnold's campaign against Quebec; long and well-written entries about camp life, his own work, and the progress of the campaign.

The Journal of Isaac Senter (Philadelphia, 1846) 40 pp.; reprinted in *Mag. Hist.* Extra No. 42 (Tarrytown, 1915) 60 pp.; Kenneth Roberts (ed.), *March to Quebec* (New York, 1938) 197–241.

SHAW, Thomas (*b.* 1753) of Standish, Me.

Private and military diary, 1775–1837; scattered notes; recollections of his youth; service at Boston, Ticonderoga, Lake George.

W. Daggett, *A Down East Yankee* (Portland, 1920) 58–61; and in I. B. Choate, *Thomas Shaw, a Down-East Homer, Mag. Hist.* Extra No. 116 (Tarrytown, 1926) 5–20.

SQUIER, Ephraim (1748–1841) of Ashford, Conn.

Military journal, September–November 1775; expedition against Quebec; fair interest.

Mag. Amer. Hist. II (1878) Part II 685–694; Kenneth Roberts (ed.), *March to Quebec* (New York, 1938) 619–628; *Mag. Hist.* Extra No. 160 (Tarrytown, 1930) 39–48.

2. Military journal, September–November 1777; march to Albany, at Stillwater, and Burgoyne's surrender.

Mag. Amer. Hist. II (1878) Part II 685–694.

STEVENS, James (1749–1834) of Andover, Mass.

Military journal, April 1775–April 1776; marches around Boston and Andover; notes on camp life, personal affairs; moderate interest, some linguistic value.

Essex Inst. Hist. Colls. XLVIII (1912) 41–71. Account and quotations in Albert Annett and Alice Lehtinen, *History of Jaffrey, N. H.* I (Jaffrey, 1937) 826–840.

STOCKING, Abner (*b.* 1753) of Chatham, Conn.

Military journal, September 1775–October 1776; Arnold's campaign; capture at Quebec; fairly interesting, but written up.

An Interesting Journal of Abner Stocking (Catskill, N.Y., 1810) 36 pp.; *Mag. Hist.* Extra No. 75 (Tarrytown, 1921) 36 pp.; Kenneth Roberts (ed.), *March to Quebec* (New York, 1938) 545–569.

STORRS, Lieut. Col. Experience (1734–1801) of Mansfield, Conn.

Military journal, June 1775 (extracts); at Cambridge, siege of Boston, Bunker Hill, etc.

Massachusetts Hist. Soc. Proc. 1st Ser. XIV (1875–1876) 84–87; *Mag. Amer. Hist.* VIII (1882) Part I 124.

TENNENT, Rev. William, of South Carolina.

Political diary, August–September 1775; journey to South Carolina to persuade Tories to join the Revolution; travel, religious work, propaganda, military affairs around Charleston; varied, and interesting.

R. W. Gibbes, *Documentary History of the American Revolution* I (1855) 225–239.

THACHER, Dr. James (1754–1844) *b*. Barnstable, Mass., physician and historian.

Military journal, January 1775–January 1783; mainly deals with the Revolutionary War; good picture of army life and hardships; detailed description of men and events.

A Military Journal during the American Revolutionary War (Boston, 1823) 603 pp.; frequently reprinted.

THAYER, Capt. Simeon (1737–1800) of Providence, R.I.

Military diary, September 1775–August 1776; Arnold's expedition; brief, mediocre prison notes.

Rhode Island Hist. Soc. Colls. VI (1867) 1–45; Kenneth Roberts (ed.), *March to Quebec* (New York, 1938) 247–294.

TILGHMAN, Lieut. Col. Tench (1744–1786) of Baltimore, Md.

1. Treaty journal, August–September 1775; secretary of Indian commission to treat with Six Nations at German Flats, N.Y.; largely social aspects of ceremonies.

2. Military journal, September–October 1781; military details of siege of Yorktown.

Memoir of Lieut. Col. Tench Tilghman (Albany, 1876) 81–101, 103–107.

[TOLMAN, Ebenezer (1748–1838).]

Military journal, September 1775–September 1776; Arnold's march; Cambridge to Quebec. Previously attributed to Joseph Ware and Ebenezer Wild, *q.v.*; but Justin H. Smith has shown that they were not in Arnold's army and that the author was probably Tolman (*Arnold's March*, 1903, 44–51).

Massachusetts Hist. Soc. Proc. 2d Ser. II (1885–1886) 267–275 (here wrongly ascribed to Ebenezer Wild); reprinted in *Mag. Hist.* Extra No. 134 (Tarrytown, 1927) 37–47. Another and very similar version, erroneously attributed to Joseph Ware, in *New England Hist. Geneal. Reg.* VI (1852) 129–150; reprinted in *Mag. Hist.* Extra No. 134 (Tarrytown, 1927) 5–35.

TOPHAM, Capt. John (1743–1792) of Newport, R.I.

Military journal, September 1775–May 1776; Arnold's expedition against Quebec; sufferings, and imprisonment; disjointed but interesting notes with some spellings of interest.

Rhode Island Sons Revolution Pubs. (1902); *Mag. Hist.* Extra No. 50 (Tarrytown, 1916) 46 pp.

TREVETT, Lieut. John (1747–1823) of Newport, R.I., U.S.N.
  1. Sea journals, November 1775–December 1776; on board sloop "Carea" during Revolutionary War; off New England; engagements, cruise, some personal notes; full and well-written.
  2. Sea journal, June–July 1778; cruise to Charlestown.
  Rhode Island Hist. Soc. Mag. VI (1885) 72–74, 106–110, VII (1887) 194–199, 271–278.

TRUMBULL, Rev. Benjamin (1735–1820) of North Haven, Conn.
  1. Chaplain's journal, July–November 1775; Montgomery's march, and siege of St. John's.
  2. Military journal, July 1776–November 1777; expedition near New York; battles of Long Island and White Plains; succinct and factual account.
  Connecticut Hist. Soc. Colls. VII (1899) 137–218; first journal also in *Bull. Fort Ticonderoga Museum* I (1927) 11–18, 15–30, 26–33, (1928) 21–35.

TULLY, Samuel (1750–1827) of Saybrook, Conn.
  Private diary, July 1775–September 1815; scattered notes of war news, local events, weather, and some personal affairs.
  History of Middlesex County, Connecticut (New York, 1884) 458, 467–468.

WARE, Pvt. Joseph (1753–1805) of Needham, Mass.
  See 1775: TOLMAN.

WARREN, Dr. John (1753–1815) of Boston.
  Surgeon's journal, April 1775–May 1776; Lexington, Bunker Hill, etc.; military and camp details, war news; full but rather dull.
  John C. Warren, *Genealogy of Warren* (Boston, 1854) 85–98.

WELLS, Sergt. Bayze (1744–1814) of Farmington, Conn.
  Military journal, May 1775–February 1777; march to Ticonderoga and Canada; naval operations on Lake Champlain; brief entries, with fairly good narrative; interesting spellings.
  Connecticut Hist. Soc. Colls. VII (1899) 241–296.

WILD, Lieut. Ebenezer (1758–1794) of Braintree and Boston.
  See 1775: TOLMAN.

WILLIAMS, Maj. Ennion, of Pennsylvania.
  Military journal, October 1775; journey to camp at Cambridge, via Connecticut; some social notes, and skirmishes; fair interest.
  Pennsylvania Archives 2d Ser. XV 7–20.

WRIGHT, Pvt. Aaron, of Reading, Pa.
  Military journal, June 1775–July 1776; siege of Boston, Cambridge; notes on camp life.
  Boston Transcript (April 11, 1862); *Hist. Mag.* VI (1862) 208–212.

1776

ANON. (lieutenant in Connecticut regiment).

Military journal, January–April 1776 (extracts); evacuation of Boston by British; camp life; minute details.

Hist. Mag. VIII (1864) 326–332.

ANON.

Weather diary, April–May 1776; kept at Quebec during the siege; some general notes of the siege.

Lit. Hist. Soc. Quebec Trans. No. 22 (1898) 45–49.

ANON. (officer in Specht's regiment of Brunswick mercenaries).

Travel diary, May–September 1776; voyage from Hanover to Quebec; except for a few days at Portsmouth, it was kept entirely at sea; long entries and good narrative.

Published at Frankfurt and Leipzig (1776). Translated, *New York State Hist. Assoc. Quar. Jour.* VIII (1927) 323–351.

ANON. (Pennsylvania soldier).

Military journal, July–December 1776; campaign around New York and retreat through New Jersey; lively account of engagements; interesting spellings.

Bull. New York Pub. Lib. VIII (1904) 547–549.

ANON. (private soldier).

Military journal, July–December 1776; operations around New York; brief and scattered notes; interesting spellings and vocabulary.

Hist. Mag. VII (1863) 366–368.

ALLEN, Daniel (1744–1777) of Cornwall, Conn., tailor.

Military and prison diary, August (?) 1776–January 1777; brief notes of marches; tailoring for soldiers; interesting spellings.

Edward C. Starr, *A History of Cornwall, Connecticut* (New Haven, 1920) 252–254.

ATLEE, Col. Samuel John.

Military journal, August 1776 (extract); battle of Long Island.

Pennsylvania Archives 2d Ser. I 509–516.

BAMFORD, Capt. William (*b.* 1727 or 1728) of British Army.

Military journal, January–December 1776; at Boston; New York campaign; brief notes, largely of movements.

Maryland Hist. Mag. XXVII (1932) 240–259, 296–314, XXVIII (1933) 9–26.

BANGS, Lieut. Isaac (1752–1780) of Eastham, Mass., and Cary's Massachusetts militia.

Army surgeon's journal, April–July 1776; siege of Boston, New York campaign; notes of army movements, description of towns and estates, Dutch and

Jewish customs, visits to Schuyler family, notes of his own affairs; fairly interesting.

Edward Bangs (ed.), *Journal of Lieutenant Isaac Bangs* (Cambridge, 1890) 70 pp. Extracts in *New Jersey Hist. Soc. Proc.* VIII (1856–1859) 120–125; *Hist. Mag.* n.s. IV (1868) 305–306.

BARBER, Rev. Daniel (1756–1834).
Military journal, 1776; siege of Boston; description of officers in Humphrey's company of Connecticut regiment.
The History of My Own Times (Washington, 1827–1832), three vols.

BAYLEY, Ens. Frye (1749–1787) of Newbury, Vt.
Military journal, June 1776–April 1783, and a few later entries; brief notes during campaign against Quebec.
F. P. Wells, *History of Newbury, Vermont* (St. Johnsbury, 1902) 382–384.

BEATTY, Capt. William (1758–1781) of Maryland Line.
Military journal, June 1776–January 1781; New York, Valley Forge, Southern campaign; brief notes.
Maryland Hist. Mag. III (1908) 104–119; *Hist. Mag.* n.s. I (1867) 79–85.

BEEBE, Dr. Lewis (1749–1816) *b.* Salisbury, Conn., of Sheffield, Mass.
Surgeon's military journal, April 1776–January 1777; expedition against Canada; lively account of Arnold's campaign; vigorous notes on failings of officers, hatred for Arnold; good description of smallpox epidemics and bad conditions; verse epigrams.
Pennsylvania Mag. Hist. Biog. LIX (1935) 321–361.

BERRY, Joshua (1755–1826) *b.* Greenland, N.H., of Pittsfield, N.H.
Military journal, November 1776 (extract); journey from Portsmouth to Albany with munitions; brief notes.
Mag. New England Hist. II (1892) 192–193.

BIGELOW, Maj. John.
Military journal, July–August 1776 (abstract); Ticonderoga to St. John's with message from Continental Congress to Burgoyne; report.
Amer. Hist. Rec. I (1872) 438–440.

BLAKE, Maj. Henry (1755–1833) of Hopkinton, N.H.
Military journal, March–October 1776; march through Connecticut and New York; Ticonderoga, Crown Point, Chamblée, Sorel; return to Castleton, Vt.
*Worcester Spy, October 25, 1903. [Forbes.]

BROWN, Obadiah.
Military journal, January 1776–January 1777; around Boston and New York; battle of Bunker Hill; movements, fatigues, guards, weather; very interesting linguistically.
Quar. Bull. Westchester Co. Hist. Soc. IV (1928) 67–72, V (1929) 10–20.

CARROLL, Charles (1737–1832) of Carrollton, Md.

Official travel journal, April–June 1776; visit to Canada as commissioner from Congress; New York to Montreal; notes on scenery of Hudson, etc.; impersonal.

Maryland Hist. Soc. Pubs. (1845) 84 pp., reprinted (1876) 110 pp.; Kate M. Rowland, *The Life of Charles Carroll of Carrollton* (1898) I App. 363–400; L. A. Leonard, *Life of Charles Carroll of Carrollton* (New York, 1918) 277–313.

CHANDLER, Abiel (1760–1833) of Andover, Mass.

Military journal, December 1776–April 1777; service as fifer in New York State; interesting linguistically.

Essex Inst. Hist. Colls. XLVII (1911) 181–186.

CLAP, Ens. Caleb (1752–1812) of Sudbury, Mass.

Military journal, March–October 1776; with Baldwin's Massachusetts Line; siege of Boston, New York campaign.

Hist. Mag. 3d Ser. III (1874–1875) 133–137, 247–251.

CLARK, Col. George Rogers (1752–1818) *b.* Charlottesville, Va., frontier soldier.

1. Journal, December 1776–March 1778; brief scattered notes; Indian skirmishes, general news, and miscellaneous.

2. Journal, February 1779; march to Kaskaskia and activities in the Illinois country.

Illinois Hist. Soc. Colls. VIII (1912) 20–28, 164–168; second journal also in *Amer. Hist. Rev.* I (1895) 90–94.

CLITHERALL, Dr. James, of Charleston, S.C.

Travel diary, May–July 1776 (extracts); fairly interesting account of journey from South Carolina to Philadelphia and New York.

Pennsylvania Mag. Hist. Biog. XXII (1898) 468–474.

COOKE, Capt. Silas (*d.* 1792) of Newport, R.I., merchant.

Private diary, December 1776–October 1779; memoranda relating to his sufferings during British occupation of Newport; interesting spellings.

Rhode Island Hist. Soc. Colls. XXXI (1938) 110–116.

CORBETT, Pvt. Ichabod (1756–1829) of Mendon, Mass.

1. Military journal, December 1776–March 1777; march to Providence; very brief notes of army work, and some private items.

2. Military journal, January–April 1778; march with Craggin's company and return; brief notes; list of payments; doggerel poem on Revolutionary generals.

Worcester Soc. Antiq. Proc. XIX (1903) 171–183.

CUTLER, Samuel (1752–1832) of Newburyport, Mass.

Prison diary, November 1776–December 1777; American prisoner in Mill Prison, Eng.; not so racy as some of the other prison journals but fairly interesting.

New England Hist. Geneal. Reg. XXXII (1878) 42–44, 184–188, 305–308, 395–398.

DANFORTH, Col. Joshua (1759–1837) of Warren, Mass.

Military journal, March–October 1776; extracts relating to events in the war; brief and rather dull.

Amer. Monthly Mag. I (1892) 619–620.

DAVIS, Moses (1743–1824) of Edgecomb, Me., judge.

Private diary, May 1776–March 1823; extracts of marriages, deaths, funerals, etc.; genealogical interest.

New England Hist. Geneal. Reg. LXXXIII (1929) 414–421.

DEWEY, Pvt. John (1754–1821) of Westfield, Mass., and Leyden, N.Y., clothier.

Military journal, April 1776–February 1777; with 3d Massachusetts Regiment; march from Roxbury and campaign in New York; battle of Trenton; brief notes of marches, etc.

A. M. and L. M. Dewey, *Life of George Dewey* (Westfield, 1898) 278–281.

DEWEY, Adjt. Russell (1755–1827) of Westfield, Mass.

Military journal, January–April 1776; march with Porter's regiment on expedition against Canada; Ticonderoga, Crown Point; military details, camp life, sickness, news; interesting spellings.

John H. Lockwood, *Westfield and Its Historic Influences* (1922) 590–596; A. M. and L. M. Dewey, *Life of George Dewey* (Westfield, 1898) 266–271.

DIGBY, Lieut. William, of Shropshire Regiment.

Military journal, April 1776–October 1777; voyage to Canada and narrative of campaigns of 1776 and 1777; with Burgoyne; battle of Hilberton; compilation made by a British officer.

J. P. Baxter (ed.), *The British Invasion from the North* (Albany, 1887) 412 pp.

DUNCAN, Capt. Henry (1735–1814) *b.* Scotland, R.N.

Naval journals, February 1776–September 1782; early portions concern operations around New York.

The Naval Miscellany, Navy Rec. Soc. XX (1902) 105–219.

DU ROI, Lieut. Augustus Wilhelm, of Prince Friedrich's Regiment.

Hessian military journal, February 1776–March 1779; largely descriptive of service with British forces in North America; notes on topography, military affairs, sociology. Translated.

Charlotte S. J. Epping (ed.), *Journal of Du Roi the Elder* (Univ. Pennsylvania, 1911) 189 pp.; also in *German-American Annals* XIII (1911) 40–64, 77–128, 131–239.

FLANDERS, John (1752–1827) of Boscawen, N.H.

Prison diary, January–April 1776; in prison in Quebec; notes on weather largely; some interesting spellings.

C. C. Coffin, *History of Boscawen and Webster* (Concord, N.H., 1878) 250–251.

FRENCH, Maj. Christopher, of 22d British regiment.

Prison diary, January–September 1776; kept while author was prisoner in Hartford Jail; a lively and amusing record, with longish entries.

Connecticut Hist. Soc. Colls. I (1860) 189–225.

GAY, Col. Fisher (1733–1776) of Farmington, Conn.

Military journal, February–March 1776; brief extracts relating to march to Boston.

Mag. Amer. Hist. VIII (1882) 127–129.

GERRISH, Col. Jacob (1739?–1817) of Newbury, Mass.

Military journal, August–November 1776; Flatbush, White Plains; brief scattered military notes.

Putnam's Monthly Hist. Mag. III (1895) 220–223.

GOODWIN, Lieut. John (1745?–1828) of Marblehead, Mass.

Military journal, December 1776–March 1777; expedition in Rhode Island; visits to taverns; military details; brief notes, but some interesting spellings.

Essex Inst. Hist. Colls. XLV (1909) 205–211.

GRAVES, Daniel (1757–1828) of Reading, Mass.

Military journal, December 1776–March 1777; with Foster's company; campaign around New York; Tarrytown, White Plains, Chatham; brief entries; interesting spellings.

Westchester Co. Hist. Soc. Bull. X (1934) 45–48.

GUILD, Capt. Joseph (1735–1794) of Dedham, Mass.

Military journal, March 1776–July 1777 (extracts); march from Cambridge to Ticonderoga; movements; smallpox epidemic; moderate.

Dedham Hist. Reg. VII (1896) 45–47.

HADDEN, Lieut. James Murray (*d.* 1817) of Royal Artillery.

Military journal, March 1776–September 1777; kept during Burgoyne's campaign; lengthy military notes, of fair interest.

Horatio Rogers (ed.), *Hadden's Journal and Orderly Books* (Albany, 1884) 1–166.

HAGEN, Dr. Edmund (1732–1777) of Scarborough, Me.

Prison diary, October–December 1776; voyage on privateer, capture, and subsequent imprisonment on prison ship "Boulogne"; brief and rather dull extracts.

Amer. Monthly Mag. XXIV (1904) 14–16, 110–111.

HASBROUCK, Col. Abraham, of Kingston, N.Y.

Private diary, October 1776–November 1777 (extracts); fire at his house; burning of farm buildings by British.

Olde Ulster IV (1908) 147–149.

HETH, Lieut. William (1750–1807) *b.* Pennsylvania, of Morgan's Virginia Rifle Regiment.

Military journal, January–August 1776; march from Winchester, Va., to Quebec; full and fairly lively entries, mostly written in prison in Quebec—he was captured when Arnold attacked; mostly military details, but some personal items; typical prison details; some interesting spellings.

Winchester Hist. Soc. Annual Papers (Va.) I (1931) 27–118.

HILDRETH, Lieut. Micah (1749–1826) of Dracut, Mass.

Military journal, August–October 1776; march to Ticonderoga; details of smallpox epidemic; food; military notes; scrappy.

Silas R. Coburn, *History of Dracut, Mass.* (Lowell, 1922) 147–152.

HOZEY, Peleg, master of sloop "Independent."

Sea journal, July–August 1776; log details of cruise off Rhode Island; interesting spellings and language.

Rhode Island Hist. Soc. Colls. XXXI (1938) 82–89, 122–123.

IRVINE, Col. William (1741–1804) of Philadelphia and 7th Pennsylvania Regiment.

Military journal, May–June 1776; expedition to Canada; capture; brief notes.

Hist. Mag. VI (1862) 115–117.

JAMES, Adm. Bartholomew (1752–1828) of England.

Military journal, January 1776–October 1798; with earlier autobiographical notes; written up from memoranda; in Boston and Rhode Island; surrender at Yorktown; Portland Harbor, and on the Kennebec in 1791; activities of British army.

Navy Rec. Soc. Pubs. VI (1896) 390 pp.

JAMISON, Capt. John.

Military journal, October 1776–December 1779; very brief and rather dull notes.

Amer. Monthly Mag. XXIII (1903) 12–13.

KIMBALL, Capt. Peter (1739–1811) of Boscawen, N.H.

1. Military journal, September–December 1776; marches from New Hampshire to New York; notes on camp life; interesting spellings.

Granite Monthly IV (1881) 230–233.

2. Military journal, July–September 1777; brief notes of military movements.

C. C. Coffin, *The History of Boscawen and Webster* (Concord, 1878) 261–264.

KRAFFT, Lieut. John Charles Philip von (1752–1804) *b*. Dresden, of Georgetown, Pa.

Hessian military journal, May 1776–January 1784; detailed and extensive account of service during the whole war; first as corporal with Von Donop's regiment, and from December, 1782, in Von Bose's regiment; long descriptions, mostly of personal affairs during the war; many minor details; a most interesting journal. Translated from the German.

New York Hist. Soc. Colls. (1882) 1–200.

LAMB, Sergt. Roger (*b.* 1756) of Dublin, 9th Foot Regiment.

Military journal, April 1776–January 1784; voyage from Cork to Quebec; Burgoyne's campaign and surrender; surrender of Cornwallis; battle of Hubbardton; descriptions of New England towns; imprisonment at Rutland; interesting details of life of British soldiers.

An Original and Authentic Journal of Occurrences during the Late American War (Dublin, 1809) 438 pp.

LENOIR, William (1751–1839) of Caldwell Co., N.C.

Military journal, August–October 1776; Rutherford's campaign against Cherokee Indian towns; bare details; interesting spellings.

Jour. Southern Hist. VI (1940) 247–257.

LINCOLN, Capt. Rufus (1751–1838) of Wareham, Mass.

Military journal, June 1776–November 1780; prisoner on parole in Long Island; camp life in New York; siege of Charleston, S.C.; battle of Long Island; Jersey campaign; Saratoga; Burgoyne's surrender; actions of Congress; followed by several poems by himself and his comrades. Disjointed notes; some interesting spellings.

James M. Lincoln (ed.), *The Papers of Captain Rufus Lincoln* (Cambridge, Mass., 1904) 3–115.

LOXLEY, Capt. Benjamin, of Philadelphia Artillery.

Military journal, July–August 1776; in Pennsylvania and New Jersey; campaign to Amboy, etc.

Pennsylvania Hist. Soc. Colls. I (1853) 223–236.

McMICHAEL, Lieut. James, of 13th Pennsylvania Regiment.

Military journal, May 1776–May 1778; in Pennsylvania, Delaware, New Jersey, New York; Valley Forge; some bad verses; fair interest.

Pennsylvania Mag. Hist. Biog. XVI (1892) 129–159; *Pennsylvania Archives,* 2d Ser. XV 195–218. Extracts in *Mag. Hist.* VI (1907) 210–211.

McPHERSON, Lieut. William.

Military journal, 1776; campaign around New York and Brooklyn; brief notes.

Long Island Hist. Soc. Colls. III (1878) Part II 168–169.

MARSTON, Col. Benjamin (1730–1792) of Marblehead.

Loyalist diary, June 1776–June 1787; fragmentary notes, partly biography, partly diary selections; descriptions of New England; verses; quite entertaining; *passim* quotations in articles.

New Brunswick Hist. Soc. Colls. No. 4 (1899) 95–108, No. 7 (1907) 79–112, No. 8 (1909) 204–277.

MELSHEIMER, Rev. Frederick Valentine (1749–1814) *b.* Regenborn, Germany, chaplain to Duke of Brunswick's Dragoons.

Hessian chaplain's journal, February–August 1776; account of voyage from Wolfenbüttel to Quebec; description of Quebec and environs; translated.

Lit. Hist. Soc. Quebec Trans. No. 20 (1891) 137–178.

MIDDLETON, Capt. Charles S., of Georgia militia.

Military journal, December 1776–January 1777; military activities of Southern troops in South Carolina and Georgia; substantial entries of fair interest.

R. W. Gibbes, *Documentary History of the American Revolution* II (1857) 47–54.

MINER, Thomas, and WHEELER, Ezekiel.

Scouting journal, July–August 1776; expedition from the lower Cohoos to Cohoos Falls, under orders of John Hurd; brief surveying notes.

State Papers, New Hampshire, XVII 69–71.

MORRIS, Margaret (1737–1816) of Burlington, N.J.

Quaker diary, December 1776–June 1778; kept for information of her sister; long serious descriptions and reflections on events of war at Burlington; some exciting personal adventures.

Private Journal by Margaret Morris (Philadelphia, 1836) 31 pp.; reprinted, edited by J. J. Smith (New York, 1865) 36 pp.; *Bull. Friends' Hist. Soc. Philadelphia* IX (1919) 2–14, 65–75, 103–114.

MUDGE, Simon (1748–1799) of Danvers, Mass.

Military journal, July–November 1776; march to Ticonderoga and camp there; fair general interest, and linguistically interesting.

Alfred Mudge, *Memorials* (Boston, 1868) 204–205; *Danvers Hist. Soc. Colls.* XXVII (1939) 40–43.

MUHLENBERG, Rev. Henry Melchior (1711–1787) *b.* Germany, of Philadelphia.

Lutheran clergyman's journal, July 1776–December 1777; church work, and some war news.

Pennsylvania Hist. Soc. Colls. I (1853) 147–186. Extracts in notes to *Life of Major-General Peter Muhlenberg* (Philadelphia, 1849).

NASH, Pvt. Solomon (1753–1778) of Abington, Mass.

Military journal, January 1776–January 1777; brief, fragmentary notes, military, personal, weather, camp life; siege of Boston, Roxbury, Cambridge, White Plains; interesting spellings.

Charles I. Bushnell (ed.), *Journal of Solomon Nash* (New York, 1861) 65 pp.; Charles I. Bushnell, *Crumbs for Antiquarians* I (New York, 1864) 5–46.

NEW YORK MORAVIAN CONGREGATION.

Congregational journal; extracts commencing in 1776; some very good passages describing naval and military engagements around New York and a good account of the fire.

Pennsylvania Mag. Hist. Biog. I (1877) 133–148, 250–262.

NICE, Capt. John (1739–1806) of Germantown, Pa.

Military journal, August–December 1776 and June 1778 (extracts); with 13th Pennsylvania Regiment; battle of Long Island, Valley Forge; prisoner; moderate interest.

Pennsylvania Mag. Hist. Biog. XVI (1892) 399–411.

PAINE, Samuel.

Scouting journal, July–August 1776; expedition under John Hurd from the lower Cohoos to Cohoos Falls; brief surveying notes.

State Papers, New Hampshire, XVII 72.

PARKER, Ens. Benjamin (*b.* 1743) of Kittery, Me.

Military journal, December 1776–March 1777; march from Kittery to Kingsbridge, N.Y.; brief notes; interesting language.

Old Eliot VI (1903) 148–151.

PAUSCH, Capt. Georg (*d.* 1796?) of Hesse-Hanau Artillery.

Hessian military journal, May 1776–October 1777; journey from Hanau to America; military life in Canada; Burgoyne's campaign; battle of Bennington; naval action on Lake Champlain; personal ill-treatment by British soldiers.

William L. Stone (trans.), *Journal of Captain Pausch* (Albany, 1886) 185 pp. Extract in A. B. Hart, *Source Book of American History* (New York, 1925) 154–157.

PEALE, Capt. Charles Wilson (1741–1827) of Pennsylvania militia, painter.

Military journal, December 1776–January 1777; in militia at Philadelphia; New York campaign; life on march; some general and personal notes; fairly good narrative, with some extended entries.

Pennsylvania Mag. Hist. Biog. XXXVIII (1914) 271–286.

PELL, Joshua, Jr. (British officer).

Military journal, April 1776–October 1777; military notes at Crown Point, Ticonderoga, Saratoga, etc.

Mag. Amer. Hist. II (1878) Part I 43–47, 107–112; *Bull. Fort Ticonderoga Museum* I (1929) 2–19.

PORTER, Col. Elisha (1742–1796) of Hadley, Mass.

Military journal, January–August 1776; march to relief of forces besieging Quebec; fairly interesting.

Mag. Amer. Hist. XXX (1893) 187–205.

[PORTERFIELD, Charles (1750–1780) of Frederick Co., Va.?]

Prison diary, March–July 1776; captured in Arnold's attack on Quebec; in prison there; full entries on the daily life of the prisoners, news, food, etc.; fairly good.

Southern Hist. Assoc. Pubs. VI (1902) 113–131, 199–209, 295–303, 400–407. Extracts in *Virginia Mag. Hist. Biog.* IX (1901–1902) 144–152; and *Mag. Amer. Hist.* XXI (1889) 318–319.

PYNCHON, William (1723–1789) of Salem, Mass.

Private diary, January 1776–March 1789 (with a year's gap); valuable and interesting account of social and political affairs in Salem; gossip, meals, war news, etc.

Fitch E. Oliver (ed.), *The Diary of William Pynchon of Salem* (Boston, 1890) 349 pp.

QUINCY, Samuel (1735–1787) of Boston, solicitor general of Massachusetts.

London diary, October 1776–March 1777 (fragments); interesting notes on social, artistic, and political affairs in London; musical notes especially interesting.

Massachusetts Hist. Soc. Proc. 1st Ser. XIX (1881–1882) 211–223.

RAINSFORD, Col. Charles, "commissary for embarking foreign troops in the British service from Germany."

Military journal, February–April 1776; in Holland raising troops to fight in America; some social notes.

New York Hist. Soc. Colls. (1879) 317–334.

ROBBINS, Rev. Ammi Ruhamah (1740–1813) of Norfolk, Conn.

Chaplain's journal, March–October 1776; northern campaign against Canada; Chamblée, Lake George, retreat; notes on services, personal affairs, army movements, hospital visits and comforting sick, weather, etc.; gloomy comments, but interesting reading.

Journal of the Rev. Ammi R. Robbins (New Haven, 1850) 48 pp.; T. W. Crissey, *History of Norfolk* (Everett, Mass., 1900) 97–121.

ROBERTS, Lieut. Algernon, of Lower Merion, Pa.

Military journal, August–September 1776; campaign from Philadelphia to Paulus Hook; fair narrative, with many interesting spellings.

Pennsylvania Mag. Hist. Biog. VII (1883) 456–463.

RODNEY, Capt. Thomas (1744–1811) of Dover (Md.) Light Infantry.

Military journal, December 1776–January 1777; campaign around New York and Brooklyn; battle of Princeton, Morristown; substantial entries.

Delaware Hist. Soc. Papers No. 8 (1888) 11–50. Extract (battle of Trenton) in *Long Island Hist. Soc. Mems.* III (1878) Part II 158–162.

ROGERS, Rev. William (1751–1824) of Newport and Philadelphia.

1. Travel diary, April–June 1776; visits from Philadelphia to Rhode Island; travel notes, preaching, social, weather, etc.; moderate interest.

Rhode Island Hist. Soc. Colls. XXXII (1939) 117–128.

2. Chaplain's journal, July–September 1779; with Hand's brigade during Sullivan's expedition; solid entries of clerical and military affairs.

Rhode Island Hist. Tracts No. 7 (1879) 136 pp. Partly in *Amer. Universal Mag.* I (1797) 390–399, II (1797) 86–91, 200–206; *Pennsylvania Archives* 2d Ser. XV 257–288; F. Cook, *Journals of the Military Expedition of Major-General John Sullivan* (Auburn, N.Y., 1887) 246–265.

3. Travel diary, August–October 1781; preaching tour in Connecticut and Massachusetts; similar to (1).

Rhode Island Hist. Soc. Colls. XXXIII (1940) 39–44, 65–72.

SELLERS, Nathan, of Pennsylvania, Quaker.

Military journal, August 1776–1778 (extracts); war in Pennsylvania, New Jersey, Long Island, North Carolina; moderate interest.

Pennsylvania Mag. Hist. Biog. XVI (1892) 191–196.

SERLE, Ambrose (1742–1812), secretary to Lord Howe.

American journal, May 1776–July 1778; travel, general descriptions and comments; talks with loyalists and comments on war; a valuable civilian journal of the Revolution.

E. H. Tatum (ed.), *The American Journal of Ambrose Serle* (San Marino, Calif., 1940) 369 pp.

SEWALL, Gen. Henry (1752–1845) of Augusta, Me.

Military journal, March 1776–November 1783; siege of Boston, Newburg, Saratoga, Valley Forge; campaigns in New England and New York; notes on camp life.

*A Maine Farmer (Augusta, 1872). Extract in *Hist. Mag.* n.s. X (1871) 128–137.

SHEPARD, Samuel, of Virginia.

Loyalist diary; extracts given under years 1776, 1777, 1784, 1785; return of a loyalist from Europe to Virginia; trouble at public meetings.

William and Mary Coll. Quar. 2d Ser. XV (1935) 408–412.

SLADE, William (1753–1826) of New Canaan, Conn., and Cornwall, Vt.

Prison diary, November 1776–January 1777; kept while author was on prison ship "Grosvenor"; notes of daily life, hardships; human and naïve; quite interesting; some interesting spellings.

Danske Dandridge, *American Prisoners of the Revolution* (Charlottesville, Va., 1911) App. 494–501.

SMITH, Sergt. John, of Rhode Island.

Military journal, September?–December 1776; with Col. Lippitt's company in campaign with Washington; New York and retreat through New Jersey; excellent picture of life of a resourceful and humorous common soldier; hardships, thieving, adventures; colloquial style.

Mississippi Valley Hist. Rev. XX (1933–1934) 247–270.

STEVENS, Pvt. Benjamin (1754–1838) of Canaan, Conn.

Military journal, February–May 1776; in Burrall's regiment on Arnold's expedition; march via Albany, Saratoga, etc.; mostly minor personal adventures; moderate interest.

D.A.R. Mag. XLV (1914) 137–140.

STIMSON, Dr. Jeremy (1751–1821) of Hopkinton, Mass.

Surgeon's military journal, September–October 1776; White Plains, Horseneck, etc.; brief notes on sick and wounded.

Massachusetts Hist. Soc. Proc. XLVI (1912–1913) 251–252.

STONE, Capt. Enos (1744–1822) of Lenox, Mass.

Military journal, November 1776–December 1777; expedition against Canada; Ticonderoga, Lake Champlain, battle of Hubbardstown; long but scattered entries, mainly of military matters; interesting spellings.

New England Hist. Geneal. Reg. XV (1861) 299.

TEN BROECK, Col. Abraham (1734–1810) of Albany, N.Y., jurist.

Journal 1776; kept with member of general assembly of New York; miscellaneous jottings; account with quotations.

Americana XVIII (1924) 169–173.

TOMPSON, Nathaniel.

Sea journal, October 1776; brief account of capture of a schooner; interesting spellings.

Maine Hist. Geneal. Recorder I (1884) 41–42.

VERNON, Thomas (1718–1784) of Newport, R.I.

Loyalist diary, June–October 1776; notes of country life kept while author was in exile in Gloucester, R.I., some political comments, but mostly notes of eating, gardening, walks, etc.; a pleasing record of enforced country life.

Rhode Island Hist. Soc. Tracts No. 13 (1881) 116 pp.

VOSE, Lieut. Col. Joseph (1738–1816) of Milton, Conn.

Military journal, April–July 1776; expedition from Cambridge to reinforce Montgomery's troops in Canada; in letter form addressed to his wife; fair details of movements and camp life; some linguistic interest.

Col. Soc. Massachusetts Pubs. VII (1900–1902) 248–262.

WALDECK, Rev. Philipp, of 3d Waldeck Regiment.

Hessian chaplain's journal, May 1776–July 1778; journey from Germany to America; account of campaigns.

Translated extracts in *Union County Hist. Soc. Proc.* II (1934) 137–143; German text, edited by M. D. Learned, in *Americana Germanica Monograph Ser.* No. 6 (Univ. Pennsylvania) 168 pp.

WEBB, Samuel Blachley (1753–1807) of Wethersfield, Conn.

Military journals, March 1776–December 1788 (with large gaps); aide to Washington in New York; in camp at Cambridge; bombardment of Boston; war news at New York; military affairs at New Haven, Fort Montgomery, and Staten Island; journey to New Haven, Boston, and New York; journey from New York to Boston and back; earlier part military, later part inclined to politics.

Worthington C. Ford (ed.), *Correspondence and Journals of Samuel Blachley Webb* (New York, 1893), three vols. Extract from military section in *Amer. Hist. Rec.* I (1872) 445–448.

WHEELER, Lieut. Rufus, of Rowley, Mass.

Military journal, July–December 1776; march from Boxford to Ticonderoga; military happenings there; march back; brief entries; interesting spellings.

Essex Inst. Hist. Colls. LXVIII (1932) 371–377.

WHITCOMBE, Lieut. Benjamin (1755–1828) of Henniker, N.H.

Scouting journal, July 1776; short scouting expedition from Crown Point to St. John's, Chamblée, etc.; no particular interest, apart from account of his shooting Gen. Gordon.

Amer. Hist. Rec. I (1872) 437–438.

WHITTALL, Job (1743–1797) of Gloucester Co., N.J.

Private diary, February 1776–December 1777; notes on activities of British and American soldiers in neighborhood, and his differences with them. Summary and extracts.

F. H. Stewart, *Notes on Old Gloucester County, New Jersey* I (1917) 255–261.

WIEDERHOLD, Capt. Andreas, Hessian soldier.

Military journal, November 1776; with Knyphausen Regiment; capture of Fort Washington, N.Y.

Pennsylvania Mag. Hist. Biog. XXIII (1899) 95–97.

WIGGLESWORTH, Col. Edward (1742–1826) of Newburyport, Mass.

Military journal, October–November 1776 (extracts); with Arnold's fleet; near Schuyler's Island; engagement on Lake Champlain; Ticonderoga and Crown Point.

Euphemia Vale Smith, *History of Newburyport* (Newburyport, 1854) 357–359.

WILD, Corp. Ebenezer (1758–1794) of Braintree, Mass.

Military journal, August 1776–December 1781; Ticonderoga campaign against Burgoyne, Rhode Island campaign, Yorktown; military affairs and personal items; a good, varied diary, with some excellent sections; interesting linguistically.

Massachusetts Hist. Soc. Proc. 2d Ser. VI (1890–1891) 78–160.

WILLIAMS, Adjt. Elisha (1757–1845) of Beverly, Mass.

Military journal, September–November 1776; with Ward's Regiment in Washington's army; mostly orderly book; New York, Harlem.

Pennsylvania Mag. Hist. Biog. XLVIII (1924) 334–353, XLIX (1925) 44–60.

YOUNG, Sergt. William.

Military journal, December 1776–January 1777; New Jersey campaign; fairly interesting account of military life, hardships, etc.

Pennsylvania Mag. Hist. Biog. VIII (1884) 255–278.

ANON.   1777

Military journal, 1777; Howe's proceedings; detailed eyewitness account, apparently by an officer of the British general staff; moderate interest.

Amer. Antiq. Soc. Proc. n.s. XL (1930) 69–92.

ANON.

Naval journal, 1777; loglike details of cruise and engagement of privateer "Oliver Cromwell" (Capt. Thomas Simmonds, of Beverly, Mass.); a poem.

Essex Inst. Hist. Colls. XLV (1909) 245–255.

ANON. (of Col. Gansevoort's regiment).

Military journal, April–August 1777; events leading to, and siege of Fort Schuyler; Indian atrocities; some interesting spellings.

Mag. Hist. III (1906) 90–104.

ALLAN, Col. John (1746–1805) of Machias, Me.

Official military journal, May 1777–January 1778; record of superintendent of Indians in Maine; expedition to St. John's River against Indians of Maine; military movements; return; quite interesting.

Frederic Kidder, *Military Operations in Eastern Maine and Nova Scotia* (Albany, 1867) 91–163.

ALLEN, Rev. Thomas (1743–1810) of Northampton, Mass.

Private diary, February 1777–August 1780; brief and rather dull notes of domestic life, prices, etc., during Revolution.

J. E. A. Smith, *History of Pittsfield, Mass., 1734–1800* (1869) 470–475.

ANDRÉ, Maj. John (1751–1780), British soldier, hanged as spy.

Military journal, 1777–1778; British army under Howe and Clinton.

Henry Cabot Lodge (ed.), *André's Journal* (Bibliophile Soc., Boston, 1903) two vols.; *Major André's Journal* (Tarrytown, 1930) 128 pp.

AUSTIN, Col. Jonathan Loring (1748–1826) of Boston.

Foreign travel journal, October–November 1777 (extracts); carrying dispatches from America to France with news of Burgoyne's surrender.

Edward E. Hale and E. E. Hale, Jr., *Franklin in France* (Boston, 1887) 156–164; *Collector* XXI (1908) 123–125, XXII (1909) 3–4.

BACKUS, Elijah (*b.* 1759) of Norwich, Conn.

College diary, January–December 1777; fairly interesting short diary of a Yale student; social life and study; verses.

Connecticut Quar. I (1895) 355–361 ("Yale Boys of the Last Century").

BARTLETT, Lieut. Israel (1748–1837) of Haverhill, Mass.

Military journal, October–November 1777; brief, moderate notes; troop movements; Burgoyne's surrender.

George W. Chase, *History of Haverhill, Mass.* (Haverhill, 1861) 401–402.

BATES, Ambrose (1758–1833) of Cohasset, Mass.

Military journal, August–December 1777; Burgoyne's surrender; brief notes of prisoners and march; very interesting spellings.

E. V. Bigelow, *A Narrative History of the Town of Cohasset* (Cohasset, 1898) 299–303.

BLAKE, Lieut. Thomas (1752–1840) of Lebanon, N.H.

Military journal, May 1777–October 1780; Sullivan's expedition; Ticonderoga, Burgoyne's campaign, Hudson campaign; fair interest.

F. Cook, *Journals of the Military Expedition of Major-General John Sullivan* (Auburn, N. Y., 1887) 38–41; Frederic Kidder, *History of the First New Hampshire Regiment* (Albany, 1868) 25–56.

BOARDMAN, Oliver (1758–1826) of Middletown, Conn.

Military journal, September–October 1777; fairly interesting journal of Sullivan's campaign; Saratoga, Burgoyne's surrender.

Connecticut Hist. Soc. Colls. VII (1899) 221–237.

CALFE, Capt. John, of Hampstead, N.H.

Military journal, February–August 1777; military details at Ticonderoga; marches, excursions, etc.

H. E. Noyes, *A Memorial of the Town of Hampstead* (Boston, 1899) I 288–294.

CHILTON, Capt. John (*d.* 1777) of 3d Virginia Regiment.

Military journal, January–September 1777; with 3d Virginia Regiment; movements, camp life, some personal items; fair interest.

Tyler's Quar. Hist. Geneal. Mag. XII (1931) 283–289.

CLARK, Joseph (1751–1813) of New Jersey militia.

Military journal, May 1777–November 1778; seminarrative of service in New Jersey, Pennsylvania, New York; Valley Forge, Brandywine.

New Jersey Hist. Soc. Proc. VII (1853–1855) 93–110.

CONNOR, Timothy (1748–1823), seaman.

Prison diary, June 1777–July 1779; captured on brigantine "Rising States," imprisonment in Forton Prison, Eng.; excellent details of hardships, attempted escapes, food, etc.; colloquial and humorous.

New England Hist. Geneal. Reg. XXX (1876) 175–177, 343–352, XXXI (1877) 18–20, 212–213, 284–288, XXXII (1878) 70–73, 165–168, 280–285.

CORNELIUS, Dr. Elias (1758–1823) of Long Island.

Surgeon's journal, August 1777–March 1778; service with Angell's Long Island regiment; captured and imprisoned in New York; escape to Norwalk; verses; quite interesting.

Journal of Dr. Elias Cornelius (Washington, 1903) 3–14.

COWAN, Capt. John.

Military journal, March–September 1777; brief, moderate notes on Indian affairs and skirmishes in Kentucky.

Willard R. Jillson, *Tales of the Dark and Bloody Ground* (Louisville, 1930) 63–68.

CRAFT, Maj. Eleazer (1743–1793) of Manchester, Mass.

Military journal, September–December 1777; march from Manchester to the Hudson, and return to Worthington; account of Burgoyne's surrender; moderate notes of stages of march.

Essex Inst. Hist. Colls. VII (1864) 194–198; J. M. and W. F. Crafts, *The Crafts Family* (Northampton, 1893) App. 689–693.

CROSS, Lieut. Col. Ralph (1738–1811) of Newburyport, Mass.

Military journal, August–December 1777; with Essex Regiment; Bemis Heights, Saratoga, Burgoyne's surrender.

Hist. Mag. n.s. VII (1870) 8–11.

CROWNINGSHIELD, Benjamin, seaman on frigate "Boston."

Sea journal, July 7, 1777 (extract); account of fight of the "Boston" with the "Fox."

New Hampshire Geneal. Rec. IV (1907) 37.

ELLERY, Hon. William (1727–1820) of Dighton, Mass., congressman.

Travel diaries, October–November 1777, June–July 1778, October–November 1778, and July 1779; entertaining notes kept on various horseback journeys, in Massachusetts, Connecticut, New York, New Jersey, Pennsylvania; mostly on way to and from Congress; notes on taverns, persons seen, some notes on political events and famous political figures; written in a Shandean style.

Pennsylvania Mag. Hist. Biog. XI (1887) 318–329, 476–481, XII (1888) 190–199.

ELMER, Dr. Ebenezer (1752–1843) of New Jersey.

1. Surgeon's journal, September 1777; a moderate account of the battle of Brandywine.

Pennsylvania Mag. Hist. Biog. XXXV (1911) 103–107.

2. Military journal, March 1776–June 1783; fair narrative of expedition against Canada.

New Jersey Hist. Soc. Proc. II (1846–1847) 95–146, III (1848–1849) 21–56, 90–102; extra entries, *ibid.* n.s. X (1925) 410–424.

3. Military journal, June–August 1779; lengthy and detailed notes on Sullivan's expedition.

New Jersey Hist. Soc. Proc. II (1846–1847) 43–50; F. Cook, *Journals of the Military Expedition of Major-General John Sullivan* (Auburn, N.Y., 1887) 80–85.

FELL, John (1721–1798) of New York City, merchant and judge.

1. Prison diary, April 1777–November 1778; kept while in Provost Jail, New York City; brief and moderate notes.

Danske Dandridge, *American Prisoners of the Revolution* (Charlottesville, Va., 1911) 112–122.

2. Political diary, 1778–1779; rather dull notes covering his career in Congress; extracts.

Mag. Hist. XXI (1915) 257–260.

FITTS, Lieut. Abraham (1736–1808) of Camden, N.H.

Military journal, September–November 1777; march from Candia to Saratoga; battles of Stillwater and Saratoga, and Burgoyne's surrender; brief notes; interesting spellings.

J. Bailey Moore, *History of the Town of Candia* (Manchester, N.H., 1893) 81–84.

GARRETTSON, Freeborn (1752–1827) of Rhinebeck, N.Y., printer and clergyman.

Clergyman's journal, June 1777–June 1826; his experiences as an itinerant preacher, in the South, Nova Scotia, and New England; prepared at the request of Wesley.

The Experience and Travels of Mr. Freeborn Garrettson (1791) two vols. Nathan Bangs's life of Garrettson (New York, 1829) is based on these and on unpublished journals.

GREEN, Dr. Ezra (1746–1847) of Dover, N.H.

Naval surgeon's journal, November 1777–September 1778; bare details of naval actions during the Revolution; aboard the "Ranger"; engagement with British sloop; cruise to Belle Isle, Quiberon, Brest, and Ireland; under John Paul Jones.

New England Hist. Geneal. Reg. XXIX (1875) 13–24; reprinted with additions as *Diary of Ezra Green, M.D.* (Boston, 1875) 28 pp.

[GREENE, Fleet S. (*b.* 1753) of Newport, R.I.]

Military diary, June 1777–October 1779; British occupation of Newport; daily events and news, from American viewpoint; good descriptions of state of people of Newport. Published anonymously; Mrs. Forbes ascribes it to Greene.

Hist. Mag. IV (1860) 1–4, 34–38, 69–72, 105–107, 134–137, 172–173.

HERBERT, Charles (1757–1808) of Newburyport, Mass.

Prison diary, January 1777–August 1780; capture at sea, transfer to Mill Prison, Eng.; account of lengthy prison life; perhaps the most detailed and interesting record of prison life during the Revolution; vivid picture of diarist and his companions, hardships, illnesses, endless attempted escapes, hopes and despairs, news, etc.

A Relic of the Revolution (Boston, 1847) 258 pp.; Rev. R. Livesey (comp.), *The Prisoners of 1776* (Boston, 1854) 264 pp.; names of prisoners in *D.A.R. Mag.* LVIII (1924) 625–629.

HITCHCOCK, Dr. Enos (1744–1803) of Providence, R.I.

Chaplain's journal, April 1777–August 1779; lengthy journal of military events and news; Massachusetts, Vermont, Burgoyne's campaign, New York campaign; detailed, but rather dull.

Rhode Island Hist. Soc. Pubs. n.s. VII (1899) 106–134, 147–194.

JENNISON, Lieut. William (1757–1843) of Milford, Mass.

Naval journal, December 1777–June 1780; brief notes of a marine during the Revolution; moderate interest.

Pennsylvania Mag. Hist. Biog. XV (1891) 101–108.

JOSLIN, Joseph, Jr. (*b.* 1759) of South Killingly, Conn.

Military diary, March 1777–August 1778; life as a teamster in the Revolutionary army; Connecticut and Rhode Island; very little of army affairs, but a most entertaining diary of country life, written in colloquial dialect and with almost pastoral quaintness.

Connecticut Hist. Soc. Colls. VII (1899) 297–369. Normalized extracts in *Connecticut Quar. Mag.* II (1896) 50–52.

LAWSON, Capt. Thomas (1727–1804) of Union, Conn.

Military journal, October 1777 (extracts); march from Tolland, Conn., to Stillwater; second battle of Stillwater.

Harvey M. Lawson, *The History of Union, Conn.* (New Haven, 1893) 125.

LEE, Capt. Andrew.

Military journal, August–December 1777; brief military details of Sullivan's expedition.

Pennsylvania Mag. Hist. Biog. III (1879) 167–173.

McKENDRY, Col. William (1751?–1798) of Stoughton, Mass.

Military journal, October 1777–June 1780; brief military and personal notes; New York campaign; Cherry Valley Massacre; Sullivan's expedition; some topographical description and account of Moravian life.

Massachusetts Hist. Soc. Proc. 2d Ser. II (1885–1886) 442–478; F. Cook, *Journals of the Military Expedition of Major-General John Sullivan* (Auburn, N.Y., 1887) 198–212.

MERRICK, Pvt. Samuel F. (1751–1835) of Wilbraham, Mass.

Military journal, September–October 1777; at Saratoga and the surrender of Burgoyne; brief and rather dull notes.

Chauncey E. Peck, *The History of Wilbraham* (1913) 136–138; Rufus P. Stebbins, *An Historical Address Delivered at the Centennial Celebration of the Town of Wilbraham* (Boston, 1864) 238–240.

MORTON, Robert, of Philadelphia.

Private diary, September–December 1777; a civilian's account of the occupation of Philadelphia by the British; fairly good.

Pennsylvania Mag. Hist. Biog. I (1877) 1–39.

NORTON, George (*b.* 1739) of Ipswich, Mass.

Military journal, January 1777–February 1780; very brief notes of marches, weather, expenses; a few interesting spellings.

Essex Inst. Hist. Colls. LXXIV (1938) 337–349.

PARKMAN, Anna Sophia (1755–1783) of Westborough, Mass.

Private diary, November 1777–July 1778 (extracts); notes of her social life, domestic affairs, and visits; a pleasant picture of life in a clergyman's home.

Harriette M. Forbes, *The Hundredth Town* (Boston, 1889) 83–89.

PAWLING, Capt. Henry, of Ulster Co., N.Y.

Prison diary, October 1777–February 1778; capture by British at King's Ferry; life aboard a prison ship; notes of escapes, food, treatment by British; well written and amusing.

Olde Ulster I (1905) 335–338, 361–365, II (1906) 18–25.

PERCIVAL, Benjamin (1752–1817) of Sandwich, Mass.

Private diary, January 1777–April 1817; extracts mainly of genealogical interest, but some personal, farming, local affairs.

Pilgrim Notes and Queries I (1913) 53–56, 73–76, 87–89, 112–113, II (1914) 27–29, 36–40.

POPP, Stephen (*b.* 1755?) of Bayreuth Regiment (Hessian).

Hessian military journal, January 1777–December 1783; a not very remarkable record of military services during the Revolution.

Pennsylvania Mag. Hist. Biog. XXVI (1902) 25–41, 245–254.

RIEDESEL, Frederike von Massow, Baroness (1746–1808); of Hesse.

Private diary, April 1777–autumn 1783; narrative and day-to-day entries, and some letters; social and army life in Canada and New England with her husband, who was with Burgoyne's army; a very readable and enlightening diary. Translated from the German.

Letters and Memoirs Relating to the War for Independence (New York, 1827) 323 pp.; *Letters and Journals Relating to the American Revolution* (Albany, 1867) 235 pp. Selection in Mark Van Doren, *An Autobiography of America* (New York, 1929) 122–136. Pages of journal per se in 1827 edition, *Letters and Memoirs:* 103–116, 120–136, 164–300.

SMITH, Jacob (1756–1844) of Smith's Bridge, Delaware-Pennsylvania boundary.

Military journal, November 1777–December 1785; very brief and scattered notes of no great interest; an American-born Swede serving with the British.

Pennsylvania Mag. Hist. Biog. LVI (1932) 260–264.

SMYTH, Capt. John Ferdinand Dalziel, of the Queen's Rangers.

Loyalist journal, last date March 1777; really a recollected narrative; indignant narrative of an indignant loyalist; adventures, escapes from rebels, imprisonment at Philadelphia; in southern Maryland, Mississippi, Philadelphia, Baltimore, New York.

A Tour in the United States (London, 1784) two vols. Extracts in *Pennsylvania Mag. Hist. Biog.* XXXIX (1915) 143–169.

STEVENS, Elisha (1752–1813) of Glastonbury, Conn.

Military diary, October 1777–August 1778; Brandywine, Germantown, Valley Forge; personal accounts, poem by Wigglesworth, some interesting spellings.

Elisha Stevens, Fragments of Memoranda (Meriden, Conn., 1922) 22 leaves, facsimile.

STEVENS, Enos (1739–1808) of Charleston, N.H., and Barnet, Vt.

Loyalist military journal, May 1777–February 1785 (fragment); loyalist serving with British; brief notes, war news, personal affairs, expedition up West River and to Fort Massachusetts; interesting spellings.

New England Quar. XI (1938) 374–388.

SULLIVAN, Sergt. Thomas, of 49th Foot Regiment (British).

Military journal, July–September 1777 (extracts); before and after the battle of Brandywine; fairly interesting.

Pennsylvania Mag. Hist. Biog. XXXI (1907) 406–418, XXXIV (1910) 229–232.

VANDERSLICE, Henry (1726–1797) of Berks Co., Pa., wagon master.

Military journal, March 1777–June 1778; expenses, purchases of supplies, notes on destruction; wagon master with Washington's army during New York campaign; varied but disjointed; interesting spellings and language.

Howard Vanderslice and H. N. Monnett, *Van der Slice and Allied Families* (Los Angeles, 1931) 140–161.

VARNUM, John (1705–1785) of Dracut, Mass.

Private diary, January 1777–December 1781 (extracts); brief notes, personal and social affairs at Dracut; fishing, weather, war news.

Silas R. Coburn, *History of Dracut, Mass.* (Lowell, 1922) 327–328; John M. Varnum, *The Varnums of Dracutt* (Boston, 1907) 54–64.

WALDO, Dr. Albigence (1750–1794) of Pomfret, Conn.

Surgeon's military journal, November 1777–January 1778; kept at Valley Forge; long entries, with vivid description of hardships and yearnings of troops; partly direct observation, partly tinged by Sterne-like sentiment; a good diary.

Hist. Mag. V (1861) 129–134, 169–172; *Pennsylvania Mag. Hist. Biog.* XXI (1897) 299–323; *Annals Med. Hist.* X (1928) 486–497.

WARREN, Capt. Benjamin (1740–1825) of Plymouth, Mass.

Military journals, July–October 1777, and July–November 1778; the first describes Saratoga campaign and battle, the second describes Cherry Valley massacre; vivid and very well told.

Jour. Amer. Hist. III (1909) 202–216, 378–384.

WEARE, Lieut. Nathan (1747–1798) of Hampton Falls, N.H.

Military journal, April–June 1777; Ticonderoga and retreat; marches, camp life, discipline, some personal notes; moderate interest.

Warren Brown, *History of the Town of Hampton Falls* (Manchester, N.H., 1900) 244–249.

WEBB, Sergt. Maj. Nathaniel, of 2d New York Regiment.

Military journal, October 1777–August 1779 (with gaps); burning of Kingston, Sullivan's expedition; quite interesting.

F. Cook, *Journals of the Military Expedition of Major-General John Sullivan* (Auburn, N.Y., 1887) 285–287; completed in *New York Hist. Assoc. Proc.* VI (1906) 87–93. Extracts in *Olde Ulster* X (1914) 209–212.

WHEELER, Maj. Bennett (*d.* 1806) of Providence, R.I.

Military journal, January 1777; extract concerning British in Rhode Island. *Rhode Island Hist. Soc. Pubs.* n.s. VI (1898) 91.

WHIPPLE, William (1730–1785) of Dighton, Mass.

Private diary, June 1777–July 1779 (with gaps); journey between Dighton and Philadelphia, accompanying William Ellery; notes on places and people, including congressmen; fair interest.

Pennsylvania Mag. Hist. Biog. X (1886) 366–374.

WISTER, Sally (1761–1804) of Philadelphia.

Private diary, September 1777–June 1778; kept on farm near Valley Forge; a most entertaining, lively journal of social life; flirtations of a young Quaker girl with officers of the Revolutionary army; witty, with many excellent scenes and conversation pieces, and some poems.

Howard M. Jenkins, *Historical Collections Relating to Gwynedd* (Philadelphia, 1897) 312–348; *Pennsylvania Mag. Hist. Biog.* IX (1885) 318–333, 463–478, X (1886) 51–60; Albert C. Myers (ed.), *Sally Wister's Journal* (Philadelphia, 1902) 224 pp.

1778

ALLAIRE, Lieut. Anthony (1755–1838) of Fredericton, N.B.

British military journal, March–November 1780; campaign in South Carolina; battle of King's Mountain; personal and military details; good, lively narrative, with full entries.

Lyman C. Draper, *King's Mountain and Its Heroes* (New York, 1929) 484–515; extract in *Tennessee Hist. Quar.* VII (1921) 104–106.

ALMY, Mrs. Mary, of Newport, R.I.

Private diary, July–August 1778; an account of the bombardment of Newport by the French fleet; fears for her family and herself; written in a sentimental style.

Newport Hist. Mag. I (1880–1881) 17–36.

ANGELL, Col. Israel (1740–1832) of Providence, R.I.

Military journals, August 1778–April 1781; commanding second Rhode Island regiment; siege of Boston, Peekskill, Brandywine, Red Bank, Valley Forge, Monmouth, Springfield; mainly notes of his own activities and the general affairs of military life.

Edward Field (ed.), *Diary of Colonel Israel Angell* (Providence, 1899) 149 pp.

BELL, Andrew, secretary to Gen. Clinton.

Military journal, June–July 1778; march of British army through New Jersey; impersonal military notes, mostly statistics.

New Jersey Hist. Soc. Proc. VI (1851–1853) 15–19.

BENJAMIN, Lieut. Samuel (1753–1824) of Livermore, Me.

Military journal, May 1778–December 1781; campaigns in New York, New Jersey, and Maryland; an uninspired brief military record.

Mary L. Benjamin, *Genealogy of the Family of Lieut. Samuel Benjamin* (n.p., 1900) 24–38.

BERKENHOUT, Dr. John (1730?–1791) of Leeds, Yorkshire, physician.

Travel diary, August–September 1778; New York to Philadelphia, as member of peace delegation; conversations with congressmen; notes on Revolutionary forces; latter part describes his arrest and imprisonment by Pennsylvania Supreme Council.

Newton D. Mereness, *Travels in the American Colonies* (New York, 1916) 574–582; *Pennsylvania Mag. Hist. Biog.* LXV (1941) 79–92.

BOARDMAN, Timothy (1754–1838) of Ipswich, Mass.

Sea journals, April 1778 and July–September 1778; on board privateer "Oliver Cromwell"; cruising from New London to Charleston, S.C.; return and skirmish with a British ship.

S. W. Boardman (ed.), *Log-book of Timothy Boardman* (Albany, 1885) 85 pp.

COOK, Capt. James (1728–1779), British explorer.

Sea journal, February 1778 (extract); description of Oregon coast.

Oregon Hist. Quar. XXIX (1928) 266–277.

DENNIS, Joseph (1759–1807) of Portsmouth, R.I.

Private diary, May–August 1778 (fragment); kept at Portsmouth; visits, social life, amusements, farming; activities of a young Quaker; British at Portsmouth.

Newport Hist. Mag. II (1881) 46–52.

FOOT, Caleb (1750–1787) of Salem, Mass.

Sea journal, July 1778–January 1782; narrative of two journeys, one to Canada and another to Europe; prisoner in England, escape to Holland; seminarrative.

Essex Inst. Hist. Colls. XXVI (1889) 104–119.

GALLOWAY, Grace Growden (*d.* 1789) of Philadelphia.

Loyalist diary, June 1778–July 1779; woman's life in Philadelphia during the Revolution; a good lively journal, with detailed and lengthy entries; mostly her own actions and difficulties, and the affairs and conversation of her friends.

Pennsylvania Mag. Hist. Biog. LV (1931) 32–94, LVIII (1934) 152–189.

GIBBS, Maj. Caleb (1748–1818) of Newport, R.I.

Military journal, August 1778; at Providence and Newport.

Pennsylvania Archives, 1st Ser. VI 734–736.

GILE, Maj. Ezekiel (1743–1828) of Plaistow, N.H.

Military journal, May 1778–June 1780; brief entries of military affairs in Rhode Island; interesting spellings.

Boston Transcript, December 4, 1905.

GOODWIN, Col. Ichabod (*b.* 1743) *b.* Berwick, Me.

Military journal, April–June 1778; at Boston; combination of orderly book and notes of military affairs, discipline, etc.

Maine Hist. Soc. Colls. and Proc. 2d Ser. V (1894) 36–71.

GREENE, William, of Boston.

Personal and travel diary, March–September 1778; American in London and Paris; apparently a prisoner released on exchange; London, Brighton, Dieppe, Rouen, Paris; accounts of his family and life; meeting with Franklin and others; social life in Paris; journey to America on man-of-war; carefully written in great detail.

Massachusetts Hist. Soc. Proc. LIV (1920–1921) 84–138.

GRIMKÉ, Maj. John Foucheraud (1752–1819) of Charleston, S.C., jurist.

Military journal, May–July 1778; campaign to the southward, expedition against British in Florida; some topographical notes. Partly written by his clerk.
South Carolina Hist. Geneal. Mag. XII (1911) 60–69, 118–134, 190–206.

HAMILTON, Lieut. Gov. Henry.

Travel journal, October–November 1778 (extracts); journey along Wabash route upon Vincennes; quotations.
A. B. Hulbert, *Historic Highways of America* VII (Cleveland, 1903) 170–175.

HAZARD, Thomas Benjamin, "Nailer Tom" (1756–1845) of South Kingston, R.I.

Farming diary, June 1778–1840; brief notes of personal, local, social, farming matters; its enormous length, persistency, and detail make it a very valuable record of local New England life; it is extremely interesting linguistically.
Caroline Hazard (ed.), *Nailer Tom's Diary* (Boston, 1930) 808 pp. Extracts in *Narragansett Hist. Reg.* I (1882–1883) 28–41, 91–106, 167–179, 277–285.

HOLTEN, Dr. Samuel (1738–1816) of Danvers, Mass., congressman.

Political diary, May 1778–August 1780; activities of Congress, news, social affairs, journeys.
Essex Inst. Hist. Colls. LV (1919) 161–176, 249–256, LVI (1920) 24–32, 88–97; *Danvers Hist. Soc. Colls.* VII (1919) 59–67, VIII (1920) 97–130. Brief extracts in *Massachusetts Hist. Soc. Proc.* 2d Ser. X (1895–1896) 463.

JENKINS, Lieut. John (1751–1827) of New London, Conn.

Military journal, June 1778–February 1781; Sullivan's campaign; battle of Newton; fair.
F. Cook, *Journals of the Military Expedition of Major-General John Sullivan* (Auburn, N.Y., 1887) 169–177.

MIX, Capt. Jonathan (1753–1817) of New Haven, Conn.

Sea journal, September–December 1778; on board "Marlborough," pursuing Jamaica fleet; log items.
William P. Blake, *A Brief Account of Jonathan Mix* (New Haven, 1886) 32–40.

NEISSER, Rev. George, of York, Pa.

Moravian journal, January–December 1778; religious work and life of the Moravian minister of York, Pa.
Pennsylvania Mag. Hist. Biog. XVI (1892) 433–438.

NUTTING, William (1752–1832) of Groton, Mass.

Diary, September 1778–March 1783 (extracts); notes relating to Revolution; references to Groton Library; funerals.
Samuel A. Green, *Groton Historical Series* III (1893) 383–399.

SHARPE, Robert (1743–1798) of Brookline, Mass.

Farming journal, April–August 1778; mostly accounts and farm details.
Brookline Hist. Soc. Pubs. No. 2 (1895) 12–13.

SPROAT, Rev. Dr. James (1722–1793) of Guilford, Conn.

Chaplain's journal, April–October 1778; visits as hospital chaplain in Philadelphia and district; brief notes.

Pennsylvania Mag. Hist. Biog. XXVII (1903) 441–445; James E. Gibson, *Dr. Bodo Otto* (Springfield, 1937) 325–336.

STONE, Stephen (1761–1782) of Guilford, Conn.

Military journal, June 1778–May 1781; brief notes of his military career; White Plains, Peekskill, etc.; partly domestic notes.

William L. Stone, *The Family of John Stone* (Albany, 1888) 30–33.

TURNOR, Philip (*b. ca.* 1752) of Laleham, Middlesex, Eng., and Hudson's Bay Company, surveyor.

1. Travel log, September 1778–September 1779; surveying from York Fort to Cumberland House and return; in this journal and the rest details of topography, navigation, etc., form bulk of entries, with occasional notes on his daily life and adventures, Indians, weather.

2. Travel log, September 1779–September 1780; surveying journey from York Fort to Albany and Moose Forts.

3. Travel log, December 1780–August 1781; travel around Albany and Moose Forts.

4. Travel log, June 1790–May 1791; with Mitchel Oman; occurrences at Cumberland House.

5. Travel log, September 1790–July 1792; travel from Cumberland House toward the Athapiscow country, and back to York Factory.

6. Travel log, July–August 1792; from York Factory to Port Nelson River (North River).

J. B. Tyrrell (ed.), *Journals of Samuel Hearne and Philip Turnor* (Toronto, 1934) 195–491, 557–577.

VAILL, Rev. Joseph (1751–1838) of Hadlyme, Conn.

Religious diary, November 1778–December 1823; religious meditations, reform, revivals, etc.; interesting.

Isaac Parsons, *Memoir of Rev. Joseph Vaill* (New York, 1839) 86–156 *passim*.

VAN SCHAACK, Peter (1747–1832) of New York City.

Private diary, October 1778–March 1782 (extracts); voyage to England; exile there, and travels about England; touristic and antiquarian notes on churches, buildings, etc.; note on Fielding; political speculations, reading, surgical operation. Quite good.

Henry C. Van Schaack, *The Life of Peter Van Schaack* (New York, 1842) 132–277 *passim*.

WEEKS, Rev. Joseph Wingate (1738–1806) of Marblehead, Mass.

Loyalist diary, June 1778–May 1779; adventures of the loyalist rector of St. Michael's; escape to Newport; bombardment of Newport, journey to New York, and voyage to London; scandals and excitements of voyage; social life in London; very lively and entertaining.

　Essex Inst. Hist. Colls. LII (1916) 1–16, 161–176, 197–208, 345–356.

WELLS, Louisa Susannah (1755?–1831) of Charleston, S.C.

　Loyalist travel diary, May–August 1778; daily notes of a voyage from Charleston, S.C., to London; really written up in the following year, but follows day-to-day pattern.

　Journal of a Voyage from Charlestown, S.C., to London (New York, 1906) 121 pp.

1779

ANON.

　Military journal, July–August 1779; Penobscot expedition; cruise from Nantasket, and military operations in Maine; long and fairly detailed notes.

　Hist. Mag. VIII (1864) 51–54.

ANON.

　Military journal, July–August 1779; rebel attack on British ships and troops in Penobscot Bay; details of bombardment.

　Nova Scotia Gazette, September 14, 1779; reprinted in *Maine Hist. Soc. Colls.* 1st Ser. VII (1876) 123–126.

ANON. (French naval officer).

　Naval journal, July–November 1779; siege of Savannah; details of action with D'Estaing's fleet; ship movements, bombardments, etc.

　The Siege of Savannah in 1779 (Albany, 1874) 9–52.

ANON. (British naval officer?)

　Sea and military journal, November–October (*sic*) 1779; siege of Savannah.

　Hist. Mag. VIII (1864) 12–16.

ANON.

　Military journal 1779; Western expedition.

　*Hill's *New Hampshire Patriot,* September 16, 1843. [Forbes.]

BARR, Ens. John, of 4th New York Regiment.

　Military journals, 1779–1782; mostly brief notes of marches and military affairs; illustrates campaigns of New York Regiment.

　A. W. Lauber (ed.), *Orderly Books of the 4th New York Regiment* (Albany, 1932) 787–865.

BARTON, Lieut. William, of Monmouth Co., N.J.

　Military journal, June–October 1779 (extract); with Maxwell's New Jersey brigade on Sullivan's expedition; fairly good narrative.

　New Jersey Hist. Soc. Proc. II (1846) 22–42; F. Cook, *Journals of the Military Expedition of Major-General John Sullivan* (Auburn, N.Y., 1887) 3–14.

BEATTY, Lieut. Erkuries (1759–1823), paymaster of Western Army.

　1. Military journal, June–October 1779; Sullivan's expedition, and Clinton's march down the Susquehannah; moderate interest.

Pennsylvania Archives 2d Ser. XV 219–253; *Cayuga County Hist. Soc. Pubs.* I 61–81; F. Cook, *Journals of the Military Expedition of Major-General John Sullivan* (Auburn, N.Y., 1887) 18–37.

2. Military journal, May 1786–June 1787; kept while author was paymaster of Western Army; journey to Kentucky and Ohio; notes on Indian affairs, town and pioneer life; travels to Philadelphia and New York on official business; return journey.

Mag. Amer. Hist. I (1877) Part I 175–179, 235–243, 309–315, 380–384, Part II 432–438.

BEEKMAN, Lieut. Tjerck, of 2d New York Regiment.

Military journal, May–September 1779; Sullivan's expedition; Pennsylvania and New York.

Mag. Amer. Hist. XX (1888) 127–136.

BOWEN, Edward (*b.* 1755) of Marblehead, Mass.

Private diary, September 1779–February 1780; brief notes of weather, shipping at Marblehead, etc.

S. Roads, *The History and Traditions of Marblehead* (Boston, 1880) 391.

BOWMAN, Major Joseph (1752–1782) b. Virginia, associate of George Rogers Clark.

Military journal, January–March 1779; news of capture of Vincennes and Clark's march on the post.

Illinois Hist. Soc. Colls. VIII (1912) 20–28; *Col. George Rogers Clark's Sketch of His Campaign in the Illinois* (Cincinnati, 1907) 82–94.

BURROWES, Capt. John, of 5th New Jersey Regiment.

Military journal, August–October 1779; brief notes on Sullivan's expedition.

F. Cook, *Journals of the Military Expedition of Major-General John Sullivan* (Auburn, N.Y., 1887) 43–51.

BUTLER, Capt. Walter N. (*ca.* 1750–1781) of Johnston, N.Y.

Military travel journal, March 1779; march with British corps of rangers along northern shore of Lake Ontario, from Niagara; brief topographical notes.

Trans. Canadian Inst. IV (1892–1893) 279–283; *Canadian Hist. Rev.* I (1920) 386–391.

CALEF, Dr. John (1726–1812) of St. Andrew's, N.B.

Military journal, June–August 1779; siege of Penobscot, from British side; notes written up as journal.

The Siege of Penobscot by the Rebels (London, 1781); G. A. Wheeler, *History of Castine, Penobscot, and Brooksville, Me.* (Bangor, 1875) 290–303; reprinted in *Mag. Hist.* Extra No. 11 (New York, 1910) 303–333.

CAMPFIELD, Dr. Jabez, of 5th New Jersey Regiment.

Surgeon's military journal, May–October 1779; kept during Sullivan's expedition; descriptions of country, and Indian towns.

New Jersey Hist. Soc. Proc. 2d Ser. III (1872–1874) 115–136; *Wyoming County Democrat* (Pa.), December 31, 1873, January 28, 1874; F. Cook, *Journals of the Military Expedition of Major-General John Sullivan* (Auburn, N.Y., 1887) 52–61.

CRUGER, Col. John Harris.
Military journal, September–October 1779; brief account, siege of Savannah. *Mag. Amer. Hist.* II (1878) 489–492.

DONELSON, John (1718–1785) of Pittsylvania Co., Va.
Travel journal, December 1779–April 1780 (extracts); river voyage as one of a party of emigrants to North Alabama.
S. C. Williams, *Early Travels in the Tennessee Country* (Johnson City, 1928) 233–242; *Who's Who on the Ohio River* (Cincinnati, 1931) 21–27.

ELD, Lieut. Col. George (*d.* 1793) of Coldstream Guards.
Military journal, May 1779–March 1780 (extracts); activities of his regiment, especially in the Jerseys, and some personal notes.
Massachusetts Hist. Soc. Proc. 1st Ser. XVIII (1880–1881) 73–79.

FAIRLIE, Lieut. James, of 2d New York Regiment.
Military journal, August–September 1779; Sullivan's Indian expedition; brief notes of the campaign.
The Sullivan-Clinton Campaign in 1779 (Univ. State New York, Albany, 1929) 175–178.

FELLOWS, Sergt. Moses (1755-1846) of Salisbury, Vt.
Military journal, June–September 1779; moderate account of Sullivan's expedition.
F. Cook, *Journals of the Military Expedition of Major-General John Sullivan* (Auburn, N.Y., 1887) 86–91.

FISHER, Samuel Rowland (1745–1834) of Philadelphia.
Prison diary, March 1779–September 1781; trial for espionage, life in prison; good, substantial entries about prison life.
Pennsylvania Mag. Hist. Biog. XLI (1917) 145–197, 274–333, 399–457.

FLEMING, Col. William (1729–1795) *b.* Jedburgh, Scotland, of Montgomery Co., Va.; soldier and statesman.
1. Travel journal, November 1779–May 1780; in Kentucky on commission to adjust land claims; notes on topography, natural history, trade; some personal details, illness, hunting, persons met, etc.; a good journal.
2. Diary, January–April 1783; kept in Kentucky.
Newton D. Mereness, *Travels in the American Colonies* (New York, 1916) 619–655, 661–674.

GOOKIN, Ens. Daniel (1756–1831) of Hampton, N.H.
Military journal, May–September 1779; moderately interesting account of Sullivan's expedition.

New England Hist. Geneal. Reg. XVI (1862) 27–33; F. Cook, *Journals of the Military Expedition of Major-General John Sullivan* (Auburn, N.Y., 1887) 102–106.

GORE, Lieut. Obadiah (1744–1821) of Wyoming Valley, Pa.

Military journal, July–September 1779; Sullivan's expedition; march to Genesee River; military details, and some notes on camp life; fair interest.

Wyoming Hist. Geol. Soc. Proc. and Colls. XIX (1926) 219–235; *The Sullivan-Clinton Campaign in 1779* (Univ. State New York, Albany, 1929) 179–188; *Bull. New York Pub. Lib.* XXXIII (1929) 711–742.

GRANT, Sergt. Maj. George, of 3d New Jersey Regiment.

Military journal, May–December 1779; fairly interesting account of Sullivan's campaign.

Hazard's Register XIV (1834) 72–76; F. Cook, *Journals of the Military Expedition of Major-General John Sullivan* (Auburn, N.Y., 1887) 107–114. Extract concerning Butler's march along Lake Cayuga in *Cayuga County Hist. Soc. Colls.* I (1879) 73–75.

GRANT, Thomas, surveyor.

Military journal, July–September 1779; kept during Sullivan's expedition; surveying route to Genesee River from Easton, Pa.

Hist. Mag. 1st Ser. VI (1862) 233–237, 273–276; F. Cook, *Journals of the Military Expedition of Major-General John Sullivan* (Auburn, N. Y., 1887) 137–144. Extracts in *Cayuga County Hist. Soc. Colls.* I (1879) 70–72.

GREELE, Thomas, of Newburyport, master of the "General Arnold."

Sea journal, March–June 1779; very brief notes of cruise of the "General Arnold"; engagements with British ships.

J. J. Currier, *History of Newburyport* (Newburyport, Mass., 1906) 631–632.

HALSEY, Zephaniah, and RAMSEY, Archibald, of Quartermaster's Dept., U.S.A.

Military journal, May 1779–December 1782; kept by quartermasters in charge of horses; New Jersey, Hudson River, New York, Yorktown, etc.

Pathfinder Mag. (Washington) September 8, 15, 22, 29, 1894.

HARDENBURGH, Lieut. John L., of Rosendale, N.Y.

Military journal, May–October 1779; Sullivan's expedition; usual military details; moderate general interest.

F. Cook, *Journals of the Military Expedition of Major-General John Sullivan* (Auburn, N.Y., 1887) 116–136; *Cayuga County Hist. Soc. Colls.* I (1879) 23–59.

HARDY, Capt. Joseph, in command of marines on frigate "Confederacy."

Military journal, December 1779–February 1780; cruise off New England coast; nautical, with some personal and social details.

J. L. Howard, *Seth Harding, Mariner* (New Haven, 1930) 213–277.

HINRICHS, Capt. Johann, engineer in the Hessian Jaeger Corps.

Hessian military journal, December 1779–June 1780; voyage from New York to Georgia; some description of Georgia; expedition to South Carolina; landing in North Edisto; siege and reduction of Charleston; voyage to Phillipsburgh; descriptions and comments in South Carolina. Extracts from German text, with English translation.

Bernhard A. Uhlendorf, *The Siege of Charleston* (Ann Arbor, 1938) 104–363.

HUBLEY, Lieut. Col. Adam (1740–1793) of Philadelphia.

1. Military journal, 1779; with 11th Pennsylvania Regiment; commencing at Wyoming; military notes and topography; fairly good.

Pennsylvania Mag. Hist. Biog. XXXIII (1909) 129–146, 279–302, 409–422.

2. Military journal, July–October 1779; journal of Sullivan's campaign; fairly good.

F. Cook, *Journals of the Military Expedition of Major-General John Sullivan* (Auburn, N.Y., 1887) 145–167; Charles Miner, *History of Wyoming* (Philadelphia, 1845) App. 82–104; Oscar E. Rising, *A New Hampshire Lawyer in General Washington's Army* (Geneva, N.Y., 1915) 43–95.

LAWRENCE, Sergt. William (*d.* 1845) of Castine, Me.

Military journal, July–August 1779; account of Penobscot expedition and siege of Majabiguaduce, from British side; fair interest.

G. A. Wheeler, *History of Castine, Penobscot, and Brooksville, Me.* (Bangor, 1875) 314–320.

LIVERMORE, Capt. Daniel (1749–1798) of Concord, N.H.

Military journal, May–December 1779; fairly good account of Sullivan's campaign; military details, engagements; fair narrative, and interesting spellings.

New Hampshire Hist. Soc. Colls. VI (1850) 308–335 (normalized). Partly in F. Cook, *Journals of the Military Expedition of Major-General John Sullivan* (Auburn, N.Y., 1887) 178–191.

LOVELL, Gen. Solomon (1732–1801) of Weymouth, Mass.

Military journal, July–August 1779; kept during Penobscot expedition; moderate notes on cruise, and military details.

Weymouth Hist. Soc. Pubs. No. 1 (1881) 93–105.

MACHIN, Capt. Thomas, of 2d New York Artillery.

Military journal, April 1779; Van Schaick's expedition against the Onondagas; brief notes.

Mag. Amer. Hist. III (1879) Part II 688–689; F. Cook, *Journals of the Military Expedition of Major-General John Sullivan* (Auburn, N.Y., 1887) 192–194.

McNEILL, Samuel (1753–1817) of Hand's Brigade, quartermaster.

Military journal, August–September 1779; kept during Sullivan's expedition; mostly a quartermaster's orderly book.

Pennsylvania Archives 2d Ser. XV 753–759.

MATHEW, Lieut. George, of Llandaff, Wales, and the Leeward Islands.
Military journal, March 1779–January 1781; voyage to New York; notes on hardships of military life; account of André-Arnold affair; monthly post facto entries.
Hist. Mag. I (1857) 102–106.

MOODY, William (1756–1821) of Falmouth, Me.
Military diary, July–August 1779; brief notes kept by a carpenter during the Bagaduce expedition; moderately interesting military details, movements, etc.
Maine Hist. Soc. Colls. 2d Ser. X (1899) 144–148.

NORRIS, Capt. James (1739–1816) of Epping, N.H.
Military journal, June–October 1779; with the 3d New Hampshire Regiment during Sullivan's expedition; long entries and good descriptions; some interesting spellings.
Buffalo Hist. Soc. Pubs. I (1879) 217–252. Partly in F. Cook, *Journals of the Military Expedition of Major-General John Sullivan* (Auburn, N.Y., 1887) 223–239.

NUKERCK, Capt. Charles, of 2d New York Regiment.
Military journal, May 1779–December 1780; Sullivan's expedition; campaign around Hudson River.
F. Cook, *Journals of the Military Expedition of Major-General John Sullivan* (Auburn, N.Y., 1887) 214–222.

PAGE, Capt. Samuel (1753–1814) of Danvers, Mass.
Military journal February–June 1779; with 11th Massachusetts Regiment; details of camp life, orders, etc.; formal journal.
Essex Inst. Hist. Colls. IV (1862) 241–249, V (1863) 1–9.

PARKER, Lieut. Robert (d. 1788) of 2d Continental Artillery.
Military journal, June–December 1779; kept during Sullivan's expedition; military details, with some general notes on scenery, camp life, etc.; a poem; fairly interesting.
Pennsylvania Mag. Hist. Biog. XXVII (1903) 404–420, XXVIII (1904) 12–25; *The Sullivan-Clinton Campaign in 1779* (Univ. State New York, Albany, 1929) 188–210.

PERKINS, Col. Simeon (1735–1812) of Norwich, Conn.
Private diary, 1779–1812 (MS dates, with gaps); long notes mostly of private affairs at Liverpool, N.S.; some military and social affairs.
Acadiensis IV (1904) 96–118 ("Old Times in Liverpool, N. S.").

PITMAN, Rev. John (1751–1820) of Providence, R.I.
Clergyman's diary, April 1779–July 1822; personal affairs, preaching tours, accidents, unusual sights; brief, but interesting extracts.
New England Mag. n.s. XII (1895) 407–414 ("A Baptist Preacher and Soldier").

Prévost, Maj. Gen. Augustine (1725–1786) *b*. Geneva, British soldier.

Military journal, September 1779; purely military details of siege of Savannah, by general commanding British forces. Translated from the French.

Southern Hist. Assoc. Pubs. I (1897) 259–268.

Reidhead, William (1757–1811) of Penobscot, Me.

Military diary, July–August 1779; fairly good account of siege of Majabiguaduce, and British defense; some linguistic interest.

Bangor Hist. Mag. V (1889–1890) 226–231.

Roberts, Sergt. Thomas, of 5th New Jersey Regiment.

Military journal, May–September 1779; march from Elizabethtown; Sullivan's expedition; fair account.

F. Cook, *Journals of the Military Expedition of Major-General John Sullivan* (Auburn, N.Y., 1887) 240–245.

Russell, Capt. Peter (*d*. 1808) *b*. Ireland, of 64th Foot Regiment (British).

Military journal, December 1779–May 1780; siege of Charleston; mainly statistical and technical notes.

Amer. Hist. Rev. IV (1898–1899) 478–501.

Russell, Maj. William (1748–1784) of Boston.

Prison diary, December 1779–August 1782; kept in Mill Prison, Eng.; an interesting record of prison life, although it is not so complete or so racy as some of the other Mill Prison diaries.

Ralph D. Paine, *Ships and Sailors of Old Salem* (New York, 1909) 124–174.

Scudder, William, of Westfield, N.J.

Prison diary, August 1779–October 1782; campaigns with New York Line; capture at Fort Stanwix; daily prison life in Canada.

Journal of William Scudder (n.p., 1794) 250 pp.

Shute, Lieut. Samuel Moore, of 2d New Jersey Regiment.

Military journal, May–November 1779; details of Sullivan's Indian expedition.

F. Cook, *Journals of the Military Expedition of Major-General John Sullivan* (Auburn, N.Y., 1887) 267–274.

Smith, Gen. Daniel (1748–1818) *b*. Stafford Co., Va., later senator from Tenn.

Surveying journal, August 1779–July 1780; member of commission running boundary line of Tennessee between North Carolina and Virginia, Tennessee, and Kentucky; topographical notes of Tennessee-Cumberland region; some personal notes.

Tennessee Hist. Mag. I (1915) 40–65.

Van Hovenburgh, Lieut. Rudolphus, of 4th New York Regiment.

Military journal, June–December 1779; kept on Sullivan's expedition and on march to Pompton, N.J.

F. Cook, *Journals of the Military Expedition of Major-General John Sullivan* (Auburn, N.Y., 1887) 275–284.

Von Huyn, Maj. Gen. Johann Christoph (1720–1780).

Hessian military journal, December 1779–May 1780; expedition to South Carolina and siege of Charleston. German text, with English translation.

Bernhard A. Uhlendorf, *The Siege of Charleston* (Ann Arbor, 1938) 367–397.

1780

Anon.

Military journal, August 1780–May 1781 (extracts); pages from the diary of a common soldier; notes on patriotism, discipline, religion, personal items, camp life; moderate interest.

Atlantic Monthly CXXXIV (1924) 459–463.

Anderson, Lieut. Thomas, of Delaware Regiment.

Military journal, May 1780–April 1782 (extracts); Southern campaign, Delaware, Virginia, South Carolina; some interesting language.

Hist. Mag. n.s. I (1867) 207–211.

Baldwin, Samuel (*b.* 1754) of Newark, N.J.

Schoolmaster's diary, March–April 1780; kept during siege of Charleston, S.C.; mainly military details.

New Jersey Hist. Soc. Proc. II (1846–1847) 77–86.

Blanchard, Claude (1742–1802) of French auxiliary army in the United States.

Military journal, March 1780–July 1783; military, social. and political affairs during the Revolution; description of Washington and other outstanding figures; notes on American customs and characteristics; an interesting and important journal. Translated.

William Duane (trans.) and Thomas Balch (ed.), *The Journal of Claude Blanchard* (Albany, 1876) 207 pp.

Buell, Capt. John Hutchinson, of 4th Connecticut Regiment.

Military journal, 1780–1783; fragment of journal describing military affairs in New Jersey, Hudson River region, Connecticut.

*Published at Brattleboro, Vt. (1887) 25 pp.

Carpenter, John (of Barnard, Vt.?).

Scouting journal, 1780 (extracts); scouting trip from Barnard through Middlesex, Brookfield, Deerfield, and Northfield.

William M. Newton, *History of Barnard, Vt.* (Montpelier, 1928) II 71–72.

Cowdrey, Capt. Nathaniel (1759–1841) of Reading, Mass.

Military journal, July–December 1780; at West Point and King's Ferry; bald military details; some bad verses; very interesting spellings.

Amer. Monthly Mag. IV (1894) 412–416.

De Brahm, French Engineer.

Military journal, February–May 1780; siege of Charleston; engineering and artillery notes. Translated.

R. W. Gibbes, *Documentary History of the American Revolution* II (New York, 1857) 124–128.

De Gálvez, Don Bernardo.

Military journal, October 1780–May 1781; official report of successful operations against Pensacola; translated from the Spanish.

Louisiana Hist. Quar. I (1917) 44–84.

Deux Ponts, Count Guillaume de Forbach (*b.* 1754) of France.

Military journal, March 1780–November 1781; kept mostly in New England; long description of Revolutionary affairs. French and English texts.

Samuel A. Green (ed.), *My Campaigns in America* (Boston, 1868) 176 pp.

Drowne, Dr. Solomon (1753–1834) of Mount Hygeia, R.I.

1. Sea journal, October 1780; cruise from Providence in sloop "Hope," privateer; poetical quotations and literary effusions.

Journal of a Cruise in the Fall of 1780 (New York, 1872) 27 pp. Extract in *Rhode Island Hist. Mag.* V (1884) 1–8.

2. Travel journal, November 1788–June 1789; kept in Marietta, O.; description of ceremonies at Indian treaty of Fort Harmar.

Mag. Amer. Hist. IX (1883) 285–286.

Ewald, Capt. Johann (1744–1813) of 2d Hessian Jaegers.

Hessian military journal, March–June 1780; expedition to Charleston and siege. German text, with English translation.

Bernhard A. Uhlendorf, *The Siege of Charleston* (Ann Arbor, 1938) 30–101.

Hawes, Matthias (1754–1828) of Union, Me.

Private diary, March 1780–April 1786 (extracts); brief notes of weather, personal, local affairs.

J. L. Sibley, *A History of the Town of Union* (Boston, 1851) 7, 50, 51, 58, 107, 161.

[Heckewelder, Christian?]

Moravian travel journal, October 1780; with Bishop Reichel and his wife from Salem to Littitz; travel notes.

Newton D. Mereness, *Travels in the American Colonies* (New York, 1916) 603–613.

Hope (N.C.) Moravian Congregation.

Congregational journal, January–December 1780; items from the *Extract der Diarii der Gemeiner in der Wachau;* usual Moravian life and work. For other extracts, cf. under 1781: Friedland Congregation. (For analysis of type, see 1753: Bethabara.)

Adelaide L. Fries (ed.), *Records of the Moravians in North Carolina* (Raleigh, 1922–1941) IV 1654–1655.

Hopkins, Thomas.

Private diary, August 1780; brief business notes, while author was employed by Friendship Salt Co. of New Jersey; personal and war matters.

Pennsylvania Mag. Hist. Biog. XLII (1918) 46–61.

HUBLEY, John.
Journal, July 2, 1780 (extract); statistics on volunteers from Pennsylvania.
Pennsylvania Archives 1st Ser. VIII 401.

KIRKWOOD, Capt. Robert (1756–1791) of White Clay Creek, Del.
Military journal, April 1780–April 1782; with Delaware Regiment in southern campaign; Charleston, Delaware, Maryland, Virginia, Carolinas; only military details.
Delaware Hist. Soc. Pubs. VI (1910) (Paper LVI) 277 pp.

LEE, Rev. Jesse (1758–1816) of Prince George County, Va.
Personal and religious diary, July 1780–November 1815; scattered notes of service in army, and work as itinerant Methodist minister; forming Methodist societies in Connecticut, Maine, Massachusetts; travel and preaching notes.
Minton Thrift, *Memoir of the Rev. Jesse Lee* (New York, 1823) 26–335 *passim.*

McCLELLAN, Capt. Joseph, of 9th Pennsylvania Regiment.
Military journal, August 1780–April 1782 (with gap); campaigns in New York and the South; revolt of the Pennsylvania Line.
Pennsylvania Archives 2d Ser. XI 601–614 (diary) 659–706 (diary, letters, etc.) 709–762 (mélange of diaries of McClellan and Lieut. William Feltman).

PENNINGTON, Lieut. William Sandford (1757–1826) of Newark, N.J., jurist, later governor of New Jersey.
Military journal, May 1780–March 1781; with 2d Continental Artillery under Knox; campaigns in New Jersey and New York; military and social notes of fair interest.
Jour. Military Service Inst. IV (New York, 1883) 314–329.

REICHEL, Johann Friedrich, of Littitz, Pa., Moravian bishop.
Moravian travel journal, May–October 1780; from Littitz to Salem and return; travel and religious notes.
Newton D. Mereness, *Travels in the American Colonies* (New York, 1916) 586–599; Adelaide L. Fries (ed.), *Records of the Moravians in North Carolina* (Raleigh, 1922–1941) IV 1893–1895.

SEYMOUR, Sergt. Maj. William, of Delaware Regiment.
Military journal, April 1780–January 1783; southern campaign, New Jersey, North Carolina, South Carolina, Maryland; spellings normalized.
Pennsylvania Mag. Hist. Biog. VII (1883) 286–298, 377–394.

SMITH, Josiah (1731–1826) of Charleston, S.C., merchant.
Prison diary, August 1780–December 1782; surrender of Charleston; civilian prisoner on prison ship; exile at St. Augustine; exchanged and sent to Philadelphia; a rather good journal.
South Carolina Hist. Geneal. Mag. XXXIII (1932) 1–28, 79–116, 197–207, 281–289, XXXIV (1933) 31–39, 67–84, 138–148, 194–210.

TALLMADGE, Capt. Samuel (1755–1825) of Brookhaven, L.I.

Military journal, December 1780–July 1782; campaigns of the 4th New York Regiment; mostly brief notes, military, weather, personal; some poems.

A. W. Lauber, *Orderly Books of the 4th New York Regiment* (Albany, 1932) 739–785.

WEARE, Jeremiah (1757–1845) of York, Me.

Private diary, 1780–July 1817 (with many gaps); mostly notes on births, deaths, etc., with some general notes on weather, farming, and personal affairs; some interesting spellings.

New England Hist. Geneal. Reg. LV (1901) 55–58, LXIII (1909) 296–297, LXIV (1910) 180–182, LXVI (1912) 77–79, 155–160, 261–265, 311–315.

1781

ANON. (soldier of Wayne's force, from Pennsylvania Line).

Military journal, May 1781–July 1782; "itinerary of the Pennsylvania Line from Pennsylvania to South Carolina"; mostly bare details of marches and hardships.

Pennsylvania Mag. Hist. Biog. XXXVI (1912) 273–292.

ANON. (French engineer).

Military journal, September–October 1781; siege of Yorktown; tactical and statistical details; added to Du Bourg's journal. Translated.

Mag. Amer. Hist. IV (1880) 449–452.

ANON. (chaplain with American Army).

Chaplain's journal, September–October 1781; journey from Elk River; siege of York, Va.; general military details; description of Williamsburg; moderate interest.

Massachusetts Hist. Soc. Colls. IX (1804) 102–108.

ALLEN, Gen. Ira (1751–1814) of Burlington, Vt.

1. Official journal, May 1781; report of conference with British about union between Vermont and Canada.

Vermont Hist. Soc. Colls. II (1871) 109–119.

2. Travel journal, December 1795–August 1796; journey to England, negotiations for trade treaty between Vermont and Canada.

The Vermonter X (1904) 210–211, 239–243.

ANDERSON, Lieut. Isaac (1758–1839) *b.* Ireland, of Butler Co., O.

Military journal, August 1781–July 1782; mainly an account of Lochry's expedition into Ohio; Indian ambush; captivity; list of prisoners; bare details.

James McBride, *Pioneer Biography* I (Cincinnati, 1869) 278–285. Partly in *Pennsylvania Archives* 2d Ser. XIV 685–689; *Ohio Archaeol. Hist. Soc. Pubs.* VI (1898) 389–392.

ATKINS, Josiah (*d.* 1781) of Waterbury, Conn.

Military journal, January–October 1781 (extracts); enlistment, service in Philadelphia, New York, and Maryland, and discharge; full entries; highly critical of Continental Army; comments on leaders, social and camp conditions, and intersectional rivalries; poetical quotations; highly interesting for its individuality.

Joseph Anderson, *The Town and City of Waterbury, Conn.* (New Haven, 1896) I 472–480.

BROWN, Rev. John (1724–1791) of Cohasset, Mass.

Clergyman's journal, October–December 1781; brief notes, personal, clerical; funerals, etc.

Edwin V. Bigelow, *A Narrative History of the Town of Cohasset* (Cohasset, 1898) 312.

BUTLER, Col. Richard (1743–1791) *b.* Ireland, of Pennsylvania, Indian trader.

1. Military journal, September–October 1781; siege of Yorktown; details of strategic operations; with 5th Pennsylvania Regiment.

Virginia Hist. Mag. VIII (1864) 102–112.

2. Military journal, September 1785–February 1786; kept during expedition from Carlisle, Pa., to hold treaty with the Miami Indians at Fort McIntosh; substantial descriptive notes of journey and treaty proceedings; fairly interesting.

N. B. Craig, *The Olden Time* (Pittsburgh, 1847, reprinted Cincinnati, 1876) II 433–464, 481–525, 529–531.

COBB, Lieut. Col. David (1748–1830) of Gouldsborough, Me.

1. Military journal, October–November 1781; Yorktown campaign; Maryland, Pennsylvania, New Jersey, New York; brief military notes.

Massachusetts Hist. Soc. Proc. XIX (1881–1882) 67–72.

2. Private diary, December 1795–December 1797; social life in military and political circles; visits to Penobscot, Machias, Boston; many notes about building, farming, and other work on his estate; quite interesting.

Bangor Hist. Mag. V (1889–1890) 49–57, 69–76, 116–120, 134–139.

DE GALLATIN, Baron Gaspard, of Switzerland.

Military journal, October 1781; siege of Yorktown; brief military details, followed by statistics. Translated from the French.

Journal of the Siege of York-town (Washington, D.C., 1931) 48 pp.

DENNY, Maj. Ebenezer (1761–1822) of Pittsburgh.

1. Military journal, May 1781–April 1783; with 4th Pennsylvania Regiment; Yorktown campaign; southern campaign; full but impersonal military details.

Pennsylvania Hist. Soc. Mems. VII (1860) 237–257.

2. Military letter-journal, July–October 1791; report to Maj. Gen. Butler, President of Court of Inquiry, concerning Harmar's unsuccessful expedition against Indians in Ohio country; careful analysis and a valuable account.

Basil Meek, "General Harmar's Expedition," *Ohio Archaeol. Hist. Soc. Pubs.* XX (1911) 102–108.

Du Bourg, Baron Cromot (1756–1836), aide to Rochambeau.

Travel journal, March–November 1781; voyage to America, travel in Rhode Island, Pennsylvania, New York, Maryland; interesting comments on and descriptions of people and places. Translated.

Mag. Amer. Hist. IV (1880) 205–214, 293–308, 376–385, 441–449.

Duncan, Capt. James (1756–1844) of Philadelphia.

Military journal, October 1781; fairly good account of the siege of Yorktown; army movements, firing, etc.

W. H. Egle's Notes and Queries (Pa.) 3d Ser. III (1896) 368–372, 376–380; *Mag. Hist.* II (1905) 408–416; *Pennsylvania Archives* 2d Ser. XV 743–752; *Old Northwest Geneal. Quar.* VII (1904) 152–159.

Dyott, Gen. William (1761–1847) of Staffordshire, Eng.

Military journal, February 1781–April 1845; includes visit to Halifax, N.S., in 1783, with descriptions of the town, notes on character of Prince William Henry, prices, etc.

Reginald W. Jeffery (ed.), *Dyott's Diary, 1781–1845* (London, 1907) two vols. (American sections, I 25–70).

Farmar, Ens. Robert Adolphus (*d.* 1804) of Birdsboro, Pa.

Loyalist military journal, March–June 1781; with 6th Foot Regiment of Royal Americans; fall of Pensacola; military and naval actions; graphic and fairly detailed.

Hist. Mag. IV (1860) 166–171; Charles F. Billopp, *A History of Thomas and Anne Billopp Farmar* (New York, 1907) 110–114.

Feltman, Lieut. William, of 1st Pennsylvania Regiment.

Military journal, May 1781–April 1782; journey from Pennsylvania to siege of Yorktown; southern campaign. See also 1780: McClellan.

Pennsylvania Hist. Soc. Colls. I (1853) 303–348. Extract concerning battle of Yorktown, in *Amer. Hist. Rec.* I (1872) 254–256.

Friedland (N.C.) Moravian Congregation.

Congregational journals; usual details of Moravian life and work. (For analysis of type, see 1753: Bethabara.)

Adelaide L. Fries (ed.), *Records of the Moravians in North Carolina* (Raleigh, 1922–1941).

January–December 1781 (with Hope), items from *Extract der Diarii der Gemeiner in der Wachau,* IV 1780–1783, January–December 1782 (with Hope) items, *idem,* IV 1831–1833; April–December 1783, IV 1872–1875, January–December 1784, V 2065–2066; January–December 1785, V 2115–2116; January–December 1786, V 2163–2164; January–December 1787, V 2209–2210; February–December 1789, V 2290–2291; February–December 1790, V 2317–2318; January–December 1791, V 2344–2346.

HARROW, Capt. Alexander, commander of the "Angelica" and "Dunmore."

Sea journal, August–November 1781 (extracts); visits to the king's shipyard at Detroit; extracts of local interest.

Burton Hist. Soc. Coll. Leaflets II (1924) 26–29.

JOHNSON, Col. Thomas (1742–1819) of Newbury, Vt.

Prison diary, March–October 1781; capture, and imprisonment in Canada; release and journey home; interesting brief notes.

F. P. Wells, *History of Newbury, Vermont* (St. Johnsbury, 1902) 384–393.

McDOWELL, Lieut. William, of 1st Pennsylvania Regiment.

Military journal, May 1781–December 1782; southern campaign and siege of Yorktown; notes of distances.

Pennsylvania Archives 2d Ser. XV 297–340.

MATHIS, Samuel (1760–1823) of Camden, S.C.

Private diary, March–August 1781; short notes of unimportant public and private affairs at Camden; brief notes of campaign with Colonel Marion.

Thomas J. Kirkland and Robert M. Kennedy, *Historic Camden* (Columbia, S.C., 1905) I 400–403.

MENONVILLE M. de, aide-major général.

Military journal, October 1781; siege of Yorktown; brief notes on tactics and statistics. Added to Du Bourg's journal. Translated.

Mag. Amer. Hist. VII (1881) 283–288.

RAWLE, Anna, of Philadelphia.

Private diary, October 1781; extracts describing wild rejoicing in Philadelphia after Cornwallis' surrender; loyalist's record.

Pennsylvania Mag. Hist. Biog. XVI (1892) 103–107.

ROBIN, Abbé Claude C. (*b. ca.* 1750), chaplain to French Army in America.

Chaplain's diary, June–November 1781; campaign from Rhode Island to Virginia; travel in Rhode Island, Connecticut, Pennsylvania, Maryland, Virginia; details about American troops and domestic life in Connecticut; in letter form.

Translated by Philip Freneau, *New Travels through North-America* (Philadelphia, 1783) 112 pp.; reprinted 1784. Extracts in *Granite Monthly* IV (1881) 424–428; A. J. Morrison, *Travels in Virginia in Revolutionary Times* (Lynchburg, 1922) 31–37.

SANDERSON, Lieut. Reuben (1755–1822) of East Haddam, Conn.

Military journal, July–December 1781 (extracts); march from Hudson River to Yorktown and return; marches and notes of camp life.

H. P. Johnston, *The Yorktown Campaign* (New York, 1881) 170–173.

SHUTE, Dr. Daniel (1756–1829) of Hingham, Mass.

Physician's journal, August 1781–April 1782; brief notes, mainly about his movements with the army during the Revolution.

New England Hist. Geneal. Reg. LXXXIV (1930) 383–389.

TILDEN, Lieut. John Bell (1761–1838) of 2d Pennsylvania Regiment.
Military journal, August 1781–December 1782; southern campaign, Virginia, Yorktown, North and South Carolina, Maryland, Pennsylvania.
Pennsylvania Mag. Hist. Biog. XIX (1895) 51–63, 208–233.

TRUMBULL, Jonathan (1710–1785) of Lebanon, Conn., governor.
Political diary, March 1781–October 1782 (extracts); scattered brief notes; consultation with Washington; journey to Danbury with his family; war news; work at Assembly.
Isaac W. Stuart, *Life of Jonathan Trumbull, Sen.* (Boston, 1859) 528–562 *passim.*

TUCKER, St. George (1752–1828) *b.* Bermuda, of Richmond, Va.
Military journal, September–October 1781; at Williamsburg; military details, sorties, bombardments, Cornwallis' surrender.
Mary H. Coleman, *St. George Tucker* (Richmond, Va., 1938) 72–78.

WIDGER, William (1748–1823) of Marblehead, Mass., seaman.
Prison diary, January–December 1781; kept in Mill Prison, Eng.; notes on food, escapes, news from home, etc.; fairly good of its kind; interesting language.
Essex Inst. Hist. Colls. LXXIII (1937) 311–347, LXXIV (1938) 142–158.

1782

ANON. (Irishman).
Travel diary, October 1782–February 1783; scattered but interesting notes on voyage to America, touristic notes on New York City, its people, and social amenities.
Bull. New York Pub. Lib. XXVII (1923) 891–895.

BALDWIN, Simeon (1761–1851) of Norwich and New Haven, Conn.
Private diary, August 1782–September 1785 (account and extracts); journey of a recent Yale graduate to Albany to take up teaching post; picture of Albany and its inhabitants, Dutch customs, social life; tutor at Yale; reading, taverns, journeys, social life; fairly interesting.
New Haven Col. Hist. Soc. Papers IV (1888) 193–208. Extracts in S. E. Baldwin, *Life and Letters of Simeon Baldwin* (New Haven, n.d.) 22–231 *passim.*

DAVIS, Capt. John (*d.* 1827) of 1st Pennsylvania Regiment.
Military journal, May 1781–January 1782; in Pennsylvania and at siege of Yorktown.
Pennsylvania Mag. Hist. Biog. V (1881) 290–310; *Virginia Mag. Hist. Biog.* I (1893) 2–16.

FAIRBANKS, John (1755–1796) of Lincoln County, Mass.
Sea journal, July–September 1782; movements and engagements of privateer "Wasp" off coast of Maine; interesting linguistically.
Maine Hist. Soc. Colls. 2d Ser. VI (1895) 139–144.

INMAN, Lieut. George (1755–1789) of Cambridge, Mass.

Private diary, February 1782–January 1789 (extracts); notes of a Tory's life in Massachusetts after the Revolution.

Cambridge Hist. Soc. Pubs. XIX (1926) 61–77.

JAY, John (1745–1829) *b.* New York City, statesman and diplomat.

Diary, June–December 1782; kept during the peace negotiations in Paris.

Frank Monaghan (ed.), *The Diary of John Jay* (New Haven, 1934) 17 pp.

[ORR (Lee), Lucinda, of Virginia.]

Private diary, September–November 1782; kept on a visit to her relatives, the Lees, Washingtons, and other families in Virginia; social details; written for a friend, Polly Brent.

Emily V. Mason (ed.), *Journal of a Young Lady of Virginia* (Baltimore, 1871) 56 pp.

ROSENTHAL, Baron ("John Rose") (*d. ca.* 1830) of St. Petersburg, Russia.

Military journal, May–June 1782; account of an unfortunate expedition to Sandusky; some interesting spellings.

Pennsylvania Mag. Hist. Biog. XVIII (1894) 129–157, 293–328.

SCATTERGOOD, Thomas (1748–1814) of Philadelphia.

Quaker journal, December 1782–July 1813; notes of experiences, travels, and work in most of the Quaker settlements in New England and the Atlantic and Southern states; journey to England and Scotland; a good deal of personal and social matter, with some literary allusions (Cowper, etc.); quite interesting extracts.

Friends' Library VIII (Philadelphia, 1844) 1–225.

THOMAS, Isaiah (1749–1831) of Worcester, Mass.

1. Notebook, July 1782–September 1804 (quotations); notes of expenses mostly.

2. Private diary, January 1805–December 1828 (with gap 1808; and a few notes 1796–1797); notes on social and domestic life, and local affairs; clubs and societies; journeys in New England; scholarly and antiquarian interests; extensive and interesting.

Amer. Antiq. Soc. Trans. IX and X (1909) 414 and 381 pp. Extracts from above, with diary for 1808, in *Amer. Antiq. Soc. Proc.* n.s. XXVI (1916) 58–79.

WALTERS, Michael (1760–1818) of Fayette Co., Pa.

Military journal, May–October 1782; Sandusky expedition; capture by Indians; only brief notes of distances.

Western Reserve Hist. Soc. Tract No. 89 (1899) 177–188.

1783

BRONSON, Deacon Isaac (1761–1845) of Southington, Conn.

Private diary, August 1783–October 1802 (extracts); religious introspection; some original hymns and poems.

, Samuel Orcutt, *History of the Town of Wolcott* (Waterbury, Conn., 1874) 289–291.

CONSTANT, Rev. Silas (1750–1825) *b.* Waterbury, Conn.

Clergyman's journal, April 1783–August 1801; notes of personal affairs, religious work, and parish affairs, chiefly at Blooming Grove, N.Y.

The Journal of the Reverend Silas Constant (Philadelphia, 1903) 561 pp.

FRENCH, Lieut. G.

Canadian exploration journal, September–October 1783; exploration of lands on Ottawa River from Carillon to Rideau and from mouth of the river to its source; thence to Ganonoucoué River and St. Lawrence; notes on timber.

Rept. Canadian Archives 1890 (Ottawa, 1891) 67–70.

FROST, Mrs. Sarah (1754–1817) of Stamford, Conn.

Sea journal, May–June 1783; aboard the "Two Sisters" during voyage to Nova Scotia; hardships of a loyalist.

J. C. Frost, *The Frost Genealogy* (New York, 1912) 396–397.

HALLOCK, Rev. Jeremiah (1758–1826) of Ware, Mass., and Canton, Conn.

Clergyman's diary, August 1783–May 1826; notes, personal reflections, and social affairs; two missions to Vermont; visits, sermons, prayers, fasting; reading.

Cyrus Yale, *Life of Rev. Jeremiah Hallock of Canton* (New York, Boston, 1854) 31–301 *passim.*

HEATH, Betsey (1769–1853) of Brookline, Mass.

Private diary, May–December 1783 and December 1790–January 1791; entertaining diary of family, social, and personal affairs; parties, dresses, meals, junketings; second diary describes celebrations at her brother's wedding; a good diary.

J. M. and W. F. Crafts, *The Crafts Family* (Northampton, 1893) 694–699.

KÖHLER, Rev. John Daniel, of Salem, N.C.

Moravian travel diary, September 1783–June 1784; a short account of the voyage and shipwreck of the Single Brethren; Amsterdam to America; storm, shipwreck off West Indies, refuge in Barbados; journey to Philadelphia, Wilmington, and Bethlehem.

Adelaide L. Fries (ed.), *Records of the Moravians in North Carolina* (Raleigh, 1922–1941) V 1964–1975.

LEWIS, Joseph, of Morristown, N.J.

Private diary, November 1783–November 1795; mainly notes of business, legal, and farming affairs; some notes on weather, social, and family matters.

New Jersey Hist. Soc. Proc. LIX (1941) 155–173, 263–282, LX (1942) 58–66, 124–137, 199–209, 254–269, LXI (1943) 47–56, 115–129, 194–200, LXII (1944) 35–53, 106–117, 167–180, 217–236.

LIVINGSTON, Mrs. Anne Home, neé Shippen (1763–1841) of Philadelphia.

Private diary, April 1783–December 1791 (with gaps); an excellent lively record of her social life, love affairs, and tragic marriage; rattling style, gossipy notes of belle of Philadelphia.

Ethel Armes (ed.), *Nancy Shippen, Her Journal Book* (Philadelphia, 1935) 349 pp. (including letters and editorial commentary).

MACAULAY, Alexander (*d.* 1798) of Yorktown, Va.

Private diary, February–March 1783; kept at Yorktown; an interesting, flippant account of life in the South; shows influence of the Sterne school of sentimentalists.

William and Mary Coll. Quar. XI (1902–1903) 183–191.

McCULLY, George (*d.* 1793) of Pittsburgh, etc.

Travel diary, June–July 1783 (fragment); itinerary of Ephraim Douglas to Detroit; council with Indians at the Delaware town.

C. M. Burton, "Ephraim Douglas and His Times," *Mag. Hist.* Extra No. 10 (New York, 1910) 39–49.

SCHNEIDER, Martin (1756–1806) of Wachovia, N.C.

Moravian travel journal, December 1783–January 1784; from Salem to Long Island, and thence to the Upper Cherokee towns on the Tennessee River; notes on travel difficulties, companions, religion, Indians and their customs.

S. C. Williams, *Early Travels in the Tennessee Country* (Johnson City, 1928) 250–265; Adelaide L. Fries (ed.), *Records of the Moravians in North Carolina* (Raleigh, 1922–1941) V 1976–1988.

SCHOEPF, Johann David (1752–1800) *b.* Weinsiedel, Germany.

Travel diary, 1783–1784; travel in the Confederation as far as Pittsburgh, and thence to Florida; narrative and scenery notes; fairly interesting. Translated.

A. J. Morrison (ed.), *Travels in the Confederation* (Philadelphia, 1911) two vols.

SMITH, Rev. James (1757–1800) of Powhatan Co., Va.

1. Travel diary, October–December 1783; from Powhatan County to Kentucky, with his brother George; notes on scenery, hazards, sickness, disappointment over Kentucky, antislavery sentiments.

2. Travel diary, October–December 1795; through Kentucky and the old Northwest; Gallipolis, Blue Licks, Lexington, Cincinnati, Great Miami, Frankfort, Cumberland Gap; many notes on scenery and natural phenomena; some character sketches and pleasant details of minor adventures; an interesting diary.

3. Travel diary, August–November 1797; into Kentucky and the Northwest; Ohio, Plainfield, Little Miami, Columbia, Chillicothe, Deerfield, Lexington; pleasant descriptions.

Edited by J. Morrow, *Ohio Archaeol. Hist. Quar.* XVI (1907) 352–401.

1784

ANON.

Sea journal, March–September 1784; voyage of ship "United States" (Capt. Thomas Bell) from Philadelphia to China and Pondicherry; said to be first American voyage to India; more general notes than usual log entries; descriptions of Sumatra, Pondicherry, etc., and natural history.

Pennsylvania Mag. Hist. Biog. LV (1931) 225–258; *Americana* (*Amer. Hist. Mag.*) XXXII (1938) 284–304.

ADAMS, Abigail (1765–1813) of Braintree, Mass.

Travel diary, August 1784–November 1787; social life in Europe; a very pleasant feminine journal.

Journal and Correspondence of Miss Adams (New York, 1841) 1–96. Selection in Mark Van Doren, *An Autobiography of America* (New York, 1929) 188–191.

BADCOCK, Rev. Josiah (1752–1831) of Andover, N.H.

Clergyman's diary, November 1784–June 1818; brief scattered notes of local, family, church, and personal matters.

J. R. Eastman, *History of the Town of Andover* (Concord, N.H., 1910) 313–314.

COKE, Rev. Dr. Thomas (1747–1814), Methodist bishop. ·

Travel journal, September 1784–June 1790; travel and Methodist meetings in New England and Atlantic states; five visits to America (although second, third, and fifth were to West Indies).

Extracts of the Journals of the Rev. Dr. Coke's Five Visits to America (London, 1793) 195 pp.

COWDIN, Capt. Thomas (1720–1792) of Fitchburg, Mass.

Legal diary, May–June 1784; attendance at the General Court, and notes of proceedings; very interesting spellings.

Fitchburg Hist. Soc. Colls. I (1892–1894) 137–146.

EVANS, Griffith (1760–1845) of Warwick, Pa.

Treaty journal, September 1784–January 1785 (extract); kept while he was clerk to the Pennsylvania commissioners at Fort Stanwix and Fort McIntosh, making treaties with Indians; notes on travel, private affairs, places, people, etc.; full and good entries.

Pennsylvania Mag. Hist. Biog. LXV (1941) 202–233.

EWING, Rev. Dr. John (1732–1802) of Philadelphia, provost of University of Pennsylvania.

Travel journal, May–July 1784; memorandum book of journey to settle Pennsylvania boundary; surveying and topographical notes.

Pennsylvania Archives, 6th Ser. XIV 3–20.

GUEST, Moses (*b.* 1755) of Cincinnati, O.

Travel diary, March 1784–November 1817 (extracts); travel in West Indies, Bermuda, etc.; journey from New Jersey to Montreal and Quebec; description of trade, etc., of Cincinnati; notes on scenery and towns.

Poems on Several Occasions (Cincinnati, 1823) 83–160; reprinted (Cincinnati, 1824).

LAWRENCE, Miss Love (1754–1803) of Lincoln, Mass.

Sea diary, July 1784; letter-journal written during trip to England; good picture of ocean voyage.

Jour. Amer. Hist. III (1909) 441–446.

LEADBEATER, Mary (1758–1826) of Ballitore.

Travel diary, March 1784–December 1820 (brief, scattered extracts); notes of American visitor to Friends in Ireland; personalia.

Jour. Friends' Hist. Soc. XXXVII (1940) 25–28.

LEE, Arthur (1740–1792) of Richmond, Va.

Treaty journal, November–December 1784; journey to treat with northwestern Indians, beginning from Carlisle to Pittsburgh, Pa.; account of treaty; literary style, with quotations from Milton and Pope; fairly interesting.

R. L. Lee, *Life of Arthur Lee* II (Boston, 1829) 377–399; N. B. Craig, *The Olden Time* (Pittsburgh, 1847, reprinted Cincinnati, 1876) II 334–344.

LIPSCOMB, John, of Halifax, N.S., merchant.

Travel journal, June–August 1784; from Halifax to Cumberland Co., N.C.; lively and interesting notes; some interesting language.

S. C. Williams, *Early Travels in the Tennessee Country* (Johnson City, 1928) 272–279.

MINOT, George Richards (1758–1802) of Boston, judge.

Private diary, December 1784–January 1800 (extracts); notes on Shays' Rebellion, and public affairs.

Massachusetts Hist. Soc. Colls. 1st Ser. VIII (1802) 93–95.

MUHLENBERG, Gen. John Peter Gabriel (1746–1807) of Woodstock, Va., and Philadelphia.

Travel diary, February–June 1784; trip to Kentucky to look after bounty lands of himself and friends; notes on travel, towns, topography, weather; with letters.

H. A. Muhlenberg, *The Life of Major-General Peter Muhlenberg* (Philadelphia, 1849) App. 425–453.

ROBERTSON, Capt. Daniel, of 48th Regiment.

Travel journal, June 1784; from Michilimackinac to Lake Superior.

Michigan Pioneer Colls. IX (1886) 643–646.

SAILLY, Peter (1754–1826) of Plattsburg, N.Y.

Travel diary, May–August 1784; Philadelphia, Albany, Johnstown, Fort Stanwix, Lake Schuyler, Fort Edward, Crown Point, Isle aux Noix, St. John; notes on scenery, visits, fishing, etc.

New York State Lib. Hist. Bull. No. 12 (1919) 58–70 ("Peter Sailly; a pioneer of the Champlain Valley").

SARGENT, Winthrop (1753–1820) of Gloucester, Mass.

1. Journal, 1784; minutes of the general meeting, Society of the Cincinnati.

Pennsylvania Hist. Soc. Memoirs VI (1858) 57–115.

2. Military journal, October–December 1791; St. Clair's disastrous expedition against the Indians; full, and very critical notes; lengthy account of the defeat.

Diary of Col. Winthrop Sargent (Wormsloe, N.C., 1851) 58 pp.; reprinted in *Ohio Archaeol. Hist. Quar.* XXXIII (1924) 237–273.

3. Private diary, October 1793–December 1795 (extracts); items of general interest, weather, social, etc.; visit to Washington at Mount Vernon and to Philadelphia; notes on Indian hostilities and difficulties at Cincinnati; horticultural notes.

Ohio Archaeol. Hist. Quar. XXXIII (1924) 273–282.

SCOTT, Rev. Job (1751–1793) *b.* Providence, R.I.

Quaker missionary journal, June 1784–November 1793; religious reflections and self-criticism; visits to Friends in New York State, Pennsylvania, and New Jersey; trials and illnesses; visit to southern states; wife's sickness; visit to Connecticut; tour in England and Ireland.

Journal of the Life, Travels, and Gospel Labours of . . . Job Scott (Warrington, 1798) 93–268.

SHAW, Maj. Samuel (1754–1794) of Boston, first American consul at Canton.

Consular journal, February 1784–July 1789; first and second voyages to Canton, visit to Bengal, return to Canton, and voyage home; partly diary, partly narrative; valuable details of American commerce with China and the East, a good picture of Chinese life; formal style.

The Journals of Major Samuel Shaw (Boston, 1847) 131–334.

SHOEMAKER, Samuel (*d.* 1800) of Philadelphia.

Private diary, October 10, 1784 (extract); a loyalist's conversation with George III.

Pennsylvania Mag. Hist. Biog. II (1878) 35–39.

WHITE, Nancy (1768–1832) of Brookline, Mass.

Schoolgirl's diary, January 1784–July 1785; notes of social life and school work of a young girl at Brookline.

The Sagamore (Brookline High School) I (n.d.) 21–24, 53–56, 87–90, 123–126, 157–160, 191–194, II 22–25, 53–56, 87–90.

1785

ALLING, Jeremiah (1763–1830) of Hamden, Conn.

Weather journal, April 1785–March 1811; brief notes, mainly of weather at Hamden, Conn.

A Register of the Weather (New Haven, 1810) 84 pp.

BENTLEY, Rev. Dr. William (1759–1819) of Salem, Mass.

Private diary, April 1785–December 1819; extensive and varied notes on his life in Salem; personal affairs, reading, weather, social affairs, local news, shipping, etc.; a most valuable and interesting diary.

The Diary of William Bentley, D.D. (Salem, 1905–1914), four vols. Extracts relating to Topsfield in *Topsfield Hist. Soc. Colls.* XX 49–66. Accounts of the diary, with extracts, in *Essex Inst. Hist. Colls.* LIV (1918) 1–21; *Harvard Theol. Rev.* IX (1916) 84–107.

BUELL, Sergt. Joseph (*d.* 1812) of Killingworth, Conn.

Military journal, December 1785–September 1787 (fragments); brief notes of military movements and happenings on frontier, in region from Fort McIntosh to Post Vincent on the Wabash.

S. P. Hildreth, *Pioneer History* (Cincinnati, 1848) 140–164.

FISH, Elisha (1762–1833) of Portsmouth, R.I.

Private diary, April 1785–December 1799; brief scattered notes; mainly visits to Friends' meetings; Quaker affairs at Newport and other Rhode Island towns; necrology.

New England Hist. Geneal. Reg. LVI (1902) 121–132.

FORD, Timothy (1762–1830) *b.* Morristown, N.J., of Charleston, S.C.

Travel diary, October 1785–November 1786 (extracts); group notes for October 1785, describing journey from New York to South Carolina; then scattered notes describing the South.

South Carolina Hist. Geneal. Mag. XIII (1912) 132–147, 181–204.

HADFIELD, Joseph (1759–1851) of Manchester, Eng.

Tourist's journal, June–October 1785; tour from New York to Canada, Montreal, Niagara, Quebec; return to Boston; meetings with distinguished people; quite interesting.

D. S. Robertson (ed.), *An Englishman in America* (Toronto, 1933) 232 pp.

HAYNES, Rev. Lemuel (1753–1833) of Rutland, Vt., and Granville, N.Y.

Travel diary, July–August 1785; travel in Vermont, preaching, and visits.

Timothy M. Cooley, *Sketches of the Life and Character of the Rev. Lemuel Haynes* (New York, 1839) 73–76.

HEART, Capt. Jonathan (1748–1791) of Farmington, Conn.

Military journal, September–October 1785; march from New Windsor, N.Y., to Fort Pitt, via Easton, Reading, Carlisle, Bedford, etc.; mainly notes of marches.

C. W. Butterfield (ed.), *Journal of Capt. Jonathan Heart* (Albany, 1885) 1–26.

HUNTER, John (Englishman).

Travel diary, November 1785 (extract); visit to Washington at Mount Vernon.

Pennsylvania Mag. Hist. Biog. XVII (1893) 76–82.

MONTGOMERY, Samuel.

Travel journal, August–October 1785; travels of a government agent through Indian country beyond Ohio River; impersonal and formal notes.

Mississippi Valley Hist. Rev. II (1915–1916) 261–273.

OCCOM, Samson (1723–1792) of Lebanon, Conn.

Missionary journal, October 1785–November 1787 (extracts); travel and missionary work among Oneida and Connecticut Indians; journeys, meetings, sermons, etc.; a good journal, with some interesting spellings.

W. DeLoss Love, *Samson Occom* (Boston, 1899) 249–275.

Porter, Gen. Andrew (1743–1813) of Worcester, Pa., surveyor.

Travel and surveying journals, May–September 1785 and July–September 1786 (extracts); fixing western boundary of Pennsylvania.

Pennsylvania Mag. Hist. Biog. IV (1880) 268–285 ("A Sketch of the Life of Gen. Andrew Porter").

Ravenel, René (1762–1822) of Pooshee, S.C.

Private diary, April 1785–November 1821; brief notes of journeys, visits, family affairs, deaths, work, education of children, etc.

Henry E. Ravenel, *Ravenel Records* (Atlanta, 1898) 225–251.

Van Cleve, Benjamin (1773–1821) of Dayton, O.

1. Personal and travel diaries, November 1785–April 1786; scattered extracts included among his memoirs; migration from New Jersey to Pennsylvania; journey from Fort Washington to Philadelphia on official business; military career (including trial for making soldiers drunk); surveying and farming in Ohio; life in Cincinnati and Dayton; grocery work at Greenville; politics; a varied and interesting record.

B. W. Bond (ed.), *"Memoirs of Benjamin Van Cleve," Quar. Pubs. Ohio Hist. Philos. Soc.* XVII (1922) 11–14, 30–41, 45–58.

2. Travel diary, May–June 1794; journey to Fort Massac and vicinity.

Illinois Hist. Soc. Trans. (1903) 62–64.

1786

Dunlap, William (1766–1839) of New York City, playwright and painter.

Private diary, November 1786–December 1834 (with large gaps); activities as playwright and painter; personal and domestic entries; journeys to New England and Canada; a valuable diary for its picture of Dunlap and his circle.

New York Hist. Soc. Colls. (1929, 1930, 1931) three vols.

Haldimand, Gen. Sir Frederick (1718–1791), Governor General of Canada.

Private diary, January 1786–August 1790; deals largely with "the busy occupations of an idle man"; visiting; card playing, etc.; a good gossipy journal, quite frank and intimate, affording a picture of aristocratic and political life; kept in England. French with English translation.

Report on Canadian Archives, 1889 (Ottawa, 1890) 124–299.

Hull, Henry (1765–1834)of Stanford, N.Y.

Quaker journal, March 1786–October 1813; conversion, travels, and religious experiences of a ministering Quaker; southern states, Ireland, New York, Canada, Ohio, etc.; notes on slavery, social conditions, Popery, education, child labor; interesting for reformist aspects of Quakerism.

Friends' Library IV (Philadelphia, 1840) 242–304.

JUDD, Eben (1761–1837) of Guildhall, Vt.

Surveying journal, September 1786–April 1787 (extracts); surveying in Essex County, Vt.; meetings, Thanksgiving celebrations; scattered and rather dull entries.

Vermont Hist. Gazetteer I (1867) 944–946.

MATTHEWS, John (*b.* 1765) of New Braintree, Mass.

Private diary, July 1786–April 1788; journey from Massachusetts to Ohio; incidents in survey of Seven Ranges, Ohio; topographical and surveying notes; some social and Indian notes.

S. P. Hildreth *Pioneer History* (Cincinnati, 1848) 170–192.

RUSSELL, Gilbert (1760–1829) of New Bedford, Mass.

Quaker travel journal, October–December 1786; account and extracts; in Connecticut, New York, and Massachusetts; notes on travel, taverns, food, meetings.

Daniel Ricketson, *The History of New Bedford* (New Bedford, 1858) 169–175.

SEWALL, Rev. Jotham (1760–1850) of Chesterville, Me.

Religious journal, May 1786–September 1850 (copious extracts); lengthy notes of missionary journeys, religious meditations, social affairs, etc.; used as basis for biography.

Jotham Sewall, *A Memoir of Rev. Jotham Sewall* (Boston, 1853) 408 pp. *passim.*

STEVENS, James, of Halifax Co., Va.

Travel diary, May–October 1786 and January 1787 (fragments); voyage from Norfolk, Va., to Scotland; Glasgow; visits to friends, relatives, court of law in Scotland; amusing notes.

Virginia Mag. Hist. Biog. XXIX (1921) 387–400.

TRUMBULL, John (1756–1843) of Lebanon, Conn., painter.

Travel diary, August–October 1786; visit to France, Germany, and Flanders; impressions of paintings, etc.

Autobiography, Reminiscences, and Letters of John Trumbull (New Haven, 1841) 101–146.

WARDER, Mrs. Ann (*ca.* 1758–1829) *b.* London, of Philadelphia.

Private diary, June 1786–October 1788; life at Philadelphia; social and personal notes; very lively style and varied details of the social round of a young matron; visits, parties, dinners.

Pennsylvania Mag. Hist. Biog. XVII (1893) 444–461, XVIII (1894) 51–63.

1787

ADAMS, John Quincy (1767–1848) of Braintree, Mass., sixth President of the United States.

1. Private diary, August 1787–September 1789; social life in Newburyport; detailed picture of life in a small New England town; notes on some journeys.

Massachusetts Hist. Soc. Proc. (1902) 295–462; also in *Life in a New England Town* (Boston, 1903) 204 pp. Extracts relating to Samuel Putnam, *Danvers Hist. Soc. Proc.* XXVIII (1940) 37–45.

2. Private diary, June 1794–January 1848; personal and political affairs; an extensive and invaluable record.

Charles F. Adams (ed.), *Memoirs of John Quincy Adams, Comprising Portions of His Diary from 1795 to 1848* (Philadelphia, 1874–1877) twelve vols. One-volume selection edited by Allan Nevins (New York, 1928) 585 pp.

ATTMORE, William (*d.* 1800) of Philadelphia, merchant.

Travel diary, November–December 1787; voyage and tour in Virginia and North Carolina; long entries; entertainments, horse races, social affairs; very lively and amusing picture of the Old South.

Edited by L. T. Rodman, *James Sprunt Hist. Pubs.* XVII (1922) 46 pp.

CLINTON, Cornelia, second daughter of Gov. George Clinton.

Diary *ca.* 1787; extract relating to her visit to the governor.

New York Geneal. Biog. Rec. XX (1889) 40–41.

COGSWELL, Dr. Mason Fitch (1761–1830) of Canterbury, Conn.

Travel diary, November–December 1787; horseback journeys through Connecticut; entertaining social observations, combined with reminiscences.

Connecticut Mag. V (1899) 532–537, 562–569, 606–614.

DEWEES, Mrs. Mary, of Philadelphia.

Travel diary, September 1787–January 1788; from Philadelphia to Kentucky by road and flatboat; lively descriptions.

Pennsylvania Mag. Hist. Biog. XXVIII (1904) 182–198. Extract in John W. Harpster, *Pen Pictures of Early Western Pennsylvania* (Pittsburgh, 1938) 177–185.

DICKINSON, Rebecca (*b.* 1738) of Hatfield, Mass.

Private diary, July 1787–August 1802; a good diary of a spinster's personal life; visits, social affairs, deaths, illnesses, opinions.

D. W. Wells, *History of Hatfield* (Springfield, 1910) 206–207.

ENYS, Capt., of 29th Regiment.

Travel diary, July 1787; visit to Niagara, and long description of the Falls.

Rept. Canadian Archives, 1886 (Ottawa, 1887) ccxxvi–ccxxxiii; C. M. Dow, *Anthology and Bibliography of Niagara Falls* (Albany, 1931) I 74–89.

HARDY, Capt. Phineas (1763–1829) of Bradford, Mass.

Military journal, January–February 1787; notes of a march from Andover, to suppress Shays' Rebellion; very brief.

New England Hist. Geneal. Reg. VII (1853) 352.

KINGSBURY, Col. Jonathan (1751–1806) of Needham, Mass.

Military journal, January 1787–June 1788; notes on Shays' Rebellion, and some courts-martial.

Needham Epitaphs 41. [Forbes.]

LITTLE, Rev. Daniel (*d.* 1801) of Wells-Kennebunk, Me.

Diary, September 1787; extract describing fight with a drunken fur trader at Condeskeeg, Me.

Bangor Hist. Mag. V (1889–1890) 168–169.

PRESTON, Samuel, of Pennsylvania, surveyor.

Surveying journal, June–July 1787 (extracts); journey to survey lands in Pike County, Pa.; a good journal, with stories of Indian captures, etc.

Pennsylvania Mag. Hist. Biog. XXII (1898) 350–365.

1788

BACKUS, James (1764–1816) of Marietta, O.

Travel diary, April 1788–May 1791; journey from Pennsylvania to Marietta and private life there; clearing for farm; good picture of pioneer life, settlers, Indians and their customs, hunting, weather, journeys, organization of community; work as agent for the Ohio Company.

William W. Backus, *A Genealogical Memoir of the Backus Family* (1889) 16–102.

BRISSOT DE WARVILLE, Jacques Pierre (1754–1793) of France.

Travel diary, May–November 1788; in letter form; journey through New England and some southern states. Translated.

New Travels in the United States of America (London, 1792) 483 pp., and published separately in same year at Dublin and New York; reprinted New York (1794); Boston (1797) 276 pp., Bowling Green, O. (1919) 544 pp. Extracts relating to Boston in 1788 in *Old South Leaflets* VI (1902) No. 126.

BULFINCH, Hannah (1768–1841) of Boston, Mass.

Private diary, 1788–October 1815; brief, scattered quotations of little value.

Ellen S. Bulfinch, *Life and Letters of Charles Bulfinch* (Boston, 1896) 91, 104–109, 141–143, 187–190.

COPLAND, Charles, of Virginia, lawyer.

Private diary, December 1788–June 1823; unmethodical register of domestic events, expenses, journeys, etc.; scrappy, but with occasional amusing or interesting items, such as theater fire at Richmond, and canal trip to Ohio.

William and Mary Coll. Quar. 1st Ser. XIV (1905–1906) 44–50, 217–230.

DAY, Rev. Jeremiah (1737–1806) of New Preston, Conn.

Clergyman's journal, September–October 1788; preaching tour in Vermont; travel notes, visits; brief notes.

Vermont Hist. Soc. Proc. n.s. I (1930) 169–176. Extracts in Ellen D. Putnam, *Some Chronicles of the Day Family* (Cambridge, Mass., 1893) 15–17.

HAMTON, James (1764–1792) of Wrightstown, Pa.

Quaker journal, January 1788–1789; schoolmastering and Quaker introspection; meetings.

Friends' Miscellany I (1831) 223–240.

HASWELL, Robert, second mate on "Columbia."

Sea journal, August 1788–May 1789; notes of Gray's voyage, exploring north-west coast; aboard "Columbia Rediviva" and "Washington"; brief notes.

Hubert H. Bancroft, *History of the Northwest Coast* I 187–207 *passim* (in his *Works*, San Francisco, 1886, XXVII).

McCLELLAN, John (1767–1858) of Woodstock, Conn.

Travel diary, May–June 1788; horseback journey from Lebanon to Albany and return; notes on scenery and taverns; fair interest.

Connecticut Mag. IX (1905) 185–189.

MAY, Col. John (1748–1812) of Boston and Portland.

Travel diary, April–August 1788; a good diary; business journeys, with goods and employees, in Pennsylvania and across grade roads to Marietta, O.; notes on hunting, personal affairs, incidents of journeys, life of first settlers of Ohio, etc.

W. M. Darlington (ed.), *Journal and Letters of Col. John May of Boston* (Cin-cinnati, 1873) 160 pp. Extracts published in *Pennsylvania Mag. Hist. Biog.* XLV (1927) 101–179; *New England Hist. Geneal. Reg.* XXX (1876) 43–49.

PENN, John (1760–1834) of London, Eng., "miscellaneous writer."

Travel diary, April 1788; visit to Reading, Pa., etc.; pleasant descriptions; visit to Muhlenberg and Gen. Mifflin.

Pennsylvania Mag. Hist. Biog. III (1879) 284–295; James B. Nolan, *Early Narratives of Berks County* (Reading, 1927) 121–130.

PRICE, Joseph (*b.* 1753) of Merion, Pa.

Private diary, December 1788–April 1810 (extracts); notes on gossip, morals, services, local affairs, deaths, weddings; fairly good, with interesting spellings.

Bull. Hist. Soc. Montgomery County (Pa.) I (1937) 55–66.

SAUGRAIN DE VIGNI, Antoine François (1763–1821) of Paris and Lexington, Ky., scientist and physician.

Travel diary, May–July 1788; Louisville to Philadelphia; descriptions of towns and route. Translated from the French.

Amer. Antiq. Soc. Proc. n.s. XIX (1908–1909) 230–238.

SHREVE, Col. Israel (1739–1799) of Mansfield, N.J.

Travel diary, July–August 1788; journey from Jersey to Rottroven on the Monongahela; difficulties of travel with family and cattle; a fairly good diary with some interesting spellings.

Pennsylvania Mag. Hist. Biog. LII (1928) 193–204; *Mag. Amer. Hist.* II (1878) Part II 741–748; L. P. Allen, *The Genealogy and History of the Shreve Family* (Greenfield, Ill., 1901) 603–611.

WILLIAMS, Timothy (1764–1849) of West Woodstock, Conn.

1. Private diary, July–August 1788; personal and local affairs, and notes of important public matters.

2. April–March 1815; sermons, texts, and notes.

Putnam Patriot. [Forbes.]

1789 '

ANON.

Surveying journal, June–August 1789; survey of the south shore of Lake Erie; little except surveying measurements, topography, etc.

Buffalo Hist. Soc. Pubs. VII (1904) 365–376.

CLARKE, Mrs. Aletta, of Sussex Co., Del.

Private diary, April 1789–February 1793; brief notes of family affairs, visits, domestic details; quite interesting for everyday life; some interesting words.

C. H. B. Turner, *Some Records of Sussex County, Delaware* (Philadelphia, 1909) 350–369.

COLNETT, Capt. James (*ca.* 1752–1806) *b.* Plymouth, Eng., R.N.

Sea and trading journal, January 1789–November 1791; in command of trading expedition of United Merchants to China aboard "Prince of Wales" and "Princess Royal" and trading voyage in the "Argonaut" to the northwest coast of America; latter journey is greatest part of diary; largely deals with capture of his vessels by the Spaniards in Nootka Sound, and relative documents; valuable historically for Spanish-American-British political and trading relations.

Judge F. W. Howay (ed.), *The Journal of Captain James Colnett* (Toronto, 1940) 328 pp.

DAVIS, Samuel (1765–1829) of Plymouth, Mass.

Travel diary, August–September 1789; horseback journey from Plymouth to Fairfield, Conn., and by water to New York; good observations of people and places.

Massachusetts Hist. Soc. Proc. 1st Ser. XI (1869–1870) 9–32.

HAY, Maj. Henry (*b.* 1765) of Detroit.

Travel diary, December 1789–April 1790; journey from Detroit to the Miami and winter at Fort Wayne; excellent picture of pioneer life in the old Northwest, among French settlers; border forays and horrors; social life and customs, fur trade, dances and amusements, music, games, etc.; vivid picture.

Edited by M. M. Quaife, *Wisconsin Hist. Soc. Proc.* (1914) 208–261; reprinted in *Indiana Hist. Soc. Pubs.* VII (1923) 295–361.

MACKENZIE, Sir Alexander (1763–1820) *b.* Stornoway, Scotland, of Northwest Company.

Exploring journals, June–September 1789, and October 1792–August 1793, expeditions on behalf of Northwest Fur Company; the first from Fort Chippewayan on Lake Athabasca, to the Arctic, which settled "the dubious point of a Northwest passage"; the second, an expedition to the Pacific. The classic of pioneer exploration in this area and, like most of the Canadian exploration journals, exceedingly good reading; written in simple style with good details and descriptions.

Voyages from Montreal, on the River St. Lawrence, through the Continent of North America to the Frozen and Pacific Oceans, in 1789 and 1793 (London, 1801) 412 pp.

MACLAY, William (1734–1804) *b.* New Garden, Pa., senator.

Political diary, April 1789–March 1791; political details of the first three sessions of first Congress; valuable and lively picture of debates, ceremonies, and accompanying social and personal activities; good pictures of contemporary politicians and of himself; important and highly interesting.

E. S. Maclay (ed.), *The Journal of William Maclay* (New York, 1890, 1927) 429 pp. Short selection in Mark Van Doren (ed.), *An Autobiography of America* (New York, 1929) 174–187.

MEACHAM, James (1763–1820) of Mecklenburg Co., Va.

Travel diary, May–August 1789, July–December 1791, February–November 1792, October–December 1796, January–June 1797 (extracts); travels in Virginia of an itinerant Methodist minister; antislavery sentiments.

Trinity Coll. Hist. Soc. Papers IX (1912) 66–95, X (1914) 87–102.

MORRIS, Gouverneur (1752–1816) of Westchester, N.Y., minister to France.

Political and social diary, March 1789–January 1793; the great American diary of the French Revolution; a splendid work for both historian and general reader.

Anne Cary Morris (ed.), *The Diary and Letters of Gouverneur Morris* (New York, 1888) two vols., containing letters and items from later years of the diary, embedded in biography (so also, Jared Sparks, *The Life of Gouverneur Morris* [Boston, 1832] Vol. I). New and complete edition, Beatrix C. Davenport (ed.), *A Diary of the French Revolution* (Boston, 1939) two vols.

PERKINS, Rev. Nathan (1749–1838) of Hartford, Conn.

Travel journal, April–June 1789; through Connecticut, Massachusetts, and Vermont, to Burlington, and return; descriptions and opinions of the new settlements; lively and frank uncensored opinions; very interesting.

A Narrative of a Tour through the State of Vermont (Woodstock, Vt., 1920) 31 pp.

PERKINS, Thomas Handasyd (1764–1854) of Boston.

Foreign-travel diaries, July 1789–September 1835 (with gaps); in Batavia, with lengthy description of places and customs; events in Paris in spring of 1795; travel through France and Holland; travel in England; general travel in Europe in 1835; full descriptions of places, people, and customs, largely in style of travel book; fairly interesting.

Thomas G. Cary, *Memoir of Thomas Handasyd Perkins* (Boston, 1856) 304 pp. *passim.*

POWELL, Ann (*b.* 1769) of Montreal.

Travel diary, May–June 1789; tour from Montreal to Detroit; seminarrative, with irregular dates; description of St. Lawrence, Lake Ontario, Niagara Falls; camping, and touristic observations.

Mag. Amer. Hist. V (1880) 37–47; W. R. Reddell, *The Life of William Dummer Powell* (Lansing, 1924) 60–73. Extracts in C. M. Dow, *Anthology and Bibliography of Niagara Falls* I (Albany, 1921) 89–91.

1790

ANON. (member of firm, Reed and Forde, of Philadelphia).

Travel diary, October 1790–January 1791; notes of a journey from Philadelphia to New Madrid, Tenn.; difficulties of navigation on the Ohio and Mississippi.

Pennsylvania Mag. Hist. Biog. XXXVI (1912) 209–216.

ARMSTRONG, Capt. John, of U.S. Army.

Military journal, September–October 1790; Harmar's punitive expedition against Indians above the Wabash headquarters; troop movements from Fort Washington; defeat by Indians; fair interest.

Basil Meek, "General Harmar's Expedition," *Ohio Archaeol. Hist. Quar.* XX (1911) 79–84; John B. Dillon, *History of Indiana* (Indianapolis, 1859) 245–248.

BLOUNT, William (1749–1800), territorial governor of Tennessee.

Official journal, October 1790–January 1796; administrative and military details.

Amer. Hist. Mag. (Nashville) II (1897) 213–277.

BROWN, William.

Travel diary, August–November 1790; from Hanover County to Kentucky, along the Ohio route; notes of distances, etc.

T. Speed, *The Wilderness Road, Filson Club Pubs.* II (1886) 56–63.

CHAPLIN, Rev. Ebenezer (1733–1822) of Sutton, Mass.

Clergyman's diary, October 1790–January 1794 (extracts); brief notes of parish and church work, personal affairs, and weather.

H. L. Shumway, "An Old-Time Minister," *Worcester Soc. Antiq. Proc.* V (1882) 44–66.

FERRIS, Zachariah (1716–1803) of Wilmington, Del.

Quaker travel diary, October 1790–February 1791; visits to Quaker meetings, in journeys from Wrightsborough, Ga., to Wilmington; preceded by brief memoranda of meetings visited on journey southward from Gaines River, Va.; interesting spellings.

Bull. Friends' Hist. Soc. XXII (1933) 58–70.

FULLER, Miss Elizabeth (1775–1856) of Princeton, Mass.

Private diary, October 1790–December 1792; a charming record of the minutiae of a girl's domestic and social life in Princeton; cookery, housewifery, visits, education; some doggerel verses; interesting vocabulary.

Frances E. Blake, *History of the Town of Princeton* (Princeton, Mass., 1915) 302–322.

HARMAR, Gen. Josiah (1753–1813) of Philadelphia.

Military journal, September–November 1790; unsuccessful punitive expedition against Indians above Wabash headquarters; troop movements around Little and Great Miami, etc.

Basil Meek, "General Harmar's Expedition," *Ohio Archaeol. Hist. Quar.* XX (1911) 89–96.

HEWARD, Hugh (*d.* 1803) of Detroit, fur trader.

Travel journal, March–May 1790; from Detroit to the Illinois by canoe; full details of travel; impersonal but interesting.

M. M. Quaife (ed.), *The John Askin Papers* I (Detroit, 1928) 339–360.

L'HOMMEDIEU, Mrs. Abigail (1774–1851) of Norwich, Conn.

Private diary, 1790–1841 (extracts undated); fragmentary but interesting notes; personal, social, love affairs, journeys.

Mary E. Perkins, *Old Houses of the Antient Town of Norwich* (Norwich, 1895) 26–30.

MACLAY, Samuel (1741–1811) of Buffalo Valley, Pa., senator.

Surveying journal, April–September 1790; on the Susquehannah to examine headwaters of the Susquehannah, and streams of northwestern Pennsylvania territory recently purchased; stages, weather, taverns, adventures, camp life, relations with settlers; rather impersonal, but quite interesting.

The Historical Journal (Williamsport, Pa.) I (1887) 137–151, 169–187, 201–216; published separately as *Journal of Samuel Maclay* (Williamsport, 1887) 63 pp.

MARSHALL and BENZIEN, of Salem, N.C., Moravians.

Travel journal, November 1790–December 1791 (extracts); journey by the authors, accompanied by a Negro "Brother Johann Samuel"; inspecting lands given by Henry Laurens; observation of the land, seeking opportunities for the brethren.

Adelaide L. Fries (ed.), *Records of the Moravians in North Carolina* (Raleigh, 1922–1941) V 1989–1997.

POPE, Col. John (1770–1845) of Lexington, Ky., senator.

Travel diary, June 1790–August 1791; travel through southern and western states; Mississippi and Ohio valleys; notes on Creek Indians, scenery, towns, social customs; literary style; fair.

A Tour through the Southern and Western Territories (Richmond, 1792), reprinted (New York, 1888) 104 pp. Extracts relating to Tennessee in S. C. Williams, *Early Travels in the Tennessee Country* (Johnson City, 1928) 318–319.

SEVIER, John (1745–1815) *b.* Augusta, Va., first governor of Tennessee.

Personal diary, May 1790–September 1815; mostly line-a-day; details of ordinary daily routine and thought; weather, chief public and social affairs; some linguistic interest.

Tennessee Hist. Mag. V (1919) 156–194, 232–264, VI (1920) 18–60; S. G. Heiskel, *Andrew Jackson and Early Tennessee History* (Nashville, 1920) II 503–614.

SMITH, William Loughton (1762–1812) of Charleston, S.C.

1. Political diary, August–September 1790; while member of House of Representatives; visit to Rhode Island when it came into Union; return to New York; descriptions of people and places.

2. Travel diary, April–May 1791; Philadelphia to Charleston; detailed description of historic sights on way, Mount Vernon, etc.

New York *Evening Post*, April 14, 21, 28, May 5, June 2, 1888; *Massachusetts Hist. Soc. Proc.* LI (1917–1918) 20–76, where earlier text is corrected.

STANLEY, Maj. William (*d.* 1814) of Cincinnati, O.

Private diary, November 1790–October 1809; mainly concerned with his business and journeys, as one of principal merchants of Cincinnati; hurried, brief entries, but gives good picture of frontier trade; some interesting spellings.

Quar. Pubs. Hist. Philos. Soc. Ohio XIV (1919) 19–32.

WALCUTT, Thomas (1758–1840) of Boston, Mass.

Travel diary, January–April 1790; travel to Marietta, O., via Virginia route, and return to Philadelphia; substantial entries; interesting details of public and social affairs of the new settlements; pleasant travel notes; taverns, food, etc.

Massachusetts Hist. Soc. Proc. 1st Ser. XVII (1879–1880) 174–206 (normalized); A. B. Hulbert, *Historic Highways of America* XII (Cleveland, 1904) 43–63.

1791

AUPAMUT, Capt. Hendrick ("chief of the remnant of the tribe by some called *Mohicans*").

Travel journal, May–October 1791; written up from notes; journey to western Indians; conferences. Interesting as an Indian's description of his people and his opinions on their treatment by the white men; speaks for United States against Britain.

Pennsylvania Hist. Soc. Memoirs II (1827–1830) 76–131.

BRADLEY, Capt. Daniel (*d.* 1825) of Fairfield, Conn.

Military journals, August 1791–January 1795; expeditions of St. Clair and Wayne against Maumee Indians; marches, skirmishes, some notes on countryside and garrison life.

Frazer E. Wilson (ed.), *Journal of Capt. Daniel Bradley* (Greenville, O., 1935) 75 pp.

CAMPBELL, Patrick (*d.* 1823), formerly of 42d Regiment.

Travel journal, June 1791–December 1792; from Scotland to St. John's, Fredericton, Quebec, Montreal, Niagara, Genesee, Albany, New York, New Jersey, St. John's, Scotland; notes on farming, Indians, soil, climate, social affairs, politics; good observations in simple style.

Travels in the Interior Inhabited Parts of North America (Edinburgh, 1793) 387 pp.; edited by H. H. Langton and W. F. Ganong (Toronto, 1937) 326 pp. Extract for November 1791 in *Ontario Hist. Soc. Papers and Recs.* XXI (1924) 91–98.

CRESSON, Caleb (1742–1816) of Philadelphia.

Private diary, January 1791–December 1792; notes on life in Philadelphia; journey to New England, with good descriptions and accounts of historic scenes.

Diary of Caleb Cresson (Philadelphia, 1877) 214 pp.

FIDLER, Peter, of Hudson's Bay Company, surveyor's assistant.

Canadian exploration journal, September 1791–April 1792; journey with Chippewa Indians to Slave Lake and east and west of Slave River; many notes of travel, personal observations, Indian affairs and customs, and stories; a very entertaining journal of fur-trading life.

J. B. Tyrrell (ed.), *Journals of Samuel Hearne and Philip Turnor* (Toronto, 1934) 493–555.

GREEN, Rev. Ashbel (1762–1848) of Philadelphia and College of New Jersey.

Travel diary, June–July 1791 (extracts); preaching, work as pastor of Second Presbyterian Church in Philadelphia; journeys into New England, etc.; work as president of College of New Jersey.

Joseph H. Jones, *The Life of Ashbel Green* (New York, 1849) 204–472 *passim*.

INGRAHAM, Capt. Joseph (1714–1799) of Boston.

Sea journal, April 1791 (extracts); journey of the brigantine "Hope" from Boston to the northwest coast of America.

Massachusetts Hist. Soc. Colls. II (1793) 20–24.

KERSHAW, James (*b.* 1764) of Camden, S.C.

Private diary, April 1791–June 1815 (extracts); very brief notes of social affairs at Camden; lively details of amusements, fashions, people, plays, etc.

Thomas J. Kirkland and Robert M. Kennedy, *Historic Camden* (Columbia, S.C., 1905) I 404–413.

LINCKLAEN, John (*b.* 1768) of Cazenovia, N.Y.

Travel journals, August 1791–October 1792 (with gaps); journeys on behalf of Holland Land Company, in Pennsylvania, New York, Vermont; descriptions of places; professional and a little dull.

Travels in the Years 1791 and 1792 (New York and London, 1897) 162 pp.

MAIR, John (1744–1830) of Iron Acton, Eng.

Travel diary, January–July 1791; visit to United States and Canada; London to Charleston, Philadelphia, New York, Boston, Hartford, Albany, Fort George, Montreal, Quebec; good descriptions of a "civilised" man looking at strange people in a strange country.

Amer. Hist. Rev. XII (1906–1907) 77–94.

MARTIN, Rev. Isaac (1757–1828) of Rahway, East Jersey.

Quaker journal, June 1791–June 1823; notes on church work, travels, religious reflections, reading.

A Journal of the Life, Travels, Labours, of Isaac Martin (Philadelphia, 1834) 160 pp.

NEWMAN, Capt. Samuel (*d.* 1791) of Boston and 2d Regiment.

Military journal, July–October 1791; St. Clair's campaign against northwestern Indians; good picture of army life; journey with his company to Philadelphia, thence to Cincinnati, and advance northward; highly personal, with excellent details of deplorable moral and disciplinary state of army.

Wisconsin Mag. Hist. II (1918–1919) 40–73.

[O'BRIEN, Joseph, of Newburyport, Mass.?]

Private diary, December 1791–1815; brief notes of outstanding personal, local, and public events around Newburyport.

Essex Inst. Hist. Colls. XLIV (1908) 332–337.

PROCTOR, Col. Thomas (1739–1806) of Philadelphia.

Commissioner's journal, March–May 1791; official report of journey from Philadelphia to Buffalo Creek and around Lake Erie; accounts of Indians and their customs; treaty with Six Nations; carefully written official report.

Pennsylvania Archives 2d Ser. IV 465–524; William Ketchum, *An Authentic and Comprehensive History of Buffalo* (Buffalo, 1864–1865), I 413–426, II 305–318.

RAMSAY, Martha Laurens (1759–1811) of Charleston, S.C.

Private diary, July 1791–June 1808; religious reflections and self-analysis, self-abasements; ejaculatory style; a few notes of illnesses, deaths, church services.

David Ramsay, *Memoirs of the Life of Martha Laurens Ramsay* (Boston, 1812) App. V 122–208; reprinted Philadelphia (1845).

SAUNDERS, Daniel, of Salem, Mass.

Seaman's journal, May 1791–August 1794; narrative, partly in diary form; escapes and sufferings in the Arabian desert.

A Journal of the Travels and Sufferings of Daniel Saunders (Salem, 1794) 128 pp.; reprinted (Leominster, Mass., 1797) 104 pp.; again (Salem, 1824) 48 pp.; again (Exeter, N.H., 1830) 71 pp. A long selection in Ralph D. Paine, *Ships and Sailors of Old Salem* (New York 1909) chaps. xiii and xiv, 252–287.

SIMCOE, Mrs. Elizabeth Posthuma (1766–1850) *b.* Whitchurch, Herefordshire, wife of lieutenant governor of Upper Canada.

Private diary September 1791–October 1796; begins just before her departure from England for Quebec and covers the four years of her husband's tenure of the lieutenant governorship; simple and charming notes on her life at Niagara and York; good picture of pioneer life in Canada; interesting drawings.

J. R. Robertson (ed.), *The Diary of Mrs. John Graves Simcoe* (Toronto, 1911) 440 pp. Extracts in article, *Niagara Hist. Soc. Pubs.* No. 36 (1924) 38–54.

1792

ANON. (member of crew of the "Chatham").

Sea journal, March–October 1792; kept during Vancouver's voyage to northwest coast; accounts of Nootkas, etc., descriptions of country, and movements of expedition; possibly by Edward Bell, clerk.

Washington Hist. Quar. V (1914) 129–137, 215–224, 300–308, VI (1915) 50–68.

CARPENTER, Capt. Benjamin, of Salem.

Sea journal, May 1792; voyage of the "Hercules" from Boston to the East Indies; notes on ports and trade; selections.

Ralph D. Paine, *Ships and Sailors of Old Salem* (New York, 1909) chap. xxi 417–439 *passim*.

CUTTING, Nathaniel (*d.* 1822) of Newburyport and Brookline, Mass.

1. Travel diary, September 1792–January 1793 (extract); visit to Boston from Providence; extensive notes describing sights, places, social life of Boston; well written and interesting.

Massachusetts Hist. Soc. Proc. 1st Ser. XII (1871–1873) 60–67.

2. Travel diary, August 1793–February 1794 (with gap); voyage from Lisbon to Algiers, with embassy under Col. David Humphreys.

Hist. Mag. IV (1860) 262–265, 359–363.

FARIS, William (1728–1804) *b.* London, of Annapolis, Md.

Private diary, January 1792–August 1804 (extracts); gossipy record of life, death, etc., in Annapolis; brief notes, but quite interesting.

Maryland Hist. Mag. XXVIII (1933) 197–244.

FRYE, Joseph, of Fryeburg, Me., town clerk.

Private diary, September 1792–March 1797 (extracts); brief notes of his doings in Fryeburg; musters, church, journeys, weather, etc.

John S. Barrows, *Fryeburg, Maine* (Fryeburg, 1938) 46–48.

HALL, Rev. Rufus (*b.* 1744) of Northampton, N.Y.

Quaker journal, October 1792–January 1814; preceded by autobiographical entries; whole is partly autobiography, partly journal; usual Quaker journal, meetings and travel in New York, New England, Upper Canada, etc.

A Journal of Rufus Hall (Byberry, Pa., 1840).

HECKEWELDER, John (1743–1823) *b.* Bedford, Eng., of Bethlehem, Pa.

1. Moravian missionary journal, May–December 1792; journey from Bethlehem to the Wabash on peace mission to the Indians; detailed descriptions of river route and settlements; inclined to narrative. Translated from the German.

Johann Heckewälders Reise (Halle, 1797); *Pennsylvania Mag. Hist. Biog.* XI (1887) 466–475, XII (1888) 34–54, 165–184.

2. Travel journal, April–July 1797; from Bethlehem to Gnadenhuetten on the Muskingum, and return; with others to survey lands for Christian Indians; journey and surveying described in interesting detail.

Pennsylvania Mag. Hist. Biog. X (1886) 125–157.

LEE, Benjamin (1765–1828), captain of the "Fair American."

1. Journal of voyage of the "Fair American," January 1792–February 1793.

Mrs. Theodore Roosevelt and Kermit Roosevelt, *American Backlogs* (New York, 1928) 52–64 *passim*.

2. Journal of voyage from New York to China, February–May 1796 (extracts). *Ibid.*, pp. 66–77 *passim*.

MENZIES, Archibald (1754–1842) *b*. near Aberfeldy, Scotland; botanist and surgeon in Royal Navy.

Scientific travel journal, April–October 1792; scientist on George Vancouver's voyage off northwest coast; general diary of happenings, with natural history, general notes, and scientific appendix.

C. F. Newcombe (ed.), "Menzies Journal of Vancouver's Voyage," *Archives Brit. Columbia, Memoir* V (Victoria, 1923) 171 pp.

MICKLE, Samuel (1746–1830) of Woodbury, N.J.

Merchant's diary, March 1792–July 1829; brief entries, personal and local, literary and genealogical; factual but interesting.

F. H. Stewart, *Notes on Old Gloucester County, N.J.* I(1917) 157–253. Extracts in *Year-Book of New Jersey Soc. Pennsylvania* 1921–1924; *Friends' Hist. Soc. Jour.* XXII (1925) 78–79.

PUGET, Lieut. Peter (*ca.* 1764–1822).

Sea journal, May–June 1792 (extract); aboard Vancouver's flagship "Discovery" during exploration of Puget Sound from Port Discovery to Birch Bay; full notes on topography, natural history; historical rather than general interest.

Pacific Northwest Quar. XXX (1939) 177–217.

REID, John, second mate of the "Fair American."

Ship's log, January 1792; cruise from Boston to East Indies; mutiny, ship life; interesting spellings.

Mrs. Theodore Roosevelt and Kermit Roosevelt, *American Backlogs* (New York, 1928) 50–52.

RUSH, Dr. Benjamin (1745–1813) of Philadelphia.

Private diary, March 1792–January 1813; notes of public affairs and public business; visits and social matters; meetings with various eminent scientists (Priestley, etc.); short biographies; a useful record.

Louis A. Biddle, *A Memorial of Dr. Benjamin Rush* (Lanoraie, 1905) 133–215.

VANCOUVER, Capt. George (*ca.* 1758–1798) of the British Navy.

Travel journal, April–October 1792; relating to discovery of Puget Sound; notes on Oregon coast, Indians, etc.; official report.

Whole (April 1791–October 1795) published as *Voyage of Discovery to the North Pacific Ocean and Round the World* (London, 1798) three vols. Extracts relating to Oregon in Edward S. Meany, *Vancouver's Discovery of Puget Sound* (New York, 1907) 61–334, and in *Oregon Hist. Quar.* XXX (1929) 33–42.

1793

BLANCHARD, Jean Pierre.

Journal, January 9, 1793; record of balloon ascension at Philadelphia.

Journal of My Forty-fifth Ascension (Philadelphia, 1793) 27 pp.; *Mag. Hist.* Extra No. 64 (1918) 22 pp.

ELLIOT, James (1775–1839) of Guilford, Vt., and Gloucester, Mass.

Military journal, 1793–1796; kept during Whiskey Rebellion and Indian warfare in the old Northwest, Pennsylvania, and Ohio.

The Poetical and Miscellaneous Works of James Elliot (Greenfield, Mass., 1798) Bk. 3; J. W. Harpster, *Pen Pictures of Early Western Pennsylvania* (Pittsburgh, 1938) 168–175.

Foss, John (1744–1800) of Newburyport, Mass.

Prison diary, July 1793–August 1797; captivity and imprisonment at Algiers; mainly narrative, with vivid description of treatment of American captives by Algerines.

A Journal of the Captivity and Sufferings of John Foss (2d ed., Newburyport, 1798?) 189 pp.

HEMPHILL, James (1774–1833) of Wilmington, Del.

Sea journals and letters, July 1793–1797; extracts in biographical article, describing voyages from Wilmington to Europe and Asia.

Delaware Hist. Soc. Papers VII (1914) Paper No. LXIV.

HUTCHINSON, Jeremy (1738–1805) of Danvers, Mass.

Travel diary, May–June 1793; journey afoot to Danville to visit his daughter; notes on distances, crops, farming, weather; interesting vocabulary.

Danvers Hist. Soc. Colls. XXVIII (1940) 64–69.

LINCOLN, Gen. Benjamin (1733–1810) of Hingham, Mass.

Treaty journal, April–September 1793; treaty negotiations with Indian tribes northwest of Ohio River; journey from Philadelphia to Detroit via Albany and Niagara; negotiations and speeches; return via Montreal; many pleasant notes on travel and social affairs.

Massachusetts Hist. Soc. Colls. 3d Ser. V (1836) 107–176. Extracts in C. M. Dow, *Anthology and Bibliography of Niagara Falls* I (Albany, 1921) 94–97.

LINDLEY, Jacob (1774–1857) of Chester Co., Pa.

1. Travel and treaty journal, April–September 1793; Quaker peace commissioner's journey to Philadelphia, and thence to Sandusky, to attend peace negotiations with Indians; long notes of scenic and social observations, customs of Indians, and interviews with them; travels around Detroit; sympathy toward Indians; a well-written and valuable journal.

Originally published in *Friends' Miscellany* II (Philadelphia, 1836) 50–156; reprinted in *Michigan Pion. and Hist. Colls.* XVII (1890) 565–632.

2. Travel journal, October–November 1797; mission to Friends in Canada and to the Seneca Indians around Buffalo Creek and Niagara; mostly notes of travel and scenery.

Buffalo Hist. Soc. Pubs. VI (1903) 169–182.

LITTLEHALES, Maj., secretary to Governor Simcoe.

Travel journal, February–March 1793; journey with Simcoe through southern Ontario between Niagara and Detroit; notes on Moravians, Indian villages, etc.

London and Middlesex Hist. Soc. Trans. VIII (1917) 6–14 (reprinted from *Canadian Literary Messenger,* 1833).

MACDONELL, Hon. Alexander (1762–1842) of Scotland and Toronto.

1. Canadian travel diary, September–October 1793; kept while author was accompanying Simcoe on journey from Humber Bay to Matchetache Bay.

Canadian Inst. Trans. I (1889–1890) 128–139.

2. Private diary, January 1799; domestic and business life in York (Toronto); political and police interests.

J. E. Middleton and Fred Landon, *The Province of Ontario* (Toronto, 1927) II App. A 1246–1250.

MACDONELL, John (1768–1850) of the Northwest Company.

1. Fur-trading journal, May–October 1793; first trading journey from Lachine to a post on the Upper Assiniboine River; valuable for account of canoe journey from Grand Portage to Lake of the Woods and for notes on life and customs of the voyageurs; good narrative.

Charles M. Gates (ed.), *Five Fur-Traders of the Northwest* (Univ. Minnesota, 1933) 63–119.

2. Fur-trading journal, October 1793–June 1795; brief extracts to illustrate type of journal kept by a clerk of Northwest Company.

L. R. Masson, *Les Bourgeois de la Compagnie du Nord-Ouest* (Quebec, 1889) I 283–295.

MICHAUX, André (1746–1802), French diplomat and botanist.

Travel diary, July 1793–April 1796 (extract); some notes on diplomatic and public affairs, but mainly notes of travel and botanical observations.

This portion translated from the French in R. G. Thwaites (ed.), *Early Western Travels* III (Cleveland, 1904) 27–104; the complete journal in French first published in *Amer. Philos. Soc. Proc.* XXVI (1889) 8–145, covering period April 1787–January 1797.

MOORE, Rev. Joseph (1732–1793) of Flemington, N.J.

Travel and treaty journal, April–September 1793; Quaker peace commissioner's journey from Philadelphia to Sandusky and Detroit to attend peace negotiations with Indians; supplements Jacob Lindley's journal, although it is less complete and less interesting.

Michigan Pion. and Hist. Colls. XVII (1890) 632–666.

PRINCE, Hezekiah (1771–1840) of Kingston, Mass.

Travel journal, November 1793–January 1794; partly narrative; from Kingston to Virginia, 1,200 miles on horseback; notes on scenery, people, places, sights, some social comments; touristic notes, but fairly interesting.

New England Mag. n.s. IX (1893–1894) 723–734.

SAVERY, William (1750–1804) of Philadelphia.

Quaker journal, July 1793–November 1798; travels and work of a ministering Quaker; among Indians around Great Lakes and in Virginia; voyage to and work in England, Ireland, Germany, France; in addition to the usual Quaker notes, it has much description of European places and persons, which is of considerable interest.

Jonathan Evans (ed.), *A Journal of the Life, Travels, and Religious Labours of William Savery* (London, 1844) 316 pp.; *Friends' Library* I (Philadelphia, 1837) 327–459.

WARD, Mrs. Susanna (1779–1860) of Salem, Mass.

Private diary, February 1793–September 1856; brief notes on family, personal, social, and local affairs, and journeys and visits; fair interest.

G. F. Dow (ed.), *The Holyoke Diaries* (Salem, 1911) 175–188.

WILLIAMS FAMILY of Chelsea, Mass.

Diary, April 1793–April 1801 (extracts); apparently kept by the daughters of Henry Howell Williams (1736–1802); social affairs in and around Boston.

William H. Sumner, *A History of East Boston* (Boston, 1858) 331–339.

YARNALL, Rev. Peter (1754–1798) of Byberry, Pa.

Quaker travel journal, May–December 1793; visit to New York and Massachusetts; journey, meetings, visits to Friends; long but impersonal notes.

Mary T. Seaman, *Thomas Richardson of South Shields* (New York, 1929) 176–196. See also, *Friends' Miscellany* II (1832) 253–308.

1794

BALDWIN, John (*b.* 1772) of Newlin, Pa.

Quaker journal, May 1794–December 1798; Quaker introspection, schooling, meetings, personalities.

Friends' Miscellany V (Philadelphia, 1834) 249–269.

BAYARD, Mrs. Martha.

Journal, 1794–1797; kept in London; fashionable social life.

S. Bayard Dod (ed.), *Journal of Martha Pintard Bayard* (New York, 1894) 141 pp.

BOYER, Lieut. John, of Virginia, and 2d Infantry Regiment.

Military journal, July–November 1794; Wayne's campaign against the northwestern Indians; purely military details, mainly of movements of American forces.

A Journal of Wayne's Campaign (Cincinnati, 1866) 23 pp.; extracts in *Michigan Pion. and Hist. Colls.* XXXIV (1904) 539–564.

BROWN, John, of Lewistown, Pa.

Travel diary, December 1794–July 1795; journey in western North Carolina; interesting spellings.

North Carolina Hist. Rev. XI (1934) 284–313.

CAZENOVE, Theophile (1740–1811) of Amsterdam, Holland.

Travel journal, October–November 1794; travels through New Jersey and Pennsylvania, as agent of the Holland Land Company; shrewd, valuable observations on the land and its people; good descriptions of Moravians. Translated from the French.

Haverford Coll. Stud. XIII (1922) 103 pp. Extracts relating to Berks Co., in James B. Nolan, *Early Narratives of Berks County* (Reading, 1927) 157–165.

[CHEW, John, officer of British Indian Dept. for Upper Canada?]

Military journal, June 1794; expedition of Indians against Fort Recovery, U.C.

Mag. Western Hist. XI (1889–1890) 383–388; *Amer. Hist. Mag.* III (1908) 639–643.

CLARK, Lieut. (later, General) William (1770–1838) *b.* Caroline Co., Va.

1. Military journal, July–October 1794; Wayne's campaign against the Shawnee Indians in Ohio; interesting spellings.

Mississippi Valley Hist. Rev. I (1914–1915) 418–444.

2. Travel journal, August–September 1808; journey from St. Louis to Fort Osage trading post; fair picture of the country; many interesting spellings.

K. L. Gregg (ed.), *Westward with Dragoons* (Fulton, Mo., 1937) 21–48.

COOKE, Capt. John (1766–1824) of Northumberland, Pa.

Military journal, July–November 1794; Wayne's campaign; from Greenville, O.; valuable account of movements, marches, fort building; impersonal, plain notes.

Amer. Hist. Rec. II (1873) 311–316, 339–345.

DICKINSON, Rev. Timothy (1761–1813) of Holliston, Mass.

Clergyman's journal, January 1794–November 1808 (with gaps); religious work and reflections, local and general news and comments, visits to Boston, etc.; moderate interest.

Worcester Soc. Antiq. Proc. VI (1883) 67–89.

Dow, Lorenzo (1777–1834) of Coventry, Conn., revivalist.

Religious diary, June 1794–April 1816, with earlier autobiographical entries; account of his life as a Methodist circuit rider in United States, Canada, England, and Ireland; six trips to Mississippi Territory; preaching, camp meetings, spiritual visitations, etc.; long, loud, and lively; a valuable picture of religious zeal and of a great eccentric.

Frequently published under different titles, e.g.: *Perambulations of a Cosmopolite* (Rochester, 1842) 421 pp.; *The Dealings of God, Man, and the Devil* (New York, 1854) two vols. in one. The handiest version is, perhaps, *History of a Cosmopolite* (Cincinnati, 1859) 9–349.

FORD, Capt. David (*d.* 1835) of Morristown, N.J.

Military journal, September–October 1794; the Whiskey Rebellion; expedition into Pennsylvania from New Jersey; descriptions of towns; good accounts of "rebels."

New Jersey Hist. Soc. Proc. VIII (1856–1859) 75–88.

GOULD, Maj. William, of New Jersey Infantry.

Military journal, September–November 1794; the Whiskey Rebellion; march into Pennsylvania from Trenton, N.J.; orders and movements.

New Jersey Hist. Soc. Proc. III (1848–1849) 173–191.

M'GILLIVRAY, Duncan (*d.* 1808) *b.* Inverness-shire, partner in Northwest Company.

Fur-trading journal, July 1794–May 1795; mostly journey to and winter at Fort St. George, Saskatchewan; account of trade and conduct of Indians; a very interesting picture of the character and life of the Indians and of their relation to the traders.

A. S. Morton (ed.), *The Journal of Duncan M'Gillivray* (Toronto, 1929) 79 pp.

MICHAEL, William (1768–1823) of Lancaster, Pa.

Military journal, October–November 1794; march to western Pennsylvania to suppress Whiskey Rebellion; marches, army life, personal adventures; all rather comic, although unintentionally; a long, sad narrative of an unfortunate lady and her troubles is interpolated; literary allusions.

Hist. Reg. (Pa.) I (1883) 64–74, 134–147; *Lancaster Co. Hist. Soc. Papers* (Pa.) XXV No. 7 (1921) 69–77.

NEEDHAM, Parry, of Adams Co., O.

Travel diary, May–June 1794; prospecting journey to the West by boat, with saddles to trade for expenses; Wheeling, Muskingum, Galliopolis, Lexington, Georgetown, Frankfort, Springfield, Cynthiana, Danville, Abington, Shelbyville, etc.; notes on persons, places, soil, etc.; colloquial.

Kentucky Hist. Soc. Reg. XXXIV (1936) 379–391.

PARKIN, Thomas (1774–1797) of Baltimore.

Travel diary, November 1794–October 1795 (extracts); voyage from Baltimore to London; description of London sights; Paris; tour through England; return to U.S.; interesting picture of a young American doing his "Grand Tour."

Maryland Hist. Mag. VII (1912) 356–374.

PLUMER, William (1759–1850) of Epping, N.H., governor.

Private and political diary, April 1794–June 1842 (extracts); personal and public affairs; business in Congress; journeys; notes on health, political views, reading, etc.

William Plumer, Jr., *Life of William Plumer* (Boston, 1857) 543 pp. *passim,* contains copious extracts; Everett S. Brown (ed.), *William Plumer's Memorandum of Proceedings in the United States Senate, 1803–1807* (New York, 1923) 673 pp.; extracts relating to varied subjects in *Amer. Hist. Rev.* XXII (1917) 340–364, and in *Jour. Amer. Hist.* XVIII (1924) 51–53.

POPE, Amos (1772–1837) of Danvers, Mass.

Private diary, February 1794–October 1807; brief almanac notes; weather, domestic affairs, deaths, sermons, local events.

Danvers Hist. Soc. Colls. X (1922) 103–114.

PUTNAM, Israel (1766–1824) of Marietta, O.

Travel diary, March 1794–January 1795 (extracts); journey from Brooklyn, Conn., to his brother at Belpré, O., and later return to New Jersey; colloquial notes on travel; pleasant enough.

New England Mag. n.s. XIII (1895–1896) 642–651.

ROUTH, Martha (1743–1817) *b.* Stourbridge, Eng.

Quaker journal, July 1794–November 1797 (extracts); journey to America; work in New England, Pennsylvania, and southern States; return to England; second visit to America; usual notes on journeys, meetings, religion.

Friends' Library XII (Philadelphia, 1848) 424–472.

TRUDEAU (or Truteau), Jean Baptiste (1748–1827) *b.* Montreal, Indian trader.

Travel journal, June 1794–1795; journey in Upper Missouri as a company agent. Translated from the French.

South Dakota Hist. Colls. VII (1914) 403–474; first part (in French) in *Amer. Hist. Rev.* XIX (1914) 299–333; second part (translated) in *Missouri Hist. Soc. Colls.* IV (1912) 9–48.

WANSEY, Henry (1752?–1827) of Warminster, Eng., clothier.

Travel diary, March–July 1794; an Englishman's journey, mostly in Pennsylvania and New York, and New England; descriptions of towns and sociological observations.

Journal of an Excursion to the United States of North America in the Summer of 1794 (Salisbury, 1796) 290 pp.; 2d ed. (Salisbury, 1798) 270 pp. Extract in Allan Nevins, *American Social History as Recorded by British Travelers* (New York, 1923) 44–57.

WELLFORD, Dr. Robert (1753–1823) *b.* England, of Fredericksburg, Va.

Military surgeon's journal, September–December 1794; kept during march of Virginia troops from Fredericksburg to Fort Pitt, to suppress the Whiskey Rebellion; medical work, scenery, weather, strong opinions, social life; fairly good.

William and Mary Coll. Quar. 1st Ser. XI (1902) 1–19.

1795

ANDERSON, Dr. Alexander (1775–1870) of New York City.

Private diary, January–November 1795 (extract); early work as an engraver, but mostly life as medical student at Columbia College; amusing details of study, social life, reading; an intimate and interesting diary.

Old New York I (1889) 46–55, 85–93, 197–204, 233–253, II (1890) 88–105, 184–192, 217–226, 289–301, 428–436.

BAYARD, Samuel (1767–1840) of Princeton, N.J., judge.

Travel diary, May 1795–December 1796; kept in London; political and legal notes, notes on political figures; account of Ireland forgeries; fairly good.

New Jersey Hist. Soc. Proc. 2d Ser. VIII (1884–1885) 203–216; account and extracts in *New York Hist. Biog. Rec.* XXIII (1892) 1–14.

CHAPMAN, Thomas, of Elizabethtown, N.J.

Travel diaries, September 1795–November 1796; travels through the eastern United States; descriptions of towns, taverns, etc.

Hist. Mag. n.s. V (1869) 357–368, VI (1869) 70–75, VII (1870) 17–19.

CONDICT, Dr. Lewis (1772–1862) of Morristown, N.J.

Travel diary, June–December 1795; horseback journey from Morristown to Kentucky and part of return; scenery and towns; comments on manners and morals of citizens of Wheeling, Pittsburgh, and Cincinnati.

New Jersey Hist. Soc. Proc. n.s. IV (1919) 108–127.

HINSDALE, Rev. Theodore (1738–1818) of Hinsdale, Mass.

Clergyman's journal, May 1795–January 1797 (account and extracts); church affairs at Hinsdale; courtship of congregation; account of parish.

History of Berkshire County, Massachusetts (New York, 1885) II 82–86.

PIERCE, Rev. Dr. John (1773–1849) of Brookline, Mass.

1. Travel journal, September 1795; journey to Providence and New Haven; inauguration of Timothy Dwight as president of Yale; notes on taverns, accident, etc.; fair interest.

Massachusetts Hist. Soc. Proc. 2d Ser. III (1886) 40–52.

2. Private diary, August 1803–August 1848 (extracts); all the extracts describe and comment on annual commencement exercises at Harvard; presumably of interest to Harvard alumni.

Ibid. 2d Ser. V (1889–1890) 167–263.

3. Travel journal, December 1812–January 1813; from Brookline to Washington, via New York, Philadelphia, Baltimore; meeting with Madison; return; mostly account of churches and sermons; dull.

Ibid. 2d Ser. XIX (1905) 366–383.

SILLIMAN, Benjamin (1779–1864) of New Haven, Conn.

1. College diary, August 1795–January 1796; kept at Yale; a good picture of college studies and social life.

George P. Fisher, *Life of Benjamin Silliman* (New York, 1866) I 29–44.

2. Travel diary, 1805–1806; tours in England, Holland, Scotland; two transatlantic journeys.

A Journal of Travels (New Haven, 1820), three vols.

TWINING, Thomas (1776–1861).

Travel diary, November 1795–May 1796; seminarrative; India to England by way of United States; journal concerning life in United States; Wilmington, Philadelphia, Baltimore, Washington, New York; notes on men and manners; particularly interesting account of George Washington.

Travels in America 100 Years Ago (New York, 1894) 180 pp.

WHITTEKER, William (1775–1853) *b.* Princeton, Mass., of Charleston, W. Va., saltmaker and carpenter.

Business journal, April 1795–1810; memoranda of travels to Java and West

Indies from Baltimore and Philadelphia; notes on East Indian trade; trading and travel on the frontier; salt drilling; an unusual, varied, and interesting journal.

West Virginia Hist. I (1939–1940) 207–224, 283–292.

1796

ALLEN, Samuel, of Montville, Conn.

Letter-journal, November 1796; journey from Alexandria and Cumberland to the Ohio via Braddock's Road; interesting spellings.

A. B. Hulbert, *Historic Highways of America* XII (Cleveland, 1904) 65–77.

AUDRAIN, Peter.

Military journal, June 1796–August 1797; a few entries describing army movements about Pittsburgh, Greenville, Forts Defiance and Miami, and Detroit.

Michigan Pion. Colls. VIII (1885) 444–447.

AUSTIN, Moses (1761–1821) of Missouri and Texas, merchant.

1. Travel diary, December 1796–March 1797; journey to the lead fields of southeastern Missouri.

Amer. Hist. Rev. V (1899–1900) 518–542.

2. Travel diary, April–May 1801; voyage down the Mississippi; traffic on Mississippi and Ohio.

Amer. Hist. Assoc. Ann. Rep. (1919), *The Austin Papers* I 69–74.

BAILY, Francis (1774–1844) of England, F.R.S.

Travel journal, October 1796–1797; tour from Washington to Pittsburgh via Pennsylvania Road; good observations on a leisurely tour.

Journal of a Tour in the Unsettled Parts of North America (London, 1856) 439 pp. Extracts relating to Pennsylvania and Ohio in A. B. Hulbert, *Historic Highways of America* XI (Cleveland, 1904) 106–150; extracts relating to Tennessee in S. C. Williams, *Early Travels in the Tennessee Country* (Johnson City, 1928) 387–430.

CHAMBERS, Charlotte (*d.* 1821) of Chambersburg, Pa.

Private diary, December 1796–April 1821; scattered extracts from diary of social life and religious work at Ludlow Station, O., Cincinnati; work for Bible Society in Ohio; fair of its kind.

Lewis H. Garrard, *Memoir of Charlotte Chambers* (Philadelphia, 1856) 135 pp. *passim.*

CLEAVELAND, Gen. Moses (*ca.* 1755–1806) of Canterbury, Conn.

Surveying journal, July 1796 (extracts); brief notes of surveying around Cleveland, O.

Charles Whittlesey, *Early History of Cleveland, Ohio* (Cleveland, 1867) 181–184.

DUFOUR, Jean Jacques (*d.* 1827) of Switzerland Co., Ind.

Daybook, March 1796–June 1816; financial records mainly; French and English text.

Indiana Hist. Colls. XIII (1925) 234–347 ("The Swiss Settlement of Switzerland County, Indiana").

ELLICOTT, Andrew (1754–1820) of Fountainville, Pa., surveyor.

Official journal, September 1796–May 1800; determining boundary between United States and French possessions; mainly journey down Ohio and Mississippi and proceedings in lower Mississippi Valley; occasional topographical and sociological notes; written up from notes.

The Journal of Andrew Ellicott (Philadelphia, 1803, 1814) 1–299.

HOLLEY, John Milton, of Salisbury, Conn.

Surveying journal, April–October 1796; from Dover to Canandaigua and Western Reserve; surveying for Cleveland Land Co.; notes on topography, natural history, etc.

Charles Whittlesey, *Early History of Cleveland, Ohio* (Cleveland, 1867) 192–202, 206–207, 215–223, 242–249.

LATROBE, Benjamin Henry (1764–1820) of Philadelphia, architect and engineer.

Travel journal, June 1796–1820; comments and sketches of Virginia, Virginians, and Virginian insects, education, etc.; notes on Louisiana; extensive descriptions.

J. H. B. Latrobe (ed.), *The Journal of Latrobe* (New York, 1905) 269 pp.

LEE, William (1772–1840) of Boston.

Travel diary, January 1796–June 1798; to France, Holland, London, and return; a few sample extracts.

William Lee, *John Leigh of Agawam* (Albany, 1888) 233–237.

McKAY, Capt. James (1759–1822) b. Scotland, of St. Louis, Mo.

Travel journal, June 1796 etc.; extracts from notes of travel and exploration in the upper Missouri region; partly diaristic; possibly drawn up for Lewis and Clark.

Wisconsin Hist. Soc. Proc. (1915) 186–210.

PEASE, Seth (1764–1819) of Suffield, Conn.

Surveying journals, May 1796–February 1798 (with gaps); journey to Western Reserve and surveys on behalf of Connecticut Land Co.; from Cleveland to Canandaigua, N.Y.; from Canandaigua to Suffield; to New Connecticut; life on Western Reserve; return to Connecticut; notes of surveys, and general comments on people and places.

Charles Whittlesey, *Early History of Cleveland, Ohio* (Cleveland, 1867) 178–181, 277–287; *Western Reserve Hist. Soc. Tract* No. 94 (1914) 27–124.

PETERS, John, of Blue Hill, Me., surveyor.

Surveying journal, September–November 1796; brief notes of Peters-Hedden survey of the lower Magaguadavic and Lake Utopia.

New Brunswick Hist. Soc. Colls. No. 8 (1909) 173–174; and insertions in the Campbell journal, *ibid.* 174–203.

POWELL, Cuthbert (*b.* 1779) of Alexandria, Va.

Sea journal, September 1796–July 1801; mainly notes of voyages, storms, trade at Alexandria.

William and Mary Coll. Quar. 1st Ser. XII (1903–1904) 221–231, XIII (1904–1905) 53–63.

ROBBINS, Rev. Thomas (1777–1856) of Sheffield, Mass.

Private diary, January 1796–February 1854; an extremely long and detailed diary of great value; life as teacher and preacher in Massachusetts and Connecticut; begun when author was student at Williams College; weather, Federalist politics; local affairs, church work; mostly brief notes, but its span and consistency put it in the same class as Hempstead's and Hazard's diaries as a reflection of the author's own life and the life of his community.

Increase N. Tarbox (ed.), *Diary of Thomas Robbins, D.D.* (Boston, 1886) two vols.

SHELDON, Charlotte (1780–*ca.* 1840) of Litchfield and Hartford, Conn.

Private diary, May–September 1796 (extracts); notes on school life, personal, and local affairs.

Emily E. Vanderpoel, *Chronicles of a Pioneer School* (Cambridge, Mass., 1903) 10–17.

WILLISTON, Rev. Dr. Seth (1770–1851) *b.* Suffield, Conn., of Durham, Conn.

Presbyterian clergyman's journal, July 1796–February 1800; interesting and valuable account of Presbyterians in Connecticut and missionary work in New York State; reading, sermons, parish work, travel; in addition, a good deal of private life; reading, weather, illnesses, politics, spiritual experiences, notes on weather, etc.

Edited by J. Q. Adams, *Jour. Presbyterian Hist. Soc.* VII (1913–1914) 175–208, 234–254, VIII (1915–1916) 40–48, 123–144, 184–192, 226–235, 316–330, IX (1917–1918) 25–40, 368–383, X (1919–1920) 24–35, 130–141.

1797

CAMPBELL, Dugald, of New Brunswick, surveyor.

Surveying journal, May–August 1797; almost wholly surveying notes of the Campbell-Peters surveying of Magaguadavic and Lake Utopia.

New Brunswick Hist. Soc. Colls. No. 8 (1909) 174–203.

COMLY, Mrs. Rebecca (*b.* 1773) of Byberry, Pa.

Quaker journal, March 1797–January 1829 (extracts); brief notes of Quaker work and travels; usual material.

Journal of the Life and Religious Labours of John Comly (Philadelphia, 1853) 493 pp.

COWLES, Julia (1785–1803) of Farmington, Conn.

Private diary, June 1797–January 1803; social and school life at Litchfield; records of private and school reading; long entries; well written, entertaining.

Laura H. Moseley, *The Diaries of Julia Cowles* (New Haven, 1931) 94 pp. Extracts in Emily N. Vanderpoel, *Chronicles of a Pioneer School* (Cambridge, 1903) 17–19.

FRENCH, Samson (1742–1834) of Southwick, Mass.

Business journal, November 1797–January 1833; few extracts, mostly notes of purchases, with some diary entries; rather dull.

M. Q. Beyer, *Genealogical History of the French and Allied Families* (Cedar Rapids, Ia., 1912) 132–135.

FROST, Rev. Amriah (1750–1819) of Milford, Mass.

Travel diary, June 1797; journey from Milford to Virginia; visit to Mount Vernon and reception by Washington.

Amer. Antiq. Soc. Proc. (1879) 71–79.

GILMOR, Robert (1774–1848) of Baltimore, Md.

1. Travel diary, July–August 1797; memoranda of journey through Mid-Atlantic and New England states; seminarrative; entertaining.

Bull. Boston Pub. Lib. (1892) 72–92.

2. Personal and travel diary, December 1826–June 1827; domestic and business life in Baltimore; voyage to New York, Philadelphia, and return to Baltimore; an intimate picture of the life and hypochondria of a "first citizen."

Maryland Hist. Mag. XVII (1922) 231–268, 319–347.

GRIFFIN, Rev. Edward Door (1770–1837) *b*. East Haddam, Conn., of Newark.

Clergyman's journal, July 1797–August 1805; resolutions, self-analysis, moral reflections, devotions, self-abasement; long and dull entries.

William B. Sprague, *Memoir of the Rev. Edward D. Griffin* (New York, 1839) 12–88.

HARRISON, Deacon Aaron (1726–1819) of Wolcott, Conn.

Religious diary, October 1797–July 1812 (extracts); sudden deaths, religious introspection, church admissions.

Samuel Orcutt, *History of the Town of Wolcott* (Waterbury, Conn., 1874) 327–328.

HAWKINS, Benjamin (1754–1818) of North Carolina, senator.

Surveying journal, March 1797; in western South Carolina; largely technical notes; brief extracts.

S. C. Williams, *Early Travels in the Tennessee Country* (Johnson City, 1928) 370–372.

JORDAN, Richard (1756–1826) *b*. Elizabeth, Va., of Newton, N.J.

Quaker journal, March 1797–1825; travels and experience as a preacher in the American states; antislavery sentiment; ministry in Maryland, Pennsylvania, Connecticut, and New Jersey; visits to Ireland, Holland, and France.

A Journal of the Life and Religious Labours of Richard Jordan (London and Philadelphia, 1829) 188 pp.; reprinted in *Friends' Library* XIII (Philadelphia, 1849) 292–349.

STEARNS, Rev. Samuel (1770–1834) of Bedford, Mass.

Religious journal, May 1797–June 1798; fragmentary notes; presents (mainly food) he received during first year as a minister.

A. E. Brown, *History of the Town of Bedford* (Bedford, 1891) 61–62.

SWAN, Maj. Caleb (*d.* 1809) *b.* Maine, paymaster of Western Army.

Military travel journal, August 1797; round trip from Detroit through north-western country; brief notes on topography and Indians.

Mag. Amer. Hist. XIX (1888) 74–77.

TOWNSEND, Ebenezer, Jr., of New Haven, Conn., merchant.

Sea journal, January 1797–July 1799; supercargo aboard sealing ship "Neptune"; sealing voyage from New York to South Pacific, Hawaii, and Canton; in letter addressed to his brother; hunting, trading, elaborate descriptions of places and people; a full and very interesting journal.

New Haven Col. Hist. Soc. Papers IV (1888) 1–115.

1798

ADAMS, Thomas Boylston (1772–1832) of Quincy, Mass.

Political diary, January–December 1798; diplomatic and social life in Berlin.

Bull. New York Pub. Lib. XIX (1915) 803–843.

CORSER, David (1754–1828) of Boscawen, N.H.

Private diary, April 1798–May 1800; brief notes on personal affairs; sufferings from Tory neighbors.

Genealogy of the Corser Family in America (Concord, N.H., 1902) 150 pp.

FULLER, Hon. Timothy, Jr. (1778–1835) of Cambridge, Mass.

1. Private diary, August 1798–July 1801; kept while author was student at Harvard; student and social life; reading, debates, etc.; interesting.

Cambridge Hist. Soc. Pubs. XI (1916) 33–53.

2. Personal and political diary, January–March 1818 (extracts); kept while author was member of Congress; political and social life in Washington.

New England Quar. XII (1939) 521–529.

HUMPHRIES, Clement, of Philadelphia; envoy to France.

Travel diary, March–October 1798; rather dull account of services.

Pennsylvania Mag. Hist. Biog. XXXII (1908) 34–53.

LEVY, Isaac H., of New York.

Travel diary, January 1798–March 1799 (fragment); voyage from New York to Madras and Calcutta; mainly log entries, but some general descriptions.

American-Jewish Hist. Soc. Pubs. XXVII (1920) 239.

MATTHEWS, Dr. Increase (1772–1856) *b.* New Braintree, Mass., *d.* Putnam, O.

Travel diary, June–September 1798; journey from Oakham, Mass., to the Ohio country; mainly travel notes, with some notes on sects and politics, and character sketches; fairly interesting.

New England Hist. Geneal. Reg. LXXXVI (1932) 33–43.

[O'CONWAY, Mathias James.]

Diary, August–September 1798; kept during plague of yellow fever at Philadelphia; deaths, flights, statistics.

American Cath. Hist. Soc. Philadelphia Recs. XIII (1902) 486–493.

STANFORD, Rev. John (1754–1834) *b.* Wandsworth, Eng., of New York City.

Chaplain's journal, March 1798–January 1834 (extracts); religious reflections, work as chaplain in the orphanages, humane and criminal institutions in New York City.

Charles G. Sommers, *Memoir of the Rev. John Stanford* (New York, 1835) 62–314 *passim.*

1799

ANON. (fur trader, of Rocky Mountain Fort on Peace River).

Fur-trading journal, October 1799–April 1800; life at the Rocky Mountain Fort; brief but entertaining notes.

Washington Hist. Quar. XIX (1928) 250–270.

AVERY, Rev. Joseph (*b.* 1743) of Tyringham, Mass.

1. Travel journal, June–September 1799; journey of a Presbyterian clergyman to the Genesee country to form churches; return to Greenbush; preaching and religious work; details of sects.

New York State Hist. Assoc. Quar. Jour. II (1921) 251–266.

2. Travel journal, August–September 1805; visit to Buffalo and vicinity; preaching, notes on families, Niagara, etc.

Buffalo Hist. Soc. Pubs. VI (1903) 223–230.

BATEMAN, Dr. Ephraim (1780–1829) of Fairfield, N.J., senator.

Social and personal diary, June 1799–December 1806; "written for my own amusement and profit"; family and schooling details, work as teacher; church work and politics; introspection and health; brief notes of fair interest.

Vineland Hist. Mag. XIII (1928) 55–64, 80–89, XIV (1929) 106–114, 127–135, 154–162, 174–182, XV (1930) 210–217, 235–246.

DEVEREUX, John William, of Milledgeville, Ga.

Travel diary, June–November 1799; interesting account of a journey from Georgia to New York.

Georgia Hist. Quar. XV (1931) 46–80.

EMERSON, Rev. John (1745–1826) of Conway, Mass.

Private diary, December 1799–October 1800 (extracts); very brief notes of local affairs and payments.

Benjamin K. Emerson, *The Ipswich Emersons* (Boston, 1900) 133.

GOSHEN (Ind.) MORAVIAN CONGREGATION.

1. Congregational journals, May 1799–August 1800 (extract); extract of the community of brethren on the Muskingum River concerning the founding of

the White River Mission; November 1800–March 1801, life and work of the Goshen community. Translated from the German.

Indiana Hist. Colls. XXIII (1938) 23–37, 53–62.

2. Congregational journal, January–December 1812; usual details of Moravian life and work; kept in English by Rev. Benjamin Mortimer.

Ohio Archaeol. Hist. Soc. Pubs. XXII (1913) 205–266.

GRANGER, Erastus (1765–1826) of Suffield, Conn., judge.

Travel diaries, March 1799–March 1804; horseback journeys from Suffield to Virginia and West Virginia, investigating land titles.

Connecticut Mag. III (1897) 100–105, 190–198.

HILL, Thomas (*d.* 1828) of New Brunswick, N.J.

Travel diary, June–July 1799 (extract); horseback journey from New Brunswick to Wyoming Co., Pa.

Pennsylvania Mag. Hist. Biog. XIV (1890) 189–198.

HUNT, Benjamin (1766–1812) of Westtown, Pa.

Private diary, April 1799–February 1812; short daily notes of personal, family, and local affairs; mainly where he went and what he did; varied and interesting for local affairs; some interesting spellings and vocabulary.

Chester Co. Hist. Soc. Bull. (Pa.) (1898) 1–20 (reprinted from *Daily Local News*).

McKENZIE, James, bourgeois of the Northwest Company.

Fur-trading journal, October 1799–August 1800 (extracts); kept at and about Fort Chippewan in the Athabasca district; valuable for notes of competition and business methods; notes of social affairs, lives of employees; very interesting for its personality and ironical humor.

L. R. Masson, *Les Bourgeois de la Campagnie du Nord-Ouest* II (Quebec, 1889) 371–399.

MANNING, James (1738–1791) of Elizabethtown, N.J., president of Brown University.

Travel diary, April–September 1779; trip to New York, New Jersey, and Philadelphia; observations on estates, taverns, scenery, crops, historical incidents, social and private matters; terse but copious.

Reuben A. Guild, *Life, Times, and Correspondence of James Manning* (n.p., 1864) 266–286.

PREBLE, Commodore Edward (1761–1807) *b.* Falmouth, Me., of the "Essex."

1. Sea journal, October 1799–November 1800; convoying from Salem; voyage around Cape Horn to Batavia and return to New York; mainly log entries.

Essex Inst. Hist. Colls. X (1869) 60–85.

2. Memorandum diary, June 1803–April 1805; expedition to Mediterranean; movements of "Constitution" and American Navy about Tripoli, return to America; brief notes.

Amer. Hist. Rec. I (1872) 53–58; *Mag. Amer. Hist.* III (1879) Part I 182–193.

STEINER, Abraham (1758–1833) of Bethlehem, Pa.

Moravian travel journal, November–December 1799; visit with F. C. de Schweinitz to the Cherokees and Cumberland settlements; visits, social and general observations; formal but interesting.

S. C. Williams, *Early Travels in the Tennessee Country* (Johnson City, 1928) 448–525.

STROTHER, John.

Surveying journal, April–May 1799; survey of North Carolina and Tennessee boundary; interesting for language and details of discomforts of commissioners.

Tennessee Hist. Mag. VI (1920) 49–57.

1800

CLEVELAND, William, of Salem, Mass.

Sea journal, July–November 1800 (extract); account of Japanese topography and customs; author was clerk on the "Massachusetts."

Ralph D. Paine, *Ships and Sailors of Old Salem* (New York, 1909) chap. xviii 352–375.

COMLY, John (1773–1850) of Byberry, Pa.

Quaker journal, September 1800–June 1832; spiritual life, and notes of travels and religious work; with autobiography and memoirs.

Journal of the Life and Religious Labours of John Comly (Philadelphia, 1853) 69–488.

DAVIS, John Russell (*b.* 1775) of Massachusetts.

Travel diary, May–June 1800; journey through Massachusetts, Vermont, and eastern New York; notes on sights, scenes, inns; religious qualms and comments.

Vermont Hist. Soc. Proc. (1919–1920) 160–180.

HARMON, Daniel Williams (1778–1845) *b.* Vergennes, Vt., partner in the Northwest Company.

Private diary, April 1800–August 1819; voyages from Montreal to the Pacific Northwest; half of it kept west of the Rockies; a very interesting journal of the general life of a trader; Lake Winnipeg, the Assiniboine, Fort William, Athabasca, Fort Vermilion, New Caledonia, Stuart's Lake, Fort William.

A Journal of Voyages and Travels in the Interior of North America (Andover, 1820) 25–432. Account with quotations in *Manitoba Hist. Scient. Soc. Trans.* No. 9 (1883–1884) 7 pp.

HAYWARD, Jonathan (1788–1813) of Danvers, Mass.

Private diary, February 1800–April 1808; occasional brief notes on local events at Danvers, deaths, etc.

Danvers Hist. Soc. Colls. III (1915) 53–58.

HENRY, Alexander (*d.* 1814) of the Northwest Company.

Travel and fur-trading journals, July 1800–May 1814; exploration in the Great Northwest; journey from Lake Superior to Lake of the Woods, Winnipeg River,

Red River, mouth of Park River; building trading post and its establishment; realistic accounts of journeys, business, Indian life, personal affairs, while author was in charge of the company's business in Minnesota, North Dakota, and Manitoba area; from 1808, author in charge of posts in Saskatchewan; long overland and river journeys; journey to Astoria and minute account of life at mouth of Columbia River in 1813–1814, with occasional journeys up the Columbia and Willamette rivers. A most valuable and interesting journal, although somewhat formal in style.

Standard edition by Elliott Coues, *New Light on the Early History of the Greater Northwest* (New York, 1897), three vols., based on the Coventry manuscript copy. Extracts relating to Red River Valley in *North Dakota Hist. Soc. Colls.* III (1910) 360–368; extracts edited by C. N. Bell in *Manitoba Hist. Scient. Soc. Trans.* No. 31 (1887–1888) 9 pp.

JOHNSON, William (1779–1828) of Sussex Co., N.J., and New York, merchant.
   1. Travel diary, September 1800–July 1801 (extracts with editorial narrative); from New Jersey to New Orleans; overland to Natchez and then voyage to New Orleans; stormy return voyage to New York.
   New Jersey Hist. Soc. Proc. n.s. VII (1922) 49–59, 122–134. Extract concerning New Orleans and voyage to New York in *Louisiana Hist. Quar.* V (1922) 34–50.
   2. Personal and business diary, June 1802–February 1813 (extracts with editorial narrative); business, social life, amusements, in New York and New Jersey; valuable picture of life and tastes of a successful businessman.
   New Jersey Hist. Soc. Proc. n.s. VII (1922) 211–216, 305–314, VIII (1923) 150–154, 219–225, 313–320.

KLUGE, John Peter (1768–1849), Moravian missionary.
   Missionary travel journals, October–November 1800, March–May 1801, September–November 1806; from Bethlehem to Goshen on the Muskingum, from Goshen to White River, and from White River to Bethlehem; travel, and notes on Moravian life and work.
   Lawrence H. Gipson (ed.), *The Moravian Indian Mission on White River*, Indiana Hist. Colls. XXIII (1938) 39–52, 67–101, 455–465.

Low, Rufus, sailing master of U.S.S. "Essex."
   Sea journal, December–November 1800; log notes of cruise of the "Essex" to Batavia.
   Essex Inst. Hist. Colls. X (1869) Part III 70–85; reprinted from *Journal Kept on Board the United States Ship Essex* (Boston, 1799).

McLEOD, Archibald Norman, partner in Northwest Company.
   Diary of a bourgeois, November 1800–June 1801; in charge of Swan River Dept., supervising fur trading between Lake Winnipeg and the Assiniboine River; weather and social details; most interesting account of life of fur traders.
   Charles M. Gates (ed.), *Five Fur-Traders of the Northwest* (Univ. Minnesota, 1933) 123–185.

[MAUDE, John, Englishman.]

Travel diary, June–October 1800; trip from New York through Upper Canada to Niagara and return to New York; long entries in travel-book style; tourist's adventures and impressions of scenery, towns, people, etc.

Published anonymously as *Visit to the Falls of Niagara* (London, 1826) 3–279 (Maude says it is a faithful copy of a "gentleman's journal"). Extracts in C. M. Dow, *Anthology and Bibliography of Niagara Falls* I (Albany, 1921) 115–122.

THORNTON, Mrs. Anna Maria (*b.* 1774?) of Washington, D.C.

1. Personal diary, January–December 1800; social and domestic life in Washington; account of friendship with George and Martha Washington, visits to Mount Vernon, etc.; detailed and factual.

2. Personal diary, August–September 1814; good description of capture of Washington by the British.

Columbia Hist. Soc. Recs. X (1907) 88–226, XIX (1916) 172–182.

WILLCOCKS, Joseph (*d.* 1814) of Ontario, Canada, politician and journalist.

Personal and domestic diary, February 1800–February 1803; domestic and social life in York (Toronto); principally notes on meals, gossip, reading; fairly interesting.

J. E. Middleton and Fred Landon, *The Province of Ontario* (Toronto, 1927) II App. B 1258–1322.

1801

ASSHETON, Susannah (*b.* 1767) of Philadelphia.

Diary ("Susan Assheton's Book"), April 1801–August 1832; brief, occasional memoranda of national, international, and family affairs; comments on dead friends.

Pennsylvania Mag. Hist. Biog. LV (1931) 174–186.

BADGER, Rev. Joseph (1757–1846) of Austinburg, O.

Presbyterian religious journal, August 1801–September 1807; missionary work, mainly in Western Reserve settlement at Austinburg; missionary tours in Ohio, Virginia, Pennsylvania; meetings, preaching; among Wyandots and in Sandusky Mission.

A Memoir of Rev. Joseph Badger (Hudson, O., 1851) 27–167.

BUCKNER, Philip (1747–1820) of Bracken Co., Ky.

Private diary, February–June 1801 (extract); journey from Bracken to Natchez by water; return by land; bare details of places and incidents.

William and Mary Coll. Quar. 2d Ser. VI (1926) 173–207.

DE SMET, Father Pierre Jean (1801–1873), Jesuit missionary.

Narrative and journal of missionary work, 1801–1873; labors and adventures among the North American Indians; minute descriptions of manners, customs, games, warfare, legends, traditions; collected during missionary journeys; sketches of country from St. Louis to Puget Sound and the Altrabasca; mostly narrative.

H. M. Chittenden and A. T. Richardson (eds.), *Life, Letters, and Travels of Father Pierre-Jean de Smet, S.J.* (New York, 1905) four vols.

ELLICOTT, Joseph, (1760–1826), *b.* Bucks Co., Pa., agent of the Holland Land Company.

Business journal, January 1801–January 1802 (extracts); early real estate operations at Buffalo Creek (New Amsterdam).

William Ketchum, *An Authentic and Comprehensive History of Buffalo* (Buffalo, 1865) II 146–150.

HASWELL, William, first officer of "Lydia," barque, of Boston.

Sea journal, October 1801–January 1802; voyage from Manila to Guam; full and good descriptions of Zamboanga and Guam; resources, government, religion, customs, etc.

Essex Inst. Hist. Colls. LIII (1917) 193–214. Extracts in Ralph D. Paine, *Ships and Sailors of Old Salem* (New York, 1909) chap. xix 380–393.

HOLYOKE, Margaret (1763–1825) of Salem, Mass.

Private diary, January 1801–October 1823; brief notes of social, personal, and local affairs; quite interesting.

G. F. Dow (ed.), *The Holyoke Diaries* (Salem, 1911) 139–174.

PICKERING, John (1777–1846) of Boston.

Travel diary, April–May 1801; visit to Holland; Leyden, Amsterdam; notes on theaters, buildings, museums; return to England.

Mary O. Pickering, *Life of John Pickering* (Boston, 1887) 189–196.

QUINCY, Josiah (1772–1864) of Boston.

Travel diary, June 1801; tour from Boston through southeastern New England; descriptions of Providence, Tiverton, Martha's Vineyard, and notes on persons; a pleasant diary.

Massachusetts Hist. Soc. Proc. 2d Ser. IV (1887–1889) 123–135.

SHELDON, Lucy (1788–1889) of Litchfield, Conn.

School diary, December 1801–February 1802 and January–March 1803 (extracts); studies and social life at Litchfield School.

Emily Vanderpoel, *Chronicles of a Pioneer School* (Cambridge, Mass., 1903) 43–53.

[SIEBENTHAL, François, of Switzerland?]

Travel journal, March–April 1801; Atlantic voyage of Swiss colonists from Vevey; France to Norfolk, Va.

Indiana Mag. Hist. XXXV (1939) 189–194.

VAN METER, Isaac, of Hampshire Co., Va. (now Hardy Co., W.Va.)

Travel diary, April–May 1801; tour through western Virginia; notes on scenery, towns, settlements, farming; sale and purchase of lands.

Trans-Allegheny Hist. Mag. I (1901–1902) 96–105.

WHITE RIVER (Ind.) MORAVIAN CONGREGATION.

Congregational journals, 1801–1808 (with gap); record of life and work of the Little Indian Congregation on White River; interesting details of Moravian missionary work and life, Indian life, weather, social affairs, etc. Translated from the German.

Lawrence H. Gipson (ed.), *The Moravian Indian Mission on the White River, Indiana Hist. Colls.* XXIII (1938) 102–465.

1802

BACON, Mary Ann (1787–1815) of Roxbury, Conn.

School diary, June–September 1802 (extracts); a charming record of school life at Litchfield, Conn.

Emily Vanderpoel, *Chronicles of a Pioneer School* (Cambridge, Mass., 1903) 66–71.

EATON, Gen. William (1764–1811) U.S.A., *b.* Woodstock, Conn.

Military diary, December 1802–December 1804, and March–May 1805; notes on Tunisian pickpockets, cruise to Malta, social notes at Cairo, march from Alexandria to Barca Desert, with notes on difficulties of journey.

Charles Prentiss, *The Life of the Late Gen. William Eaton* (Brookfield, 1813) 237–238, 268–277, 301–335.

GILPIN, Joshua (1765–1841) of Philadelphia.

1. Travel diary, October 1802; from Wakefield to Bethlehem via Germantown, Easton, Stroudsburg; full descriptions of everything he saw; expenses; farming conditions; a long account of the Moravian settlement at Bethlehem.

Pennsylvania Mag. Hist. Biog. XLVI (1922) 15–38, 122–153.

2. Travel diary, September–October 1809; tour from Philadelphia through western Pennsylvania, visiting Lancaster, York, Bedford, Washington, Pittsburgh, etc.; comments on towns and trade of Ohio; very full descriptions and comments.

Ibid. L (1926) 64–78, 163–178, 380–382, LI (1927) 172–190, 351–375, LII (1928) 29–58.

LITTLE, Nathaniel W. of Blandford, Mass.

Travel diary, July–October 1802; from Blandford to northwestern Ohio, via New York, Princeton, Philadelphia, Lancaster, Pittsburgh, Chillicothe, Muskingum, Greensburg, etc.; ordinary travel observations of moderate interest.

Old Northwest Geneal. Quar. X (1907) 237–245.

SIBLEY, Dr. John (1757–1837) of Natchitoches, Va.

Travel diary, July–October 1802; voyage from Charleston, S.C., to New Orleans, up Mississippi to Washington (Mississippi Territory); descriptions of New Orleans and surrounding country.

Louisiana Hist. Quar. X (1927) 474–497.

TAYLOR, Rev. John (1762–1840) of Westfield and Deerfield, Mass.

Travel diary, July–October 1802; from Deerfield to the Mohawk and Black River country of New York; missionary journey; lengthy descriptive notes.

E. B. O'Callaghan, *Doc. Hist. State New York* III (1850) 673–696; extract in Joel Munsell, *Annals of Albany* VI (1855) 219–222.

TUCKER, Mrs. Mary Orne (1775–1806) of Haverhill, Mass.

Private diary, April–May 1802; domestic and social life in Essex County; notes on reading; full and well-written entries of considerable interest.

Essex Inst. Hist. Colls. LXXVII (1941) 306–338.

TURNER, Charles (1760–1839) of Scituate, Mass.

Surveying journal, August–October 1802 (extract); surveying grants and sales of land in Nova Scotia; Campobello, Grand Manan, etc.; some general and social notes.

Massachusetts Hist. Soc. Proc. 1st Ser. XVII (1879–1880) 206–216.

WILLIAMS, William (1763–1824) *b.* Chatham Co., N.C., of Whitewater, Ind.

Quaker journal, March 1802–December 1822; journeys and visits to Friends' meetings in southern states; tours in Atlantic and trans-Allegheny states; removal to Indiana and work there, with various tours in the East; usual Quaker entries.

Journal of the Life, Travels, and Gospel Labours of William Williams (Cincinnati, 1828) 272 pp.

1803

BUCKMINSTER, Rev. Joseph Stevens (1784–1812) of Boston.

Private diary, December 1803–August 1806; first part is a record of studies modeled on Gibbon's journal; notes on reading, mainly religious and philosophical; journey to Europe; notes on literary acquaintances in London; and at Strasbourg.

Eliza B. Lee, *Memoirs of Rev. Joseph Buckminster* (Boston, 1849) 237–278.

COVELL, Rev. Lemuel.

Baptist travel journal, September–November 1803; tour in western New York and Canada; attendance at meetings; comments on Indians.

Buffalo Hist. Soc. Pubs. VI (1903) 207–216.

COWDERY, Dr. Jonathan (1767–1852) *b.* Sandisfield, Mass., surgeon's mate on the "Philadelphia."

Captive's diary, December 1803–June 1805; capture and captivity in Tripoli; medical work in Bashaw's family; daily life of the American prisoners, etc.

American Captives in Tripoli (Boston, 1806) 34 pp.

CUROT, Michel, fur trader in Wisconsin.

Fur-trading journal, July 1803–June 1804; in charge of Yellow River Post in northern Wisconsin; travels, trade, daily life, notes on Indians; quite interesting. Translated from the French.

Wisconsin Hist. Soc. Colls. XX (1911) 396–471.

FORBES, John.

Journal, May 1803; Indian affairs in Florida; seizure of leader of Indians, William Augustus Bowles.

Florida Hist. Soc. Quar. IX (1931) 279–289.

HARRIS, Rev. Dr. Thaddeus Mason (1768–1842) *b.* Charlestown, Mass., of Boston, minister and antiquarian.

Travel journal, March–June 1803; from Lancaster, Pa., to Ohio, via Strasbourg, Shippensburg, Marietta, and return via Wheeling, Somerset, Bedford, Yorktown; notes on geography, topography, and historical account of Ohio.

The Journal of a Tour (Boston, 1805) 11–85; R. G. Thwaites, *Early Western Travels* (Cleveland, 1904) III 309–382.

IRVING, Washington (1783–1859), writer and traveler.

Travel diaries; detailed descriptions, notes on persons, places, tales, etc.; of special interest as noted below.

1. July–August 1803; journey to Ogdensburg (Oswegatchie) with Josiah Hoffman, Thomas Ogden, and others, and into the Black River country; juvenile, romantic observations on the frontier.

Stanley Williams (ed.), *Journal, 1803* (New York, 1934) 48 pp.

2. July 1804–1805; young Irving on his European travels; France, Italy, Switzerland, Greece, Germany, Belgium.

W. P. Trent (ed.), *Mr. Irving's Notes and Journal of Travel in Europe 1804–1805* (New York, 1920) three vols.

3. July–August 1815; travels in Wales.

W. P. Trent and G. S. Hellman (eds.), *The Journals of Washington Irving* (Boston, 1919) I 3–18.

4. June 1817; journey from Liverpool to Runcorn, with William C. Preston.

Stanley Williams (ed.), *Tour in Scotland 1817* (New Haven, 1927) 75–79.

5. August–September 1817; London to Edinburgh and tour through Scotland; interesting notes on people, places, and tales.

Ibid. 21–72.

6. August–November 1820; undated notes in France.

Trent and Hellman, I 19–48.

7. August 1822–July 1823; Germany, Austria, Bohemia.

Ibid. I 49–225.

8. July 1823–August 1824; kaleidoscopic notes in England, France, Germany, Holland.

Stanley Williams (ed.), *Journal of Washington Irving (1823–1824)* (Cambridge, Mass., 1931) 244 pp.

9. August 1824–February 1826; France.

Trent and Hellman, II, 199 pp.

10. February–April 1826; Spain.

Ibid. III 1–63.

11. March–April 1828; Spain; Irving's first stay in Granada; part of journey from Madrid into southern Spain; completes records of other diaries in Spain.

Stanley Williams (ed.), *Journal of Washington Irving 1828 and Miscellaneous Notes on Moorish Legend and History* (New York, 1937) 1–65.

12. April 1828–February 1829; journey from Madrid into southern Spain; generally brief notes.

Clara Louise Penny (ed.), *Washington Irving Diary, Spain 1828–1829* (New York, 1926) 142 pp.

13. July–August 1829; Spain, Granada to Gerona.

Trent and Hellman, III 65–100.

14. September–November 1832; journey in western America, making notes for *A Tour on the Prairies.*

Ibid. III 101–186.

15. September 1833; New York State, Esopus, and Dutch tour.

Ibid. III 187–196.

16. April–July 1842; New York to Spain.

Ibid. III 196–220.

JEWITT, John Rodgers (1783–1821) of Boston.

Captive's diary, March 1803–July 1805; survivor of ship "Boston," capture by Nootka Indians; brief notes of daily life in Indian fashion; written in Defoe-like style; apparently written by Richard Alsop, "who drew from Jewitt his story, during repeated interviews."

Norman L. Dodge (ed.), *A Journal Kept at Nootka Sound* (Boston, 1931) 84 pp.; originally published with this title at Boston (1807) and frequently reprinted with varying titles.

SELKIRK, Douglas Thomas, fifth Earl of (1771–1820), philanthropist.

Diaries, November 1803–December 1804 (extracts); kept in Upper and Lower Canada; brief extracts relating to foundation of his Red River settlement; moderate interest.

Royal Soc. Canada Proc. and Trans. 3d Ser. VI (1912) Sec. II 3–9.

SWEARINGEN, Lieut. James Strode.

Travel journal, July–August 1803; from Detroit to Chicago; brief notes on topography, weather, etc.

M. M. Quaife, *Chicago and the Old Northwest* (Univ. Chicago, 1913) 373–377.

WEIR, James (1777–1845) of Greenville, Ky.

Travel diary, March–July 1803; voyage and travel; Natchez, Baton Rouge, New Orleans, Philadelphia, Pittsburgh; imprisonment by Spaniards at Baton Rouge; notes on towns, waterspout, etc.; fairly good.

O. A. Rothert, *A History of Muhlenberg County* (Louisville, 1913) 443–448.

WHITE, Mary Wilder (1780–1811) of Concord, Mass.

Private diaries, December 1803–January 1805; scattered extracts (indexed under "Journals"); religious and social life at Concord.

Mary W. Tileston, *Memorials of Mary Wilder White* (Boston, 1903) 409 pp. *passim*.

YARNALL, Mrs. Hannah Haines (1765–1822) of Byberry, Pa.

Quaker travel journal, September–November 1803; visit to Friends in Canada; meetings, work, weather, religious reflections; notes on Indians and Methodist rivalries.

Mary T. Seaman, *Thomas Richardson of South Shields* (New York, 1929) 197–222.

1804

CAMERON, Duncan, *b.* Schenectady, employee of Northwest Company.

Fur-trading journal, August–December 1804 (extracts); kept while author was in the Nipigon Department, between Lake Superior and Hudson's Bay; travel about the territory, establishment of fort, criticism of Indians, rivalry with Hudson's Bay Company; very interesting.

L. R. Masson, *Les Bourgeois de la Compagnie du Nord-Ouest* (Quebec, 1889) II 267–300.

[CONNOR, Thomas?], employee of Northwest Company.

Fur-trading journal, September 1804–April 1805; winter in region of Cross Lake and Snake River; building of trading post; trading activities and varied work around post; notes on Indian customs and habits; a most interesting narrative, with some linguistic interest.

Charles M. Gates (ed.), *Five Fur-Traders of the Northwest* (Univ. Minnesota, 1933) 245–278.

DUNBAR, William (1749–1810) of Natchez, Miss.

Travel journal, October 1804–January 1805; surveying and exploration journey from St. Catherine's Landing to Hot Springs; Red, Black, and Washita rivers.

Documents Relating to the Purchase and Exploration of Louisiana (Boston, 1904) 7–189; D. Rowland, *Life, Letters and Papers of William Dunbar* (Jackson, Miss., 1930) 216–320.

FARIES, Hugh, employee of Northwest Company.

Fur-trading journal, July 1804–May 1805; author in charge of fur trading around Rainy Lake post during absence of supervisor; work and life around the post; valuable and highly interesting notes on social life of the voyageurs.

Charles M. Gates (ed.), *Five Fur-Traders of the Northwest* (Univ. Minnesota, 1933) 189–241.

FLOYD, Sergt. Charles (*ca.* 1781–1804) of Kentucky.

Exploration journal, March–August 1804; entertaining record of a sergeant on the Lewis and Clark expedition; bare details of the expedition; interesting spellings.

Amer. Antiq. Soc. Proc. n.s. IX (1893–1894) 238–252; R. G. Thwaites (ed.), *Original Journals of the Lewis and Clark Expedition* VII (New York, 1905) 3–26.

FOORD, James (1761–1821) of Milton and Dedham, Mass.

Travel diary, January–May 1804; business trip from Massachusetts to Kentucky to investigate titles; Boston, New York, Philadelphia, Frankfort, Ohio Valley, by stage and horseback; notes on stages, inns; brief entries, with some social interest.

Pennsylvania Mag. Hist. Biog. LXIV (1940) 1–21.

GASS, Sergt. Patrick (1771–1870) *b.* Falling Springs, Pa.

Exploration journal, May 1804–September 1806; kept while author was a member of the Lewis and Clark expedition; the first published account of the expedition; very good reading, although journal was polished for publication.

A Journal of the Voyages and Travels of a Corps of Discovery, under the Command of Captain Lewis and Captain Clarke (Pittsburgh, 1807) 262 pp.; frequently reprinted; J. K. Hosmer (ed.), *Gass' Journal of the Lewis and Clark Expedition* (Chicago, 1904) 298 pp.

HOPKINS, Gerard T.

Quaker travel journal, May 1804; visit to Buffalo; account of the country and notes on farming.

Buffalo Hist. Soc. Pubs. VI (1903) 217–222.

JOHNSTON, John (1781–1851) *b.* Scotland, of New York, merchant.

Business journals, May 1804–1847; scattered extracts; business life in New York, travel abroad; moderate interest.

Emily J. de Forest, *John Johnston of New York, Merchant* (New York, 1909) 196 pp. *passim.*

LEWIS, Capt. Meriwether (1774–1809) of Virginia, explorer.

1. Exploration journal, August–December 1803; down Ohio River and up the Mississippi; mainly topographical notes.

Wisconsin Hist. Soc. Pubs. XXII (1916) 31–76.

2. Exploration journal, January 1804–September 1806; extensive account of the exploration to the Northwest with William Clark; distances, topography, etc.

R. G. Thwaites (ed.), *Original Journals of the Lewis and Clark Expedition* I–V (New York, 1904–1905).

LOOMIS, Hezekiah (1779–1862) of Tolland Co., Conn., and Dayton, O.

Sea journal, November 1804–November 1805; aboard U.S. brig "Vixen"; cruise in Mediterranean; ship movements and work as steward; some social details.

Essex Inst. Hist. Colls. LXIII (1927) 285–308, LXIV (1928) 33–48, 129–144, 225–230.

MALHIOT, François Victor (1776–1840), clerk of Northwest Company.

Fur trader's journal, July 1804–June 1805; in charge of Fond du Lac Department, south of Lake Superior; repairing and rebuilding post; interesting notes on life of fur trader; good source for economics of fur trade. Translated from the French-Canadian patois.

Wisconsin Hist. Colls. XIX (1910) 163–215.

MASON, Hon. Jonathan (1756–1831) of Boston, senator.

Travel diary, November 1804–April 1805; horseback journey from Boston to Savannah; comments and descriptions, people, places, social life, theaters; expense list; pleasant journal.

Massachusetts Hist. Soc. Proc. 2d Ser. II (1885–1886) 5–34.

ORDWAY, Sergt. John (*ca.* 1775–*ca.* 1817) *b.* Bow, N.H., of the Lewis and Clark expedition.

Exploration journal, May 1804–September 1806; kept on the Lewis and Clark expedition; River Dubois, Floyd's Creek, Teton River, Fort Mandan, Marias River, Great Falls, Great Divide, down Columbia River to Pacific; at Fort Clatsop, Walla Walla River, headwaters of Missouri River.

Wisconsin Hist. Soc. Pubs. XXII (1916) 79–402.

SCOTT, George.

Missionary journal, 1804; mission with John Bruce to Sandusky, Brownstown, and vicinity.

Western Missionary Mag. (1803) 1–13.

SHALER, William (1778?–1833).

Travel journal, February 1804–November 1805; voyage from Canton to California; Gulf of California, Fonseca Bay, Santa Catalina Island, Cape San Lucas, Hawaiian Islands, Canton; personal observations and material derived from travel books.

Lindley Bynum (ed.), *Journal of a Voyage between China and the North-Western Coast of America* (Claremont, Calif., 1935) 109 pp.; first published in *Amer. Reg.* III Part I (1808). Extracts in R. G. Cleland, *A History of California* (New York, 1922) 470–482.

SUTCLIFF, Robert, of Sheffield, Eng.

Travel diary, May 1804–October 1806; from England to New York, and extensive travels in Pennsylvania, New Jersey, New York, Virginia; touristic and travel notes, scenery, occupations, people, customs; pleasant, journalistic style.

Travels in Some Parts of North America (Philadelphia, 1812) 289 pp.

TILLINGHAST, Capt. William E., of Providence, R.I.

Travel diary, August–October 1804; journey from Providence through New York State to Saratoga and Lake George; notes on towns, scenery, taverns, farming; fair interest; interesting spellings.

Rhode Island Hist. Soc. Colls. XXXII (1939) 8–16, 80–84.

WHITE, Hon. Ebenezer (1727–1817) of Portland, Conn.

Private diary, September–July 1804; brief, scattered notes, personal, local, farming, sermons, weather.

History of Middlesex County, Connecticut (New York, 1884) 501–502.

WHITEHOUSE, Pvt. Joseph, of Kentucky.

Exploration journal, May 1804–November 1805; with the Lewis and Clark expedition; "a Minute relation of the various transactions and occurrences which took place dureing a Voiage of [blank in MS] years from the United States to the Pacific Ocean through the interior of the conti[nent] of North America"; a useful supplement to the better-known journals of the expedition; some linguistic interest.

R. G. Thwaites (ed.), *Original Journals of the Lewis and Clark Expedition* VII (New York, 1905) 29–190.

1805

ANON.

Travel diary, April 1805; trip from Bardstown, Tenn., to Washington, D.C.; notes on scenery and towns, taverns; general comments; full entries of fair interest.

Amer. Hist. Mag. (Nashville) VIII (1903) 91–100.

ANTHOLOGY SOCIETY (Boston).

Journal, October 1805–July 1811; journal of the society conducting the *Monthly Anthology and Boston Review*; impersonal, but a valuable literary record.

Journal of the Proceedings of the Society (Boston Athenaeum, 1910) 35–258.

AYER, Mrs. Sarah Connell (1791–1835) of Portland, Me.

Private diary, November 1805–March 1835; extensive notes on religious and social life in Andover and Newburyport, Mass., Concord and Bow, N.H., Portland and Eastport, Me.; an attractive diary beginning with the trivial visits, reading, and chitchat of a child, and developing into a dominantly religious record in later years.

Diary of Sarah Connell Ayer (Portland, 1910) 404 pp.

BARTLETT, Henry, of Frederick Co., Va.

Travel journal, April–June 1805; journey to Ohio and Kentucky from Virginia; expenses and brief descriptive notes; good narrative of a backwoods preacher appended.

Virginia Mag. Hist. Biog. XIX (1911) 68–86.

BIGELOW, Timothy (1767–1821) of Worcester, Mass., lawyer.

1. Travel diary, July–August 1805; trip to Niagara, via Massachusetts and New York; return via Montreal, Lake Champlain, Vermont, and New Hampshire; good, full notes on topography, towns, taverns, agriculture, etc.

Journal of a Tour to Niagara Falls (Boston, 1876) 121 pp. Extract in A. B. Hulbert, *Historic Highways of America* XII (Cleveland, 1904) 116–142.

2. Travel diary, July 1815; trip to Newport, New York, Philadelphia; general travel details and descriptions.

Diary of a Visit to Newport (Cambridge, Mass., 1880) 29 pp.

BURR, Isaac, of Delaware Co., N.C.

Travel diary, September–November 1805; journey through New York and Atlantic states to Virginia; notes on travel difficulties, taverns, expenses.

Jour. Amer. Hist. III (1909) 447–452.

Espy, Josiah (1771–1847) of Columbus, O.

Travel diary, June–November 1805; tour from Bedford, Pa., into Ohio and Kentucky; visits to relations; description of springs, scenery, Cincinnati, Louisville, New Lancaster.

Ohio Valley Hist. Soc. Misc. (Cincinnati, 1871) No. 1, 28 pp.

Hooker, Edward (1785–1846) of Farmington, Conn.

Political diary, November 1805–December 1808 (extracts); graduation at Yale, journey to Charleston, S.C., tutorship at Caroline College, Columbia; experiences in South; extracts relate mainly to political history of South, with a few social and general items.

Amer. Hist. Assoc. Ann. Rep. 1896 I (Washington, 1897) 842–929.

Kenny, Rev. Patrick (1763–1840) *b.* Dublin, pastor of St. Peter's, Wilmington, Del.

Clergyman's diaries, March 1805–March 1833 (with some gaps); details of Catholic missions at Coffee Run, West Chester, Wilmington, churches of St. Mary and Holy Trinity, Philadelphia; many private notes of expenses, opinions of people, social affairs, parish and farm work, his daily life and infirmities, and the weather; touched with sarcastic and whimsical humor; a most interesting diary.

Amer. Cath. Hist. Soc. Philadelphia Recs. VII (1896) 94–137, IX (1898) 64–128, 223–256, 305–337, 422–458.

Larocque, François Antoine, of Montreal, clerk of Northwest Company.

Fur trader's diary, June–October 1805; journey from Fort de la Bosse trading post on Assiniboine, to the Yellowstone; notes on fur trade and trapping; earliest account of the Crow Indians; notes on daily life, country, fur trade; full and clear narrative, with many lively incidents.

French text edited by L. J. Burpee, *Canadian Archives Pubs.* (1910) No. 3, 82 pp.; translated and edited by Ruth Hazlitt, *Frontier and Midland* (Mont.) XIV (1933–1934) 241–247, 332–339, XV (1934–1935) 67–75, 88, and this reprinted as *Sources of Northwest History* No. 20, 27 pp. Extracts in L. R. Masson, *Les Bourgeois de la Compagnie du Nord-Ouest* (Quebec, 1889) I 299–313.

Levy, Aaron, of New York.

Private diary, September 1805–May 1834 (extracts); entries relating to Jews in New York; business, service as paymaster in army, necrology.

American-Jewish Hist. Soc. Pubs. XXVII (1920) 336–344.

Payson, Rev. Edward (1783–1827) of Portland, Me.

Clergyman's journal, July 1805–February 1825 (extracts); religious reflections, self-analysis and exercises, resolves, prayers, religious reading, health, hopes, and despairs.

Asa Cummings, *A Memoir of the Rev. Edward Payson* (New York, 1830) 35–436 *passim*.

Pike, Zebulon Montgomery (1779–1813) *b*. Lamberton, N.J.

Exploring journal, 1805–1807; expeditions to sources of the Mississippi, through Louisiana to sources of Arkansaw, Kans, La Platte, and Pierre Jaun rivers; tour through New Spain; official exploring expedition.

An Account of Expeditions to the Sources of the Mississippi (Philadelphia, 1810); often reprinted. The standard edition is: Elliott Coues (ed.), *The Expeditions of Zebulon Montgomery Pike, to Headwaters of the Mississippi River, through Louisiana Territory, and in New Spain, during the Years 1805–6–7* (New York, 1895), three vols. Part relating to southern Louisiana Purchase boundary line (July 1806–February 1807) in S. H. Hart and A. B. Hulbert, *Overland to the Pacific* I (Denver, 1932) 200 pp., and part relating to the tour of New Spain (February–July 1807) *ibid*. II 203–280; part relating to the voyage up the Mississippi (August 1805–1806) abstracted as *An Account of a Voyage up the Mississippi River* (Washington, 1807) 68 pp. and published in part in *Minnesota Hist. Soc. Colls.* I (1902 reprint) 302–342. Part also published (omitting Mississippi journey) as Milo M. Quaife (ed.), *The Southwestern Expedition of Zebulon M. Pike* (The Lakeside Classics) (Chicago, 1925) 239 pp.

Putnam, Archelaus (1787–1818) of New Mills (Danversport), Mass.

Private diary, January 1805–June 1817; interesting and varied details of local affairs, personal matters, work as apothecary, religious introspection, literary ambitions; a poem.

Danvers Hist. Soc. Colls. IV (1916) 51–72, V (1917) 49–69, VI (1918) 11–29.

Ratcliff, Mrs. Mildred (1773–1847) of Brownsville, Pa.

Quaker journal, November 1805–August 1833 (extracts); travels and work in Virginia, Carolinas, Ohio; visits to Baltimore, Philadelphia; meetings west of Alleghenies and in South; religious exercises, travel notes, introspection, etc.

Memoranda and Correspondence of Mildred Ratcliff (Philadelphia, 1890) 38–172 *passim*.

Smith, Lydia, of Boston.

Travel diary, December 1805–January 1806 (fragment); kept irregularly and sent to America in letters; social life in London; very literary and stylish; revealing picture of well-bred young American.

Massachusetts Hist. Soc. Proc. XLVIII (1914–1915) 508–534.

White, Tryphena Ely (*b*. 1784) of Genesee St., N.Y.

Private diary, June–September 1805; kept during first months of family's settlement at Genesee St.; housework, gardening, meals, layout of farms, roads, etc.; religious services, housebuilding, neighbors; very interesting diary of woman's side of pioneer life.

Tryphena Ely White's Journal (New York, 1904) 46 pp.

1806

AIKINS, Charles, of Sandwich, Ont.
Canadian travel diary, June–July 1806; journey from Sandwich to York; notes on settlements and mills.
Ontario Hist. Soc. Papers and Recs. VI (1905) 15–20.

ASHE, Thomas (1770–1835), English traveler.
Travel diary, October–November 1806; travel book and general gazetteer arranged as a diary; impersonal descriptions; from Pittsburgh to New Orleans; sociological and economic observations.
Travels in America (London, 1808) three vols.

ATKINS, Quintius F. (1782–1859) of Ohio.
Missionary journal, April 1806–August 1807; missionary to Wyandot Indians on Sandusky River; mostly summary; useful as historical record.
Western Reserve Hist. Soc. Tracts L (1879) 110–113.

HENKEL, Rev. Paul (1754–1825) of New Market, Va.
Lutheran missionary journal, July–September 1806; journey from New Market to Point Pleasant, O.; visits to German community; preaching and accounts of country and co-religionists; good details of German settlers; a solid and pleasant diary.
Ohio Archaeol. Hist. Soc. Quar. XXIII (1914) 162–218.

INGERSOLL, Henry, of Massachusetts.
Travel diary, March 1806–May 1808; scattered entries with *post facto* narrative; Miranda's expedition to South America; travel; imprisonment at Cartagena.
Amer. Hist. Rev. III (1897–1898) 681–684.

ROE, Capt. Daniel (1740–1820) of Brookhaven, L.I.
Farming diary, February 1806–January 1808; mainly notes on weather, farming, crops, household, and family affairs; interesting spellings.
Alfred S. Roe (ed.), *The Diary of Captain Daniel Roe* (Worcester, 1904) 64 pp.

1807

BALDWIN, Rev. Benjamin.
Baptist journal, October–December 1807; missionary tour on Susquehannah River and vicinity.
Massachusetts Baptist Missionary Mag. II (1808) 37–43.

BEDFORD, Dr. John R. (1782–1827) of Florence, Ala.
Travel diary, January–March 1807; tour from Nashville to New Orleans, down Cumberland, Ohio, and Mississippi rivers; scenery and character sketches; personal and social items; fairly interesting.
Tennessee Hist. Mag. V (1919) 40–63, 107–122.

BLENNERHASSETT, Harman (1765–1831) *b*. England, associate of Aaron Burr.

Private diary, August–November 1807; minute narrative of the incidents which occurred from the time of his arrest in Kentucky until his discharge in Richmond, Va.

William H. Safford (ed.), *The Blennerhassett Papers* (Cincinnati, 1864) 303–507.

CASE, Rev. Isaac (1762–1852) of Readfield, Me.

Baptist journals, May–November 1807 and May 1808–January 1809; preaching tours in Monmouth, Canaan, Islesboro, Fairfield, Harmony, etc.; meetings, visits, etc.

Massachusetts Baptist Missionary Mag. II (1808–1809) 14–18, 161–166. Scattered extracts in Henry S. Burrage, *History of the Baptists in Maine* (Portland, 1904).

CLUBB, Capt. Stephen (*b*. 1762) of Saco, 2d mate of the "Hyades."

Prison diary, December 1807–June 1809; capture by French while sailing from Charleston; imprisonment with his wife at Arras; long notes on travels and prison experiences, comments on French people and customs, teaching English, etc.; quite interesting.

A Journal; Containing an Account of the Wrongs, Sufferings, and Neglect Experienced by Americans in France (Boston, 1809) 60 pp., reprinted *Mag. Hist.* Extra No. 51 (Tarrytown, 1916) 59 pp.

EARLY, John (1786–1873) *b*. Bedford Co., Va., bishop of Methodist Episcopal church.

Private diary, May 1807–February 1812 (extracts); experiences and travels mainly in Virginia; preaching on various circuits; notes on religion and politics; moderate general interest.

Virginia Mag. Hist. Biog. XXXIII (1925) 166–174, 283–287, XXXIV (1926) 130–137, 237–251, 299–312, XXXV (1927) 7–12, 280–286, XXXVI (1928) 175–179, 239–248, 328–332, XXXVII (1929) 130–138, 256–260, XXXVIII (1930) 251–258, XXXIX (1931) 41–45, 146–151, XL (1932) 70–74, 147–154 (incomplete).

IRVING, Peter (1771–1838) of New York, elder brother of Washington Irving.

Travel diaries, April–September 1807 (incomplete and with gap); travel in France, Italy, Switzerland, England, and Scotland; long and matter-of-fact notes of a "Grand Tour"; mostly formal and Baedeker-like in style; notes on paintings, buildings, scenery, towns, etc.; varied by occasional personal items and literariness.

Edited by L. B. Beach, *Bull. New York Pub. Lib.* XLIV (1940) 591–608, 649–670, 745–772, 814–842, 888–914.

JACKSON, John Richard (1787–1847) *b*. Alexandria, Va., Catholic priest of Montreal.

Religious journal, July 1807–September 1808 (extracts); his journey to Montreal and his conversion to Catholicism; scenic description with mystical aspects; fair interest.

United States Cath. Hist. Mag. I (1887) 92–100.

MORSE, Rev. Asahel.

Baptist journal, August–October 1807; preaching tour in northwestern New York and Upper Canada.

Massachusetts Baptist Missionary Mag. II (1809) 149–155.

PURSH, Frederick (1774–1820) *b.* Siberia, of Philadelphia.

Botanical journal, May–October 1807; expedition in northeastern Pennsylvania and New York; travel and scientific notes; followed by report.

William M. Beauchamp (ed.), *Journal of a Botanical Excursion* (Syracuse, 1923) 113 pp.

STONE, John (1781–1849) of Salem, Mass.

"Diary or Memorandum Book," April 1807–September 1847; kept while author was deacon of First Church, Salem; religious and some social affairs of the church.

Essex Inst. Hist. Colls. LXI (1925) 97–112, 259–264.

SWIFT, Gen. Joseph Gardner (1783–1865), U.S.A., *b.* Nantucket, Mass.

Diaries, July 1807–January 1865; partly written up as memoirs; military life, engineering, politics, agriculture, history, antisecessionist politics; private and family affairs; extensive and varied observations and reflections.

The Memoirs of Gen. Joseph Gardner Swift (Worcester, 1890) 9–289.

1808

BURR, Aaron (1756–1836), Vice-President of the United States.

Foreign diary, June 1808–June 1812 (with gaps); kept during author's residence in Europe, especially at London and Paris; opening as diaristic jottings, diary develops as daily narrative; private and social affairs, visits, comments on people and places; an important record.

M. L. Davis, *The Private Journal of Aaron Burr* (New York, 1838) two vols., mostly correspondence. Davis' text is a poor one; the best text is *The Private Journal of Aaron Burr* (Rochester, N.Y., 1903) two vols., reprinted from the original MS.

CLAUS, Col. William.

Treaty journal, May–August 1808; at and about Amherstburg; negotiations and other dealings with Ottawas, Hurons, etc.

Michigan Pion. and Hist. Colls. XXIII (1893) 47–60.

CRAM, Rev. Jacob (1762–1833) of Exeter, N.H.

Missionary journal, June 1808–February 1809; Congregational minister's tour through settlements of northern New Hampshire and Vermont; horseback rides, meetings, notes on religious provision of towns.

Journal of a Missionary Tour (Rochester, 1909) 37 pp.

CURTIS, Holbrook (1787–1858) of Watertown, Mass., judge.

Private diary, September 1808–March 1813 and August 1821–June 1822; journeys in Connecticut, weather, news, reading, visit to Philadelphia, philosophical and religious reflections; interesting self-portrait.

Elizabeth Curtis (comp.), *Letters and Journals* (Hartford, Conn., 1926) 49–53, 64–77.

FRASER, Simon (1776–1862) *b*. Bennington, N.Y., of Northwest Company.

Exploration journal, May–August 1808; journey mainly by canoe from Fraser's River in the Rocky Mountains to the Pacific coast; well-written narrative, with interesting details of Atmah and Chilkotin Indians and adventures.

L. R. Masson, *Les Bourgeois de la Compagnie du Nord-Ouest* (Quebec, 1889) I 157–221.

HARTWELL, Jesse, of New Marlborough, Mass.

Baptist journal, September–November 1808; preaching tour in Connecticut, New York, Delaware.

Massachusetts Baptist Missionary Mag. II (1810) 302–307.

IRISH, Rev. David, of Aurelius, N.Y.

Baptist journal, November–December 1808; preaching tour in Massachusetts.
Massachusetts Baptist Missionary Mag. II (1809) 238–243.

MASSIE, Capt. Henry (*b*. 1784) of Falling Springs Valley, Va.

Travel diary, April–June 1808; journey with friend from Fredericksburg, Va., to Boston; rather dull touristic notes.
Tyler's Quar. Hist. and Geneal. Mag. IV (1922) 77–86.

PILLSBURY, Phinehas (*b*. 1767) of Nobleboro, Me.

Diary, beginning in July 1808; mainly genealogical interest; deaths, births, etc.
New England Hist. Geneal. Reg. LXIII (1909) 373–379, LXIV (1910) 75–76, 154–157, 374–375, LXVI (1912) 274–281, 359–366.

ROWLEY, Rev. Samuel, of Granville, N.Y.

Baptist journal, August–October 1808; preaching on west side of Lake Champlain, in Essex, Franklin, and St. Lawrence counties.
Massachusetts Baptist Missionary Mag. II (1809) 169–172.

SUMMERS, Lewis (1778–1843) of Kanawha Co., Va., judge.

Travel diary, June–August 1808; from Alexandria, Va., through Valley of Virginia, down New and Kanawha rivers, to Gallipolis, O.; seeking location for his father; notes on character of the land, descriptions of towns; some political notes, visits, farming notes; a useful journal, with some interesting Southern locutions.
Southern Hist. Mag. I (1892) 49–81.

WILLISTON, Josiah, of Boston.

Private diary, December 1808–August 1814; selections of genealogical interest, deaths, births, etc.
New England Hist. Geneal. Reg. LXV (1911) 366–371.

1809

ARNOLD, Seth Shaler (1788–1871) of Westminster, Vt.

Private diary, September 1809–March 1850 (extracts); a varied journal, selected for facts and views of social, economic, industrial, and religious life of Vermont; account of silkworm industry; great local interest.

Vermont Hist. Soc. Proc. n.s. VIII (1940) 107–186.

BRADBURY, John, *b.* Scotland, botanist of London.

Travel journal, December 1809–January 1811; narrative with day-to-day entries; travel in Louisiana, Ohio, Kentucky, Indiana, Tennessee, Illinois, and Western territories; notes on places, Indians, botany; Osage word list.

Travels in the Interior of America (Liverpool, 1818) 364 pp., reprinted with additions (London, 1819) 346 pp.; R. G. Thwaites (ed.), *Early Western Travels* (Cleveland, 1904) V 320 pp., reprinting 1819 edition.

COLBY, Rev. John (1787–1817) *b.* Sandwich, N.H., *d.* Norfolk, Va.

Baptist journal, November 1809–October 1817; travel and preaching in Vermont, New Hampshire, Maine, Rhode Island, and Ohio; partly narrative and autobiography; left unfinished.

The Life, Experience and Travels of John Colby (3d ed., Cornish, Me., 1829) two vols. in one, reprinted (Lowell, Mass., 1838).

CUTLER, Hon. Ephraim (1767–1853) of Marietta, O.

1. Travel journal, July–September 1809; driving cattle from Ohio River to Baltimore; some pleasant notes on visits, taverns, towns, and farms; a good picture of country life.

2. Travel journal, May–December 1837; travel notes in Connecticut, while author was delegate to Presbyterian Assembly at Philadelphia.

Julia P. Cutler, *Life and Times of Ephraim Cutler* (Cincinnati, 1890) 90–103, 229–238.

Foss, Daniel, of Elkton, Md.

Castaway's diary, September 1809–1814; sole survivor of wreck of brig "Negociator"; five years' life alone on Pacific island; occasional notes of a Robinson Crusoe-like life.

A Journal of the Shipwreck and Sufferings of Daniel Foss (Boston, 1812) 24 pp.; another edition (Boston, 1816) is reprinted in *Mag. Hist.* Extra No. 28 (New York, 1914) 29–51.

GALE, William A., captain's assistant on the "Albatross."

Sea journal, June 1809; day-by-day account of efforts to find a trading post on the Columbia River.

H. H. Bancroft, *History of the Northwest Coast* II 133–134 (in *Works*, San Francisco, 1886).

JONES, Peter, secretary to commissioners.

Treaty journal, September 1809; proceedings for Indian treaty of Fort Wayne.
John L. Heineman (ed.), *Journal of the Proceedings* (Connersville, Ind., 1910)
24 pp.

ROBBINS, Caira (1794–1881) of East Lexington, Mass.

Private diary, July 1809–May 1823 (account and extracts); brief notes on
schooling, domestic, and social affairs; literature, theaters, journeys; fairly interesting.
Lexington Hist. Soc. Proc. IV (1905–1910) 61–81, including letters.

SHORT, Maj. Peyton (1761–1825) *b.* Spring Garden, Va., of Kentucky.

Travel diary, November–December 1809; tour through part of Mississippi Territory; Mobile, Pensacola, etc.; notes on soil, climate, scenery, social and commercial conditions; some estimates of persons; fairly interesting.
Ohio Hist. and Phil. Soc. Quar. Pubs. V (1910) 3–15.

THOMPSON, David (1770–1857), astronomer and geographer of Northwest Company.

Travel journals (extracts); in Oregon, Washington, and Idaho; notes on
topography, geography, navigation; valuable, but dull reading.
1. September 1809–March 1812; in Idaho. *Washington Hist. Quar.* XI (1920)
97–103, 163–173.
2. September–October 1809; Pend Oreille country. *Ibid.* XXIII (1932) 18–24.
3. April–May 1810; Pend Oreille country. *Ibid.* XXIII (1932) 88–93.
4. June–August 1811; Spokane country. *Ibid.* IX (1918) 11–16.
5. June 1811; Pend Oreille country. *Ibid.* XXIII (1932) 173–176.
6. June 1811; Spokane country. *Ibid.* VIII (1917) 183–187.
7. July–August 1811; down the Columbia. *Oregon Hist. Soc. Quar.* XV (1914)
39–63, 104–125.
8. August 1811; Spokane country. *Washington Hist. Quar.* VIII (1917) 261–
264.
9. November 1811; Spokane country. *Ibid.* IX (1918) 169–173.
10. October–November 1811; Spokane country. *Ibid.* IX (1918) 103–106.
11. March 1812; Spokane country. *Ibid.* X (1919) 17–20.
See also J. B. Tyrrell (ed.), *David Thompson's Narrative of His Explorations*
(Toronto, 1916) 582 pp.; and Elliott Coues (ed.), *New Light on the Early History of the Greater Northwest* II (New York, 1897), which has digests of Thompson's journals for 1808–1811.

1810

ANON.

Sea journals, September 1810–June 1812; from New York to mouth of Colum-
bia River; an account based on diaries now lost.
P. A. Rollins (ed.), *The Discovery of the Oregon Trail* (New York, 1935)
App. A 267–280 (translated from a French translation).

DWIGHT, Margaret Van Horn (1790–1834) of New Haven, Conn., and Warren, O.

Travel diary, October–November 1810; from Milford, Conn., to Warren, O.;
addressed to her cousin Elizabeth; long, lively entries in rattling style, describing
adventures, inns, characters; a good diary.

Max Farrand (ed.), *A Journey to Ohio in 1810* (New Haven, 1912) 64 pp.
Extract in James B. Nolan, *Early Narratives of Berks County* (Reading, 1927)
57–67.

McBRIDE, James (1788–1859) of Hamilton, O.

Letter-journal, June–July 1810; brief notes on journey to Lexington, Ky.
Ohio Hist. and Phil. Soc. Quar. Pubs. V (1910) 21–27.

1811

BAKER, Rev. Daniel (1791–1857) *b.* Midway, Ga., of Austin, Tex.

Religious journals, August 1811–September 1848 (extracts); notes while
author was student at Hampden Sidney College, work at Winchester, Va., work
for formation of religious college at Austin, Tex., work at Holly Springs; mission
to Texas.

William M. Baker, *The Life and Labours of the Rev. Daniel Baker* (3d ed.,
Philadelphia, 1859) 35–343 *passim*.

BRACKENRIDGE, Henry Marie (1786–1871) *b.* Pittsburgh.

Travel journal, April–August 1811; up the Missouri River, travels in Louisiana from St. Charles to Manuel Lisa's fort near Mandan village; residence and
return; accompanied Lisa in pursuit of the Astorians.

First published in his *Views of Louisiana* (Pittsburgh, 1814) 198–268; expanded version, called second edition, published separately as *Journal of a Voyage
up the River Missouri in 1811* (Baltimore, 1815) 247 pp.; latter reprinted in R. G.
Thwaites (ed.), *Early Western Travels* (Cleveland, 1904) VI 21–166.

HUNT, Wilson Price (1783–1842) of Trenton, N.J.

Travel and exploration journal, July 1811–February 1812; overland trip with
companions from St. Louis to mouth of Columbia River by a new route across
the Rockies; notes on adventures, topography, natural history; good reading.

P. A. Rollins (ed.), *The Discovery of the Oregon Trail* (New York, 1935)
App. A 281–308.

HYDE, Miss Nancy Maria (1792–1816) of Norwich, Conn.

Private diary, February 1811–September 1812; work as teacher in a girls'
school; full entries in literary style; Christian reading, literary reading (Scott,
Rogers, Burns, etc.), sermons, gardening, social life, reflections; many original
verses; a rather interesting, genteel diary.

The Writings of Nancy Maria Hyde (Norwich, Conn., 1816) 27–210.

MACLEAN, William (1756–1825) of Lincoln Co., N.C., physician.

Travel diary, May–June 1811; from Lincolnton, N.C., to Nashville, Tenn.; notes of inns, people, towns, expenses; lively record.

North Carolina Hist. Rev. XV (1938) 378–388.

TAYLOR, Rowse, of Newport, R.I.

Travel journal-letter; July–December 1811; Quaker family's journey by carriage from Newport to Ohio; notes on scenery, towns, local customs, horrors of taverns; settlement and farming at Smithfield, O.

Bull. Friends' Hist. Soc. Philadelphia VIII (1918) 90–100, IX (1919) 18–26.

TIPTON, John (1786–1839) of Harrison Co., Indiana, senator.

1. Military journal, September–November 1811; Tippecanoe campaign; interesting spellings.

Indiana Mag. Hist. II (1906) 170–184; reprinted from *Indianapolis News,* May 5, 1879.

2. Surveying journal, May–June 1820; journey to locate site for state capital.

Ibid. I (1905) 9–15, 74–79; reprinted from *Indianapolis News,* April 17, 1879.

WALKER, Adam, of 4th U. S. Infantry Regiment.

Military journal, April 1811–May 1812; two campaigns of the Fourth Infantry Regiment in Michigan and Indiana; fairly good narrative but written up from notes.

A Journal of Two Campaigns (Keene, N.H., 1816) 143 pp., *Indiana Hist. Colls.* VII (1922) 693–710; *American State Papers, Military Affairs* I 268–295.

WARDEN, David Bailie (1774–1845) *b.* Ireland, professor and statesman.

Sea journal, August–September 1811; aboard frigate "Constitution," cruise from Annapolis to Cherbourg.

Maryland Hist. Mag. XI (1916) 127–141, 204–217.

1812

ANON. (scout of 17th U. S. Infantry Regiment).

Military journal, August–September 1812; notes on border warfare; relief of Detroit and Fort Wayne.

Mississippi Valley Hist. Rev. I (1914–1915) 272–278.

ASKIN, Capt. Charles (*b.* 1780) *b.* Detroit, of Canadian militia.

Military diary, July–September 1812 (extracts); service during war; surrender of Detroit; account of Fort Dearborn Massacre; much of it personal.

Canadian Archives Pubs. No. 7 (1912) 235–248; extract concerning Dearborn Massacre in *Mississippi Valley Hist. Rev.* I (1914–1915) 561–565.

ASKIN, John.

Diary, June 1812–March 1815; scattered, brief, and miscellaneous entries, mainly news and events of the war.

Michigan Pion. and Hist. Colls. XXXII (1902) 468–474.

AUSTIN, Stephen Fuller (1793–1836), founder of Texas.

1. Travel diary (May 1812)–February 1813; observations on Mississippi River navigation, effects of earthquake at New Madrid, travel in Mississippi.

Amer. Hist. Assoc. Ann. Rep., The Austin Papers II (1919) Part I 205–209.

2. Travel diary, June–September 1821; first trip to Texas; exploration for site of the colony; from New Orleans to "Nachitoches" by boat and then inland; mainly impersonal descriptions.

Texas Hist. Assoc. Quar. VII (1903–1904) 286–307.

3. Military diary, August–September 1824; campaign against the Karankaways.

Amer. Hist. Assoc. Ann. Rep., The Austin Papers II (1919) Part I 885–887.

4. Prison diary, December 1833–April 1834; Mexico; observations on the Catholic church; descriptions of Salamanca, León, San Luis Potosí, etc.; arrest and imprisonment; philosophizing.

Texas Hist. Assoc. Quar. II (1898–1899) 184–210.

BEALL, William K., of Kentucky, assistant quartermaster general, United States Army.

Military diary, July–August 1812; in the Ohio country under Hull; capture by the British; comic-opera plot.

Amer. Hist. Rev. XVII (1911–1912) 783–808.

CARR, Francis, of Bangor, Me., congressman.

Political diary, May–July 1812; kept during author's service as congressman; brief notes, mainly political.

Bangor Hist. Mag. II (1886–1887) 214–216.

DARNELL, Elias, of Kentucky.

Military journal, August 1812–February 1813; Winchester's expedition against Canada with Kentucky volunteers and regulars; hardships, battles, suffering, captivity.

A Journal, Containing an Accurate and Interesting Account etc. (Philadelphia, 1854) 98 pp.; *Mag. Hist.* Extra No. 31 (New York, 1914) 1–53.

EVANS, Amos Alexander (1785–1848), U.S.N., surgeon.

Sea journal, June 1812–February 1813; cruise on the "Constitution."

Pennsylvania Mag. Hist. Biog. XIX (1895) 152–169, 374–386, 468–480. Extracts in *Patriotic Marylander* III (1917) 177–186.

FLAGET, Benedict Joseph (1763–1850), first Catholic bishop of Bardstown, Ky.

Catholic churchman's journal, January–November 1812; diocesan work of bishop of Kentucky; journey to Baltimore; mostly brief, formal notes of his work, but more expansive at Baltimore. Translated from the French.

Edited by W. J. Howlett, *Amer. Cath. Hist. Soc. Philadelphia Recs.* XXIX (1918) 37–59, 153–169, 231–249.

HEALD, Maj. Nathan (*b.* 1775) of New Ipswich, N.H.

Military journal, August 1812–January 1822; march from Chicago to Detroit; attack by Indians; miscellaneous biographical notes; brief scattered notes.

M. M. Quaife, *Chicago and the Old Northwest* (Univ. Chicago Press, 1913) 402–405.

HORRY, Gen. Peter (1747–1815) of Winyah Bay, S.C.

Personal diary, June–October 1812; plantation and domestic details; work, relaxation, musings; good picture of an elderly, well-to-do, active Southerner.

South Carolina Hist. Geneal. Mag. XXXVIII (1937) 81–86, 116–119, XXXIX (1938) 46–49, 96–99, 125–128, 157–159, XL (1939) 11–14, 48–51, 91–96, 142–144, XLI (1940) 15–18, XLII (1941) 8–11, 72–75, 118–121, 189–193, XLIII (1942) 57–60, 125–128, 181–184, 251–255, XLIV (1943) 55–58, 124–129, 196–199, 255–257, XLV (1944) 51–55, 116–119, 177–181, 222–225, XLVI (1945) 54–56 (in progress).

HUNTINGTON, Mrs. Susan (1791–1823) of Boston.

Private diary, March 1812–December 1822 (extracts); a record of the Lord's dealings with her, reflections on religion and her own life, family notes in this light, self-analysis.

Benjamin B. Wisner, *Memoirs of the Late Mrs. Susan Huntington* (Boston, 1826) 62–353 *passim.*

LUCAS, Capt. Robert (1781–1853) of Scioto Co., O., governor.

Military journal, April–September 1812; disastrous Hull campaign of the volunteers in Ohio up to surrender of Detroit; return across Lake Erie and down Ohio to Portsmouth; valuable account of military affairs; interesting spellings.

Iowa Jour. Hist. Pols. IV (1906) 343–437.

LUTTIG, John C. (*d.* 1815), clerk of Missouri Fur Company, of St. Louis.

Fur-trading journal, May 1812–March 1813; fur-trading expedition on the upper Missouri; extremely interesting in parts for social life of traders and Indians; some German-English features in spelling and syntax.

Stella M. Drumm (ed.), *Journal of a Fur Trading Expedition* (Missouri Hist. Soc., St. Louis, 1920) 192 pp.

M'KEEVOR, Dr. Thomas, of Dublin, Ireland.

Travel diary, June–August 1812; doctor with Earl of Selkirk's expedition to Hudson's Bay; notes on voyage, weather, natural history, language, Eskimo life.

A Voyage to Hudson's Bay (London, 1819) 76 pp.

PORTER, Capt. David (1780–1843), U.S.N.

Sea journal, October 1812–August 1814; cruise aboard the "Essex" in Pacific Ocean, Galápagos Islands, Marquesas Islands; description and travel notes.

Journal of a Cruise Made to the Pacific Ocean (Philadelphia, 1815) two vols. in one; reprinted (New York, 1822) two vols.

REYNOLDS, Dr. James, surgeon's mate.

Prison journal, July–October 1812; with Hull's expedition against Canada;

capture with his patients near Fort Malden; journey to Quebec; on prison ship at Quebec; patriotic and antimonarchistic notes of moderate interest; some interesting spellings.

G. M. Fairchild (ed.), *Journal of An American Prisoner* (Quebec, 1909) 32 pp.

ROACH, Maj. Isaac (*d.* 1848) of Philadelphia, soldier and politician.

Military journal, July 1812–April 1824; war services around Buffalo and the Lakes; Battle of Lake Erie; notes on later army life; moderate interest and apparently inaccurate.

Pennsylvania Mag. Hist. Biog. XVII (1893) 129–158, 281–315.

STUART, Robert (1785–1848) *b.* Callander, Scotland, later of Michilimakinac Co., Mich., employee of Northwest Company.

Journal of fur trading and exploring, June 1812–May 1813; journey, mainly by canoe, up Columbia River from Astoria, via Tongue-Point, Klickitat River, Walla Walla River, Vinson Wash, American Falls, McCoy Creek, Moody Creek, Sweetwater River, North Platte, Neb., Wyoming, Nebraska, St. Louis; horseback journey from St. Louis to Green River, Ky.; accounts of his adventures, with notes on scenery, natural history, Indians, etc.; extensive entries; a good example of a journal of exploration.

P. A. Rollins (ed.), *The Discovery of the Oregon Trail* (New York, 1935) 391 pp.

WALL, Garrett, of Pittsburgh.

Military journal, October 1812–April 1813; brief notes of marches and encampment at Sandusky; little interest.

W. H. Egle's Notes and Queries (Pa.) (1900) 165–166.

[WATERHOUSE, Dr. Benjamin (1754–1846) of Harvard and Brown.]

1. Prison journal, December 1812–April 1815; capture at sea by the British and imprisonment at Melville Island, Halifax, and later at Chatham and at Dartmoor, Eng.; an extensive, literary diary, recounting daily life and news but with a great deal of general comment and reflection; fairly vivid but too literary.

A Journal of a Young Man of Massachusetts (Boston, 1816), reprinted *Mag. Hist.* Extra No. 18 (New York, 1911) 272 pp.

2. Diary, 1828 and 1835–April 1844 (extracts); reminiscences, reflections, and memoranda; extracts relating to Harvard and the diarist's character.

Cambridge Hist. Soc. Pubs. IV (1909) 25–37.

1813

BAYARD, James Asheton (1767–1815) *b.* Bohemia Manor, senator from Delaware.

European travel diary, May 1813–September 1814; commissioner in negotiations with Great Britain; at Gothenburg, St. Petersburg, Riga, Berlin, Holland, London, Brussels, etc.; greater part in Russia at time when Alexander I was attempting mediation; very interesting details and impressions of diplomatic and aristocratic life and characters.

Elizabeth Donnan (ed.), *Papers of James A. Bayard, Amer. Hist. Assoc. Ann. Rep.* II (1913) 385–516.

BEAUMONT, William (1785–1853), army doctor and physiologist.

1. Military-medical diary, March–May 1813; medical notes of a surgeon's mate in the War of 1812; battle of Little York; storming of Fort George.

Jesse S. Myer, *Life and Letters of Dr. William Beaumont* (St. Louis, 1912) 38–47.

2. Travel diary, May–September 1820 (extracts); Plattsburg to Mackinac; descriptions; long quotations from Benjamin Franklin.

Ibid. 74–85.

BONNER, Capt. James.

Military journal, October 1813–April 1814 (extracts); events in the war; Upper Sandusky and Fort Meigs, O.; Indian notes.

Western Reserve Hist. Tracts No. 49 (1879) 103–104.

CHEVER, Capt. James, Jr. (1791–1857) of Salem, privateersman.

Sea journal, December 1813–April 1814 (extracts); cruise of the "America."

Ralph D. Paine, *Ships and Sailors of Old Salem* (New York, 1909) chap. xxiv 489–495.

CRAWFORD, William Harris (1772–1834) of Americus, Ga., diplomat.

Private diary, June–November 1813; journey from Washington to Pennsylvania; minister at French Court; meetings with famous politicians and statesmen, notes on places, social affairs, reading, plays, etc.; interesting diary.

Edited by Daniel C. Knowlton, *Smith Coll. Stud. Hist.* XI No. 1 (1925) 9–52. Extracts in J. E. D. Shipp, *Giant Days* (Americus, Ga., 1909) 101–115.

Dow, Peggy (1780–1820), wife of Lorenzo Dow.

Journal of vicissitudes, January 1813–July 1816; notes on camp-meeting religion, as "supplementary reflections to the journey of her life."

Forms second part of Lorenzo Dow, *The Dealings of God, Man, and the Devil* (1854), and his *History of Cosmopolite* (Cincinnati, 1859) 663–708.

[EGERTON, Charles Calvert.]

*The Journal of an Unfortunate Prisoner on Board the British Prison Ship "Loyalist" (Baltimore, 1813). [Sabin.]

FOGG, Rev. William (1790–1859) of Kittery, Me.

Clergyman's journal, April 1813–August 1821; brief notes on weather, local affairs at Kittery, marriages, deaths, war news, church affairs, farming, parish meetings, fashions, journeys; description of President Monroe; verses.

Old Eliot III (1899) 7–9, 15–19, 33–36, 41–43, 76–80, 108–112, 124–127, 138–139, 164–168, 178–184, 195–198.

GALLATIN, James (1796–1876), statesman.

Political diary, March 1813–October 1827; Russian offer of mediation, Treaty of Ghent, treaty of commerce; author's ministry in France; restoration of Bourbons, assassination of Duc de Berri; return to America; special mission to England; intimate picture of family; valuable politically and personally.

A Great Peacemaker (New York, 1914) 314 pp., reprinted as *The Diary of James Gallatin* (New York, 1916) 314 pp. Résumé by C. C.Maconochie in *Blackwood's Mag.* CXCVII (1915) 311–324.

GERRY, Elbridge, Jr. (1791–1883).

Travel diary, May–July 1813; horseback journey, Ohio, Virginia, Washington, Pennsylvania; notes on social life of Washington; descriptions of Moravians; detailed and interesting notes.

Claude G. Bowers (ed.), *The Diary of Elbridge Gerry, Jr.* (New York, 1927) 222 pp. Extract in *Massachusetts Hist. Soc. Proc.* XLVII (1914) 523–528.

HAMTON, Aaron, of New Jersey, Quaker.

Travel journal, May–June 1813; New Jersey to Holland Purchase in New York State; notes on taverns, town, people, Indians; original verses.

New York Hist. XXI (1940) 324–334, 431–442.

HARTSELL, Capt. Jacob (1786–1843) of Cherokee Creek, Washington Co., Tenn., farmer.

Military diary, October 1813–January 1814; military movements, camp life, comments on Indians; many personal notes and comments; farmer's interests; many interesting incidents and good picture of diarist; some poems.

Mary H. McCown (ed.), "The J. Hartsell Memora," *East Tennessee Hist. Soc. Pubs.* XI (1939) 93–115, XII (1940) 118–146.

HICKS, Rev. Elias (1748–1830) *b.* Hempstead, L.I., of Jericho, N.Y.

Quaker journal, March 1813–January 1820; introduced and followed by autobiography and memoirs; private life and religious work at Jericho; journeys and preaching in middle and southern states, New York, New England, Pennsylvania, Ohio, etc.; more general in interest than the usual Quaker journal, with many notes of social life, reading, domestic work, etc.

Journal of the Life and Religious Labours of Elias Hicks (New York, 1832) 132–387.

HOWE, Rev. Joseph P. (*d.* 1830) of West Lexington, Ky.

Missionary journals, October–December 1813 and September–October 1814; horseback journeys, preaching at various Presbyterian meetings in Kentucky.

Jour. Presbyterian Hist. Soc. XVI (1934–1935) 373–388.

INDERWICK, James (*d.* 1815), naval surgeon.

Sea diary, July–August 1813 (extracts); naval warfare; raiding English shipping off English and Irish coasts; defeat and capture of H.M.S. "Pelican."

Bull. New York Pub. Lib. XXI (1917) 395–405.

LEE, Mrs. Mary (1783–1860) of Boston and Brookline, Mass.

Private diary, January 1813–April 1816; kept for her husband during his absence in India; family news, public affairs, religious reading, views on war and Napoleon.

Frances R. Morse (ed.), *Henry and Mary Lee, Letters and Journals* (Boston, 1926) 167–226.

MORRELL, James.

Travel diary, August 1813; Philadelphia to Ballston and Saratoga Springs; detailed and dull.

Pennsylvania Mag. Hist. Biog. XXXIX (1915) 425–433.

PALMER, Benjamin Franklin (1793–1824) of Stonington, Conn.

Prison diary, December 1813–April 1815; kept while author was aboard British warships, in prison at Melville Island and at Dartmoor; detailed accounts of prison life, often in a literary manner modeled on Sterne; descriptions, philosophizing; an excellent prison diary; poem, letters, prison regulations appended.

The Diary of Benjamin Franklin Palmer (*Acorn Club Pubs.* No. 11) (New Haven, 1914) 274 pp.

PECK, John Mason (1789–1857) *b.* Litchfield, Conn.

Baptist missionary journals, June 1813–February 1857; extensive missionary journeys in trans-Allegheny region, mostly Illinois and Missouri; wide interests and good observation; much of it is a general diary of everyday affairs, weather, adventures, social conditions; one of the very best missionary journals.

Rufus Babcock, *Forty Years of Pioneer Life* (Philadelphia, 1864) 360 pp.

RODNEY, Capt. Daniel (1764–1846) of Lewes, Del., judge.

Military and private diary, March 1813–April 1829; ship movements mostly; earlier part kept while author was destroying British cruisers in the Delaware; business notes.

C. H. B. Turner (ed.), *Rodney's Diary and Other Delaware Records* (Philadelphia, 1911) 3–14.

SCHILLINGER, Ens. William, of Ohio militia.

Military journal, February–August 1813; with Hosbrook's company of Ohio militia, mainly at Fort Amanda building boats; garrisoning and provisioning of stockade and general work; news of siege of Fort Meigs; dislike of Kentucky troops; some interesting spellings.

Ohio Archaeol. Hist. Quar. XLI (1932) 51–85.

TAIT, James A. (1791–1855) of Dry Fork, Ala., judge.

Military diary, August 1813–March 1814; with Capt. Smith on military expedition against Creek Indians; portraits of officers; battle of Auttose; Indian notes.

Georgia Hist. Quar. VIII (1924) 229–239.

VALPEY, Joseph, Jr. (1792–1816) of Salem, Mass., seaman.

Prison diary, November 1813–April 1815; capture on the "Monkey" of Boston; imprisonment at Halifax and subsequently at Dartmoor, Eng.; notes on prison conditions, daily activities; moderate interest; highly interesting linguistically, and includes many "poems" by himself and his comrades.

Journal of Joseph Valpey, Michigan Soc. Col. Wars (1922) 71 pp.

WINSLOW, Mrs. Harriett Lathrop (1796–1833) *b.* Norwich, Conn.

Missionary journal, November 1813–December 1832 (extracts); religious self-analysis, some social items, reflections on heathen; teaching in school for the poor; journey to New England; marriage; voyage to Calcutta and Jaffna; thirteen years as a missionary in Ceylon.

Miron Winslow, *Memoir of Mrs. Harriett L. Winslow* (New York, 1840) 24–441 *passim.*

YOST, Robert.

Military journal, December 1813–January 1814; march from St. Clearsville, O., to Fort Detroit; general comments on proceedings, places, and people; some interesting spellings.

Ohio Archaeol. Hist. Quar. XXIII (1914) 150–161.

1814

ANDERSON, Capt. Thomas Gummersall (1779–1875) *b.* Sorel, Lower Canada, Indian agent.

Military journal, August–November 1814; at Fort McKay, Prairie du Chien, Wis.; military affairs, and dealings with Fox, Sauk, Puan, Sioux Indians; interesting and valuable journal.

Wisconsin Hist. Colls. IX (1909, reprint of 1882 vol.) 207–251, with letters.

BAXLEY, Rev. John (d. 1849) of Baltimore, Md.

Private diary, September 1814; account of British fleet off Baltimore, and bombardment of Fort McHenry.

William G. Hawkins, *Life of John H. W. Hawkins* (Boston, 1863) 11–14.

CALLAWAY, James (1783–1815) of Missouri.

Military diary, August–September 1814; Taylor's expedition against Sac and Fox Indians; from Cap au Gris; battle of Credit Rock; fairly good diary with some interesting spellings.

Missouri Hist. Soc. Colls. V (1927–1928) 74–77.

CAROW, Isaac, of New York City.

Travel diary, December 1814–June 1815 and April 1827–October 1828; the first section relates to a voyage from New York to England and touring there; the second relates to travel in England, France, Switzerland, and Germany; interesting picture of a "Grand Tour"; lively touristic details, with some literary interests, and notes of customs, meals, inns, etc.

Mrs. Theodore Roosevelt and Kermit Roosevelt, *American Backlogs* (New York, 1928) 202–230.

DARLINGTON, Maj. William (1782–1863) of Philadelphia, botanist.

Military diary, September–December 1814; with Pennsylvania Volunteer Light Infantry; marches; Darlington's court-martial for objecting to regular army discipline; peaceful life of amateur soldiers.

Western Pennsylvania Hist. Mag. XX (1937) 197–214.

DULLES, Joseph Heatly (1795–1876) of Philadelphia, and Charleston, S.C.

Travel diary, August 1814; a young Yale man's jaunt to Plattsburg and Burlington.

Pennsylvania Mag. Hist. Biog. XXXV (1911) 276–289.

ELLIS, William, of Mobile, Ala.

Captive's diary, August–September 1814; capture by British and Creek Indians; removal to Pensacola.

Aurora (Philadelphia), January 4, 1815.

EVANS, Rev. William (1787–1867) of Philadelphia.

Quaker journal, May 1814–May 1862; set in autobiography; very detailed and extensive journal of Quaker travels and religious work.

Journal of the Life and Religious Services of William Evans (Philadelphia, 1870) 710 pp.

MERRITT, Capt. William Hamilton (1793–1862) *b.* Bedford, N.Y., Canadian statesman.

Prison diary, July–December 1814; march as captive from Buffalo to Cheshire, N.Y., and imprisonment there; social life and general war news; a very pleasant and entertaining diary.

Select British Documents of the Canadian War of 1812 III (Toronto, 1928) 623–648.

MURPHY, Pleasants (1786–1863) of Tazewell Co., Va.

Private and military diary, December 1814–January 1815; mostly notes of parades and marches.

William and Mary Coll. Quar. 2d Ser. III (1923) 231–238.

NAPIER, Lieut. Henry Edward (1789–1853) of London, Eng.

Naval journal, March–September 1814; blockade of New England; lieutenant on H.M.S. "Nymphe"; spirited journal; begins at Halifax, off Massachusetts coast; notes on attitude of New Englanders and relations of Quakers with British; weather, ship movements, amusements and horseplay; good, full entries.

Walter M. Whitehill (ed.), *New England Blockaded in 1814* (Salem, 1939) 3–58.

PIERCE, Capt. Nathaniel (1795–1823) of Newburyport, Mass.

Prison diary, November 1814–July 1815; capture at sea by British and imprisonment at Dartmoor; notes on daily activities, weather, food, escapes, release; fairly good of its kind with some interesting spellings.

Essex Inst. Hist. Colls. LXXIII (1937) 24–59.

PLEASANTS, Thomas Franklin (1790–1817) of Philadelphia and New Orleans, lawyer.

Military diary, April–December 1814 (extracts); activities as member of Philadelphia militia; camp life, detailed account of an affair of honor; unintentionally comic.

Pennsylvania Mag. Hist. Biog. XXXIX (1915) 322–336, 410–424.

STEVENS, Joseph Lowe (1790–1879) of Castine, Me.

Naval surgeon's journal, March–July 1814; aboard privateer "Yankee," off Madeira, etc.; mainly general memoranda.

Rhode Island Hist. Soc. Colls. XII (1919) 76–83.

TATUM, Maj. Howell (*d.* 1823) of Nashville, Tenn., "principal topographical engineer of Tennessee volunteers under Maj.-Gen. Jackson."

Military exploration journal, August 1814–January 1815; first part describes survey of Alabama River, with good topographical details; remainder gives details of the New Orleans campaign until just before capture of Fort Bowyer by the British; latter part has full descriptions of narrative type and contains some matters of general interest and historical importance.

Edited by John S. Bassett, *Smith Coll. Stud. Hist.* VII No. 1 (1921–1922) 138 pp.; extract in *Alabama Hist. Soc. Pubs.* II (1898) 130–177.

1815

CHESTER, Caroline (1801–1870).

School diary, November 1815–January 1816 (extract); detailed account of a fourteen-year-old's struggles at Litchfield School.

Emily Vanderpoel, *Chronicles of a Pioneer School* (Cambridge, Mass., 1903) 150–154.

COTTON, Dr. John (*b.* 1792) *b.* Plymouth, Mass.

Travel diary, September–November 1815; from Rhode Island to Ohio; to New York by boat, then through New York, Pennsylvania, and Ohio; general, social, and touring notes; fairly interesting.

Jour. Amer. Hist. XVI (1922) 36–49, 249–260. Extracts in *Old Northwest Geneal. Quar.* XIII (1910) 59–67.

DE MUN, Jules.

Travel journals, September–November 1815, February–April 1816, June–August 1816; from St. Louis to upper Arkansas River, from Huerfano Creek to Gasconade River, from St. Louis to lower Kansas River; trading expeditions. Translated from the French.

Missouri Hist. Soc. Colls. V (1927–1928) 167–208, 311–326.

GREEN, Capt. Nathan (1787?–1825) of Salem, privateersman.

Sea journal, March–April 1815 (extracts); cruise aboard the "Grand Turk," privateer.

Ralph D. Paine, *Ships and Sailors of Old Salem* (New York, 1909) chap. xxiv 500–503.

HILL, Capt. Samuel (*b.* 1777) of Boston.

Sea journal, March 1815–February 1817; voyage of "Ophelia" from Boston to Canton; fitting out ship; sailing details; life and work aboard ship; Valparaiso, Sandwich Islands, South Seas, Batavia, etc.; detailed descriptions.

New England Quar. X (1937) 355–380.

KENNEDY, Albert (1792–1864) of Madison Co., Va., teacher.

Private diary, January 1815–January 1829 (summary and extracts); various trips to Kentucky, visits; brief notes of genealogical interest.

William E. Brockman, *History of the Hume, Kennedy, and Brockman Families* (Washington, 1916) 128–130.

McKENZIE, Lieut. M., of the British Navy.

Sea journal, January 1815; notes kept while author was reconnoitering in Mobile Bay.

Tennessee Hist. Mag. I (1915) 66–69.

MILLS, Rev. Samuel J. (1783–1818) b. Torringford, Conn.

Religious journal, February 1815–May 1818; missionary work in New Orleans, distributing Bibles among American soldiers and British prisoners; voyage to Africa and missionary work and travel in West Africa around Sierra Leone; notes on scenery, sites, dealings with natives, schools in Freetown.

Gardiner Spring, *Memoirs of the Rev. Samuel J. Mills* (New York, 1820) 74–217 *passim*.

PLESSIS, Joseph Octave (1763–1825), Catholic bishop of Quebec.

Catholic journal, August–September 1815; pastoral visitation along St. Lawrence; visit to Indian mission at Point Pleasant, Me., and return via Portland, Boston, Worcester, Hartford, New Haven, Albany, Lake Champlain; extracts relating to Catholicism in New England. Translated from the French.

Amer. Cath. Hist. Soc. Philadelphia Recs. XV (1904) 377–402.

REICHEL, Rev. Gotthold Benjamin (1785–1833) b. Nazareth, Pa.

Moravian travel journal, September–October 1815; journey from Friedenstadt, N.C., to Bethlehem and Nazareth, Pa.; pleasant, full descriptions of places and co-religionists; translated from the German.

Moravian Hist. Soc. Trans. IV (1895) 125–161.

ROBERTSON, Thomas Bolling (1779?–1828), congressman.

Travel diary, June–July 1815; an American in Paris during the accession and abdication of Napoleon.

Journal of Events in Paris (Philadelphia, 1815) 80 pp.; enlarged edition, *Letters from Paris* (Washington, 1816) 101 pp.

TICKNOR, George (1791–1871) of Boston, scholar and author.

Personal and travel diaries, May 1815–August 1857; travel to England and France, study in Göttingen, Italy, Spain, England; residence in England, with travels and visits; professorship at Harvard; efforts for reform there; studies in English and Italian; further extensive travels in Europe; notes on literary and scholarly affairs and persons and on public figures and literary men; extensive and important diary.

George S. Hillard, *Life, Letters, and Journals of George Ticknor* (Boston, 1877) two vols. *passim;* best edition Boston (1909) two vols.

1816
ANON.

Travel diary, May 1816; journey afoot through Vermont and New England.
North American Rev. IV (1817) 175–186.

BRECKENRIDGE, Richard (1781–1840) of Marengo Co., Ala.

Travel diary, August–September 1816 (fragment); account of hardships of
journey in Tennessee River country; good narrative.
Alabama Hist. Soc. Trans. (1898–1899) 142–153.

BROWN, Uria (*b.* 1769) of Chester Co., Pa., and Baltimore.

Travel and business diary, June 1816–March 1817; journey from Baltimore to
Pennsylvania, Virginia, Ohio, and Maryland; settling land claims; amusing
adventures along the Cumberland Road.
Maryland Hist. Mag. X (1915) 262–283, 344–369, XI (1916) 42–49, 142–157,
218–237, 348–375.

CHAMBERLAIN, Eli (1795–1817) of Lebanon, Me.

Sea journal, January 1816–January 1817 (with gap); voyage of the "Gentoo"
from Salem to Calcutta via Cape of Good Hope and return; nothing remarkable.
Essex Inst. Hist. Colls. LXVI (1930) 479–493, with letters.

FLOWER, George (*ca.* 1780–1862) *b.* Hertfordshire, Eng., of Albion, Ill., colonist.

Travel diary, August–November 1816 (extracts); a young Englishman's journey through New York, Pennsylvania, Ohio, Kentucky, Virginia; observations
of Negroes, frontier life, taverns, etc., and notes on towns; interesting extracts.
Mississippi Valley Hist. Rev. XIV (1927–1928) 137–155.

GILLIAM, James Skelton, of Petersburg, Va.

Travel diary, July–September 1816; trip to Saratoga via Philadelphia and New
York; mainly at Saratoga and New York; travel and social notes. Account with
running extracts.
Tyler's Quar. Hist. Geneal. Mag. II (1920) 294–309.

HIGBEE, William F., of Cumberland Co., N.J.

Travel diary, December 1816–August 1817; journey from Cumberland Co. to
Kittanning, western Pennsylvania, to survey his father's property; return to
Somerset via Indiana; brief notes of no great interest, apart from expense list and
some spellings.
Pennsylvania Mag. Hist. Biog. XLVII (1923) 80–84.

MERCER, William Newton (1792–1869) of Natchez and New Orleans, surgeon
and planter.

1. Travel diary, July–September 1816; Baltimore to Louisville by stage, flatboat, and horseback; notes on strange sights and characters, scenery, medicinal
springs, and Indian mounds; rather interesting.
Ohio Archaeol. Hist. Quar. XLV (1936) 351–364.

2. Travel diary, September–October 1816 (continuation of above); from Louisville to New Orleans by steamboat.

Jour. Southern Hist. II (1936) 390–402.

MILLS, Robert (1781–1855) of Baltimore, architect.

Personal and business diary, January–December 1816; brief notes.

Maryland Hist. Mag. XXX (1935) 257–271.

NORTH, Asahel (1782–1846) of Windsor, Vt., and Greene Co., Ill.

Travel diary, June–July 1816; from Windsor to the Illinois Territory; names of towns, and distances.

Illinois Hist. Soc. Jour. XV (1922–1923) 679–687.

OGDEN, Eliza.

School diary, July 1816–January 1818 (extracts); lengthy accounts of classes and sermons at Litchfield School.

Emily Vanderpoel, *Chronicles of a Pioneer School* (Cambridge, Mass., 1903) 160–176.

ROBERTSON, Powhatan.

Private diary, May–July 1816 and one entry in September 1818; student at William and Mary; social life, cutting classes, studies.

William and Mary Coll. Quar. 2d Ser. XI (1931) 61–68.

SEELY, Miss Catharine (1799–1838) of Darien, Conn.

Religious diary, January 1816–June 1838; religious self-analysis, prayers, self-abasement, illnesses, occasional family notes.

Memoirs of Catharine Seely (New York, 1843) 16–208 *passim*.

TAYLOR, Rev. Oliver Alden (1801–1851) of Manchester, Mass.

Religious journals, February 1816–December 1851 (extracts); at Union College, theological studies at Andover, pastoral life at Manchester; reflections on backslidings, notes on public and local affairs, Gold Rush, parish trials; better than usual clerical journal.

Timothy A. Taylor, *Memoir of the Rev. Oliver Alden Taylor* (Boston, 1854) 26–519 *passim*.

THOMAS, David (1776–1859) of New York State.

Travel diary, May–July 1816; journey through western New York, Pennsylvania, West Virginia, southern Ohio, Kentucky, Indiana, Wabash region; pleasant touristic notes, social life, taverns, customs, topography, Indians of Ohio Valley; followed by notes on western country.

Travels through the Western Country in the Summer of 1816 (New York, 1817, 1819) 320 pp. Extract relating to Indiana in Harlow Lindley, *Indiana as Seen by Early Travelers* (Indianapolis, 1916) 42–135.

WALKER, James, of Buckingham Co., Va.

Private diary, March–June 1816; work as manager of Wilderness Road; travel in Kentucky; inns, prices, camping, riding.

Kentucky State Hist. Soc. Reg. XXXIX (1941) 224–229.

1817

ANON. (of Salem, Mass.)

Travel diary, September 1817–February 1818; a mechanic's notes of a journey to Ohio, via Bedford and Pittsburgh, and return to New England; an excellent, lively account of the journey and criticism of what he saw.

Essex Inst. Hist. Colls. VIII (1866) 226–249.

BIRKBECK, Morris (1764–1825) of England, and Edwards Co., Ill., colonist.

Travel diary, April–August 1817; land-hunting journey with George Flower from Richmond, Va., through Pennsylvania, Ohio, Indiana, and Illinois; day-by-day narrative of adventures; notes on taverns, characters, towns and critical commentary by a keen observer; valuable for its picture of frontier life.

Notes on a Journey in America (2d ed., Philadelphia, 1818) 163 pp. Extracts relating to Indiana in Harlow Lindley, *Indiana as Seen by Early Travelers* (Indianapolis, 1916) 171–190.

CHESEBROUGH, Silas (1796–1845) of Stonington, Conn., and Syracuse, N.Y.

Travel diary, September–November 1817 (extracts); from Stonington to Ohio Territory, via New Jersey and Pennsylvania; descriptions of route.

Amer. Hist. Rev. XXXVII (1931–1932) 65–88.

COBBETT, William (1763–1835), British author, politician, and agriculturist.

Travel diary, May 1817–April 1818; a year's farming on Long Island; notes on soil, farming, economics, expenses, manners and customs, political and religious institutions.

A Year's Residence in the United States of America (New York, 1818) reprinted (London, 1819) in three parts. Modern edition, *A Year's Residence in America* (London, 1922) 1–205. Extracts relating to the Birkbeck settlement in Harlow Lindley, *Indiana as Seen by Early Travelers* (Indianapolis, 1916) 508–521.

DEAN, Thomas (1783–1844) of Deansboro, N.Y.

Travel diary, May–October 1817; journey to Indiana to get lands for Brother-town Indians; accompanied by representative Indians; by boat to Lake Ontario and through Lakes, portage to mouth of Wabash; by canoe and afoot in southern Indiana; return from Fort Wayne to Detroit; good practical details of country and matter-of-fact description of difficulties.

Indiana Hist. Soc. Pubs. VI (1918) 273–345.

FLÜGEL, J. G. (*d.* 1855) *b.* Germany, trader.

Travel journal, January–June 1817 (section kept in English); down the Mississippi to New Orleans; account of New Orleans after the battle.

Louisiana Hist. Quar. VII (1924) 414–440.

FORDHAM, Elias Pym (*b.* 1763), English farmer.

English immigrant diary, December 1817–February 1818; daily happenings at English Prairie, Ill.; trip down the Patoka; winter work; journey to Kentucky;

trip across the Wabash in search of lands; interesting account of Birkbeck settlement.

F. A. Ogg (ed.), *Personal Narrative by Elias Pym Fordham* (Cleveland, 1906) 136–169.

KEYES, Willard, of Newfane, Vt.

Travel diary, June 1817–July 1819; canoe journey to Wisconsin with Peters colony and two years at Prairie du Chien; schoolteaching, milling, logging; valuable diary of early Wisconsin life; mainly brief notes of his own doings.

Wisconsin Mag. Hist. III (1919–1920) 338–363, 443–464.

LAFITTE, Jean (*fl.* 1809–1821) of Louisiana, pirate.

Travel diary, March–May 1817; voyage from New Orleans to Galveston; privateers at Galveston; Lafitte in service of Spain. Translated from the Spanish.

Louisiana Hist. Quar. XXI (1938) 1102–1107.

LANGSLOW, Capt. Richard, of the East India Service.

Travel diary, September–October 1817; from New London to New York by steamboat, by coach to Albany, Utica, Buffalo, Niagara, Batavia, Utica, and return; tourist's notes on inns, food, places, Falls, scenery, etc.; expense list; fairly interesting.

Buffalo Hist. Soc. Pubs. V (1902) 111–133.

LIPPINCOTT, Thomas (1791–1869) of Sullivan Co., N.Y., and Milton, Ill.

Travel diary, November 1817–February 1818; journey with wife and baby, via Easton, Steubenville, Marietta, Maysville, Augusta, St. Louis; notes on companions, conditions of travel, places, etc.; good narrative.

Mrs. Charles P. Noyes (ed.), *A Family History in Letters and Documents* (St. Paul, 1919) 331–342; *Illinois Hist. Soc. Jour.* X (1917–1918) 237–255; first printed in *Presbytery Reporter* (Alton, Ill.) January 1870.

LONG, Col. Stephen H. (1784–1864) of Corps of Topographical Engineers.

Travel journal, July–August 1817; by skiff from Prairie du Chien to Falls of St. Anthony; long descriptions of places and antiquities.

Minnesota Hist. Soc. Colls. II (1889 reprint of 1860–1867) 9–83.

LYE, Joseph (1792–1834) of Lynn, Mass., shoemaker.

Private diary, November 1817–September 1832; work as shoemaker and notes on weather, church and local affairs, reading, fishing, camp meetings; fairly interesting. Original diary in twelve volumes.

Lynn Hist. Soc. Reg. XIX (1915) 41–53. Excerpts from first four volumes.

PALMER, John, of Lynn, Eng.

Travel diary, March–October 1817; voyage to New York; by stage to Pittsburgh, via Bedford, Stoyestown, and Greensburg, and by boat down the Ohio; followed by a description of Ohio, Indiana, Illinois, and Missouri, "and a variety of other useful information" on land prices, economics, towns, etc.

Journal of Travels in the United States of North America (London, 1818) 456 pp.

SEWALL, William (1797–1846) of Augusta, Me.

Private diary, January 1817–March 1846 (extracts); extensive daily record; travels in Augusta, Me., Maryland, Virginia, and Illinois; schooling, farming, weather, visits, church and local matters, courtship; the diary has no sparkle, but its extent and detail make it an interesting record of country life.

John Goodell (ed.), *Diary of William Sewall* (Beardstown, Ill., 1930) 283 pp.

SMITH, Richard (1784–1824) b. Farley, Eng.

Quaker journal, January 1817–July 1824; from 1817 to 1820 he was in Ohio, where he joined the Friends; journey to New York through Pennsylvania; in Ohio and Kentucky; trade, religion, and journeys.

Jour. Friends' Hist. Soc. XIII (1916) 49–58, 89–97, 129–139, XIV (1917) 15–23, 59–69, 108–118 (biography and extracts from journal).

SOULT, Marshal.

Extracts from the Journal of Marshal Soult, Addressed to a Friend and by Whom Translated Is Not a Subject of Enquiry (Newburyport, 1817). Ascribed to Samuel Lorenzo Knapp by Mrs. E. Vale Smith, *Hist. Newburyport* 327. [Forbes.]

1818

ANON., missionary of A.B.C.

Official missionary journal, January 1818–April 1823; kept at Brainerd mission in Cherokee Nation; at Hoyt, Butrick, and Chamberlain; interesting details of Indians and missionary work, social life and visits.

Missionary Herald XIV (1818) 200–204, 213–216, 242–245, XV (1819) 17–22, 154–159, 176–182, XVI (1820) 34–39, 49–53, 87–92, 145–149, XVII (1821) 21–23, 43–49, 71–74, 284–287, 305–307, 337–342, XVIII (1822) 13–16, 105–107, 284–287, 305–309, XIX (1823) 44–46, 169–172, 341–343.

BACON, Rev. Samuel (1781–1820) of Worcester, Mass.

Clergyman's journal, November 1818–April 1820 (extracts); work in Sunday school movement in New York, and later as minister; work for African agency of Bible Society; journey to Africa on behalf of African slaves; work and death in Sierra Leone.

J. Ashmun, *Memoir of the Rev. Samuel Bacon* (Washington City, 1822) 138–274 *passim*.

BRIDGHAM, Eliza Williams (1799–1882) b. Providence, R.I., of Newport.

Travel diary, July–August 1818; in New England and New York; descriptions of places and social details; written for her sister.

Mag. Hist. II (1905) 14–27, 90–95.

BUTLER, Robert S., secretary to Indian treaty commission.

Treaty journal, September–October 1818; treaty with Chickasaw Indians at Old Town (near Tuscumbia, Ala.); conferences, etc.

S. C. Williams, *Beginnings of West Tennessee* (Johnson City, 1930) App. A 283–300.

CARY, Anne M., of Chelsea, Mass.

Letter-diary, July 1818; touristic notes of a journey to Canada; Albany, Schenectady, Lake Ontario.

Caroline G. Curtis (ed.), *Cary Letters* (Cambridge, 1891) 247–269.

CLARK, Mrs. Laura (1798–1863) of Wakeman, O.

Personal diary, June–October 1818; valuable and intimate record of pioneer life in Firelands, O., area; domestic details; loneliness and nostalgia of a doctor's wife; excellent and detailed diary.

The Firelands Pioneer (Norwalk, O.) n.s. XXI (1920) 2308–2326.

CUTLER, Benjamin Clarke (1798–1863) of Brooklyn, N.Y.

Private and religious diary, October 1818–August 1860 (extracts); college life, religion, work and reflections; rector of St. Ann's, Brooklyn; typical clerical journal notes.

Horatio Gray, *Memoirs of Rev. Benjamin C. Cutler* (New York, 1865) 16–334 *passim*.

ENDICOTT, Mary (1800–1871?) of Danvers, Mass.

Private diary, April 1818–January 1866 (extracts); selected mainly for genealogical interest; births, deaths, marriages, some local affairs and general notes.

Salem Press Hist. Geneal. Rec. II (1892) 112–122, 171–176, continued in *Putnam's Monthly Hist. Mag.* I (1892–1893) 28–31, 61–63, 125–127, 250–253.

FAUX, William, English farmer.

Travel diary, November 1818–July 1820; journey to America to ascertain prospects for British emigrants, especially in Birkbeck settlement; Boston, Charleston, Washington, Philadelphia, New York; Illinois, English Prairie; return to England; satirical, abusive picture of American life and domestic manners; amusing or annoying according to taste and tolerance.

Memorable Days in America (London, 1823) 488 pp.; reprinted in R. G. Thwaites (ed.), *Early Western Travels* (Cleveland, 1905) XI 16–305, XII 11–138. Extracts relating to Indiana in Harlow Lindley, *Indiana as Seen by Early Travelers* (Indianapolis, 1916) 290–326.

GILMAN, Mrs. Rebecca (1746–1823) of Marietta, O., and Philadelphia.

Private diary, October 1818–November 1819 (fragments); visit to Providence, reading, domestic affairs; moderate interest.

Mrs. Charles P. Noyes (ed.), *A Family History in Letters and Documents* (St. Paul, 1919) I 351–352.

GUILD, James (1797–1841) of Tunbridge, Vt., peddler.

Travel diary, October 1818–1824; travels as peddler and Jack-of-all-trades in various states, Vermont, New York, Pennsylvania, etc.; journey to England; occasional work as tinker, schoolmaster, portrait painter; experiences and impressions from time to time; occasional verses; a most unusual and entertaining diary with some linguistic interest.

Vermont Hist. Soc. Proc. n.s. V (1937) 249–314.

HITCHCOCK, Maj. Gen. Ethan Allen (1798–1870) of Vergennes, Vt.

1. Military diary, January 1818–April 1868; life at West Point; Florida wars, Mexican War, Civil War; abundant nonmilitary notes, travel abroad, comments on literature, philosophy, etc. Extracts with running editorial narrative.

W. A. Croffut (ed.), *Fifty Years in Camp and Field* (New York, London, 1909) 514 pp.

2. Sociological diary, November 1841–April 1842; kept during investigation on Indian Territory of the charges of fraud and profiteering against contractors who removed Indians to the west of the Mississippi River; private notes of what he saw and heard and his impressions; a valuable account of the seamier side of frontier life and the misfortunes of the Indians.

Grant Foreman (ed.), *A Traveler in Indian Territory* (Cedar Rapids, 1930) 262 pp.

HULME, Thomas, English farmer.

Travel diary, September 1818–August 1819; tour in Ohio, Indiana, and Illinois; by stage, by an ark on the Ohio, and return overland; describes English settlement in Illinois.

Journal Made during a Tour in the Western Countries of America (London, 1828), forming Part III of William Cobbett's *A Year's Residence in the United States of America*; reprinted in R. G. Thwaites, *Early Western Travels* (Cleveland, 1904) X 17–84.

NUTTALL, Thomas (1786–1859) *b.* Yorkshire, of Philadelphia, botanist.

Travel diary, October 1818–February 1820; a naturalist's travels down the Ohio and in the Arkansas country; Fort Smith to the Red River, Cave-in-Rock, Shawneetown, etc.; valuable botanical and ethnological notes.

A Journal of Travels in the Arkansa Territory (Philadelphia, 1821) 296 pp.; R. G. Thwaites (ed.), *Early Western Travels* (Cleveland, 1905) XIII 364 pp.

OWEN, John (1786–1848) of Tuscaloosa, Ala.

Travel diary, October–December 1818; removal of house and family from Norfolk Co., Va., to Tuscaloosa; brief notes of stages and minor hardships.

Southern Hist. Assoc. Pubs. I (1897) 89–97.

PINCKNEY, Charles Cotesworth (1746–1825) of South Carolina, soldier, statesman, planter.

Plantation diary, April–December 1818; kept at Pinckney Island; work on the plantation; farming records.

South Carolina Hist. Geneal. Mag. XLI (1940) 135–149.

RUSSELL, Jonathan (1771–1832) *b.* Providence, R.I., diplomat.

Travel diary, October 1818–May 1819; journey from Stockholm to Berlin, Vienna, and through Italy; meetings with important Europeans (Metternich, etc.); opinions of objets d'art, ruins, towns, customs, religion, etc.; intelligent American appraisals; lengthy notes.

Massachusetts Hist. Soc. Proc. LI (1917–1918) 369–498.

SCHOOLCRAFT, Henry Rowe (1793–1864), explorer.

1. Travel journal, 1818; daily notes of journey up Mississippi, from mouth of Ohio to St. Louis, with notes on mineralogy, geography, sociology, etc.

A View of the Lead Mines of Missouri (New York, 1819) 299 pp. A variant journal of the same trip is printed in his *Scenes and Adventures in the Semi-Alpine Region of the Ozark Mountains* (Philadelphia, 1853) 256 pp.

2. Travel journal, November 1818–February 1819; from Potosi in Missouri Territory through Missouri and Arkansas toward the Rockies; long descriptions of geography, topography, and people, and personal adventures; interesting.

Journal of a Tour into the Interior of Missouri and Arkansaw (London, 1821) 102 pp.

3. Exploration journal, March–September 1820; description and travel in the old Northwest from Detroit through the Lakes to the sources of the Mississippi; with Governor Cass's expedition.

Narrative Journal of Travels through the Northwestern Regions of the United States (Albany, 1821) 419 pp. Slightly different version in *Summary Narrative of an Exploratory Expedition to the Sources of the Mississippi River* (Philadelphia, 1855) 596 pp. Chap. xxv abridged in *Iowa Hist. Rec.* XVI (1900) 100–106.

4. Exploration journal, 1821; with General Cass on expedition down Wabash and Ohio rivers to Shawneetown, by wagon across southern Illinois to St. Louis, up Mississippi and Illinois rivers to Peoria, and by horseback to Chicago; Indian treaty; notes on geography, and natives.

Travels in the Central Portions of the Mississippi Valley (New York, 1825) 459 pp.

1819

ANON., missionary of A.B.C.

Official missionary journal, March 1819–December 1822; kept at Elliott among the Choctaw nation; farming and mission work, journey to found a new mission; very interesting.

Missionary Herald XV (1819) 220–225, XVI (1820) 1–5, 149–155, 169–176, XVII (1821) 48–52, 74–76, 287–292, 307–313, 342–344, XVIII (1822) 76–80, 179–182, 378–379, XIX (1823) 114–116.

BAGLEY, Lowell (1784–1860) of Amesbury, Mass.

Private diary, February 1819–October 1850; notes of local affairs, family, weather, Boston visits and news, natural history study, farm work, circus, and quacks; a very pleasant diary of a very peaceful life.

Mary B. Longyear, *The History of a House* (Brookline, 1925) 12–32.

BROWN, Gen. Jacob (1775–1828), U.S.A.

Military journal, May–July 1819; inspection tour (with his wife) around garrisons of Great Lakes via Brownsville, Oswego, Genesee, Niagara, Fort George, Buffalo, Detroit, Mackinac, Green Bay, etc.; mostly descriptions of scenery and social notes; fairly interesting.

Buffalo Hist. Soc. Pubs. XXIV (1920) 296–323.

ELLIS, Ira I., of Pittsylvania Co., Va.

Travel diary, May–June 1819; Pittsylvania County to Kentucky, on horseback, and return; notes en route.

Virginia Mag. Hist. Biog. XLI (1933) 33–40.

FORSYTH, Maj. Thomas (1771–1833) *b*. Detroit, Mich., fur trader at Peoria, Ill.

Travel diary, June–September 1819; Leavenworth's expedition to establish Fort Snelling; by water from St. Louis to Falls of St. Anthony and return; interesting details, especially about the lead mines and the Indians of the upper Mississippi.

Wisconsin Hist. Colls. VI (1872, reprinted 1908) 188–219; reprinted in *Minnesota Hist. Soc. Colls.* III (1870–80) 139–167.

GOLDIE, James (1792–1886) *b*. Scotland, of Ayr, Ont., botanist.

Travel diary, 1819; journey, mostly afoot, through Eastern Canada and New England; mostly botanical and travel notes with a few political entries and echoes of the War of 1812.

*Diary of a Journey through Upper Canada (Toronto, 1897).

GREENLEAF, Miss Mary Coombs (1800–1857) *b*. Newburyport, Mass.

Religious journal, July 1819–January 1857 (extracts); notes on religious life and reflections, health, family; missionary work among Chickasaw Indians.

Life and Letters of Miss Mary C. Greenleaf (Boston, 1858) 20–340 *passim*.

HALLOCK, Rev. William Allen (1794–1880) *b*. Plainfield, Mass.

Religious journal, November 1819–May 1851; life in seminary at Andover, preaching tours, foundation of American Tract Society and his work for it as secretary, family notes.

Helen C. Knight, *Memorial of Rev. William A. Hallock* (New York, 1882) 13–75 *passim*.

HAWKINS, Rev. John Henry Willis (1797–1858) *b*. Baltimore.

Clergyman's journal, April 1819–February 1842; tour from Baltimore through western states, Ohio, Pennsylvania; work in Massachusetts, Boston, etc.

William G. Hawkins, *Life of John H. W. Hawkins* (Boston, 1863) 23–191 *passim*.

HOW, Rev. Moses (1798–1882) of New Bedford, Mass.

Clergyman's journal, August 1819–November 1826 and December 1836; work as pastor at New Bedford, local and social affairs, political notes, poems.

Diary of Rev. Moses How (New Bedford, 1932) 3–22. Undated extracts from the journal of W. S. G. Howe of New Bedford are given on pp. 25–29 of the same volume.

MASON, Dr. Richard Lee (*d*. 1824) of St. Louis, Mo., physician.

Travel diary, October–December 1819; from Pennsylvania to Illinois through Ohio, Kentucky, and Indiana, to locate bounty land near Alton, Ill.; acute observations on people and customs; somewhat impersonal but quite interesting.

Narrative of Richard Lee Mason in the Pioneer West (New York, 1915) 74 pp. Extracts relating to Indiana in Harlow Lindley, *Indiana as Seen by Early Travelers* (Indianapolis, 1916) 235–238.

OTIS, Harriet, of Chelsea, Mass. (?)
  Letter-diary, July–August 1819; touristic notes of a journey to Saratoga Springs; social and literary details.
  Caroline G. Curtis (ed.), *Cary Letters* (Cambridge, 1891) 269–281.

RICHARDSON, Jacob, Jr., of New Hampshire.
  Travel and frontier diary, August 1819–June 1821 (account and extracts); journey from New Hampshire to Arkansas, via Cincinnati; life as schoolmaster in Arkansas and Natchez; notes on Indians.
  Hyde Park Hist. Rec. IV (1904) 49–67.

SLADE, Gen. Jeremiah, of Martin Co., N.C.
  Travel diary, June 1819; from Martin Co., N.C., to Nashville, Tenn.; hospitality on way; flowery descriptions.
  Trinity Coll. Hist. Papers VI (1906) 37–56.

WATSON, William (1773–1836) of Hartford, Conn.
  Private diary, February 1819–October 1836; extracts mainly of genealogical interest, births, deaths, etc.
  New England Hist. Geneal. Reg. LXXIX (1925) 298–310, 401–409, LXXX (1926) 54–72.

YARNALL, Elias (1757–1847) of Philadelphia.
  Quaker travel journal, November–December 1819 (fragment); journey from Philadelphia to Charleston, S.C., as member of a committee to investigate condition of Friends there; mainly details of voyage.
  Bull. Friends' Hist. Soc. Philadelphia IX (1920) 118–127.

1820

AUDUBON, John James (1785–1851), naturalist.
  1. Botanical journal, October 1820–December 1821; journal of his trip to New Orleans; bird life, hunting.
  Howard Corning (ed.), *Journal of John James Audubon, Made during His Trip to New Orleans* (Boston, 1921) 1–225, reprinted (Cambridge, Mass., 1929).
  2. Travel journal, July 1840–October 1843; journey while Audubon was gathering subscriptions for his "Birds of America"; travel and description in United States and Canada.
  Howard Corning (ed.), *Journal of John James Audubon ... 1840–1843* (Cambridge, Mass., 1929) 179 pp. Extracts relating to visit to Iowa in 1843 in *Annals of Iowa* 3d Ser. XVI (1928) 403–419; general extracts in Maria R. Audubon, *Audubon and His Journals* (New York, 1897) two vols.

BENTON, Henry P., deputy surveyor of public lands in Indiana.

Surveying journal, February–April 1820; surveying boundaries of Big Miami Reserve, south of Wabash River; surveying details, notes on weather, camps, etc.
Indiana Mag. Hist. XXXVII (1941) 387–395.

CUTLER, George Younglove, law student at Litchfield, Conn.

Private diary, May–December 1820 (extracts); an amusing account of social life in Litchfield, especially in relation to the young ladies of Litchfield School.
Emily Vanderpoel, *Chronicles of a Pioneer School* (Cambridge, Mass., 1903) 193–207.

DOTY, James Duane (1779–1865) b. Salem, N.Y., governor of Wisconsin Territory.

Official travel journal, May–August 1820; expedition with Cass and Schoolcraft to Lake Superior and sources of the Mississippi; investigation of northern Indians, topography, and resources; impersonal but has some general interest.
Wisconsin Hist. Colls. XIII (1895) 163–219.

EMERSON, Ralph Waldo (1803–1882), poet, essayist, lecturer.

Journals, January 1820–December 1875; entries often irregular; "records of local and provincial fact, of his contemporaries, . . . of his reading, of his thoughts, of material for future poems or essays, of solitary ecstasies in the presence of beauty, of valiant voyages of an exploring soul" (Bliss Perry). More a commonplace book than a journal.

E. W. Emerson and W. E. Forbes, *Journals of Ralph Waldo Emerson* (Boston, 1914) ten vols.; an excellent one-volume selection is Bliss Perry, *The Heart of Emerson's Journals* (Boston, 1926) 357 pp.

ENGLAND, Rt. Rev. John (1786–1842) b. Cork, Ireland, first Catholic bishop of Charleston, S.C.

Diocesan journal, July 1820–December 1823; account of his church and diocesan work during his first three years as bishop in America.
Amer. Cath. Hist. Soc. Philadelphia Recs. VI (1895) 29–55, 184–224; separately printed as *Diurnal of the Right Rev. John England* (Philadelphia, 1895) 68 pp.

FITCH, Jeremiah, of Boston and Bedford.

Travel diary, July–August 1820; journey from Boston to Saratoga Springs, N.Y., and return; pleasure jaunt, with notes on inns and sights on way.
Massachusetts Hist. Soc. Proc. L (1916–1917) 189–196.

FORSTER, William (1784–1854) b. England, ministering Quaker.

Travel journal, 1820–1825; travel in New England, Canada, New York, New Jersey, Pennsylvania, Delaware, Maryland, Ohio, Indiana, and Illinois; travel, work, meetings.
Benjamin Seebohm (ed.), *Memoirs of William Forster* (London, 1865) two vols.; extracts relating to Indiana in Harlow Lindley, *Indiana as Seen by Early Travelers* (Indianapolis, 1916) 256–268.

HAWLEY, Zerah, of New Haven, Conn.

Travel diary, September 1820–September 1821; tour through Connecticut, Massachusetts, New York, northern Pennsylvania, and Ohio; a year's residence in Western Reserve; interesting notes on many towns, scenery, crops, trade, etc.

A Journal of a Tour (New Haven, 1822) 158 pp.

KEARNY, Capt. Stephen Watts (1794–1848) *b.* Newark, frontier soldier.

Military exploration journal, July–August 1820; Council Bluffs–St. Peters expedition, between upper Missouri and Mississippi River to open up route between Camp Missouri (near Omaha) and Camp Cold Water (near Minneapolis); describes forts, towns, Indian villages, geography; some personal items.

Missouri Hist. Soc. Colls. III (1908–1911) 8–29, 99–131; *Annals of Iowa* 3d Ser. X (1912) 343–371.

LEWIS, Jane R., and LEWIS, Mary Ann.

School diary, "Summer, 1820"; brief notes on daily studies at Litchfield School.

Emily Vanderpoel, *Chronicles of a Pioneer School* (Cambridge, Mass., 1903) 221–225.

NETTLETON, Rev. Asahel (1783–1844) *b.* North Killingworth, Conn.

Clergyman's journal, April–June 1820; religious work in Nassau (near Albany); meetings in schools, taverns, etc.; revival meetings.

Bennett Tyler, *Memoir of the Rev. Asahel Nettleton* (Hartford, 1844) 108–123.

SIMPSON, George (1792–1860) *b.* Loch Broom, Scotland, governor of Hudson's Bay Company.

1. Fur-trading journal, July 1820–June 1821; begins at Rock Depot on Hayes River; mostly in Athabasca Department; business details, his own activities in the early days of his service; highly personal and revealing; an important journal.

E. E. Rich (ed.), *Journal of Occurrences in the Athabasca Department* (Toronto, 1938) 498 pp.

2. Fur-trading journal, August 1824–June 1825; voyage from York Factory to Fort George and return; very important in Northwest history.

Frederick Merk (ed.), *Fur Trade and Empire, Harvard Hist. Stud.* XXXI (1931) 3–174.

3. Travel journal, 1841–1842; tour of inspection of properties of Hudson's Bay Company; includes four chapters on California, and notes of a world tour.

Narrative of a Journey Round the World (London, 1847) two vols.

WEST, Rev. John (1775?–1845) *b.* Farnham, Eng., chaplain to Hudson's Bay Company.

Religious and missionary journal, May 1820–October 1823; journey from England to Winnipeg; residence as chaplain at Red River colony; daily events, with accounts of the country, Indians, missionaries, and state of religion; return to London; an interesting journal.

The Substance of a Journal (London, 1824) 326 pp., reprinted (Montreal, 1866). Extracts in *North Dakota Hist. Soc. Colls.* III (1910) 441–490.

WOODS, John (*d.* 1829), "a well-to-do English farmer."

Travel and emigrant diary, June 1820–July 1821; very full account of his life and prospects and the progress of Birkbeck's settlement in Illinois; travel notes and comments on agriculture, towns and villages, American customs, etc.; a valuable and interesting diary.

Two Years' Residence in the Settlement on the English Prairie (London, 1822) 310 pp.; reprinted in R. G. Thwaites (ed.), *Early Western Travels* X (Cleveland, 1904) 177–357.

ANON.   1821

Travel diary, June–November 1821; from Charleston, S.C., to Rhode Island, Massachusetts, New Hampshire, Vermont, Canada, New York, Maine, and return to Charleston; usual travel notes.

Prominent Features of a Northern Tour (Charleston, 1822) 48 pp.

BECKNELL, Capt. Thomas.

1. Travel journal, September 1821–September (?) 1822; *post facto* and dated irregularly; Boone's Lick, Mo., to Santa Fe; description of Santa Fe; return; account of second expedition over similar route.

2. Travel journal, November–December 1824? (undated and written up for newspaper article); Santa Cruz to the Green River "several hundred miles from Santa Fé"; descriptions of country and Indians.

Missouri Hist. Rev. IV (1909–1910) 65–81, 81–84 (reprinted from the *Missouri Intelligencer,* April 22, 1823, and June 25, 1825); first journal reprinted in A. B. Hulbert, *Southwest on the Turquoise Trail* (Denver, 1933) 56–68.

CROSWELL, Rev. Harry (1778–1858) of New Haven, Conn.

Clergyman's diary, October 1821–May 1848; extracts arranged to illustrate his parish work, character, congregational thought, politics, interest in New Haven, etc.

New Haven Col. Hist. Soc. Papers IX (1918) 46–69; reprinted in F. B. Dexter, *A Selection from the Miscellaneous Historical Papers of Fifty Years* (New Haven, 1918) 349–365.

FOWLER, Maj. Jacob (1765–1850) *b.* New York, of Covington, Ky.

Travel diary, September 1821–July 1822; from Arkansas through Indian Territory, Oklahoma, Kansas, Colorado, and New Mexico to the sources of the Rio Grande; valuable geographically; impersonal, but very interesting for spellings and language.

Elliott Coues (ed.), *The Journal of Jacob Fowler* (New York, 1898) 183 pp. Section relating to Oklahoma (September–October 1821) in *Chrons. Oklahoma* VIII (1930) 181–188.

GARRY, Nicholas, deputy governor of Hudson's Bay Company.

Travel diary, March–November 1821; from England to New York (meeting with Astor), Montreal; visiting posts of Hudson's Bay Company in Northwest

Territories; descriptions, often social and scenic; return voyage to England; well written and entertaining.

Edited by F. N. A. Garry, *Royal Soc. Canada Proc. and Trans.* 2d Ser. VI (1900) Sec. II 73–204.

HARRIS, Rev. Thompson S., missionary of A.B.C.

Missionary journals, November 1821–November 1828; work among the Senecas at Buffalo Creek and Cattaraugus reservations; rather impersonal account of religious and school work, with some religious reflections and moralizing.

Missionary Herald XXIII (1827) 248–250; *Buffalo Hist. Soc. Pubs.* VI (1903) 281–378.

PEARSON, John, of Ewell, Surrey, England.

Travel diary, 1821; intention to settle on farm; after trip to western Pennsylvania he returned to England; vigorous and lively abuse of Americans, Scotsmen, innkeepers, dogs, towns, etc.; entertaining or annoying according to taste and tolerance.

Notes Made during a Journey in 1821 in the United States of America (London, 1822) 72 pp. Extract in J. W. Harpster, *Pen Pictures of Early Western Pennsylvania* (Pittsburgh, 1938) 277–285.

RODMAN, Samuel (1792–1876) of New Bedford, Mass.

Private diary, December 1821–April 1829; long and detailed record of life in New Bedford; regular notes of work, social affairs, and church life; reading and reflections; valuable and interesting.

Z. W. Pease (ed.), *Samuel Rodman Diary* (New Bedford, 1927) (reprinted from *The Morning Mercury*) 349 pp. Section, 1827, missing from 1927 edition, published as Bradford Swan (ed.), *New Bedford in 1827* (New Bedford, 1935) 32 pp.

TEAS, Thomas Scattergood (*b.* 1796) of Philadelphia.

Travel diary, July 1821 (extracts); journey afoot from Philadelphia to Indiana by way of Pittsburgh; long descriptive entries, details of Indians, scenery, towns, etc.

Harlow Lindley, *Indiana as Seen by Early Travelers* (Indianapolis, 1916) 246–255.

VAN LIEW, Elizabeth (1790–1873) of Middlebush, N.J.

Private diary, September 1821–September 1856; arranged by editor as jottings on Six Mile Run, N.J., weather, necrology, family visits to West and lake country.

Somerset Co. Hist. Quar. (Somerville, N.J.) VII (1918) 55–61, 123–127.

WHITALL, John M. (1800–1877) of Philadelphia.

Private diary, October 1821–April 1867; scattered extracts on religion, reflections, life as sailor; becomes Quaker; captain of an East Indiaman; mainly notes on his shortcomings and on business life in Philadelphia and mission work there.

Hannah W. Smith, *John M. Whitall: The Story of His Life* (Philadelphia, 1879) 112–287 *passim*.

WILLIAMSON, Hon. William D. (1779–1846) of Bangor, Me., congressman and
    governor.
    Travel diary, November 1821–May 1822; journey from Bangor to Washington
to attend 17th Congress; brief travel and political notes.
    New England Hist. Geneal. Reg. XXX (1876) 189–191, 429–431; *Bangor Hist.
Mag.* VIII (1893) 50–54.

1822

ANON. ("Committee" of American Literary, Scientific, and Military Academy of
    Middletown, Conn.).
    1. School travel journal, June 1822; excursion made by cadets of the American
Literary, Scientific, and Military Academy, under Capt. Alden Partridge; from
Norwich, Vt., to Concord, N.H., via Enfield and Salisbury, and return through
Hopkinton, Hillsborough, and Newport; notes on countryside, drills, etc.
    A Journal of an Excursion (Concord, N.H., 1822) 38 pp.
    2. School travel journal, November 1826; from Middletown, Conn., to Pough-
keepsie, West Point, and New York City.
    Journal of an Excursion (Middletown, Conn., 1826) 22 pp.
    3. School travel journal, December 1826; from Middletown to Washington,
D.C.
    Journal of a Tour of a Detachment of Cadets (Middletown, 1827) 100 pp.

ANON.
    Travel diary, October–December 1822; journey from Horsham, Pa., to New
Lisbon, O., mainly over the Erie Pike; return by southern route to Pittsburgh and
Pennsylvania way; notes on taverns, food, towns, and minor adventures; fair
interest, with some interesting spellings.
    Pennsylvania Mag. Hist. Biog. XLIX (1925) 61–74.

BRINCKLÉ, Rev. Samuel C. (1796–1863) of Radnor, Pa.
    Clergyman's diary, January 1822–December 1832; kept while author was
rector of Radnor Church and St. Peter's Church, Chester Valley; extracts relating
to churches, sermons, vestry meetings, parish work.
    The History of Old St. David's Church (Philadelphia, 1907) App. 198–206.

COLLINS, Stephen (1797–1871) of Philadelphia, physician.
    Private diary, July 1822–April 1860; religious life after his conversion; un-
varied notes on religion, reflection, prayer, self-abasement, etc.
    The Autobiography of Stephen Collins (New York, 1872) 235 pp. *passim.*

HADLOCK, Capt. Samuel, Jr. (1792–1833) of Cranberry Isles, Me., showman.
    Travel journals, 1822–1826; extended travel in Europe, Ireland, England, Ger-
many, France; social life, travel notes, verses, many interesting spellings; extracts
in biographical setting; so interesting as to suggest desirability of straight publication as diary.
    Rachel Field, *God's Pocket* (New York, 1934) 163 pp. *passim.*

LAY, John, of Buffalo, merchant.

Travel diaries, August 1822–January 1824; extracts relating to travel in Scotland and England, where he met some famous literary men; return to Boston and comments on theater, etc.

Buffalo Hist. Soc. Pubs. IV (1896) 125–145 ("The Journeys and Journals of an Early Buffalo Merchant").

LIEBER, Dr. Francis (1800–1872) *b.* Berlin, Germany, of New York City.

Scholar's diary, June 1822–October 1857; journal kept in Greece, early life in Germany and London, emigration to America; notes on study and reading and journeys; tours in Europe, where he had many eminent acquaintances in the literary world; teaching and scholarship at Columbia University; social and artistic life in New York.

Thomas S. Perry (ed.), *The Life and Letters of Francis Lieber* (Boston, 1882) 44–296 *passim*.

RAVENEL, Dr. Henry (*b.* 1790) of Pooshee, S.C.

Private diary, September 1822–March 1853; brief notes of family affairs, work, journeys, weather; continues his father's diary.

Henry E. Ravenel, *Ravenel Records* (Atlanta, 1898) 251–253.

ROBERTS, Deborah S. (*b.* 1802) of Darien, Conn., and New York City.

Religious journal, June 1822–May 1838; reflections on God and herself, Negroes, morals, Christian consolation; self-abasement and afflictions, illness; recluse-like.

Memoirs of Catherine Seely (New York, 1843) 216–250.

ROSATI, Joseph (1789–1843) *b.* Sora, Italy, of Baltimore, Catholic archbishop.

Catholic diocesan journal, August 1822–December 1826; travel and daily work of archbishop; detailed but impersonal.

St. Louis Cath. Hist. Rev. III (1921) 311–369, IV (1922) 76–108, 165–184, 245–271, V (1923) 60–88.

STEWART, Rev. Charles Samuel (1795–1870), American missionary.

Missionary journal, November 1822–July 1825; voyage from Philadelphia to Sandwich Islands around Cape Horn; missionary work in the islands, with notes on manners and customs of the inhabitants, account of Lord Byron's visit and description of interment of king and queen on island of Oahu; linguistic, anthropological, and social notes; literary style.

Journal of a Residence in the Sandwich Islands (London, 1828) 406 pp.; published with different introductory material as *Private Journal of a Voyage to the Pacific Ocean and Residence at the Sandwich Islands* (New York, 1828) 406 pp. Prior publication in *Christian Advocate* (Philadelphia) II (1824) 277–283, 320–324, III (1825) 216–222, 266–270, 314–319, 359–363, 407–408, 452–455, 552. Long review and excerpts in *Amer. Quar. Rev.* III (1828) 342–369.

STOCKTON, Betsey, Negro missionary.

Missionary journal, November 1822–July 1823; voyage from Philadelphia around Cape Horn to Sandwich Islands; good descriptions of cruise, fishing, ceremonies, social life, arrival at Hawaii, description of island; an interesting journal.

Christian Advocate (Philadelphia) II (1824) 232–235, 564–566, III (1825) 36–41.

SUMNER, Gen. William H. (1780–1861), U.S.A., of Massachusetts.

Private diary, November 21, 1822 (extract); incidents in the life of John Hancock as related by his widow to Gen. Sumner.

Mag. Amer. Hist. XIX (1888) 504–510.

WILBOR, Mary L. (*b.* 1806).

School diary, May–August 1822; studies and social life at Litchfield School.

Emily Vanderpoel, *Chronicles of a Pioneer School* (Cambridge, Mass., 1903) 234–241.

1823

ANTHONY, Joseph (*b.* 1797) of New Bedford, Mass.

Private diary, January 1823–June 1824; full and varied diary, social and local affairs, reading, trips to New York, business, ship affairs; an intimate and very interesting record of a small New England town.

Zephaniah Pease (ed.), *Life in New Bedford a Hundred Years Ago* (New Bedford, 1922) 91 pp.

BROOKS, William G., cadet of the American Literary, Scientific and Military Academy, Norwich, Vt.

School travel journals, September and October 1823; excursion to Manchester, Vt., and to Windsor, Vt.; formal style, but interesting picture of military school life.

Vermont Hist. Soc. Proc. (1915–1916) 95–107.

BUTRICK, Rev. Daniel S. (1789–1851) of Windsor, Mass.

Missionary journal, February–August 1823; travel and missionary work among the Cherokees.

Missionary Herald XX (1824) 8–14.

JOHNS, James (1797–1874) of Huntington, Vt., writer.

Private and business diaries, 1823–1826; notes on happenings in a little Vermont town; births, deaths, marriages, accidents; a seizure by the Devil, rape, court battles, jail break, celebrations, later notes on beginning of Civil War; entertaining, sympathetic, and observant notes.

Vermont Hist. Soc. Proc. n.s. IV (1936) 69–88.

KENNERLY, James (1792–1840) of St. Louis, sutler at Council Bluffs.

Business diary, November 1823–January 1826 (early entries retrospective); business records, life at the post, weather; good picture of life and work.

Missouri Hist. Soc. Colls. VI (1928–1931) 41–97.

LONG, Zadoc (1800–1873) of Buckfield, Me.

Private diary, April 1823–May 1860 (extracts); local life in Maine; trade, weather, family, religion, journeys, accidents and providences, prices; mostly impersonal, but interesting.

A. Cole and C. F. Whitman, *A History of Buckfield* (Buckfield, 1915) 469–508; Pierce Long (ed.), *From the Journal of Zadoc Long* (Caldwell, Ida., 1943), gives a delightful selection.

RAVENSCROFT, John Stark (1772–1830) *b.* Petersburg, Va., first Protestant Episcopal bishop of North Carolina.

Visitation journal, June–July 1823; first visitation of North Carolina; sharp and fairly entertaining comments.

Protestant Episcopal Church Hist. Mag. V (1936) 42–46.

SIMMONS, Dr. W. H., commissioner.

Travel journal, September–October 1823; journey from St. Augustine to Tallahassee to choose site for capital; member of commission.

Florida Hist. Soc. Quar. I (April, 1908) 28–36.

STOW, Rev. Baron (1801–1869) *b.* Croydon, N.H., of Boston.

Clergyman's journal, June 1823–December 1866 (copious extracts); student life at Columbia College, preaching tour in Virginia, ministry at Portsmouth and Boston; parish work and religious reflections; as secretary of triennial convention; revival meetings; trip to Europe, Italy, Switzerland, Germany, England.

John C. Stockbridge, *A Model Pastor* (Boston, 1894) 392 pp. *passim.*

TAYLOR, Rev. James Brainerd (1801–1829) *b.* Middle Haddam, Conn.

Religious journals, May 1823–October 1828 (extracts); religious exercises, self-analysis and prayers, illness; study at Nassau Hall (Princeton) and in theological seminary; preaching in South Carolina.

John H. and Benjamin H. Rice, *Memoir of James Brainerd Taylor* (New York, 1833) 131–405 *passim.*

TODD, Rev. John (1800–1873) of Pittsfield, Mass.

Clergyman's journal, February 1823–May 1871 (extracts); parochial life at Andover, Groton, and Northampton; personal and family affairs; full and well-written notes.

John E. Todd (ed.), *John Todd, the Story of His Life* (New York, 1876) 529 pp. *passim.*

WILLIAMS, John Lee, commissioner.

Travel journal, October–November 1823; sea journey from Pensacola to St. Mark's; selection of Tallahassee as site for capital.

Florida Hist. Soc. Quar. I (April 1908) 37–44 (July 1908) 18–27.

WORK, John (1791?–1861) *b.* Northern Island, chief trader for Hudson's Bay Company.

Trading journals; richly descriptive accounts of fur trading and exploration; business details; important as records of the fur trade of the Northwest at the time of its greatest prosperity.

1. July 1823–November 1824; first journey, with Peter Skene Ogden, from York Factory to Columbia River; journeys to and from Spokane House and Fort Astoria; account and extracts.

Canadian Hist. Assoc. Ann. Rep. (1929) 21–29.

2. November–December 1824; Fort George to the Fraser River and return.

Washington Hist. Quar. III (1912) 198–228.

3. June 1825–September 1826; trading on the Columbia.

Ibid. V (1914) 83–115, 163–191, 258–287, VI (1915) 26–49.

4. April–May 1830; Snake River fur brigade; Fort Colville to Fort Vancouver.

Oregon Hist. Soc. Quar. X (1909) 296–313.

5. August 1830–July 1831; Snake River expedition.

Ibid. XIII (1912) 363–371, XIV (1913) 280–314.

6. August 1831–July 1832; expedition from Fort Vancouver to the Flatheads and Blackfeet of the Pacific Northwest.

W. S. Lewis and P. C. Phillips (eds.), *Journal of John Work* (Cleveland, 1923) 209 pp.

7. May–July 1834; Fort Vancouver to the Umpqua River and return.

Oregon Hist. Soc. Quar. XXIV (1923) 238–268.

1824

ANON., missionary of A.B.C.

Missionary journal, July 1824–March 1825; kept at Dwight among the Cherokees of Arkansas.

Missionary Herald XXI (1825) 48–51, 175–176, 244–248.

ADAMS, Riley M. (1808–1894) of Vineland, N.J.

Schoolboy's diary, August–December 1824; at Norwich Military Academy; substantial entries describing excursion of cadets to the White Mountains and camping there; fairly interesting.

Vineland Hist. Mag. IV (1919) 10–15, 33–36, 56–60, 74–78, 85–87, 107–110, 127–130, 153–159.

ASHLEY, William Henry (1778–1838) of Powhatan Co., Va., and St. Louis, Mo.

Exploration journal, November 1824–August 1825; tour in the Rocky Mountains from Fort Atkinson; narrative partly in journal form; notes on topography, etc.

H. C. Dale (ed.), *The Ashley-Smith Explorations and the Discovery of a Central Route to the Pacific, 1822–1829* (Cleveland, 1918) 117–161.

BETHUNE, Mrs. Joanna (*b.* 1770) of New York City.

Private diary, September 1824–August 1847; religious reflections and prayers; some domestic and family notes; work for infant schools.

George W. Bethune, *Memoirs of Mrs. Joanna Bethune* (New York, 1864) 125–250.

DOBBIN, William (1771–1858) *b.* Ireland, of Jackson, N.Y.

Travel diary, July–August 1824; voyage from Ireland to Montreal; notes on seasickness, religious and social life afloat; lengthy entries.

William J. Foster, *John Dobbin of Connagher* (Schenectady, 1936) 75–82.

DOUGLAS, David (1798–1834) of London Horticultural Society.

Travel journals, 1824–1834; two journeys to the Pacific Northwest on behalf of the Horticultural Society of London; first journey was to the mouth of the Columbia River, with various journeys in Oregon, etc.; overland trip with McLoughlin via Red River settlement and York Factory; return to England in October 1829; the second trip to the Northwest (January–December 1830) includes journey to California; trip from Columbia River to Sandwich Islands, October 1833–January 1834.

Extracts edited by Sir W. J. Hooker in *Companion to the Botanical Magazine* (London) II (1835–1836) 79–182; *Oregon Hist. Soc. Quar.* VI (1905) 76–97, 206–227, 288–309, 417–449; see also *Journal Kept by David Douglas during His Travels in North America, 1823–1827* (London, 1914) 364 pp.

DUNCAN, Mrs. Elizabeth Caldwell (1808–1876) of Jacksonville, Ill., wife of the governor.

Private diary, November 1824–February 1825; May 1828–January 1848; early school life in Newark; domestic and social life in Illinois; rather dull.

Illinois Hist. Soc. Jour. XXI (1928–1929) 1–91, supplemented in *Illinois Hist. Soc. Trans.* No. 26 (1919) 126–127, 164–167, 177–178.

HESS, John W. (*b.* 1824) of Salt Lake City.

Journal and autobiography, August 1824–March 1855 (extracts); mainly narrative of his service with the Mormon Battalion in 1846.

Utah Hist. Quar. IV (1931) 47–55.

MARMADUKE, Meredith Miles (1791–1864) of Sabine Co., Mo., governor of Missouri.

Travel diary, May–August 1824 and May 1825; from Franklin, Mo., to Santa Fe and return next year; brief notes, mainly of stages; notes on people and customs of New Mexico.

Missouri Hist. Rev. VI (1911–1912) 1–10; A. B. Hulbert, *Southwest on the Turquoise Trail* (Denver, 1933) 69–77; first published in *Missouri Intelligencer,* September 2, 1825.

OWEN, William (1802–1842) *b.* Scotland, of New Harmony, Ind.

Private diary, November 1824–April 1825; visits to New York, Philadelphia, Washington, Cincinnati, Pittsburgh; mainly kept at New Harmony; full and well-written entries, mostly of social life and work there; normal nonsociological approach; visits, friends, church activities, amusements, etc.; a pleasant and intelligent diary.

Indiana Hist. Soc. Pubs. IV (1906) 134 pp.

PAINE, Mrs. Abiel Ware (1787–1852) of Winslow, Mass.

Private diary, April 1824–November 1851 (extracts); family and domestic affairs, religious life, visits; an intimate and pleasant record of feminine interests and religious life, mainly at Winslow.

Lydia A. Carter, *The Discovery of a Grandmother* (Newtonville, Mass., 1920) 76–131.

PORTER, Moses (1794–1858) of Putnamville, Mass.

Private diary, January–December 1824; daily work and social life of a farmer; markets and prices; notes on Danvers and Salem; a pleasant diary.

Danvers Hist. Soc. Colls. I (1913) 31–51, II (1914) 54–63.

Ross, Alexander (1783–1856) *b.* Scotland, of Hudson's Bay Company.

Travel journal, February 1824–March 1825; Snake River country expedition; notes on hunting, Indians, and interesting account of trouble with Piegans.

Oregon Hist. Soc. Quar. XIV (1913) 366–388.

SCOULER, Dr. John (1804–1871), of Hudson's Bay Company, surgeon.

Travel journal, July 1824–March 1826; from England to the Columbia aboard the Hudson's Bay Company's "William and Anne"; Vancouver, Nootka Sound; zoölogical notes.

Oregon Hist. Soc. Quar. VI (1905) 54–75, 159–205, 276–287; first published in *Edinburgh Jour. of Science* V (1826) and VI (1827).

1825

ANON.

Exploration journal, May–October 1825; official journal of the Atkinson-O'Fallon expedition, up the Missouri from St. Louis to the mouth of the Yellowstone; careful details of movements, mileage, topography, etc.; useful geographically.

North Dakota Hist. Quar. IV (1929) 5–56.

DEADERICK, David Anderson (1797–1873) of Jonesboro, Tenn.

Public journal, September 1825–October 1872; notes on chief public events, especially those relating to East Tennessee; journalistic and impersonal, arranged as annals.

East Tennessee Hist. Soc. Pubs. VIII (1936) 121–137, IX (1937) 93–110.

FINAN, P. (of Newry, Mass.?)

Travel journal, April–August 1825; voyage to Quebec, combined with recollections of Canada during the War of 1812.

Journal of a Voyage to Quebec (Newry, 1828) 400 pp.

HOWE, Samuel Gridley (1801–1876) of Boston.

Private diary, April 1825–April 1829 (extracts); Byronic adventures in Greece during the Revolution; account of whole war, Missolonghi, siege of Athens; philanthropic work in Greece at Corinth; literary and romantic interests.

Laura E. Richards (ed.), *Letters and Journals of Samuel Gridley Howe: The Greek Revolution* (Boston, 1909) 419 pp. *passim.*

JONES, Rev. Peter (1802–1856) *b*. Burlington Bay, Canada West, Chippewa chief and Wesleyan missionary.

Methodist missionary journals, April 1825–June 1856; extensive and detailed notes of work and life, mainly among Chippewa Indians, of whom he was chieftain, and also among Moravian and Munceytown Indians.

Life and Journals of Kah-ke-wa-quo-nā-by (Toronto, 1860) 424 pp.

LONGACRE, James B. (1794–1869) of Philadelphia, engraver.

Private diary, July–August 1825 (extracts); journey from Philadelphia to New York; art in New York; voyage to Albany and Boston; descriptions; art in Boston; travel in Rhode Island, Connecticut, and return to New York.

Pennsylvania Mag. Hist. Biog. XXIX (1905) 134–142.

OGDEN, Peter Skene (1794–1854) *b*. Quebec, chief factor of Hudson's Bay Company.

Travel journals, November 1825–July 1829; reports of Snake River expeditions; notes on fur trapping, Indian affairs, statistics; important geographically.

Oregon Hist. Soc. Quar. X (1909) 331–365, XI (1910) 201–222, 355–396.

PAINE, Albert Bulkeley (1807–1885) of Randolph, Vt., farmer.

Farmer's diary, September 1825–January 1828; farming work, weather, visits, illness, family affairs; interesting.

Albert P. Paine, *History of Samuel Paine, Junior* (1923) 92–100.

QUINCY, Eliza Susan.

Diary, June 1825 and 1828–1829; brief extracts relating to Harvard.

Cambridge Hist. Soc. Pubs. IV (1909) 90–92.

REED, Rev. Isaac, of Owen Co., Ind.

Travel journal, 1825; in Indiana and eastern Illinois; trip to Paris, Ill., to organize Presbyterian church.

*The Christian Traveller (New York, 1828). Quoted in *Illinois Hist. Soc. Trans.* No. 22 (1916) 74–76.

SIBLEY, Gen. George Champlain (1782–1863) *b*. Great Barrington, Mass., factor at Fort Osage, Mo.

Exploration journal, October 1825–March 1826; early part devoted to a survey of the Santa Fe Trail, beginning at Rabbit Ear Creek; later part, personal, business, and some social items; moderate interest.

A. B. Hulbert, *Southwest on the Turquoise Trail* (Denver, 1933) 133–174 (reprinted from *Western Journal* V [1852] 178 ff.)

UNDERWOOD, Joseph Rogers (1791–1876) of Bowling Green, Ky., politician.

1. Diary, November 1825–December 1826 (fragments); entries relating to the Old and New Court contest.

Filson Club Hist. Quar. XIII (1939) 202–210.

2. Political diary, September 1832 (fragment); interviews with President Jackson.

Ibid. XV (1941) 41–44.

1826

ALCOTT, Amos Bronson (1799–1888) *b.* Wolcott, Conn., author and mystic.

Private diary, September 1826–October 1882; "beginning as a schoolmaster's record of daily events in the school-room and of nightly resolves and aspirations, they soon open out to include domestic, civic, and natural affairs, religion and philosophy, science and art, records of travel, proposals for reform, comments upon hundreds of books and upon hosts of men and women. As compared with the Journals of Emerson and Thoreau they are not only much greater in bulk but far more extensive in range and topic." (Shepard)

Odell Shepard (ed.), *The Journals of Bronson Alcott* (Boston, 1938) 559 pp.

ARNETT, Thomas (1791–1877) *b.* Guilford Co., N.C.

Quaker journal, April 1826–August 1861; religious life, work, and travels of an itinerant Quaker minister; conventional entries, set in autobiography.

Journal of the Life, Travels and Gospel Labors of Thomas Arnett (Chicago, 1884) 422 pp.

CLINTON, George W.

Travel diary, April–June 1826; excursion of the Rensselaer School from Albany to Lake Erie, by the Erie Canal; in large part, natural history notes and botanical nomenclature.

Buffalo Hist. Soc. Pubs. XIV (1910) 277–305.

LYON, Capt. George Francis (1795–1832), R.N., F.R.S.

Travel journal, January–December 1826; tour and residence in Mexico; notes of unusual places, people, and customs, with emphasis on mines and mining.

Journal of a Residence and Tour in the Republic of Mexico (London, 1828) two vols.

ROGERS, Harrison G. (*d.* 1828), clerk with Smith, Jackson, and Sublette, fur traders.

1. Travel journal, November 1826–January 1827; on J. S. Smith's southwestern expedition; San Gabriel and San Bernardino; interesting details of Spanish life and religion; some linguistic interest.

2. Travel journal, May–July 1828; march through northern California and southern Oregon; detailed account of Indians and the country; many personal items; an interesting journal.

H. C. Dale, *The Ashley-Smith Explorations and the Discovery of a Central Route to the Pacific 1822–1829* (Cleveland, 1918) 197–228, 237–271. Partly in John G. Neihardt, *The Splendid Wayfaring* (New York, 1920) 262–268.

SHILLITOE, Rev. Thomas (1754–1836) *b.* London, Eng., ministering Quaker.

Religious journal, July 1826–August 1829 (section relating to his tour in the United States); voyage from Liverpool; New York, Canada, Buffalo, New York, New England, Baltimore, Philadelphia, New Jersey, Ohio, Indiana, Kentucky;

travels and religious work, visits to Indians, the President, prisons, and Moravians; account of Hicksites; comments on slavery; considerable general interest.

Friends' Library III (Philadelphia, 1839) 342–478.

SPARKS, Jared (1789–1866) of Baltimore, historian.

Travel diary, March–October 1826; notes of a tour from Boston to South Carolina, Virginia, Pennsylvania, Delaware, and return; visits to friends, notes of research in New York and New England.

Herbert B. Adams, *The Life and Writings of Jared Sparks* (Boston, 1893) I 415–545.

VAN VLECK, Rev. Charles A. (1794–1845) of Bethania, N.C., Moravian.

Travel journal, October 1826; from Salem, N.C., to Bethlehem, Pa.; difficulties of travel *en famille*.

North Carolina Hist. Rev. VIII (1931) 187–206.

WHITALL, Hannah (*d.* 1848) of Philadelphia.

Private diary, August 1826–October 1844 (extracts); notes on family and personal affairs, deaths, religious reflections, work as schoolmistress.

Hannah W. Smith, *John M. Whitall: The Story of His Life* (Philadelphia, 1879) 42–58.

1827

ANON. (army officer).

Private diary, September 1827–March 1828 (account and quotations); politics, social life, plays, in Washington; kept by a young army officer.

Lynn Hist. Soc. Reg. No. 25 Part II (1923–1928) 121–123.

AIME, Valcour (1798–1867) of St. James plantation, La.

Plantation journal, 1827–1853; notes on the pioneer operations of the St. James sugar plantation, near New Orleans.

*Plantation Diary of the Late Mr. Valcour Aime (New Orleans, 1878).

B., J., Esq.

Travel journal, July 1827–July 1828; from England to America and return; New York, down the Ohio and Mississippi to New Orleans; rather dull travel notes, revised for publication.

The English Party's Excursion to Paris . . . to Which Is Added a Trip to America (London, 1850) 152–440.

BOLLING, Col. William (*b.* 1777) of Bolling Hall, Goochland Co., Va.

Private diary, January 1827–June 1828; details of running three farms; trips to Fredericksburg for church convention and to Richmond for anti-Jackson convention; primarily a farming diary, with valuable details of large-scale agriculture.

Virginia Mag. Hist. Biog. XLIII (1935) 237–250, 330–342, XLIV (1936) 15–24, 120–128, 238–245, 323–334; XLV (1937) 29–39, XLVI (1938) 44–51, 146–152, 234–239, 321–328, XLVII (1939) 27–31.

CLOPPER, Joseph Chambers (1802–1861) of Cincinnati, O.

Travel diary, November 1827–October 1828; no regular entries, but memoranda and recollections; journey from Cincinnati to Texas, New Orleans, Galveston, Harrisburg; observations of "rustics"; journey to San Antonio; the Brazos; an interesting diary in literary and highfalutin' style.

Texas Hist. Assoc. Quar. XIII (1909–1910) 44–80.

ERMATINGER, Edward (1797–1876) *b.* Island of Elba, of Hudson's Bay Company.

Fur-trading journal, March 1827–October 1828; York Factory express journal; journeys between Fort Vancouver and Hudson's Bay; mainly brief, undeveloped notes of stages, weather, hunting, etc.

Edited by C. O. Ermatinger and J. White, *Royal Soc. Canada Proc. and Trans.* 3d Ser. VI (1912) Sec. II 67–127.

HIGGINSON, Mrs. Louisa S. (mother of Thomas Wentworth Higginson).

Private diary, October 1827–March 1828 (extracts from diary-letters); social life and gossip at Cambridge, Mass., while her husband was Steward and Patron at Harvard; quite entertaining.

Cambridge Hist. Soc. Pubs. II (1906–1907) 20–32.

HOBBIE, Miss Hannah (1806–1831) *b.* Northeast, N.Y.

Religious journal, August 1827–January 1831 (extracts); religious reflections, self-abasement, consolations, illnesses, ejaculations; family notes and religious visits.

Robert G. Armstrong, *Memoir of Hannah Hobbie* (New York, 1837) 32–225 *passim.*

IDE, Simeon (1794–1889) *b.* Shrewsbury, Mass., of Windsor, Vt., printer.

Diary, 1827–February 1878 (scattered extracts in biography); biographical and social notes from journals of a yeoman, freeman, and pioneer printer.

Louis W. Flanders, *Simeon Ide* (Rutland, Vt., 1931) 347 pp. *passim.*

JUDAH, Dr. Samuel (*b.* 1777) of New York City.

Travel diary, October–December 1827; from New York to Vincennes, Ind., to visit his lawyer son, and return; unremarkable travel details and comments.

Indiana Mag. Hist. XVII (1921) 338–352.

MITCHELL, Dr. Elisha (1783–1857) of the University of North Carolina.

Geological journal, December 1827–August 1828; in a series of diary-letters to his wife; partly personal but mostly scientific; kept during vacation, while he was doing field work in North Carolina, etc.

James Sprunt Hist. Mono. No. 6 (1905) 73 pp.

SÁNCHEZ, José María, draftsman.

Travel journal, November 1827–June 1828; draftsman to a commission to arrange boundary between Mexico and the United States; Laredo, Bejar, Austin, Nacogdoches; details of Indians; historical notes. Translated from the Spanish.

Southwestern Hist. Quar. XXIX (1925–1926) 249–288.

SMITH, Jedediah (1798–1831) *b*. Bainbridge, N.Y., trader and explorer.

Travel journal, June 1827–July 1828; travels in and west of the Rockies; fur trade; walk across Utah desert; second journey into California; escapes from Mojaves and adventures in California and Oregon; fair details of general life of a trader and of Indian life; an important journal.

M. S. Sullivan (ed.), *The Travels of Jedediah Smith* (Santa Ana, Calif., 1934) 1–105, partly narrative and editorial comment.

SNELLING, Col. Josiah (1782–1828) of Fort Snelling, Minn.

Journal, April 1827–June 1828 (quotations); his activities at Fort Snelling. In article by H. D. Dick, *Minnesota Hist.* XVIII (1937) 399–406.

WOODRUFF, Samuel, of Windsor, Conn.

Travel diary, October 1827 (extract); Saratoga, reflections on Burgoyne's campaign; dull.

William L. Stone, *Life of Joseph Brant* (New York, 1838) I App. l–lvii; reprinted (Albany, 1865).

1828

BAILLIE, Col. John (1772–1833), British Orientalist and member of Parliament.

Travel diary, November 1828–March 1829; tour of America from Washington to Vera Cruz; highly critical notes of Americans and their inns, travel facilities, manners, and food; route down the Mississippi to New Orleans and voyage to Vera Cruz.

Mag. Amer. Hist. XIX (1888) 331–338, 424–428, 511–512, XX (1888) 61–64.

COOPER, James Fenimore (1789–1851), novelist.

1. Travel diary, July–August 1828; tour in France; Paris to Switzerland, with notes on towns and scenery.

2. Travel diary, September 1830; in Paris; visits with Lafayette; critique of Jefferson's letters.

Putnam's Mag. (1868) 730–737, 167–172.

3. Personal diary, January–May 1848; personal and domestic life at Cooperstown; record of work, reading, weather, etc.; brief, but gives intimate picture of Cooper's home life.

James F. Cooper (ed.), *Correspondence of James Fenimore Cooper* (New Haven, 1922) II App. 727–752; first published as *A Journal Kept by James Fenimore Cooper*, in *A Daily Memorandum Book* (New York, 1848).

DUFFIELD, George (1794–1868) of Carlisle, Pa., and Detroit, Presbyterian minister.

Clergyman's diary, November 1828–June 1868 (extracts); conduct of ministry; religious, business, and political notes; mostly summaries, valuable only historically.

Mississippi Valley Hist. Rev. XXIV (1937–1938) 53–67.

ERMATINGER, Frank (1798–1857) *b.* Lisbon, clerk of the Hudson's Bay Company.

Military journal, June–July 1828; McLeod expedition against the Clallam Indians of Puget Sound; Fort Vancouver; good narrative.

Washington Hist. Quar. I (January 1907) 16–29.

GRIMKÉ, Angelina (1805–1879) of Charleston, S.C.

Private diary, winter 1828–May 1835 (extracts); reflections on slavery and work against it.

Catherine H. Birney, *The Grimké Sisters* (Boston, 1885) 55–123 *passim.*

HEAD, Sir George (1782–1855) of Carshalton, Surrey, Eng., soldier and author.

Private travel diary, December 1828–July 1829; Halifax, N.S., to Presque Isle, thence to Rivière de Cape, and York, Upper Canada; four months' residence in the woods on border of Lakes Huron and Simcoe; journey from Lake Simcoe to Quebec via Niagara; usual touristic notes.

Forest Scenes and Incidents in the Wilds of North America (London, 1829) 362 pp.

HENSHAW, Capt. Levi (1769–1843) of Springfield, W.Va., miller.

Travel diary, November 1828–March 1829; journey from Mill Creek to Kentucky; notes on towns, crops, countryside, visits, local people and characters; notes of expenses.

Mabel H. and Ann H. Gardiner, *Chronicles of Old Berkeley* (Durham, N.C., 1938) 259–281.

HONE, Philip (1780–1851) of New York City.

Private diary, May 1828–March 1851; diary of a wealthy and influential citizen; politics, literature, art, industry, social life in New York; literary but intimate.

Bayard Tuckerman, *The Diary of Philip Hone* (New York, 1889) two vols.; a reworking of this edition, with additional extracts, edited by Allan Nevins (New York, 1927) two vols. Brief extracts (November 1828–September 1850) in *Old New York* I (1890) 316–331.

JUDSON, Mrs. Emily Chubbuck (1817–1854) of Hamilton, N.Y.

Private and missionary diary, April 1828–January 1833; apparently autobiography of childhood, arranged as diary; followed by extracts from a missionary journal (January 1847–March 1850) kept at Maulmain, Burma.

A. C. Kendrick, *The Life and Letters of Mrs. Emily C. Judson* (New York, 1861) 16–30, 246–249, 319–328.

LUNDY, Benjamin (1789–1839) of St. Clairsville, Va., abolitionist.

1. Travel diary, May–October 1828; journey to antislavery societies in New England and New York.

The Life, Travels and Opinions of Benjamin Lundy (Philadelphia, 1847) 26–28.

2. Canadian travel diary, January 1832; tour in Upper Canada, from Queenstown to Detroit, with description of Wilberforce settlement of Negroes; propagandist journey; historically interesting.

Published in his paper *The Genius of Universal Emancipation* (Mount Pleasant, O., 1832); reprinted in *Ontario Hist. Soc. Papers and Recs.* XIX (1922) 110–133.

3. Travel diary, May 1833–July 1835; New Orleans to Texas and New Mexico; San Felipe de Austin, San Antonio de Bexar, Monclova, Laredo, Aransas Bay; return to New Orleans and Cincinnati; second journey to Texas and Mexico; notes on scenery, natural history, adventures, weather, persons, and customs; quite good narrative.

The Life, Travels, and Opinions of Benjamin Lundy (Philadelphia, 1847) 32–186.

McCoy, Rev. Isaac (1784–1846) *b.* Uniontown, Pa., *d.* Louisville, Ky., Baptist missionary.

1. Exploration journal, July–October 1828; exploring expedition west of Mississippi, with Indian tribes to be emigrated; Michigan to St. Louis and first tour with northern Indians; highly interesting details of Indians and some personal notes.

2. Exploration journal, August–November 1830; tour to survey lands assigned to emigrated Delawares near Topeka.

Kansas Hist. Quar. V (1936) 227–277, 339–377.

McDonald, Archibald, chief factor of Hudson's Bay Company.

Travel journal, July–October 1828; canoe voyage from Hudson's Bay to the Pacific, accompanying Sir George Simpson.

Malcolm McLeod (ed.), *Peace River* (Ottawa, 1872) 1–39.

Mayo, Mrs. Abigail (1761–1843) *b.* Elizabethtown, N.J., of Richmond, Va.

Foreign diary, July 1828–August 1829; aristocratic social life in Paris; visits, meetings with Lafayette and diplomats; notes on monuments, museums, galleries, plays, operas, balls; moderate interest.

Mary M. Crenshaw (ed.), *An American Lady in Paris* (1927) 144 pp.

Stark, Frederick G., of Manchester, N.H., merchant.

Travel diary, October 1828; business trip from Manchester to Philadelphia; by stage to Providence, steamer to New York, stage to Trenton, steamer to Philadelphia; substantial entries describing towns, scenery, etc.

Granite Monthly V (1882) 42–46.

Wetmore, Maj. Alphonso (1793–1849) of Boone's Lick Co., Mo., lawyer.

Travel journal, May–August 1828 (extract); from Franklin, Mo., to Santa Fe; a lively and flippant narrative in a letter to the Secretary of War.

Missouri Hist. Rev. VIII (1913–1914) 184–195; A. B. Hulbert (ed.), *Southwest on the Turquoise Trail* (Denver, 1933) 182–195; first published as *Sen. Exec. Doc.* 90, 22d Cong. 1st sess.

1829

ABEEL, David (1804–1846) *b.* New Brunswick, missionary to China.

Missionary journal, October 1829–May 1833; irregular day-by-day entries; China, Singapore, Siam; moral, social, and religious discussions; an "enlightening" journal by one of the first American missionaries in China; Dutch Reformed Church.

Journal of a Residence in China (New York, 1834) 398 pp.; reprinted (New York, 1836) 398 pp. Cf. also *Missionary Herald* XXVII–XLII *passim.*

ALEXANDER, William Patterson (1805–1884) *b.* Cherry Valley, Ky., missionary.

Private and religious diary, February 1829–October 1872 (extracts); begun at Princeton; religious reflections; marriage; voyage on whaling ship round Cape Horn to the Marquesas; work as missionary in the Marquesas, Waioli, Lahainaluna, and Wailuku.

Mary C. Alexander, *William Patterson Alexander* (Honolulu, 1934) 516 pp. *passim.*

BALDWIN, Christopher Columbus (1800–1835) of Worcester, Mass.

Private diary, January 1829–August 1835 (lacking year 1832–1833); notes of the librarian of the American Antiquarian Society; antiquarian and bibliographical interests, general reading, notes on life and work of his friends and acquaintances, weather, natural history, visits, his work on the catalogue of the society; a fairly interesting scholar's record.

Diary of Christopher Columbus Baldwin (*Amer. Antiq. Soc. Trans. and Colls.* VIII, Worcester, 1901) 380 pp. Extracts in *Amer. Antiq. Soc. Proc.* (1812–1849) 314–320; *Americana* (*Amer. Hist. Mag.*) XXVIII (1934) 319–341.

BAYFIELD, Adm. Henry Wolsey (1795–1885) *b.* Hull, Eng.

Surveying journals, July 1829–July 1853; surveying coasts and harbors, mainly around St. Lawrence River.

Lit. Hist. Soc. Quebec Trans. No. 28 (1910) 27–95 (quotations in a paper by Capt. Boulton).

BROWNELL, Thomas Church (1779–1865) *b.* Westport, Mass., Protestant Episcopal bishop of Connecticut.

1. Missionary journal, November 1829–March 1830; journey via Philadelphia, Pittsburgh, Cincinnati, Louisville, Lexington, New Orleans, Mobile, and return; notes on preaching, people and places, and the dioceses.

2. Missionary journal, November 1834–April 1835; journey to New Orleans; mostly comments on church there.

Protestant Episcopal Church Hist. Mag. VII (1938) 303–322.

DUNCAN, Joseph (1794–1844) *b.* Paris, Ky., of Jacksonville, Ill., governor of Illinois.

Political diary, February 1829–March 1830; notes on politics at Washington while author was member of Congress; personal affairs in Kentucky and Illinois.

Illinois Hist. Soc. Trans. No. 26 (1919) 180–187. Extract (February–July 1829) in article in *Tennessee Hist. Mag.* VII (1922) 245–249.

FOSTER, Rev. Absalom, of Willington, S.C.

Missionary journal, December 1829–May 1830; letter-journal to American Home Mission Society; report on missionary activities at Pendleton, S.C.

Presbyterian Hist. Soc. Jour. XIII (1928–1929) 289–296.

GREEN, Rev. Jonathan S.

Exploring and missionary journal, March–October 1829; tour on barque "Volunteer," work on Pacific Northwest coast; New Archangel, Kiganee, Norfolk Sound; and in California; descriptions of country, government, Russian settlements, northern Indians, California missions, his own adventures; religious commentary; an important and interesting journal.

Missionary Herald XXVI (1830) 343–345, 369–373, XXVII (1831) 33–39, 75–79, 105–107; *Journal of a Tour on the Northwest Coast of America* (New York, 1915) 105 pp., prefaced by notes assembled from the *Missionary Herald* (1831). Extracts in A. B. Hulbert, *The Oregon Crusade* (Denver, 1935) 45–78.

HILLARD, Mrs. Harriet (1809–1877) of Salem, Mass.

Private diary, May 1829–September 1834 (extracts); voyage from Salem to Manila, life there and in Macao, return to England and thence to the United States; notes on social life in stations, parties, reading; good picture of tedium of formal social life.

Katharine Hillard (ed.), *My Mother's Journal* (Boston, 1900) 320 pp.

JONES, Alexander (1764–1840) of Providence, R.I.

1. Travel diary, May 1829; from Providence to New York via Hartford and New Haven; interesting notes on churchmen; also travel and social notes.

Protestant Episcopal Church Hist. Mag. X (1941) 6–13.

2. Travel diary, August 1829; from Providence to New York and Philadelphia to attend convocation of Protestant Episcopal Church as delegate from Rhode Island; similar to (1).

Ibid. X 18–29.

3. Travel diary, October–November 1832; from Providence to New York to attend triennial convention of his church as a lay deputy; account of debates; unusual and interesting diary.

Ibid. I (1932) 6–18.

LONGFELLOW, Henry Wadsworth (1807–1882), poet.

Private diaries, May 1829, July 1835, February 1838–June 1840, October 1845–April 1881; journey in Germany; in Stockholm; reading, translations, lectures, visits with literary men, Emerson's lectures, reflections, writing and college work, social affairs, some verses, literary plans, literary friendships; a valuable and interesting record of a literary and scholarly life.

Samuel Longfellow, *Life of Henry Wadsworth Longfellow* (Boston, 1886) I chaps. xix–xxi, II chaps. i–xxii, III chaps. i and v–xiv. *Life* reprinted in Longfellow's *Works* (Boston, 1886) XII–XIV.

PAINE, Horace Hall (1810–1864) of East Randolph, Vt., merchant.

Private diary, December 1829–January 1830; first kept while author was clerk in a dry goods store in New York City; fire; impressions of New York; brief but interesting.

Albert P. Paine, *History of Samuel Paine, Jr.* (n.p. 1923) 85–88.

RILEY, Maj. Bennet (1787–1853) *b*. St. Mary's Co., Md., of 6th Infantry Regiment, U.S.A.

Military journal, May–November 1829 (evidently written by Lieut. James F. Izard on behalf of the Major); expedition from Jefferson Barracks, Mo., to the crossing of the Arkansas River by the Santa Fe Trail, via Leavenworth; official journal; interesting account of encounter with raiding Indians.

New Mexico Hist. Rev. III (1928) 267–300.

STONE, Col. William Leete (1792–1844) of New York, editor.

Travel diary, September–October 1829; trip from New York City to Niagara, partly by Erie Canal; careful observations and humorous reflections; literary style.

Buffalo Hist. Soc. Pubs. XIV (1910) 207–272. Extensive extracts in *Mag. Amer. Hist.* XX (1888) 316–324, 395–399, 489–494, XXI (1889) 46–49.

WILLIAMS, Rev. L. S.

Missionary journal, February 1829 (extracts); life and work among the Choctaw Indians.

Missionary Herald XXV (1829) 251–253.

1830

BACKHOUSE, Hannah Chapman (1787–1850) *b*. Norwich, Eng.

Quaker journal, August 1830–February 1835 (extracts relating to America); voyage to the United States, Philadelphia, Baltimore, New York, Ohio, Indiana, New England, New York, South Carolina, Tennessee, Kentucky; travels and visits to Friends and their meetings; a good deal of pleasant general description and comment on scenery, men, and institutions.

Extracts from the Journal and Letters of Hannah Chapman Backhouse (London, 1858) 78–185.

BALLANCE, Charles (1800–1872) of Peoria, Ill., lawyer.

Travel journal, December 1830–January 1843; irregular entries; business records, travel in Kentucky and Illinois, description of Peoria, events.

Illinois Hist. Soc. Jour. XXX (1937–1938) 70–84.

CAMPBELL, William M. (1805–1849) *b*. Lexington, Va., of St. Charles, Mo., lawyer.

Travel diary, April–May and December 1830; business and prospecting trip in Missouri; St. Charles Co. to Jefferson City, Booneville, Chariton, Howard, Callaway counties, etc.; notes on places, soil, etc.

Missouri Hist. Soc., Glimpses of the Past III (1936) 138–150.

COLLINS, Daniel Lake (1808–1887) of Great Egg Harbor, N.J., farmer and
surveyor.

Travel diary, August 1830–February 1831; journey to the west and return;
New York State, Buffalo, Pennsylvania, Ohio, Ohio Canal, Cincinnati, Kentucky, Indianapolis, Wabash, down Mississippi to New Orleans, by sea to New
York; notes on scenery, social life, economic conditions; mostly narrative written
up from diary.

Arthur Adams and Sarah A. Risley, *A Genealogy of the Lake Family* (1915)
App. VI 280–293.

DAVIS, Hannah, of Shiloh, N.J.

Travel diary, August 1830; journey to Alford and Friendship, N.Y., with five
companions; brief notes of daily journeys.

Vineland Hist. Mag. XVII (1932) 164–165.

EARLE, Dr. Pliny (1809–1892) of Northampton, Mass., alienist.

Private diary, May 1830–February 1864 (copious extracts); travels, work, and
social observations in New England and Philadelphia; travel and residence in
England, France, Switzerland, Italy; work with the insane; work in South Carolina; visit to Cuba; residence in New York and Washington; comments on the
Civil War; a very detailed and interesting diary of social life and work in Europe
and America of a man with wide interests and interesting friends.

Franklin B. Sanborn (ed.), *Memoirs of Pliny Earle* (Boston, 1898) 409 pp.

FERRIS, Warren Angus (1810–1873) of Reinhardt, Tex., explorer.

Fur-trading journal, February 1830–November 1835; life in the Rockies,
about the sources of the Missouri, Columbia, and Colorado, while author was
employee of American Fur Company; trapping, trading, clerking; told in narrative form; interesting for life of fur trader and Indian affairs.

P. C. Phillips, *Life in the Rocky Mountains* (Denver, 1940) 365 pp.; originally
published in *Western Literary Messenger* (Buffalo) II (January 1843), III (May
1844).

FOWLER, John, Englishman.

Travel diary, June–December 1830; tour in New York State; Flushing, Albany,
Buffalo, Niagara, Rochester, New Hartford, Poughkeepsie, New York City; shipwreck; return by western islands; fairly well-written observations and narrative;
notes for settlers, scenery, travel facilities.

Journal of a Tour in the State of New York (London, 1831) 333 pp.

GREENE, Dr. Roland (1770–1859) of Cranston, R.I.

Quaker travel journal, July 1830; journey from Barton, Vt., to East Farnham,
Canada; notes on scenery and farms.

Bull. Friends' Hist. Soc. Philadelphia II (1908) 119–121.

HALSEY, Jacob (*d.* 1842) of New Jersey, partner in American Fur Company.

Fur-trading journal, January 1830–June 1833 (abstract, with gaps); records of
Fort Tecumseh and Fort Pierre on Upper Missouri, near mouth of Teton River;

brief notes describing life of fort, arrivals and departures of traders and trappers; many famous persons mentioned.

South Dakota Hist. Colls. IX (1918) 69–167.

HENSHAW, Capt. Hiram, of Berkeley Co., W.Va.

Travel diary, January–May 1830; journey from Berkeley County to Kentucky via Ohio; notes on scenery, farming, mills, towns, visits, expenses.

Mabel H. and Ann H. Gardiner, *Chronicles of Old Berkeley* (Durham, N.C., 1938) 282–314.

HERR, Benjamin.

Travel diary, September–October 1830; Strasburg, Pa., to Philadelphia, New York City, Saratoga, Schenectady, Buffalo, Sandusky; Ohio, Illinois, Kentucky, Virginia, Pennsylvania, Strasburg; touristic notes.

German-American Annals V (1903) 8–31.

HEWINS, Amasa (1795–1855) of Boston, portrait painter.

Foreign travel diary, August 1830–June 1833; travel and study of painting in Europe, mostly in Italy; notes on travel conditions, galleries, paintings, sculpture; also travel in Spain, France, and England.

Francis H. Allen (ed.), *Hewins's Journal* (Boston, 1931) 145 pp.

KENRICK, Rt. Rev. Francis Patrick (1796–1863), Catholic bishop of Philadelphia.

Diary and visitation journal, February 1830–March 1852; diocesan work, religious reflections; administration; some travel notes and reflections on Mexican War.

E. F. Tourscher (ed.), *Diary and Visitation Record* (Lancaster, Pa., 1916) 29–267.

McCALL, James (1774–1856) b. Lebanon Springs, N.Y., senator from New York.

Official journal, June–September 1830; visit to Wisconsin to settle differences between Winnebagos and Menominees; first part at Detroit; voyage to Green Bay; interviews with Indians; return; some good description.

Wisconsin Hist. Colls. XII (1892) 177–204.

NORTHRUP, Enos.

Travel diary, May–June 1830; from Hinckley, O., to Gull Prairie, Mich.; brief notes of stages.

Michigan Pion. Colls. V (1882) 69–70.

PHELPS, Mrs. Caroline, of Lewiston, Ill.

Diary, 1830–1840; narrative with few dates, "journal of my life"; pioneering in Illinois; interesting account of woman on the frontier.

Illinois Hist. Soc. Jour. XXIII (1930–1931) 209–239.

POOR, Mary (1747–1834) of Indian Hill Farm, Mass.

Private diary, June 1830–September 1834 (extracts); brief notes of weather, and social and family life of an old lady; pleasant.

New England Mag. n.s. XIII (1895–1896) 316–322.

WYATT, Col. Richard Ware (1806–1881) of Louisa Co., Va.

Travel diary, 1830 (daily entries but without dates); horseback journey into western country; Blue Ridge, Ohio River, Kentucky, etc.; notes on scenery, towns, people; fair interest.

Kentucky State Hist. Soc. Reg. XXXIX (1941) 106–115.

1831

BURGESS, Rt. Rev. George (1809–1866), first bishop of Maine.

European travel diary, April 1831–April 1834 (extracts); university life in Göttingen, Bonn, and Berlin, and travel in other parts of Germany; notes on universities, lectures, literary figures, scenery; religious inclination.

Alexander Burgess, *Memoir of George Burgess, D.D.* (Philadelphia, 1869) 33–47.

COLE, Thomas (1801–1848) *b.* Bolton, Eng., of Philadelphia and New York, painter.

Travel diaries, August 1831–February 1848 (extracts); travel in Italy, New York State and Catskills, another visit to Europe, England, Switzerland, Italy, and again in Catskills; notes on painting and painters, scenery, poetry, etc.

Louis L. Noble, *The Life and Works of Thomas Cole* (3d ed., New York, 1856) 132–380 *passim.*

CROOK, John (*b.* 1831) *b.* Trenton, Lancashire, of Provo, Ut.

Autobiography and journal, October 1831–September 1863; emigration; joins Mormons at Salt Lake in 1856; notes on farming, hardships, development of Provo Valley, etc.

Utah Hist. Quar. VI (1933) 51–62, 110–112.

FLOYD, John (1751–1837) of Montgomery, Va., governor of Virginia.

Social and political diary, March 1831–February 1834; public, political, and social life in Virginia; national and international news; his activities in Washington in the Jacksonian period, while he was governor of Virginia; mainly political interest, with notes on many eminent national figures.

Charles H. Ambler, *The Life and Diary of John Floyd* (Richmond, 1918) 123–237.

FOWLER, Thomas, Englishman.

Travel journal, summer 1831; tour through Canada to Niagara Falls; descriptions of country, towns, manners, customs, scenery.

The Journal of a Tour through British America (Aberdeen, 1832) 288 pp.

HALL, Rev. Sherman (1800–1879) *b.* Weathersfield, Vt., missionary of A.B.C.

Missionary travel journal, August 1831–January 1833; among the Ojibways; journey from Mackinaw to St. Mary's River, to south shore of Lake Superior; visit to Lac du Flambeau.

Missionary Herald XXIX (1833) 410–414, 472–473, XXX (1834) 24–27.

HUNTINGTON, Charles P., of Northampton and Boston, judge.

Private diary, January 1831–November 1834 (extracts); political, literary, and social opinions; domestic affairs, gossip, political maneuverings in state legislature; shrewd comments of a man with a "latent streak of radicalism."

Massachusetts Hist. Soc. Proc. LVII (1923–1924) 244–269.

KUHN, Hon. George Horatio (1795–1879) of Boston, manufacturer.

Business journal, January–November 1831; extracts relating to early manufacturing in Dedham, Mass., and vicinity; projects for factories, etc.

Dedham Hist. Reg. VIII (1897) 91–94.

LAPHAM, Increase Allen (1811–1875) of Milwaukee, Wis., engineer.

Private diaries, January 1831–March 1832 (scattered extracts); life in Ohio; notes of little value.

Ohio Archaeol. Hist. Soc. Pubs. XVIII (1909) 45.

McLEOD, Alexander Roderick, of Hudson's Bay Company.

Travel journal, September–December 1831; from Fort Vancouver southward to recover property of Jedediah Smith taken by Indians after the massacre on Umpqua River.

M. S. Sullivan (ed.), *The Travels of Jedediah Smith* (Santa Ana, Calif., 1934) 112–135.

MOTTE, Jacob Rhett (1811–1868) of Charleston, S.C., student.

College diary, May–September 1831; kept while author was junior at Harvard; full and highly entertaining notes on college life and work; sprightly and intimate; interesting for Harvard personalities and curriculum; some notes on Town as well as Gown.

Arthur H. Cole (ed.), *Charleston Goes to Harvard* (Cambridge, Mass., 1940) 108 pp.

O'BRYAN, William (1778–1868) of Shebear, Devon, Eng.

Travel diary, August 1831–June 1834; voyage from Liverpool to New York and extensive travels in New York, New Jersey, Pennsylvania, Ohio, etc.; personal adventures and general description; less literary than is usual for this type of journal, more varied, and truer to diary style; manners, institutions, advice to settlers.

A Narrative of Travels in the United States of America (London, 1836) 419 pp.

ROEBLING, Johann August (1806–1869) b. Thuringia, engineer, of Pittsburgh.

Travel diary, May–August 1831; Thuringia, Bremen, life at sea, Philadelphia; detailed descriptions and accounts; rather formalized but interesting. Translated.

Edward Underhill (trans. and ed.), *Diary of My Journey* (Trenton, N.J., 1931) 124 pp.

STRANG, James Jesse (1813–1856) b. Scipio, N.Y., of Voree.

Mormon diary, May 1831–May 1836; early days at Hanover, N.Y., reading, debating, religious life, school work, and personal affairs, escape from drowning.

M. M. Quaife, *The Kingdom of St. James* (New Haven, 1930) 195–234.

ANON.   1832

Indian diary, April–May 1832; details of Black Hawk War; brief notes of Indian activities.

Iowa Jour. Hist. Pol. VIII (1910) 265–269.

BALL, John (*b.* 1794) of Lansingburgh, N.Y.

Travel journal, March 1832–November 1833 (extracts); with Wyeth's expedition; Baltimore to Oregon and life in Oregon; adventures and incidents of journey; notes on Indians, scenery, natural history, climate; moderate interest.

"Across the Continent Seventy Years Ago," *Oregon Hist. Soc. Quar.* III (1902) 82–106.

BETTLE, Mrs. Jane (1773–1840) of Pennsbury, Pa., and Philadelphia.

Quaker journal, August 1832–March 1840; wholly concerned with her bodily and spiritual conditions, and implorings and thanks to the Lord.

Extracts from the Memorandums of Jane Bettle (London, 1845) 13–66.

BIGGS, Asa (1811–1878) of Williamston, N.C., judge.

Travel diary, April–May 1832; trip from Williamston, N.C., to New York and return; Mount Vernon, Washington, Baltimore, Philadelphia, New York; some lively descriptions of places and of the proceedings of the Senate; fair interest.

R. D. W. Connor (ed.), *Autobiography of Asa Biggs* (Raleigh, 1915) 41–51.

BOUTWELL, Rev. William T., missionary at Leech Lake, Minn.

Travel journal, June–August 1832; in company with H. R. Schoolcraft, from Mackinaw through Lake Superior region and Ojibway country to headwaters of Mississippi River; good descriptions of country and notes on forts, etc.

Missionary Herald XXX (1834) 132–136, 177–180, 222–223, 259–262; *Minnesota Hist. Soc. Colls.* I (1902 reprint of 1850–1856 vol.) 121–140.

BROWNING, Orville Hickman (1806–1881), senator.

1. Military diary, April–May 1832; march to Yellow Banks during Black Hawk War; brief notes of movements.

Frank E. Stevens, *The Black Hawk War* (Chicago, 1903) 117–118.

2. Private diary, June 1850–July 1881; a huge and regularly kept record; work as lawyer; gallantries, social life, marriage; work and politics in the Senate; life in Quincy; opinions on slavery; a very important diary.

The Diary of O. H. Browning, Illinois Hist. Soc. Colls. XX (1925) XXII (1933).

CAMPBELL, Robert (1808–1894) of Perthshire, and Red River Colony.

Travel diary, November 1832–September 1833; journey to Kentucky to buy sheep for Red River Colony.

North Dakota Hist. Quar. I (1926) 35–45.

CARR, Lieut. George Kirwan, of the Rifle Brigade, Halifax, N.S.

Travel diary, October–December 1832; tour through United States and Canada along St. Lawrence and Hudson; Baltimore, Philadelphia and return; notes on scenery, taverns, customs, fashions, persons; full, pleasant daily entries, apparently written up after return.

Bull. New York Pub. Lib. XLI (1937) 743–774.

CHAMBERLAIN, Ebenezer Mattoon (*b.* 1805) of Orrington, Me.

Travel diary, June 1832–December 1835; journey from Maine to Indiana; description of natural history, manners, customs; two poems; flowery style.

Indiana Mag. Hist. XV (1919) 233–259.

CLAYBROOKE, Thomas W. (*b. ca.* 1800) of Brookeville, Va.

Travel diary, October–November 1832; Virginia to Tennessee; mostly brief details of the trip; some personal notes, descriptions, expenses.

William and Mary Coll. Quar. 2d Ser. XIII (1933) 163–169.

FOLTZ, Surgeon General Jonathan M. (1810–1877), U.S.N.

Diaries, January 1832–June 1867 (extensive quotations in biography); lively and entertaining notes on adventures in naval cruises and expeditions; his personal affairs, reading, jottings on history and scenery, Civil War, Indies, South America, etc.

Charles S. Foltz, *Surgeon of the Seas* (Indianapolis, 1931) 35–300 *passim.*

GRATIOT, Henry, "sub-Indian agent."

Indian journal, January–June 1832; events and proceedings with the Winnebago Indians at Rock River; Black Hawk War; vaccination of Indians; speeches.

Mississippi Valley Hist. Rev. XII (1925–1926) 396–407.

KEMBLE, Frances Anne (Butler) (1809–1893), actress and writer.

Travel journal, August 1832–July 1833; travel in and description of mid-Atlantic and New England cities; largely social and theatrical notes.

Journal of a Residence in America (London and Philadelphia, 1835) two vols.

KING, William C., of Detroit, carpenter.

Private diary, January–September 1832 (extracts); brief notes of work during a cholera epidemic; social and public affairs; fairly interesting.

Michigan Hist. Mag. XIX (1935) 65–70.

MARSH, Rev. Cutting (1800–1873) *b.* Danville, Vt., Congregational missionary to Stockbridge Indians.

Missionary journal, June–July 1832 (extracts); incidents in the Black Hawk War in Wisconsin; his emotions; descriptions of Indians.

Wisconsin Hist. Soc. Colls. XV (1900) 60–65.

MEEKER, Rev. Jotham (1804–1855) *b.* Hamilton Co., O., printer and missionary in Kansas Territory.

Missionary journal, November 1832–January 1855; brief notes of his work as missionary and printer for Baptist mission in Kansas; notes on farming, printing, binding, translations into Ottawa, etc.

Douglas C. McMurtrie and Albert H. Allen, *Jotham Meeker* (Chicago, 1930) 45–126.

MILLER, Aaron.

Travel diary, April–June 1832; in Ohio looking for a farm; through Williamsport, Brownsville, Zanesville, Columbus, Urbana, Cincinnati, Chillicothe, Wheeling, Winchester; general comments on soil and developments.

Ohio Archaeol. Hist. Soc. Pubs. XXXIII (1924) 69–79.

PRATT, Orson (1811–1881) *b.* Hartford, N.Y., of Salt Lake City, Mormon apostle.

1. Private diary and autobiography, February 1832–June 1844 (dates of diary extracts); notes on religious, business, social, domestic activities; dull as a journal but valuable as a collection of dates, facts, etc.

Utah Geneal. Hist. Mag. XXVII (1936) 117–124, 163–169, XXVIII (1937) 42–48, 92–96, 118–125, XXIX (1938) 34–36; first printed in *Deseret News Weekly* VIII (1858), June 2, 9.

2. Private diary, March–July 1846 (extracts); journey of Mormons from Nauvoo to Great Salt Lake, founding of the city; long detailed entries; an excellent record of the migration.

Utah Geneal. Hist. Mag. XV (1924) 55–59, 104–109, 166–171, XVI (1925) 19–24, 71–76, 118–123, 160–167, XVII (1927) 118–126, 209–214.

PROUDFOOT, Rev. William (1787–1851) *b.* Scotland, of London, Ont.

1. Presbyterian clergyman's diary, June 1832–September 1834; daily life at and around London; clerical and secular; interesting, solid entries, with some Scottish locutions.

London and Middlesex Hist. Soc. Trans. VI (1915) 6–70, VIII (1917) 20–30, XI (1922) 5–93.

2. Diary, March 1833–December 1835; church work, visits, journeys, comments on church and secular matters, including agriculture, military training, drinking, sectarian rivalries, journey to the United States to collect funds, some personal items; a good diary of parochial life among Scotch Canadians.

Ontario Hist. Soc. Papers and Recs. XXVI (1930) 498–572, XXVII (1931) 435–496, XXVIII (1932) 71–113, XXIX (1933) 141–159. Extract relating to journey to New York in *Mississippi Valley Hist. Rev.* XVIII (1931–1932) 378–396.

SMITH, Mrs. Abigail Tenney (1809–1885) *b.* Hardwick, Mass.

Missionary journal, December 1832–1885 (extracts); educational work in connection with her husband's mission at Kaumakapili, Sandwich Islands.

Mary D. Frear, *Lowell and Abigail* (New Haven, 1934) 39–279 *passim*.

SMITH, Lowell (1802–1891) *b.* Heath, Mass.

Missionary journal, December 1832–*ca.* 1885; missionary work as pastor of Kaumakapili Church, Sandwich Islands.

Mary D. Frear, *Lowell and Abigail* (New Haven, 1934) 39–283 *passim*.

WYETH, Nathaniel Jarvis (1802–1856), explorer.

Exploration journals, June 1832–September 1833 (lacking first portion, May–June), and May 1834–April 1835; two exploring expeditions in Oregon territory; the first across Nebraska, Wyoming, Idaho, and Oregon to the mouth of the Columbia; the second around the Columbia; detailed notes of movements, topography, etc.; and very fine descriptions of Indians.

F. G. Young (ed.), *Sources of the History of Oregon* I Nos. 3–6 (1899) 155–219, 221–256. The first journal in A. B. Hulbert, *The Call of the Columbia* (Denver, 1934) 112–153.

1833

ANON. (of Fort Nisqually).

Fur-trading journals, May 1833–April 1835, March 1849–December 1852, May–June 1870 (last kept by Edward Huggins); occurrences at Fort Nisqually; trading, Indians, farming; work at the Fort; rather poor text.

Washington Hist. Quar. VI (1915) 179–197, 264–278, VII (1916) 59–75, 144–167 (edited by Clarence B. Bagley). *Ibid.* X (1919) 205–230, XI (1920) 59–65, 136–149, 218–229, 294–302, XII (1921) 68–70, 137–148, 219–228, 300–303, XIII (1922) 57–66, 131–141, 225–232, 293–299, XIV (1923) 145–148, 223–234, 299–306 (edited by Victor J. Farrar). *Ibid.* XXV (1934) 60–64. Extract of this text, 1833–1835, in F. I. Trotter and J. R. Loutzenhiser (eds.), *Told by Pioneers* (n.p., 1937) I 7–67.

ABDY, Edward Strutt (1791–1846), Fellow of Jesus College, Cambridge.

Travel diary, April 1833–October 1834; tour in Canada and the United States, New England, Canada, Washington, D.C., the southern and western states; caustic antislavery and anti-American comments.

Journal of a Residence and Tour (London, 1835) three vols.

BACK, Sir George (1796–1878), R.N.

Exploration journal, February 1833–September 1835; narrative and daily entries; expedition to the mouth of the Great Fish River and along the shores of the Arctic Ocean; geographical interest.

Narrative of the Arctic Land Expedition (London, Philadelphia, 1836).

BOTSFORD, Jabez Kent, of Newton.

Travel diary, April–August 1833 (extracts); social life in Newton; visit to New York, theaters; journey to Chicago by Erie Canal, Lake steamers; travel notes; pleasant diary.

Eli H. Botsford, *Adventures in Ancestors* (n.p., 1936?) 61–75.

DAVID, George (Englishman?).

Travel diary, September–October 1833 (extracts); trip from Sandusky through Michigan, Indiana, Illinois, to Chicago; comments on farms, forests, taverns, American institutions; lively, varied, critical, and entertaining.

Michigan Hist. Mag. XVIII (1934) 53–66.

ELDRIDGE, Charles William (1811–1883) of Hartford, Conn.

Travel diary, June–August 1833; tour through Connecticut, Vermont, Montreal, Quebec; amateur painter's observations of country and people; heavily literary, with many literary allusions, and inclined to narrative.

Vermont Hist. Soc. Proc. II (1931) 53–82.

EVANS, Sergt. Hugh (1811–1836) of Clark Co., Ind., and U.S. Dragoons.

1. Military journal, October 1833–September 1834; mainly notes on first summer campaign of U.S. Dragoons to Rocky Mountains; an ordinary soldier's account of what is covered in Dodge's diary.

Chrons. Oklahoma III (1925) 175–215.

2. Military journal, May–August 1835; Dodge's expedition to the Rocky Mountains; long notes on march, military life, Indians; good solid entries; some interesting spellings.

Mississippi Valley Hist. Rev. XIV (1927–1928) 192–214.

HARRIS, Mrs. Dilue (*b.* 1825) of Houston, Tex.

Diary, April 1833–April 1837; monthly entries, largely reminiscence; begun by Dr. Pleasant W. Rose and continued by his daughter Mrs. Harris; life in Harrisburg, Texas; interesting.

Texas Hist. Assoc. Quar. IV (1900–1901) 85–127, 155–189.

LEE, Rev. Jason (1803–1845) *b.* Quebec, missionary in Oregon.

Personal and travel diary, August 1833–July 1838; from Canada to Liberty, Mo., thence overland to Fort Vancouver; unusual point of view, life on the trail as seen by a troubled missionary.

Oregon Hist. Soc. Quar. XVII (1916) 116–146, 240–266, 397–430. Partly in *Christian Advocate* (New York) October 3 and 30, 1834; and A. R. Hulbert, *The Oregon Crusade* (Denver, 1935) 147–160, 167–184.

MERRILL, Rev. Moses (1803–1840) *b.* Sedgwick, Me., missionary to Oto Indians.

Missionary journal, July 1833–August 1839 (extracts); work among the Oto Indians in the Platte River country; interesting details of Oto life and customs, religious work and education, personal affairs and adventures.

Nebraska Hist. Soc. Trans. IV (1892) 160–191.

OTEY, Rt. Rev. James Hervey (1800–1863), first Episcopal bishop of Tennessee.

Clergyman's diary, March 1833–January 1863 (extracts); diocesan work, visitations, journeys in the South, religious reflections, affairs of his family, illnesses, weather, gossip; quite interesting.

William M. Green, *Memoir of the Rt. Rev. James Hervey Otey* (New York, 1885) 151–169.

PORTER, Charles Henry (1811–1841) of Norwich, Conn.

Religious journal, May 1833–August 1841 (extracts); preparation for college; study at Westfield Academy, Mass.; religious reflections and resolves; visits to sick; meetings; preaching.

E. Goodrich Smith, *Memoir of Charles Henry Porter* (New York, 1849) 13–151 *passim*.

PURCELL, John Baptist (1800–1883), Catholic bishop of Ohio.

Private diary, November 1833–April 1836; journey to his diocese; lively commentary on local conditions; comments and gossip on nuns, bigotry, drunkenness, his work; intimate, personal, and highly amusing.

Cath. Hist. Rev. V (1919) 239–255.

SHAFTER, Oscar Lovell (1812–1873) *b.* Athens, Vt.

Diary 1833–April 1863; extracts from the diary of a justice of the supreme court of California; migration and early life in California; quotations in a tiresome mélange of quotation and comment.

Flora H. Loughead (ed.), *Life, Diary, and Letters of Oscar Lovell Shafter* (San Francisco, 1915) 323 pp. *passim.*

STEELE, Millicent Pollock, of Toronto (and Ellen Frances Steele).

Travel diary, April–August 1833 (letter diaries); description of a journey from London to Simcoe Co., Upper Canada, via New York; lively details of social life aboard ship; details of American and overland journey, clearing site, homemaking, and social affairs; lively and amusing.

Ontario Hist. Soc. Papers and Recs. XXIII (1926) 483–510.

STEINES, Hermann, *b.* Germany, of Franklin Co., Mo.

Travel and personal diary, July 1833–December 1837 (with large gaps); journey from Baltimore to Pittsburgh; searching in Missouri for land on which to settle; life in Missouri with other German political refugees, followers of Gottfried Duden.

"The Followers of Duden," *Missouri Hist. Rev.* XIV (1919–1920) 56–59, 436–443, 443–446.

TOLMIE, Dr. William Fraser (1812–1886) b. Inverness, Scotland, surgeon and
     trader at Fort Vancouver.

Travel diary, April–May 1833; excellent descriptions of Fort Vancouver and Indians thereabouts; botanical notes; a good diary.

Washington Hist. Quar. III (1912) 229–241.

VAILL, Rev. William F., missionary of A.B.C.

Missionary journal, May 1833; travel and preaching in the principal Osage villages; interesting details of Osage customs.

Missionary Herald XXIX (1833) 366–371.

WALKER, Mary Richardson (1814–1897) of Walla Walla, Wash.

Missionary journal, January 1833–July 1850 (extracts); marriage to Elkanah Walker; travel to Oregon Territory; missionary work among the Spokanes; domestic details.

Clifford M. Drury, *Elkanah and Mary Walker* (Caldwell, Ida., 1940) 250 pp. *passim.* Part published in *The Frontier* (Montana) XI (1931); reprinted as No. 15 of *Sources of Northwest History,* 19 pp.

1834

Anon. (of Willamette Valley, Ore.).

Missionary journal, April 1834–December 1838; hardships of Methodist missionaries; work and worship; notes on Indians; intimate portrait of the mission; marriage records, etc., appended.

Oregon Hist. Soc. Quar. XXIII (1922) 230–266.

Anon. (officer of 1st U.S. Dragoons).

Military journals, May–September 1834 and May–August 1835; marches of the Dragoons in the Mississippi Valley; to Pawnee, Pict, and Comanche villages on Red River; from Fort Gibson to Des Moines; from Des Moines to near mouth of Boone River and to Minnesota; second journey is a good narrative, the first, only brief notes.

Iowa Jour. Hist. Pol. VII (1909) 331–378.

Anon. ("Citizen of Edinburgh").

Travel diary, March–June 1834; travel mainly in New York State; conventional descriptions and hints for emigrants.

Journal of an Excursion to the United States and Canada (Edinburgh, 1835) 168 pp.

Allis, Rev. Samuel, missionary of A.B.C.

Missionary journal, October 1834; travel to the Pawnee Indians; details of his work and comments on the Pawnees.

Missionary Herald XXXII (1836) 68–70.

Anderson, William Marshall (1807–1881) of Louisville, Ky.

Travel diary, May–June 1834; journey from Chimney Rock, Neb., to the Green River rendezvous, Wyo.; brief but racy diary.

Edited by A. J. Partoll, *Frontier and Midland* (Montana) XIX (1938) 54–63; reprinted as No. 27 of *Sources of Northwest History* (Univ. Montana) 12 pp.; originally printed in *Circleville Democrat and Watchman* September 29, October 13, 1871.

Chardon, Francis Auguste (*d.* 1848), fur trader in Upper Missouri.

Fur trader's journal, June 1834–May 1839; fur trade at and around Fort Clark in the Upper Missouri country among the Mandans, Gros Ventres, and their neighbors; very detailed account of work and private life and Indian affairs; vivid picture of the smallpox epidemic of 1837; an excellent journal.

A. H. Abel (ed.), *Chardon's Diary at Fort Clark* (Pierre, S.D., 1932) 458 pp. Extract which includes the description of the smallpox epidemic in *Mississippi Valley Hist. Rev.* XVII (1930–1931) 278–299.

Clarke, Rev. James Freeman (1810–1888) of Newton, Mass., and Louisville, Ky.

Clergyman's journal, November 1834–November 1861; scattered notes on church affairs and theology; Civil War news.

Edward E. Hale (ed.), *James Freeman Clarke: Autobiography, Diary and Correspondence* (Boston, 1891) 107–275.

DODGE, Col. Henry (1782–1867) *b.* Vincennes, Ind., of U.S. Dragoons.

1. Military exploration journal, June–August 1834; exploration on the south-western plains; mainly councils with Indians at the Toyash village.

Annals of Iowa 3d Ser. XVII (1930) 173–197; *American State Papers, Military Affairs* V 373–382; *House Exec. Doc.* No. 2, 23d Cong., 2d sess. 70–91.

2. Military journal, May–August 1835; with detachment of Dragoons in the Rockies; journey from Fort Leavenworth; among Pawnees.

House Exec. Doc. 181, 24th Cong., 1st sess. (1836) 38 pp.

DUNBAR, Rev. John, missionary of A.B.C.

Missionary journal, June 1834–April 1835; journey from Fort Leavenworth to Indian villages between the Platte and Missouri rivers; at Grand Pawnee village; interesting details of Pawnee customs and habits.

Missionary Herald XXXI (1835) 343–349, 376–381, 417–421.

FRASER, Rev. William (*b.* 1808) *b.* Pictou Co., N.S., of Bond Head, Simcoe Co., U.C.

Presbyterian clergyman's journal, August 1834–July 1835; experiences from time of his ordination in Pictou until his settlement at Bond Head; full notes of church work, visits, journeys, religious reflections, etc.

London and Middlesex Hist. Soc. Trans. XIV (1930) 80–156 (with a long introduction on early Presbyterianism in Western Ontario by H. E. Parker).

HEYWOOD, Robert, of The Pike, Bolton, Lancs.

Travel diary, May–October 1834; voyage from Liverpool to New York; tour by stage and steamer; New York, Philadelphia, Washington, Maysville, Lexington, Louisville, Cincinnati, Columbus, Pittsburgh, Erie, Buffalo, Niagara, Montreal, Quebec, Albany, Boston, New York, Philadelphia, Liverpool; sightseeing, descriptions of eminent persons, scenery, taverns, costs, customs, etc.; full entries; an interesting diary.

A Journey to America in 1834 (Cambridge, Eng., 1919) 112 pp.

INCHES, James.

Travel diary, 1834.

*Journal of an Excursion in the Year 1834 (1835).

INGALLS, Charles Francis, of Abington, Conn., and Lee Co., Ill.

Travel diary, April–May 1834; Abington, Conn., to Buffalo, Erie, Detroit, Chicago; statistical.

Illinois Hist. Soc. Jour. XVIII Part I (1925) 417–420.

JARRETT, David, of Upper Providence, Pa.

Travel diary, May–June 1834; overland trip to the West, with a party from Montgomery Co., Pa.; Ohio and Virginia; notes on distances, towns, character of roads, country, inns; at Richmond, Somerset, Wheeling, Shippensburg, Carlisle, etc.

Montgomery Co. Hist. Soc. Hist. Sketches VI (1929) 121–136.

KEMPER, Jackson (1789–1870) *b.* Pleasant Valley, N.Y., Protestant Episcopal bishop of Wisconsin.

1. Travel journal, 1834; trip of inspection to the Green Bay mission, Wisconsin; very detailed and extensive entries; religious, personal, society, education, scenery, Indians; very interesting.

Wisconsin Hist. Colls. XIV (1898) 394–449.

2. Travel journal, July–August 1838; trip in Wisconsin, from Dubuque to Fond du Lac; first visitation of Wisconsin.

Wisconsin Mag. Hist. VIII (1924–1925) 423–445.

3. Diocesan journal, January 1841–June 1859 (with gaps); notes on his diocesan work.

Nashotah Scoliast I (1883–1884) Nos. 1–8.

4. Travel journal, 1843; visit to Minnesota; with extracts from his letters.

Minnesota Hist. VII (1926) 264–273.

5. Diocesan journal, 1856; visitation of Nebraska and Kansas; notes of visits, and brief comments.

Protestant Episcopal Church Hist. Mag. IV (1935) 231–234.

KENNEDY, Alexander.

Fur trader's journal, May–June 1834 (fragment); journal kept at Fort Clark, Mo., among Mandan Indians; little except weather notes.

A. H. Abel (ed.), *Chardon's Journal at Fort Clark* (Pierre, S.D., 1932) App. A 323–330.

KERR, Rev. J.

Missionary journal, May–August 1834; brief notes of work among the Shawnee Indians.

Christian Advocate (Philadelphia) XII (1834) 517–519.

PRESTON, Mrs. William, of Virginia.

Private diary, May 1834–March 1838 (extracts); notes on eminent men, Calhoun, Webster, *et al.*

The Land We Love (Charlotte, N.C.) III (1867) 334–336, 419–422, 512–514, IV (1868) 402–404, V (1869) 119–122.

RUSSELL, Osborne (1814–*ca.* 1865) of Maine, employee of Northwest Company.

Fur trapper's journal, April 1834–June 1843; in the Rocky Mountains; mainly in Yellowstone country, Snake Valley, Great Salt Lake, Green River; among Crow and Blackfeet Indians; meeting with Oregon missionaries; good narrative of his experiences and details of trapper's life and Indians.

L. A. York (ed.), *Journal of a Trapper* (Boise, Ida., 1914) 105 pp. Extracts in A. B. Hulbert (ed.), *Where Rolls the Oregon* (Denver, 1933) 177–219.

TOWNSEND, John Kirk (1809–1851) of Philadelphia, physician and naturalist.

Travel journal, July–September 1834; with party led by Nuttall across the Rockies to the headwaters of the Columbia River.

Extracts in *Waldie's Select Circulating Library* Part II (1835) 427–432;

reprinted in A. B. Hulbert (ed.), *The Call of the Columbia* (Denver, 1934) 188–226. This journal was the basis for the first part of Townsend's *Narrative of a Journey across the Rocky Mountains* (Philadelphia, 1839), the rest being an account of a journey to the Sandwich Islands and South America. The *Narrative* was reprinted with a few changes as *Sporting Excursions to the Rocky Mountains* (London, 1840). The Western American portion of the Philadelphia edition is reprinted in R. G. Thwaites (ed.), *Early Western Travels* (Cleveland, 1905) XXI 107–369.

UNDERWOOD, Ammon (1810–1887) of Columbia, Tex., merchant and legislator.

Private diary, January 1834–February 1838; voyage from Boston to Texas; social, political, and business life in Texas; Texas-Mexican War; Texas Republic; interesting spellings, especially of Spanish names.

Southwestern Hist. Quar. XXXII (1928–1929) 124–151.

WHEELOCK, Lieut. Thompson B., of U.S. Dragoons.

Exploration journal, June–August 1834; Dodge's expedition from Fort Gibson to the Pawnee Pict village, Toyash village; council with Indians.

Sen. Exec. Doc. 1, 23d Cong., 2d sess. (1834) 73–93; *American State Papers, Military Affairs* V 373–382.

1835

ALLING, Prudden (1809–1879) of Norwalk, O.

Travel diary, May–June 1835 (incomplete); trip from Norwalk to Chicago; adventures with a coach from Detroit, Ypsilanti, Michigan, Indiana, Chicago, Ottawa, Ill.; comments on trade, prospects, unusual events, land values in Chicago; fair interest.

The Firelands Pioneer (Norwalk, O.) n.s. XX (1918) 2016–2024.

BOYNTON, Lucien C. (1811–1886) of Boston, teacher and lawyer.

Private diary, November 1835–June 1853 (extracts); lively notes on his education, reading, love affairs, American life; honest and observant appraisal of American life from Boston to Richmond.

Amer. Antiq. Soc. Proc. n.s. XLIII (1933) 329–380.

BRADLEY, Cyrus Parker (1818–1838) of Concord, N.H.

Travel diary, June 1835; college student's holiday tour in Ohio and Michigan; long entries at Ohio, Marietta, Cincinnati, Portsmouth, Chillicothe, Circleville, Columbus, Sandusky City, Lake Erie, Pontiac, Cleveland; a lively picture of social and political conditions and descriptions of scenery, people, towns, inns; humorous style.

Ohio Archaeol. Hist. Soc. Quar. XV (1906) 207–270.

BRUNSON, Alfred (1793–1886) *b.* Danbury, Conn., of Prairie du Chien, Wis.

Methodist travel journal, September–December 1835; horseback tour from Meadville, Pa., to Wisconsin; religious comments, and general descriptions of country, etc.; fairly interesting.

Wisconsin Hist. Colls. XV (1900) 264–291.

DEAS, Lieut. Edward (*b. ca.* 1812) of South Carolina.

Official journal, December 1835–February 1836; account of occurrences during emigration of Creek Indians from Alabama to Arkansas; hardships, mishaps; fair reading, official style.

Jour. Southern Hist. VII (1941) 225–242.

DE LA SAGRA, Ramón, of Havana, botanist.

Travel diary, July–August 1835 (extracts); in New York, West Point, Schenectady, Utica, Erie Canal, Rochester, Albany, Genesee; careful travel-book descriptions. Translated from the Spanish.

New York Hist. XIX (1938) 407–418; further extracts, partially overlapping, in *Rochester Hist. Soc. Pubs.* XVIII (1940) 106–117.

FORD, Capt. Lemuel (1788–1850) of 1st U.S. Dragoons.

Military journals, May–September 1835 and February 1836–September 1837; first section includes Dodge's expedition to the Rocky Mountains, a 1,600-mile march through Nebraska, Colorado, Kansas, with notes on Indians and traders; second section includes visits to his home in Indiana; Fort Leavenworth; recruiting service in Indiana; resignation from the army.

Mississippi Valley Hist. Rev. XII (1925–1926) 550–579. Ford used this journal as the basis for his narrative, *A Summer upon the Prairie, Army and Navy Chronicle* II and III (1836), which is reprinted in A. B. Hulbert (ed.), *The Call of the Columbia* (Denver, 1934) 228–305.

GAGE, John (1802–1890) of Litchfield and Watertown, N.Y.

Travel diary, April 1835–May 1836; tour in New York, Pennsylvania, Maryland, and Michigan; visits to principal towns, smelting works, the new industrial scene; social descriptions in Washington, Baltimore, and Chicago; building flour mill at Chicago; an interesting diary.

Vineland Hist. Mag. IX (1924) 177–183, 188–191, 216–220, X (1925) 29–31, 47–51, 66–68, 229–232.

HOPKINS, Mrs. Louisa (1812–1862) of Portland, Me.

Private diary, November 1835–January 1840 (brief extracts); literary notes, reading, meeting with Dana.

George L. Prentiss, *The Life and Letters of Elizabeth Prentiss* (New York, 1882) 203–206.

KINGSBURY, Lieut. Gaines Pease, of U.S. Dragoons.

Military exploration journal, May–September 1835; from Fort Leavenworth up the South Platte, Fountain Creek, Manitou, Bent's Fort, down Arkansas River, Santa Fe Trail, Fort Leavenworth; topographical details, etc.

Sen. Exec. Doc. 209, 24th Cong., 1st sess. (1836).

LINCOLN, William (1802–1843) of Worcester, Mass., lawyer.

Private diary, November 1835 and January 1841; introspective observations, notes on politics; extracts to illustrate character.

Amer. Antiq. Soc. Proc. n.s. VII (1890–1891) 434–435.

McPHAIL, Dr. Leonard (*d.* 1867) of Maryland, surgeon.

Surgeon's military journal, June–August 1835; journey from Fort Gibson into the Indian country with the Dragoons; completion of treaty with Comanches and return.

Chronicles of Oklahoma XVIII (1940) 281–292.

PAINE, Albert Ware (1812–1907) of Bangor, Me., lawyer.

Private diary, August 1835–June 1836; long, well-written notes; comments on slavery, French war, political news, Mexican War, Indian warfare in Southwest, Deposit Bill; public, personal, social life in Bangor; militia, theaters, clubs, Daniel Webster, temperance and church work; an interesting and useful diary.

Lydia A. Carter, *The Discovery of a Grandmother* (Newtonville, Mass., 1920) 202–244.

PARKER, Rev. Samuel (1779–1866) *b.* Ashfield, Mass., Congregational missionary.

Missionary journal, March 1835–May 1837; overland journey via St. Louis, Independence, Colorado, Columbia River, Fort Vancouver; notes on scenery, Nez Percé Indians, Indian vocabularies and notes on Indian life; return via Sandwich Islands. Parker was first A.B.C. missionary to go to this area.

Journal of an Exploring Tour beyond the Rocky Mountains (Ithaca, 1838) 371 pp. His report of this tour, which is more diaristic in style and content, is published in A. B. and D. P. Hulbert (eds.), *Marcus Whitman, Crusader* (Denver, 1936) Part I 89–135.

PATTERSON, Gen. Robert (1792–1881) of Philadelphia.

Travel diary, May–June 1835 (extracts); Philadelphia to the upper Mississippi; visit with Jackson to Washington's birthplace; to Monticello; travel on Mississippi; dignified observations.

Jour. Amer. Hist. I (1907) 653–668.

POOLE, Caroline B. (1802–1844) of Cambridge, Mass., and Monroe, La.

Private diary, August 1835–May 1837; a Yankee schoolteacher in Louisiana; voyage from Boston to New Orleans; up the Mississippi, Red, and Black rivers; school work at Monroe; trip to Louisville in summer of 1836; school again; an effective picture of Yankee loneliness in the midst of Southern hospitality.

Louisiana Hist. Quar. XX (1937) 651–679.

SPENCER, Caroline.

Travel diary, July 1835; trip to Niagara; a lively and interesting record.

Mag. Amer. Hist. XXII (1889) 331–342.

WHITMAN, Rev. Marcus (1802–1847) *b.* Rushville, N.Y., missionary and doctor.

Missionary travel journal, May–October 1835; exploration with the Rev. Samuel Parker beyond the Rocky Mountains; Liberty, Mo., Bellevue, Neb., Fort Laramie, the old Oregon Trail; mostly religious and Indian notes.

Oregon Hist. Quar. XXVIII (1927) 239–257; a slightly different text in A. B. and D. P. Hulbert (eds.), *Marcus Whitman, Crusader* (Denver, 1936) Part I 146–165.

1836

BRADLEY, Rev. Caleb (1772–1854) of Westbrook, Me.

Diary, January 1836–March 1861 (extracts); a few interesting extracts relating to Fourth of July celebrations from 1836 to 1860; local, social, and personal notes.

Atlantic Monthly XCIV (1904) 108–113, XCV (1905) 83–90.

BURCHARD, George (1810–1880) of Greenbush, Wis.

Whaling journal, September 1836 onward (extracts); aboard the "Columbia" of Newark, N.J., around Cape Horn and in the Pacific; return to New York; some interesting hunting and social details.

Wisconsin Mag. Hist. XVIII (1934–1935) 422–441, XIX (1935–1936) 103–107, 227–241, 342–355.

CONANT, Augustus Hammond (1811–1863) *b*. Brandon, Vt., of Desplaines River, Ill.

Private diary, January 1836–June 1857 (extracts); notes of farming, reading, Methodist preaching, studies and writing sermons, household work; missionary work and study.

Robert Collyer, *A Man in Earnest* (Boston, 1868) 43–110 *passim;* abridged as *Augustus Conant* (Boston, 1905) 31–55 *passim.*

DAVIDSON, James D. (*ca.* 1810–1882) of Lexington, Va., lawyer.

Travel diary, October–December 1836; tour in Ohio, Indiana, Kentucky, Louisiana, Alabama, Georgia, South Carolina; down Ohio and Mississippi and up Atlantic coast; frank, lively views on slavery, morals, northern and southern cities; an excellent diary.

Jour. Southern Hist. I (1935) 345–377. Extracts (October 1836, Indiana) in *Indiana Mag. Hist.* XXIV (1928) 131–134.

DAWSON, James William (1808–1880) of Wilmington, Del.

Sea journal, January 1836–May 1839 (extracts); notes kept during whaling voyages from Wilmington to the Pacific.

Samuel Lamborn, *The Genealogy of the Lamborn Family* (Philadelphia, 1894) 118–119.

GRAY, William Henry (1809–1889) *b*. Fairfield, N.Y., of Portland, Ore.

1. Travel journal, July–September 1836 (extract); in a letter, based on memoranda set down during the journey; from Rendezvous to Fort Walla Walla; some interesting spellings.

Oregon Hist. Quar. XXXVIII (1937) 355–369.

2. Travel journal, December 1836–October 1837.

Whitman Coll. Quar. XVI (1913).

3. Travel journal, April–May 1838; in letter to a friend; from Independence, Mo., to Oregon; brief and statistical.

Pacific Northwest Quar. XXIX (1938) 277–282.

HARRIS, Lewis Birdsall (1816–1893) of Harrisburg, Pa., and Houston, Tex.

Travel diary, March–May 1836 (followed by undated recollections); Pennsylvania to Texas, via Pittsburgh, St. Louis, New Orleans, Galveston; arrival in Galveston at period of Alamo, etc.; Sam Houston after defeat of Santa Anna; interesting descriptions.

Southwestern Hist. Quar. XXV (1921–1922) 63–71, 131–140.

LUARD, Capt. Thomas W., of Canadian militia.

Military diary, 1836–1838; militia service during the Upper Canada rebellion; Navy Island campaign.

R. and K. M. Lizar, *In the Days of the Canada Company* (Toronto, 1936).

McLEOD, Maj. Martin (1813–1860) b. L'Original, near Montreal, of Minnesota.

Private diary, July 1836–May 1841; mainly relates to a filibustering trip across Minnesota in fall of 1836; adventures told with considerable verve; original poems, and quotations from Shakespeare and the romantic poets; a very interesting diary.

Minnesota Hist. Bull. IV (1921–1922) 351–439. Extracts in John H. Stevens, *Personal Recollections of Minnesota and Its People* (Minneapolis, 1890) 345–357.

MINOR, Lucian (1802–1858) of Louisa Co., Va., professor at William and Mary College.

Travel diary, November–December 1836; from Charlottesville, Va., to junction of Ohio and Wabash rivers; substantial and well-written entries; scenery, social and personal comments; a good deal of literary interest (Dickens, Johnson, Congreve, etc.); a very pleasant diary.

Massachusetts Hist. Soc. Proc. 2d Ser. VII (1891–1892) 263–294.

PRENTISS, Mrs. Elizabeth (1818–1878) of New York, and Dorset, Mass.

1. Literary diary, January 1836–December 1839; in Dana's class; wide reading and criticism; German classics; romantic emotionalism.

2. Private diary, October 1840–August 1856 (extracts); life at Richmond, schoolteaching, reading, nature notes and moralizing, effect of Byron; domestic work, ill health, marriage; diary about her son Edward.

George L. Prentiss, *The Life and Letters of Elizabeth Prentiss* (New York, 1882) 50–154 *passim*.

RIEGER, Rev. Joseph (1811–1867) b. Bavaria, of St. Louis, Mo.

Private diary, November 1836–August 1837 (extract); life of a Christian missionary in Illinois, Iowa, and Missouri.

"The Followers of Duden," *Missouri Hist. Rev.* XVIII (1923–1924) 216–225.

WHITMAN, Mrs. Narcissa (1808–1847), missionary.

1. Travel journal, June–September 1836; in a letter; from Liberty, Mo., to Fort Hall; descriptions and notes on domestic life of the missionaries.

Oregon Pion. Assoc. Trans. 19th Ann. Reunion (1891) 40–68.

2. Domestic journal, March 1842; in a letter; the happy but difficult life of the missionaries at Wailatpu.

Ibid. 21st Ann. Reunion (1893) 143–153. Extracts in: Mary O. Douthit, *The Souvenir of Western Women* (Portland, Ore., 1905) 19–21, and in T. C. Elliott, *The Coming of the White Women, 1836* (Portland, Ore., 1937).

WOODCOCK, Thomas Swann (1805–1863) of Manchester, Eng., and New York, engraver.

Travel diary, May 1836; trip from New York to Niagara Falls and return; description of Falls, but mainly notes on trade, manufactures, and land values.
Bull. New York Pub. Lib. XLII (1938) 675–694.

ZAHM, Matthias (1789–1874) of Lancaster Co., Pa.

Private diary, January 1836–August 1849; scattered notes of events in Lancaster; too brief to be of much interest.
Lancaster Co. Hist. Soc. Papers XII (1908) 184–194.

1837

ANON. (young girl of the Hopkins family of Swanton, Vt.).

Travel diary, June–July 1837; in a letter describing a wagon trip from Keene, O., across Illinois, via Paris, Springfield, and Beardstown; interesting feminine and domestic details.
Jour. Amer. Hist. III (1909) 511–516.

ANON. ("committee" of cadets of Norwich University).

School travel journal, July 1837; excursion to the Franconia Mountains, under Capt. Alden Partridge.
Journal of an Excursion to the Franconia Mountains (Northfield, Vt., 1837) 14 pp.

BACKUS, Captain Electus (1804–1862) *b.* New York City.

Military journal, November 1837–April 1838; bare notes of a campaign against Indians in Florida.
Hist. Mag. X (1866) 279–285.

DALLAS, George Mifflin (1792–1864), United States minister to Russia and England.

Diplomat's diary, July 1837–July 1839 and December 1856–May 1861; first part kept while author was minister in Russia; second part while he was at the Court of St. James's; very pleasant and readable diaries; discreet, modest general entries in political setting; court and national news and comments, social life, some gossip and comments on famous people; many items of literary interest and some original verse.
Susan Dallas (ed.), *Diary of George Mifflin Dallas* (Philadelphia, 1892) 443 pp.

DAUBNEY, Dr. Charles Bridle (1795–1867) of Oxford, Eng., naturalist.

Travel diary, July 1837–July 1838; through United States and in Canada; along east side of Mississippi River to St. Louis; later up Mississippi and Ohio;

visits to American scientists and scholars; notes inclined to scientific matters; literary style; quite interesting.

Journal of a Tour (Oxford, 1843) 231 pp.

DAYTON, Mrs. Maria Annis Tomlinson (*b.* 1815) *b.* Rhinebeck, N.Y.

Private diary, November 1837–September 1882 (extracts); very pleasant notes on social and domestic life, family, children, etc.; verses.

Laura D. Fessenden, *Genealogical Story (Dayton and Tomlinson)* (Cooperstown, N.Y., 1902) 90–103.

DWINNELL, Joseph Porter (1820–1839) of Danvers, Mass.

Private diary, January 1837–August 1838; brief notes of local affairs, work, carpentry, reading, and education; an interesting record of country life.

Danvers Hist. Soc. Colls. XXVI (1938) 23–41.

EDWARDS, Philip Leget (1812–1869) *b.* Kentucky, of Sacramento, Calif., lawyer.

Travel diary, January–September 1837; account of a cattle drive along the Pacific coast; with Willamette Cattle Company from Des Sables, Willamette, Fort George, Port Bodega, voyage to San Francisco; early account of San Francisco; Monterey; an interesting diary of California before the Gold Rush days; vigorous and personal.

California in 1837 (Sacramento, 1890) 47 pp.; republished (San Francisco, 1932) 47 pp.

FARNHAM, Mrs. Jerusha Loomis (*b.* 1804) *b.* Andover, Conn., schoolteacher.

Travel diary, May–July 1837; from Tully, N.Y., to the Gale colony at Log City, Ill.; significant happenings during journey, and pious reflections; weather, activities of her children, farming, domestic activities; a pleasant diary of a woman pioneer.

E. E. Calkins (ed.), *Log City Days* (Galesburg, Ill., 1937) 11–57.

FEATHERSTONHAUGH, George William (1780–1866), British geologist.

Travel diary, 1837; by canoe in Wisconsin Territory; very full entries in literary vein; topography and scenery, mineralogy, customs, adventures, Indians and Indian life.

A Canoe Voyage up the Minnay Sotor (London, 1847) two vols. Extracts describing trip through the Tennessee Valley in *Tennessee Hist. Mag.* 2d Ser. III (1932) 45–58.

FOULKE, Joseph (1786–1863) of Gwynedd, Pa., schoolmaster.

Travel diary, May–June 1837; visit with family to Friends on Long Island; visits, meetings, notes on scenery and social life; seminarrative.

Bull. Friends' Hist. Soc. Philadelphia XX (1931) 27–31.

FOWLER, Littleton (1802–1846), of Sabine Co., Tex.

Missionary journal, August 1837–April 1838 (extracts in narrative); Methodist missionary in Texas; religion and politics, with some personal religious items.

Texas Hist. Assoc. Quar. II (1898–1899) 73–84.

GARRIOCH, Peter (*b.* 1811) of St. Peters, Minn.

Travel diary, July–November 1837 (extracts); from Red River Colony to St. Peter's by cart and canoe; negotiations with Chippewas; account of Kaposia mission and Falls of St. Anthony.

"Peter Garrioch at St. Peters," *Minnesota Hist.* XX (1939) 119–128.

GIROD, Amury (*d.* 1837) of Varennes, Lower Canada, adventurer.

Political journal, November–December 1837; political affairs among the French in Quebec. Translated from the German and Italian.

Canadian Pub. Archives Rep. 1923 (Ottawa, 1924) 370–380.

HACKER, Jeremiah (1801–1895) of Portland, Me.

Religious journal, July 1837–November 1844; lively account of religious life, meetings, and revivals in Portland; temperance work; editorship of "The Portland Pleasure Boat."

Vineland Hist. Mag. XVII (1932) 204–211, XVIII (1933) 232–237, 268–275, 305–312, 340–343, XIX (1934) 22–27.

HAWTHORNE, Nathaniel (1804–1864), novelist.

1. Travel journals and notebooks, July 1837–June 1853; primarily observations of New England life; "a repository not only of seminal ideas for stories, but also of descriptions of actual places, persons, and incidents" (Stewart); indispensable to an understanding of Hawthorne's literary method.

Randall Stewart (ed.), *The American Notebooks* (New Haven, 1932) 350 pp.

2. Travel journals and notebooks, August 1853–May 1860; England, France, Italy; careful descriptive notes and observations; "sketches of places and men and manners, many of which would doubtless be very delightful to the public" (Hawthorne).

English Note-Books (with *Our Old Home*) and *French and Italian Note-Books,* forming Vols. VII, VIII, and X of the Riverside Edition of Hawthorne's *Works* (Boston, 1883). Mrs. Hawthorne's bowdlerized version of the English journal (1853–1857) is replaced by Randall Stewart (ed.), *The English Notebooks,* Mod. Lang. Assoc. Amer., Gen. Ser. XIII (New York, 1941) 667 pp.

An early undated diary referring to boyhood in Maine, adventures, games, reading, etc., was published as S. T. Pickard (ed.), *Hawthorne's First Diary* (Boston, 1897) 49–99; the authenticity of this is accepted by Austin Warren [*Nathaniel Hawthorne,* New York, 1934, p. 76].

A selection from the journals is Newton Arvin (ed.), *The Heart of Hawthorne's Journals* (Boston, 1929), of which the text is not reliable.

HIGBEE, Miss Lucy Ann, of Trenton, N.J.

Private diary, May–July 1837; diary of a spinster of about forty, taking her niece from Richmond, Va., to Ohio by stage and steamer; notes on scenery, Niagara, social affairs; pleasant touristic diary.

The Diary of Lucy Ann Higbee (Cleveland, O., 1924) 57 pp.

JUDD, Rev. Sylvester (1813–1853) of Augusta, Me.

Private diary, August 1837–January 1841 (extracts); life in divinity school at Harvard, appointment to pastorate at Augusta, Me., and notes of work there.

Arethusa Hall, *Life and Character of the Rev. Sylvester Judd* (Boston, 1854) 113–185 *passim*.

LILLYBRIDGE, Dr. C., of New York, physician.

Travel journal, March 1837; accompanying emigrating Cherokees; Tennessee, Ohio, Mississippi, and Arkansas rivers; data on health of Indians; official and impersonal but unusual and interesting.

Mississippi Valley Hist. Rev. XVIII (1931–1932) 232–245.

NYE, Thomas (1801–1877) of Montreal, lawyer.

Travel diary, October–December 1837; journey from Montreal to Chicago, by stage to Ontario, by steamer through the Lakes; return with his bride, overland to Detroit, steamer to Cleveland, and thence overland to Montreal; brief notes of things done, seen, and heard; good picture of prairie fire; notes on inns; moderate interest.

Hugh McLellan (ed.), *Journal of Thomas Nye* (Champlain, N.Y., 1932) 30 pp.

PEAKE, John (1756–1841) of Fairfax Co., Va., and Sangamon Co., Ill.

Private diary, January–December 1837; brief notes of daily occupations, devotions, etc.

Illinois Hist. Soc. Jour. VIII (1915–1916) 114–131.

PORTER, Mrs. Deborah H. (1809–1847) of Bangor, Me.

Religious journal, June 1837–June 1845 (extracts); parson's wife's notes, self-analysis, lamentations, trials, meetings, contemplations of God, prayers, omens, consolations and despairs, relations with preachers.

Anne T. Drinkwater, *Memoir of Mrs. Deborah H. Porter* (Portland, 1848) 34–226 *passim*.

RANKIN, Charles (*d.* 1886) of Ontario, surveyor.

Canadian surveying journal, May–June 1837; exploration for road from Oakville, on north side of Lake Ontario, to Owen Sound on Lake Huron; some general notes.

Ontario Hist. Soc. Papers and Recs. XXVII (1931) 497–510.

ROGERS, Lieut. Col. Robert D. (1809–1885) *b.* Haldimand, Ont., of Cobourg Rifles.

Canadian military journal, December 1837–January 1838 (fragment); movements of militia during rebellion of 1837; brief notes.

Canadian Hist. Rev. XIII (1932) 429–430.

SMITH, Joshua Toulmin (1816–1869) of Birmingham, Eng., lawyer.

Travel diary, August 1837–July 1838 (first part written by his wife); England to New York, Albany, Utica, Buffalo, Detroit; account of Detroit and Michigan; disappointment at not finding Utopia; return to Utica. Notes on American "bar-

barisms," prisons, elections, American women, cookery, linguistics; a carefully written analysis in lively and provocative vein.

Floyd B. Streeter (ed.), *Journal in America, 1837–1838* (Metuchen, N.J., 1925) 54 pp., forming No. 41 of Heartman's Historical Series.

SMITH, William Rudolph (1787–1868) of Montgomery Co., Pa., and Wisconsin.

Travel diary, July–October 1837; by canal and river from Pennsylvania to Wisconsin, via Pittsburgh, Steubenville, Wheeling, Marietta, Cincinnati, Louisville, Evansville, St. Louis, Alton, Dubuque, Prairie du Chien; and part of return journey; notes on towns and incidents of journey, social and general observations; quite interesting.

Wisconsin Mag. Hist. XII (1928–1929) 192–220, 300–321; *Incidents of a Journey from Pennsylvania to Wisconsin Territory, in 1837* (Chicago, 1927) 27–72.

STEBBINS, Salmon (1795–1882) *b.* Plainfield, N.H., Methodist preacher.

Methodist journal, May 1837–August 1838; journey to Wisconsin; travel and preaching there; simple, direct notes of work, etc.

Wisconsin Mag. Hist. IX (1925–1926) 188–212.

SUMNER, Charles (1811–1874) of Boston, lawyer and politician.

. Foreign travel diary, December 1837–April 1838; voyage across Atlantic; in France, Rouen, Paris, and study at Ecole de Droit; theaters, museums, English and American colony, trials; detailed and interesting notes of life of Americans in Paris.

Edward L. Pierce, *Memoirs and Letters of Charles Sumner* (Boston, 1877) I 213–286.

THOREAU, Henry David (1817–1862), essayist and transcendentalist.

Personal journal, October 1837–November 1861; distinctly a "literary" journal and commonplace book; "a daily record of things thought, seen, and felt . . . If a man is curious to know what such an original, plain-spoken, perfection-seeking, convention-despising, dogma-disbelieving, wisdom-loving, sham-hating, Nature-worshipping, poverty-proud genius was in the habit of confiding to so patient a listener at the close of the day, he has only to read the book" (Torrey).

Edited by Bradford Torrey, in *The Writings of Henry David Thoreau* (Boston, 1906) Vols. VII–XX. Portions published separately as, *Early Spring in Massachusetts* (Boston, 1881), *Summer* (Boston, 1884), *Winter* (Boston, 1888), *Autumn* (Boston, 1892). A fine selected edition is, Odell Shepard (ed.), *The Heart of Thoreau's Journals* (Boston, 1927) 348 pp.

WARREN, Dr. John Collins (1778–1856) of Boston, surgeon.

Diaries, June 1837–April 1856; voyage to Europe, England, Ireland, France, Italy; touristic travels and notes, visits to medical schools and doctors; journal of professional life and work in Boston; some domestic and social items; further travel in Europe.

Edward Warren, *The Life of John Collins Warren* (Boston, 1860) two vols., *passim.*

WILLS, Rev. William Henry (1809–1889) of Tarboro, N.C.

1. Travel diary, April–May 1837; drive by sulky from Tarboro, through Florida, Georgia, and Alabama, looking for site for home; comments on taverns, food, sectarians, farming, towns; detailed list of expenses; long entries, personal and amusing.

Southern Hist. Assoc. Pubs. VI (1902) 471–483, VII (1903) 7–16, 79–84, 187–192.

2. Travel diary, April–May 1840; by hack from Tarboro to Washington, train to Baltimore; over mountains to Cumberland, Wheeling, Ohio, Kentucky, Illinois, Tennessee, Mississippi, Alabama, and return; vigorous and amusing comments on social habits, institutions, and places.

Southern Hist. Assoc. Pubs. VII (1903) 349–352, 427–432, VIII (1904) 23–39, 129–138.

1838

ANON. (English farmer).

Travel diary, April–November 1838; from England to New York, New Jersey, and Pennsylvania; farming in Murray Valley, Pa., beginning of voyage home; moderate interest.

Lycoming Hist. Soc. Occasional Paper No. 6 (1928); *Now and Then* V (1936) 151–169.

ALLEN, Rev. William Y. (1805–1885) of Texas, and Rockville, Ind., chaplain of the Congress of the Texas Republic.

Private diary, March 1838–October 1839 (extracts); notes of his experiences in Texas, religious affairs, Indians.

Southwestern Hist. Quar. XVII (1913–1914) 43–60; reprinted from *Texas Presbyterian,* March 19, April 16 and 30, May 7, August 6 and 20, October 8 and 29, December 31, 1880, March 4, December 23, 1881, March 31, 1882, January 26, June 29, December 14, 1883.

BAKER, Charles Minton (*d.* 1872) *b.* New York, of Lake Geneva, Wis.

Travel diary, September–October 1838; from Hortonville, Vt., to Wisconsin; notes on towns, inns, canals; moderate interest.

Wisconsin Mag. Hist. V (1921–1922) 389–401.

BARRETT, Selah Hibbard (*b.* 1822) of Rutland, O.

Religious journal, February 1838–February 1872; self-educated Methodist; ministerial labors and travels in Ohio and occasional missions in other parts of the United States and Canada; revival meetings; work for religious press.

Autobiography of Selah Hibbard Barrett (Rutland, O., 1872) 396 pp.

COOMBE, George, Scotch phrenologist.

Travel diary, September 1838–February 1840 (extracts); Albany, New York, and environs; description of Shakers, Albany politics, and manners, etc.

Notes in the United States of North America (Edinburgh, 1841) three vols. Extracts in *Munsell's Colls. on Hist. Albany* (Albany, 1867) II 343–353.

DEARBORN, Henry Alexander (1783–1851) of Roxbury, Mass.

1. Travel diary, August–October 1838; journey to Niagara frontier to negotiate treaties with Seneca and Tuscarora Indians; Roxbury, Albany, Buffalo, Genesee, Nunda Falls, Niagara, Buffalo Creek, Lewiston, Rochester, Oswego, Kingston, Ogdensburg, Rossie lead mines, Montreal, Burlington; very extensive entries, with descriptions of scenery, Indians and their customs, myths and sports, and notes on farming, fortifications, etc.; illustrated.

2. Travel diary, November–December 1838; mission to Buffalo to negotiate treaty of emigration with Seneca Indians; mainly personal, weather, reading, and general comments on politics, Red Jacket, etc.

3. Travel diary, August 1839; journey from Boston to Cattaraugus by railroad, to attend council of Six Nations.

Buffalo Hist. Soc. Pubs. VII (1904) 39–183, 185–217, 219–225.

EELLS, Myra E. (a missionary).

Travel diary-letter, March–September 1838; New England, Ohio, St. Louis, in the Rockies; Englishwoman's observation of Americans—Negro, Indian, and white—and their customs; religion in the Rockies.

Oregon Pioneer Assoc. Trans., 17th Ann. Reunion (1889) 54–88a.

GREY, Louise Elizabeth (*d.* 1841), wife of John George, first Earl of Durham, governor of British North America.

Private diary, April–December 1838; voyage to Canada; notes on official, private, and social life of the governor-general and his family; much personal matter; good of its kind.

Lit. Hist. Soc. Quebec 9th Ser. (1915) 7–61.

MILLER, Henry B. (1814–1847) of York Co., Pa.

Private diary, January 1838–January 1839; St. Louis; descriptions of political and social life; trip to Iowa and Illinois; Natchez; a fairly interesting diary, but "trivial or merely personal" matter has been omitted by the editor.

Missouri Hist. Soc. Colls. VI (1928–1931) 213–287.

OLIN, Dr. Stephen (1797–1851) *b.* Leicester, Vt., president of Wesleyan University.

Foreign travel diary, November 1838–August 1840; travel in France, Italy, Ireland, Germany; inspecting antiquities, scenery, crops, business; down the Danube to Turkey; general social and touring observations.

The Life and Letters of Stephen Olin (New York, 1853) I 223–345, II 10–28.

PETERS, John (1812–1871) of Brooklyn, N.Y., and Vicksburg, Miss., merchant.

Private and business diary, November 1838–March 1841; business life in Vicksburg and his attempt to recover his fortunes after the panic of 1837; a few personal details.

Mississippi Valley Hist. Rev. XXI (1934–1935) 529–542.

POLKE, William, of Plymouth, Ind.

Travel journal, August–November 1838; journey in charge of party of Potta-wattomie Indians who "emigrated" from Twin Lakes, Marshall Co., Ind., to the Osage River in Western Territory; events during the march, deaths and sickness; details of Indian life and travel; an interesting journal.

Indiana Mag. Hist. XXI (1925) 316–336.

SANDERS, Cyrus (1817–1887) of Johnson Co., Iowa.

Travel diary, December 1838–January 1845; journey from Ohio to Johnson Co., Iowa; interesting details, taverns, cooking, gambling, dentists, etc.; work as surveyor; interesting general diary, with some literary allusions.

Iowa Jour. Hist. Pols. XXXVII (1939) 52–88.

STERNE, Adolphus (1801–1852) *b.* Cologne, Germany, of Nacogdoches, Tex.

Private and business diary, November 1838–November 1851; records of deaths, taxes, politics, early life in Texas; an interesting, extensive, and valuable record of early Texas.

Southwestern Hist. Quar. XXX (1926–1927) to XXXVIII (1934–1935) *passim.*

STEVENS, Henry (1791–1867) of Burlington, Vt., founder of Vermont Historical Society.

Private diary, January 1838–August 1842; farming, everyday life, politics; brief entries.

Vermont Hist. Soc. Proc. II (1931) 115–128.

SUTTER, Johann August (1803–1880) of California.

Private diary, April 1838–1856; only partly diary and mostly relating to 1849; account of his career; some interesting spellings reflecting German-English pro-nunciation.

The Argonaut (San Francisco) January 26, February 2, 9, 16, 1878; reprinted as, Douglas S. Watson (ed.), *The Diary of Johann August Sutter* (San Francisco, 1932) 56 pp.

SWARTZELL, William.

Diary May–August 1838; journal of residence in Missouri, written by a former Mormon deacon; *chronique scandaleuse.*

Mormonism Exposed (Pekin, O., 1840) 48 pp.

WEBSTER, Daniel (1782–1852), statesman.

Diary, July 1838–January 1839 (fragments never before published); personal and autobiographical; visits to Eliot, Me.

Old Eliot VIII (1908) 29–32.

WHEELER, Daniel (1771–1840) *b.* London, ministering Quaker.

Quaker journal, December 1838–October 1839 (American section); visits to Quaker meetings at Philadelphia, Baltimore, in New York, New England, Nova Scotia, and Ohio; impersonal.

Friends' Library VII (Philadelphia 1843) 290–305.

YOUNG, Dr. John A. (1812–1873) of Monmouth, Ill., physician.

Private diary, December 1838–April 1839; to Cincinnati on Ohio steamer; flirtations, Booth's performance of *Julius Caesar* and *Richard III;* journey to Monmouth to begin practice, trip to St. Louis, general social entries; a frank and fairly amusing diary.

Annals of Iowa 3d Ser. XIX (1933) 139–145.

BENEDICT, J. W.   1839

Military journal, September–November 1839; campaign against the Comanches in Texas; little contact with Indians; description of country.

Southwestern Hist. Quar. XXXII (1928–1929) 300–310.

BREWER, Henry Bridgeman (1813–1886) of Wilbraham, Mass.

Sea journal, September 1839–April 1840; voyage of the "Lausanne"; with his family from New York round Cape Horn to Fort Vancouver; reinforcing Oregon Mission at The Dalles; notes on weather, cruise, religious life on board, reading; fair interest.

Oregon Hist. Quar. XXIX (1928) 189–208, 288–310.

BROWNELL, George (1793–1872) of Thompson, Conn., and Waltham, Mass.

Foreign travel diary, February–May 1839; visit to England to study industrial methods and conditions; out by sailing ship and home by steamship; interesting details of travel and of industrial and social life in England; good picture of an early industrialist.

Lowell Hist. Soc. Pubs. II (1926) 325–371.

CROSBY, Jesse W. (1820–1893) *b.* Yarmouth, N.S., of Salt Lake and St. George, Ut.

Mormon diary, April 1839–April 1858 (with many gaps and added biographical matter); his life as a Mormon; joining Mormons in Missouri during "Mormon War"; missionary journeys in British provinces, and later in England; the Mormon migration to Utah and building of Salt Lake; governmental troubles; an excellent picture of western America and some interesting details of Victoria's England.

Annals Wyoming XI (1939) 145–218.

HAMILTON, John (*b.* 1800?) of Lock Haven, Pa.

Travel diary, November–December 1839; Pine Creek, Clinton Co., to Philadelphia by Union Canal and return; fair descriptions.

Hist. Jour. (Northwestern Pa.) I (1887) 110–118.

HASKEW, Rev. Peter (*b.* 1803) of Alabama, Methodist Episcopalian.

Missionary journal, April–December 1839; while author was serving with St. Joseph Mission, Fla., and Apalachicola Mission; religious and mission work; personal and domestic details, and comments on Negroes; fairly interesting.

Florida Hist. Soc. Quar. XVII (1938–1939) 132–151.

KNOWLES, David E. (1801–1848) *b*. Orange, Mass., of East Farnham, Quebec.

Quaker travel journal, November 1839–September 1840; journey to the Chero-kees, mainly by horse and coach from East Farnham to Cincinnati, Arkansas, Indiana; stages, visits to Friends and meetings, and Cherokee missions.

Bull. Friends' Hist. Soc. VI (1915) 70–78, VII (1916) 15–21, 42–50.

MUNGER, Asahel, and Eliza.

Travel diary-letter, May–September 1839; Ohio to Oregon; notes on travel and religion and criticism of fur companies.

Oregon Hist. Soc. Quar. VIII (1907) 387–405.

SMITH, E. Willard (*b*. 1814) *b*. Albany, of Washington, D.C., architect and civil engineer.

Travel diary, August 1839–July 1840; journey into the Rocky Mountains with the fur traders Vasquez and Sublette; descriptions of the Indians and renegade whites.

Oregon Hist. Soc. Quar. XIV (1913) 250–279; extracts in *Annals Wyoming* XI (1939) 33–41.

1840

CURTIS, William Edmund (1823–1880), New York jurist.

Private diary, January 1840–1880; begun at Washington (Trinity) College, Hartford, Conn.; college work, reading, and criticisms, with some verses; social life; travels with usual touristic notes; work as lawyer and judge; an interesting diary of a man of wide interests.

Elizabeth Curtis, *Letters and Journals* (Hartford, 1926) 93–347, interspersed with letters.

DOUGLAS, Sir James (1803–1877) of the Hudson's Bay Company, Pacific Depart-ment, later governor of British Columbia.

Travel journal, December 1840–January 1841; voyage from Fort Vancouver to California; Monterey; account of political organization of whole of California; inland journey to Santa Clara Valley.

California Hist. Soc. Quar. VIII (1929) 98–115.

FROST, Rev. John H. (*d*. 1863–1866), Methodist missionary in Oregon.

Missionary journal, May 1840–November 1843 (extracts); Fort Vancouver; life in a mission on the Clatsop Plains; note of return to Boston via San Francisco and Oahu; partly narrative.

Oregon Hist. Quar. XXXV (1934) 50–73, 139–167, 235–262, 348–375.

GREGG, Josiah (1806–1850) *b*. Overton Co., Tenn., of Independence, Mo.

Private diary, February 1840–January 1847; end of life as trader on Santa Fe Trail; trips into Texas, medical studies; service with Arkansas Volunteers and with Wool's column in Mexico; visits to Monterrey and Saltillo; a fine diary.

Maurice G. Fulton (ed.), *Diary and Letters of Josiah Gregg* (Norman, Okla., 1941) 413 pp., with letters inserted at appropriate dates in the diary. The second volume (1944) extends to 1850.

LAUGHLIN, Samuel H. (*b.* 1796), editor of the *Nashville Union*.

1. Political diary, April–May 1840, journey from McMinnville, Tenn., to Washington and Baltimore as delegate to Democratic National Convention; interesting for travel details and politics of Andrew Jackson and J. K. Polk.

2. Political diary, September–November 1843; while author was member of Tennessee Senate and of "the immortal thirteen"; valuable, detailed account of procedure of legislators.

Tennessee Hist. Mag. II (1916) 45–55, 55–85.

LOVELL, Mrs. Lucy Buffum, of Bellingham, Mass.

Private diary, October 1840–June 1843; domestic notes of the Quaker wife of a Baptist minister; birth of children and their upbringing; pleasant reading.

M. R. Lovell (ed.), *Two Quaker Sisters* (New York, 1937) 49–109.

LOWE, Rev. Charles (1828–1874) b. Portsmouth, N.H., of Boston.

Private diaries, September 1840–June 1872 (copious extracts); early studies at Harvard, general and religious reading in the divinity school; parish work in New Bedford; Sunday-school work; journey to Europe, Egypt, and Near East; parish work in Boston; further travels in England and Europe; travel, reading, church; a journal of wide interests.

Martha P. Lowe, *Memoir of Charles Lowe* (Boston, 1884) 5–514 *passim.*

MARSTON, Maj. David, of Hampton, N.H.

Journal of events, May 1840–1879; outstanding events, providences, weather, etc.

Joseph Dow, *History of the Town of Hampton* (Salem, Mass., 1893) 579–580.

MORRISON, Mrs. Anna R. (*b.* 1820) of Jacksonville, Ill.

Private and travel diary, November 1840–March 1841; New York to Jacksonville, Ill., rather dull notes.

Illinois Hist. Soc. Jour. VII (1914) 34–50.

MOTT, Mrs. Lucretia (1793–1880) of Philadelphia and Roadside, Pa.

Quaker travel journal, May–September 1840; journey from New York to Liverpool; World's Convention in London; travel through England, Ireland, Scotland; visits to Quaker meetings and schools.

Anna D. Hallowell (ed.), *James and Lucretia Mott* (Boston, 1884) 146–175.

PHILIPS, Dr. Martin W. (1806–1889) of Hinds Co., Miss., physician and planter.

Plantation diary, January 1840–January 1863; largely records of Log Hall cotton plantation, Miss.; crops, planting, etc., with a few personal entries; interesting as a clear, factual record of a "progressive" Southern planter; little about the Civil War.

Mississippi Hist. Soc. Pubs. X (1909) 305–481.

REATH, B. B., of Philadelphia.

Travel diary, August 1840; visit to Wilkes-Barre; conventional literary descriptions; notes on gallantries; good picture of the diarist.

Wyoming Hist. Geol. Soc. Proc. and Colls. XV (1917) 157–172.

STARIN, Frederick J., of Fultonville, N.Y.

Travel diary, May 1840–October 1841 (with a few entries in 1847); journey from Montgomery Co., N.Y., to Milwaukee, thence to East Troy, Whitewater, Madison, Fort Madison, etc.; valuable picture of early settlements in south and southeast Wisconsin; fair reading.

Wisconsin Mag. Hist. VI (1922–1923) 73–94, 207–232, 334–345.

STICKNEY, Mrs. Elizabeth (1781–1868) of Newburyport, Mass.

Private diary, November 1840–January 1842 (extracts); social life, reading, antislavery interests; kept at Philadelphia.

A. L. Marston (ed.), *Records of a Californian Family* (San Diego, 1928) 10–11.

SUTHERLAND, John (1819–1886) of La Porte, Ind.

Private diary, May 1840 (extract); Whig gathering at Tippecanoe; detailed; interesting spellings and word formations.

Mississippi Valley Hist. Rev. IV (1917–1918) 362–370.

1841

ALLAN, George T., of Cathlamet, Ore., of Hudson's Bay Company.

1. Travel diary, March–July 1841; voyage from Fort Vancouver to York Factory on Hudson's Bay with Ermatinger; narrative style.

2. Travel diary, November 1841; brief account of horseback trip through the Willamette Valley.

Oregon Pioneer Assoc. Trans., 9th Annual Reunion (1881) 38–55, 56–59.

BIDWELL, John (1819–1900) of New York, N.Y., and Chico, Calif.

Travel diary, May–November 1841; with Captain Bartleson's California party from Independence, Mo., to California; first emigrant train to California; descriptions of country, natural history, crops, weather, social conditions, incidents; rather impersonal.

A Journey to California (1842) 32 pp.; reprinted, edited by H. I. Priestley (San Francisco, 1937) 48 pp., which includes the marginalia made by George McKinstry on the copy he used as a guidebook; original also in Charles C. Royce, *John Bidwell* (Chico, Calif., 1906) 8–37.

BRACKENRIDGE, William Dunlop (1810–1893) b. Scotland, horticulturist on the Wilkes expedition.

Travel journal, April–October 1841; in Oregon and California; descriptions and horticultural notes.

Washington Hist. Quar. XXI (1930) 218–229, 298–305, XXII (1931) 42–58, 129–145, 216–227.

BURRITT, Elihu (1810–1879) b. New Britain, Conn., blacksmith.

Private diaries, August 1841–January 1858 (extracts); his reading and languages, crusades for world peace and penny postage in America and Europe, work in antislavery movement.

Merle Curti (ed.), *The Learned Blacksmith* (New York, 1937) 11–138.

EMMONS, Lieut. George Foster (1811–1884), U.S.N.

Naval exploration journal, July–August 1841; scattered notes of government exploration; Fort Vancouver; descriptions and diagrams.

Oregon Hist. Soc. Quar. XXVI (1925) 263–273.

EWING, Thomas (1789–1871) of Ohio, secretary of the treasury in Tyler's cabinet.

Political diary, August–September 1841 (extract); account of breach between Tyler and his cabinet.

Amer. Hist. Rev. XVIII (1912–1913) 97–112.

FALCONER, Thomas (1805–1882) *b.* Bath, Eng., judge.

Travel diary, August–October 1841; account of what befell the main party of Texans left behind when Cooke set out in search of the settlements of New Mexico; long, interesting entries; the diary supplements his "narrative" of the expedition.

F. W. Hodge (ed.), *Thomas Falconer's "Letters and Notes on the Texan Santa Fe Expedition 1841–1842"* (New York, 1930) App. 105–118.

HAYES, Rutherford Birchard (1822–1893), nineteenth President of the United States.

Private and political diary, June 1841–January 1893; begun at Kenyon College and continued until his death; study at Kenyon, Columbus, and Harvard Law School; law practice at Sandusky; work in Cincinnati; service in Civil War; governorship of Ohio; Presidency; an extensive and valuable record of public life with a good deal of private and general matter.

Charles R. Williams (ed.), *Diary and Letters of Rutherford Birchard Hayes* (Ohio State Archaeol. Hist. Soc., 1922–1926) five vols.

LYELL, Sir Charles (1797–1875) of England, F.R.S.

1. Travel diary, July 1841–August 1842; travel in New England, Nova Scotia, Canada; geological, topographical observations; notes on society and customs, meetings with prominent Americans, etc.

Travels in North America (London, 1845) two vols.

2. Travel diary, September 1845–June 1846; Liverpool to Halifax; New England; down Atlantic coast to Louisiana; up the Mississippi; geological and social observations; rather impersonal.

A Second Visit to North America (London, 1849) 2 vols; often reprinted.

PRITCHARD, Rev. John Lamb (1811–1862) of Wilmington, N.C.

Baptist journal, July 1841–May 1861 (extracts); meetings, preaching, visits, travels, sermons, weather, reading, some political notes; less formalized than usual religious journal.

J. D. Hufham, *Memoir of Rev. John L. Pritchard* (Raleigh, 1867), 32–133 *passim*.

SWAN, Lansing B. (1809–1861) of Rochester, N.Y.

Travel diary, June 1841; trip from Rochester to Michigan by stage, steamer, and railroad; lively, full descriptions of towns, countryside, hardships of travel, etc.

Journal of a Trip to Michigan in 1841 (Rochester, 1904) 53 pp.

VAN LENNEP, Mrs. Mary Elizabeth (1821–1844) *b.* Hartford, Conn.

Religious journals, April 1841–August 1844 (extracts); mainly religious reflections, emotions, and weather; some notes on domestic and local affairs, sickness, preparation for missionary career, marriage, voyage to Turkey, and missionary work there.

Louisa Hawes, *Memoir of Mrs. Mary E. Van Lennep* (Hartford, 1847) 84–320 *passim*.

WILKES, Lieut. Charles (1798–1877), U.S.N., *b.* New York City.

Naval exploration journal, May–August 1841; government exploring expedition in the Northwest; very good descriptions of places and Indians.

Washington Hist. Quar. XVI (1925) 49–61, 137–145, 206–223, 290–301, XVII (1926) 43–65, 129–144, 223–229; this diary was the basis for his *Narrative of the United States Exploring Expedition* (Philadelphia, 1845) five vols.

WILLIAMS, Joseph (*b.* 1777) of Cumberland Co., Pa.

Travel diary, April 1841–October 1842; journey from Ripley Co., Ind., to Oregon Territory; with early wagon train to Oregon, and a later journey from thence to the Southwest; full of notes of accidents and incidents, especially of a sordid kind; notes on Indians (heathens), scenery, natural history, immorality of Indians and whites, estimates of farming possibilities; valuable historically, and very good journalistic reading.

Narrative of a Tour from the State of Indiana (Cincinnati, 1843) 48 pp.; reprinted, edited by J. C. Bell (New York, 1921) 95 pp.

1842

ANON. ("clerical supernumerary" on U. S. frigate "United States").

Sea journal, January 1842–August 1844; cruise in Pacific Ocean; routine descriptions of voyage; South America, Mexico, Hawaii, etc.; important because Herman Melville was also on this cruise.

Charles R. Anderson (ed.), *Journal of a Cruise to the Pacific* (Durham, N.C., 1937) 21–67.

CHASE, Samuel Worcester (*b.* 1811) of North Yarmouth, Me.

Whaling journal, September 1842–1845; first mate of the "Arab"; hunting, hardships, places visited, etc.; interesting account and extracts.

William H. Rowe, *Shipbuilding Days in Casco Bay* (Yarmouth, 1929) 172–186.

CRAWFORD, Medorem (*d.* 1891) *b.* New York, of Yamhill Co., Oregon.

Travel diary, March–October 1842; with Elijah White's party; New York to St. Louis and across the plains to Oregon; mainly statistical.

Sources of the History of Oregon in *Oregon Hist. Soc. Pubs.* I Part I (1897) 5–28.

FRÉMONT, Col. John Charles (1813–1890), explorer.

Travel journal, May 1842–August 1844; report of the exploring expedition in the Rocky Mountains in 1842 and to Oregon and California in 1843–1844.

Sen. Doc. 174, 28th Cong. 2d sess. (Washington, 1845) 294 pp.; often reprinted, usually as *Narrative of the Exploring Expedition.*

HUTCHINSON, Anderson (1798–1853) of Austin, Tex., judge.

Prison diary, September 1842–June 1843; capture by Mexicans at Behar, travel to Mexico, and imprisonment at Perote Castle; return by boat to the United States; brief factual entries, but rather interesting.

Texas Hist. Assoc. Quar. XIII (1909–1910) 294–311.

PREBLE, Adm. George Henry (1816–1885) *b.* Portland, Me.

Travel diary, February–April 1842; Rodgers' canoe expedition across the Everglades of Florida, around Lake Okeechobee, and up and down the connecting rivers and lakes; stages, topography, natural history, some personal adventures and comments; supplements Rodgers' official report; quite interesting.

The United Service (Philadelphia) VIII (1883) 358–376.

SCOTT, Rev. James Leander, Seventh-Day Baptist missionary.

Missionary journal, January–July 1842; through Pennsylvania, Ohio, Indiana, Illinois, Iowa, Wisconsin, and Michigan; descriptions of scenery, climate, emigration prospects, religious conditions; poetical quotations; a useful journal.

Journal of a Missionary Tour (Providence, 1843) 203 pp.

TRUEHEART, James L. (1815–1882) of San Antonio, Tex.

Prison diary, September 1842–April 1844; capture by Mexicans at Behar, journey to Mexico, and imprisonment at Perote Castle; much general description, besides notes of hardships, some lively characterizations and shrewd observations; highly interesting.

F. C. Chabot (ed.), *The Perote Prisoners* (San Antonio, 1934) 344 pp.

1843

ALCOTT, Louisa May (1832–1888) *b.* Germantown, Pa., author.

Private diary, July 1843–July 1886 (with gaps; copious extracts); early diary kept at Fruitlands, reading, schooling; personal, domestic, and social affairs; many notes on her reading, writing, and literary interests and friendships; much of it revised but still a pleasant and interesting record of a literary life.

Ednah D. Cheney (ed.), *Louisa May Alcott: Her Life, Letters and Journals* (Boston, 1889) 404 pp. *passim;* reprinted (Boston, 1928).

BOARDMAN, John (1824–1883) *b.* Cazenovia, N.Y., of Makawao, Island of Maui, farmer.

Travel diary, May–November 1843; from Shawnee Mission (near Westport, Kans.) to Oregon, via Laramie, Fort Hall, Fort Boise, Vancouver; brief matter-of-fact notes on the route, Indians, missionaries, buffalos, scenery.

Utah Hist. Quar. II (1929) 99–121.

BOONE, Capt. Nathan (1782–1857) *b.* Kentucky, of U.S. Dragoons, son of Daniel Boone.

Military travel journal, May–July 1843; expedition from Fort Gibson over the southwestern prairies; mainly historical and topographical notes; Indians, buffalo hunting, note on how to prepare buffalo meat; impersonal.

Louis Pelzer, *Marches of the Dragoons in the Mississippi Valley* (Iowa City, 1917) 189–237; *Chrons. Oklahoma* VII (1929) 63–105.

BRIDGE, Horatio (1806–1893), U.S.N.

Travel journal, June 1843–October 1844; touristic notes on the Canaries, Liberia, Sierra Leone, and the African west coast.

Nathaniel Hawthorne (ed.), *Journal of an African Cruiser* (New York, 1845) 1–179.

COOKE, Col. Philip St. George (1809–1895) *b.* near Leesburg, Va., *d.* Detroit.

1. Official military journal, May–July 1843; "journal of an expedition of a detachment of U.S. Dragoons from Fort Leavenworth—to protect the annual caravan of traders, from Missouri to the Mexican boundary on the road to Santa Fe."

Mississippi Valley Hist. Rev. XII (1925–1926) 72–98, 227–255.

2. Official military journal, October 1846–January 1847; march from Santa Fe to San Diego, in command of the Mormon Battalion.

Sen. Exec. Doc. 2, 30th Cong. spec. sess. (Washington, 1849) 85 pp.; the text of this is inaccurate; and the text of the original MS is published in R. P. Bieber (ed.), *Exploring Southwestern Trails* (Glendale, Calif., 1938) 65–240.

CROCKER, Alvah (1801–1874) of Fitchburg, Mass.

Private diary, October 1843–October 1845 (extracts); brief reports of activities in connection with Fitchburg, and Vermont and Massachusetts railroads; travels and surveys, and religious notes.

William B. Wheelwright, *Life and Times of Alvah Crocker* (Boston, 1923) 29–36.

ELDREDGE, Joseph C., general superintendent of Indian affairs for the Republic of Texas.

Travel journal, May–August 1843; meeting with Comanches to form friendly relations for government of Texas; official report to Sam Houston.

West Texas Hist. Assoc. Year Book IV (1928) 114–139.

HECKER, Rev. Isaac Thomas (1819–1888) *b.* New York City, Catholic missionary.

Private and religious diary, April 1843–June 1845; early part kept at Brook Farm; religious interests, spiritual disquiet, and struggles; life in Concord; notes on the various influences on his religious life.

Walter Elliott, *The Life of Father Hecker* (New York, 1891) 61–193 *passim;* reprinted (New York, 1894).

JOHNSON, Overton, and WINTER, William H. (1819–1879).

Travel journal, May 1843–June 1845; a travel narrative written up from notes; conventional travel book; people, places, customs, sights; across Rocky Mountains; description of Oregon and California; only Winter was in California (although "we" is used).

Route across the Rocky Mountains (Lafayette, Ind., 1846) 152 pp.; reprinted (Princeton, N.J., 1932) 199 pp.; *Oregon Hist. Soc. Quar.* VII (1906) 62–104, 163–210, 291–327.

LAWRENCE, Amos Adams (1814–1886) of Boston.

Business diary, May 1843–December 1883 (scattered extracts); business life in Boston, work as treasurer of Harvard, news of war, personal affairs.

William Lawrence, *Life of Amos A. Lawrence* (Boston, 1888) 50–273 *passim*.

NESMITH, James W. (*b.* 1820) *b.* Maine.

Travel diary, May–October 1843; from Independence, Mo., to Oregon, in Marcus Whitman's party; notes on hunting.

Oregon Hist. Soc. Quar. VII (1906) 329–359.

NEWBY, William T. (1820–1884) *b.* Warren Co., Tenn., of McMinville, Ore.

Travel diary, May–November 1843 and one entry for February 1845; from Dadeville, Mo., to Independence and thence to Oregon City; brief notes of travel, distances, and some descriptions; many interesting spellings.

Oregon Hist. Quar. XL (1939) 219–242.

PARRISH, Rev. Edward Evans (1791–1874) *b.* W. Va., of Linn Co., Ore.

Travel diary, October 1843–July 1845; Ohio, Kentucky, Missouri, overland to Oregon; usual travel notes, Indians, hunting, sights, etc.; fair interest.

Oregon Pioneer Assoc. Trans. 16th Annual Reunion (1888) 82–122.

READING, Pierson Barton (1816–1869) *b.* New Jersey.

Travel diary, May–December 1843; Westport, Mo., to Monterey, Calif.; account of route, hardships, organization of party, Sutter's estates; down Sacramento River to San Francisco; brief account of voyage to Monterey.

Soc. California Pioneers Quar. VII (1930) 148–198.

SALTER, William (*d.* 1910) of Burlington, Ia., Congregational minister.

1. Missionary journal, November 1843–January 1846; work in Jackson County, Iowa, and adjoining country; observations of the frontier and pioneers; personal and critical estimates, opposition to slavery and liquor, fostering education; good frontier material.

Annals Iowa 3d Ser. XIX (1933–1935) 539–553, 592–613, XX (1935–1937) 26–49; a memoir based on this in *Annals Iowa* 3d Ser. VII (1906–1907) 592–607 and reprinted in *Jackson Co. Annals* (Ia.) No. 4 (1907) 42–54.

2. Almanac diary, January–December 1846; kept at Maquoketa, Ia., and Burlington; brief notes of weather, clerical visits, etc.

Annals Iowa 3d Ser. XVII (1930) 466–469.

SUBLETTE, William Lewis (1799?–1845) of St. Louis, Mo., fur trader.

Diary, May–June 1843; account of a hunting trip in Missouri with Sir William Drummond Stewart.

Mississippi Valley Hist. Rev. VI (1919–1920) 99–110.

SYLVESTER, Avery, of Deer Island, Me., ship's captain.

Sea journals, August 1843–May 1846 (extracts); four voyages of the brigs "Pallas" and "Chenamus" between Oahu and Oregon; notes on Indians, settlers, trading, country, etc.

Oregon Hist. Quar. XXXIV (1933) 259–272, 359–371.

TALBOT, Theodore (d. 1862) of Kentucky.

1. Travel journal, April–October 1843; with the Frémont expedition to map the country from Missouri to the Oregon coast; exploration of Oregon Territory; full descriptions of scenery; written for his mother and fuller than the following.

2. Travel journal, November 1848–December 1852; with the first military company in Oregon Territory; voyage to Oregon, service during Gold Rush period, notes on desertions.

Charles H. Carey (ed.), *The Journals of Theodore Talbot* (Portland, 1931) 153 pp.

TIBBETTS, Capt. John C. (1798–1862) of Brooklin, Me.

Sea journal, July–August 1843; voyage of brig "Gulnare" from Antwerp to New York; details of sailing, interesting observations on passengers; philosophizing and piety; poems; an excellent self-portrait of an actively religious Yankee seaman.

New England Quar. XI (1938) 154–165.

WHIPPLE, Henry Benjamin (1822–1901), first Protestant Episcopal bishop of Minnesota.

Travel journal, October 1843–May 1844; voyage from New York, overland through Florida, Georgia, Mississippi, Louisiana, up the Mississippi to St. Louis, up the Ohio, overland through Ohio, Pennsylvania, Delaware, Virginia, Maryland; acute observations and comments on social and religious conditions and slavery; long and very interesting entries.

Lester B. Shippee (ed.), *Bishop Whipple's Southern Diary 1843–1844* (Minneapolis, 1937) 208 pp.

YOUNG, John Edward (1824–1904) of Indian Point, Ill.

Travel diary, September 1843–January 1844; Illinois to the Shenandoah Valley by horseback; principally descriptions of farming and crops in Illinois, Indiana, Kentucky, Ohio, West Virginia, and Virginia.

Illinois Hist. Soc. Jour. XXV (1932–1933) 167–189.

Anon.   1844

Journal of a Wanderer; Being a Residence in India and Six Weeks in North America (London, 1844) 250 pp.

Allen, Capt. James (1806–1846) *b*. Ohio, of 1st U.S. Dragoons.

Military journal, 1844; march into the Indian country in northern Iowa Territory.

House Exec. Doc. 168, 29th Cong. 1st sess. (1845); parts relating to Iowa (August–October) in *Iowa Jour. Hist. Pols*. XI (1913) 68–108; parts relating to South Dakota in *South Dakota Hist. Colls*. IX (1918) 347–368.

Baxter, Henry, of Friendship, N.Y.

Private diary, April–November 1844; rafting lumber on the Allegheny and Ohio rivers, and selling it; full daily narrative of his work and personal life, with accounts of towns, industries, and social life; comments on reading and religion; a very good diary.

Pennsylvania Mag. Hist. Biog. LI (1927) 27–78, 143–171, 207–243.

Clyman, James (1792–1881) *b*. Fauquier Co., Va., of Napa, Calif.

1. Travel diary, May 1844–July 1846; journey from Independence, Mo., to Oregon along Oregon Trail to Willamette Valley and thence to Napa Valley; travels in California; return to Missouri; a simple straightforward diary with some literary allusions; interesting for the lore of plains and mountains, written with good humor and common sense; some interesting spellings and words.

California Hist. Soc. Quar. IV (1925) 307–360, V (1926) 48–84, 110–138, 255–282, 378–401; Charles L. Camp (ed.), *James Clyman, American Frontiersman* (San Francisco, 1928) 59–235.

2. Farming diary, January–December 1871; brief notes concerning his daily occupations and farming.

California Hist. Soc. Quar. VI (1927) 64; in Camp's edition, 242–243.

Gary, Rev. George (1793–1855) *b*. Middlefield, N.Y., missionary.

Missionary travel journal, April 1844–January 1848; voyage from New York to Oregon via Honolulu; missionary work, notes on people, places, sermons, etc.; return to New York.

Oregon Hist. Quar. XXIV (1923) 68–105, 153–185, 269–333, 386–433.

Harris, N. Sayre, secretary of Protestant Episcopal Church.

Missionary travel journal, beginning March 1844; from New Orleans by steamer up Mississippi to Fort Towson; tour via Forts Smith, Gibson, and Scott, the Shawnee Mission, and Fort Leavenworth; inspection of missionary posts in Indian Territory, among Choctaws, Seminoles, Creeks, Cherokees, Osages, etc.; valuable comments and criticisms on work of missions and much general and social matter; quite interesting.

Journal of a Tour in the "Indian Territory" (New York, 1844) 74 pp. Partly in *Chrons. Oklahoma* X (1932) 219–256.

MARTIN, Col. William (1765–1846) of Dixon Springs, Tenn.

Political diary, April 1844 (extracts); kept during attendance at Whig Convention; nomination of Clay; brief notes.

Lucy H. Horton, *Family History* (Franklin, Tenn., 1922) 137.

MOORE, George (1806–1876), Englishman.

Travel diary, August–November 1844; voyage from Great Britain to New York; travel in Canada and United States; New York, Baltimore, Washington, Niagara and return; rather dull notes on towns, scenery, etc.

Journal of a Voyage across the Atlantic (London, 1845) 96 pp.

WHARTON, Maj. Clifton (*d.* 1847) *b.* Pennsylvania, of 1st U. S. Dragoons.

Military journal, August–September 1844; march from Fort Leavenworth to Pawnee villages on Platte River; thence to country of the Otos, Pottawatomies, Ioways and Sauks, on Missouri River, and return to Fort Leavenworth; purpose to reconcile Pawnees and Sioux and to impress the natives; notes on country and councils; literary style.

Kansas Hist. Soc. Colls. XVI (1923–1925) 272–305.

1845

ABERT, Lieut. James William, of Corps of Topographical Engineers.

1. Military exploration journal, June 1845; expedition from Bent's Fort to St. Louis; scientific details and notes on journey.

H. Bailey Carroll (ed.), *Guádal P'a* (Canyon, Texas, 1941) 121 pp., reprinted from *Sen. Exec. Doc.* 438, 29th Cong. 1st sess., 75 pp.

2. Military exploration journal, June 1846–March 1847; exploration of New Mexico; mainly notes on topography, natural history, etc.; some personal items.

Sen. Exec. Doc. 41, 30th Cong. 1st sess. (1848) 417–546. Earlier part in William H. Emory, *Notes of Travel in California* (New York, 1849) App. 72–83.

BROWN, William Reynolds (1816–1874) *b.* near Urbana, O., of Kaposia, Tenn.

Farming diary, October 1845–June 1846; small details of farming, domestic, social work, and life in Minnesota; a valuable and highly interesting record of pioneer farming.

R. C. Loehr (ed.), *Minnesota Farmers' Diaries* (St. Paul, 1939) 37–82.

DUERST, Mathias, *b.* Switzerland, of New Glarus, Wis.

Travel diary, April–August 1845; across Atlantic and overland journey to Wisconsin; daily narrative; quite interesting. Translated.

Wisconsin Hist. Colls. XV (1900) 292–337.

EWBANK, Thomas (1792–1870).

Travel diary, December 1845–August 1846; narrative and daily entries of "whatever interested me, and that, in sooth, with nearly everything, arts, manners, customs," *ad infin.;* voyage to Brazil; mainly detailed notes on Brazilian life.

Life in Brazil (New York, 1856) 469 pp.

HARRITT, Jesse (*b.* 1818) *b.* Indiana, of Oregon.

Travel diary, April–October 1845; from Missouri River along Oregon Trail to The Dalles; mainly notes on stages and difficulties of journey; some Oregon prices.

Oregon Pioneer Assoc. Trans., 38th and 39th Annual Reunion (1910–1911) (Portland, 1914) 506–526. Partly in "Route of the Meek Cut-off," *Oregon Hist. Quar.* XXXV (1934) 2–6.

HICKS, Elijah, missionary to Indians.

Missionary journal, December 1845–June 1846; travel through Oklahoma; work and council among Comanches; official journal.

Chrons. Oklahoma XIII (1935) 68–99.

HOWELL, John Ewing (1806–1885?) *b.* West Virginia, of Clark Co., Mo.

Travel diary, April–October 1845; from Jackson Co., Mo., to Oregon City; mainly description of route, scenery, etc.

Washington Hist. Quar. I (1906–1907) 139–158.

KERN, Edward M.

Travel journal, November 1845–February 1846; with Frémont's party in exploration of Mary's or Humboldt River, Carson Lake, Owens River and Lake; notes on topography, scenery, hunting, etc.

James Hervey Simpson, *Report of Explorations across the Great Basin of the Territory of Utah* (Washington, D.C., 1876) 486 pp. Journal, App. Q 477–486.

LYMAN, Prof. Chester Smith (1814–1890) *b.* Manchester, Conn., of Yale.

Travel diary, October 1845–June 1850; voyage around Cape Horn to the Sandwich Islands, Honolulu, Hawaii; thence to San Francisco and the gold mines; work as missionary, surveyor, gold digger; vivid account of life in the islands and the mines, with good account of the debauchery of San Francisco and the gold fevers; an excellent diary.

F. J. Teggart (ed.), *Around the Horn to the Sandwich Islands* (New Haven, 1924) 328 pp. Extracts relating to the Gold Rush in *California Hist. Soc. Quar.* II (1923–1924) 181–202.

NEWTON, Rev. Alonzo (1822–1891) of Lima, N.Y.

Religious journal, January–July 1845; kept while author was attending theological seminary at Lima; study and later religious work, illness, sensibility.

Claire A. Newton, *The Colchester, Conn., Newton Family* (Naperville, Ill., 1911) 109–114.

PALMER, Joel (1810–1881) *b.* Canada, of Laurel, Ind.

Travel diary, April 1845–July 1846; over Rocky Mountains to the mouth of the Columbia River; travel-book material and narrative written up from notes; observations of Nez Percé Indians and helpful notes for emigrants; Chinook and Nez Percé vocabularies; one of the best journals of the Oregon Trail.

First published as *Journal of Travels* (Cincinnati, 1847) 189 pp.; reprinted (Cincinnati, 1851, 1852); R. G. Thwaites (ed.), *Early Western Travels* (Cleveland, 1906) XXX 311 pp.

POLK, James Knox (1795–1849), eleventh President of the United States.

Personal and political diary, August 1845–June 1849; his presidency; Mexican War, acquisition of Oregon, conquest of California and the Southwest; an intimate picture of Polk's likes and dislikes, political and personal; an exceedingly valuable political document, with long, detailed, and carefully written entries.

Milo M. Quaife (ed.), *The Diary of James K. Polk* (Chicago, 1910) four vols.; extracts edited by Allan Nevins as, *Polk: The Diary of a President* (New York, 1929) 412 pp.

SNYDER, Jacob R. (1812–1878) *b.* Philadelphia, of St. Louis and San Francisco.

Travel diary, May–October 1845; from Independence, Mo., to California; routine descriptions.

Soc. California Pioneers Quar. VIII (1931) 224–260.

STEELE, John (*b.* 1821) *b.* Ireland, of Salt Lake City.

Mormon diary, September 1845–May 1877 (preceded and followed by autobiographical notes); with the Nauvoo Legion; defense against mob, journey to Salt Lake, building of city, plague of crickets, work in church, mission to England; a good narrative.

Utah Hist. Quar. VI (1933) 3–28.

TURNER, Lieut., and FRANKLIN, Lieut., of Corps of Topographical Engineers.

Military exploration journals, summer 1845 (abstracts); with Colonel Kearny; up Platte River to Laramie, South Pass, Green River, return to Bent's Fort and Fort Leavenworth.

Sen. Exec. Doc. 1, 29th Cong. 1st sess. (1845) 214–217.

WALKER, William (1800–1874) *b.* Wayne Co., Mich., *d.* Kansas City, Mo., provisional governor of Nebraska Territory.

Private diary, March 1845–June 1854; personal and family life, weather, public work, reading, people and places, social affairs, early life in Nebraska Territory; easy, chatty style, with some literary allusions; a lively and interesting diary.

W. E. Connelley (ed.), *The Provisional Government of Nebraska Territory* (Lincoln, Neb., 1899) 153–406.

WOOD, William (1809–1894) of New York City, school commissioner.

Travel diaries, April–October 1845 and March 1846–March 1848; journey from Fort Smith to New Orleans and New York; descriptions of scenery, meals, hotels, towns; life in New York City; death of his wife; journey to England and travel there; remarriage, and life in New York City.

Autobiography of William Wood (New York, 1895) II 39–79, 249–298.

1846

ADAMS, Lieut. J. J., and DUNBAR, Lieut. H. C., U.S.A.

Military journal, June 1846–June 1847; Mexican War; descriptions of people and country; siege and surrender of Vera Cruz. Combination of two diaries with much editorial summarizing.

W. W. Bishop (ed.), *Journal of the Twelve Months' Campaign of Gen. Shields's Brigade* (St. Louis, 1847) 3–46.

BARBOUR, Mrs. Martha Isabella Hopkins (1824–1888) *b.* Henderson, Ky.

Private diary, July–October 1846; kept while author was staying with Mrs. Lucy Jones at Galveston, Texas; pleasant notes of domestic and social life and longings for her husband's safety during the Mexican War.

R. van B. T. Doubleday (ed.), *Journals of Philip Norbourne Barbour and His Wife* (New York, 1936) 111–166.

BARBOUR, Maj. Philip Norbourne (1813–1846) *b.* Henderson, Ky.

Military diary, March–September 1846; service in Mexican War to time of his death; general notes on army life; moderate interest.

R. van B. T. Doubleday (ed.), *Journals of Philip Norbourne Barbour and His Wife* (New York, 1936) 17–108.

BIGLER, Henry William (1815–1900) *b.* Harrison Co., W. Va., of Salt Lake City.

Mormon diary, June 1846–April 1891 (only a few extracts after 1850); with Mormon Battalion; mining at Sutter's mill; journeys in Utah and California; meetings with eminent Mormons and pioneers; a personal and lively journal with some interesting language.

Utah Hist. Quar. V (1932) 35–64, 87–112, 134–160. Extracts in *Overland Monthly,* September 1887.

BLISS, Robert S. (*b.* 1805) of Salt Lake City.

Military diary, August 1846–January 1848; with the Mormon Battalion in march from Kansas to California, return to Missouri River, and back again to Utah; notes of army movements, scenery, Indians and their customs, religious and personal affairs; a very readable diary, with some linguistic interest.

Utah Hist. Quar. IV (1931) 67–96, 110–128.

BREEN, Patrick, *b.* Ireland, of the Donner party.

Travel diary, November 1846–March 1847; snowbound in Sierra Nevada with the Donner party; weather, deaths; brief matter-of-fact entries; historical interest; some interesting spellings.

Edited by F. J. Teggart, *Acad. Pacific Coast Hist. Pubs.* I (1910) 271–284. Shortened version in *California Star,* May 22, 1847, and *Nashville Whig,* September 4, 1847. Frequently reprinted, e.g., in Edwin Bryant, *What I Saw in California* (New York, 1848) 256–260; of which most recent reprint is edited by Marguerite E. Wilbur (Santa Ana, Calif., 1936) 232–237.

BRYANT, Edwin (1805–1869) of Lexington, Ky., journalist.

Travel diary, April 1846–August 1847; tour of the emigrant route to California, through Rockies and the desert, in California, and return overland; colorful, journalistic descriptions and comments; clever observations, analyses; an excellent literary diary.

What I Saw in California (New York, 1848) 455 pp.; frequently reprinted; most recently edited by Marguerite E. Wilbur (Santa Ana, Calif., 1936) 481 pp.

CLAYTON, William (1814–1879) *b.* Lancashire, of Salt Lake City, historian and Mormon high priest.

Official Mormon journal, February 1846–October 1847; substantial daily entries, recording the journey of the original company of Mormon pioneers from Nauvoo, Ill., to the valley of the Great Salt Lake; very good, simple narrative of the great migration, with many intimate minutiae, descriptions of scenery, natural history, daily activities of the company, mob violence, factionalism, and personalities.

William Clayton's Journal (Salt Lake City, 1921) 376 pp.; much of it is combined with Orson Pratt's journal in a serial article, "The Pioneers of 1847," in *Hist. Rec.* (Salt Lake City) IX (1890).

COLTON, Rev. Walter (1797–1851), U.S.N., alcalde of Monterey, Calif.

Travel journal, July 1846–June 1849; embellished with sketches, recollections, etc.; realistic and lively account of work and conditions of the gold fields; notes on social life and military affairs in California and his administration of Monterey; rather formalized and historical, but valuable.

Three Years in California (New York, 1850) 456 pp.

EDWARDS, Pvt. Marcellus Ball (*b.* 1828) of Saline Co., Mo.

Military journal, June 1846–April 1847; with the Missouri Volunteers on Kearny's march from Fort Leavenworth to New Mexico, and Doniphan's expedition against the Indians of New Mexico; marches, military movements, camp life, hunting, private affairs; literary style, with some verses.

Ralph P. Bieber (ed.), *Marching with the Army of the West* (Glendale, Calif., 1936) 107–280.

EMORY, Lieut. Col. William Hemsley (1811–1887) of Corps of Topographical Engineers.

Military exploration journal, August 1846–January 1847; military reconnaissance with advanced guard of the Army of the West; from Bent's Fort to San Diego, including part of the Arkansas, Del Norte, and Gila rivers; topography, scenery, scientific details.

Exec. Doc. 7, 30th Cong. 1st sess. (1848) 15–126; republished as *Notes of Travel in California* (New York, Philadelphia, 1849) 1–275. Section relating to journey to Santa Fe in *Niles Reg.* LXXI (1846) 138, 154, 174.

FOOTE, Sarah, of Wellington, O.

Travel diary, April–May 1846; wagon journey from Wellington, O., to Winnebago Co., Wis.; girl in her teens with her family; pleasant full notes of an unexciting journey.

Wisconsin Hist. Soc. Proc. (1911) 188–200 (reprinted from private edition, 1905); *Jour. Amer. Hist.* XV (1921) 25–36.

FURBER, Pvt. George C., of Germantown, Pa., lawyer.

Military journal, May 1846–May 1847; with the Tennessee Cavalry Regiment in the Mexican War; camp life, social affairs, duties, hardships; description of

Texas and Mexico; manners, customs, religion of Mexicans; military operations; written up for publication as a historical work.

The Twelve Months' Volunteer (Cincinnati, 1850) 640 pp.

GIBSON, Lieut. George Rutledge (*ca.* 1810–1885) *b.* Montgomery Co., Va.

Military journal, June 1846–April 1847; in the Mexican War, under Kearny and Doniphan; march from Fort Leavenworth to New Mexico; Santa Fe, El Paso del Norte, Chihuahua; Battle of Sacramento; army life; descriptions of people, places, customs; good observations in Mexico.

Ralph P. Bieber (ed.), *Journal of a Soldier under Kearny and Doniphan* (Glendale, Calif., 1935) 363 pp.

HOLLINGSWORTH, Lieut. John McHenry (1823–1889), U.S.A., *b.* Baltimore.

Military and travel diary, September 1846–August 1849; voyage of the "Susan Drew" from New York to California with soldiers; a very good picture of tension among soldiers on the long voyage; service in California; military and social life and adventures in mining country; interspersed letters and newspaper clippings; a highly interesting and lively diary.

California Hist. Quar. I (1923) 207–270; *The Journal of Lieutenant John McHenry Hollingsworth* (San Francisco, 1923) 61 pp.

HUGHES, John Taylor (1817–1862), soldier.

Military journal, August 1846–May 1847; Doniphan's expedition, in Texas, New Mexico, and Mexico; notes on topography, dealings with Indians, camp life, etc.; some interesting Southern locutions.

William E. Connelley, *Doniphan's Expedition and the Conquest of New Mexico* (Topeka, 1907) 59–111; Hughes used the diary for the notes in his *Doniphan's Expedition* (Cincinnati, 1847).

JOHNSTON, Capt. Abraham (1815?–1846) *b.* Upper Piqua, O., of 1st Dragoons.

1. Military journal, June–August 1846; march with Kearny's Army of the West from Fort Leavenworth to Santa Fe; military details, descriptions, and some general notes.

Ralph P. Bieber (ed.), *Marching with the Army of the West* (Glendale, Calif., 1936) 73–104.

2. Military journal, September–December 1846; march from Santa Fe to Southern California.

House Exec. Doc. 41, 30th Cong. 1st sess. (1848) 567–614.

JONES, Nathaniel Vary (1822–1863) of Salt Lake City.

Military journal, July 1846–August 1847 (extracts); with Mormon Battalion on march to California by Santa Fe Trail; later member of guard for Frémont, from California to Missouri; rather bald details of army life and movements.

Utah Hist. Quar. IV (1931) 3–23.

KANE, Paul (1810–1871) *b.* Mallow, Ireland, of York, Canada, painter.

Travel diary, May 1846–October 1848 (preceded by narrative of a previous journey); journeys of a painter among the North American Indians; Toronto,

Mackinaw, Sault Ste Marie, Fort William, Kaministikwia route to Fort Alexander, Winnipeg, Saskatchewan River, Edmonton, Athabasca Pass, Columbia, Fort Vancouver, Oregon City, Fort Vancouver again, and return to the East; notes of adventures, characters, Indian life and customs, hardships; a good diary, but written up in touristic style.

Wanderings of an Artist among the Indians of North America (London, 1859) 455 pp.; reprinted with introduction by L. J. Burpee (Toronto, 1925) 329 pp.

KENLY, Capt. John Reese (*b.* 1822) of Baltimore, Md., and Eagle Artillery Company.

Military diary, June 1846–July 1848; presented as memoirs, but the author says they are taken from notes, letters, and diary, mostly made and written as the events occurred.

Memoirs of a Maryland Volunteer (Philadelphia, 1873) 521 pp.

LANMAN, Charles (1819–1895) *b.* Monroe, Mich., traveler and writer.

1. Travel diary, June–August 1846; canoe voyage up Mississippi and around Lake Superior; St. Louis, Sault Ste Marie, Prairie du Chien, St. Peter's River, Crow Wing Lake, Winnipeg; literary touristic descriptions.

A Summer in the Wilderness (New York, 1847) 208 pp.

2. Travel diary, May–August 1847; tour across New York, in Catskills and Adirondacks, to Lake Champlain, Montreal, Quebec, Saguenay River; fishing and sealing on St. Lawrence; Labrador, New Brunswick, St. John's River, Penobscot River; literary travel notes.

A Tour to the River Saguenay (Philadelphia, 1848) 231 pp.

LARCOM, Miss Lucy (1824–1893) of Beverly, Mass.

Private diaries, April 1846–September 1891; journey from Massachusetts to Illinois; difficulties of travel; work as teacher in Norton, Mass.; romantic jottings, nature worship, reading, poets, history, visits, and journeys, reflections and philosophizings; an interesting and intelligent diary.

Daniel D. Addison (ed.), *Lucy Larcom: Life, Letters, and Diary* (Boston, 1894) 21–272 *passim.*

LAWRENCE, Amos (1786–1852) of Groton, Mass.

Private diary, February 1846–December 1852 (extracts); notes on the pious life of a prominent Massachusetts citizen; dulled by editorial interpolations; extracts from letters.

William Lawrence (ed.), *Extracts from the Diary and Correspondence of the Late Amos Lawrence* (Boston, New York, 1855) 369 pp.

LEE, John Doyle (1812–1877) *b.* Randolph Co., Ill., of Utah.

1. Mormon diary, November 1846–July 1847; record of personal missions for Brigham Young; life at winter quarters; emigration to Utah; Harmony.

2. Mormon diary, May–July 1859 (fragment); "underground" after the Mountain Meadows Massacre, for which he was executed in 1877.

Charles Kelly (ed.), *Journals of John D. Lee* (Salt Lake City, 1938) 244 pp.

LINDSEY, Robert (1801–1863) *b*. Gildersome, Yorkshire.

Quaker travel journal, December 1846–July 1851 (extracts); travel in various parts of the world; this section describes visits to many parts of the United States where there were Friends' meetings.

Travels of Robert and Sarah Lindsey (London, 1886) 11–53.

McCLELLAN, Gen. George Brinton (1826–1885) of Philadelphia.

Military journal, September 1846–December 1852; few scattered entries about Mexican War; mostly general notes, vivaciously written; interesting for character of McClellan as a youth and the lively descriptions of Mexico and Mexicans, military life and discipline, and siege of Vera Cruz.

W. S. Myers (ed.), *The Mexican War Diary of George B. McClellan* (Princeton, 1917) 97 pp.

McCLINTOCK, William A. (*d*. 1847) of Bourbon Co., Ky.

Military journal, September 1846–January 1847; letter-diaries to parents, etc.; Mexican War, march to Texas and northern Mexico; Little Rock, San Antonio, Corpus Christi, Brownsville, Monterrey; a few military details; mostly notes on people and places; author killed at battle of Buena Vista.

Southwestern Hist. Quar. XXXIV (1930–1931) 21–37, 141–158, 231–256.

McKINSTRY, George.

Travel diary, November 1846–March 1847; Reed and Donner emigration party to California; hardships while party was entrapped in Sierra Nevada; rescue and arrival at Sutter's Fort.

Journal Kept by a Suffering Emigrant on the California Mountains (West Hoboken, N.J., 1917) broadsheet; John C. Power, *History of the Early Settlers of Sangamon County, Ill.* (Springfield, 1876) 604–607; originally published in *St. Louis Reveille* (1847).

MAGOFFIN, Susan Shelby (1827–1855) *b*. Arcadia, Ky.

Travel diary, June 1846–September 1847; from Independence, Mo., down Santa Fe Trail and into Mexico; a newly married gentlewoman's account of her adventures; descriptions of scenery, adventures, social life, gossip, recipes, etc.; a delightful diary, in easy style.

Stella M. Drumm (ed.), *Down the Santa Fé Trail and into Mexico* (New Haven, 1926) 294 pp.

OSWANDEL, Jacob, of 1st Pennsylvania Volunteers.

Military journal, December 1846–July 1848; kept during Mexican War; arranged with letters and historical extracts about Mexico, etc.; revised by author.

Notes of the Mexican War (Philadelphia, 1885) 642 pp.

PRINGLE, Virgil K. (of Hickory Grove, Ill.?).

Travel diary, April–November 1846; with his family from Hickory Grove to the Willamette Valley, Ore., via Oregon Trail; ordinary notes of natural history, scenery, hardships; inclined to farmer's viewpoint; moderate interest.

Oregon Pioneer Assoc. Trans., 48th Annual Reunion (1920) 281–300.

QUITMAN, Maj. Gen. John Anthony (1798–1858) of Monmouth, Miss., governor of Mississippi.

Military journal, July–August 1846; notes on journeys in connection with military affairs to Mexico, etc.; family notes.

John F. Claiborne, *Life and Correspondence of John A. Quitman* (New York, 1860) I 236–240.

RICHARDSON, Pvt. William H., of West River, Md.

Military journal, August 1846–July 1847; with Doniphan's expedition; quite good account of daily camp life, troubles and pleasures of ordinary soldiers; battle of Bracito.

Journal of William H. Richardson (Baltimore, 1847) 84 pp.; reprinted (Baltimore, 1848) 96 pp.; again (New York, 1849) 96 pp.

ROBINSON, Jacob S., of Portsmouth, N.H.

Military journal, June 1846–June 1847; with Doniphan's expedition; more concerned with social life and scenery than with military affairs; daily camp life of common soldier; some interesting spellings of Mexican names.

Sketches of the Great West (Portsmouth, 1848); reprinted, *Mag. Hist.*, Extra No. 128 (Tarrytown, 1928) 58 pp.; again, edited by Carl L. Cannon (Princeton, 1932) 96 pp.

ROGERS, Col. William P. (1819–1862) of Aberdeen, Miss., and Houston, Tex.

Military journal, July 1846–May 1847; Mexican War; battle of Monterrey; accounts of marches and camp life; philosophizing.

Southwestern Hist. Quar. XXXII (1928–1929) 257–285.

SAFFORD, Daniel (1792–1856) *b.* Hamilton, Mass., of Boston.

Travel journal, May 1846–October 1853 (with letters); tour in Europe as delegate to World's Evangelical Convention in London; Scotland, England, France, Germany, Switzerland; travel in Canada and Europe for health; general touristic notes.

Ann E. Safford, *A Memoir of Daniel Safford* (Boston, 1861) 172–217.

SANBORN, Prof. Francis Gregory (1838–1884) of Andover, Mass.

Private diary, December 1846–March 1858 (extracts); details of his education and school life.

Worcester Soc. Antiq. Proc. VI (1884) 164–168.

[SCRIBNER, Benjamin Franklin (1825–1900) of New Albany, Ind.]

Military journal, July 1846–June 1847; from New Albany to Mexico; in Mexican War with the "Spencer Greys"; camp life, personal experiences and sentiments, and unvarnished account of army life during the war; Buena Vista; written up in journalistic style.

Camp Life of a Volunteer (Philadelphia, New Albany, 1847) 75 pp., reprinted under title *A Campaign in Mexico by "One who was thar'"* (Philadelphia, 1850) 75 pp.

STANDAGE, Pvt. Henry (1818–1899) *b.* London, Eng., of Mormon Battalion.

Military journal, July 1846–July 1847; enlisted with Mormon Battalion at Council Bluffs; journey to Los Angeles; abundant details and many personal items; long account of Pueblo (Los Angeles); a good, simple journal; inserted letters.

Frank A. Golder (ed.), *The March of the Mormon Battalion* (New York, 1928) 138–238.

WHEATON, Ellen Birdseye (1816–1858) of Syracuse, N.Y.

Private diary, October 1846–June 1857 (with letters); domestic and social life of a woman about Syracuse; home life, reading, antislavery meetings; voluminous and informative, if rather dull.

The Diary of Ellen Birdseye Wheaton (Boston, 1923) 420 pp.

WILLARD, Daniel, of Hartford, Conn.

Private diary, 1846 (extracts with no days marked); visit to Washington; brief notes on political leaders; rather dull.

Massachusetts Hist. Soc. Proc. LII (1918–1919) 99–100.

1847

ANON.

*Journal of the Route from New York to Real del Monte by Way of Tampico (1847). (Sabin.)

ARMITAGE, Theodore.

Travel diary, March–April 1847; by flatboat from Pittsburg, Ind., to New Orleans.

Indiana Mag. Hist. IX (1913) 273–275.

ATKINSON, Rev. George Henry (1819–1889) *b.* Newburyport, Mass., missionary in Oregon.

1. Sea journal, October 1847–July 1848; from Boston to Portland, Ore., round Cape Horn and via Sandwich Islands; good descriptions of places and social observations; personal and religious reflections; good reading.

Myron Eells (ed.), *Biography of Rev. G. H. Atkinson* (Portland, Ore., 1893) chaps. iii, v, and vii.

2. Missionary travel journal, June 1848–June 1858 (extracts); Vancouver to Oregon City; organization of mission and schools, religious work, sermons; personal notes and some good descriptions of people and places.

Oregon Hist. Quar. XL (1939) 52–63, 168–187, 265–282, 345–361, XLI (1940) 6–33, 212–226, 288–303, 386–404.

AYERS, Elisha.

*A Journal of Travel . . . "in different parts of the United States, including anecdotes, remarks, adventures, criticisms, geography, mineralogy, history, curiosities, antiquities, poetry, observations, etc." (Preston, Conn., 1847) 52 pp.

BAILEY, Thomas, of 5th Regiment Indiana Volunteers, musician.

Military journal, October 1847–July 1848; kept during Mexican War; some general descriptions of places; moderate interest.

Indiana Mag. Hist. XIV (1918) 134–147.

BERNARD, Jesse Talbot (1829–1909) *b.* Portsmouth, Va., of Newnansville, Fla., lawyer.

Travel diary, September 1847–January 1857; brief and scattered notes; visit to Philadelphia and later to Florida; mediocre.

Florida Hist. Quar. XVIII (1939) 115–126.

BLANCHET, Augustine Magloire Alexandre (*b.* 1797), Catholic bishop of Walla Walla, Wash.

Travel journal, April–September 1847 (in a series of six letters); journey of missionaries over Oregon Trail from Pittsburgh to Walla Walla; notes on places, missions, people, difficulties of travel, entertainments, scenery; lively and entertaining notes.

French text in *Rapport sur les missions du Diocèse de Québec* IX (1851) 1–28; translation in *Illinois Cath. Hist. Rev.* IX (1927) 208–222.

COLLINS, Lieut. Francis (1820–1882) b. Lowville, N.Y., of Columbus, O.

Military journal, January 1847–August 1848 (with preceding autobiographical notes); service with 4th Artillery Regiment during the Mexican War, beginning at Tampico; mostly nonmilitary, although he describes marches and actions; social, camp life, scenery, Mexican customs, towns; very well written and readable.

Ohio Hist. Philosophical Soc. Quar. Pubs. X (1915) 37–109.

CROSS, William Berry (*d.* 1891) of Sacramento, Calif.

Sea journal, February 1847–February 1853; brief extract for 1850 describing voyage of the "Crescent" from Salem to California.

New England Hist. Geneal. Reg. XC (1936) 38–41.

DIEDERICHS, Johannes Fr., of Eberfeld, Germany, and Manitowoc, Wis.

Travel diary, August 1847–May 1848; from Eberfeld to Bremen, New York, and Milwaukee; settlement at Manitowoc; good narrative. Translated.

Wisconsin Mag. Hist. VII (1923–1924) 218–237, 350–368.

EGAN, Maj. Howard (*b.* 1815).

Travel diary, April 1847–September 1855; scattered notes combined with memoirs of son and grandson; notes on pioneer life in the West, Indians, pony express, Mormons, cattle ranching, etc., confused in an amateur editorial mélange.

W. M. Egan (ed.), *Pioneering the West, 1846–1878* (Richmond, Utah, 1917) 302 pp. *passim.*

FERGUSON, Pvt. Philip Gooch (*b.* 1824) of St. Louis, Mo.

Military travel diary, June 1847–July 1848; march with reinforcements of Missouri Volunteers to Santa Fe; Indian warfare; expedition against Chihuahua;

battle of Santa Cruz de Rosales; notes on events of march, soldier's life, Mexican scenery, people, places, customs; more personal than most of the Mexican War journals.

Ralph P. Bieber (ed.), *Marching with the Army of the West* (Glendale, Calif., 1936) 283–361.

HARTMAN, Pvt. George W. (*b.* 1828) of Westmoreland Co., Pa., and 2d Pennsylvania Regiment.

Military journal, January 1847–July 1848; Mexican War; New Orleans, Vera Cruz, Perote; battles of Churubusco and Molino del Rey; Mexico City; mainly military details, but some notes on the life of the common soldier.

A Private's Own Journal (Greencastle, Pa., 1849) 35 pp.

HASTINGS, Loren B. (1819–1881) *b.* St. Johnsbury, Vt., of Port Townsend, Ore.

Travel diary, April–December 1847; overland from Illinois to Oregon via St. Joseph and Oregon Trail; notes on stages, Indian encounters; some good narrative passages.

Oregon Pioneer Assoc. Trans., 51st Annual Reunion (1923) 12–26.

HOFFMAN, Mrs. Virginia Haviside (1832–1855) *b.* Glastonbury, Conn.

Religious and missionary journal, December 1847–April 1855; religious reflections and self-abasement; with Protestant Episcopal mission among the Kroos in West Africa; mission at Cavalla and Rocktown; details of missionary life, customs of natives; a year in the United States, and return to Africa.

George D. Cummins, *Life of Mrs. Virginia Hale Hoffman* (Philadelphia, 1859) 31–161 *passim.*

INGERSOLL, Chester.

Diary letters, May–September 1847; written while author was on journey from Independence, Mo., to California, along Oregon Trail; largely descriptions of scenery and natural phenomena.

Joliet Signal, May 18–August 29, 1848; reprinted, edited by D. C. McMurtrie, *Overland to California in 1847* (Chicago, 1937) 50 pp.

KIMBALL, Heber Chase (1801–1868) *b.* Sheldon, Vt., of Salt Lake City, Mormon apostle.

Mormon travel journal, April–June 1847; full and excellent notes kept during progress of the pioneer company of Mormons from winter quarters on the Missouri to the Salt Lake Valley; good record of struggles of the Mormon pioneers.

Originally published in 1854; reprinted in *Utah Geneal. Hist. Mag.* XXX (1939) 9–19, 76–85, 140–149, 204–211, XXXI (1940) 18–24, 80–87, 150–158, 211–218.

KURZ, Rudolph Friederich (1818–1871) of Berne, Switzerland, painter.

Private diary, January 1847–September 1852 (extracts); experiences among the fur traders and Indians during a stay at western posts of fur companies on the Mississippi and upper Missouri; from New Orleans to St. Louis and Fort Union; sometimes employed as clerk at Forts Union and Berthold; comments on Gold

Rush and Mexican War; intimate acquaintance with traders and Indians and great sympathy for latter; extensive notes on Indian life and customs; a most valuable diary of Indian life; translated from the German.

Myrtis Jarrell and J. N. B. Hewitt (eds.), *Journal of Rudolph Friederich Kurz* (Washington, D.C., 1937) 382 pp. Extracts in D. I. Bushnell, "Friederich Kurz, Artist-Explorer," *Smithson. Inst. Ann. Rep.* (1927) 507–527.

MURRAY, Alexander Hunter (1818–1874) *b.* Kilmun, Scotland, employee of Hudson's Bay Company.

Travel journal, June 1847–June 1848; voyage from Lapierre to the Yukon; building of Fort Yukon; description of visiting Indians and record of their information on furs and inhabitants; winter at the fort and return to Lapierre; meteorological notes; a substantial and often entertaining journal.

Canadian Archives Pubs. No. 4 (1910) 125 pp.

NOBLE, Mr. (with Joshua N. Saunders), overseer of El Destino plantation, Fla.

Plantation journal, January–December 1847; kept by Noble for first seven months and by Saunders for last five; careful details of plantation work at El Destino and notes on health of workers; interesting spellings and vocabulary.

U. B. Phillips and J. D. Glunt (eds.), *Florida Plantation Records, Missouri Hist. Soc. Pubs.* (1927) 209–338.

PAINE, Charles Smith, Jr. (1819–1895) of Randolph, Vt., farmer.

Private diary, January 1847–November 1879 (extracts); notes on personal, family, and town affairs; visits to neighboring towns; details of farming, religion, morals, natural history; some verses.

Albert P. Paine, *History of Samuel Paine, Jr.* (n.p. 1923) 135–159.

PIERCE, Gen. Franklin (1804–1869) *b.* Hillsborough, N.Y., fourteenth President of the United States.

Military journal, June–August 1847; brief jottings during marches and in camp; Mexican War; Mexico, Virgara, San Juan, Perote; work about camp, sickness.

Nathaniel Hawthorne, *Life of Franklin Pierce* (Boston, 1852) 68–94.

POINT, Nicolas (1799–1868) of Rocroy, France, Jesuit.

Travel journal, May–June 1847; with Father De Smet from Fort Lewis, via Missouri River, as far as Fort Union at mouth of Yellowstone; data about American Fur Company and scientific notes. Translated from the French.

Mid-America n.s. II (1931) 238–254.

REED, James Frazier.

Private diary, February–March 1847 (extracts); record of second party attempting to relieve the Donner party; brief notes of progress; some dramatic scenes.

C. F. McGlashan, *History of the Donner Party* (Truckee, 1881, fourth edition; reprinted Stanford Univ. Press, 1940) 153–158.

RITCHIE, M. D.

Private diary, February 1847; journey of first party attempting to relieve the Donner party; brief notes of progress.

C. F. McGlashan, *History of the Donner Party* (Truckee, 1881, fourth edition; reprinted Stanford Univ. Press, 1940) 119–120.

ROSENBAUM, S. E. (*b.* 1822) *b.* Bohemia, immigrant.

Immigrant's journal, May–July 1847; Jew's voyage from Germany to New York; kept in German.

Pubs. American-Jewish Hist. Soc. XXXV (1939) 63–113.

SMITH, Mrs. Elizabeth Dixon, of La Porte, Ind., and Lafayette, Wis.

Travel diary, April 1847–February 1848; journey with her family from La Porte to Oregon; brief notes, mainly of stages and natural phenomena; a few interesting mishaps, hardships, death of husband, movements in Oregon; moderate interest.

Oregon Pioneer Assoc. Trans., 35th Annual Reunion (1907) 153–176.

SMITH, Capt. Ephraim Kirby (1807–1845) of Litchfield, Conn.

Military diary, January–September 1847; included in his letters; interesting personal details and notes of military life.

Emma J. Blackwood (ed.), *To Mexico with Scott* (Cambridge, Mass., 1917) 1–218.

STEVENS, Gen. Isaac Ingalls (1818–1862) *b.* North Andover, Mass., governor of Washington Territory.

Military journal, March–December 1847; Mexican War; Jalapa, Puebla, El Peñon, Contreras, Churubusco, Molino del Rey, Chapultepec, Mexico City, return to New Orleans; in Washington; military details and notes on terrain; some notes on scenery and social life.

Hazard Stevens, *The Life of Isaac Ingalls Stevens* (Boston, 1900) I 111–224 *passim.*

THAYER, Rev. Dr., of Newport, R.I., schoolmaster.

Foreign travel diary, May–July 1847; unremarkable descriptions of a tour in Belgium, along the Rhine, and in Switzerland.

Newport Hist. Soc. Bull. No. 79 (April 1931) 7–15, No. 80 (July 1931) 14–23.

1848

ANON.

Travel diary, June–July 1848; travel in the upper Des Moines Valley; detailed and interesting notes on countryside.

Annals Iowa 3d Ser. IX (1909–1910) 94–104.

BARTLETT, John Russell (1805–1886), United States boundary commissioner.

Travel journal, August 1848–January 1853; travel in Texas, Mexico, California, Sonora, and Chihuahua in connection with the United States and Mexico boundary commission; extensive journals of adventures, with scientific data and general observations.

Personal Narrative of Explorations and Incidents (New York, 1854) two vols.; reprinted (New York, 1856) two vols. in one.

"BROOKS, J. Tyrwhitt, M.D.," of London, Eng.

Travel diary, April–October 1848; expedition from San Francisco to the gold mines; Monterey, Sacramento Valley, Mormon diggings, Bear Valley, etc.; interview with Sutter; written for amusement of family; in travel-book style; fairly interesting. This best-seller, which was translated into several languages, was actually written by Henry Vizetelly, assisted by David Bogue, neither of whom had ever visited America.

Four Months Among the Gold-Finders in California (London and Philadelphia, 1849) 1–49.

COFFIN, Elijah (1798–1862) of New Garden, N.C.

Clergyman's journal, November 1848–December 1861; meetings and religious work in Indiana and Kansas, with visits to New England, North Carolina, etc.; usual matter of a clerical journal.

Mary C. Johnson (ed.), *The Life of Elijah Coffin* (1863) 23–262.

COWLES, Helen Maria (1831–1850) of Austinburg, O.

Private diary, January 1848–March 1850 (extracts); religious and moral reflections, plans for teaching, lectures, teaching, visits, social affairs, weather, family affairs; fairly interesting.

Grace Victorious; or, the Memoir of Helen M. Cowles (Oberlin, 1856) 41–205 *passim*.

FARWELL, John Villiers (1825–1908) of Chicago, merchant.

Private diary, November 1848–August 1853 (extracts); descriptions of Chicago; news, Gold Rush, business, fire alarms, elections, family affairs, trips to the country; religion, Bible studies and moral reading, sermons, moral reflections; dull style, but an interesting picture of a Christian businessman in the making; Mr. Day and God, but no Clarence.

Abby Ferry, *Reminiscences of John V. Farwell* (Chicago, 1928) I 99–174.

HARRINGTON, Leonard Ellsworth (1816–1883) *b.* New Lisbon, N.Y., Mormon bishop, of Salt Lake City.

Mormon diary, March 1848–January 1881 (with some prior autobiographical notes); summary of march to Great Salt Lake; mostly notes of preaching and educational work in Mormon church; some verses.

Utah Hist. Quar. VIII (1940) 1–64.

JAMIESON, Milton, of Batavia, O.

Military journal, September 1847–July 1848; with Ohio volunteers during Mexican War; military details; notes on country along route of the army, and on customs and agriculture of Mexico; seminarrative.

Journal and Notes of a Campaign in Mexico (Cincinnati, 1849) 105 pp.

LEWIS, Henry (*d.* 1904) of Düsseldorf, Germany, panoramist.

Travel diary, June–August 1848; canoe journey along the Mississippi, from Falls of St. Anthony to St. Louis, while making sketches for his enormous panorama of the upper Mississippi; high-flown romantic narrative and descriptions of natural history, Indians, etc.

Bertha L. Heilbron (ed.), *Making a Motion Picture in 1848* (St. Paul, 1936) 58 pp., reprinted from *Minnesota Hist.* XVII (1936) 131–158, 288–301, 421–436.

LONG, John Davis (1838–1915) *b.* Buckfield, Me., governor of Massachusetts.

Private diary, February 1848–August 1915 (selections); boyhood in Buckfield, school days, Harvard; work as schoolmaster, lawyer, and politician; secretaryship of the Navy; reading, journeys, family and private affairs; a fairly good general diary.

Lawrence S. Mayo, *America of Yesterday* (Boston, 1923) 250 pp.

MOERENHOUT, Jacob Antoine (1796 or 1797–1879), French consul at Monterey, Calif.

Travel journal, July–August 1848; official report to French minister of tour of placer-mining country in California; careful and official observations; translated.

"The Inside Story of the Gold Rush," Document III, *California Hist. Soc. Spec. Pub.* VIII (1935) 4–40.

OBER, Merrill (1832–1853) of Monkton, Vt.

Private diary, September–November 1848; life of a boy in a Vermont village; studies, reading, music; simple entries.

New England Quar. I (1928) 32–40.

RAYMOND, Henry Jarvis (1820–1869) *b.* Lima, N.Y., editor and politician.

Public journal, January 1848–August 1866 (extracts); public and political affairs; interviews with famous politicians; with Army of Potomac in 1863; discussions of Civil War and intervention; Philadelphia convention of 1866; impersonal notes.

Scribner's Mag. XIX (1879–1880) 57–61, 419–424, 703–710, XX (1880) 275–280.

ROOT, Riley.

Travel diary, April 1848–January 1850; St. Joseph to Oregon City and California, return to East via Panama; extensive details of overland journey; thirdhand report of Whitman Massacre; a useful diary.

Journal of Travels (Galesburg, Ill., 1850) 143 pp.

THORNTON, Jessy Quinn.

Travel diary, May–November 1848 (section of travel book); Oregon and California; journey from Independence, Mo.; conventional details of route, sights, Indians; seminarrative.

Oregon and California in 1848 (New York, 1849) two vols.

1849

ANON.

Travel diary, April–August 1849; from Austin, Tex., to the gold mines of Mariposa, Calif.; notes on travel, scenery, etc.; fair.

"Sketches from the Journal of a Traveler," *Texas Monument* (La Grange) February 19, 26, March 5, 12, 1851; reprinted in L. P. Bieber (ed.), *Southern Trails to California in 1849* (Glendale, Calif., 1937) 259–280.

ANON.

Travel diary, December 1849–December 1853; brief, scattered, and rather dull notes relating to western journeys.

Verna I. Shupe, *The Argonauts and Pioneers* (Pocatello, Ida., 1931) 12–18.

ALDRICH, Lorenzo D., of Lansingburgh, N.Y.

Travel diary, April 1849–February 1850 and November–December 1850; from Albany to California via Fort Smith and Santa Fe Trail to San Diego; steamer to San Francisco, thence to Yuba City; resumes with homeward journey from San Francisco to Panama; good descriptions; fresh, lively style.

A Journal of the Overland Route to California and the Gold Mines (Lansingburgh, 1851) 46 pp.

AUDUBON, John Woodhouse (1812–1862) *b.* Henderson, Ky.

Travel journal, February 1849–May 1850; from New York to California by a new southern route; Pittsburgh, New Orleans, Brazos, Texas, Mexico, Arizona, San Diego; notes of great hardships.

Frank H. Hodder (ed.), *Audubon's Western Journal* (Cleveland, 1906) 249 pp.

BAKER, George H. (1827–1906) of Boston, Mass., and Sacramento, Calif.

Travel diary, May–August 1849; in gold country, Sacramento, San Francisco, San Jose; mining.

Soc. California Pioneers Quar. VIII (1931) 39–70.

BOWMAN, E. I. (of Jerseyville, Ill.?).

Travel diary, March–May 1849; from Jerseyville, Ill., toward California, ending at Missouri River; brief notes of stages.

Elizabeth Page, *Wagons West* (New York, 1930) 333–335.

BOYDEN, Seth (1788–1870) of Newark, N.J., inventor.

Travel diary, March 1849–March 1851 (extracts); Panama to Pacific, voyage to San Francisco, up the Sacramento, the diggings, return voyage, to Havana via Panama; a good account of mining methods; several days' entries often combined.

New Jersey Hist. Soc. Proc. n.s. XII (1927) 309–318, 455–461, XIII (1928) 70–76.

CHAPMAN, W. W., of Illinois.

Travel diary, March 1849–September 1850; from Illinois to Sacramento and the gold fields; brief, unenterprising entries; a few later entries in California relate to the timber trade.

Wyoming Hist. Dept. Quar. Bull. I (1923) No. 2, 7–9.

CHRISTMAN, Enos (*b.* 1821) of Westchester, Pa., journalist apprentice.

Travel diary, July 1849–May 1853; voyage round the Cape; work in California; long descriptions in journalistic style, often of personal affairs; quite interesting.

Florence M. Christman (ed.), *One Man's Gold: The Letters and Journal of a Forty-Niner* (New York, 1930) 278 pp.

CLARK, Bennett C. (1819–1890) of Boonville, Mo.

Travel diary, April–August 1849; Missouri, bound for California; difficulties of journey; a few personal items; ends in Nevada; fairly interesting.

Missouri Hist. Rev. XXIII (1928–1929) 3–43.

CLARK, Sterling B. F. (1825–1852) *b.* Rutland, Vt., of Hollidaysburg, Pa.

Travel diary, March–August 1849; from Hollidaysburg to St. Louis, Fort Kearny, Laramie, South Pass, Salt Lake, Sacramento; mostly bare, cryptic notes of distances.

E. S. Mighels (ed.), *How Many Miles from St. Jo?* (San Francisco, 1929) 7–28.

COKE, the Hon. Henry John (1827–1916), English traveler.

Travel diary, December 1849–November 1850, etc.; England to Charleston; St. Louis, St. Joseph's, overland to Council Bluffs, Laramie, The Dalles, California; voyage to Sandwich Islands and thence home; mostly a diary of incidents in the journey across the plains.

A Ride over the Rocky Mountains to Oregon and California (London, 1852) 388 pp.

COOK, Elliott Wilkinson (*b.* 1818) of Cumberland Hill, R.I.

Travel diary, January 1849–January 1850; voyage from Lockport to Panama; stay of eleven weeks; voyage to San Francisco; odd jobs around mines; return home; mainly dull log details.

J. J. Cook (ed.), *Land Ho* (Baltimore, 1935) 43 pp.

COUTS, Lieut. Cave Johnson (1821–1874) *b.* Springfield, Tenn., of 1st U.S. Dragoons.

Military exploration diary, September–November 1849; conducting the Whipple expedition from San Diego to the Colorado River; mostly general items, incidents, character sketches, notes on Indians; a rather interesting diary.

William McPherson (ed.), *From San Diego to the Colorado in 1849* (Los Angeles, 1932) 78 pp.

Cox, Cornelius C. (*b.* 1825) of Harrisburg, Tex.

Travel diary, April 1849–February 1850; Texas to California; Los Angeles, Stockton; difficulties; gradual disintegration of the party; notes on hunting, camping, Indians.

Southwestern Hist. Quar. XXIX (1925–1926) 36–50, 128–146, 201–212.

CROSS, Maj. Osborne (1803–1876) U.S.A., *b.* Prince Georges Co., Md.

Military journal, May–November 1849; march of Mounted Riflemen from

Fort Leavenworth to Fort Vancouver; full narrative report; marches, topography, scenery, natural history, etc.

R. W. Settle (ed.), *The March of the Mounted Rifleman* (Glendale, Calif., 1940) 33–272; *Sen. Exec. Doc.* 1, 31st Cong. 2d sess., Part 2, 126–244.

DALLAS, Lieut. Francis Gregory (1824–1890) *b.* Boston, of German and U.S. navies.

Private diary, May 1849–June 1859 (with gaps); three years' service in German navy, after dismissal from U.S.N.; reinstatement and service in U.S.N. as midshipman and lieutenant; duty in the Pacific; Indian affairs in Pacific Northwest; at Philadelphia; on west coast of Africa in suppressing slave trade; early entries are personal, but later entries tend to be log notes.

Gardner W. Allen (ed.), *The Papers of Francis Gregory Dallas, U.S. Naval Hist. Soc.* VIII (1917) 147–242.

DAMON, Rev. Samuel C. (1815–1885) *b.* Holden, Mass., of Honolulu.

Missionary travel journal, April–July 1849; from Sandwich Islands to Columbia River, Vancouver, Oregon, San Francisco, and down the Sacramento; from San Francisco to the Islands again; long entries describing scenery, social and moral conditions, chinook, etc.; good narrative, and fair general interest.

A Trip from the Sandwich Islands (Honolulu, 1849) 96 pp., reprinted from *The Friend* (Honolulu), September 1–December 20, 1849, a newspaper edited by Damon; reprinted *Mag. Hist.* Extra No. 97 (Tarrytown, 1923) 86 pp.; republished as *A Journey to Lower Oregon* (San Francisco, 1927) 86 pp.

DELANO, Alonzo (1806–1874) of New York.

Travel diary, May–September 1849; overland from St. Joseph to Shasta Co., Calif.; daily incidents, concluding with account of life in California, especially in the mines; narrative largely in diary form; extensive descriptions, and breezy and quite interesting narrative.

Life on the Plains and among the Diggings (Auburn, 1854) 384 pp., reprinted as *Across the Plains and among the Diggings* with introduction by R. R. Wilson (New York, 1936) 192 pp.

DE MASSEY, Ernest, of Passavant, France.

Travel diary, December 1849–1851; arrival from Le Havre; in San Francisco; life there and in the mines; journeys to Klamath, San Jose, and Santa Cruz; sent in sections to his relatives; largely in narrative form. Translated from the French.

M. E. Wilbur (ed.), *A Frenchman in the Gold Rush* (1927) 183 pp.

DEWOLF, Capt. David (1822–1862) *b.* Yarmouth, N.S., of Wyoming, Ill.

Travel diary, May–October 1849; overland journey to California, beginning at Lexington; Fort Kearny, Platte River, Laramie, Sweetwater, Salt Lake, Sacramento; notes on natural phenomena, Indians, Mormons; fairly interesting.

Illinois Hist. Soc. Trans. 32 (1925) 184–222, with letters.

DORE, Benjamin (1825–1906) *b.* Athens, Me., carpenter.

Travel diary, November 1849–January 1852; round Cape Horn with the Argonauts; work as carpenter in San Francisco; shipbuilding at Portland, Ore.; good observations; naïve, fresh, and humorous; several poems; interesting language.

California Hist. Soc. Quar. II (1923–1924) 90–139; reprinted as *Journal of Benjamin Dore* (Berkeley, 1923) 54 pp.

DUNDASS, Samuel Rutherford (1819–1850) of Jefferson Co., O., lawyer.

Travel diary, March 1849–January 1850; from Steubenville, O., to Independence, Platte River, Sweetwater, Salt Lake City, Pleasant Valley, California; journey to San Francisco, where he died; conventional descriptions and incidents.

Journal of Samuel Rutherford Dundass (Steubenville, O., 1857) 66 pp.; journal 7–56.

DURIVAGE, John E., correspondent of *Daily Picayune,* New Orleans.

Travel journal, March–July 1849; from New Orleans, through Mexico, to California; a series of descriptive articles in journal form.

The Daily Picayune, March–September 1849; reprinted in R. P. Bieber, *Southern Trails to California in 1849* (Glendale, Calif., 1937) 159–255.

DWINELLE, John W. (1816–1881) *b.* Cazenovia, N.Y., of Rochester, N.Y., and Oakland, Calif., lawyer.

Travel diary, August–October 1849; New York to San Francisco via Panama; begins as ship was nearing Panama; good descriptions of Chagres, Panama, Acapulco, San Diego, San Francisco, and notes on life on board ship.

Soc. California Pioneers Quar. VIII (1931) 105–129, 141–182.

EASTLAND, Thomas B., of Nashville, Tenn., and San Francisco.

Travel diary, April–December 1849; Nashville, New Orleans, Mexico, San Antonio, El Paso, to San Francisco; unusual route; lively camping details and descriptions of towns; interspersed letters.

California Hist. Soc. Quar. XVIII (1939) 99–135, 229–250.

ESBJÖRN, L. P., Swedish immigrant.

Travel diary, June–August 1849; Swedish immigrant making trip from Sweden to Newfoundland; daily life; many religious details. Translated.

Augustana Hist. Soc. Pubs. V (1935) 11–34.

FULLER, Margaret, Marchioness Ossoli (1810–1850), authoress.

Travel diary, January–April 1849; kept in Rome while it was a republic; notes on Mazzini, clericalism, political disturbances.

Jour. Modern Hist. XII (1940) 209–220.

GIBBS, George (1715–1873) *b.* Astoria, L.I.

Military diary, May–June 1849 (incomplete); civilian with the Cross expedition of Mounted Riflemen from Fort Leavenworth to Fort Vancouver; expansive narrative; scenery and general notes.

R. W. Settle (ed.), *The March of the Mounted Riflemen* (Glendale, Calif., 1940) 275–327, reprinted from *New York Journal of Commerce,* July 25, September 1, 1849.

GUNN, Lewis Carstairs (1813–1892) *b*. Bloomingdale, N.Y.

Travel diary, April 1849–April 1850; New Orleans to the Brazos, overland across Texas, voyage to San Francisco and the San Joaquin; prospecting about Jamestown; later work as a physician; a sober diary.

Anna L. Marston (ed.), *Records of a Californian Family* (San Diego, Calif., 1928) 21–84.

HACKNEY, Joseph (of Jerseyville, Ill.?).

Travel diary, May–September 1849; St. Joseph to California with the Jerseyville company; a racy and very interesting journal, with substantial and well-written entries; social life during the trip; interesting language.

Elizabeth Page, *Wagons West* (New York, 1930) 110–193.

HALE, Israel F. (1804–1891) of St. Joseph, Mo.

Travel diary, May–September 1849; St. Joseph to Sacramento Valley; description of route and sights on way, difficulties with Indians, and notes on Mormons.

Soc. California Pioneers Quar. II (1925) 61–130.

HALE, Richard Lunt, of Newburyport, Mass.

Travel diary, November 1849–May 1850; from Newburyport round Cape Horn to San Francisco; incidents of voyage; descriptions in literary vein, with long sketches of some of the crew; followed by a narrative of four years spent in California, Oregon, and South America, with journal taken up again on voyage back to Hampton Roads (February–May 1854).

C. E. Russ (ed.), *The Log of a Forty-Niner* (Boston, 1923) 17–63 and 166–180.

[HALL, John L., of Bloomfield, printer aboard the "Henry Lee."]

Travel journal, February–September 1849; voyage of the Hartford Union Mining and Trading Company aboard the "Henry Lee"; around Cape Horn to San Francisco; official journal, in interesting style, with appropriate poetical embellishments; printed on the ship.

Journal of the Hartford Union Mining and Trading Co., printed on board the "Henry Lee" (San Francisco Harbor, 1849) 88 pp.; reprinted (Wethersfield, Conn., 1898) 252 pp; reprinted, with an introduction by Oscar Lewis (Grabhorn Press, San Francisco, 1928) 127 pp.

HALSEY, Dr. Gaius Leonard (*d*. 1891) of Unadilla, N.Y.

Travel diary, February–November 1849; from Plainville to New York, Panama, and California, and return; brief travel notes.

Francis W. Halsey, *The Pioneers of Unadilla Village* (Unadilla, N.Y., 1902) 289–302.

HAWKS, James D.

Travel diary, August–October 1849; from Point San Domingo, Lower Calif., to San Diego; good account of hardships, hunger, thieves; brief account of voyage from San Diego to San Francisco.

Soc. California Pioneers Quar. VI (1929) 83–98.

HAYES, Benjamin Ignatius (1815–1877) b. Baltimore, of Los Angeles, district judge.

Travel diary, September 1849–March 1875; journey overland from Socorro to Warner's ranch; incidents during journey, and account of life in southern California; varied, with ample entries and descriptions; notes written for his wife.

Marjorie T. Wolcott (ed.), *Pioneer Notes from the Diaries of Judge Benjamin Hayes* (Los Angeles, 1929) 307 pp.

HESLEP, Dr. Augustus M. (b. 1806) of Jacksonville, Ill., physician.

Travel diary and letters, May 1849–January 1850; along Santa Fe Trail from Independence, Mo., to San Jose, Calif.

L. P. Bieber (ed.), *Southern Trails to California in 1849* (Glendale, Calif., 1937) 353–386, reprinted from *Daily Missouri Republican* May 24, July 4, 24, September 12, 1849, and January 28, 1850.

HIGGINSON, Thomas Wentworth (1823–1911) of Boston, Mass.

Private diary, 1849–April 1906; literary and social life in Boston; travels; military career during Civil War; intimate self-portrait. Text much edited and arranged; with letters.

Letters and Journals of Thomas Wentworth Higginson 1846–1906 (Boston, 1921) 358 pp. *passim.*

HOFFMAN, Benjamin, of Shepherdstown, W.Va.

Travel diary, June–September 1849; overland journey from West Virginia to California; brief and undistinguished notes.

West Virginia Hist. III (1941) 59–75.

HOSFORD, Rev. Benjamin Franklin (1817–1864) b. Thetford, Vt., of Haverhill, Mass.

Clergyman's journal, January 1849–June 1852; religious reflections, illness, reading (Coleridge, etc.), sermons, etc.; rather dull.

A Memorial of Rev. Benjamin F. Hosford (Cambridge, Mass., 1866) 25–47.

HOSPERS, John (b. 1801) b. Amsterdam, of Pella, Ia., schoolmaster.

Travel diary, May–August 1849; emigration from Holland to Pella; across America by steamer on the Lakes and canals, and by stage in Iowa; pleasant, simple notes on the journey. Translated from the Dutch.

Iowa Jour. Hist. Pols. X (1912) 363–382.

JOHNSTON, William Graham (b. 1828) of Pittsburgh.

Travel diary, March–July 1849; journey across plains with the first wagon train to enter San Francisco in 1849; six weeks' camping on Missouri frontier; narrative of life in mines; interesting for its fullness and detail; written up from notes.

Experiences of a Forty-Niner (Pittsburgh, 1892) 23–247.

KENDALL, Joseph (1803–1864) b. Bicester, Eng., of New York City.

Travel diary, May–July 1849; begun after a month at sea on the brig "Canton," and ends just after the ship rounded Cape Horn; long details about himself and his companions; a good journal, with some excellent descriptive writing.

A Landsman's Voyage to California (San Francisco, 1935) 23-103.

KERR, Thomas (1825-1888) *b.* county Louth, Ireland, of San Francisco.

Travel and private diary, October 1849-March 1852; Ireland to California; London, San Francisco; amusing notes on sailors, passengers, ship life, San Francisco during the Gold Rush, mining country; Eliza City; working for Captain Sutter; work as builder in San Francisco; a long diary, valuable for its detailed picture of places and customs; very interesting spellings of Spanish words, a kind of interlingual folk etymology.

California Hist. Soc. Quar. VII (1928) 203-227, 395-404, VIII (1929) 17-25, 167-182, 262-277.

KING, Timo, of Clarksville Co., Ark.

Travel diary, April-September 1849 (extracts, with narrative introduction); diary kept during trip of first wagon train to California during the Gold Rush; some very long narrative entries; murder and execution, trials, character sketches.

Bancroft Library, Berkeley, Calif., has eleven galley proofs prepared by S. H. Logan of Clarksville, Ark., in 1939.

KINGSLEY, Nelson (*d.* 1852) of New Milford, Conn.

Travel diary, February 1849-March 1851; around Cape Horn; work in the diggings; good account of everyday life; some linguistic interest.

Diary of Nelson Kingsley, Acad. Pacific Coast Hist. Pubs. III (1914) 179 pp.

LASSELLE, Stanislaus, of Logansport, Ind.

Travel diary, March-August 1849; overland to California along or near Santa Fe Trail; notes on camps, Indians; some rather good observation and interesting spellings.

Seymour Dunbar, *A History of Travel in America* IV (Indianapolis, 1915) App. M 1427-1443.

LOWELL, Mrs. Ellen Bancroft (1837-1894) of Boston.

Private diary, October 1849; brief notes on domestic affairs, school work, reading, music.

Ella L. Cabot, *Arthur Theodore Lyman and Ella Lyman* (1932) I 242-245.

LYMAN, Albert, of Hartford, Conn.

Travel diary, February 1849-February 1850; member of Connecticut Mining and Trading Company; journey to California around Cape Horn, and mining; account of life in the diggings; voyage to the Sandwich Islands.

Journal of a Voyage to California (Hartford, 1852) 192 pp.

McCALL, Ansel J. (*b.* 1816) of Bath, N.Y., lawyer.

1. Travel diary, April-September 1849; from St. Joseph to Sacramento via South Pass; long entries in literary style, with poetical quotations and allusions.

The Great California Trail in 1849 (Bath, N.Y., 1882) 86 pp., reprinted from the *Steuben Courier Journal,* pp. 8-85.

2. Gold miner's diary, September–November 1849; prospecting in California; notes on mining procedure, character of miners, their lives, and fortunes; literary style.

Pick and Pan (Bath, N.Y., 1883) 46 pp., reprinted from the *Steuben Courier Journal,* pp. 5–42.

MARCY, Capt. Randolph Barnes (1812–1887) *b.* Greenwich, Mass., frontier soldier.

1. Military exploration journal, September–October 1849; reconnaissance in northern and western Texas; working over route for travelers; description of topography, Indians, etc.; official report.

First published in *Sen. Exec. Doc.* 64, 31st Cong. 1st sess. (1850). Combined with extracts from newspapers in Grant Foreman, *Marcy and the Gold Seekers* (Norman, Okla., 1939) 152–371 *passim.* Extensive extracts in *West Texas Hist. Assoc. Year Book* I (1925) 30–54.

2. Military exploration journal, May–July 1852; official report on exploration of headwaters of the Red River, La.; good descriptions of region and Indians; well written and very readable.

Sen. Exec. Doc. 54, 32d Cong. 2d sess. (1853) 10–82; *West Texas Hist. Assoc. Year Book* III (1927) 78–117; Grant Foreman, *Adventure on Red River* (Norman, Okla., 1937) 12–134.

MARCY, William Learned (1786–1857) *b.* Southbridge, Mass., secretary of war in Polk's cabinet.

Private and political diary, December 1849–July 1851 and March–April 1857 (extracts); politics in Washington, estimates of politicians; good political diary.
Amer. Hist. Rev. XXIV (1918–1919) 444–462, 641–653.

MELVILLE, Herman (1819–1891), novelist and traveler.

1. Travel diary, October–December 1849; voyage to England; life on board ship; troublesome contacts with publishers in London; the Continent.
Raymond M. Weaver, *Herman Melville, Mariner and Mystic* (New York, 1921) 284–304 *passim.*

2. Travel diary, October 1856–May 1857; tour in Europe and Asia Minor; analytic notes on places seen and books read.
Raymond M. Weaver (ed.), *Journal up the Straits* (New York, 1935) 182 pp. For notes on Weaver's "probable" errors in transcribing the journal, see review by Robert S. Forsythe, *Amer. Lit.* VIII (1936–1937) 85–96.

3. Travel diary, May–August 1860 (fragment); voyage on the clipper "Meteor" around Cape Horn; weather and sailing notes.
New England Quar. II (1929) 120–125.

MORGAN, William Ives (1826–1869) of Bristol, Conn.

Travel diary, July 1849–February 1853 (extracts); around Cape Horn to California; prospecting; notes on politics and trade; entertaining extracts.
Harper's Mag. CXIII (1906) 920–926 ("The Log of a Forty-Niner").

PALMER, Robert, of Philadelphia.

Travel diary, August–December 1849; voyage in barque "Maria" from Delaware Bay around Cape Horn to San Francisco; description of San Francisco; followed by letter giving narrative of a five weeks' "voyage of discovery" up the Pacific coast; mediocre.

A Voyage round Cape Horn (Philadelphia, 1863) 31 pp.

PARRY, Charles Christopher (1823–1890) of Davenport, Ia., botanist.

Travel journal, March–April 1849; journey to intercept escort of Major Emory's Mexican boundary expedition; travel notes from Davenport to Natchez, Cincinnati, Albany, etc.

Mississippi Valley Hist. Rev. XXVII (1940–1941) 435–441.

PIERCE, Hiram Dwight (*b.* 1810) of Troy, N.Y., blacksmith.

Travel diary, March 1849–January 1851; from New York to Panama, overland, and voyage to San Francisco; good account of Chagres, old Panama, and Tecamos, and some good observations on bad manners of passengers; less interesting in California; return via Panama; interesting linguistically.

Sarah W. Meyer (ed.), *A Forty-Niner Speaks* (Oakland, Calif., 1930) 74 pp.

POOLE, Fitch (1803–1873) of Danvers, Mass.

Social diary, January 1849–March 1870; brief, scattered notes; work as leather currier, librarian, author; mainly local news and notes about his writing and library.

Danvers Hist. Soc. Colls. XIV (1926) 41–62.

POWELL, H. M. T., of Greenville, Ill.

Travel diary, April 1849–March 1852; Illinois to California; Gold Rush days, particularly at Mariposa; travel in California and return to Illinois; Santa Fe, Gila, and Colorado trails; an exceptionally good Gold Rush diary; illustrated.

D. S. Watson (ed.), *The Santa Fe Trail to California* (San Francisco, 1931) 272 pp.

PRITCHARD, Capt. J. A., of Petersburgh, Ky.

Travel diary, April–May 1849 (extract); Kentucky to St. Louis by boat, overland through Missouri; descriptions of Missouri towns.

Missouri Hist. Rev. XVIII (1923–1924) 535–545.

SIMPSON, Lieut. James Hervey (1813–1883), Topographical Engineers.

Military exploration journal, 1849; reconnaissance from Santa Fe to the Navajo country under command of Col. John M. Washington.

Sen. Exec. Doc. 12, 31st Cong. 1st sess.; reprinted as *Journal of a Military Reconnaissance* (Philadelphia, 1852) 140 pp.

SITGREAVES, Capt. Lorenzo (1811–1888) *b.* Philadelphia, of Corps of Topographical Engineers.

Military exploration journal, September–November 1849; expedition down the Zuñi and Colorado rivers; Indian customs.

Sen. Exec. Doc. 59, 32d Cong. 2d sess. (1853) 4–21.

SMITH, W. C. S., of Napa City, Calif.

Travel diary, April–June 1849; overland journey from San Jose to San Diego; valuable account of hardships of gold seekers, and descriptions of Lower California missions.

Robert G. Cleland, *A History of California* (New York, 1922) 483–495; reprinted separately (Napa City, n.d.) 36 pp.

STANSBURY, Capt. Howard (1806–1863) of Corps of Topographical Engineers.

Military exploration journal, June 1849–September 1850; report to Col. Abert on his daily activities during expedition to Utah; geography, natural history, minerals, water supply, etc.; account of Mormon settlement and Indians; extensive and detailed.

An Expedition to the Valley of the Great Salt Lake (Philadelphia, 1852) 1–267; also printed as *Sen. Exec. Doc.* 2, 32d Cong. special sess. (1851) 1–303.

STUART, Jacob, of Washington Co., Tenn.

Travel diary, November 1849–July 1850 (with large gap); journey from Knoxville to Sonora, Calif., with Tennessee party under Gen. Anderson; failure in gold seeking; change to lumbering; fair.

Tennessee Hist. Mag. 2d Ser. I (1931) 279–285.

STUART, Joseph Alonzo (*b.* 1825).

Travel journal, May 1849–April 1867 (with brief introductory narrative); across the plains to California, with an account of mining life and life as sailor during Civil War; lively but written up for publication.

My Roving Life (Auburn, Calif., 1895) two vols.

THORNTON, Maj. John, Englishman.

Travel diary, June–October 1849; voyage to New York, through New York State; Tarrytown, Ithaca, Buffalo, Niagara; and in Canada; Queenstown, Guelph, Montreal, Quebec; return to New York; fairly lively touristic notes.

Diary of a Tour through the Northern States of the Union and Canada (London, 1850) 120 pp.

THURSTON, Samuel Royal (1816–1851) *b.* Kennebec Co., Me., delegate to Congress for the Oregon Territory.

Political diary, November 1849–August 1850; political efforts for Oregon in Washington, D.C.

Oregon Hist. Soc. Quar. XV (1914) 153–205.

UPHAM, Samuel Curtis (1819–1885) of Philadelphia, bank clerk.

Travel diary, January–August 1849 (followed by description of San Francisco and California); voyage from Philadelphia around Cape Horn, Rio de Janeiro, Chile to San Francisco and Sacramento; expenses, life on ship; lively but apparently written up.

Notes of a Voyage to California (Philadelphia, 1878) 594 pp., diary itself pp. 23–217.

WATSON, William J.

Travel diary, May–September 1849; with wagon train from St. Joseph via Oregon Trail, to Oregon City; notes on scenery, topography, distances, etc.

Journal of an Overland Trip to Oregon (Jacksonville, 1851) 48 pp.; only known copy owned by Mr. Coe. [Wagner.]

WEBSTER, Kimball (1828–1916) of Pelham, N.H., surveyor.

Travel diary, April–October 1849; by railroad and steamer to Chicago; down Illinois and Mississippi rivers by steamer to Independence; overland to Sacramento Valley, taking the Cherokee (or "Greenhorn's") cutoff on Humboldt River (urged on emigrants by Lassen, for not disinterested reasons); continued as narrative of two years' residence in California and three years in Oregon; mediocre.

The Gold Seekers of '49 (Manchester, N.H., 1917) 33–99.

WHITING, William Henry Chase (1824–1865) *b.* Biloxi, Miss., engineer.

1. Military travel journal, February–May 1849; survey for route between El Paso and Gulf of Mexico by way of Austin or San Antonio; topography, etc., and some exciting adventures and personal notes.

R. P. Bieber (ed.), *Exploring Southwestern Trails 1846–54* (Glendale, Calif., 1938) 241–350.

2. Military journal, February–April (1850); difficult march from Fredericksburg, Tex., to El Paso del Norte; meeting with Apaches; formalized, but unusually good descriptions for a military journal.

Southern Hist. Assoc. Pubs. IX (1905) 361–373, X (1906) 1–18, 78–95, 127–140.

WILLIAMS, Maj. William (*d.* 1874) of Westmoreland Co., Pa., sutler at Fort Dodge, Ia.

Military travel journal, May–July 1849; experiences and impressions during trip from St. Louis to Fort Snelling, Minn., and return to Westmoreland Co., Pa.; guidebook type of notes, with accounts of towns, Mormons, etc.

Annals Iowa 3d Ser. XII (1921) 241–281.

WOODS, Daniel B., of Philadelphia.

Travel diary, July 1849–November 1850 (preceded by narrative of voyage to San Francisco); work in the gold mines, mining processes, wages, conditions, news of strikes, details of prospectings at Salmon Falls, Mariposa, Tuolumne, Stanislaus, Hart's Bar, etc.; many religious reflections; a fairly good diary.

Sixteen Months at the Gold Diggings (New York, 1851) 49–166.

1850

ANON.

Travel diary, 1850; tour in North and South America.

*Journal of a Tour in North and South America (London, 1852). [Sabin.]

ABBEY, James, of New Albany, Ind.

Travel diary, April–September 1850; from St. Joseph across the plains and mountains to California; personal items, descriptions of adventures, scenery, Indians, difficulties, etc.; a very good narrative with solid and well-written entries.

A Trip across the Plains (New Albany, Ind., 1850) 64 pp.; reprinted *Mag. Hist.* Extra No. 183 (Tarrytown, 1933) 63 pp.

BARRINGTON, Alexander, of St. Mary's, O.

Travel diary, April–December 1850; to California aboard the barque "Paoli"; miner's life, Nevada City region; brief and fairly interesting notes.

A California Gold-Rush Miscellany (San Francisco, 1924) 3–9.

BENNETT, James (1813–1869) of New Harmony, Ind.

Travel diary, April–September 1850; overland journey from New Harmony to Carson Valley, Calif.; substantial descriptions, including social and camp scenes, quarrels, deaths, Indian trade, hunting, impressions of the great migration; fairly interesting.

New Harmony Times, March 16 to August 3, 1906; reprinted as *Overland Journey to California* (New Harmony, 1906) 45 pp.

BROWN, John Lowery (*ca.* 1770–1852), half-breed Cherokee, of Willistown in Cherokee Nation.

Travel diary, April–November 1850; journey from Grand Saline (C.N.) to Carson's Creek, Calif.; brief notes of distances, some dramatic passages of dialogue, notes of difficulties in the desert; some interesting spellings.

Chrons. Oklahoma XII (1934) 177–213.

BROWN, Warren, of Hampton Falls, N.H.

Diary and journal of events, April 1850–December 1898; weather, farming, public events; done in connection with a history of Hampton Falls.

Warren Brown, *History of the Town of Hampton Falls* (Manchester, N.H., 1900) 483–499.

CLAPP, John T., of Kalamazoo, Mich.

Travel diary, beginning March 1850; Kalamazoo to Sacramento via Chicago, Iowa City, Council Bluffs; return in November via Panama; a fairly good day-by-day narrative.

A Journal of Travels to and from California (Kalamazoo, 1851) 67 pp.; only known copy owned by Mr. Graff. [Wagner.]

CULBERTSON, Thaddeus A.

Official travel journal, 1850; to the Mauvaises Terres and upper Missouri; valuable details of forts, Indians, and natural history of South Dakota and upper Missouri.

Smithson. Inst. Pubs. 5th Ann. Rep. (1850) App. IV 84–145; *Sen. Exec. Doc.* No. 1, 32d Cong. special sess. (1851) 84–132.

DUTTON, Jerome (1826–1893) *b.* Afton, N.Y., of Olive, Ia.

Travel diary, March–September 1850; overland from Scott Co., Ia., to Sacramento, Calif.; an undistinguished journal, including letters.

Annals Iowa 3d Ser. IX (1909–1910) 447–483.

EDMUNDSON, William, of Oskaloosa, Ia.

Travel diary, May–October 1850; an undistinguished account of a journey from Oskaloosa to Placerville, Calif.

Annals Iowa 3d Ser. VIII (1907–1908) 516–535.

EVANS, Robert Frank, of Shelbyville, Tenn.

Travel diary, April–August 1850; from Shelbyville to California; by steamer down the Mississippi to New Orleans; voyage to Chagres; across Panama; voyage to San Francisco; joshing and overwritten journalistic style, with verses.

Notes on Land and Sea, 1850 (Boston, 1922) 140 pp.

FRINK, Mrs. Margaret Alsip (of Martinsville, Ind.?).

Travel diary, March–September 1850; journey across the plains from Martinsville to Sacramento.

Journal of the Adventures of a Party of California Gold-Seekers (Oakland, 1897) 121 pp., reprinted from a privately printed edition (1850).

GAYLORD, Orange (*b.* 1823) *b.* Tioga Co., Pa., carpenter.

1. Travel diary, March 1850–September 1851; journey from Marshall Co., Ill., to California and Oregon via Oregon Trail; Carson Valley, Placerville, voyage to Oregon, voyage down coast to San Francisco and San Diego, across Panama and voyage to New York; brief notes, with longer ones on natural phenomena.

2. Travel diary, March–August 1853; brief notes of a journey from Magnolia, Ill., to Oregon City.

Oregon Pioneer Assoc. Trans., 45th Annual Reunion (1917) 403–439.

GLISAN, Dr. Rodney (*b.* 1827) *b.* Linganore, Md., assistant surgeon, U.S. Army.

Military journal, January 1850–November 1858 (extracts); notes on Oregon and Washington Indian wars; literary narrative.

Journal of Army Life (San Francisco, 1874) 511 pp.

HAILMAN, James W., of Pittsburgh, ironmaster.

Travel diary, January–February 1850; trip from Pittsburgh to St. Louis and return; longish, critical travel and social notes; moderate interest.

Western Pennsylvania Hist. Mag. XXIII (1940) 175–181.

HARLAN, Aaron Word (1811–1911) of Croton (Mich.?).

Travel diary, May–September 1850; from Athens, Mo., to the California gold mines, via Council Bluffs, Platte River, Laramie; descriptions of prairie and mountains; unadventurous; the desert section is the most interesting; poem.

Annals Iowa 3d Ser. XI (1913) 32–62.

HEWITT, Henry Leeds, of Erie Co., O.

1. Travel diary, March–June 1850; overland from Ohio to California; a dull account.

2. Travel diary, May 1853–March 1856; arrivals and departures; San Francisco to Ohio via Panama and return; San Francisco to Puget Sound and return; mainly statistical.

Washington Hist. Quar. XXIV (1933) 135–141, 142–146.

INGALLS, Eleazar Stillman (1820–1879) of Antioch, Ill., lawyer.

Travel diary, March 1850–August 1851; from Lake Co., Ill., to Hangtown (Placerville), Calif., by the overland route; account of the mines, hardships, and a stampede; lively journalistic style.

Journal of a Trip to California (Waukegan, 1852) 51 pp.

JACKSON, Alfred T., of Norfolk, Conn.

Mining diary, May 1850–June 1852; work at Rock Creek, Nevada Co., Calif.; simply told details of work of placer miners, daily life and relaxations; quite interesting, although a made-up journal (see a review in *Nation,* March 28, 1907); some linguistic interest.

Chauncey de L. Canfield (ed.), *The Diary of a Forty-Niner* (New York, San Francisco, 1906) 231 pp.

LAIRD, John Chamberlain (1825–1902) of Winona, Wis.

Travel diary-letter, October–November 1850; steamboat journey on upper Mississippi; descriptions of Galena, St. Anthony Falls, and aspects of life in Iowa, Illinois, and Wisconsin; superficial but pleasant.

Minnesota Hist. XII (1931) 157–167.

LANGWORTHY, Franklin (1798–*ca.* 1855) of Mount Carroll, Ill.

Travel diary, April 1850–May 1853; overland route to California via Great Salt Lake; two years' residence in California; return by Pacific Ocean and Central America; journey of more than 9,000 miles; impersonal, scientific observations with philosophical comments; careful descriptions of scenery.

Scenery of the Plains, Mountains, and Mines (Ogdensburgh, N.Y., 1855) 324 pp.; reprinted, edited by P. C. Phillips (Princeton, 1932) 292 pp.

LOOMIS, Leander Vaness (1827–1909) *b.* Fredonia, N.Y.

Travel diary, April–August 1850; from Birmingham, Ia., to Sacramento, Calif., via Council Bluffs, Fort Laramie, and Fort Hall; with Birmingham emigrant party; matter-of-fact style, with social interest; interesting spellings.

Edgar M. Ledyard (ed.), *A Journal of the Birmingham Emigrating Company* (Salt Lake City, 1928) 198 pp.

McKEEBY, Lemuel Clarke (1825–1915) *b.* New York City, of Milwaukee, Wis., and Los Angeles.

Travel diary, May–August 1850; from Council Bluffs to California; routine descriptions of route, Salt Lake City, and mining country; concluded by long narrative; may have been written much later.

California Hist. Soc. Quar. III (1924) 45–72, 126–170.

MAYNARD, Dr. David Swinson (1808–1873) *b.* Rutland Co., Vt., of Cleveland, O., and Seattle, Wash.

Travel diary, April–November 1850; from Ohio to the Puget Sound country; travels in Puget Sound country; a physician's notes on the health of the emigrants.

Thomas W. Prosch, *David S. Maynard and Catherine T. Maynard* (Seattle, 1906) 8–23. Extract in *Washington Hist. Quar.* I (1906) 50–62.

MILES, William, of Carlisle, Pa.

Travel diary, May–December 1850; with Captain French's overland party, by sea from New York City to New Orleans, thence overland to San Diego, and by sea to San Francisco; chief interest lies in the trouble with mules and with the nefarious Captain French.

Journal of the Sufferings and Hardships of Captain Parker H. French's Overland Expedition (Chambersburg, Pa., 1851) 24 pp.; reprinted (Cadmus Bookshop, N.Y., 1916) 26 pp.

NORELIUS, Eric (1833–1862) of Columbus, O., and Minnesota.

Travel diary, July 1850–1854 (combined with memoirs); begins with voyage to America and continues with notes of life of Swedish immigrants; schools, churches, attendance at Columbus College; interesting for development of the Middle West. Translated.

Early Life of Eric Norelius, Augustana Hist. Soc. Pubs. No. 4 (1934) 320 pp.

PANGBOURN, David Knapp.

Travel diary, June–August 1850 (extract); from New York to San Francisco by sea; description of Panama.

Amer. Hist. Rev. IX (1903–1904) 104–115.

READ, Dr. George Willis (1819–1880) of Greene Co., Pa., physician.

Travel diary, May–August 1850; with Greene County party, from Independence to Hangtown (Placerville), Calif.; account of the diggings and mining; account of a journey from New York to California in 1862; substantial and clearly written notes; moderate interest.

Georgia W. Read, *A Pioneer of 1850* (Boston, 1927) 17–100.

SAWYER, Lorenzo (1820–1891) b. Le Roy, N.Y., of San Francisco, later chief justice of Supreme Court of California.

Travel diary, May–July 1850; from St. Joseph to California; conventional notes on route, scenery, sights; solid entries but lacking in spontaneity.

Edward Eberstadt (ed.), *Way Sketches, Containing Incidents of Travel across the Plains* (New York, 1926) 125 pp.

SHOTTENKIRK, D. G., of Mount Carroll, Ill., schoolmaster.

Travel diary, June–July 1850 (fragment); on the road to California about Green River.

Appendix to P. C. Phillips' edition of Franklin Langworthy's *Scenery of the Plains, Mountains, and Mines* (Princeton, 1932) 280–285.

SMITH, Charles W., of Victor, N.Y.

Travel diary, April–August 1850; from Centerville, Ida., to Weber Creek, Calif.; unexciting, but better written than the usual Gold Rush journal; journalistic, with poetical quotations.

R. W. G. Vail (ed.), *Journal of a Trip to California* (New York, 1920) 79 pp.

STEELE, John (1832–1905) *b.* Middleton Co., N.Y., of Wisconsin, soldier and minister.

Travel diary, April–September 1850; from Wisconsin to California; extensive, well written, but conventional, notes; original poems.

Joseph Schafer (ed.), *Across the Plains in 1850* (Chicago, 1930) 234 pp.; first published in *Lodi Valley News* (Wis.) April 8–November 18, 1899.

STIMSON, Fancher (1828–1902) of Council Bluffs, Ia.

Travel diary, April–July 1850; from Palmyra, Wis., to California, via Council Bluffs, Platte River, South Pass; moderate interest.

Annals of Iowa 3d Ser. XIII (1922) 408–423.

TAYLOR, Col. Marion C. (*d.* 1871) of Shelby Co., Ky., lawyer.

Military diary, April–June 1850; with López Cárdenas' expedition against Cuba; enlistment at Louisville; voyage, description of islands, guards; return to Louisville; quite interesting.

Kentucky Hist. Soc. Reg. XIX (1921) 79–89.

THISSELL, G. W., of Bellefontaine, Ia.

Travel diary, March–September 1850; with an ox team from Missouri River to California via Oregon Trail; early summary of discovery of gold, interposed editorial comment, and narrative of other pioneers; journalistic, but fair interest.

Crossing the Plains in '49 (Oakland, 1903) 176 pp.

UDELL, John (*b.* 1795) of Jefferson, O., and New York City.

1. Travel diary, January 1850–July 1855; overland to California along the Oregon Trail; work in Placerville and Yuba; return via Panama; second trip to California in 1852, stay until 1854, and return; many religious reflections; quite interesting.

Incidents of Travel to California (Jefferson, O., 1856) 302 pp. The formal diary is on pp. 9–106; on pp. 114–239 is an autobiography, which draws largely from his diary (January 1833–October 1855), concerning his work in the Baptist church, and his farming, domestic life, and travel east of the Mississippi; these extracts, although very scattered, give an interesting picture of pioneer life.

2. Travel diary, 1858–1859; journey from Jefferson to Los Angeles along Santa Fe trail; winter in Albuquerque; account of massacre of part of the party by Mojaves.

Journal of John Udell (Jefferson, O., 1868) 47 pp.

WILLIAMS, John T. (1825–1881) of Clinton Co., Ind.

Travel diary, March–September 1850; from Indiana to Parks (*sic*) Bar, Calif.; notes on distances, Indians, and accidents.

Indiana Mag. Hist. XXXII (1936) 393–409.

WOOD, John (1825–1896) of Greenfield, O., lawyer, merchant, teacher.

Travel diary, April–September 1850; from Cincinnati to the gold mines of California; notes on route, hardships, difficulties, prices.

Journal of John Wood (Chillicothe, O., 1852) 76 pp.; reprinted (Columbus, O., 1871) 112 pp.

WOODWARD, Thomas (1806–1878) *b*. Stockton-on-Tees, Eng., of Highland, Wis.

Travel diary, May–July 1850 (incomplete); from St. Joseph to California via Platte River and South Pass; very good details of things seen and felt; one of the best of the western travel diaries.

Wisconsin Mag. Hist. XVII (1933–1934) 345–360, 433–446.

WORTLEY, Victoria Stuart (1837–1912).

Travel diary, May 1850–May 1851; tour in North and South America; the diary of a fascinated child; observations on people, customs, slang, etc.

A Young Traveller's Journal (London, 1852) 58 pp.

1851

BARBOUR, George W., of Kentucky.

Official journal, May–October 1851; Indian affairs of California; member of commission to formulate "a definite policy with regard to the aboriginal tribes of California."

Southwestern Hist. Quar. XL (1936–1937) 145–153, 247–261.

CRAWFORD, P. V.

Travel diary, March–September 1851; from Madison, Ind., to St. Joseph and thence to Oregon; a conventional overland diary with notes on route, sights, Indians, etc.

Oregon Hist. Soc. Quar. XXV (1924) 136–169.

DAVIS, Alvah Isaiah (*b*. 1825) *b*. Geauga Co., O., of Linn Co., Ore.

1. Travel diary, December 1851–October 1852; brief notes of farming and weather near Lockport, Ill.; at Chicago; journey across Iowa along Oregon Trail to Willamette; quite interesting, especially for unusual entries indicating genesis of the desire to emigrate.

Oregon Pioneer Assoc. Trans., 37th Annual Reunion (1909) 355–381.

2. Private diary, October 1852–April 1854; farming in Oregon; brief notes of work and weather; some personal notes, and prices.

Oregon Pioneer Assoc. Trans. 38th and 39th Annual Reunion (1910–1911) 444–476.

EVANS, John, overseer of Chemonie plantation, Fla.

Plantation journal, January–December 1851 and January–August 1856 (written by A. R. and B. S. McCall after January 21); careful details of work about the Chemonie plantation; health and discipline of slaves; interesting linguistically.

U. B. Phillips and J. D. Glunt (eds.), *Florida Plantation Records, Missouri Hist. Soc. Pubs.* (1927) 339–509.

FLINT, Dr. Thomas (1824–1904) *b*. New Vineyard, Me.

Travel diary, May–July 1851 and December 1852–July 1855; brief notes of trip from Maine to California via Panama; full diary of round trip from California to Illinois to bring sheep and cattle into California; fairly good account of difficulties.

Hist. Soc. Southern California Ann. Pubs. XII (1923) 53–127.

GREENE, Paul, of western New York, farmer.

Travel diary, October–November 1851 (extracts); Buffalo to Toledo, the Ohio River, Cincinnati, Piqua, Louisville, Memphis; very good descriptions of cities and life on the Ohio.

History Teacher's Mag. VII (1916) 122–123.

GUNN, Elizabeth Le Breton (1811–1906).

Travel diary-letters, February–August 1851; written to her family while she was making voyage around Cape Horn to join her husband in California; interesting details of a woman's view of the voyage, cooking, social life, etc.; quite pleasant.

A. L. Marston (ed.), *Records of a California Family* (San Diego, Calif., 1928) 91–135.

HOWE, William S. G. (d. 1860) of Hanover, N.H.

Private diary, June 1851–February 1853 (extracts); social work, visits to points of interest, family and domestic notes, weather, music, installation of gas.

Diary of Rev. Moses How (New Bedford, 1932) 25–29.

LECOUVREUR, Frank (1829–1901) b. Ortelsburg, Prussia, of Los Angeles, Calif., civil engineer.

Private and travel diary, April 1851–October 1871; written in form of letters; Berlin, Hamburg, voyage to San Francisco, San Francisco, mining, Los Angeles, voyage to Germany via Panama, New York, return to Los Angeles; extensive and fairly interesting. Translated from the German.

Julius C. Behnke (comp.), *From East Prussia to the Golden Gate* (New York, Los Angeles, 1906) 355 pp.

LOBENSTINE, William Christian, b. Eisfeld, Germany, of Leavenworth, Kans.

Private diary, April 1851–August 1852, and April 1854–July 1858 (extracts); in California, and return to the East; overland journey from Wheeling to California; flatulent journalistic style, with many German constructions.

Belle W. Lobenstine (ed.), *Extracts from the Diary of William C. Lobenstine* (n.p., 1920) 101 pp.

MAYER, Frank Blackwell (1827–1899) of Baltimore, artist.

Travel diary, May–July 1851; kept while author was painting on the frontier; journey to Cincinnati, Mammoth Cave, Louisville, up Mississippi to St. Paul, among Sioux at Kaposia, at Traverse des Sioux; a full and detailed account of what he saw, with a good deal of personal matter; highly interesting.

B. L. Heilbron (ed.), *With Pen and Pencil on the Frontier in 1851* (St. Paul, 1932) 214 pp.

OWEN, Maj. John (1818–1889) of Pennsylvania, trader at Fort Owen, Ore.

Fur-trading journals, April 1851–February 1871; details of affairs at Fort Owen and of trading journeys in the vicinity; Walla Walla, The Dalles, Salmon River, Forts Vancouver and Benton, Great Salt Lake, etc.; varying style, sometimes brief notes, but often long and detailed descriptions. In addition to details of journeys and trading, much of it is personal and general description. A highly interesting record of the early Pacific Northwest and its fur trade.

S. Dunbar (ed.), *The Journals and Letters of Major John Owen* (New York, 1927) two vols.

PRATT, Parley Parker (1807–1857) *b*. Burlington, N.Y., Mormon elder, missionary, editor.

1. Travel diary, March–October 1851; from Salt Lake City to San Francisco, return to Utah; account of Mormon missions in San Francisco, Los Angeles, San Bernardino, etc.; moderate interest.

California Hist. Soc. Quar. XIV (1935) 59–73, 175–182. Extract in slightly different form, March–July 1851, in *The Autobiography of Parley Parker Pratt* (New York, 1874) 414–429.

2. Travel journal, September 1856–March 1857; Salt Lake City to the eastern United States, principally Philadelphia, as a Mormon missionary.

Autobiography, 484–494.

ROBE, Robert (1821–1908) *b*. Ohio, pioneer Presbysterian minister in Oregon.

Travel journal, April–August 1851; Washington, D.C., to St. Joseph, overland to Umatilla country; descriptions of route, Indians, difficulties; conventional, apart from religious overtones.

Washington Hist. Quar. XIX (1928) 52–63.

ROTCH, Mrs. Benjamin S., of Boston.

Private diary, December 1851–January 1853 (extracts); kept by the daughter of Abbott Lawrence, United States minister to Great Britain; a fascinated onlooker at social functions in Paris during the Second Empire.

New England Quar. VI (1933) 513–524.

SHEPHERD, Dr. J. S.

Travel diary; overland journey to California, with notes for emigrants.

Journal of Travel across the Plains to California (Racine, 1851) 44 pp.; only known copy in the Rollins collection. [Wagner.]

WOOD, Elizabeth, of Tazewell Co., Ill.

Travel diary, June–September 1851 (fragment); Fort Laramie to Oregon; conventional notes on route, scenery, Indians, etc.; literary and mediocre.

Oregon Hist. Quar. XXVII (1926) 192–203; originally published in *Peoria Weekly Republican,* January 30 and February 13, 1852.

ZEIBER, John Shunk (1803–1890) *b*. Pottstown, Pa., of Multnomah Co., Ore., journalist.

Travel diary, April–October 1851; from Peoria, Ill., to Portland, Ore.; substantial entries of journalistic type; reporting incidents of journey and remarkable sights, happenings, conditions; bright narrative and fairly interesting reading.

Oregon Pioneer Assoc. Trans., 48th Annual Reunion (1920) 301–335.

1852

ANON.

Travel diary; from Abbeville, S.C., to Ocola, Fla.; interesting observations of political conditions, etc.

*Incidents of a Journey from Abbeville (Edgefield, 1852).

ADAMS, Mrs. Cecelia Emily McMillen (1829–1867) *b.* Lodi, N.Y., of Hillsboro, Ore.

Travel diary, May–October 1852; from Missouri to Oregon; a pleasant record of an unexciting journey across the plains and mountains; personal, social, and everyday details.

Oregon Pioneer Assoc. Trans., 32d Annual Reunion (1904) 288–329.

AKIN, James, Jr. (*d.* 1852) of Henry Co., Ia.

Travel diary, April–October 1852; with his family from Salem, Ia., to the Cascades, Ore., via the Oregon Trail; brief notes of distances and incidental commonplace activities.

Oregon Pioneer Assoc. Trans., 36th Annual Reunion (1908) 259–274; *University Oklahoma Bull.* n.s. 172 (1919) 32 pp.

ANDERSON, Rev. David (1814–1885) *b.* London, Bishop of Prince Rupert's Land.

Travel journal, June–October 1852; travel and description in the Canadian northwest; notes on missionary schools and churches in Prince Rupert's Land.

The Net in the Bay (London, 1854) 276 pp.; this reprinted (London, 1873).

BIXBY, Marcellus, *b.* Maine, of Amador Co., Calif.

Travel diary, February 1852–June 1856; a rather dull account of a journey from Maine to California.

Hist. Soc. Southern California Ann. Pubs. XIII (1924–1927) 317–333.

BROWN, John W., of Princeton, Ark.

Private diary, August 1852–April 1853 (extracts); mostly travel data, with some personal affairs; to Memphis and return twice; journey to New Orleans.

Jour. Southern Hist. IV (1938) 377–383.

BUTLER, Mrs. Ashmun J. (1826–1910) *b.* Bourbon Co., Ky., of Medford, Ore.

Travel and private diary, April 1852–January 1854; from Missouri to Rogue River Valley, Ore.; hard winter spent in Yreka; life in the Rogue River Valley; domestic notes; Indian war of 1853; a good diary, with some interesting spellings.

Oregon Hist. Quar. XLI (1940) 337–366.

CONYERS, E. W., of Quincy, Ill., and Clatskanie, Ore.

Travel diary, April–September 1852; journey with emigrating party from Quincy to Oregon by Oregon Trail; written up with full detail of hardships and dramatic moments; apparently based on a diary.

Oregon Pioneer Assoc. Trans., 33d Annual Reunion (1905) 423–512.

EBEY, Col. (*b.* 1818) of Franklin Co., O., and NEFF, Mrs. Isaac (*b.* 1822) *b.* Washington Co., Va., of Whidby Island, Puget Sound.

Private diary, June 1852–October 1853; peaceful life at Whidby Island; gardening, domestic and social life; primarily the diary of Mrs. Neff.

Washington Hist. Quar. VII (1916) 239–246, 307–321, VIII (1917) 40–62, 124–152.

FRIZZELL, Mrs. Lodisa, of Effingham Co., Ill.

Travel diary, April–June 1852; from Little Wabash River to California via St. Louis, Forts Kearny and Laramie, South Pass, to Cañon Creek and the Sierra Madre; descriptions of the usual kind, with some religious and personal items; a highly interesting diary; some interesting spellings.

V. H. Paltsits (ed.), *Across the Plains to California in 1852* (New York, 1915) 30 pp.; reprinted from *Bull. New York Pub. Lib.* XIX (1915) 335–362.

GREINER, John (1810–1871) *b.* Philadelphia, senior agent for Indian affairs at Santa Fe.

Official journal, April–September 1852; systematic and detailed record of his work as superintendent of Indian affairs in New Mexico; impersonal, but valuable picture of life of Navajos, etc.

Old Santa Fe III (1916) 189–243.

HICKMAN, Richard Owen (1831–1895) of Shelby Co., Ky., and Silver Bow, Mont.

Travel diary-letter, May–December 1852; overland journey from Independence to Nevada City; excellent account of daily life and adventures en route.

The Frontier IX (1929) 242–260; reprinted in *Sources of Northwest Hist.* No. 6 (Univ. Montana) 22 pp.

HIGGINSON, Henry Lee (1834–1919) of Boston, musician.

Travel diary, June 1852–May 1863 (extracts); travel in England, Switzerland, Italy, etc., pursuing his musical studies; service as a major during the Civil War.

Bliss Perry, *Life and Letters of Henry Lee Higginson* (Boston, 1921) 27–189.

JACKSON, Mitchell Young (1816–1900) *b.* near Mount Vernon, O., of Lake St. Croix, Minn.

Farming diary, August 1852–June 1863; begins at Wabash; debate on emigrating to Oregon; journey to find location in Minnesota; removal with his brother and their families to Lake St. Croix in 1854; life on his farm there; fairly full notes of farming, weather, domestic, social, and religious affairs, opinions on slavery, etc.; an interesting diary; fuller than, but not so varied in detail as, William R. Brown's similar diary.

R. C. Loehr (ed.), *Minnesota Farmers' Diaries* (St. Paul, 1939) 85–220. Extracts in *Agricultural Hist.* IV (1930) 92–120.

KERNS, John T., of Rensselaer, Ind.

Travel diary, March–October 1852; from Rensselaer to Portland, Ore., along Oregon Trail; pleasant descriptions and narrative but no great interest.

Oregon Pioneer Assoc. Trans., 42d Annual Reunion (1914) 148–193.

LAMSON, Joseph, of Bangor, Me.

Travel diary, April 1852–April 1860; greater part describes voyage in the "James W. Paige" from Bangor to San Francisco, around Cape Horn; followed by selections describing outstanding characters, a duel, cattle-stealing, a fandango, and Yosemite; a quite amusing account of life on ship.

Round Cape Horn (Bangor, 1878) 156 pp.

LANE, William Carr (1789–1867) *b*. Pennsylvania, governor of New Mexico.

Travel diary, July 1852–February 1853; St. Louis to Santa Fe, inauguration as governor, trip to southern New Mexico; very dull, in highfalutin' style.

New Mexico Hist. Soc. Pubs. No. 20 (1917) 23–62.

LIBBEY, David (1828–1904) of Penobscot, Me.

Private diary, January 1852–December 1878 (extracts); brief notes concerning school, hunting, work on rapids; service in Civil War; timber work and carpentering in San Francisco and work in foundry; brief, simple notes.

Fannie H. Eckstorm, *David Libbey* (Boston, 1907) 28–95 *passim*.

McALLISTER, Rev. John, of Louisiana, Mo.

Travel diary, April–October 1852; overland from Missouri to Oregon via Galena and Oregon Trail; mainly devoted to notes on camping and physical conditions; rather interesting.

Oregon Pioneer Assoc. Trans., 50th Annual Reunion (1922) 471–508.

McGILL, George M. (1838–1867) of Allegheny, Pa.

Travel diary, July–August 1852; Allegheny to Lake Superior with his father; a boy fishing and "exploring"; delightful reading.

Moorsfield Antiquarian I (1937–1938) 256–266.

PAINE, Rev. Timothy Otis (1824–1895) of Joppa village.

Private diary, September 1852–October 1895 (scattered extracts); reflections, observations of nature, comments on poetry of Wordsworth and Holmes.

Lydia A. Carter, *The Discovery of a Grandmother* (Newtonville, Mass., 1920) 320–325.

PARKER, Ellen Augusta (1833–1910).

Private diary, March 1852–September 1857 (extracts); domestic life, teaching, etc., of a young Wisconsin pioneer; valuable.

Grant Showerman, *The Indian Stream Republic and Luther Parker, New Hampshire Hist. Soc. Colls.* XI (1915) 130–162.

RANDLE, William, of Henry Co., Tenn.

Travel diary, June–August 1852; from Paris, Tenn., to Trenton, Lexington, Perryville, Clifton; flippant and fairly amusing journalistic comments.

Tennessee Hist. Mag. IX (1925) 195–208.

RICHARDS, Caroline Cowles (*b*. 1842) of Canandaigua, N.Y.

Private diary, November 1852–June 1880; lively and keen observation of a young girl in New York; life with grandfather in Canandaigua; religious and careful upbringing; records of Civil War; reading novels, etc.; an interesting record of a prosperous and respectable family.

Diary of Caroline Cowles Richards (Canandaigua, 1908) 162 pp., *Village Life in America, 1852–1872* (London, 1912) 207 pp.; latter reprinted (New York, 1913) 225 pp.

RIKER, John F.

Travel diary, 1852; trip from Cincinnati to San Francisco by the overland route.

*Journal of a Trip to California (Urbana, O., 1855?) 32 pp.; only known copy discovered by E. J. Wessen. [Wagner.]

SHARP, Mrs. Cornelia A., of Jackson Co., Mo.

Travel diary, May–October 1852; from Missouri to Oregon City by Oregon Trail; brief notes of stages and the commonplaces of scenery, natural history, and mishaps.

Oregon Pioneer Assoc. Trans., 31st Annual Reunion (1903) 171–188.

SIMMONDS, James (1847–1915) of Dartmouth, N.S.

Private diary, November 1852–June 1909 (scattered extracts); notes of family and personal affairs in Nova Scotia.

Frank W. Simmonds, *John and Susan Simmonds* (Rutland, Vt., 1940) 100–104.

SPENCER, Lafayette, of Cedar, Ia.

Travel diary, May–October 1852; with emigrant train from Van Buren Co., Iowa, along Oregon Trail to Oregon City; brief and poor notes of distances, etc.

Annals Iowa 3d Ser. VIII (1907–1908) 304–310.

TERRELL, Joseph Christopher (*b.* 1831) of Boonville, Mo.

Travel diary, May–July 1852; overland trip to California; usual notes on scenery, natural history, etc.

Reminiscences of the Early Days of Fort Worth (Fort Worth, 1906) 76–91.

THOMSON, Origen.

Travel diary, 1852; journey across the plains.

*Crossing the Plains &c in 1852 (Greensburg, Ind., 1896) 122 pp.

TURNBULL, Thomas (*b. ca.* 1812) *b.* Chillingworth, Eng., of Glencoe, Ill.

Travel diary, April–August 1852; from Chicago to Hangtown, Calif., via Council Bluffs, Mormon Trail, Oregon Trail (joined at North Platte Bridge); unusual route; full entries, with good detail and good observations; farming interest; mostly impersonal, but one of the best journals of the Gold Rush by virtue of its spontaneity; some linguistic interest.

Wisconsin Hist. Soc. Proc. LXI (1913) 151–225.

1853

ANON. (woman of MacMurphy family).

Travel diary, March–October 1853; journey from Wisconsin to California; written up in romantic narrative style.

Nebraska Hist. Soc. Trans. III (1892) 270–278.

ALLYN, Henry, of Fulton Co., Ill.

Travel diary, March–September 1853; from Fulton Co., Ill., to Willamette Valley via Oregon Trail; substantial entries, topography, natural history, curiosities, from farmer's viewpoint; a good narrative and excellent picture of the great exodus; well written, with poetical allusions; one of the best diaries of the Oregon emigration.

Oregon Pioneer Assoc. Trans., 49th Annual Reunion (1921) 372–435.

AUBREY, Francis Xavier (1824–1854) *b.* Quebec, Santa Fe trader.

1. Travel diary, July–September 1853; new route from California to Albuquerque via Tejon Pass; last part of journey from San Francisco to Albuquerque.

R. G. Bieber and A. B. Bender (eds.), *Exploring Southwestern Trails 1846–1854* (Glendale, 1938) 353–377; first printed in *Santa Fe Weekly Gazette,* September 24, 1853.

2. Travel diary, July–August 1854; San Jose, Calif., to Zuñi, N.M.

Bieber and Bender, *op. cit.* 377–383; first printed in *The Daily Missouri Republican,* September 26, 1854.

BALDWIN, Charles Candee (1834–1895) of Cleveland, O.

Private diary, June 1853–1856 (extracts); includes details of work at Harvard and a poem in the meter of Longfellow's "Hiawatha."

Western Reserve Hist. Soc. Tract No. 88 (1896) 129–139.

BELSHAW, Maria Parsons.

Travel diary, August–October 1853 (extract); Lake Co., Ind., to Oregon; journey on the Snake River Trail to what is now Benton Co., Ore., and steamboat voyage on the Columbia.

Oregon Hist. Quar. XXXIII (1932) 318–333.

BLACK, Reading Wood (1830–1867) *b.* Springfield, N.J., of Uvalde, Tex.

Private diary, December 1853–February 1856; mostly kept at his ranch on the Leona; one trip of two months on a mustang chase, various business trips to Eagle Pass, San Antonio, and Austin; brief notes on trade, farming, gardening, personal affairs, visits, weather, etc.; fairly interesting general diary, with some linguistic interest.

The Life and Diary of Reading W. Black (Uvalde, Texas, 1934) 35–93.

CARLETON, Maj. James Henry (1814–1873) *b.* Maine, frontier soldier.

Military exploration journal, December 1853; "excursion to the ruins of Abó, Quarra, and Gran Quivara, in New Mexico"; archaeological descriptions.

Smithson. Inst., 9th Ann. Rep. (1854) 296–320.

DINWIDDIE (David or John) of Porter Co., Ind.

Travel diary, March–October 1853; from Porter Co., Ind., to Independence and thence to Oregon City via Nebraska, Wyoming, Utah, Idaho, Snake River; notes on scenery, expenses, etc.; fair interest.

The Frontier VIII (Montana, 1928) 115–130; reprinted in *Sources of Northwest History* No. 2 (Univ. Montana) 14 pp.

GARRARD, Charles T., of Kentucky.

Foreign-travel diary, March–June 1853; inspecting and purchasing cattle for importation into Kentucky; mostly in Yorks, Lancs, and London; return voyage; some interesting social notes.

Kentucky Hist. Soc. Reg. XXIX (1931) 402–415, XXX (1932) 37–60.

HARKER, Mary Haines.

Private diary, May–December 1853; Quaker girl's visit to Virginia; Lynchburg; visits, social affairs, varied reading, marriage; a lively feminine diary.

Virginia Quar. Rev. XI (1935) 61–81.

HEAP, Gwinn Harris (1817–1887) b. Chester, Pa., government official.

Travel diary, May–August 1853; from Westport, Mo., to Los Angeles via Council Grove, Fort Atkinson, Bent's Fort, Fort Massachusetts, Green River, Cedar City, Mohave River; expedition with E. F. Beale, the superintendent of Indian affairs in California; written up as an official journal.

Central Route to the Pacific (Philadelphia, 1854) 136 pp.

HINES, Miss Celinda E., of Hastings, N.Y.

Travel diary, February–September 1853; from New York to the Cascades, Ore., by railroad and steamboat to St. Louis and Independence, thence overland via Oregon Trail; with her family; besides the usual notes on scenery, etc., many personal, family, and social notes; a pleasant diary.

Oregon Pioneer Assoc. Trans., 46th Annual Reunion (1918) 69–125.

KAUTZ, Gen. August Valentine (1828–1895) b. Germany, frontier soldier.

Military diary, July 1853–September 1895 (extracts); service in the West; social life around Puget Sound; visits to farms, sketches of settlers, excursions on the Sound, accounts of Nootka Indians; quite interesting.

Washington Historian I (1900) 115–119, 181–186, II (1900) 12–15.

KINGSBURY, Rev. Cyrus (1786–1870) b. Alstead, N.H.

Missionary journal, January–December 1853; brief notes of work among Choctaw Indians; extracts not very illuminating.

Chrons. Oklahoma III (1925) 152–157.

KNIGHT, Mrs. Amelia Stewart, of Monroe Co., Ia., and Clark Co., W.T.

Travel diary, April–September 1853; from Iowa to near Milwaukie, Ore., via Oregon Trail; notes on daily life, mishaps, hardships; some well-told incidents and amusing comments; feminine and personal interests; one of the best among pioneer diaries written by women; very considerable general interest.

Oregon Pioneer Assoc. Trans., 56th Annual Reunion (1928) 38–53.

Long, Jonathan Dean (1819–1889) of Brookline, Mass.

Sea diary, July–August 1853; from New York to San Francisco; overland across Panama; nothing remarkable.

New England Hist. Geneal. Reg. XCI (1937) 312–319.

Longworth, Basil Nelson.

Travel diary, March 1853–January 1854; with party of preachers and their families, from New York State to Marysville, Ore., along Oregon Trail; mainly impersonal notes on stages and scenery, with some occasional unusual incidents and religious reflections.

The Diary of Basil N. Longworth (Denver, 1927) 43 pp.; mimeographed copies published by Hist. Recs. Survey of Oregon (Portland, 1938) 68 pp.

Merrimon, Augustus S. (1830–1892) of Asheville, N.C., attorney.

Business diary, October 1853–January 1854; kept on circuit; court procedure, social conditions, etc., in western North Carolina; lengthy entries of description and comment.

North Carolina Hist. Rev. VIII (1931) 300–330.

Möllhausen, Heinrich Balduin (1825–1905) *b.* Bonn, Germany, naturalist.

Travel diary, 1853–1854; naturalist with Whipple's government expedition from Fort Smith, Ark., via Indian Territory and New Mexico to San Diego; notes on Indian life and aboriginal antiquities; illustrated; more general in interest than the official journal of the expedition. Translated from the German.

Mrs. Percy Sinnett (trans.), *Diary of a Journey from the Mississippi to the Coasts of the Pacific* (London, 1858) two vols.

Stewart, Agnes.

Travel diary, March–September 1853; "Alleganey City," Pa., to St. Joseph and overland to Oregon; sentimental and descriptive; an unusual diary of an ordinary young girl.

Oregon Hist. Quar. XXIX (1928) 77–98.

Welles, C. M., of Connecticut.

Travel diary, February 1853–July 1854; travel in many parts of the world, of which the diary describes only part; he remained in California after June 1854, from which time his book is summarized from the original diary.

Three Years' Wanderings of a Connecticut Yankee (New York, 1859) 26–304 (diary section).

Whipple, Lieut. Amiel Weeks (1818–1863) *b.* Greenwich, Mass., U.S.A.

Military exploration journal, July 1853–March 1854; survey of routes in the Southwest for a railroad; Fort Smith, along Arkansas and Canadian rivers, Albuquerque, San José River, down Colorado and Chiquito, to sites of Holbrook and Flagstaff; Bill Williams River to the Colorado; Mohave River to site of Barstow; Cajon Pass to San Bernardino, Los Angeles, and San Pedro; scientific and geographical details.

Grant Foreman (ed.), *A Pathfinder in the Southwest* (Norman, Okla., 1941) 298 pp.

WILLIAMS, Mrs. Velina A., of Winnebago Co., Ill.

Travel diary, April–September 1853; with her husband and family from Mississippi River to Klamath Lake, Ore.; usual notes on Oregon Trail, but a great deal of everyday life, social items, domestic, camping, fears; feminine, and very good reading.

Oregon Pioneer Assoc. Trans. 47th Annual Reunion (1919) 178–226.

WINTHROP, Theodore (1828–1861) of New Haven, Conn., author.

Travel diary, 1853; trip by canoe and horse from Port Townsend along Columbia River and across the mountains; entertaining, humorous style.

John H. Williams (ed.), *The Canoe and the Saddle; or, Klalam and Klickatat* (Tacoma, 1913) 332 pp.; this edition has the journal and some letters in addition to the main narrative (which was originally published in 1862 and went into several editions).

1854

ANON.

Fur-trading journal, September 1854–November 1856; official record of trading at Fort Benton, Mont.; life, Indians, weather; impersonal and matter-of-fact.

Montana Hist. Soc. Contribs. X (1940) 1–99.

BECKWITH, Lieut. Edward Griffin (1818–1881) *b.* Cazenovia, N.Y., of 3d U.S. Artillery.

1. Military exploration journals, April–November 1854; exploration of route for Pacific railroad, near 38th and 39th parallels of latitude; from mouth of Kansas to Sevier River, in the Great Basin; similarly along the 31st parallel, from Salt Lake to the Pacific coast.

House Exec. Doc. 129, 33d Cong., 1st sess. (1855) 1–87.

BELL, James G., of San Antonio, Tex., and California.

Private diary, June–November 1854; "log of the Texas-California cattle drive"; from San Antonio, El Paso, Tucson, to Los Angeles, by boat to San Francisco and Sacramento; good descriptions of people, places, customs, and some personal notes; an excellent, lively diary.

Southwestern Hist. Quar. XXXV (1931–1932) 208–237, 290–316, XXXVI (1932–1933) 47–66.

BYRNE, J. H., assistant computer under John Pope of Corps of Topographical Engineers.

Military exploration journal, January–May 1854; journal of Pope's exploration for route for Pacific railroad, near 32d parallel; from Red River to Rio Grande.

House Exec. Doc. 129, 33d Cong. 1st sess. (1855); Appendix to Pope's report, 66–122.

CROSBY, Charles A. (*b.* 1835) of Texas.

Military diary, October–November 1854 (extract); in Texas with Gen. Albert Sidney Johnston; notes on stages, camps, etc.

West Texas Hist. Assoc. Year-Book XVII (1941) 100–107.

De Long, Charles E. (1832–1876) *b.* Dutchess Co., N.Y., lawyer and politician
in California and Nevada.

Private diary, January 1854–December 1862; life in California as seen and
lived by a young man developing from clerk to an important politician; movements, business, political dealings; longer later entries, in California courts and
legislature; political maneuvers, electioneering, California during Civil War; and
valuable as picture of hectic political life; a few poems.

California Hist. Soc. Quar. VIII (1929) 194–213, 337–363, IX (1930) 50–80,
129–181, 243–287, 345–397, X (1931) 40–78, 165–201, 245–297, 355–397.

Diman, Rev. Jeremiah Lewis (1831–1881) of Providence, R.I.

Private diary, August 1854–June 1856; travel in Europe, study at Halle and
Heidelberg, travel in France and England; notes on scholars, universities, and
tourist's interests; a good diary.

Caroline Hazard (ed.), *Memoirs of the Rev. J. Lewis Diman* (Boston, New
York, 1887) 64–107.

Fogle, Augustus (1820–1897) of Salem, N.C., carpenter.

Moravian travel diary, April–November 1854; from Salem, N.C., to the Cherokee Moravian mission, via New Salem, Ill.; visits to mission stations; notes of
travel difficulties, some graphic incidents and personal affairs; a good journal.

Edmund Schwarze, "History of the Moravian Missions among Southern Indian Tribes," *Moravian Hist. Soc. Trans.,* Special Ser. I (1923) 257–276.

Parke, Lieut. John Grubb (1827–1900) *b.* Coatesville, Pa., of Corps of Topographical Engineers.

Military exploration journal, January–November 1854; exploration for railroad
near 32d parallel, between Dona Ana on the Rio Grande and Pimas villages on
the Gila; scientific details.

House Exec. Doc. 129, 33d Cong. 1st sess. (1855) 3–24.

Parker, William B. (attached to Marcy's expedition).

Military exploration journal, June–October 1854; carefully detailed description
of journey through Texas; botanical and sociological notes; Indians.

Notes Taken during the Expedition Commanded by Capt. R. B. Marcy (Phila-
adelphia, 1856) 2–242. Extracts (August 1854, conference with Comanches on
Clear Fork of the Brazos), *West Texas Hist. Assoc. Year Book* I (1925) 56–72,
reprinted from chaps xv and xvi of the *Notes.*

Stuart, Granville (1834–1918), gold miner, rancher, politician.

Private diary, begun June 1854 (scattered throughout narrative); mining,
trade, ranching, politics, frontier life, mainly in Montana; kept alternately by
Granville Stuart and his brother James.

P. C. Phillips (ed.), *Forty Years on the Frontier* (Cleveland, 1925) two vols.

Swinscoe, Charles, of New York, stevedore.

Travel journal, March–May 1854 (incomplete); New York to Liverpool on clipper "Dreadnaught"; sailing details, notes on passengers, Liverpool, return; interesting picture of hard ship discipline.

Massachusetts Hist. Soc. Proc. LXV (1932–1936) 3–21.

VANDERSLICE, Maj. Daniel, Jr. (1799–1889) of Highland, Kans., Indian agent.

Treaty journal, April 1854–April 1855 (extracts); negotiations as agent of Iowa, Sac, Fox, and Kickapoo Indians; purchase of western tracts of land; journey to Washington with Indian delegates.

Howard Vanderslice and H. N. Monnett, *Van der Slice and Allied Families* (Los Angeles, 1931) 166–186.

WOODS, Rev. James (1815–1886) *b.* New Braintree, Mass., of California.

Clergyman's journal, November 1854–April 1855 (extract); record of his ministry in Los Angeles, California; preaching, visits, law cases, social commentary and news; fair local interest.

Hist. Soc. Southern California Quar. XXIII (1941) 65–86.

1855

ANON. (Mormon).

Mormon missionary journal, April 1855–January 1866; journal of Las Vegas mission; religious work and general activities.

Andrew Jensen, *History of Las Vegas Mission, Nevada Hist. Soc. Papers* (1926) 119–284.

ABBOT, Lieut. Henry Larcom (1831–1927) *b.* Beverly, Mass., of Corps of Topographical Engineers.

Military exploration journal, August–November 1855 (extracts); railroad surveys in Oregon; topographical, statistics, letters.

Oregon Hist. Quar. XXXIII (1932) 1–24, 115–133.

ANDERSON, James, chief factor of Hudson's Bay Company.

Arctic journal, July–August 1855; extract relating to search for crews of the "Erebus" and "Terror."

Royal Geog. Soc. Jour. XXVII (1857) 321–328.

BROWN, Henry Billings (1836–1913) of Detroit, judge.

Private diary, June 1855–March 1875 (extracts and summary); students at Yale, visits to Europe, journey to Detroit, reading, legal work, comments on Civil War.

Charles A. Kent, *Memoir of Henry Billings Brown* (New York, 1915) 36–72.

CHAMBERS, James H. (1820–1866?) of Montana, fur trader.

Semiofficial fur-trading diary, January 1855–October 185–?, and extract from travel journal, July–August 1856; social life of men at the fort, hunting trips; frank and quasi-literary; impressionistic hasty entries; highly personal, with incidental business entries; a most unusual and arresting diary.

Hist. Soc. Montana Contribs. X (1940) 100–187.

CHANDLESS, William, of London, Eng., wagon driver.

Travel diary, July 1855–February 1856; from Atchison to Salt Lake; account of Mormons; trip to California, via Fillmore, Cedar City, Las Vegas, San Bernardino, Los Angeles; voyage to San Francisco; entertaining, but inclined to be travel-book narrative.

A Visit to Salt Lake (London, 1857) 346 pp.

EGGE, Heinrich, of Davenport, Ia. *b.* Schleswig-Holstein.

Travel diary, May–June 1855 (extracts); Hamburg to New York and thence to Chicago; observations and descriptions of a happy and pleased German immigrant. Translated from the German.

Mississippi Valley Hist. Rev. XVII (1930–1931) 123–134.

HARRIS, Townsend (1804–1878) of New York City, first United States envoy in Japan.

Foreign diaries, August 1856–February 1858; notes on travel in Japan, India, Egypt, Sumatra, Siam, China; diplomatic and social life in Japan, descriptions of Japanese scenery, life, customs.

M. E. Cosenza (ed.), *The Complete Journal of Townsend Harris* (New York, 1930) 616 pp. Parts relating to Japan in W. E. Griffis, *Townsend Harris, First American Envoy in Japan* (Boston, 1895) 33–307.

HEMBREE, Warman C., of the Yamhill County Company, Oregon Volunteers.

Military journal, October 1855–April 1856; Yakima Indian war; brief notes of marches and encampments.

Washington Hist. Quar. XVI (1925) 273–283.

JAEGER, Louis John Frederick (*b.* 1825) *b.* Berks Co., Pa., ferryman at Fort Yuma, Calif.

Private business diary, December 1855–July 1857 (fragment); work at the ferry, trips into Mexico, San Diego, Los Angeles, San Bernardino; bare details of drunken brawls, etc.; a repetitious but interesting diary.

Southern California Hist. Soc. Pubs. XIV (1928–1930) 89–128, 213–242.

KIP, Lieut. Lawrence (1836–1899) of 3d Artillery Regiment.

1. Military journal, May–June 1855; journey from Vancouver to Walla Walla; council with Indians there; return.

F. G. Young (ed.), *Sources of the History of Oregon* I (1897) 1–26; reprinted *Mag. Hist.* Extra No. 39 (New York, 1915), 45 pp. (from a text printed but not published, San Francisco, 1855).

2. Military journal, May–October 1855; expedition against Indians of Pacific Northwest; battle of Four Lakes, Spokane Plains; councils with Indians; literary style, with much general, social, and scenic description.

Army Life on the Pacific (New York, 1859) 144 pp.; reprinted *Mag. Hist.* Extra No. 30 (New York, 1914) 117 pp.

MILLER, Joaquin (1841?–1913), poet.

Private diary, October 1855–November 1857; mining in Shasta, Calif.; notes on Indians; factual and introspective entries; poems.

John S. Richards (ed.), *Joaquin Miller: His California Diary* (Seattle, 1936) 106 pp.

MORSE, Abner (1819–1881) *b.* Randolph, Vt., of River Falls, Wis.

1. Travel diary, December 1855–March 1856; journey from New England to Wisconsin; lively social comments and observations on taverns, etc., from temperance standpoint; some linguistic notes.

Wisconsin Mag. Hist. XXII (1938–1939) 195–212, 329–343, 427–434.

2. Private diary, April 1859–March 1861; at River Falls, Wis.; interesting notes on religious revivals, building, and social activities, farming, schoolteaching; linguistic notes.

Wisconsin Mag. Hist. XXIII (1939–1940) 62–88.

PAINTER, Robert Moore (1827–1868) *b.* St. Genevieve, Mo., of 1st Regiment of
      Oregon Mounted Volunteers.

Military diary, October 1855–May 1856; Indian wars in Washington Territory; brief notes, with some longer accounts of battles.

Washington Hist. Quar. XV (1924) 13–26.

PAINTER, William Charles (1830–1900) *b.* St. Genevieve, Mo., of 1st Regiment
      of Oregon Mounted Volunteers.

Military diary, October 1855–January 1856; brief notes on Indian wars.

Washington Hist. Quar. XV (1924) 27–31.

ROBBINS, Harvey, of the Northern Battalion, Oregon Volunteers.

Military diary, October 1855–February 1856; Indian uprising on Rogue River.

Oregon Hist. Quar. XXXIV (1933) 345–358.

SESSIONS, Rev. John (1795–1884) of Vermont, California, and Honolulu.

Travel diary, July–August 1855 (extracts); notes on San Francisco, Sacramento and environs; mining; San Francisco Bay.

Soc. Californian Pioneers Quar. V (1928) 9–29.

WARREN, Lieut. Gouverneur Kemble (1830–1882) *b.* Newport, R.I., of Corps of
      Topographical Engineers.

Military exploration journal, August–November 1855; journeys in the Dakota country; Fort Pierre, Fort Kearny, Fort Laramie, Fort Pierre, Sioux City; scientific notes.

Explorations in the Dacota Country (Washington, 1856) 4–34.

WELD, Dr. Francis Minot (1840–1893) of Jamaica Plains, Mass.

Private diary, January 1855–July 1865; pleasant diary of boyhood in Jamaica Plains, sports, schooling, family, friendships; a few details of study at Harvard; work as naval surgeon and as army surgeon, especially during the Civil War.

Sarah S. W. Blake, *Diaries and Letters of Francis Minot Weld* (Boston, 1925) 11–206.

1856

BROKMEYER, Henry C. (1828–1906) *b*. Germany, of St. Louis, philosopher.

Mechanic's diary, May–November 1856; "notes of thoughts and happenings of the day, as they occurred in the life of a molder in the Mississippi Valley fifty years ago"; natural history notes, and social, political, and philosophical commentary; written with much linguistic local color and dialogue; a literary work.

A Mechanic's Diary (Washington, D.C., 1910) 239 pp.

BROWN, J. Robert.

Travel diary, April–October 1856; from St. Louis to California, via Fort Laramie, Green River, Fort Bridger, Salt Lake, Rag Town, Carson Valley; sketches of noted characters; Indian and mountain stories.

Journal of a Trip across the Plains of the United States (Columbus, 1860) 120 pp.

COLT, Miriam (*b*. 1817) of West Stockholm, N.Y.

Travel diary, January 1856–December 1857; journey of Vegetarian Company from New York to Kansas Territory; full, literary journal of the trip, and daily life of the settlement; domestic and public affairs, Indian troubles, failure of settlement; interesting.

Went to Kansas (Watertown, N.Y., 1862) 294 pp.

FOLSOM, Rev. Willis F. (*ca.* 1825–1894), a Choctaw Indian missionary.

Missionary journal, August 1856–October 1894; notes of missionary work; disappointingly conventional.

Chrons. Oklahoma IV (1926) 61–69.

GALLOWAY, Andrew, secretary of Edmundson's Mormon Company.

Travel diary, June–July 1856; with handcarts from vicinity of Iowa City across Missouri River to Florence (near Omaha); brief notes of movements.

Annals Iowa 3d Ser. XX (1935–1937) 444–449.

LEE, Robert Edward (1807–1870) of Virginia, soldier.

Military journal, March 1856–February 1861 (scattered extracts); service in Texas as colonel in 2d U.S. Cavalry; journal notes are brief and factual.

West Texas Hist. Assoc. Year Book VIII (1932) 3–24.

READER, Samuel James (1836–1914) *b*. Greenford, Pa., of Topeka, Kan.

Private diary, September 1856 (extracts); general notes, and an account of battle at Hickory Point; interesting linguistic mélange.

Kansas Hist. Quar. I (1931) 30–31.

REEDER, Andrew H. (1807–1864) *b*. Easton, Pa., first governor of Kansas.

Private diary, May 1856 (extracts); entries made while he was escaping from Kansas to Illinois in disguise after indictment for high treason; mostly in hiding in Kansas City; entertaining.

Kansas Hist. Soc. Colls. III (1881–1884) 205–223.

SAVAGE, William (1833–1908) of Cedar, Ia., farmer and painter.

Farming diary, March 1856–October 1863; daily life of a farmer and naturalist in Van Buren Co., Ia.; mostly farming details; repetitive but interesting.

Annals Iowa 3d Ser. XIX (1933–1935) 83–114, 189–220, 470–474, XX (1935–1937) 140–150, 459–471, 535–543 (incomplete).

WAILES, Benjamin Leonard Covington (1797–1861) of Washington, Miss.

Travel diary, October–November 1856; Vicksburg to Arkansas; life on river packet; inspection of property in Arkansas, Pine Bluff, Little Rock; expenditures.

Mississippi Valley Hist. Rev. XXII (1935–1936) 419–433.

WOLF, Capt. Lambert Bowman (1834–1918) *b.* Evansburg, O., of 1st U.S. Cavalry.

Military diary, December 1856–January 1861; experiences and observations of a cavalryman in Kansas; some later expansions; general notes on army life, Indian incidents, army songs; fairly interesting.

Kansas Hist. Quar. I (1932) 195–210.

1857

BANDEL, Private Eugene (1835–1889) *b.* Prussia, armorer in U.S. Infantry.

Military journal, May–November 1857; surveying Kansas boundary; military escort; diversions, hardships, Indian raids, his own affairs; substantial and very pleasant entries.

Ralph P. Bieber (ed.), *Frontier Life in the Army* (Glendale, Calif., 1932) 131–211.

BEADLE, Erastus Flavel (1821–1894) of Buffalo, N.Y.

Travel diary, March–September 1857; journey from Buffalo to preëmpted lands near Omaha; details of journey and incidents; social affairs, notes on fellow travelers, political sentiment, the great migration, life in Nebraska, and the financial panic of 1857; substantial entries, with good narrative.

To Nebraska in Fifty-Seven (New York, 1923) 89 pp., reprinted from *Bull. New York Pub. Lib.* XXVII (1923) 71–115, 171–212.

BEALE, Lieut. Edward Fitzgerald (1822–1893) *b.* D.C., commander of Wagon Route Survey and Camel Corps.

Military journal, June 1857–February 1858; San Antonio, Fort Defiance to the Colorado, Los Angeles; Fort Tejon to the Colorado and return to Fort Defiance; official report, full of notes on the route and the camels.

Lewis B. Lesley, *Uncle Sam's Camels* (Cambridge, Mass., 1929) 144–281; first printed as *House Exec. Doc.* 124, 35th Cong. 1st sess. (1858).

BURROUGHS, John (1837–1921) *b.* Roxbury, N.Y., author.

Private diary, March 1857–February 1921 (extracts); entries reflecting his mental growth and interests and rough material for his books; travel in Europe and America; reflections and introspection; nature and literature notes.

Clara Barrus (ed.), *The Heart of Burroughs' Journals* (Boston, 1928) 361 pp.

CAMPBELL, Hugh, surveyor.

Surveying journal, April–November 1857; surveying South Kansas boundary; from St. Louis to Fort Leavenworth with the astronomical party.

Kansas Hist. Quar. VI (1937) 339–377.

CARTER, William Alexander (1820–1881) *b.* Prince William Co., Va., of Fort Bridger, Wyo.

Travel diary, September–November 1857; his second western journey, from Atchison, Kans., to Fort Bridger, Utah Territory; taking up job as sutler with Johnston's forces; full entries, with a good many notes of social life, fellow travelers, Indians, natural phenomena, Mormon ruins; a good narrative on unexciting material.

Annals Wyoming XI (1939) 75–110.

DAVIDSON, Greenlee (*d.* 1863) of Lexington, Va.

Travel diary, September 1857 (extract); description of a visit to Indianapolis.

Indiana Mag. Hist. XXIV (1928) 134–136.

GOVE, Capt. Jesse, of Concord, N.H., and 10th U.S. Infantry.

Diary-letters, June 1857–June 1858; written to his wife, describing the Utah expedition; interesting descriptions.

New Hampshire Hist. Soc. Colls. XII (1928) 442 pp.

HILDT, George H. (1855–1913) of Ohio.

Frontier diary, June–December 1857; journey across Missouri to Johnson County, Kans.; life on Kansas frontier while he was overlooking lands; very interesting details of frontier life and scenes, with many sidelights on contemporary politics and persons.

Kansas Hist. Quar. X (1941) 260–298.

JOHNSTON, Col. Joseph Eccleston (1807–1891) *b.* Cherry Grove, Va., of U.S. Cavalry.

Surveying journal, May–October 1857; surveying southern Kansas boundary line; mainly topographical notes.

Kansas Hist. Quar. I (1932) 104–139.

"MAY, Anna," of New Hampshire.

Private diary, February–July 1857; kept while author was senior student at New Hampton Institute, N.H.; interesting in relation to the English and classical courses of "Female Collegiate Institutes" of the day.

G. W. Robinson (ed.), *Journal of Anna May* (Cambridge, Mass., 1941) 100 pp.

PALLISER, Capt. John (1807–1887) of British Army.

Exploration journals, 1857–1860; expedition between river Saskatchewan and United States frontier, Red River and Rockies, and to the Pacific; Canada between western shore of Lake Superior and the Pacific.

Exploration—British North America (London; H.M. Stationery Office, 1863) 325 pp.

PECKHAM, E. L.

Travel diary, June 1857; Rhode Island to Iowa and return, by railroad; New Englander's annoyance with the early Middle West; entertaining.

Jour. Amer. Hist. XVII (1923) 225–235, XVIII (1924) 39–50.

REID, John C. (*b.* 1824) of Marion, Ala.

Travel diary, September 1857–July 1858; through Texas, New Mexico, Arizona, Sonora, California; topography, climate, soil, inhabitants; mostly narrative, apparently based on a diary.

Reid's Tramp (Selma, Ala., 1858) 237 pp.; reprinted (Austin, Texas, 1935) 245 pp.

RUFFIN, Edmund (1794–1865) of Prince George Co., Va., editor of *Farmer's Register*.

Private diary, January 1857–June 1865; mainly relating to Civil War, but prior entries on great storm, a visit to Washington (January–February 1857), and visit to John Tyler (November 1857) with long account of conversation with Tyler.

William and Mary Coll. Quar. 1st Ser. XIV (1905–1906) 193–211, 215, XX (1911–1912) 69–101, XXI (1912–1913) 224–233, XXII (1913–1914) 258–263, XXIII (1914–1915) 31–45, 154–171, 240–258.

STACEY, May Humphreys (1837–1886) of Chester, Pa., later Lieut. Col. U.S.A.

Travel journal, May–October 1857; Chester to Philadelphia, and California; survey of wagon route from Fort Defiance to the Colorado River, in Beale's Camel Corps; fascinated observations of a nineteen-year-old; people, places, food, etc.; a good record.

Lewis B. Lesley, *Uncle Sam's Camels* (Cambridge, Mass., 1929) 21–115.

WOOD, J. C., superintendent of San Antonio–San Diego mail line.

Travel journal, June 1857–January 1858; journey undertaken to survey condition of mail route between San Antonio and San Diego; notes on roads, terrain, pasturage, water, etc., with some personal items.

Report to Hon. A. V. Brown, Postmaster-General (Washington, 1858) 43 pp.

1858

COOPER, Douglas, of Fort Washington, United States agent for Chickasaw Indians.

Official journal, July 1858; organization of expedition against Comanche Indians; march along Beaver Creek, Wichita village; no success in finding Comanches.

Chrons. Oklahoma V (1927) 381–390.

ENGLE, F. E.

Surveying journal, October–December 1858; expedition to survey route from Fort Smith, Ark., along Canadian River, for wagon road to continue to Colorado

River (part of a series of surveys to establish route to California); general notes on topography and scenery, with some social items; well written, interesting.

Chrons. Oklahoma XII (1934) 74–96.

FELT, Andrew M. (1824–1907) of Clayton, Mich.

Travel diary, November–December 1858 (fragment); from Flushing to San Francisco; train to New York, steamer to New Orleans, across Panama, steamer to San Francisco; fair touristic and social notes.

Michigan Hist. Mag. XV (1931) 112–125.

GUTHRIE, Abelard (1814–1873) *b.* near Dayton, O., of Kansas.

Political diaries, March 1858–July 1862 (extracts); political notes relating to Quindaro and the Quindaro Company; comments on political figures of Kansas and Nebraska and on some national figures (Lincoln, etc.); many minor domestic and social items; an interesting diary.

W. E. Connelley (ed.), *The Provisional Government of Nebraska Territory* (Lincoln, Neb., 1899) 116–152.

HAMILTON, James B. (*b.* 1830) of Ansted, W.Va.

Private diary, January 1858–June 1859; brief entries; religion, farm work, surveying, fishing, and personal affairs; a few later entries relating to the Civil War.

J. B. Peters and H. B. Carden, *History of Fayette County, West Virginia* (Charleston, W.Va., 1926) 200–212.

JACKSON, George Andrew (1836–1897) of Glasgow, Mo., and Ouray, Colo.

Travel diary, December 1858–March 1859; camping and hunting journey from and around Vasquez Fork, Colo.; prospecting in Colorado gold diggings; breezy and entertaining style; a fresh, interesting, and veracious picture of a prospector's life.

Colorado Mag. XII (1935) 201–214.

JACKSON, Col. Oscar Lawrence (1840–1920) of Newcastle, Pa.

Private and military diary, September 1858–July 1865; early life as country schoolmaster in Pennsylvania; detailed account of Civil War campaigns and raids in South, siege of Vicksburg, Kenesaw Mountain, Sherman's march.

D. P. Jackson (ed.), *The Colonel's Diary* (Sharon, Pa., 1922) 232 pp.

JACOBS, William Plumer (1842–1917) of Clinton, S.C.

Private diary, January 1858–July 1917; early part deals with studies at school and in college at Charleston; religious reflections, verses, etc.; greatest part deals with his religious and philanthropic work, and the history of the Thornwell Orphanage at Clinton.

Thornwell Jacobs (ed.), *Diary of William Plumer Jacobs* (Oglethorpe Univ., Ga., 1937) 484 pp.

McDONALD, David (1803–1869) of Indianapolis, judge.

Travel diaries, December 1858–January 1859, June 1862, September 1864, December 1864; journeys to Washington, D.C.; first contains lengthy description of functioning of Supreme Court, second describes city and political figures, third recounts interview with Lincoln, fourth has political items.

Indiana Mag. Hist. XXVIII (1932) 282–306.

MULLAN, Lieut. John.

Military survey journal, July 1858; survey of military road from Fort Dalles, O.T., to Fort Walla Walla; general notes, with comments on Dr. Whitman (the missionary) and on the defeat of Gen. Steptoe.

The Frontier (Univ. Montana) XII (1931–1932) 368–375; reprinted as No. 18 of *Sources of Northwest History* (Univ. Montana) 10 pp.

PHILLIPS, Cyrus Olin.

Travel diary, July–August 1858; Sacramento to San Francisco, voyage to British Columbia; topography and statistics.

California Hist. Soc. Quar. XI (1932) 152–153.

SELDEN, John Armistead, of Richmond and Westover, Va.,

Plantation diary, July 1858–May 1864; plantation life on the Westover estate; interesting successor to Byrd's diary; practical farming and plantation details; vacation at White Sulphur Springs.

Edited by J. S. Bassett, *Smith Coll. Stud. Hist.* VI (1920–1921) No. 4, 257–330.

VORHEES, Augustus (1828–1905) *b.* New York State, of Kansas.

Travel diary, June–July 1858; journey with the Lawrence party to Pike's Peak; from Bluff Creek, Kan., to Jim's Camp; mainly notes of distances, but valuable because of rarity of diaries of Pike's Peak gold rush.

Colorado Mag. XII (1935) 41–50; Le Roy R. Hafen (ed.), *Pike's Peak Guidebooks of 1859* (Glendale, Calif., 1941) App. H 336–346.

WAY, Phocion R. (*d.* 1898) of Tucson, Ariz., and Cincinnati, O.

Travel diary, June 1858 (extract); frontier life in southern Arizona; description of Tucson and its inhabitants; Indians; an excellent extract.

Southwestern Hist. Quar. XXXVI (1932–1933) 180–188.

1859

BATES, Edward (1793–1869) of St. Louis, Mo., statesman.

Private diary, April 1859–July 1866; not consistently diary entries, for some newspaper clippings, letters, and odd printed items are included; mainly political affairs during period when he was a possible candidate for President, and while he was in Lincoln's cabinet; much of it personal and local; many literary quotations and allusions; a valuable and very interesting document.

H. K. Beale (ed.), *The Diary of Edward Bates* (Washington, 1933) 685 pp.

BOLTON, Charles E. (*b.* 1840?) of South Hadley Falls, Mass.

Travel diary, August 1859; brief journey to Maine via Boston; visit to Augusta, to Boston, and home; a country boy sightseeing; a few interesting spellings.

New England Quar. IX (1936) 119–131.

DAVIS, Sylvester (*b.* 1839?) of Massachusetts.

Travel diary, April–October 1859; Iowa to Denver, Colo.; mining in Pike's Peak country; then to Santa Fe country by way of Raton Pass; statistical.

New Mexico Hist. Rev. VI (1931) 383–416.

FONTAINE, Col. William Winstan.

Political diary, February 1859; meeting with former President Tyler, and Tyler's account of his father's description of Patrick Henry's delivery of "Give me liberty" speech.

William and Mary Coll. Quar. 1st Ser. XVI (1907–1908) 157–161.

GASS, A. M.

Travel diary, April–June 1859; the Pike's Peak gold rush; journey from Texas.

Le Roy Hafen (ed.), *Overland Routes to the Gold Fields, 1859* (Glendale, Calif., 1942) 218–231.

HALL, Susan Mitchell, *b.* New Haven, Conn., of Amador Co., Calif.

Travel diary, September 1859; from Ione, Calif., to Nevada; conventional travel notes.

California Hist. Soc. Quar. XVII (1938) 75–78.

LINDSEY, Mrs. Sarah (1804–1876) of Bolton, Eng.

Quaker travel diary, June 1859–June 1860; voyage to Panama and California; in California and thence to Honolulu; extracts descriptive of persons and social life; very pleasant.

Travels of Robert and Sarah Lindsey (London, 1886) 134–163.

McPHERSON, William Gregg (*d.* 1908) *b.* Lyme, N.Y., of Orange Co., Calif.

Travel diary, April 1859–November 1873; westward journey to Des Moines, Council Bluffs, Omaha, Laramie, South Pass, Marysville, Downieville; mining in California; a detailed and rather interesting record.

Orange News (California) August 6–12, December 16–31, 1937.

PALMER, Dr. Alonzo Benjamin (1815–1887) *b.* Richmond, N.Y., of Chicago, physician.

Foreign travel diary, April–October 1859 (extracts); in England and Scotland visiting hospitals and lectures; tourist visits to monuments, galleries, etc.; full descriptions; some social views.

Memorial of Alonzo Benjamin Palmer (Cambridge, Mass., 1890) 21–126.

PATTERSON, E. H. N. (1829–1880) of Oquawka, Ill., journalist.

Travel diary, March–June 1859; the Pike's Peak gold rush; Platte River route; the fullest diary of this journey.

Le Roy Hafen (ed.), *Overland Routes to the Gold Fields, 1859* (Glendale, Calif., 1942) 65–197.

PEASE, Edwin R., teacher of "the English branches of education."

Travel diary, April–May 1859; the Pike's Peak gold rush; St. Joseph to Fort Kearny.

Le Roy Hafen (ed.), *Overland Routes to the Gold Fields, 1859* (Glendale, Calif., 1942) 203–213.

POST, Charles C. (1831–1906) of Decatur, Ill., lawyer.
Travel diary, May–June 1859; the Pike's Peak gold rush; the Arkansas River route; detailed descriptions concerning difficulties of travel, etc.; fair.
Le Roy Hafen (ed.), *Overland Routes to the Gold Fields, 1859* (Glendale, Calif., 1942) 19–55.

RICHARDSON, Albert D., journalist.
Travel diary, May–June 1859; the Pike's Peak gold rush; the Leavenworth and Pike's Peak Express route, stagecoach journey; a good journalistic narrative.
Le Roy Hafen (ed.), *Overland Routes to the Gold Fields, 1859* (Glendale, Calif., 1942) 240–262.

SNOW, Taylor N. (*d.* 1859?) of Indiana.
Travel diary, May–August 1859; overland to California; travel notes and details of Indian raids; some interesting spellings. Diary ends abruptly, and editor supposes Snow was killed in an Indian raid.
Indiana Mag. Hist. XXVIII (1932) 193–208.

THIBODO, Dr. Augustus J. (*b.* 1834?) of Kingston, Ont.
Travel diary, June 1859–April 1860; Ontario to St. Paul, Minn.; overland to Walla Walla; long entries, with careful descriptions of people, places; scientific interest.
Pacific Northwest Quar. XXXI (1940) 287–347.

TUTTLE, Charles M. (*d.* 1906) of Union, Wis., farmer.
Travel diary, beginning April 1859; from Wisconsin to California; to Salt Lake, thence by Simpson's southern route; diary ends at Neill's Creek; interesting social comments in early and late parts of the diary.
Wisconsin Mag. Hist. XV (1931–1932) 69–85, 219–233.

WILLING, Dr. George M., of St. Louis, physician.
Travel diary-letters, May–June 1859; two letters to his wife; journey to Pike's Peak gold mines, Santa Fe Trail to Pueblo, thence to the mines; descriptions of country and mining; fair interest.
Mississippi Valley Hist. Rev. XIV (1927–1928) 360–378, reprinted from *Daily Missouri Republican,* August 9, 1859.

1860

ADAMS, Charles Francis, Jr.
Political diary, September 1860 (extracts); campaigning with William H. Seward in Minnesota.
Minnesota Hist. VIII (1927) 165–171.

ANTHONY, Webster D. (*b.* 1838) *b.* Union Springs, N.Y., first speaker of Colorado Assembly.

Travel diary, July 1860; from Denver to Oro City (Leadville); details of frontier life; literary style.

Colorado Mag. XI (1934) 228–237.

ASHE, Lieut. E. D., R.N., director of Quebec Observatory.

Scientific journal, July–September 1860; voyage from New York to Labrador to observe eclipse of sun; general notes on scenery, eclipse, etc.

Lit. Hist. Soc. Quebec Trans. (1861, reprinted 1927) 1–16.

BOND, Ens. J. Harman, of Royal Canadian Rifles.

Military travel journal, July 1860; from Kingston, Ont., to Fort Garry, Red River; brief, accurate details of movements, country, people, etc.

North Dakota Hist. Quar. VI (1932) 231–238.

BURTON, Sir Richard Francis (1821–1890), H.M. consul at Trieste, author.

English travel diary, August–October 1860; travel in Utah; extensive descriptions and comments on people and places; literary travel notes.

The City of the Saints and Across the Rocky Mountains to California (London, 1861) 707 pp; reprinted (New York, 1862) 574 pp.

CLARK, George T. (1837–1888) of Denver, Colo.

Travel diary, May–June 1860 (extract); across the plains from Iowa to Colorado; in Denver; rather dull notes.

Colorado Mag. VI (1929) 131–140.

COWELL, Emilie Marguerite.

Travel diary, January 1860–June 1861; kept during her husband's concert tour in America.

The Cowells in America (London, 1934) 409 pp.

HAWLEY, H. J. (1839–1923) of Argyle, Wis., and Central City, Colo.

Travel diary, April–May 1860; from Argyle, Wis., to Pike's Peak via Dubuque, Des Moines, Omaha, and Denver; fairly interesting travel notes, with some interesting spellings.

Wisconsin Mag. Hist. XIX (1935–1936) 319–342.

LATHAM, Milton S. (1827–1882) b. Columbus, O., senator from California.

Private diary, January–May 1860; political notes; obtaining appointment by state legislature as United States senator; political life in Washington.

California Hist. Soc. Quar. XI (1932) 3–28.

LEWIS, Edward J. (1828–1907) b. Philadelphia, of Bloomington, Ill., journalist and postmaster.

Travel diary, March–September 1860; journey with party from Bloomington to Pike's Peak area; prospecting and work in the diggings; Denver, Iowa Gulch, California Gulch, Tennessee Gulch; gambling, camp life and fare, prices; return to Bloomington; an interesting diary.

Colorado Mag. XIV (1937) 201–219, XV (1938) 20–33.

MAYNADIER, Lieut. H. E., U.S. Army.

Military exploration journal, 1860; exploration of upper Yellowstone and Missouri rivers.

Exploration of the Yellowstone River by Gen. W. F. Raynolds, 40th Cong. I Sess., *Sen. Exec. Doc.* No. 77 (Washington, D.C., 1868) 134–154. Extract relating to a boat trip to Omaha in *North Dakota Hist. Quar.* I, No. 2 (1927) 41–51.

WARD, Lester Frank (1841–1913) *b.* Joliet, Ill., sociologist and geologist.

Private diary, July 1860–December 1869 (with a year's gap from August 1862); youth and teaching in rural Pennsylvania; courtship and marriage; period of army service; government clerk in Washington; mostly weekly entries; an intimate and delightful diary of an eager, intelligent Victorian. Original written in French; translation published.

Bernhard J. Stern (ed.), *Young Ward's Diary* (New York, 1935) 321 pp.

INDEX

(References are to pages. Anonymous diaries are not indexed.)